Tuesday
Dec. 18th 7:40 - 9:20 Am

S0-AKL-011

PATTERNMAKING
for Fashion design

PATTERNMAKING
for Fashion design

HELEN JOSEPH ARMSTRONG

Los Angeles Trade-Technical College

1817

HARPER & ROW, PUBLISHERS, New York

Cambridge, Philadelphia, San Francisco,
London, Mexico City, São Paulo, Singapore, Sydney

Dedicated to my mother and father. Without them, this book would not have been written.

Sponsoring Editor: Fred Henry
Project Editor: Donna DeBenedictis
Text Design: Gayle Jaeger
Cover Concept: Helen Joseph Armstrong
Cover Execution: Gayle Jaeger
Cover Illustration: Mona Shafer Edwards and Steve Randock
Technical Illustrations: Steve Randock and James Venecia
Fashion Illustrations: Mona Shafer Edwards
Production: Debra Forrest
Compositor: ComCom Division of Haddon Craftsmen, Inc.
Printer and Binder: The Murray Printing Company

PATTERNMAKING FOR FASHION DESIGN

Copyright © 1987 by Harper & Row, Publishers, Inc.

All rights reserved. Printed in the United States of America. No part of this book may be used or reproduced in any manner whatsoever without written permission, except in the case of brief quotations embodied in critical articles and reviews. For information address Harper & Row, Publishers, Inc., 10 East 53d Street, New York, NY 10022.

Library of Congress Cataloging in Publication Data
Armstrong, Helen Joseph.
  Patternmaking for fashion design.

  Includes index.
  1. Dressmaking—Pattern design.   I. Title.
II. Title: Pattern making for fashion design.
TT520.A74 1986   646.4′072   85-8512
ISBN 0-06-040332-2

  89 9 8 7 6 5

Contents

PREFACE VII

PART I *Development of the basic patterns* 1
    1 THE WORKROOM 3
    2 FIGURE ANALYSIS 29
    3 MEASURING TECHNIQUES 43
    4 METHODS FOR MAKING BASIC PATTERNS 63

PART II *Three major patternmaking principles* 109
    (INTRODUCTION TO FLAT PATTERNMAKING)
    5 DART MANIPULATION (PRINCIPLE #1) 111
    6 TUCK-DARTS, PLEATS, FLARES, AND GATHERS 137
    7 STYLELINES 167
    8 ADDED FULLNESS (PRINCIPLE #2) 179
    9 CONTOURING (PRINCIPLE #3) 203
    10 COWLS AND BUILT-UP NECKLINES 225

PART III *Collars, skirts, sleeves, and sleeve/bodice combinations* 251
    11 COLLARS 253
    12 SKIRTS 275
    13 SLEEVES AND SLEEVE/BODICE COMBINATIONS 349

PART IV *Patternmaking details* 411
    14 BUTTONS/BUTTONHOLES AND FACINGS 413
    15 PLACKETS AND POCKETS 423

PART V *Dresses, tops, jackets, coats, capes, and hoods* 439
    (PATTERNMAKING BASED ON TORSO FOUNDATION)
    16 THE TORSO DRAFT 441
    17 DRESSES WITHOUT WAISTLINE SEAMS 447
    18 TOPS 469
    19 JACKETS AND COATS 485
    20 CAPES AND HOODS 515

PART VI *Patternmaking for bifurcated garments* 527

21 PANTS 529
22 ACTIONWEAR FOR DANCE AND EXERCISE 581
23 SWIMWEAR 595
24 ELASTIC, CROTCH LINING, AND BRA CUPS 615

PART VII *Problems and solutions* 619

25 KNITS—STRETCH AND SHRINKAGE FACTORS 621
26 PANT DRAFT ADJUSTMENT FOR PERSONAL FIT 627
27 FITTING PROBLEMS AND PATTERN CORRECTION 633

METRIC CONVERSION TABLE 687
PATTERNS
    HALF-SIZE BASIC PATTERN SET 689–699
    QUARTER-SIZE BASIC PATTERN SET 701–703
    QUARTER-SIZE TORSO 705
    FRENCH CURVE 707
GENERAL INDEX 709
INDEX TO FITTING PROBLEMS AND PATTERN CORRECTION (CHAPTER 27) 712

Preface

Patternmaking for Fashion Design was written with specific goals in mind:
- To provide a comprehensive patternmaking text that would not require supplements.
- To present clear instruction, with corresponding easy-to-follow technical illustrations and up-to-date fashion sketches, that will stimulate the creative imaginations of both technical and design-oriented students.
- To make available a reference source for the professional patternmaker and designer.
- To fill the need for standard patterns and to provide instructions for adapting them to personal fit.
- To provide a variety of instruction so that the motivated student will continue to learn long after the classroom experience.

We believe that *Patternmaking for Fashion Design* accomplishes these goals.

The book is divided into seven parts to facilitate the location of desired information. A brief description of the special features found in Parts I through VII follows.

Part I—Chapters 1 through 4—contains information that applies to all parts of the text and should be studied carefully before pattern work begins. Chapter 1, *The Workroom,* covers introductory information concerning tools, terms, definitions, symbols, and the completion of patterns. It is suggested that a tab be placed at page 20 for quick reference. Part I also features figure analysis and measuring techniques, and provides three methods for developing the basic pattern set of bodice, skirt, and sleeve. Choose the method that best satisfies your needs. Instructions are given here for standard and personal fit.

Part II—Chapters 5 through 9—is the foundation of the book. The beginning student is introduced to the flat patternmaking system and the three major patternmaking principles (dart manipulation, added fullness, and contouring). These principles form the basis for developing patternmaking techniques and skills relating to pattern designs. The slash/spread and pivotal/transfer methods are used to demonstrate pattern manipulation of the bodice. Once these techniques are learned they can be applied to all patterns and designs. It is suggested that the projects be taken in sequence, as each leads to more complex patternmaking.

Part III—Chapters 11 through 13—covers the adaptation of patterns to design variations, and has several special features. The skirt section contains new information about the slinky and one-dart working pattern that should be explored. The Circle/Cascade Radius Chart is included to expedite designs featuring circular

skirts and cascades. The chart eliminates the need for mathematical formulas, as all measurements for the radii are included. Refer to this chart when developing cascades for any section of a garment.

Part IV—Chapters 14 and 15—covers button/buttonhole placement, facings, plackets, and pockets. They are grouped together because they are all finishings and add-ons to garments. Additional fold-back facing instructions are given in Chapter 18 *(Tops),* since they apply mainly to garments of that type.

Part V—Chapters 16 through 20—features dresses without waistline seams, tops (shirts, blouses, and dartless knit foundations), jackets (including lapels, lining, and interconstruction), and coat and cape foundations. These garments are all based on the torso foundation pattern. Hoods are included here because they commonly are found with capes. This instruction, it should be noted, applies to all garments featuring hoods.

Part VI—Chapters 21 through 24—covers an exciting range of bifurcated garments (those with leg openings). Patternmaking instructions cover both standard and personal fit. The inclusion of bodysuits, leotards, and swimwear is a new and important addition. More and more manufacturers are dealing with these types of garments because of today's more active lifestyles.

Part VII—Chapters 25 through 27—deals with problems and solutions. Three different subjects are covered: adaptation of the pattern for the stretch and shrinkage factors of knits (Chapter 25); pant draft instruction for personalized fit (Chapter 26); fitting problems and pattern correction of the basic pattern set and of pants (Chapter 27).

In the back of the book the following are found:
- Metric Conversion Table
- Half-size Basic Pattern Set
- Quarter-size Basic Pattern Set
- Quarter-size Torso

(*Note:* These patterns can be cut out of the book and transferred to pattern paper or plastic for use in pattern development.)
- French Curve. If this tool cannot be purchased, cut from the text and transfer to pattern paper or plastic.
- Indexes. A general index to the entire book and a separate, detailed index for Chapter 27, Fitting Problems and Pattern Correction, is provided.

This book is based on the contributions of great patternmakers of the past; adds to them new innovations and concepts gained through years of experience in the industry and the classroom; and is comprehensive enough to be a valuable tool now and in the future regardless of fashion trends.

Every effort has been made to avoid errors; however, with a text of this magnitude, it is possible that errors may exist. Hopefully, any errors found are minor ones and will not hinder the reader's understanding of pattern development.

We acknowledge that there is more than one method for developing patterns and welcome comments and ideas from readers.

ACKNOWLEDGMENTS

I wish to express my appreciation to the following persons who contributed freely of their time to help make *Patternmaking for Fashion Design* a better book.

Special appreciation goes to Loretta Sweeney for the countless hours spent proofreading and correcting errors in the original, rough manuscript, and for typing the finished work for presentation to the publishers.

Much gratitude goes to:

■ Steve Randock and Jim Venecia, who inked my penciled technical illustrations perfectly, and who spent nights and weekends to help me meet my deadlines.

■ Mona Shafer Edwards, who traced my penciled sketches, adding beautiful faces to complete the illustrations, and who willingly resketched art pieces to meet my expectations.

■ Annette Taylor, who took time from the writing of her own book, *Discover Illustrating Fashion—The Annette Taylor Method,* to review and make helpful suggestions for the improvement of the fashion sketches in this book.

■ all the reviewers, for their helpful suggestions: Vivyanne Thomas, Woodbury University; Phyllis R. Brodsky, Fashion Institute of Technology; Gerald F. Smith, Miami-Dade Community College; Jo Wilson, Mesa Community College; Michelle A. Morganosky, University of Illinois-Urbana; Nora M. MacDonald, West Virginia University; Peyton Hudson, North Carolina State University; and especially Vivian Ray Tellefsen, The Fashion Institute of Design and Merchandising, who spent hours going over the manuscript with me and making suggestions that strengthened the text.

■ Jeanne Rea, for graciously allowing me to modify her method for developing the stretchy knit pattern for use in the text.

■ Jack Fingerman, a noted designer and production patternmaker, for his insight and suggestions for the jacket foundation and interconstruction development.

■ Samuel Schelter and Henry Heller of Catalina Swimwear, who took time to answer all my questions concerning swimwear and knits.

■ Joe and Nicky Wislocky, who worked out certain mathematical calculations on the computer, saving me countless hours of work.

■ Ron and Pat Hart of Harts' Letter Shop, for allowing me to use the photocopying machines at all hours when I needed to meet my deadlines.

■ Linda Melin, who worked with me on testing and retesting the bodice draft, and for researching the history of pants.

■ Kay Cleverly, whose encouragement and good will helped me to forge ahead.

■ my husband Chip and my son Vincent, for their patience and understanding at the times when they counted the most.

■ the countless students over the past sixteen years, who have found, as I have, the thrill and excitement of exploring the wonderful world of patterns.

I wish to say thanks to Gerber Camsco, Inc., Lance Kluger of Ben Kluger & Associates, Inc. (Pellon®), QST Industries, Inc., and Dario Grad-O-Meter, for allowing me to use them as references. I also extend thanks to Sharon Tate for the use of several photographs from her book, *Inside Fashion Design, Second Edition,* published by Harper & Row.

Last, but not least, my thanks to Fred Henry, for allowing me creative freedom and control over the direction of the text; Gayle Jaeger, for applying her creative expertise to the design of the text; and Nicole St. John, Donna DeBenedictis, Rhonda Roth, and many others at Harper & Row, for helping to make *Patternmaking for Fashion Design* a beautiful presentation.

HELEN JOSEPH ARMSTRONG

___ *part* One

DEVELOPMENT OF THE BASIC PATTERNS

1

THE WORKROOM

PATTERNMAKING TOOLS 4
Tool chart 1 4
Tool chart 2 5
Tool chart 3 6
THE INDUSTRIAL FORM 7
PATTERN PAPER 9
IX granite tag (.007) to 5X granite tag (.019) 9
1 to 5 double-duty marking paper 9
WORKROOM TERMS AND DEFINITIONS 9
Landmarks 8
Reference areas 8
Patternmaking terms 9
Balance line terms 12
Fabric terms 14
Pattern production terms 15
The cost sheet 18
The pattern chart 19
COMPLETING THE PATTERN 20
Notches 20
Punch/circles 20
Slits 20
Jog seams 20
Seam allowance 20
Pattern grainline 22
Completing darts 23
Dart shape at pattern's edge 24
Shaping dart legs 26
Pattern information 27

PATTERNMAKING TOOLS

To work efficiently, the patternmaker must have the proper tools and supplies. To communicate effectively in the workroom and to minimize errors due to misunderstanding, the patternmaker should know and understand the terminology common to the industry. This chapter is devoted to tools, supplies, and definitions of terms used in the industry in order to simplify the patternmaking process.

    The professional patternmaker arrives on the job with all the tools needed for patternmaking. Each tool is marked with an identity symbol and transported in a carrying case for convenience and protection. Tools can be purchased from apparel supply houses, art stores, department stores, and yardage stores. Some specialized tools, such as the rabbit punch used to punch pattern holes for hanger hooks, are generally supplied by the manufacturer.

TOOL CHART 1

A faint outline of a basic pattern has been included as a visual guide for some of the uses of these tools.

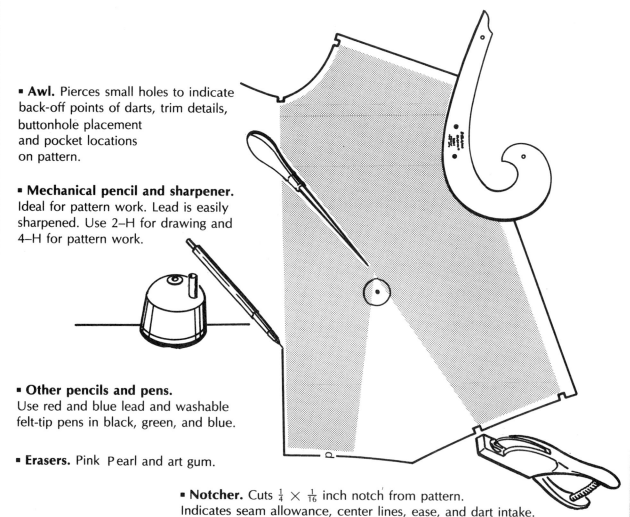

- **French curve.** Deitzgen #17 is one of several curves used for shaping armholes and necklines.

- **Awl.** Pierces small holes to indicate back-off points of darts, trim details, buttonhole placement and pocket locations on pattern.

- **Mechanical pencil and sharpener.** Ideal for pattern work. Lead is easily sharpened. Use 2–H for drawing and 4–H for pattern work.

- **Other pencils and pens.** Use red and blue lead and washable felt-tip pens in black, green, and blue.

- **Erasers.** Pink Pearl and art gum.

- **Notcher.** Cuts $\frac{1}{4} \times \frac{1}{16}$ inch notch from pattern. Indicates seam allowance, center lines, ease, and dart intake.

TOOL CHART 2

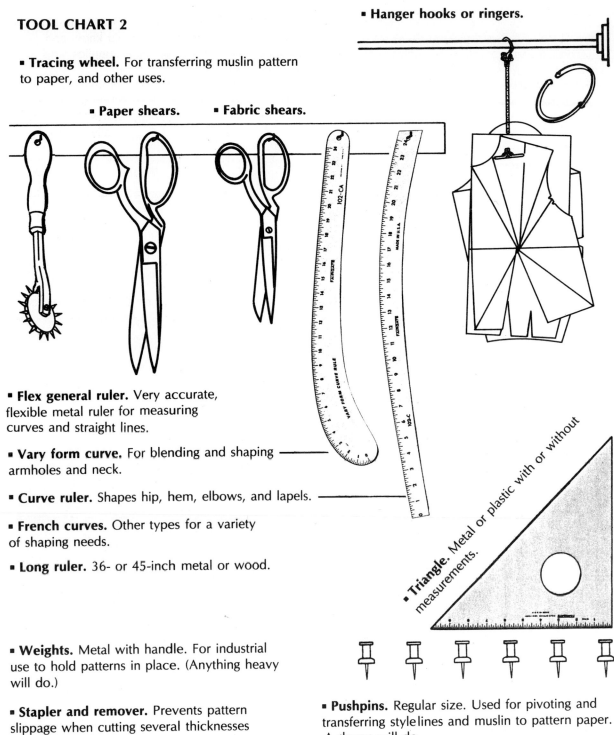

- **Tracing wheel.** For transferring muslin pattern to paper, and other uses.

- **Hanger hooks or ringers.**

- **Paper shears.** - **Fabric shears.**

- **Flex general ruler.** Very accurate, flexible metal ruler for measuring curves and straight lines.

- **Vary form curve.** For blending and shaping armholes and neck.

- **Curve ruler.** Shapes hip, hem, elbows, and lapels.

- **French curves.** Other types for a variety of shaping needs.

- **Long ruler.** 36- or 45-inch metal or wood.

- **Triangle.** Metal or plastic with or without measurements.

- **Weights.** Metal with handle. For industrial use to hold patterns in place. (Anything heavy will do.)

- **Stapler and remover.** Prevents pattern slippage when cutting several thicknesses of paper.

- **Hand punch.** Punches holes for ringers.

- **Tailor's chalk.** Black, white, and yellow, used for marking fabric (wax or chalk).

- **Tracing paper.** Transfer muslin pattern shapes.

- **Pushpins.** Regular size. Used for pivoting and transferring style lines and muslin to pattern paper. A dozen will do.

- **Cutting board.** (For cutting and a base for pushpins.)

- **Straight pins.** Dressmaker silk #17 for draping and fittings.

- **Pin cushion.** For wrist or table.

TOOL CHART 3

▪ **Tailor's square.** A 24 × 14 inch metal ruler with two arms that form a 90° angle and a scale on back side. It simultaneously measures, rules, and squares. To find a 45° angle, mark outside and inside corners. Extend line through corners.
▪ **Squaring a line.** Draw a straight line, label A–B. With arm of square *exactly* on A–B line and corner touching A, extend A to C to form 90° angle. Careless placement will cause draft to be off-balance, resulting in fitting problems.

▪ **Puzzle:** Ten squared lines complete the bodice draft. Can you find them?

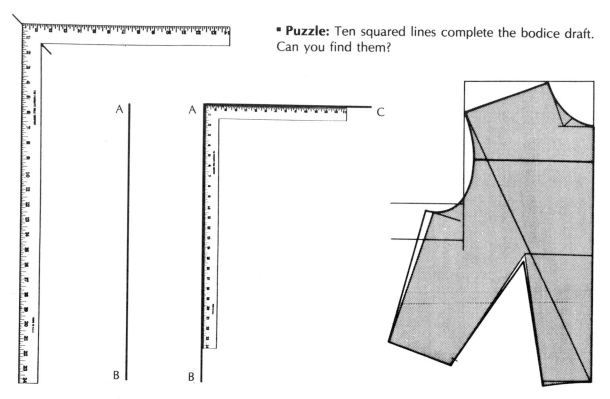

▪ **Plastic ruler.** 2 × 18 inch transparent ruler. Used for drawing straight or bias lines. Flexible enough to measure curves.

▪ **Circle template.** For drawing circles to represent buttonhole placement on patterns.

▪ **Masking tape.** For mending patterns and as a base for marking figure.

▪ **Compass.** For drawing circles and arcs.

▪ **Elastic.** $\frac{1}{4}$-inch width. Used for defining waistline and armhole. 36-inch length is adequate.

▪ **Measuring tape.** Metal-tipped, linen, or plastic. For measuring form or figure. Somewhat inaccurate.

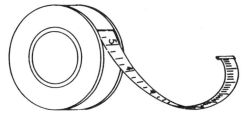

▪ **Metal tape.** $\frac{1}{4}$-inch-wide ruler in a dispenser. Convenient and flexible for measuring form or figure. Very accurate tool.

THE INDUSTRIAL FORM

During the past 140 years, industrial forms have undergone many evolutionary changes in an effort to keep pace with the changing fashion trends and silhouettes. The original forms were shapeless, willow-caned, woven mounds that were padded to individual specifications. The more recent forms are made of metal, canvas, and handmolded papier-mâché, with collapsible shoulders and armplates that allow the garment to be slipped freely over the form. Special features can be incorporated on the form upon request, such as both a right and left detachable arm. Each year the forms are altered to reflect the current fashion silhouette.

Forms come in a wide variety of styles and size ranges, including half sizes. In addition to size, form companies make forms for type of garment desired (dresses, evening, sportswear, bifurcates, skirts, children's, men's and boys', and so on), and miniature forms that are exact replicas in one-half proportions of a regular form. Other types of forms for the home sewer can be purchased in department and yardage stores.

These forms represent a composite figure type that is accepted as the standard ideal of the human torso. They serve many purposes:

- For pattern drafting and draping
- For reference measurements
- For fitting sample garments and establishing hemlines

The patternmaker should be able to identify all key landmarks. They are the *same* on the form, the figure, and the pattern.

FORM AND FIGURE COMPARISON

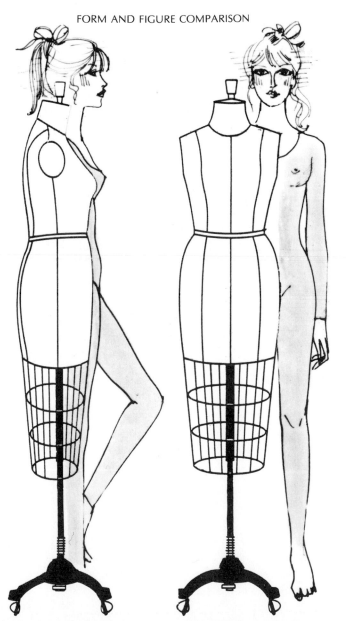

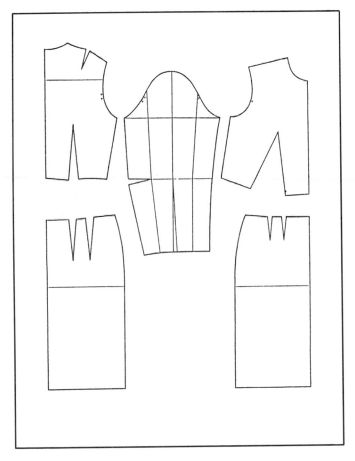

LANDMARKS

Numbers refer to both the front and back wherever indicated. Included is a symbol key.

1. Center front neck
   Center back neck
2. Center front waist
   Center back waist
3. Bust points
4. Center front bust level
   (between bust points—broken line)
5. Side front (Princess)
   Side back (Princess)
6. Mid-armhole front
   Mid-armhole back
7. Shoulder tip
8. Shoulder at neck
9. Armhole ridge or roll line
   (indicated by dotted line)
10. Plate screw
11. Armhole plate

Symbol key

- CF = Center front
- CB = Center back
- BP = Bust point
- SS = Side seam
- SW = Side waist
- SH = Shoulder
- HBL = Horizontal Balance Line

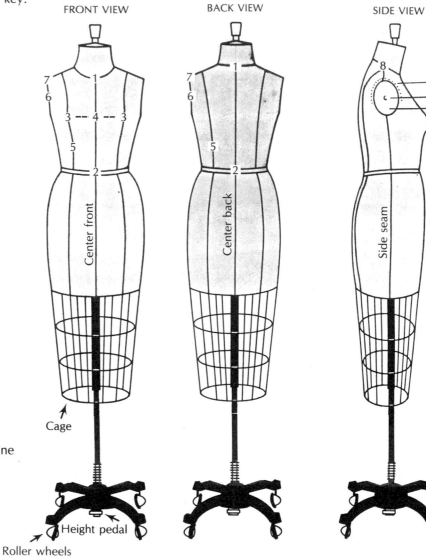

FRONT VIEW BACK VIEW SIDE VIEW

Center front

Center back

Side seam

Cage

Height pedal

Roller wheels

REFERENCE AREAS

Reference areas are indicated on forms with slash lines.

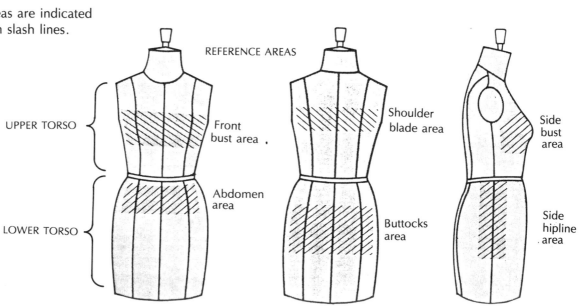

REFERENCE AREAS

UPPER TORSO

LOWER TORSO

Front bust area

Abdomen area

Shoulder blade area

Buttocks area

Side bust area

Side hipline area

PATTERN PAPER

Pattern paper comes in a variety of weights and colors, each serving a special purpose. Each paper supplier uses a code system to indicate the range of paper weights available. The manufacturer's preference is based on personal choice and the use to which it is put. The heavy pattern papers are commonly referred to as *tag board, manila,* or *hard paper,* whereas the lighter weights are called *marking paper.* Their proper coding and common usage are as follows:

IX GRANITE TAG (.007) to 5X GRANITE TAG (.019)

This heavy pattern paper can be purchased in a color-coded series; for example, green on one side and white on the other. This has several advantages. It indicates at a glance the working surface of the pattern. Companies with several divisions can color code the pattern to indicate to which division it belongs. This type of paper is usually used for the *first* pattern, and always used for the *production pattern* (the final pattern, made after the fit of the garment has been perfected and the first pattern corrected), and for *pattern grading* (developing size ranges).

1 TO 5 DOUBLE-DUTY MARKING PAPER

This light to heavy white marking paper is used for developing first patterns and for making markers (precise pattern layouts). It contains symbols as an aid for establishing true grainlines.

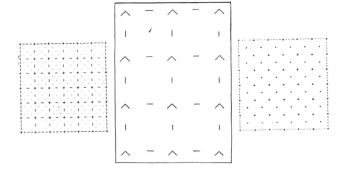

WORKROOM TERMS AND DEFINITIONS

Terms and definitions relate to the form, figure, patterns, paper, fabric, and the interrelationship among them.

PATTERNMAKING TERMS

Pattern drafting. A system of patternmaking that depends on a series of form or figure measurements to complete the paper pattern.

Pattern draping. A two-dimensional piece of fabric draped around a form or figure conforming to its shape (or arranged artistically in folds for a specific design), creating a three-dimensional fabric pattern. This muslin pattern is transferred to paper to be used for corrections and a final pattern.

Basic pattern set. A 5-piece pattern set, consisting of a front/back bodice and skirt, and a long sleeve, which represents the dimensions of a specific form or figure. It is developed without design features. It is always traced for pattern development requiring slashing and spreading, with the traced copy referred to as a *working pattern*.

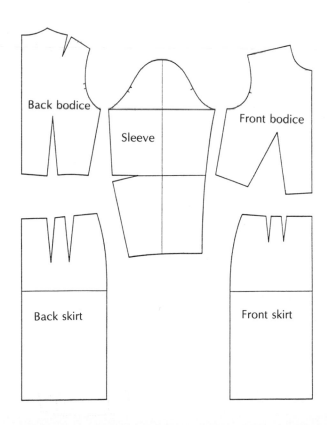

Back bodice

Sleeve

Front bodice

Back skirt

Front skirt

Landmarks. Designated points around the body that correspond with those on the form that are used for measuring the body sections when drafting and draping.

Dot mark. A pencil mark indicating a specific point on the pattern or muslin. A series of dot marks are connected to outline a shape or line on the pattern or muslin.

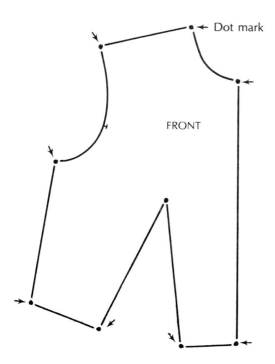

← Dot mark

FRONT

Pin marking. Placing pins through the muslin or form in a series to evaluate styleline placement.

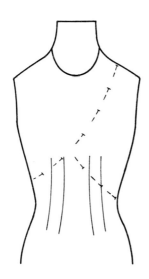

Trueing. The blending and straightening of pencil lines, crossmarks, and dot marks for the purpose of establishing correct seam lengths; example, trueing side seam having a side dart. (Trueing includes blending.)

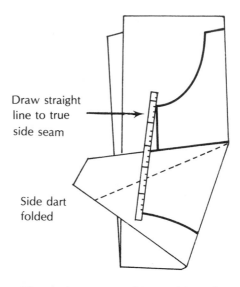

Draw straight line to true side seam →

Side dart folded

Blend. A process of smoothing, shaping, and rounding of angular lines along a seam for a smooth transition from one point to the next and for equalizing the discrepancies of joining lines and marks made on the pattern or muslin. (Blending includes trueing.)

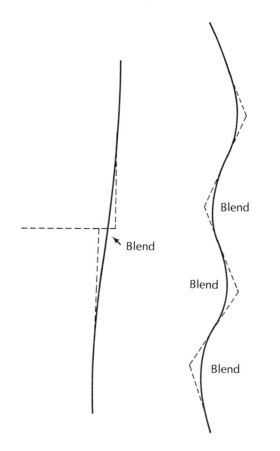

Blend

Blend

Blend

Blend

Bust point. A designated place on the bust and pattern.

Apex. The highest location of a mound (also referred to in flat patternmaking as the pivotal point).

Dart. A wedge-shape cutout in a pattern used as a means of controlling the fit of the garment.

Dart legs. Two lines forming an open space at the pattern's outline that converge at a predetermined point on the pattern (creating a wedge shape).

Dart intake. Amount of excess (or space) confined between dart legs to control the fit of the garment.

Double-ended dart. A long dart passing through the waist of a garment without a waistline seam. The dart intake is controlled by two punches and circles placed at the center fold at waist level and $\frac{1}{8}$ inch from one side of the dart leg, and $\frac{1}{4}$ to $\frac{1}{2}$ inch below and above point of dart at each end.

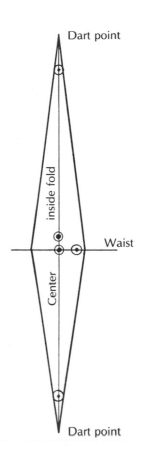

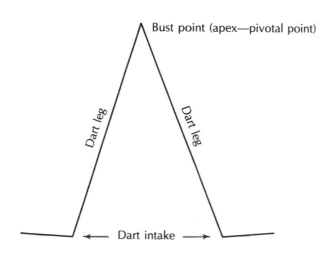

Dart point. The end of a dart.

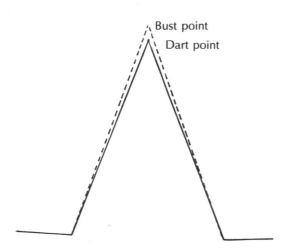

Uprighting a dart. Shifting the dart point so it is in line with the center of the dart legs.

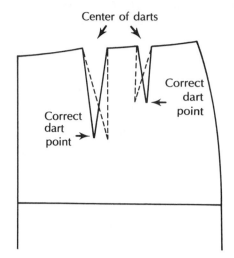

Center of darts

Correct dart point

Correct dart point

Additional dart information. Can be found on pages 23 through 26, and Part Two of this text, where information is applied to the pattern design.

Cupping the pattern. To cup a pattern, crease-fold one dart leg to dart point, then fold it over to meet the other leg. This will cause a bulge to form in the pattern. The purpose for cupping the pattern is to true dart legs and to establish the seamline shape of the dart at the pattern's edge.

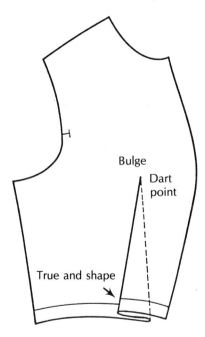

Bulge

Dart point

True and shape

Ease. The measurement added to the pattern's outline for comfort and freedom of movement. It is the even distribution of fullness without forming gathers.

Template. Patterns one-fourth or one-half the size of a regular pattern. Templates are used for patternmaking projects (at the back of the text).

To trace. To make a pencil outline of a pattern as a duplicate for pattern development or for completing a pattern.

Test fit. A muslin garment cut from a first pattern that includes the horizontal balance lines (HBL) and grainlines drawn as a guide for perfecting the fit.

BALANCE LINE TERMS

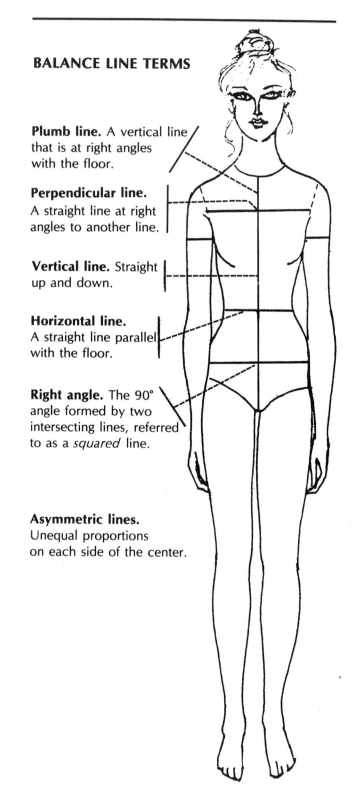

Plumb line. A vertical line that is at right angles with the floor.

Perpendicular line. A straight line at right angles to another line.

Vertical line. Straight up and down.

Horizontal line. A straight line parallel with the floor.

Right angle. The 90° angle formed by two intersecting lines, referred to as a *squared* line.

Asymmetric lines. Unequal proportions on each side of the center.

Balance. The perfect relationship between parts that when combined form a unit (or whole) in which each part is in exact proportion and harmony with all others.

Balancing a pattern. Finding and adjusting the differences between adjoining pattern parts to improve the hang of the garment.

The horizontal balance line (HBL). Fixed straight lines on given areas of the figure or form that are parallel with the floor. These lines on the pattern should correspond with those on the figure or form to balance the garment and have it hang well (Figure 1). If they do not correspond, the garment will be out-of-balance and will not hang well on the figure (Figure 2). The HBL controls the fit on standard figures or figures with asymmetric shoulders and/or hiplines (Figure 3).

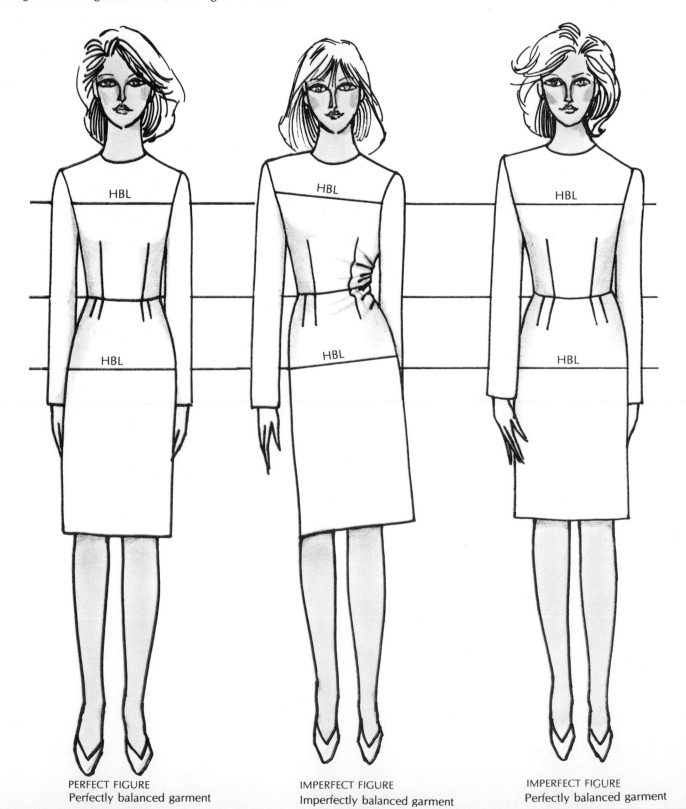

PERFECT FIGURE
Perfectly balanced garment

FIGURE 1

IMPERFECT FIGURE
Imperfectly balanced garment

FIGURE 2

IMPERFECT FIGURE
Perfectly balanced garment

FIGURE 3

FABRIC TERMS

Grain. The direction in which the yarn is woven or knit (lengthwise grain or warp, crosswise grain or weft).

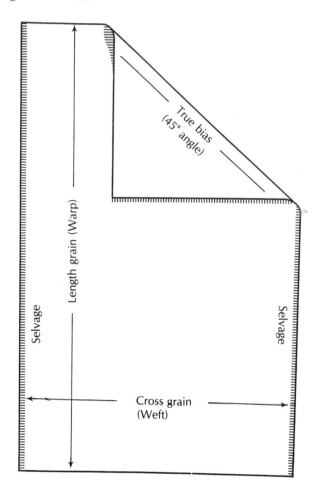

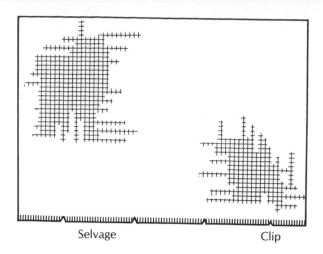

Selvage   Clip

Bias. A slanting or diagonal line cut or sewn across the weave of the cloth.

True bias (45° angle). The angle line that intersects with the length and cross grains at a 45° angle. True bias has a maximum give and stretchability, easily conforming to the figure's contours. Flares, cowls, and drapes work best when cut on true bias.

Muslin. A plain-woven fabric made from bleached or unbleached corded yarns in a variety of weights:
- *Coarse weave:* used for draping and testing basic patterns
- *Light weight:* used for softly draped garments
- *Heavy weight:* firmly woven—used for testing tailored garments, coats, and suits.

Below is an example of muslin folded on straight and crosswise grain.

Length grain (warp). Yarns parallel with the selvage and at right angles to the cross grain. This is the strongest grain and drapes best when perpendicular to the floor.

Cross grain (weft). Yarns woven across the fabric from selvage to selvage. It is the filling yarn of woven fabrics. Cross grain yields to tension.

Selvage. The narrow, firmly woven, and finished edge on both length grain sides of the woven fabric. Clip selvage to release tension.

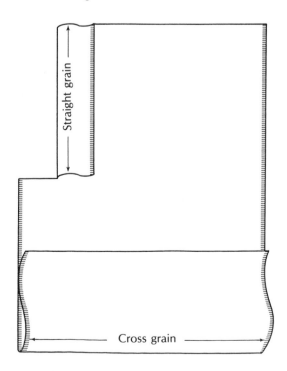

Bowing. Off-grain fabric caused by yarns that are not at true right angles with each other. To straighten for grainline accuracy, stretch the fabric diagonally from opposite ends until the yarns are at right angles to each other. Fabrics such as taffeta or those with a permanent finish cannot be adjusted.

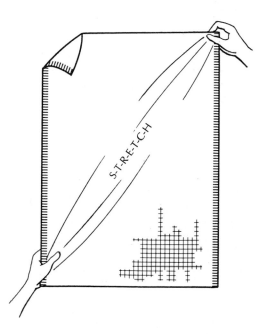

Finding the grainlines. This process can be accomplished by pulling a thread, then cutting along pulled space, or by tearing the fabric along the grainline. The fabric then can be stretched until the grains are at right angles to each other.

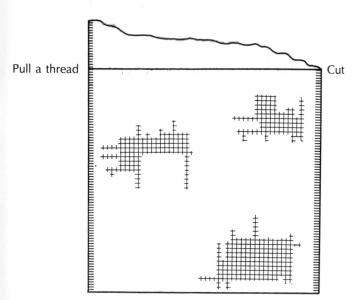

PATTERN PRODUCTION TERMS

First patterns. The original pattern developed for each design. This pattern is generally made out of marking paper and usually requires some adjustments. Unless the design is asymmetrical, only half a pattern is developed. After all corrections are complete a full production pattern is then made on granite tag paper.

Production pattern. The production pattern is a pattern set that has been test-fit, corrected, and perfected, and contains every pattern piece required to complete the garment. It is used by the grader for grading sizes within a given size range, and by the marker maker for a fabric layout. A pattern chart is placed in front of the set (see page 19).

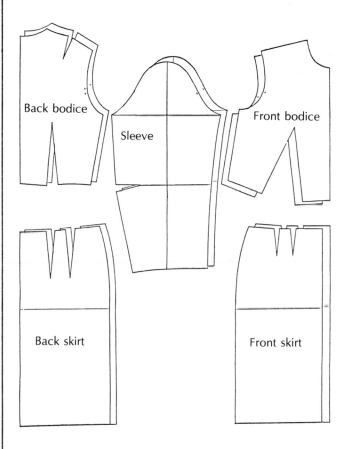

Pattern grading. Proportionately increasing or decreasing the size and shape of an original pattern within a given size range (referred to as the *pattern grade*). This is done in length, circumference, and width. Patterns are graded with the use of a grading machine, a computer, or a grading ruler, which is convenient in a design room or classroom. To purchase the grading ruler and grading text, contact Eleanor Davis, 1128 Lafayette St., San Gabriel, California 91776.

GRADING MACHINE

COMPUTER GRADING MACHINE

HINGED GRADING RULER

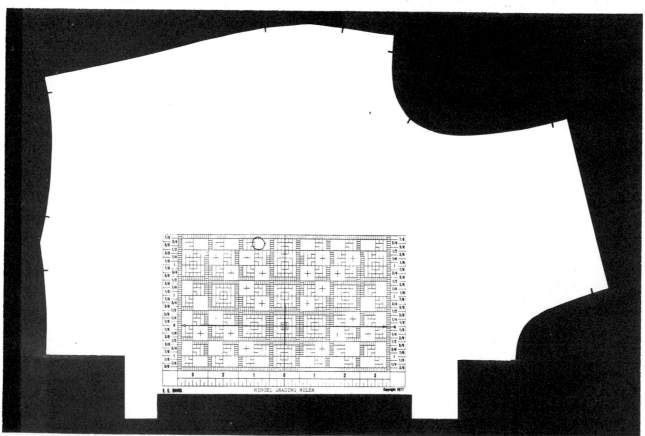

Pattern marker. A marker is a length of paper containing a copy of all pattern pieces to be cut at one time. All pattern symbols (punch marks, circles, and notches) must be indicated on the pattern, and all patterns must be interlocked and aligned on the marker paper so that when cut the grainlines will be parallel to the selvage of the fabric. *Exception:* Facings and small pieces are sometimes placed off grain to save yardage. The completed marker is placed on top of layers of fabric as a guide for the cutter. There are three methods for making markers:

▪ A pattern marker maker traces each pattern on marker paper.

▪ Patterns are photographed (photo marking) on paper as a conveyor belt carries the patterns under a photo machine.

▪ A computer with miniaturized copies of the original pattern used in the lay-up process houses the information in its memory bank until needed.

Pattern cutter. After the marker is made and laid on top of the layers of fabric, the garments are cut by the cutter or by a computer cutting machine.

PATTERN MARKER

CUTTING MACHINE

COMPUTER CUTTING MACHINE

THE COST SHEET

A cost sheet is a complete record of each design manufactured. Its purpose is for *costing* the garment and establishing the wholesale price. The top part of the form (Items 1 and 2) is filled out in the design room as completely as required. It should include the names and telephone numbers of salesmen and fabric and trim companies, as well as fabric swatches, a sketch, and special pattern information or instructions.

The original copy is for the manufacturer or production person who completes the lower part (items 3 and 4) and marks yardage. A duplicate is kept in the design room for quick reference. This provides the manufacturer with information required for his use and makes for fewer interruptions in the design department.

DATE	6-8-85	STYLE No.	#5102
DESCRIPTION	Sport Jacket, Netting Inlay	SEASON	Fall '85
		SELLING PRICE	40.95

SIZE RANGE **6/18** COLORS **Periwinkle — Fushia**

MARKERS /

MARKER YARDAGE: _____ ALLOWANCE: _____

1. MATERIAL	YARDS	PRICE	AMT
100% Cotton 60" White Sheeting	1¼	2.50	350
100% Cotton 60" White Netting	¼	6.00	2.00
Lining M.L. Tubing			
TOTAL MATERIAL COST			5.50

2. TRIMMINGS	QUANT	PRICE	AMT
Buttons			
Pads 1 pc 2 ply	1	1.20	1.20
Embroidery (Maldin Pads #716-9777 Mr. Sinke)			
Belts			
Zippers			
Pleating, Tucking			
D-Rings	6	.10	.60
Jumbo Snaps	5	30	1.50
Belt	1	1.00	1.00
Bias trim ½	2	50	1.00
⅝" Bias trim	¾	.50	40
TOTAL TRIMMINGS COST			5.70

3. LABOR			
2 hrs			8.00
Cutting 200 count			50
Labor outside work			
Dying			1.00
Bias			.10
Payroll Taxes & Health Fund			50
Trucking			
TOTAL LABOR COST			10.10

4. TOTAL COST			21.30

REMARKS

SKETCH

MATERIAL SWATCH

THE PATTERN CHART

The pattern chart is a complete record of all pattern pieces within the pattern set, and also includes swatches, sketch, and special pattern information. Each pattern shape is identified as to name and number of pieces to be cut. A color code is used to distinguish linings and interlinings from other pattern pieces. When completed, the chart is placed in front of the production pattern (see illustration) and given to the production manager.

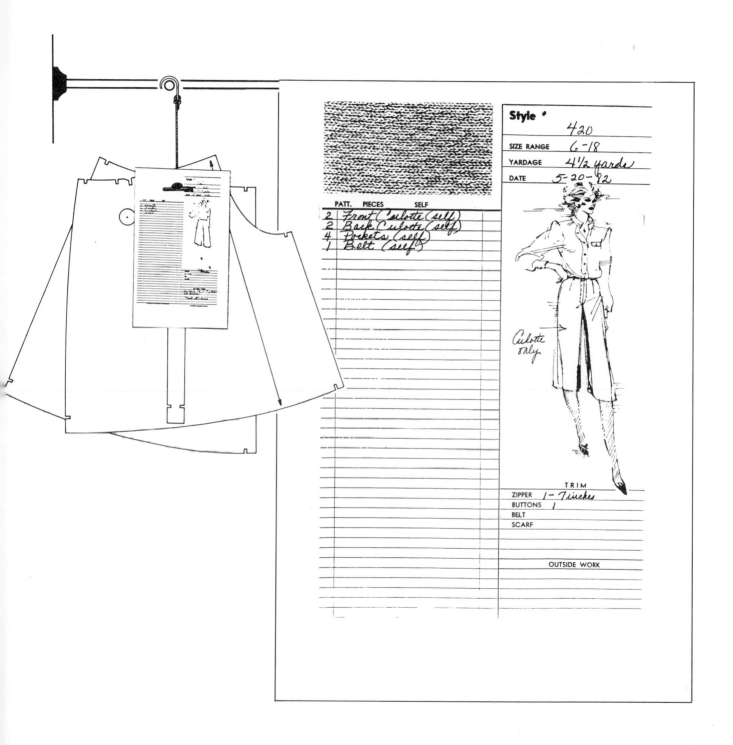

PATT.	PIECES	SELF
2	Front Culotte (self)	
2	Back Culotte (self)	
4	Pockets (self)	
1	Belt (self)	

Style # 420
SIZE RANGE 6-18
YARDAGE 4½ yards
DATE 5-20-82

Culotte only

TRIM
ZIPPER 1 - 7 inches
BUTTONS 1
BELT
SCARF

OUTSIDE WORK

COMPLETING THE PATTERN

Workroom information provided below is general information required to complete all patterns and is placed here for easy reference. This information will not be repeated in other sections and will be referred to only as *complete the pattern.* This will allow a full concentration and emphasis on the information and principles pertinent to each chapter without unnecessary repetition. The patternmaker should use the appropriate information when needed.

Patternmaking symbols, such as notches, punches, and circles, are the silent language used by the designer, patternmaker, grader, marker maker, and seamstress with regard to the pattern and garment. Missing or misplaced symbols disrupt the flow of production, costing time and money. Following are general uses for symbols. Where differences exist, the patternmaker should defer to the company's preference for method of indicating symbols.

NOTCHES

The notch symbol is illustrated on technical illustrations as it will actually appear on a pattern (Figures 1 and 2). In the text the notch is illustrated as a straight line (squared in from the pattern's edge) with a crossbar at the end. Notch placement varies but is generally placed to indicate the following:
- Seam allowances
- Center lines
- Ease and gather control
- Dart legs
- Identify front (1 notch) and back (2 notches)
- Identify joining parts (series of notches at various locations) (Figure 3)
- Zipper placement
- Foldback (facings)
- Hemlines
- Waistline (sheath)
- Inward curves (to release tension)
- Shoulder tip location for extended shoulders

PUNCH/CIRCLES

- Dart intake
- Dart back-off points
- Dart curves
- Corners
- Buttonholes/buttons
- Trimmings
- Pocket placement

SLITS

Slits are used for placket insertions or to indicate inside corners.
- Placket openings—$\frac{1}{16}$ inch wide. Fold pattern, notch a crossbar to indicate end and slit (Figure 1).
- Inside corners (Figure 2, point *X*).

JOG SEAMS

A jog seam is used to indicate a temporary change in the seam allowance. For example, side seam may be $\frac{3}{4}$ inch jogging to $\frac{1}{2}$ inch under the arm (Figure 1).

SEAM ALLOWANCE

Seam allowances vary with each company. The following information is general:
$\frac{1}{4}$ **inch**
- All faced areas
- Narrow spacing
- Extreme curves
- Sleeveless armholes
$\frac{1}{2}$ **inch**
- Side seams
- Armholes
- Waistlines
- Center lines
- Stylelines
Variable ($\frac{1}{2}$ to $1\frac{1}{4}$ inches)
- Placket or zipper openings
- Top-stitched seams
- Side seams

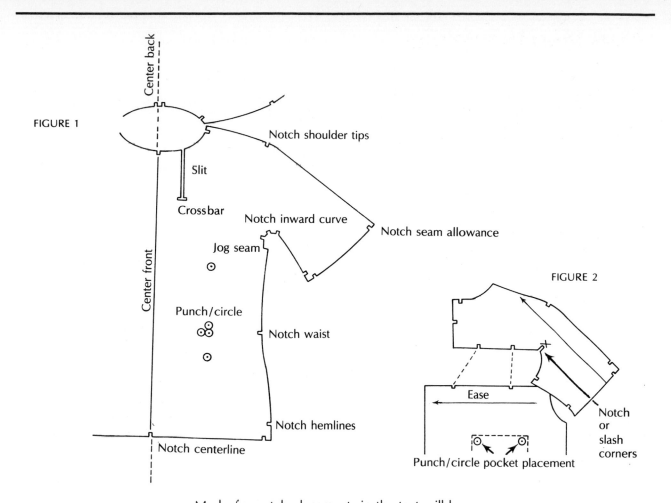

FIGURE 1

Center back

Notch shoulder tips

Slit

Crossbar

Notch inward curve

Notch seam allowance

Center front

Jog seam

Punch/circle

Notch waist

Notch hemlines

Notch centerline

FIGURE 2

Ease

Punch/circle pocket placement

Notch or slash corners

Marks for notch placements in the text will be illustrated as lines to seams (Figures 3 and 4), or as shown in Figure 5.

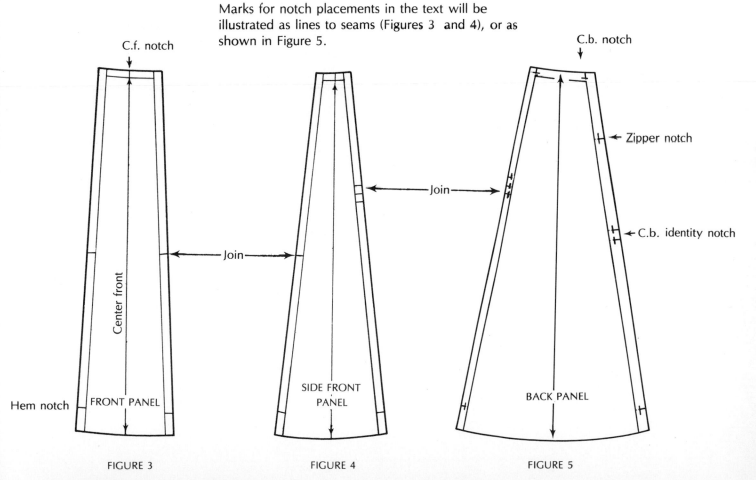

C.f. notch

Center front

Hem notch

FRONT PANEL

FIGURE 3

Join

SIDE FRONT PANEL

FIGURE 4

Join

C.b. notch

Zipper notch

C.b. identity notch

BACK PANEL

FIGURE 5

PATTERN GRAINLINE

The pattern grainline is a line drawn on each pattern piece (from end to end) to indicate the direction in which the pattern is to be placed on the grain of the fabric relative to the selvage edge. Pattern placement is illustrated in Figure 1. The effect of grainline on garments is shown in Figures 2, 3, and 4.

Direction of grainline

- Vertical grainline is drawn parallel with center line for garments to be cut on straight grain (Figure 2).
- Bias grainline is drawn at an angle with center line (45° angle for true bias) for garments to be cut on the bias (Figure 3).
- Horizontal grainline is drawn at right angles to the center line for garments to be cut on crosswise grain (Figure 4).

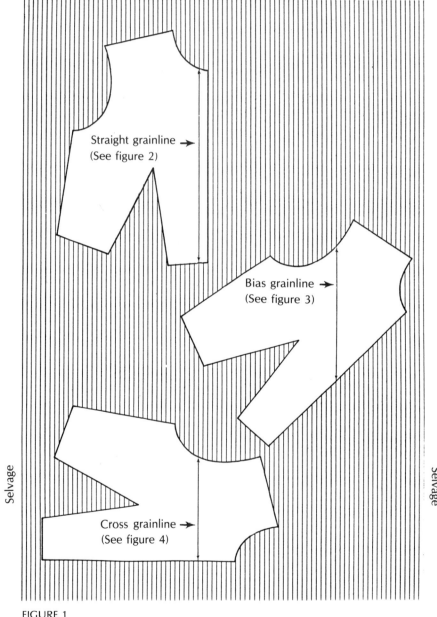

Straight grainline →
(See figure 2)

Bias grainline →
(See figure 3)

Cross grainline →
(See figure 4)

Selvage

Selvage

FIGURE 1

VERTICAL GRAIN

FIGURE 2

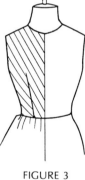

BIAS GRAIN

FIGURE 3

CROSS GRAIN

FIGURE 4

Grainline arrows

- Grainline with arrows at both ends indicates that the top of the pattern may be placed either up or down on the fabric.
- Grainline with arrow at the top *or* the bottom indicates that the pattern must be placed in one direction only.

COMPLETING DARTS

Dart points

All darts radiate from the highest part (apex) of a mound. The mounds of a figure are rounded, not pointed. If a dart is stitched to its apex (highest point), it would cause strain around the mound area (most noticeable on the bust mound). By ending the dart before it reaches the apex (such as the bust point), additional fabric is released to accommodate the rounded mound shape of the bust (or any other mound). Broken lines indicate released fabric.

Front bodice darts

FIGURE 1 *Single dart pattern:*
- *Dart point:* approximately $\frac{1}{2}$ inch from bust point (a greater distance if bust mound exceeds B-cup).

FIGURE 2 *Two-dart pattern:*
- *Waist dart:* 1 to $1\frac{1}{2}$ inches from bust point.
    Other darts (side, shoulder, or any other location): marked 1 to 2 inches from bust point.

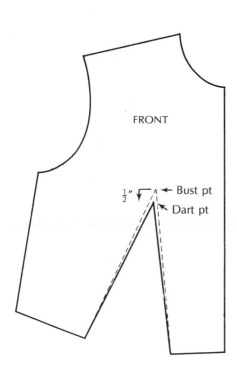

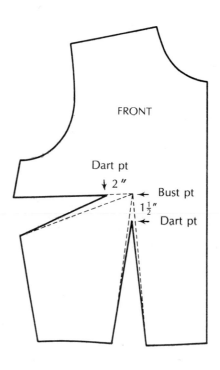

Direction of dart excess

Dart legs may be cut to within the seam allowance (e.g., $\frac{1}{2}$ inch with excess cut away) or folded. The center, or inside, fold of folded darts or seams of cut-out darts will lie toward the center front or center back when placed along the shoulder, waist, or neckline. When placed at armhole, center front, center back, and side seams, the dart excess is directed toward waistline (downward). Darts placed at the corners of a pattern (shoulder tip, shoulder at neck, sidewaist and center front waist) can be folded in either direction.

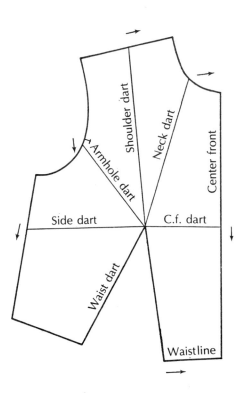

FIGURE 2
▪ Cup the pattern using the corner of the table.
▪ Fold dart leg over to meet the other dart leg. Crease and remove pattern. (Do not flatten pattern after it is cupped.)

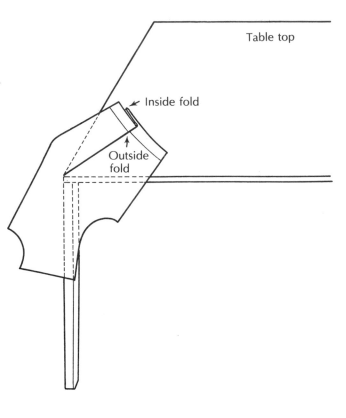

FIGURE 3
▪ With a tracing wheel, trace seamline, transferring seam shape to dart excess underneath. Pencil in perforated lines.

DART SHAPE AT PATTERN'S EDGE

Three methods for shaping the darts are shown:

Cupping the pattern   (Method 1)

FIGURE 1
▪ Crease-fold dart leg to bust point.

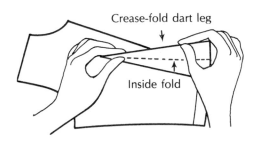

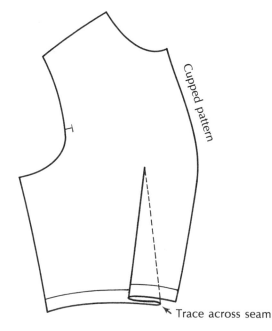

Pencil marking   (Method 2)

FIGURE 1
- Label dart point *X*.
- Draw a guideline in center of dart leg. Label *Y*.
- Measure from dart leg to Y. Record.

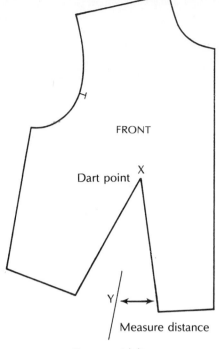

FIGURE 2
- Determine the direction the excess will lay: Using above measurement, mark a point out from dart leg. Label *Z*. Measure the distance from *X* to *Z*. Record.

FIGURE 3
- $X - Y = X - Z$. Mark and connect to dart legs.

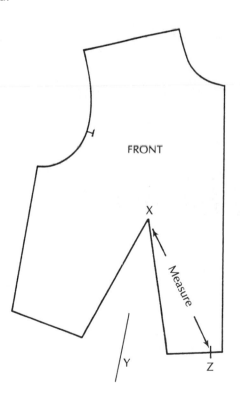

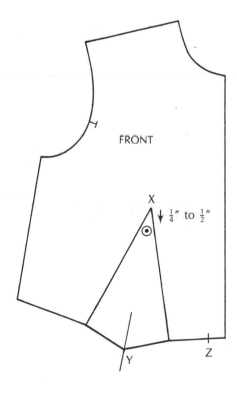

Punch and circle $\frac{1}{4}$ to $\frac{1}{2}$ inch below dart point for stitching guide.

Tissue copy of dart area   (Method 3)

FIGURE 1

▪ Trace dart and part of waist on transparent paper (shaded area).

▪ Remove paper and fold dart using method 1 as a guide.

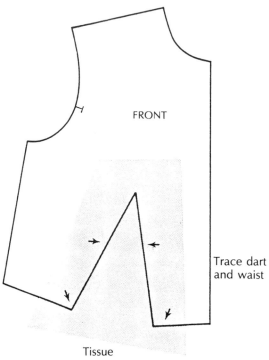

FRONT

Trace dart
and waist

Tissue

FIGURE 2

▪ Unfold, place over original pattern (shaded area).

▪ With tracing wheel, trace shape of seam edge to pattern underneath.

▪ Remove paper and pencil in perforated lines.

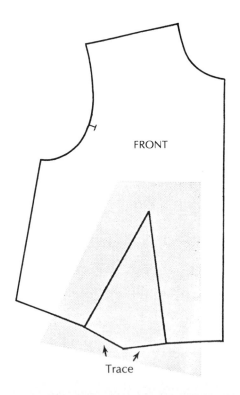

FRONT

Trace

SHAPING DART LEGS

FIGURES 1 and 2

▪ Follow illustration as a guide for shaping darts curving legs to conform to shape of bust and abdomen.

WAIST DART

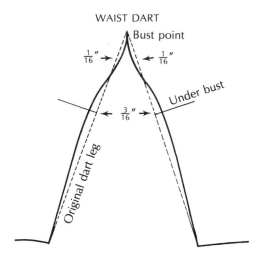

Bust point

$\frac{1}{16}$″ $\frac{1}{16}$″

$\frac{3}{16}$″   Under bust

Original dart leg

DOUBLE-ENDED DART

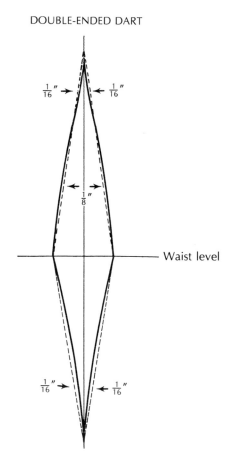

$\frac{1}{16}$″ $\frac{1}{16}$″

$\frac{1}{8}$″

Waist level

$\frac{1}{16}$″ $\frac{1}{16}$″

PATTERN INFORMATION

Using a pencil or felt-tip pen, mark each pattern accurately with sufficient information and symbols to complete the pattern for a test fit or for production. Pattern information should be grouped on the top section of each pattern, face up, where the information can be read quickly. It should be clearly written or printed.

Methods for writing this information, and what information is included, vary from company to company:
▪ Full pattern information (see illustration) can be written face up on one copy of each pattern within the set, with only the style number and grainline on each duplicate shape.
▪ Complete information can be written face up on each pattern shape and its duplicates.
▪ Selective information can be written face up, eliminating words identifying pattern pieces such as front, back, or sleeves.

BODICE SHOWN ON THE OPEN

The following examples may be used as a guide:

Grainline. Always draw grainline through length of each pattern piece.

Pattern part. Identify by name (for example, *front, back, bodice, skirt, sleeve, collar, pocket*).

Style number. Identify number used to code pattern set (for example: 3363).

Pattern size. Give specific size within given size range.

Number of pattern pieces. Identify number of pieces to be cut for each specific pattern shape.

Cut symbol. A horizontal line can be drawn between the size and the number of pieces as a symbol for the word *Cut*, or the word itself may precede the number of pieces (e.g., *Cut two*).

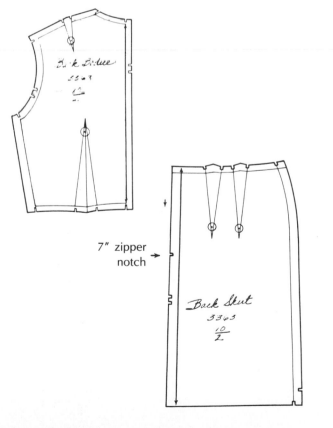

7" zipper notch →

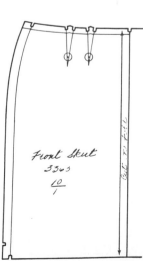

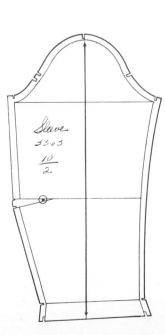

Special information

- Right-side-up (when sides differ)

Instruction applied to patterns for asymmetric designs in which the right side differs from the left side, and for patterns cut on engineered fabric types such as border prints, random-spaced flowers, geometric forms, multiple colors, and other features that repeat at great distances. Such fabrics require special pattern placement on the fabric so that the fabric design features can be arranged in the same location for all garments cut from that fabric. *Right-side-up* (RSUP) indicates to the marker maker that the pattern must be placed face up on the marker to ensure a proper lay on the marker.

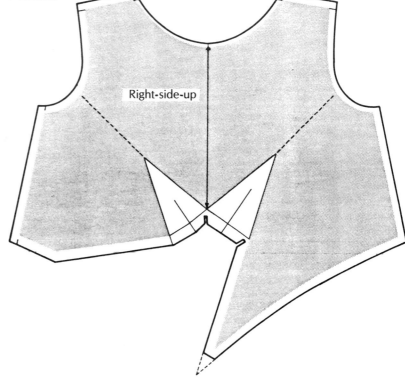

Right-side-up

- Stripe/plaid placement

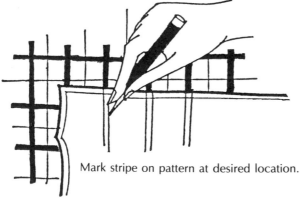

Mark stripe on pattern at desired location.

- Color block differences
- Fabric type
- Any other information special to the pattern set

Facings: For facing instructions, see Chapter 14.

THE ELUSIVE IDEAL 30
Who is this standard ideal figure? 30
Pattern industry standards 31
Department store standards 31
Other attempts at standardization 31
INDIVIDUAL FIGURE ANALYSIS 32
Comparison of individual figure versus standard 33
SUMMARY 41
Body cross-sections 41

2

FIGURE ANALYSIS

THE ELUSIVE IDEAL

WHO IS THIS STANDARD IDEAL FIGURE?

She is an ideal composite figure whose measurement standards are based upon who is listening to whom. She evolved from consumer feedback to buyer, buyer to manufacturer, and manufacturer to industrial form company. Her standards are whatever successful manufacturers, commercial pattern companies, chain and department stores, and industrial form companies say they are. She is a form, she is a figure, she is a set of measurements, and her silhouette changes at the slightest whim of fashion. She is considered "ideal" only when her measurements satisfy a majority of consumers.

Who needs her? Technicians need her dimensions for patternmaking and fittings, designers need her silhouette for creating new designs, manufacturers need her for showings, models need her dimensions for hire, and consumers need her for their representation.

Does this elusive figure have standards? Even though her dimensions vary, she does have standards. She is symmetrical, with an upright stance, and aesthetically pleasing body proportions, with a ratio of 10 to $12\frac{1}{2}$ inch difference among bust, waist, and hips. These standards are based strictly on Western world concepts as to what is ideal. There can never be a universally acceptable standard because of the variety of anatomical figure types. Other countries set their own standards based on their own regional concept of the ideal figure.

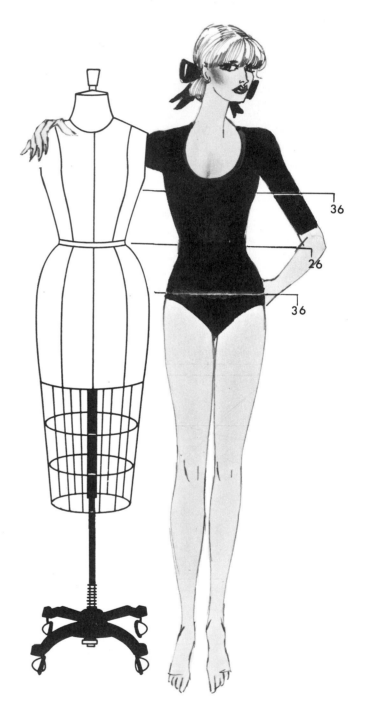

36

26

36

PATTERN INDUSTRY STANDARDS

In response to national standards and consumers' needs, the pattern industry established the Measurement Standard Committee that devised its version of figure types and sizes. The following is a composite of the pattern industry figure types. Specific measurements can be found in the back of pattern books and are not included here as they are periodically revised and updated.

DEPARTMENT STORE STANDARDS

Department stores such as Sears, J. C. Penney, Montgomery Ward, and Spiegel have developed their own strict specifications as to the ideal figure composite in an endeavor to better satisfy the needs of their buying public. Some use National Bureau of Standards' measurements, while others conduct surveys and samplings of the population by such methods as sending survey forms to their consumers requesting their measurements. After this information is compiled, specification sheets are given to the manufacturer to use when developing patterns for that particular store.

OTHER ATTEMPTS AT STANDARDIZATION

Attempts to standardize sizes in America originally began in the late 1800s when manufacturers mass-produced farm labor uniforms in small, medium, and large sizes—which proved less than ideal for those smaller or larger than this size range. The next serious effort was made by the military by their attempt to mass-produce well-fitting uniforms. In 1901, the federal government created the National Bureau of Standards (NBS), a nonregulatory agency for the purpose of standardizing measurements for science and industry. By 1970, NBS had developed complete size ranges based on frequency measurements from large population segments. Periodically, it reissues and updates these standards but can only recommend acceptance. (Write to Superintendent of Documents, U.S. Government Printing Office, Washington, D.C. 20402, to obtain a copy of SD Catalog No. C13.20/42-70, NBS Voluntary Product Standard.) Manufacturers, however, prefer having flexibility to change measurements quickly to suit consumer needs without regard to rigid standards. With world trade increasing, this creates an as yet unsatisfied need for a central data bank that could contain nonwestern regional standards for trading partners. With the age of computer technology, this may ultimately be possible.

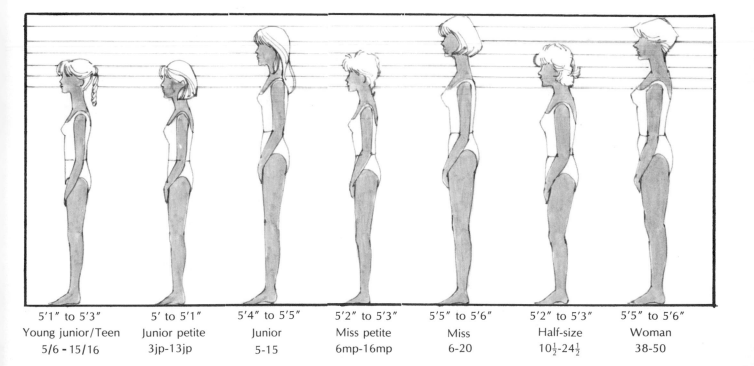

5'1" to 5'3"	5' to 5'1"	5'4" to 5'5"	5'2" to 5'3"	5'5" to 5'6"	5'2" to 5'3"	5'5" to 5'6"
Young junior/Teen	Junior petite	Junior	Miss petite	Miss	Half-size	Woman
5/6 - 15/16	3jp-13jp	5-15	6mp-16mp	6-20	10½-24½	38-50

INDIVIDUAL FIGURE ANALYSIS

An awareness of anatomical differences among humans helps explain why ready-to-wear garments cannot possibly fit all figure types perfectly. It would be impractical and expensive for manufacturers to try to satisfy the needs of those figures who fall outside of the standard range.

The purpose of analyzing your figure is to determine if, and where, your figure deviates from the standard average. The following figure series illustrates body characteristics that cause fitting problems. By selecting body parts that closely resemble yours and recording your findings on your Personal Measurement Chart under Figure Composite, they can be used in the development of your personal basic pattern. As you analyze your figure, draw your body shape, part by part, over the figure outline as a comparison with the standard. If you have figure characteristics not mentioned, record these in the space entitled Other Deviations. If while analyzing your figure you find that it is less than perfect, do not despair. It is the pattern that must be perfect, not your figure.

Preparation. With the help of a friend, analyze your figure using a doorway as a plumb line (for a profile view). For self-evaluation, draw a plumb line through the center of a mirror and view your figure (Figure 1).

Wear your usual foundation garments, or a close-fitting body suit or leotard over the foundations. Tie a string, belt, or elastic around your waist for definition.

Measure your head from the top of the crown to your chin level in preparation for the following series (Figure 2).

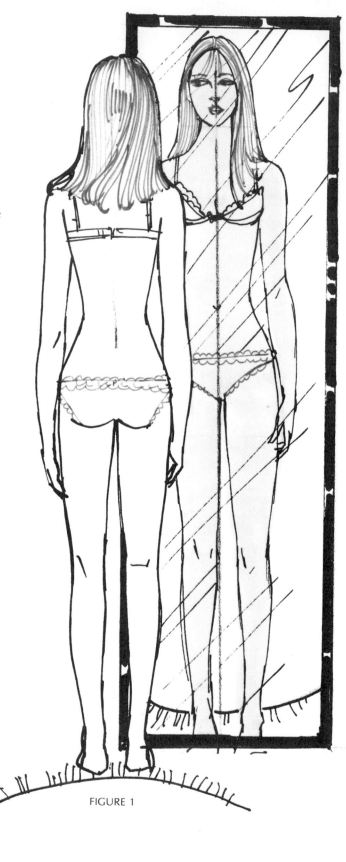

FIGURE 1

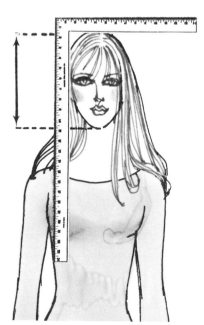

FIGURE 2

COMPARISON OF INDIVIDUAL FIGURE VERSUS STANDARD

Head height. One calculation used to determine figure proportions is the number of times the *head height* can be divided into the full length of the figure. The head count for an adult female by Western world standards is between $7\frac{1}{2}$ to 8 heads, and is used to establish bust points, waist, crotch, and knee level for a standard average figure type (Example: third figure below).

Standard body parts

- *Bust level:* Chin to bust, 1 head
- *Waist level:* Chin to waist, 2 heads
- *Crotch level:* Chin to crotch, 3 heads
- *Knee level:* Chin to mid-knee, $4\frac{1}{2}$ heads

The individual female's proportions are not as predictable between chin and ankle. (Broken lines across chart indicate the bust, waist, hip, and knee locations of each figure type and how they compare with the standard head height locations—third figure.) To find how you compare with the standard, use your head measurement to chart your personal figure composite. Place tape at chin and measure to bust point, waist, crotch, and knee bone. If the tape ends above or extends below the noted reference line by more than $\frac{1}{4}$ inch, record a minus or plus on your Personal/Model Measurement Chart under Personal Figure Composite and label high or low bust, waist, hips, and knee.

Note: Suppose "Miss Average" with perfect proportions has a 14-inch circumference difference between bust and waist, and waist and hips, and the other three figure types pictured have a super ideal 10-inch difference among bust, waist, and hips. Which do you consider more ideal?

(Chin level)

1 head
(Bust level)

2 heads
(Waist level)

3 heads
(Crotch level)

$4\frac{1}{2}$ heads
(knee bone)

Floor

Hip types
- *Ideal:* Curves outward gradually from waist and rounds over hip bone.
- *Heart-shape:* Curves outward abruptly from waist and rounds sharply inward to hips.
- *Square:* Curves outward abruptly from waist and falls straight to hip.
- *Diamond:* Curves diagonally downward from waist to hips.

Note: The hip and waist measurements could be the same, yet the shapes differ. Why?

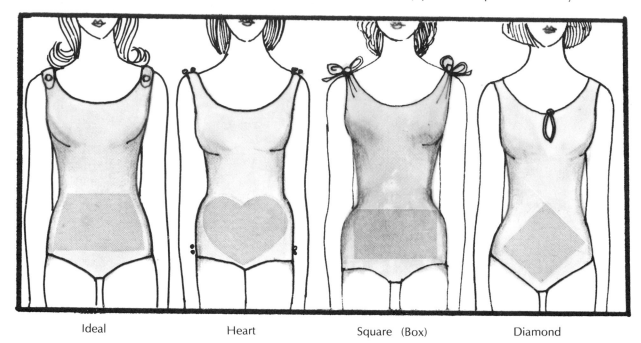

Ideal   Heart   Square (Box)   Diamond

Shoulder/hip relationships
- *Ideal:* Shoulders and hips are aligned, waist/hip difference is between 10 and 11 inches.
- *Hourglass:* Shoulders and hips are aligned, waist/hip difference is 13 inches or more.
- *Straight line:* Shoulders and hips are aligned, waist/hip difference is 8 inches or less.
- *Wide shoulders:* Shoulder width exceeds hip width.
- *Narrow shoulders:* Hip width exceeds shoulder width.

Note: Wide and narrow shoulders—waist/hip differences change the silhouette significantly.

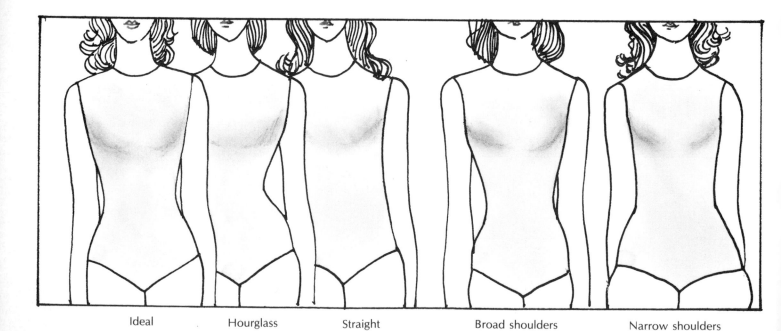

Ideal   Hourglass   Straight   Broad shoulders Small hips   Narrow shoulders Large hips

Shoulder types
- *Ideal:* Shoulders slope slightly from neck base.
- *Sloped:* Shoulders slope radically downward from neck base.

- *Square:* Shoulders level with neck base.
- *Muscular:* Fleshy shoulders around neck area.
- *Bony:* Protruding shoulder bones and clavicle.

IDEAL

SLOPED

SQUARE

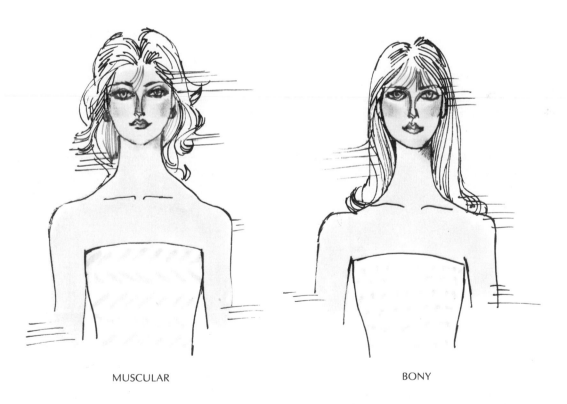

MUSCULAR

BONY

Bust/back relationship

Align your mid-ankle and mid-waist with the plumb line of a mirror or doorway. Choose figure which closely resembles yours and record type.

- *Ideal:* Slightly more view of bust than back (B-cup).
- *Large bust, small back* (C, D, or DD-cup).
- *Small bust, large back* (A-cup).
- *Hollow chest:* Concave above bust.
- *Pigeon breast:* Protruding bone above bust.
- *Other:* Large bust and large back, or a small bust and small back (not illustrated).

    Note: The following figures all have the same bust circumference, yet clothes will fit each figure in a different way. Why?

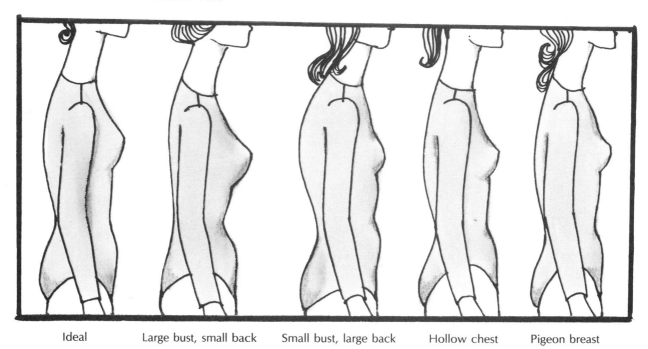

| Ideal | Large bust, small back | Small bust, large back | Hollow chest | Pigeon breast |

Back types

- *Ideal:* Back curves slightly outward.
- *Flat:* Straight back, no curve.
- *Round:* Dominant outward-curved back.
- *Dowager's hump:* A rounded protruding hump.

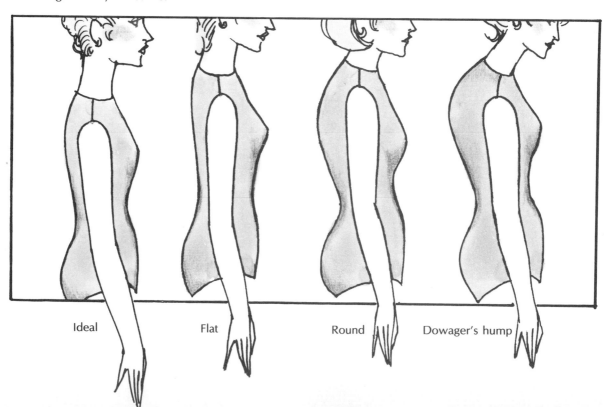

| Ideal | Flat | Round | Dowager's hump |

Arm types

▪ *Ideal:* Flesh almost straight from ball of arm to elbow, tapering to wrist.

▪ *Thin arm:* Flesh closer to skeletal structure than average (between thin and bony).

▪ *Fleshy arm:* Bulges outward just below the ball of arm.

▪ *Fleshy arm:* Bulges between shoulder tip and elbow.

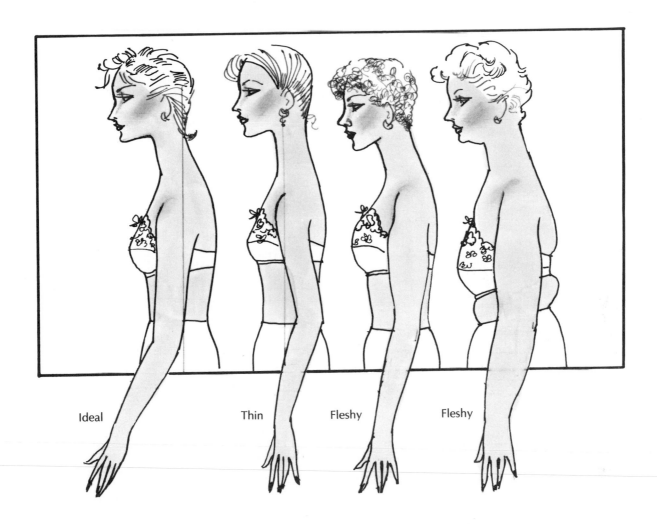

Ideal   Thin   Fleshy   Fleshy

Leg types

Choose and record your leg type using illustration as a guide.

- *Bowlegs:* Legs with outward curvature.
- *Knock-knees:* Legs bend inward and knees touch each other in walking.

- *Bird legs:* Little musclature and flesh, full hips, space between thighs.
- *Bottom-heavy:* Bulging thighs; from a front view, thighs exceed hip width.

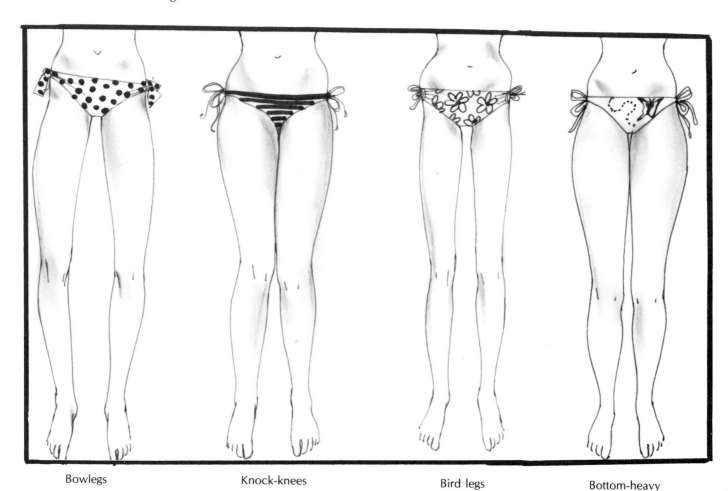

Bowlegs   Knock-knees   Bird legs   Bottom-heavy

Figure stance

Your figure stance affects the hang and balance of garments you wear. With a less than perfect stance (tilting waistline and high/low hips), hemlines ride upward or fall downward and sleeves show stress, affecting comfort and fit. This usually indicates that the balance of the garment is not in harmony with the figure's stance. To determine your stance, align your mid-ankle with the plumb line of a mirror or doorway. Record stance.

- *Perfect stance:* Ear lobe in alignment with plumb line. Wrist bone at or slightly forward of line.
- *Forward stance:* Ear lobe and wrist forward of plumb line. Elbows of stooped figures are in front of plumb line.
- *Upright stance:* (Military and arched back.) Ear lobe at or behind plumb line. Elbow and wrist slightly forward or slightly back of line.

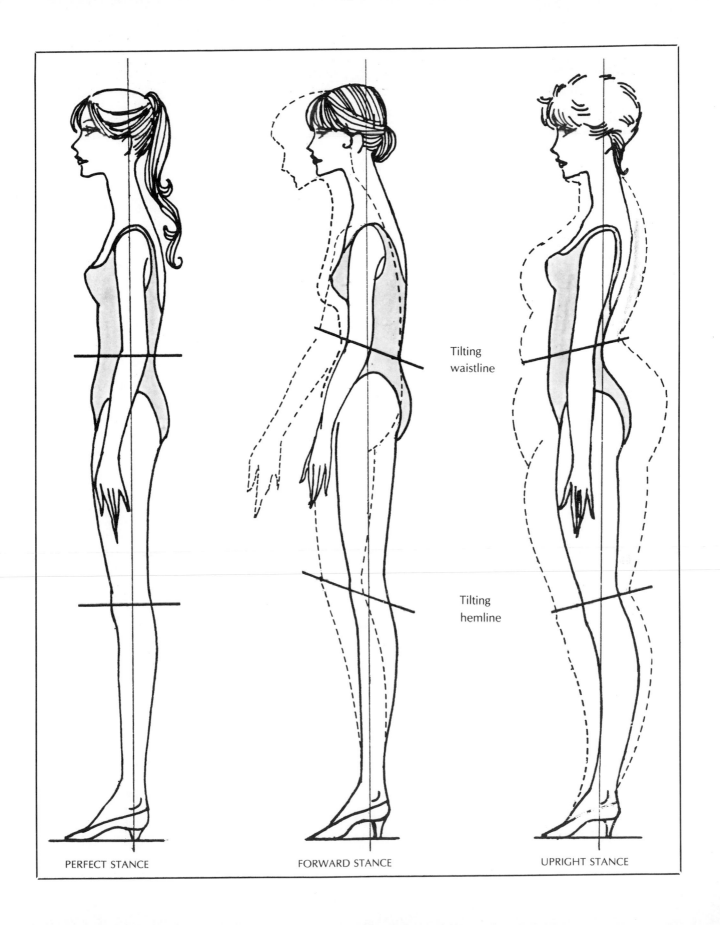

Tilting
waistline

Tilting
hemline

PERFECT STANCE   FORWARD STANCE   UPRIGHT STANCE

Abdomen/thigh relationships

- *I-Shape:* Flat buttocks, flat tummy.
- *R-Shape:* Flat and low buttocks, large tummy, well-rounded thighs.
- *S-Shape:* Large buttocks, flat tummy, large thighs.

- *Oval O-Shape:* High-protruding tummy and low-protruding buttocks.
- *O-Shape:* Abdomen and buttocks protrusion at same level.

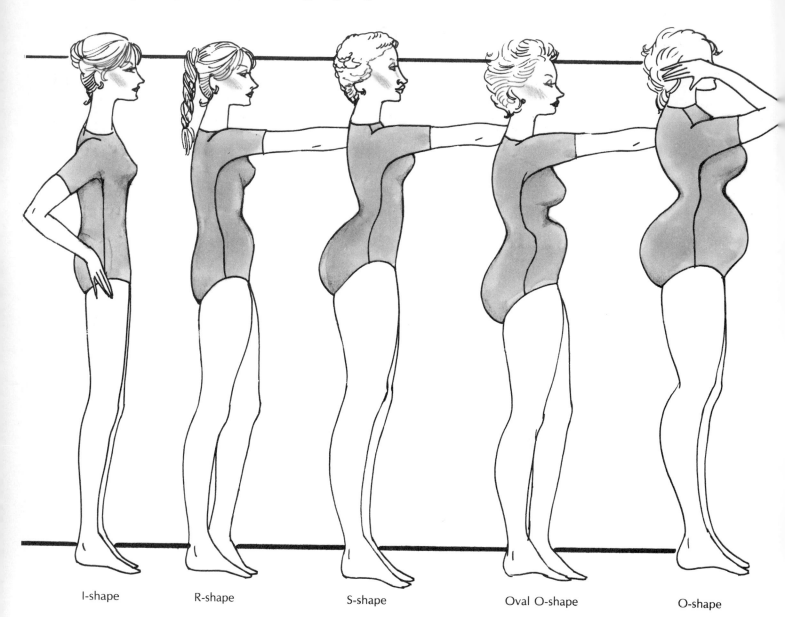

I-shape   R-shape   S-shape   Oval O-shape   O-shape

Other deviations (not illustrated)

- *Off-center neck:* Neckline is off-plumb and right shoulder length differs from left.
- *Asymmetric figures:*

Type 1—one side of figure can have larger bust mound, buttock, thigh, knee, or calf than does the other side.

Type 2—Figures with asymmetric hips or shoulders (high or low) will be determined at the time the figure is measured for pattern development.
List other variations not mentioned.

SUMMARY

The ideal figure is only an illusion. Measurements and sizes do not always determine the ideal. A figure may have ideal measurements, perfect proportions of body parts, a perfect stance, and yet clothes may not fit as well or the same as on someone else. This seeming contradiction can best be understood by viewing cross sections of body parts—buttocks, waist/abdomen, and chest/back. It is the arrangement of flesh (the thickness around the skeletal structure) that causes variations in between the chin and the ankle. Figure deviations, if any, really do not matter when you are developing a personal-fit pattern as long as the measurements taken are accurate and all fitting problems are corrected when the garment is test fit.

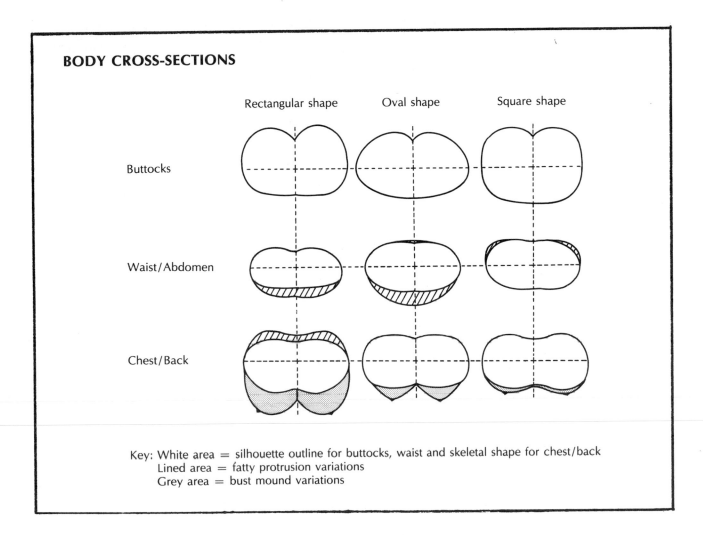

BODY CROSS-SECTIONS

Key: White area = silhouette outline for buttocks, waist and skeletal shape for chest/back
Lined area = fatty protrusion variations
Grey area = bust mound variations

Note: For those desiring to know what type of clothes to wear, see the *Fashion Coloring Book,* by Sharon Tate, published by Harper & Row, 1984.

3

MEASURING TECHNIQUES

Introduction 44
The measurement charts 44
Tools required for the measuring process 44
INDUSTRIAL FORM MEASUREMENT CHART 45
Circumference measurements 45
Upper torso (bodice) 45
Dart measurements 45
Lower torso (skirt/pant) 45
Arm measurements (sleeve) 45
PERSONAL/MODEL MEASUREMENT CHART 46
Circumference measurements 46
Upper torso (bodice) 46
Dart measurements 46
Lower torso (skirt) 46
Arm measurements (sleeve) 46
Personal figure composite 46
MEASURING THE INDUSTRIAL FORM 47
Preparing the form for measuring 47
Verifying shoulder/side seam alignment 48
Circumference measurements 48
Horizontal balance line (HBL) 49
Vertical measurements 50
Horizontal measurements 51
Additional measurements for pant draft 52
MEASURING THE HUMAN FIGURE 54
Figure preparation 54
Measuring the body to determine symmetry 55
Circumference measurements 57
Arc measurements 57
Bodice measurements 58
Measuring the arm 60
Armhole depth and cap height chart 60
Additional measurements for pant draft 61
Crotch measurements 61
Dart intake chart (21) 62

INTRODUCTION

Measurements are a major factor in the development of the basic pattern set. Measurements are a timesaving device as they:
- Serve as the foundation for pattern drafting, draping, and development of new designs
- Establish body dimensions in terms of size and shape
- Are a reference for pattern corrections
- Help determine body symmetry for a personal fit

These measurements are a timesaving device only when taken accurately. This requires maximum concentration and patience throughout the measuring process.

This chapter contains measuring techniques for the *industrial form* and the *human figure*. For easy reference, the arm for sleeve and leg for pant development is placed at the end of the measurement series. In addition, one segment of this chapter is devoted to the asymmetrical figure (in which one side of the figure differs from the other). Measurement-taking techniques determine specific asymmetry (high/low shoulder or hip) as it is the high side of the figure that is used for drafting or draping (with adjustments made at the completion of the pattern).

The patternmaker in industry should study the section on Figure Analysis (Chapter 2) thoroughly, as an understanding of the human figure will provide an increased awareness of the individual's figure deviations versus the standard ideal established by industry. He or she will better understand why the consumer complains from time to time that the garment doesn't fit well. Although the form is used to develop garments, it is the model (or individual) who must wear the garments produced.

THE MEASUREMENT CHARTS

All measurements should be recorded on the measurement charts provided prior to any pattern development. This will eliminate the necessity of remeasuring the form or figure each time a new pattern is drafted, draped, or designed. The Industrial Form Measurement Chart on page 45 and the Personal/Model Measurement Chart on page 46 can be duplicated and used for each type of industrial form, individual figure, or model. The Metric Conversion Table is located at the back of the book.

TOOLS REQUIRED FOR THE MEASURING PROCESS

- Measuring tape.
- Pencils: Washable felt-tip (to mark the body).Red pencil (to mark the form, muslin, or make corrections). Lead pencil (for recording and for pattern work).
- Masking tape (for body marking, if desired).
- Straight pins.
- The Industrial Measurement Chart (for the form) or Personal Measurement Chart (for model or personal fit).
- Flexible or plastic ruler.
- Ruler, 36 inches or longer, if desired.

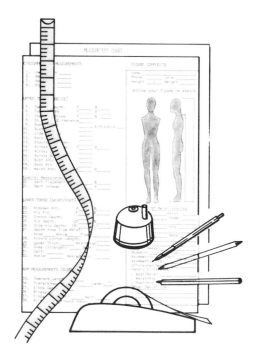

INDUSTRIAL FORM MEASUREMENT CHART

CIRCUMFERENCE MEASUREMENTS

1. Bust: _____
2. Waist: _____
3. Abdomen: _____
4. Hip: _____

Record length by setting form at height level needed. Measure as follows:
CF waist to floor: _____
CB waist to floor: _____
CB neck to floor: _____

UPPER TORSO (BODICE)

5. Center length: F _____ B _____
6. Full length: F _____ B _____
7. Shoulder slope: F _____ B _____
8. (not needed)
9. Bust depth: _____ Bust radius _____
10. Bust span: _____
11. Side length: _____
12. Back neck: _____
13. Shoulder length: _____
14. Across shoulder: F _____ B _____
15. Across chest: _____
16. Across back: _____
17. Bust arc: _____
18. Back arc: _____
*19. Waist arc: F _____ B _____

DART MEASUREMENTS

*20. Dart placement: F _____ B _____
*21. Dart intake (Standard) F _____ B _____

LOWER TORSO (SKIRT/PANT)

*22. Abdomen arc: F _____ B _____
*23. Hip arc: F _____ B _____
24. Crotch depth: _____
*25. Hip depth: CF _____ CB _____ Diff: _____
*26. Side hip depth: _____
27. Waist to: Ankle _____ Floor _____ Knee _____
28. Crotch length: _____
29. Upper thigh: _____ Mid-thigh: _____
30. Knee: _____
31. Calf: _____
32. Ankle: _____

ARM MEASUREMENTS (SLEEVE)

Standard sleeve measurements are given on page 73.
33. Overarm length: _____
34. Armhole depth: _____
35. Cap height: _____
36. (Not needed) _____
37. Biceps _____
38. (Not needed) _____
39. Wrist _____

Form make and type _____
Size _____ Year _____

*Measurements also apply to skirt and pant development.

PERSONAL/MODEL MEASUREMENT CHART

CIRCUMFERENCE MEASUREMENTS

Record lengths where indicated.

40

1. Bust: _____   3. Abdomen: _____
2. Waist: _____   4. Hip: _____

41

42

UPPER TORSO (BODICE)

5. Center length: F _____ B _____
6. Full length: F _____ B _____
7. Shoulder slope: F _____ B _____
8. Asymmetric shoulder diff.:   _____
9. Bust depth: _____ Bust radius: _____
10. Bust span: _____
11. Side length: _____
12. Neck: _____
13. Shoulder length: _____
14. Across shoulder: F _____ B _____
15. Across chest: _____
16. Across back: _____
17. Bust arc: _____
18. Back arc: _____
*19. Waist arc: F _____ B _____

DART MEASUREMENTS

*20. Dart placement: F _____ B _____
*21. Total intake: F _____ B _____
    Number of darts: F _____ B _____
    Each dart intake: F _____ B _____
    Dart spacing: F _____ B _____

LOWER TORSO (SKIRT)

*22. Abdomen arc: F _____ B _____
*23. Hip arc: F _____ B _____
24. Crotch depth: _____
*25. Hip depth: CF _____ CB _____
    Tilting waist diff.: _____
*26. Side hip depth: _____
    Asymmetric hip diff.: _____
27. Waist to: Knee _____ Ankle _____ Floor _____
28. Crotch length: _____
29. Upper thigh: _____ Mid-thigh: _____
30. Knee (straight): _____ Bent: _____
31. Calf: _____
32. Ankle: _____   Ankle/Heel: _____

ARM MEASUREMENTS (SLEEVE)

33. Overarm length: _____
34. Armhole depth: _____
35. Cap height: _____
36. Elbow depth: _____
37. Biceps: _____
38. Elbow (straight): _____ Bent _____
39. Wrist _____   Around hand _____

PERSONAL FIGURE COMPOSITE

Outline your figure characteristics on sketch:
A. Head height relationship:
   Bust: _____   Waist: _____
   Crotch: _____   Knee: _____
B. Hip type: _____
C. Shoulder/Hip relationship:
   Shoulder: _____ Hip: _____
D. Shoulder type: _____
E. Bust/Back relationship:
   Bust: _____ Back: _____
F. Back type: _____
G. Arm type: _____
H. Leg type: _____
I. Stance: _____
J. Abdomen/Thigh relationship:
   Abdomen: _____ Thigh: _____ Type: _____
K. Other deviations: _____
L. Asymmetric figure (record high side, right or left)
   Shoulder: _____ Hip: _____
M. Tilting waistline (record high/low, front and back)
   Front: _____ Back: _____
N. Bust/Waist difference: _____
   Waist/Hip difference: _____
   Bust/Hip difference: _____

Name _____ *Date* _____
Address _____ *Phone* _____
Height _____ *Weight* _____ *Size* _____

*Measurements also apply to skirt and pant development.

MEASURING THE INDUSTRIAL FORM

All measurements must be taken accurately and with care. Since forms are still made by hand, they may differ slightly on each side of the center front and back, and the shoulder and side seams may be out of alignment (adjustment will be made later to balance the form). Except for circumference measurements of the bust, waist, abdomen, and hips, measure only one-half of the form; however, the *same* half of the front and back should be used. When fitting the muslin to the form, the garment should be placed on the side measured.

When measuring the form, place the metal-tipped end of the tape on one reference point and extend it to the next reference point. Record each measurement when taken. For easy reference, instructions are followed by numbers in parentheses that correlate with those on the measurement charts (and those contained throughout the text).

• Asterisks placed by numbers apply to both skirt and pants measurements.

• Arc measurements refer to measurements taken from center lines to side seams.

• Measure the waistline from mid-tape or below-tape level. Once established, be consistent. Below-tape level is used for measurements in this book.

PREPARING THE FORM FOR MEASURING

FIGURE 1

Waistline. If the waistline tape is damaged, replace it before measuring.

Bust bridge. (The basic garment spans the bust points.) Cut a strip of cloth $1\frac{1}{2} \times 26$ inches, fold edges to the center, and fold in half again. Press and place across bust points, ending just beyond side seams, and pin. Place pin through bust points. Crossmark bust points and center line on bridge.

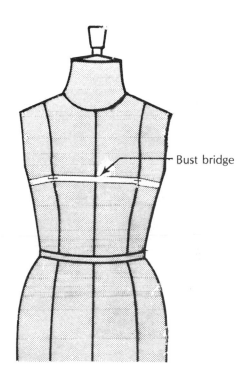

Bust bridge

VERIFYING SHOULDER/SIDE SEAM ALIGNMENT

FIGURE 2

Even with the best quality control, the shoulder and side seams of the form may be out of alignment, causing the measurements to vary from side to side. It is always best to measure one side and to fit the garment on that side consistently. Prior to draping or measuring the form for pattern development, the alignment of the form should be verified and corrected, if necessary:

- Place ruler at shoulder tip and side seam and draw line through armplate. If ruler's edge does not pass through the center of armplate screw, measure from the line to the center of the screw.
- Shift the shoulder and side seams equal to this measurement as shown:

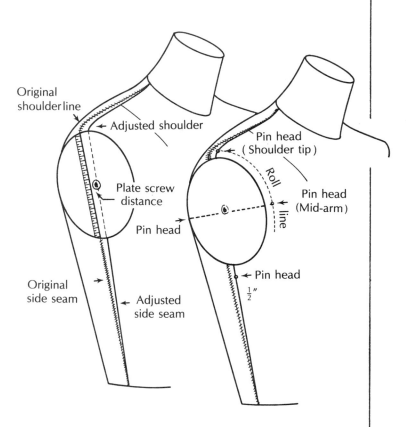

CIRCUMFERENCE MEASUREMENTS

FIGURE 3

Bust (1), across bust points and back.
Waist (2), around waist.
Abdomen (3), three inches below waist.
Hip (4), measure widest area keeping tape parallel with floor. Pin mark hip level at center front (referred to as X-point).

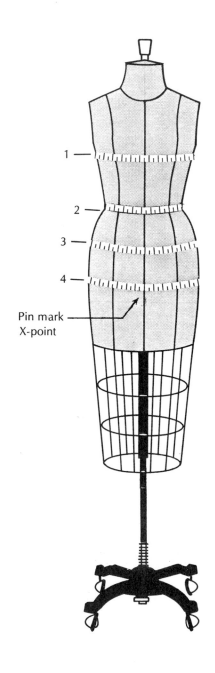

- Draw new shoulderline from shoulder tip to neck.
- Draw new side seam from armplate to side waist.
- Thrust pin into form and pin mark front and back mid-armhole on roll line on level with plate screw (broken line indicates level of plate screw).
- Pin mark shoulder tip and $\frac{1}{2}$ inch below armhole plate at side seam.

HORIZONTAL BALANCE LINE (HBL)

FIGURES 4, 5, and 6
- Measure from the floor or table top to pinmark at center front hip level (X-point) (Figure 4).
- Using this measurement, measure up from the floor or table top and mark the center back and both sides with a pin (Figures 5 and 6). Recheck before recording measurements.
- Draw a line through hip marks, using a flex or plastic ruler as a guide. (Lay the edge of the ruler on X-mark and pinmarks at side seams of form. Draw the line. Repeat until the line is drawn completely around the form.) *Note:* In industry, the standard hip depth for Misses sizes is located 8 to 9 inches down; Petites, 6 to 7 inches down; and Half sizes, to 11 inches down.

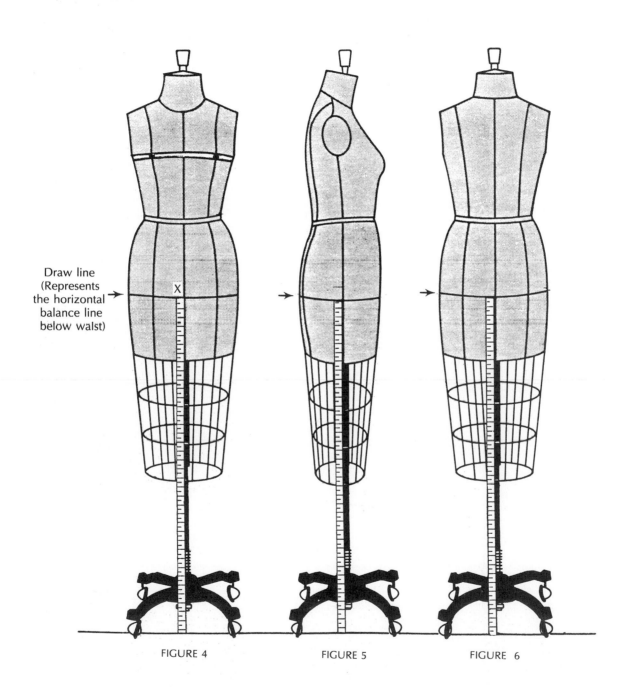

Draw line
(Represents the horizontal balance line below waist)

X

FIGURE 4   FIGURE 5   FIGURE 6

VERTICAL MEASUREMENTS

FIGURES 7 and 8

Side length (11). Armplate to side waist.

Shoulder length (13). Shoulder tip to neck.

Armhole depth (34). Shoulder tip to bottom of armhole plate.

Side hip depth (26). Side waist to HBL, on side of form being measured.

Bust radius (9). Measure from bust point ending under bust mound.

Front and back

FIGURES 9 and 10

Center length (5). Neck to waist (over bust bridge).

Full length (6). Waist to shoulder at neck, parallel with center lines.

Shoulder slope (7). Center of waist to shoulder tip (pinhead mark).

Bust depth (9). Shoulder tip to bust point.

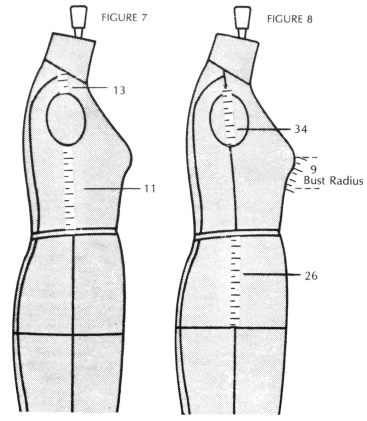

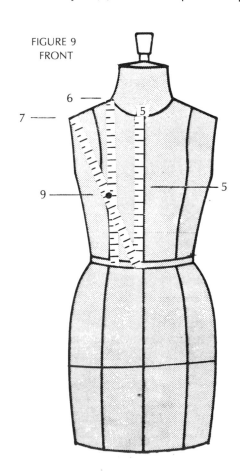

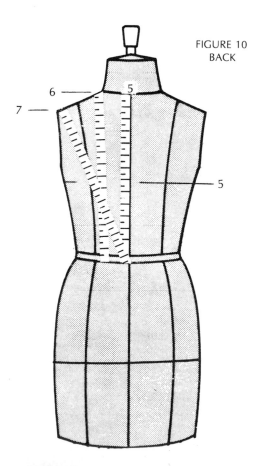

HORIZONTAL MEASUREMENTS

Front

FIGURE 11

Across shoulder (14). Shoulder tip to center front neck.

Across chest (15). Center front to mid-armhole (pinhead mark).

Bust arc (17). Center front, over bust point, ending 2 inches below armplate at side seam.

Bust span (10). Place tape across bust points, divide in half for measurement.

Waist arc (19). Center front waist to side waist seam.

***Dart placement (20).** Center front to side front (princess line).

Dart intake (21). Standard = 1 inch (two $\frac{1}{2}$-inch darts). Petite = $\frac{3}{4}$ inch (two $\frac{3}{8}$-inch darts).

***Abdomen arc (22).** Center front to side seam, starting 3 inches down from waist.

***Hip arc (23).** Center front to side seam on HBL line.

***Hip depth (25).** Center front to HBL line.

Back

FIGURE 12

Back neck (12). Center back neck to shoulder at neck.

Across shoulder (14). Shoulder tip to center back neck.

Across back (16). Center back to mid-armhole at ridge (pinhead) plus $\frac{1}{4}$ inch.

Back arc (18). Center back to bottom of arm plate.

Waist arc (19). Center back waist to side waist seam.

***Dart placement (20).** Center back waist to side back (princess line).

Dart intake (21). Standard = 2 inches (two 1-inch darts). Petite = $1\frac{3}{4}$ inches (two $\frac{7}{8}$-inch darts)

***Abdomen arc (22).** Center back to side seam, starting 3 inches down from waist.

***Hip arc (23).** Center back to side seam on HBL line.

***Hip depth (25).** Center back waist to HBL line.

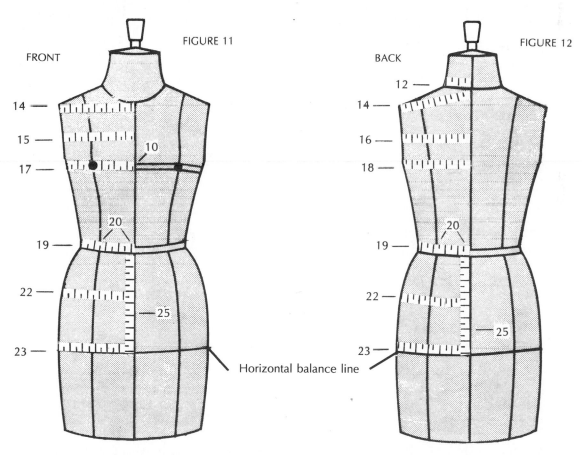

FIGURE 11

FRONT

FIGURE 12

BACK

Horizontal balance line

This completes the measuring process for the form. For the development of the basic pattern set using these measurements, refer to Chapter 4. *Note:* For sleeve development, use the

measurements given on page 73 and record them in the space provided on the chart, or measure the model's arm using instructions given on page 60.

ADDITIONAL MEASUREMENTS FOR PANT DRAFT

(For waist, hip, and abdominal measurements, see chart numbers with asterisk.)

Vertical measurements

FIGURE 13

With metal-tipped end of tape placed below waist tape at side, measure the following key locations:

    To end of leg (ankle level) (27).
    To floor (27).
    To knee (mid-knee) (27).

Circumference measurements

FIGURE 14

    Upper thigh (29). Near crotch base.
    Mid-thigh (29). Between crotch and knee.
    Knee (30). Mid-knee level.
    Calf (31). Widest part below knee.
    Ankle (32). End of form leg.

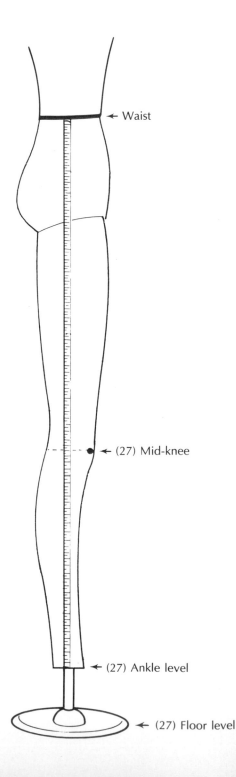

← Waist

← (27) Mid-knee

← (27) Ankle level

← (27) Floor level

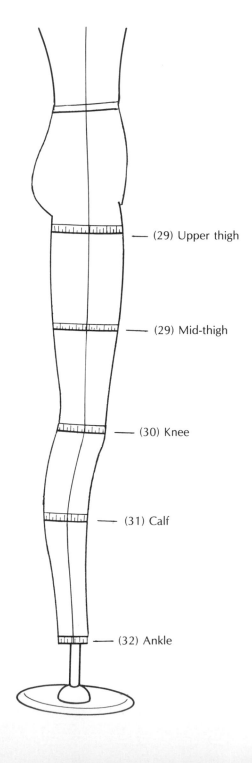

— (29) Upper thigh

— (29) Mid-thigh

— (30) Knee

— (31) Calf

— (32) Ankle

Crotch length (28)

FIGURE 15
Measure from center front waist tape under crotch base (between legs) to center back waist at tape.

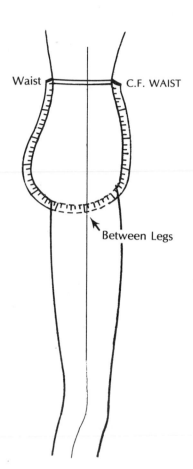

Crotch depth (24)

(Also referred to as the *rise* by tailors)

FIGURE 16
Place square rule between legs with edge of arms touching abdomen and crotch. Measure depth from waist level to crotch level.

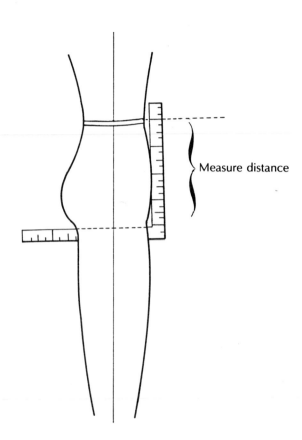

MEASURING THE HUMAN FIGURE

The model in industry is chosen to represent the manufacturer because her measurements are similar to the company's standard ideal. As such, she is used for test fitting the garment before pattern can be used for mass production. The techniques used to measure the model are the same as those used to measure an individual for a personal fit. Whether for the model or an individual, a precision fit can only be achieved with accurate measurements. These measurements are used for reference purposes when developing the basic pattern set, related foundation patterns, and other pattern designs. Measure and mark each location carefully. Recheck them and record on the Personal Measurement Chart.

Ideally, the model should stand barefoot on a flat hard surface with feet slightly apart and weight evenly distributed. She should wear a close-fitting garment (body suit or leotard) over whatever foundation she normally wears—preferably one that defines the neckline, armhole, shoulder, and side seams. Measurements should be taken in between breathing while the model maintains a natural, relaxed stance.

FIGURE PREPARATION

The body should be marked as each landmark is located by either pinning the garment or marking the body itself with a washable felt-tip pen. If an overgarment is not worn, or if the garment worn is not sectioned, indicate the neckline, sides, waist, centerline and armhole as follows:

Neckline

FIGURES 1 and 2
Place a neckchain around the neck, allowing it to encircle the neck at the neck base. With pen, draw line around neck. Crossmark in between V-shaped hollow at front of neck and nape (dominant bone) at back of neck with head bent forward.

Waistline and centerlines

FIGURES 3 and 4
Place belt, elastic, or band around waist to define the *apparent* waistline. The *actual* waistline slopes below the belt at center back and is used to develop skirts and pants. The apparent waist is used for developing the basic bodice. Place the edge of the tape on neck mark in line with navel, and draw plumb line from center front neck to navel. Repeat for back using center back neck mark and crease of buttocks as a guide.

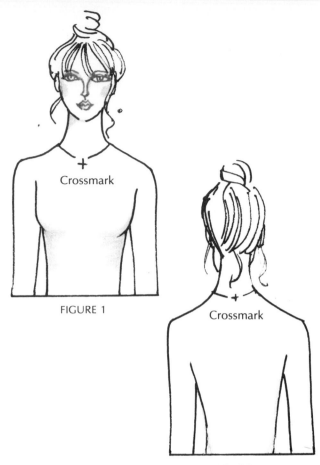

Crossmark

FIGURE 1

Crossmark

FIGURE 2

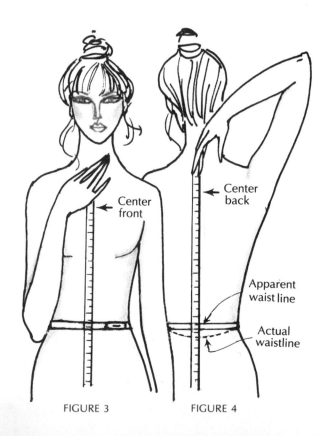

Center front

Center back

Apparent waist line

Actual waistline

FIGURE 3

FIGURE 4

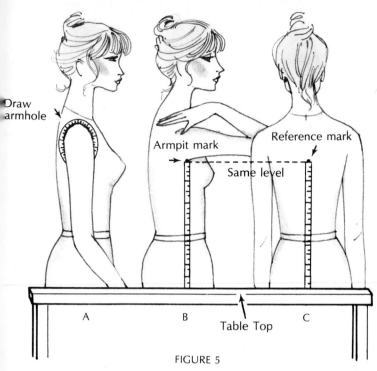

Draw armhole

Armpit mark

Reference mark

Same level

A

B

Table Top

C

FIGURE 5

Armhole and landmark

FIGURE 5a and b

Slip the measuring tape or elastic under the arm, drawing the tape or elastic up to the shoulder tip. Tie the tape away from shoulder tip and draw line around armhole. With model's arm raised, continue drawing line under arm. Remove the tape and crossmark a point on the line under the armpit.

Reference mark

FIGURE 5b and 5c

(Used only for drafting the basic pattern set.) Measure up from the floor or table top to crossmark at armpit (Figure 5b). Using this measurement, measure up from floor or table top to center back. Crossmark for reference (Figure 5c).

MEASURING THE BODY TO DETERMINE SYMMETRY

Most figures differ to some degree from side to side, having either a high and low shoulder and/or hip, or a tilting waistline. These figure deviations affect the way clothes hang on the figure, resulting in garments that show stress or strain and hemlines that tilt upward or downward.

Shoulder symmetry

FIGURE 6

Model should stand relaxed with elbows bent and fingers clasped together. Measure from the table top or the floor with either a ruler or tape to the right and left elbow bone. If the lengths differ more than $\frac{1}{4}$ inch between them, the shoulders are asymmetrical. Record the *difference* under Shoulder slope difference (8) and asymmetry under Figure Composite (L) on the Personal Measurement Chart. To improve symmetry, a shoulder pad whose width equals this difference may be attached to the low shoulder.

FIGURE 6

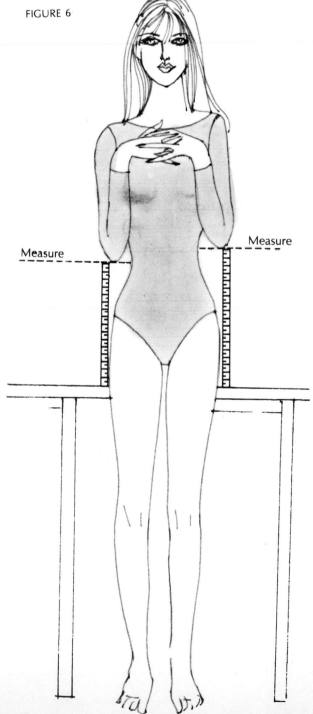

Measure

Measure

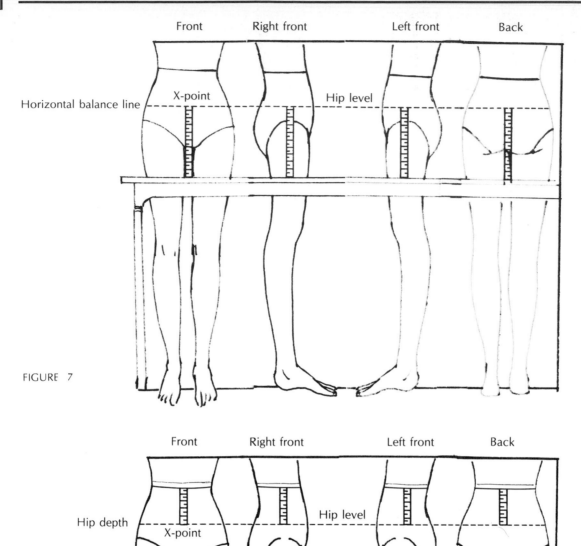

Front Right front Left front Back

Horizontal balance line — X-point — Hip level

FIGURE 7

Front Right front Left front Back

Hip depth — X-point — Hip level

FIGURE 8

Horizontal balance line (HBL)

FIGURE 7
The HBL represents the widest part of the hip. This line is always parallel with the floor. To find this line, see Hip (4) on page 57 to establish X-point. Measure up from the floor or table to this location. Using this measurement, measure up to center back and both sides of the figure and pin mark.

Waist to hip depth

FIGURE 8
Measure down from the waist to HBL marks and record measurements:

Hip depth (25)

- Center front to pin mark (X-point)
- Center back to pin mark.

Side hip depth (26)

- Right side to pin mark
- Left side to pin mark.

Asymmetric hips (high/low). Compare the right and left side hip measurements. If the difference is more than $\frac{1}{4}$ inch, hips are asymmetric. Record the *difference* (26) and high hip in space L.

Tilting waistline. If center front to HBL differs more than $\frac{1}{2}$ inch from center back to HBL, the model is considered to have a tilting waistline. Record *difference* (25) and Figure Composite under M. Instructions given for this figure type should be used for pattern development. In extreme cases, the pattern will look somewhat different than those illustrated in the text.

CIRCUMFERENCE MEASUREMENTS

FIGURE 9

Neck (12). Measure around neck. Record one-fourth of measurement.

Bust (1). Hold tape lightly and measure across bust points, under arm and across back.

Waist (2). Take a firm but not tight measurement. Remove belt while measuring, replace belt.

Abdomen (3). Measure around widest area of abdomen.

Hip (4). Place measuring tape around the widest part of the hipline. Keep the tape parallel with the floor. Pin mark center front at this level to indicate hip depth (referred to as X-point). Subtract bust from waist, waist from hip and bust and hip. Record in space N on chart.

ARC MEASUREMENTS

Circumference measurements are divided into fourths in order to establish the divisions of the figure for patternmaking. It is best to adjust those measurements after they have been divided to allow the garment to fall in better alignment with the figure's proportions (protruding bust in front, and buttocks in back). To adjust the front and back quarter measurements for bust, waist, abdomen, and hips, add to and subtract $\frac{1}{4}$ inch from each of the following locations and record on the chart in the number space indicated below:

Bust and back arc (17, 18)
- Front: $+ \frac{1}{4}$ inch
- Back: $- \frac{1}{4}$ inch

Abdomen arc (22)
- Front: $+ \frac{1}{4}$ inch
- Back: $- \frac{1}{4}$ inch

Waist arc (19)
- Front: $+ \frac{1}{4}$ inch
- Back: $- \frac{1}{4}$ inch

Hip arc (23)
- Front: $- \frac{1}{4}$ inch
- Back: $+ \frac{1}{4}$ inch

Side seam location

FIGURE 10

If the model is not wearing a garment indicating side seam, and the figure is being prepared for draping the basic garment, mark side seam as follows: To locate side seam on the figure, measure from center front to side at bust, waist, abdomen and hip levels using front arc measurements. Mark. Place ruler's edge at marks and draw line for side seam.

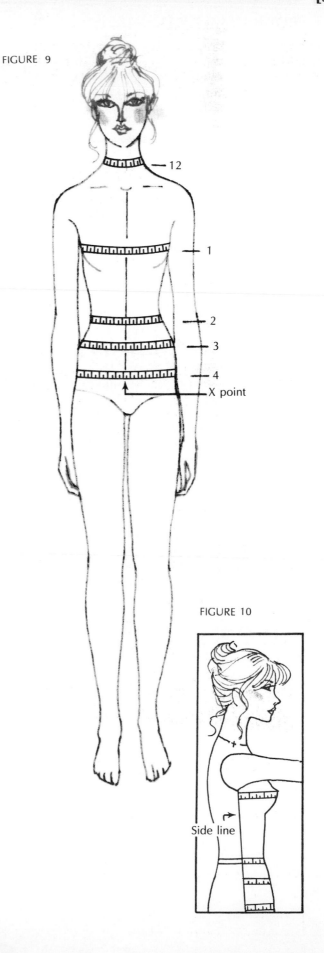

FIGURE 9

FIGURE 10

BODICE MEASUREMENTS

(Waistline ends below belt line. All measurements should start or end there.)

Special notation. For figures not wearing garments indicating shoulder, neck, and shoulder tip, follow instructions indicated by asterisk to locate them.

Back bodice

FIGURE 11a and 11b

Center length (5). Measure from center back neck to waistline. (For dominant shoulder blades, and/or full back, place a bridge across the blades. Suggestion—use a ½-inch wide flex ruler and measure over the bridge.)

Full length (6). Shoulder at neck to waist, parallel with center back.*

Shoulder slope (7). Shoulder tip to center back waist.**

* To locate shoulder at neck, use center length measurement (5), add ¾ inch (1 inch for full back). Mark this measurement on the tape. Place tape at waist in line with side neck and parallel with center back. Where the measurement intersects with neckline, crossmark for shoulder at neck location (Figure 11b). Record this measurement in space 6 (Full length).
**To locate shoulder tip, use full length measurement (6). Mark on tape. Place tape at the center back waist and where measurement on tape touches outline of armhole, crossmark for shoulder tip location (Figure 11b). Record this measurement in space 7 (Shoulder slope).

Back bodice

FIGURE 12

Across shoulder (14). Shoulder tip to center back neck.

Across back (16). Mid-armhole to center back.

Armhole depth (34). Center back neck to reference mark (used for draft only).

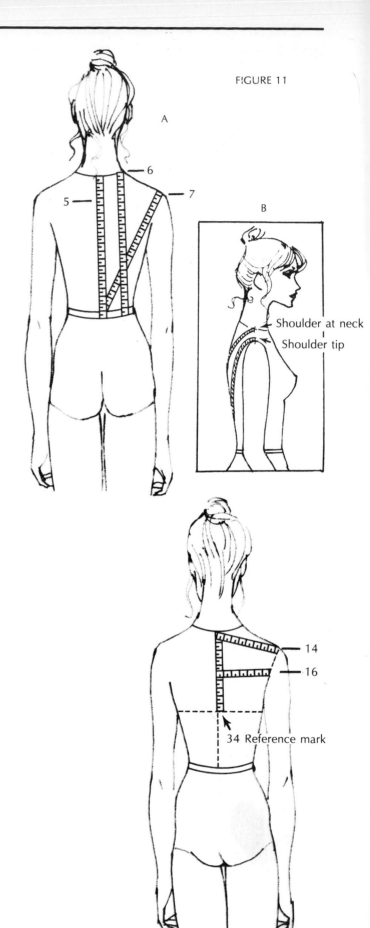

FIGURE 11

A

B

Shoulder at neck
Shoulder tip

14
16
34 Reference mark

Front bodice

FIGURE 13

Center length (5). Hold narrow ruler over bust point. Measure center front neck mark to waist over ruler.

Full length (6). Waist to shoulder at neck mark, parallel with center front.

Shoulder slope (7). Center front waist over bust point to shoulder tip mark.

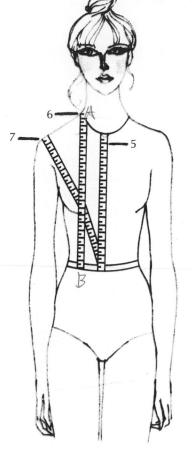

FIGURE 13

Front bodice

FIGURE 14a

Shoulder length (13). Shoulder at neck to shoulder tip.

Across shoulder (14). Shoulder tip to center front neck mark.

Across chest (15). Mid-armhole at creaseline to center front.

Bust depth (9). Shoulder tip to bust point.

Bust span (10). Bust point to bust point. Record one-half the amount.

Waist dart placement (20). Bust span less $\frac{3}{4}$ inches. Same for front and back.

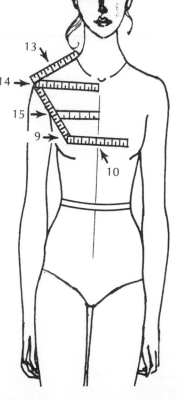

FIGURE 14

FIGURE 14b

Side length (11). Armpit mark to waist on side line.

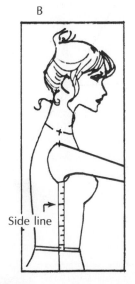

Side line

Dart chart

A personalized dart intake chart is given on page 62. Refer to it and record the dart intake for your figure at the end of the measuring process.

Figure height. Measure and record on Figure Composite on chart.

Crown to floor (40).

Center back neck mark to floor (41).

Waist to floor (42).

MEASURING THE ARM

Measurements are taken over a slightly bent arm so that the sleeve will not appear too short when the arm is fully bent or too long when in a relaxed position.

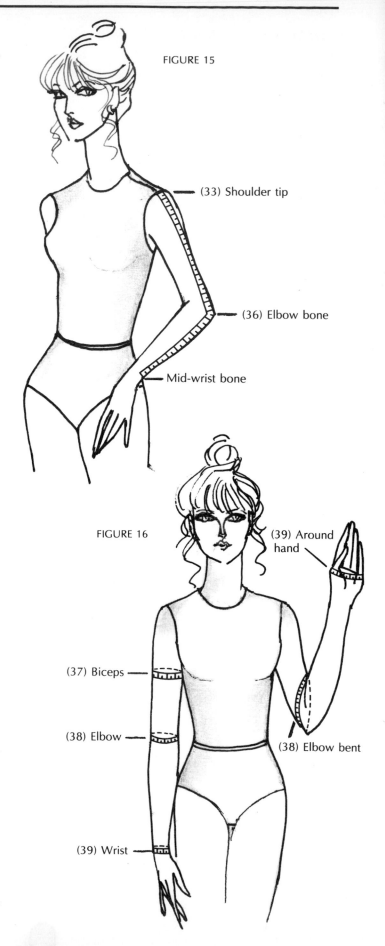

FIGURE 15

(33) Shoulder tip

(36) Elbow bone

Mid-wrist bone

Vertical measurements

FIGURE 15

Overarm length (33). Shoulder tip over elbow to mid-wrist bone.

Elbow depth (36). Shoulder tip to elbow bone.

Circumference measurements

FIGURE 16
(Taken around widest area)

Biceps (37). Add 2 inches for ease. If biceps are very large, add $1\frac{1}{2}$ inches.

Elbow (38). Straight and bent.

Wrist (39). Around wrist.

Around hand (39). With thumb placed across palm, measure around knuckle and thumb. Add $\frac{3}{8}$ inch for ease (variable).

FIGURE 16

(39) Around hand

(37) Biceps

(38) Elbow

(38) Elbow bent

(39) Wrist

ARMHOLE DEPTH AND CAP HEIGHT CHART

Choose armhole depth and cap height for your size range and record on Measurement chart. Measurements based on bodice grade for sizes. Record armhole depth in space (34), and cap height in space (35).

Size	Armhole depth (34)	Cap height (35)
6–7	4 1/2 inches	Add 1 inch to
8–9	4 5/8 inches	measurement
10–11	4 3/4 inches	and record in
12–13	4 7/8 inches	space (35).
14–15	5 inches	
16–17	5 1/8 inches	
18–19	5 1/4 inches	
20–21	5 3/8 inches	
22	5 1/2 inches	

Note: Add 1/8 inch for each size above 22, and subtract 1/8 inch for each size under 6.

ADDITIONAL MEASUREMENTS FOR PANT DRAFT

Measure the following key locations:

Vertical measurements

FIGURE 17

To below ankle bone (27).
To floor (27).
To knee (mid-knee) (27).

Circumference measurements

FIGURE 18

Upper thigh (29). Widest part below crotch.
Mid-thigh (29). Between crotch and knee level.
Knee (30). Standing. Bending.
Calf (31). Widest part below knee.
Ankle (32). Around ankle bone (reference).
Ankle/heel (32). Point toe.

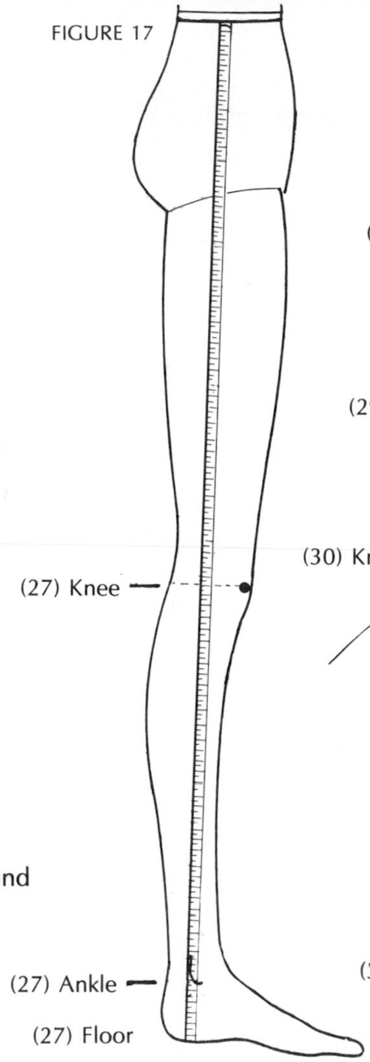

CROTCH MEASUREMENTS

Crotch length (28)

FIGURE 19

Measure from center front waist, under and around crotch (between legs), to center back waist.

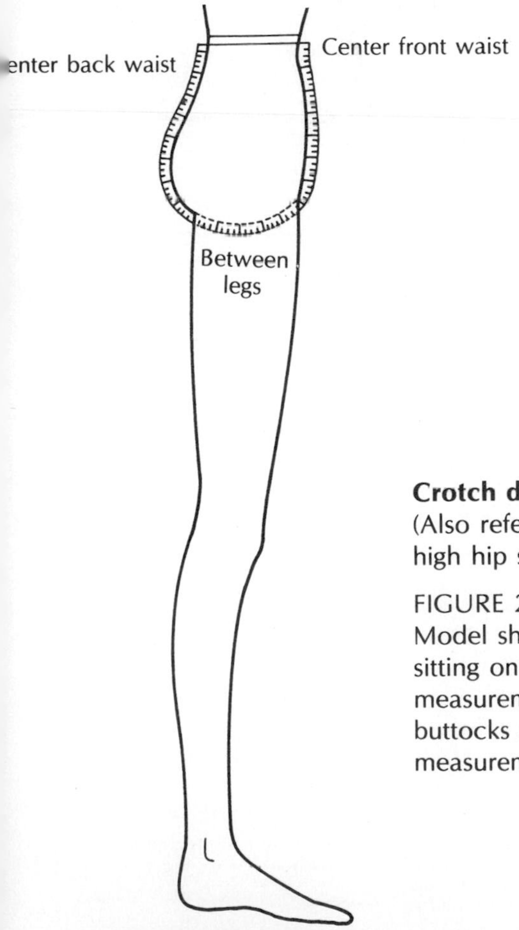

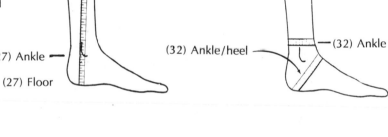

FIGURE 17

(27) Knee

(27) Ankle

(27) Floor

FIGURE 18

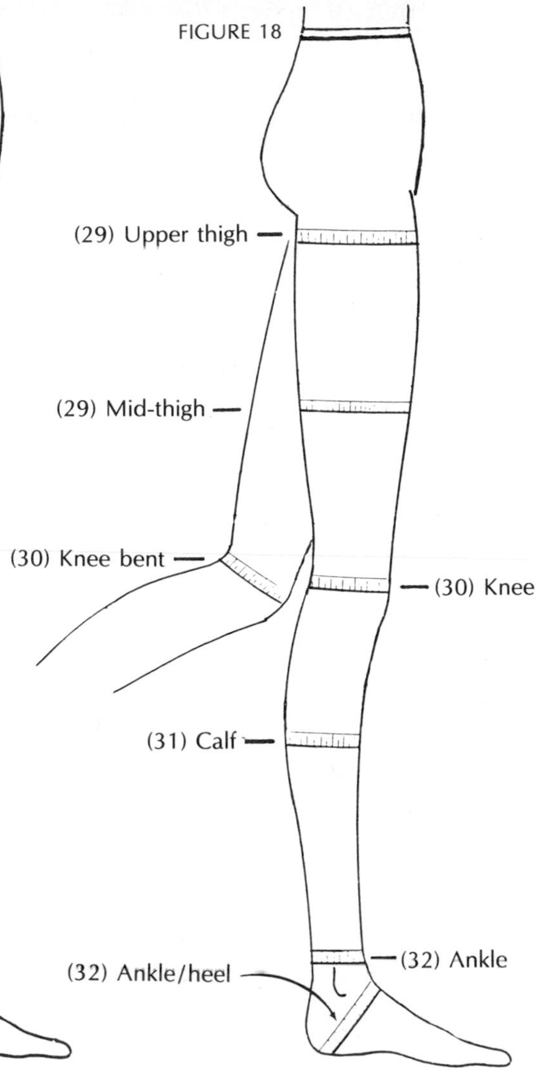

(29) Upper thigh

(29) Mid-thigh

(30) Knee bent

(30) Knee

(31) Calf

(32) Ankle/heel

(32) Ankle

Center back waist   Center front waist

Between legs

Crotch depth (24)

(Also referred to as the *rise* by tailors; taken on high hip side.

FIGURE 20

Model should assume a natural, relaxed position, sitting on a flat-based, hard chair or table when measurement is taken. *Note:* For figures with large buttocks and/or thighs, *subtract ½ inch* from measurement.

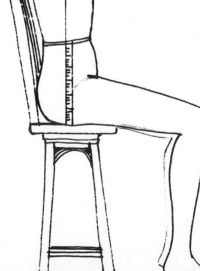

FIGURE 19

FIGURE 20

DART INTAKE CHART (21)

Waist/hip difference	Front: skirt/pant			Back: skirt/pant		
	Total intake	No. of darts	Dart intake	Total intake	No. of darts	Dart intake
4 inches	1/2 inch	1	1/2 inch	3/4 inch	1	3/4 inch
5 inches	1/2 inch	1	1/2 inch	1 inch	1	1 inch
6 inches	1/2 inch	1	1/2 inch	1 1/4 inch	1	1 1/4 inch
7 inches	1/2 inch	1	1/2 inch	1 1/2 inch	1	1 1/2 inch
8 inches	3/4 inch	2	3/8 inch	1 3/4 inch	2	7/8 inch
9 inches	3/4 inch	2	3/8 inch	1 3/4 inch	2	7/8 inch
10 inches	1 inch	2	1/2 inch	2 inch	2	1 inch
11 inches	1 1/4 inch	2	5/8 inch	2 1/4 inch	2	1 1/8 inch
12 inches	1 1/2 inch	2	5/8 inch	2 1/2 inch	2	1 1/4 inch
13 inches	1 1/2 inch	2	5/8 inch	2 3/4 inch	2	1 3/8 inch
14 inches	1 1/2 inch	2	5/8 inch	2 3/4 inch	2	1 3/8 inch

Dart spacing: 1 1/4 inch

Chart usage

The purpose of the dart intake chart is to establish the personal dart intake when developing skirt and pants and for general reference. It is included here for convenience in completing the Personal Fit Measurement Chart after the waist and hip measurements are taken.

First, subtract waist (2) and hip (4) measurements, not including ease (or use abdomen measurement if greater than hip). Find the difference in Column 1 to the nearest whole number, read across to find the total intake allotted for front and back, the number of darts and dart intake for each dart (quarter pattern). Record in space (21) on chart in order given.

S-shapes

For a better fit, S-shape figures should use only one dart in front, and all remaining excess should be combined equally with the back darts.

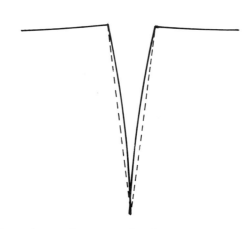

For a better fit, curve dart legs. (Broken lines indicate original dart.)

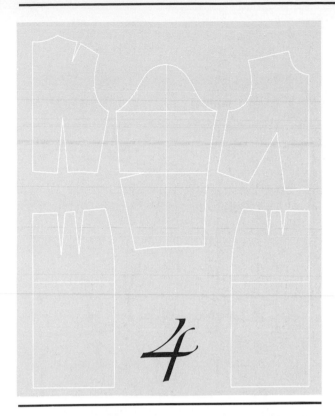

4

METHODS FOR MAKING
BASIC PATTERNS

Introduction 64

Drafting the basic patterns

THE BODICE DRAFT 66
The front bodice draft 66
The back bodice draft 68
THE SKIRT DRAFT 70
Skirt front and type 1 skirt back 70
Type 2 skirt back 72
THE SLEEVE DRAFT 73
Sleeve draft measurement chart 73
ADJUSTING SLEEVE TO ARMHOLE OF
    BODICE 76
Cap ease and armhole notch placements 76
Increasing and decreasing cap ease 78
Distributing cap ease equally 79
Armhole adjustment to eliminate puckering 80
PREPARING PATTERNS FOR TEST FIT 82
Trueing basic patterns 82
Asymmetric shoulder and/or hip 84
Muslin preparation for test fit 85

Draping the basic patterns

THE BODICE DRAPE 86
Preparation for the bodice drape 87
The front bodice drape 88
The back bodice drape 90
THE SKIRT DRAPE 93
The front skirt drape 94
The back skirt drape 95
TRANSFERRING MUSLIN DRAPE TO PATTERN
    PAPER 99

Commercial pattern adjustments

Preparation of patterns 102
Dart adjustment for bra cup sizes A,C,D,DD 102
Bra cup adjustment chart 103
Adjustments for asymmetry 104
Other adjustments 107
Muslin preparation for test fit 108
*Conversion to a one-dart bodice and seamless
    patterns 108*

INTRODUCTION

The figure you are viewing is wearing a rather plain and uninteresting dress. It has no particular style or design detail, except for a few vertical seams placed here and there. If it were hanging on a rack in a store, would you buy it? Probably not, yet this simple little basic dress is related to every garment in your clothes collection. It is related to every design created and every pattern developed. It represents the very foundation upon which patternmaking, fit, and design is based.

Let's analyze the characteristics of the dress that make it so significant. It is made up of five distinct parts consisting of a front and back bodice, a front and back skirt that hangs straight from the hip, and slim, full-length sleeves. The dress follows the figure's outline, covering the outermost parts without contouring the hollow areas. It has a series of seams directed toward the figure's bulges—the bust, abdomen, buttocks, shoulder blades, and elbows. The pattern pieces are shaped to fit the figure's dimensions, and the garment fits with comfort and ease in perfect harmonious balance with the figure's stance.

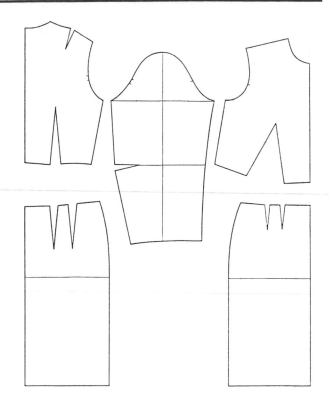

Basic pattern parts

The five pattern parts that make up the basic dress are called *basic patterns, blocks, foundations,* or *slopers.* This set serves many purposes. It clarifies and helps the patternmaker understand the fit of a garment relative to the pattern shape in the development stages of these parts. It is a record of the figure's dimensions. It is the foundation of the Flat Patternmaking System and the basis of other secondary foundation patterns such as the torso, jacket, coat, pant, jumpsuit, swimwear, and so on.

Pattern perfection

Because it is the basis for the Flat Patternmaking System, the basic patterns must be perfected to eliminate all errors that could be passed on to each new design based on it. It is well worth the time and effort spent to analyze the fit of the garment and to make all pattern corrections required to perfect it.

The shaping process

The dimensions of the figure are represented on the pattern by length, width, and depth using straight lines, curved lines, and wedge shapes. To clarify, envision the body in a transparent, cylindrical wrap:
- *Front view:* Excess beyond the figure's outline (neckline, shoulder, armhole, side, waist and hipline) is cut away (shaded areas). This creates the outer shape of the pattern.
- *Side view:* Excess remaining within the garment is stitched to conform to the outermost bulges of the figure (bust, shoulder blades, abdomen and buttocks). These confined areas form wedges and are called darts. Darts control the fit of the garment and help to create a three-dimensional form from a two-dimensional piece of cloth or paper. Since darts are an integral part of fit, they are always somewhere within the frame of the garment or pattern. Darts are also referred to as dart equivalents when the excess is used for gathers, pleats, tucks, stylelines (those crossing at, or near, a bulge), flare (when not confined by stitching), and as hidden ease (in armholes).

Patternmaking methods

This chapter covers the three methods used to develop the Basic Pattern set:
- *Drafting the basic patterns (page 66)*
- *Draping the basic patterns (page 86)*
- *Adjusting the commercial basic pattern (page 102)*
  Choose the method best suited to your needs.

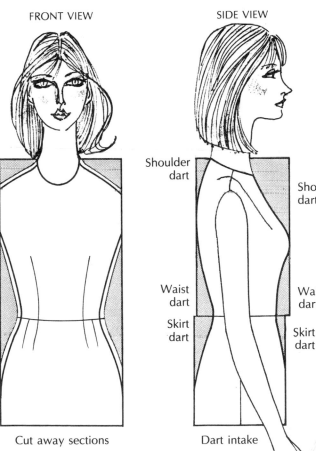

FRONT VIEW   SIDE VIEW

Shoulder dart

Shoulder dart

Waist dart

Waist dart

Skirt dart

Skirt dart

Cut away sections   Dart intake

Back measurements needed
- Full length (6) _____
- Across shoulder (14) _____
- Center back length (5) _____
- Shoulder slope (7) _____
- Back neck (12) _____
- Waist arc (19) _____
- Dart placement (20) _____
- Side length (11) _____
- Back arc (18) _____
- Across back (16) _____

THE BACK BODICE DRAFT

FIGURE 5

A–B = Full length (6).

A–C = Across shoulder (14) (square from A). Square down 7 inches from C for guideline.

B–D = Center back length (5). Mark and square out 4 inches from D for guideline.

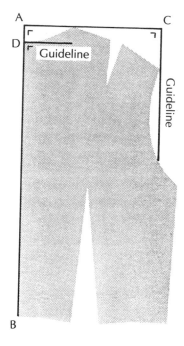

FIGURE 6

B–E = Waist arc (19) plus $1\frac{1}{2}$ inches for dart intake. Square from B. (Use 1-inch dart intake for Petites.)

E–F = $\frac{3}{16}$ inch, squared down from E.

B–G = Dart placement (20).

G–H = $1\frac{1}{2}$ inches (1 inch for Petites).

G–I = One-half of G–H.

B–J = Side length (11). (For use as guidemark.)

Personal fit: Replace B–J instruction with: D–J = armhole depth (34).

J–K = Back arc (18) plus $\frac{3}{4}$ inch (ease), squared from J.

J–L = B–I. Mark.

L–M = $\frac{3}{4}$ inch, square down from L for dart point. Draw each dart leg from M, extending line $\frac{1}{8}$ inch past points G and H. From these points, draw a slightly curved line to B and F.

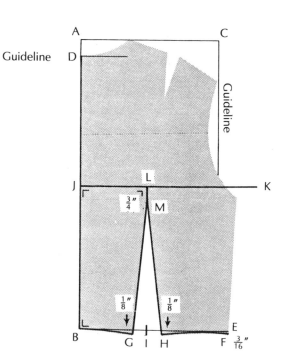

FIGURE 7

B–N = Shoulder slope (7). N touches somewhere on C guideline.

A–O = Back neck (12). Mark. Draw line from O to N. If line does not equal shoulder length, plus ½ inch for dart intake, extend or shorten length of point N until it does. (Line may extend beyond guideline.) Square down from O (on O–N line) to D guideline. Label P.

P–Q = $\frac{3}{8}$ inch diagonal line. With French curve touching D, Q, and O, draw neckline.

Shoulder dart:

O–R = One-half of O to N. Mark. With ruler touching points R and M, draw a 3-inch line down from R. Label S (dart point).

To locate T, mark ¼ inch from R and square up ⅛ inch. Connect T with O and S.

To locate U, mark ¼ inch from R and square up ¼ inch (guideline).

From S, draw dart leg to guideline equal to T-S. Connect U to N.

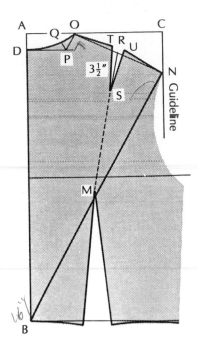

FIGURE 8

Draw a line from F to K.

K–V = ½ inch (for depth below armhole).

Personal fit: Tilting waistline—mark side seam (11) down from V. To blend waistline, see Chapter 26.

D–W = One-half of D–J, plus ¾ inch. Mark.

W–X = Across back (16) plus ⅜ inch, squared from W.

With French curve touching N, X, and V, draw armhole.

This completes the bodice draft. Do not cut patterns from paper until the sleeve has been drafted, as modifications to the bodice armhole may be required to balance the sleeve. (Sleeve draft follows skirt draft.)

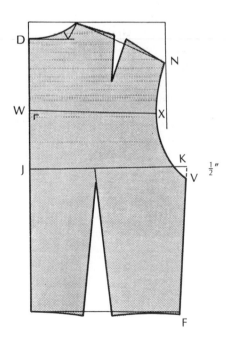

THE SKIRT DRAFT

The basic skirt draft can be developed for several uses:
- As the foundation pattern for other skirt designs
- As a suit skirt or separate skirt
- Or combined with the bodice to form a dress

Two versions of the back skirt is given, Type 1 and Type 2. They are described as follows:

Type 1. The foundation skirt is drafted with two darts of equal length and intake on the back. This simplifies the pattern manipulating process when designing skirts with flare, gathers, and pleats.

Type 2. This pattern is developed with two darts of unequal length and intake. It is used as a separate skirt for suits and for straight-line skirt designs. Because of the unequal darts on the back, this type fits the figure better.

A shaded outline of the skirt has been superimposed on the draft to visually illustrate the purpose of each line relevant to the developing draft. For quick reference, numbers from your Personal Measurement Chart or Industrial Measurement Chart are shown in parentheses in the sequence given in the draft.

For personal dart intake, see page 62 if necessary. Follow *"Personal fit:"* instructions where they apply.

Measurements needed for skirt draft				
■ Skirt length (as desired)				
■ (25) Hip depth	CF	_____	CB	_____
■ (23) Hip arc	F	_____	B	_____
■ (19) Waist arc	F	_____	B	_____
■ (20) Dart placement	F	_____	B	_____
■ (26) Side hip depth	R	_____	L	_____
■ *Personal fit: Record the following: (21)*				
Total intake	F	_____	B	_____
Number of darts	F	_____	B	_____
Each dart intake	F	_____	B	_____

SKIRT FRONT AND TYPE 1 SKIRT BACK

FIGURE 1

A–B = Skirt length desired.
A–C = Center front hip depth (25). Mark.
A–D = Back hip arc (23). Square out from A.
C–E = A–D, squared from C.
B–F = A–D, squared from B. Connect D to F.
E–G = Center back hip depth (25). Cross mark.

Personal fit: Extend line beyond D, if necessary.

A–H = Front hip arc (23).
C–I = A–H, squared from C.
B–J = A–H, squared from B. Connect J to H.

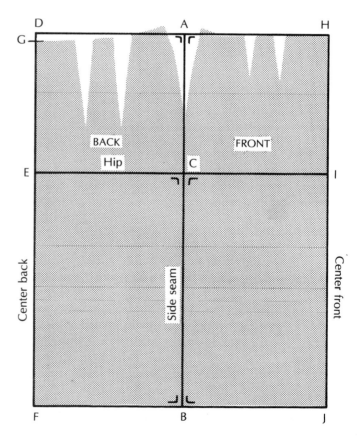

FIGURE 2

Back:

D–K = Back waist arc, plus ¼ inch ease (19).

K–L = 2 inches (dart intake).

   Personal fit: K–L = Total dart intake (21).

D–M = Dart placement (20).

   Personal fit: Apply personal dart intake and spacing starting from point M.

- Measure 1 inch from M (dart intake). Mark.
- Space 1¼ inch between darts. Mark.
- Measure 1 inch from mark (dart intake). Mark.
- Square up and down at each dart mark.
- Square up and down from point L, as shown.

Front:

H–N = Front waist arc, plus ¼ inch (19).

N–O = 1 inch dart intake.

   Personal fit: N–O = Total dart intake (21).

H–P = Dart placement (20).

   Personal fit: Apply personal dart intake and spacing starting from point P.

- Measure ½ inch from P (dart intake). Mark.
- Space 1¼ inch between darts. Mark.
- Measure ½ inch from mark (dart intake). Mark.
- Square up and down at each dart mark.
- Square up and down from point O.

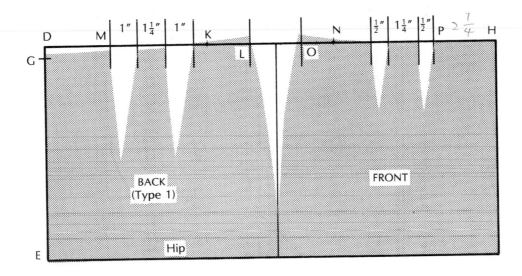

FIGURE 3

C–L and C–O = Hip depth at side seam (26).

- Draw front and back hipline curve using skirt curve ruler. Measure up from point C until the measurement touches somewhere on L and O line. Relabel points L and O.

- Draw waistline, using shallow side of curve ruler, from points G and H to hip marks L and O guidelines.

Note: This is a tentative waistline. (To shape a tilting waist, see Chapter 26.)

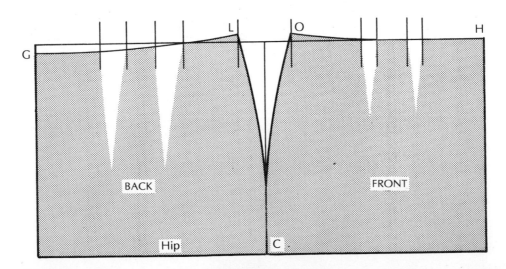

FIGURE 4

Back:
- Locate dart centers and square down $5\frac{1}{2}$ inches (5 inches for Petites) from D–H line. Draw dart legs from curve of waistline to dart points.
- True dart legs by adding to the shorter leg, blending with waistline.

Front:
- Locate dart centers and square down $3\frac{1}{2}$ inches ($3\frac{1}{4}$ inches for Petites) from D–H line.
- Draw dart legs from curve of waistline to dart points.
- True dart legs by adding to shorter leg. Blend with waistline.
- Cut skirt front and back from paper.

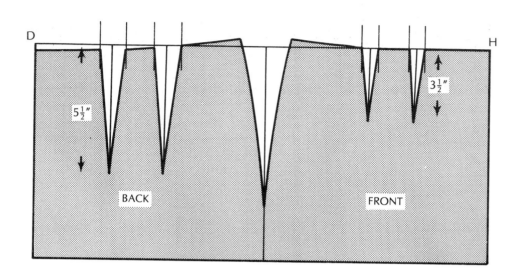

TYPE 2 SKIRT BACK (for suits and separates)

FIGURE 5

Trace the basic back skirt (Type 1), omitting darts. Crossmark dart placement (first dart leg closest to center back)

Dart information:
- Long dart: Total dart intake, less $\frac{1}{2}$ inch. (Example: $1\frac{1}{2}$ inch.) Length = $5\frac{1}{2}$ inches.
- Space: $1\frac{1}{4}$ inches.
- Short dart: Dart intake $\frac{1}{2}$ inch. Length = $3\frac{1}{2}$ inches.
- Locate dart centers. Draw dart lengths parallel with center back. Draw dart legs to dart points, true, and blend with waistline.
- Complete pattern for test fit using front skirt.

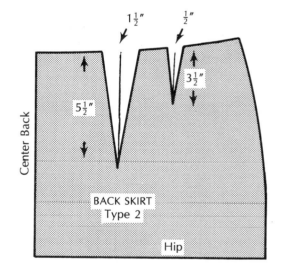

THE SLEEVE DRAFT

The arm is one of the most efficient and mobile parts of the human anatomy as it is capable of moving in every direction. When relaxed, it may lie in perfect alignment, forward or backward relative to the side. The arm can perform an infinite variety of functions, and it is this ability that places a burden on the sleeve.

The sleeve is one of the most difficult of the basic pattern pieces to fit. The well-balanced sleeve will hang on the relaxed arm without any visible puckering or stress around the cap without regard to the alignment with the side seam of the garment:

- *Perfect stance:* Center grain aligns with side seam.
- *Forward stance:* (stooped shoulders): Sleeve grain is forward of side seam.
- *Upright (military) stance:* Sleeve grain can fall back of side seam.

Perfect   Forward   Upright

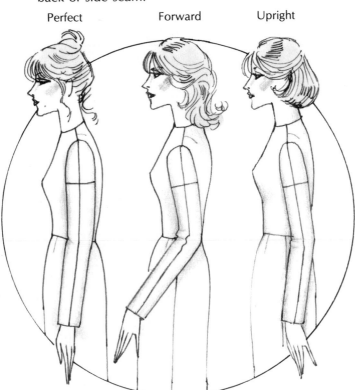

After completing the sleeve draft, and before cutting out the bodice pattern, the patternmaker should follow the instructions (given at the end of sleeve draft directions) on how to adjust the sleeve and/or bodice to achieve a perfect relationship amongst the sleeve, armhole and the arm. The completed draft is used with both the bodice draft and the bodice drape.

A shaded outline of the basic sleeve has been superimposed on the draft to illustrate visually the purpose of each line relevant to the developing draft. Using measurements previously recorded on your Personal or Industrial Measurement Chart, mark and label each line carefully (for arm measurements refer to page 60). For quick reference, numbers from the chart are shown in parentheses and are listed in sequence they are used in the draft. *Note:* The sleeve cap is developed with a shape slightly forward of the center to more accurately fit the angle of the ball of the arm.

Use *Personal fit* instructions where they apply.

Measurements needed	Additional personal fit measurements:
■ (33) Overarm length _____	
■ (35) Cap height ____	■ (36) *Elbow depth* _____
■ (37) Biceps _____	■ *(39) Around hand* _____

The following table of measurements are given as a *guide* for establishing company standards. It is possible that the patternmaker or manufacturer may wish to assign a different size to the measurements given. Elbow and wrist measurements are included in the draft process. (However, wrist measurements are listed as reference only.) Instruction is provided at the completion of the draft for increasing elbow and decreasing wrist measurements, if desired.

For sleeve sizes not listed, note measurement scale between sizes. Continue decreasing or increasing measurements until desired size is reached.

SLEEVE DRAFT MEASUREMENT CHART

Misses' and women's sizes (ease included)

Sizes	6	8	10	12	14	16	18	20
Overarm length	21 7/8	22 1/4	22 5/8	23	23 3/8	23 3/4	24 1/8	24 1/2
Cap height	5 5/8	5 3/4	5 7/8	6	6 1/8	6 1/4	6 3/8	6 1/2
Biceps	12 1/8	12 3/8	12 5/8	13	13 3/8	13 7/8	14 3/8	14 3/4
Wrist	8 1/8	8 3/8	8 5/8	9	9 3/8	9 7/8	10 3/8	10 3/4

Junior and junior petite sizes (ease included)

Sizes	5	7	9	11	13	15	17
Overarm length	21 5/8	22	22 3/8	22 3/4	23 1/8	23 1/2	2 7/8
Cap height	5 1/2	5 5/8	5 3/4	5 7/8	6	6 1/8	6 1/4
Biceps	11 7/8	12 1/8	12 3/8	12 3/4	13 1/8	13 5/8	14 1/8
Wrist	7 7/8	8 1/8	8 3/8	8 3/4	9 1/8	9 5/8	10 1/8

FIGURE 1

The sleeve frame:

A–B = Overarm length (33)
A–C = Cap height (35)
C–D = One-half of C–B minus 1 inch.

> *Personal fit: Measure down from A for elbow level.*

> Square out from both sides of A, B, C, and D.

C–E = One-half of biceps (37)
C–F = C–E.
B–G = 2 inches less than C–E.
B–H = B–G

> Connect G to E, and H to F.
> Label elbow level I and J.

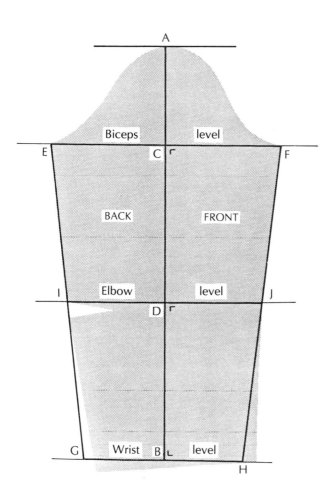

FIGURE 2

Sleeve cap:

E–K = One-fourth of E–C.
F–L = E–K.
A–M = E–K.
A–N = E–K.

Square the following points:

K = $\frac{7}{8}$ inches. Label O.
M = $\frac{5}{8}$ inches. Label P.
N = $\frac{3}{8}$ inches. Label Q.
L = $\frac{5}{8}$ inches. Label R.

> With ruler touching O–P, and Q–R, dot mark midpoints. Label S and T as shown.

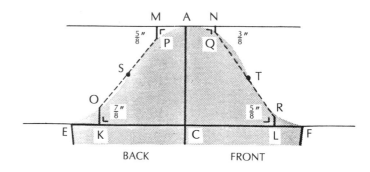

FIGURE 3

Shaping sleeve cap:

▪ Draw sleeve cap with the vary curve ruler, or French curve as illustrated.
▪ To draw curve of the sleeve, position ruler on draft so that the curve edge touches points A, Q, and T (outward curve) and points T, R, and F (inward curve). Repeat process for back sleeve cap.

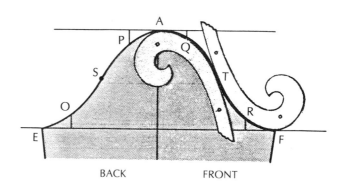

FIGURE 4

Elbow dart:

I–U = One-half of I–D.

U–V = $\frac{3}{8}$ inch, squared from U.

I–W = 1 inch (dart intake).

Connect I to V, and connect V to W equal to I–V measurement. Mark.

G–X = $\frac{5}{8}$ inch.

Draw line from W through X equal to I–G measurement plus $\frac{1}{8}$ inch (ease). Label Y.

Y–Z = G–H (Line touches somewhere on the wrist guideline). Connect Z with J.

Sleeve notches identify the back from the front sleeve (when attaching sleeve to bodice), and control the ease distribution.

• *Back sleeve:* Two notches spaced $\frac{1}{2}$ inch apart, mark first notch $1\frac{1}{8}$ inches down from point S. Square notches in from curve of cap.

• *Front sleeve:* One notch, marked 1 inch down from point T, and squared in from curve of cap.

FIGURE 5

Changing wrist measurement:

To increase or decrease wrist add or subtract from points Y and Z equally, blending to points W and J.

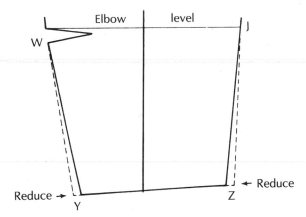

FIGURE 6

Blending elbow dart

• Extend dart legs $\frac{1}{4}$ inch and connect to E and Y to increase elbow room. (This also blends the dip at back underseam caused by dart intake.)

Adjust sleeve to armhole of bodice following instruction on page 76.

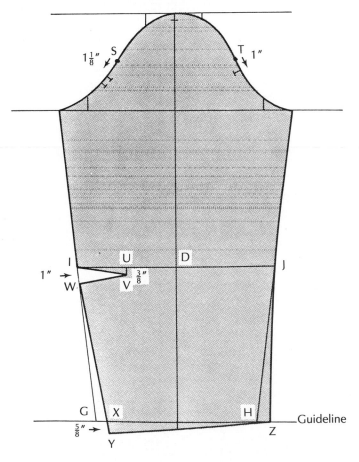

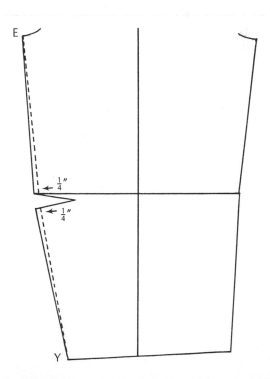

ADJUSTING SLEEVE TO ARMHOLE OF BODICE

The basic sleeve should measure approximately 2 inches more across the biceps of the pattern than the circumference of the arm. The sleeve cap should measure an average of $1\frac{1}{4}$ to $1\frac{3}{4}$ inches more than the front and back bodice armhole, with the ideal being a difference of $1\frac{1}{2}$ inches. The difference between the sleeve cap and armhole measurements is the amount of ease needed to fit over the ball of the arm. The amount of cap ease is determined by the width of the biceps, cap height, and the circumference of the front and back armhole. If any of these factors are out of harmony, it will affect the fit and appearance of the sleeve in the following ways: excessive or insufficient cap ease; cap ease unequally distributed between the front and back armhole; sleeves too tight or too loose. Incorrect placement of the shoulder and/or side seams will affect the alignment of the sleeve on the garment. It is advisable to correct these problems before attaching the sleeve to the garment in order to minimize fitting problems later.

CAP EASE AND ARMHOLE NOTCH PLACEMENTS

Method 1: walking the pattern

FIGURE 1a, 1b and 1c

- Place the front of the sleeve cap on the front armhole of bodice with the corner of the sleeve cap touching the corner of the armhole. Using a pushpin, walk (or pivot) the curve edge of the sleeve cap along the curve edge of the armhole, advancing pushpin as follows:
- Walk the sleeve around the front armhole curve to sleeve notch (Figure 1a). Mark notch of sleeve on bodice.
- Continue walking sleeve (Figure 1b) until shoulder tip of bodice is reached (Figure 1c). Mark sleeve cap at this point.
- Repeat process for back side of sleeve (not illustrated). Measure the distance between marks on sleeve cap. Record overall cap ease: _____.
- If cap ease measures less than $1\frac{1}{4}$ inches or more than $1\frac{3}{4}$ inches, adjust sleeve by following instructions on page 78.

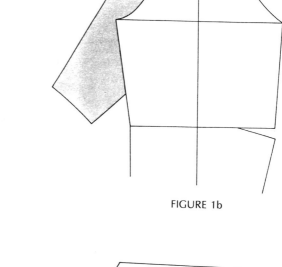

FIGURE 1b

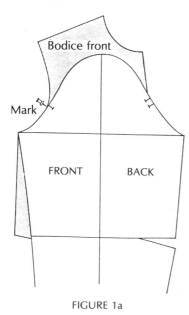

FIGURE 1a

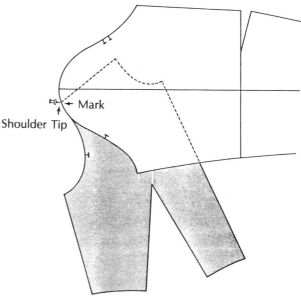

FIGURE 1c

Method 2: curving rule measurement

FIGURE 2a, 2b and 2c
■ Measure around the curve of the sleeve cap and armhole with a metal measuring tape, plastic rule, or flex rule as follows: Stand the measuring device on end and contour ruler to follow the pattern curves using both hands to control the ruler (Figure 2a). Follow the illustrations as a guide. Record measurements.
■ Measure the back armhole and use this measurement to mark the location on the sleeve (Figure 2b).
■ Repeat this process for the front armhole and sleeve cap (Figure 2c).
■ Measure the distance between marks on sleeve cap and record overall cap ease: _____.
■ If cap ease measures less than $1\frac{1}{4}$ inches or more than $1\frac{3}{4}$ inches, adjust sleeve by following instructions given on page 78.

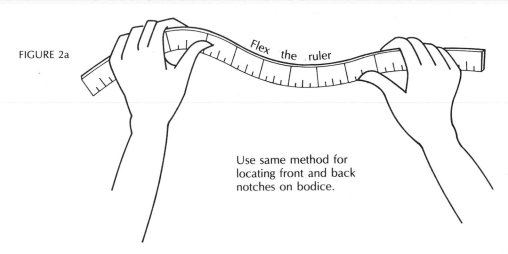

FIGURE 2a

Flex the ruler

Use same method for locating front and back notches on bodice.

Back armhole and sleeve cap:

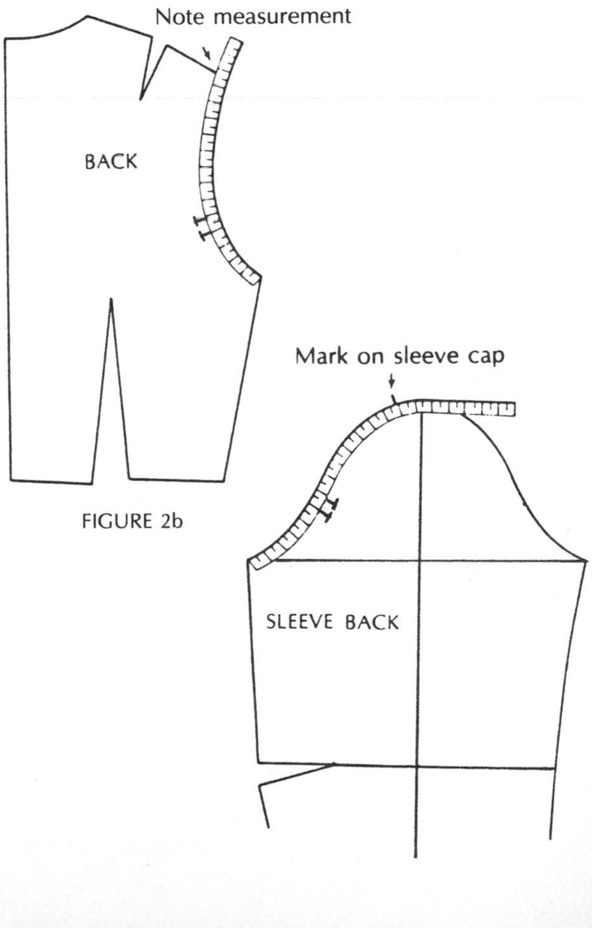

Note measurement

BACK

Mark on sleeve cap

SLEEVE BACK

FIGURE 2b

Front armhole and sleeve cap:

Note measurement

FRONT

Mark on sleeve cap

SLEEVE FRONT

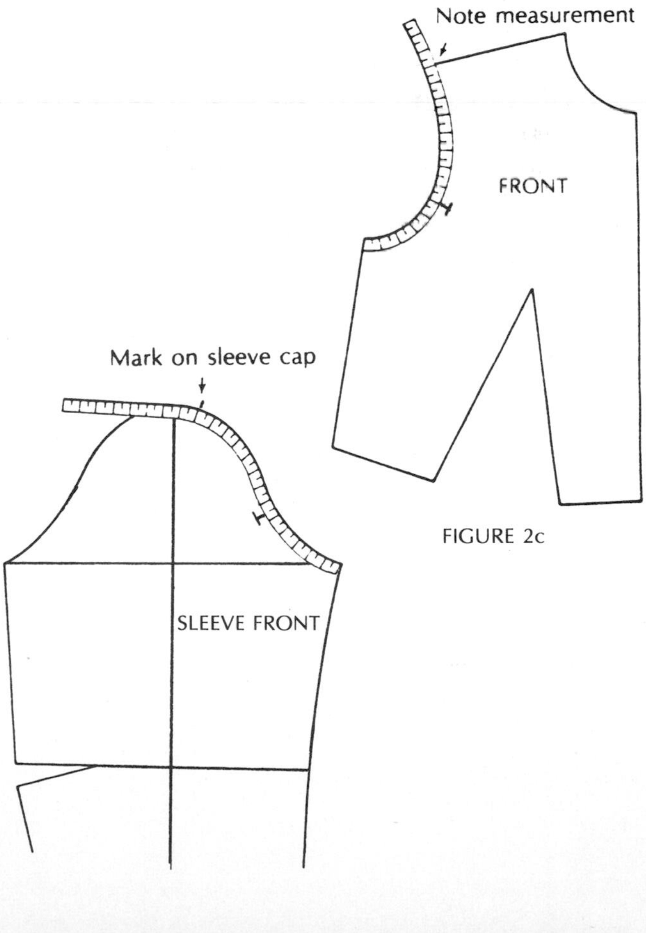

FIGURE 2c

INCREASING AND DECREASING CAP EASE

(Another version given in Chapter 27, sleeve section.)

Increasing cap ease

FIGURE 3
- Trace sleeve and all markings.
- Extend biceps lines equally out from each side indicating amount needed.
- Place sleeve pattern on top of tracing with a pushpin through corner of biceps and point of new biceps mark.
- Pivot pattern upward until sleeve caps touch. Draw and blend new cap. Pivot pattern downward until underseams touch: Draw and blend new underseam. True elbow dart.
- Repeat for front sleeve (broken lines = original pattern).
- Cut from paper.

Decreasing cap ease

FIGURE 4
- Trace sleeve and all markings.
- Measure in equally from each side of biceps indicating reduced amount. Mark.
- Place sleeve pattern on top of tracing with a pushpin through corner of bicep and point of new biceps mark.
- Pivot pattern upward until sleeve caps touch. Draw and blend new cap. Pivot pattern downward until under seams touch. Draw and blend new underseams. Remove pattern and true elbow dart (shaded areas = original pattern).
- Repeat for back sleeve.
- Cut from paper.

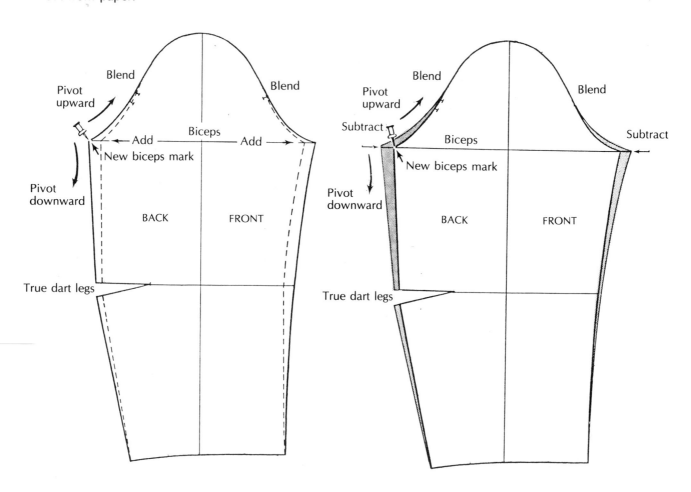

DISTRIBUTING CAP EASE EQUALLY

The perfect sleeve is stitched to the armhole with the center cap notch placed at shoulder tip, and the underseam with the side seam of the garment. If the front and back armholes are not the same measurement, or close to it, more ease will be placed on one side of the armhole than the other. This can cause fitting problems such as puckers along one side of the sleeve cap. To correct a possible problem follow the instruction given.

Shifting cap notch

• Draw a mark half the distance between front and back sleeve cap marks. Adjust as follows:
• If mark touches center grain of sleeve, place cap notch at grainline. See adjustment given for Figure 5.
• If the mark is up to $\frac{3}{16}$ inch away from the center grainline of the sleeve, place the notch at mark. See adjustment given for Figures 6a and 6b.
• If the guideline is more than $\frac{3}{16}$ inch away from the center grainline of the sleeve, it is the front and back armholes of the bodice that are adjusted. This adjustment will be made at the time of fitting, using instructions given in Chapter 27 under the sleeve correction section. Cut and stitch sleeve but do not attach to garment. Go to page 82.

Note: If cap notch is shifted more than $\frac{3}{16}$ inch away from sleeve grain, in either direction, the sleeve will fall out of alignment with side seam of the garment, and can cause fitting problems.

Equal distribution

FIGURE 5
Example: Excess (shaded area) is equally distributed, requiring no shift of the cap notch.

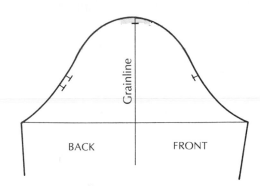

Excessive excess in front armhole

FIGURE 6a
Example: Cap ease (shaded area) is greater on the front sleeve cap.
• Shift cap notch toward front sleeve cap to equalize excess.

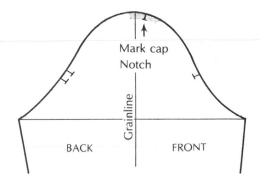

Excessive excess in back armhole

FIGURE 6b
Example: Cap ease (shaded area) is greater on the back sleeve cap.
• Shift cap notch toward front sleeve cap to equalize excess.

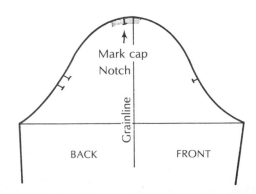

ARMHOLE ADJUSTMENT TO ELIMINATE PUCKERING

The following armhole adjustments should be made if the equalized sleeve cap excess cannot be eased into the armhole without puckering. Even though the cap ease has been equally distributed puckering can occur if the fabric is too rigid, or the seamstress is inexperienced. It is best *not* to remove cap height to decrease cap ease as it will only cause the sleeve to fall away from the side of the garment and stress lines to appear on the sleeve when the garment is on the figure. Three methods are given, but the excess distribution can usually be solved by Figure 7 instructions. If not, include Figure 8 and/or Figure 9.

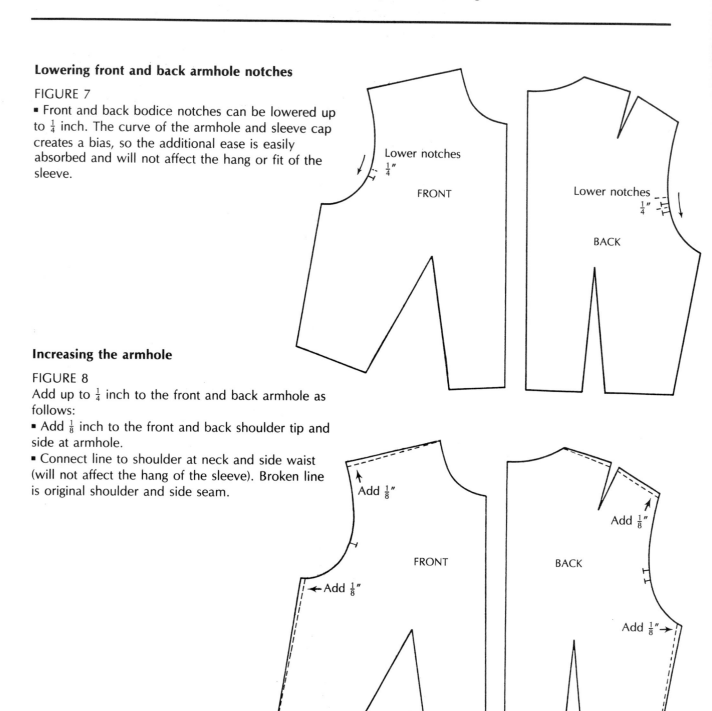

Lowering front and back armhole notches

FIGURE 7
▪ Front and back bodice notches can be lowered up to $\frac{1}{4}$ inch. The curve of the armhole and sleeve cap creates a bias, so the additional ease is easily absorbed and will not affect the hang or fit of the sleeve.

Increasing the armhole

FIGURE 8
Add up to $\frac{1}{4}$ inch to the front and back armhole as follows:
▪ Add $\frac{1}{8}$ inch to the front and back shoulder tip and side at armhole.
▪ Connect line to shoulder at neck and side waist (will not affect the hang of the sleeve). Broken line is original shoulder and side seam.

Transfer excess from darts to armhole

FIGURE 9

- Transfer up to $\frac{1}{4}$ inch to the front and back armhole from the waist and shoulder darts. Cut patterns at armhole to, not through, bust point (front bodice), and back shoulder dart to armhole. Spread patterns $\frac{1}{4}$ inch. Place paper underneath and tape across patterns. Blend armholes. Any remaining excess at the shoulder should be treated as ease. Place notches 1 inch in from shoulder at neck and shoulder tip of the front and back patterns to control ease.

Note: Also use this method for enlarging the armhole for garments requiring large shoulder pads.

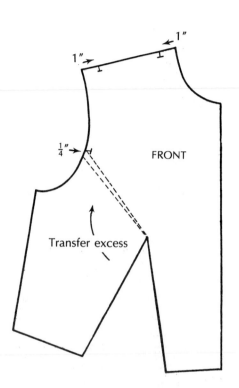

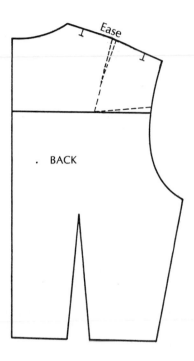

PREPARING PATTERNS FOR TEST FIT

TRUEING BASIC PATTERNS

To true, place pattern with darts on top of pattern without darts, if possible. Incorrect seams should be adjusted equally at each end and blended with seamline. Review Chapter 27 for guide on how to mend when adjusting patterns. Recheck all measurements and cut pattern from paper.

Trueing front and back bodice

FIGURE 10
▪ Place back pattern on top of front pattern (shaded area), touching shoulder neck corners and edge of pattern to shoulder dart leg. Mark dart location on front shoulder.

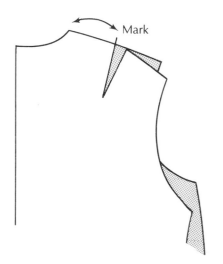

FIGURE 11
▪ Move back pattern so that other dart leg touches mark on front shoulder and pattern's edge matching to shoulder tip. Adjust shoulder, if necessary.

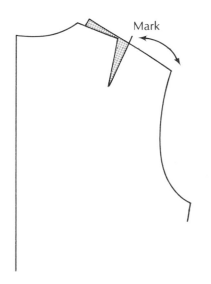

FIGURE 12
▪ Place side seams together, matching side at armhole and waist. Adjust side seam, if necessary.

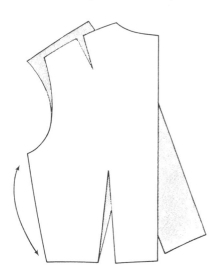

Trueing front and back skirt

FIGURE 13
▪ Place back and front (shaded area) skirts together at sides. Match HBL lines. Skirt should true to side waist and hem from the HBL. If not, recheck drape or recheck square line on draft. If correct adjust patterns above and below the HBL to true.

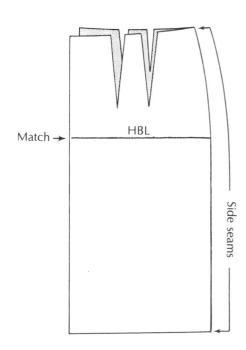

Trueing bodice with skirt

FIGURE 14
- Place center back of bodice to center back of skirt (shaded area), matching stitchline to dart leg (should match perfectly).

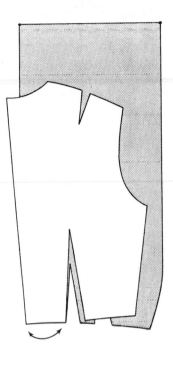

FIGURE 16
- Shift back pattern along waistline, matching mark of bodice with other dart leg on skirt. Side seams should match. If not, recheck waistline measurements and adjust.
- Repeat for front bodice and skirt (not illustrated).

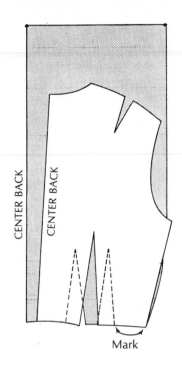

Mark

FIGURE 15
- Shift back pattern, matching other dart leg to dart leg of skirt. Broken line is skirt dart underneath. Mark location of dart leg on bodice.

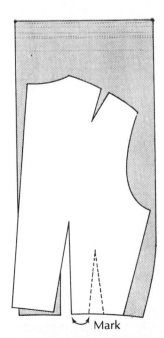

Mark

ASYMMETRIC SHOULDER AND/OR HIP

FIGURE 17
Patterns developed for figures with high and low hips and/or shoulders are cut with a full front and a full back. Make the following pattern adjustments *before* cutting a muslin.

- Draw a slash line from the low to high side of the front and back pattern. Cut slash line to, not through, pattern (hinge effect).
- Overlap pattern on the low side equal to the difference recorded. Secure with tape along cut line of both sides of pattern.
- Mend and blend lines at sides. Redraw darts on skirt.

Measurements needed
- (8) Asymmetric shoulder difference _____
- (26) Asymmetric hip difference _____

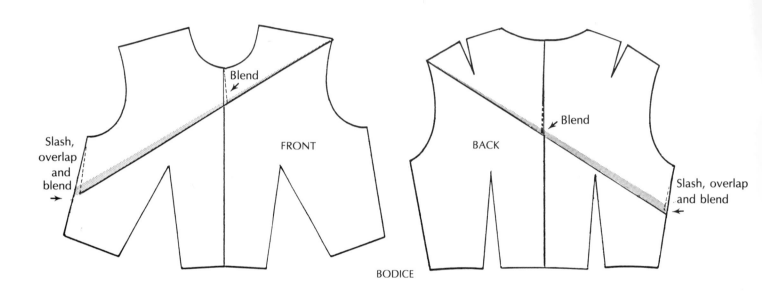

BODICE

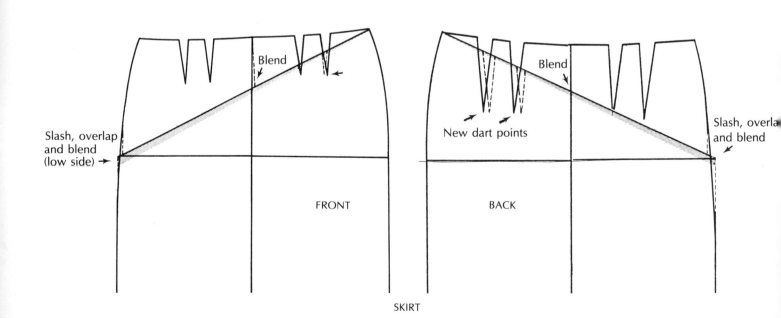

SKIRT

MUSLIN PREPARATION FOR TEST FIT

FIGURE 18

Fold muslin. Place patterns on muslin with front bodice and skirt on fold. Be sure that center back bodice, skirt, and sleeve grain are parallel with selvage as shown. Trace, include all markings. If fitting a form, cut half a muslin. Trace full patterns for figures with asymmetric shoulders and/or hiplines on *open* muslin.

Seam allowance on muslin for adjustment purposes
- $\frac{1}{4}$ inch around neckline.
- 1 inch at shoulder seams.
- $\frac{1}{2}$ inch around armhole.
- 1 inch at side seams and center back.
- $\frac{1}{2}$ inch at waistline.
- 1 inch at center front and back for half a garment.

Note: For facing instructions, see Chapter 14.

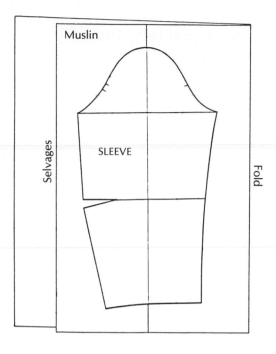

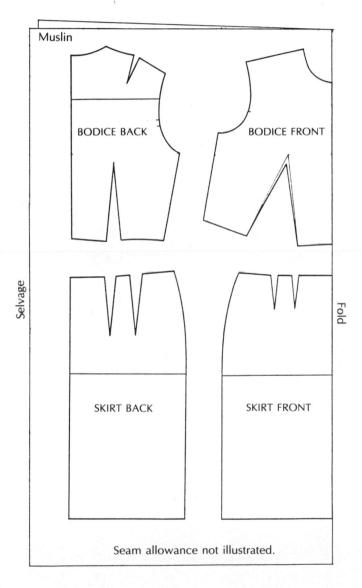

FIGURE 19

After seam allowances are added, cut garment from fabric. Fold darts and cut along waistline. Stitch and connect bodice with skirt. The sleeve is stitched to the garment *after* the test fit. When stitching the muslin, use long machine stitches for easy removal for adjusting muslin. Press seams open with a warm iron. Do not use steam. Place on form or figure. (Turn to Chapter 27 for guidance in fitting.)

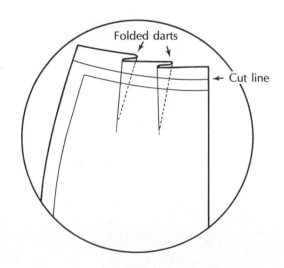

Draping the basic patterns

THE BODICE DRAPE

The art of draping lies in the skillful use of the hands. Like a sculptor, the draper uses the palm of the hand and the fingertips to gently smooth and mold the fabric on the form in an upward, outward, downward, and inward motion, always allowing the grainline to fall naturally without pulling or stretching the fabric out of shape. The draper must also maintain the balance of the garment. It should be in harmony with the natural stance of the figure; otherwise, the garment will hang off-balance on the form or figure. To control the drape, the crosswise grain (the lines drawn across the muslin referred to as the horizontal balance line (HBL)) must lie in perfect horizontal alignment with the floor. If not, gapping (misplaced excess) and strain (insufficient fabric in a given area) result.

The form or figure. Either side of the form or figure may be draped, but both the back and the front should be draped on the same side. The opposite side is completed by cutting the draped muslin on the fold. A full garment is required for fitting the figure, but only the draped half when fitting the form. Figures with asymmetric shoulders should be draped on the high side (without regard as to which side is illustrated). An illusion of symmetry can be created by placing a shoulder pad on the low side and pinning it to the bra or support

garments. It is more difficult to conceal differences for asymmetric figures with high and low hips or tilting waistlines. (These problems can usually be minimized by wearing one-piece or monochromatic garments.)

When draping the human figure, the model should wear a close-fitting garment, preferably one that defines the neckline, side seams, and center back (for example, a leotard, bodysuit, dress, or foundation garments) that will support the pins and secure the muslin. However, the model can be marked to define these locations (see page 54).

FIGURE 1a and 1b

Pinning. Joining seams and darts should be pinned perpendicular to the fold line of the muslin (Figure 1a) and not to the form or to the model's foundation garments. This will allow the drape to fall naturally when it is viewed. Parallel pinning (Figure 1b) will cause puckering and fullness, and distort the look and fit of the drape.

The sleeve. The basic sleeve is usually drafted and is not included in the drape section (see page 73 for draft).

Once the drape has been completed, it is transferred to pattern paper, trued, and test fit. Instructions for fitting corrections are contained in Chapter 27.

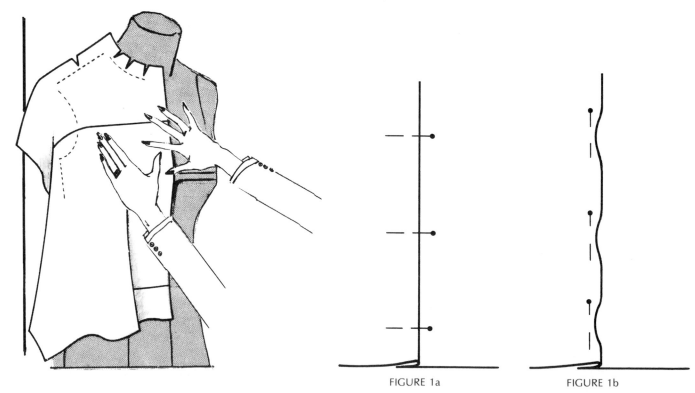

FIGURE 1a   FIGURE 1b

PREPARATION FOR THE BODICE DRAPE

Muslin needed

- Do not use more muslin than is required. Trim or slash the selvage to eliminate yarn tension, correct bowing in the fabric (see page 15 for guidance), and cut the muslin using measurements taken from the form as follows:

FIGURE 2

- *Length:* Measure front and back forms from the shoulder at neck to the waist, add 3 inches.
- *Width:* Measure from the center front and back forms across the bust and back to the side of the form, add 4 inches.

Personal fit: Add 8 inches to muslin width. Draw vertical line 5 inches in from edge of muslin to indicate center line. Follow instructions below for muslin preparation, measuring from center line (not illustrated).

FIGURE 2

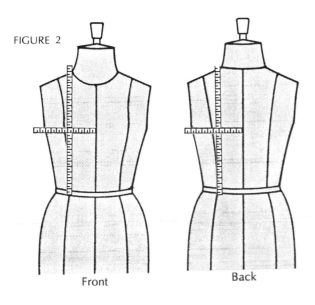

Front   Back

- Fold muslin under 1 inch along straight grain of front/back.
- Press without steam. (Avoids shrinkage and makes muslin easier to handle.)

Measurements needed
- (5) Center front length _____
- (5) Center back length _____
- (20) Dart placement _____

Muslin preparation for front drape

FIGURE 3

- Measure down 4 inches from top at fold and out $2\frac{1}{4}$ inches. Draw tentative neckline with French curve.

- Cut to within $\frac{1}{2}$ inch of line.
- Measure down 3 inches from neck and square a line from the fold across the muslin or pull a crosswise thread. (Represents the Horizontal Balance Line—HBL.)
- Measure down from the neck equal to the center front length (5). Square a line from the fold at waist equal to dart placement (20).

FIGURE 3

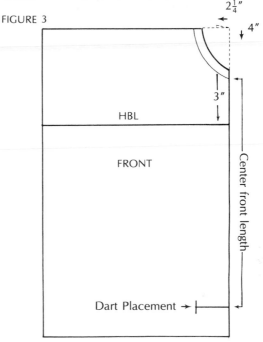

Muslin preparation for back drape

FIGURE 4

- Repeat process, using illustration and back measurements as a guide.

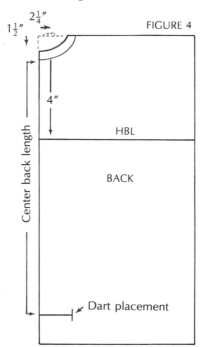

FIGURE 4

THE FRONT BODICE DRAPE

Study the illustrations and instructions before beginning the drape. Note: Holding pins are thrust into the form but should be pinned to the garment when draping the figure. When slashing to relieve muslin tension, do *not* slash inside the outline of the form or it will cause fitting problems. The armhole and neckline will be trimmed to stitchline with the armhole not being lowered until transferred to paper. This allows for better control of fit at this stage of the drape development.

FIGURE 1a and 1b

Muslin placement. Place center fold of muslin on center front of form (Figure 1a), or centerline of muslin on center front of figure (Figure 1b). Pin as follows:
- Center front neck.
- Center front bust (pin to bridge).
- Center front waist.
- Smooth muslin from center front at bridge to bust. Pin muslin at bust point, and pin dart placement mark at waist.

Personal fit: Secure muslin to undraped side as shown (Figure 1b). Continue with the following instructions.

Neckline. Starting from center front neck, smooth muslin upward along neckline toward shoulder, slashing just to neckline to relieve strain. Pin shoulder at neck.

Shoulder line. With palm of hand and fingertips resting just above bust, gently smooth muslin along shoulder line from neck to shoulder tip. Slash at an angle midway to relieve tension. Pin shoulder tip.

Mid-armhole. Allow muslin to lay over ridge of the armhole. Pin, taking care *not* to smooth out the excess from the hollow area between shoulder tip and bust. Crossmark plate at side seam.

FIGURE 2

Guidemark the following locations:
- Mid-neck.
- Shoulder at neck.
- Shoulder tip.
- Mid-armhole at ridge (pin head location).

Arm plate (armpit). With palm and fingertip resting on side of bust, continue smoothing muslin downward along armhole and outward past armplate and side seam. Pin.
Personal fit: Trim excess from upper armhole from shoulder tip to the HBL line. Raise arm and smooth muslin toward side seam. Crossmark armpit at this location and trim armhole to this mark.

Remove pins and trim neckline to within $\frac{1}{4}$ inch (tenative) and shoulder to within $\frac{1}{2}$ inch of seamline. Cut along armhole ridge from shoulder tip to plate and beyond. Repin.

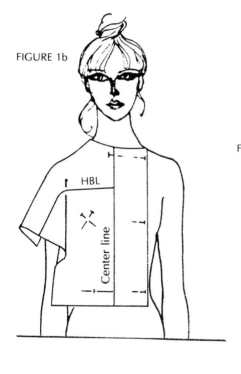

FIGURE 1b

HBL

Center line

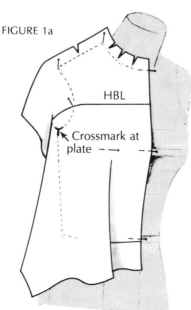

FIGURE 1a

HBL

Crossmark at plate

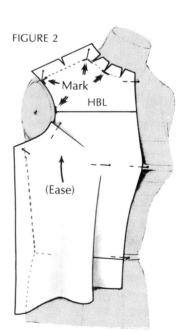

FIGURE 2

Mark

HBL

(Ease)

Ease allowance. Lift muslin approximately $\frac{1}{8}$ inch at crossmark of plate (armpit), and pin a tuck $\frac{1}{4}$ inch for ease (folds to $\frac{1}{8}$ inch) between HBL and side seam. Tuck should be directed to bust point. This ease eliminates strain in garment when arm is in a forward position and when shoulder is raised. Crossmark plate (armpit). Trim armhole to crossmark, allowing mark to show. Pin (Figure 2).

FIGURE 3a and 3b

Side seam. With palm of the hand on side of the bust and fingers extended toward the side of the form, smooth muslin downward along side to waistline. (Excess muslin will divide itself naturally.) Pin muslin at side seam of waist. Mark a guide for side seam down from crossmark. Mark corner of waist.

Waistline. Smooth muslin along waistline to approximately $1\frac{1}{2}$ inches from side waist. Pin a tuck $\frac{1}{4}$ inch (folds to $\frac{1}{8}$ inch) for waist ease. Continue smoothing muslin along waistline to side front seam of form. Crossmark. Slash along waist.

Personal fit: Pinch remaining excess between fingers at waist touching dart placement mark on muslin. Crossmark muslin at waist for dart intake.

Note: If excess folds over center front, trim surplus to within 1 inch of dart marks and bust point (Figure 3-b).

FIGURE 4

Waist dart. Fold excess into a waist dart with excess toward center line. Pin dart perpendicular to fold line. Trim excess to within $\frac{1}{2}$ inch of waistline.

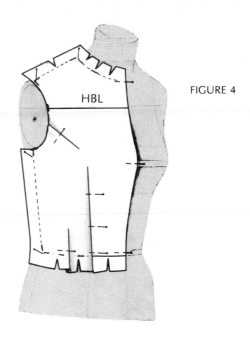

FIGURE 4

FIGURE 5a and 5b
- Trim neck to seamline.
- Measure $\frac{1}{2}$ inch out from crossmark at plate (armpit) for ease. Mark (Figure 5a). Crease-fold side seam from mark to side waist, and along shoulderline. Fold muslin over and pin as shown (Figure 5b).

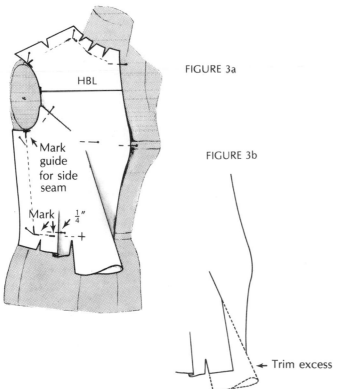

FIGURE 3a

FIGURE 3b

Mark guide for side seam

Mark $\frac{1}{4}''$

← Trim excess

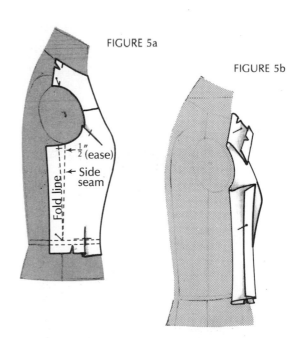

FIGURE 5a

FIGURE 5b

$\frac{1}{2}''$ (ease)

← Side seam

Fold line

THE BACK BODICE DRAPE

FIGURE 1a and 1b

Muslin placement. Place center fold of muslin on center back of form (Figure 1a), or centerline of muslin on center back of figure (Figure 1b). Pin as follows:
- Center back at neck guidemark.
- Center back at HBL line.
- Center back at waistline tape.
- Dart placement mark at waist.

Personal fit: Secure muslin to undraped side as shown. Continue with the following instructions.

- Smooth muslin across HBL (grainline parallel with the floor). Excess muslin will divide itself naturally between upper and lower bodice. Pin ridge line of armhole (pinhead location).

BACK

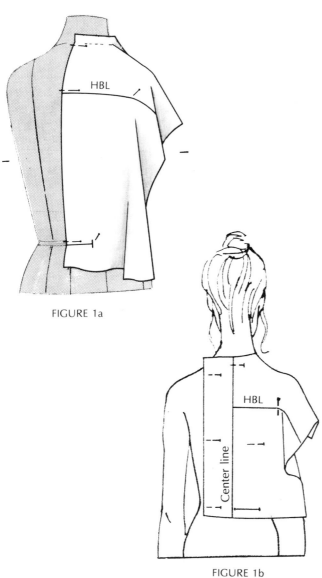

FIGURE 1a

FIGURE 1b

FIGURE 2

Neckline. Starting from the center back neck, smooth muslin along neck to shoulder. Slash to neckline to relieve strain. Pin shoulder at neck. From shoulder at neck, smooth muslin along shoulder line to side back seam (mid-shoulder). Crossmark for dart leg.

Guidemark the following locations:
- Corner of shoulder at neck
- Mid-neck

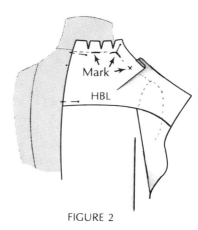

FIGURE 2

FIGURE 3

- From HBL at mid-armhole, smooth muslin upward over ridge of armhole to shoulder tip. Excess muslin will divide itself naturally. Pin shoulder tip and crossmark for guide.
- From shoulder tip, smooth excess over to side back seam (mid-shoulder). Crossmark for dart leg.

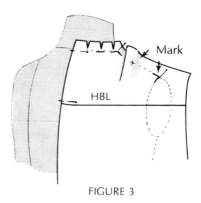

FIGURE 3

FIGURE 4

Shoulder dart. Fold remaining excess into dart (excess toward center back). *Note:* If excess is less than $\frac{3}{8}$ inch, treat it as ease. If no excess exists, recheck position of HBL or for gapping at armhole. (Model or form could have a flat back requiring no shoulder dart.)

- Unpin. Trim excess along ridge of armhole starting at HBL and to within $\frac{1}{2}$ inch of shoulderline and $\frac{1}{4}$ inch of neckline. Repin.

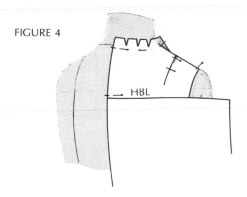

FIGURE 4

FIGURE 5

Waist dart and ease. From dart mark fold in $1\frac{1}{2}$ inches with excess toward center back (1 inch for Petites).

- Crossmark dart legs at waistline.
- Continue smoothing muslin toward side. Pin $\frac{1}{4}$-inch tuck for ease (folds to $\frac{1}{8}$ inch) between dart and side seam. Slash waistline where needed.
- Guidemark waist.

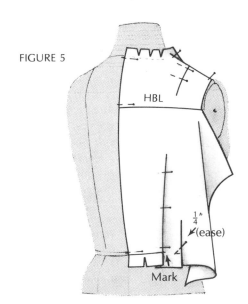

FIGURE 5

FIGURE 6a and 6b

Arm plate (armpit). Using both hands at the same time do the following: With one hand, smooth muslin downward from HBL and outward past side seam of the form. With the other hand, smooth muslin from waist outward past side seam. Pin side waist and slightly beyond arm plate. (All remaining excess is removed.)

- Crossmark armplate (armpit) at side seam and side waist. Unpin.
- From armplate (armpit) mark, measure out $\frac{1}{2}$ inch for ease. Mark (Figure 6a).
- Trim side to within 1 inch of side seam.
- Trim armhole around plate (armpit) up along armhole ridge ending at HBL.
- Trim shoulder to within $\frac{1}{2}$ inch.

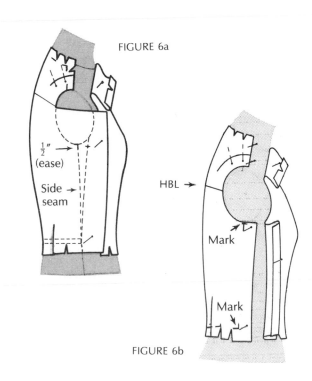

FIGURE 6a

FIGURE 6b

FIGURE 7

Join front and back drape. Pin front shoulder line over back, matching shoulder at neck and shoulder tip. Pin front side seam over back, matching ease marks at armplate (armpit) to marks at waist.
▪ Trim back neckline along guidemarks lowering front neck ⅜".

FIGURES 8, 9, 10, and 11

▪ Test: The armhole is not lowered at this time. Plate (armpit) crossmarks are needed as reference points for lowering front back armholes and seam allowances when transferring muslin to paper. Remove ease pins at waist and mid-armhole. Remove pins from center front and center back. If muslin remains in perfect alignment with center front and center back, and armhole falls away evenly from form or figure without strain or gapping, prepare for transfer to paper (see Figure 8). If drape looks like Figures 9, 10, or 11, redrape the bodice until armhole fits well and garment hangs in perfect alignment with form or figure.
▪ Remove muslin from form and prepare for skirt drape.

FIGURE 7

Gapping or strain should not appear around armhole

Trim ⅜"

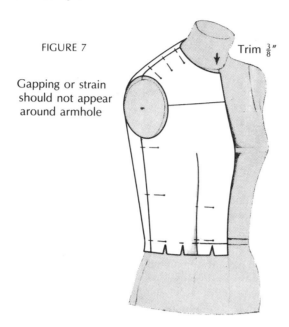

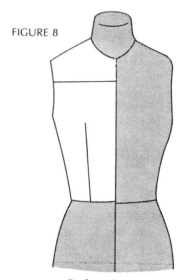

FIGURE 8

Perfect alignment

FIGURE 9

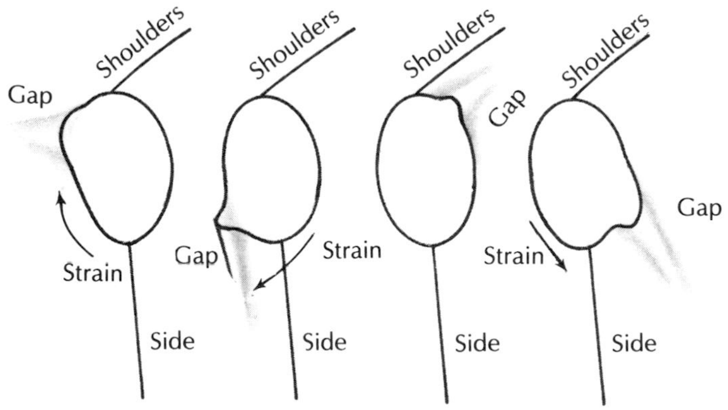

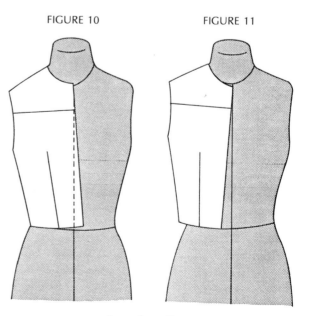

BACK ARMHOLE — FRONT ARMHOLE

Gap — Shoulders — Strain — Side

Shoulder out of alignment — Side seam out of aligment — Shoulders out of alignment — Side seam out of alignment

FIGURE 10 — FIGURE 11

Imperfect alignment

Note: Release shoulder and side seam for redraping bodice. If necessary, release darts.

THE SKIRT DRAPE

The basic skirt hangs straight downward from the widest part of the hipline. This location is marked by a line drawn across the pattern. This line is referred to as the horizontal balance line (HBL). The key to a balanced pattern and garment lies in the accurate placement of the HBL on the form, figure, muslin, and pattern. Any deviation of the HBL between front and back skirt at the *side seam* will cause fitting problems. If the HBL of either the front or back skirt of the muslin lies above the HBL mark at side seam, the dart intake will be too great, causing stress across the thigh when walking. If the line is placed below the HBL mark on the form, there will be insufficient dart intake, causing flare at the hemline.

Measurements needed
- (25) Center front hip depth _____
- (20) Dart placement _____
- (23) Hip arc F _____ B _____
- (19) Waist arc F _____ B _____ (reference only)

Muslin needed
- Cut muslin using front and back hip measurement, add 3½ inches for width, and length as desired.
- Trim or clip selvage. Straighten muslin grain if bowed (see page 15 for guidance).
- Fold under 1 inch along straight grain and press *without* steam.

Personal fit: Add 6 inches to width and place a vertical line for center front through length 3 inches in from muslin edge. Continue with instructions given.

Muslin preparation for skirt drape

FIGURE 1
- Measure down from fold equal to center front hip depth, plus 2 inches. Mark and square across muslin *carefully* (or pull grain to define line). This represents the HBL.
- Measure out from fold on HBL line to equal hip arc measurement. Crossmark. Measure over ½ inch for ease. Mark. Measure over 1 inch for seam allowance and mark.
- Square up and down from HBL at each mark.
- Measure up from HBL at center front equal to the center front depth (25), and square across equal to the dart placement (20).
- Cut excess away from side (broken line).
- Repeat for back using back measurements (not illustrated).

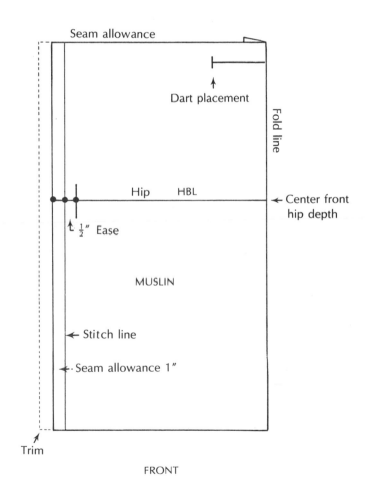

FRONT

THE FRONT SKIRT DRAPE

The basic skirt front will be developed with two back skirts both of which are commonly used for designing garments:

- Type 1 for skirt designs. Darts are of equal length and intake.
- Type 2 for suit skirts or separates. Darts are of unequal length and intake.

FIGURE 1a and 1b
- Place square line of muslin (HBL) on the HBL line of the form (Figure 1a) and figure (Figure 1b) aligning the center front of the muslin with the center front.
- Pin HBL at center front and side seam at crossmark of muslin.
- Pin center front at waistline.
- Pin at dart placement.

Personal fit: Pin excess to other side of figure to secure muslin while draping.

- With palm of the hand on hipbone, and finger tips touching side hip, move hand upward smoothing muslin along side seam to waistline.
- Crossmark side waist and pin.

FIGURE 2

- From side waist, smooth muslin along waistline approximately 1 inch, and pin $\frac{1}{4}$ inch tuck for ease (folds $\frac{1}{8}$ inch). Mark for waistline guide.
- Remove pin from HBL at side seam, and repin at second guideline mark on muslin (ease). Smooth upward from HBL to waist and pencil rub side seam so that the hipline shape will show on muslin.

Personal fit: Place plastic ruler along hipline to side waist and draw hip shape.

Dart information:
- Divide excess into two darts.

Personal fit: If remaining excess is $\frac{5}{8}$ inch or less, drape one dart. If more than $1\frac{3}{8}$ inch, drape three darts and space 1 inch apart.

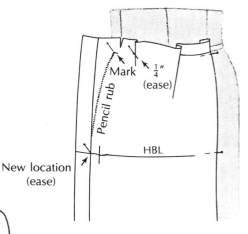

New location (ease)

FIGURE 2

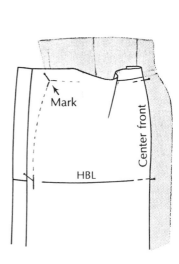

Mark

HBL

Center front

FIGURE 1a

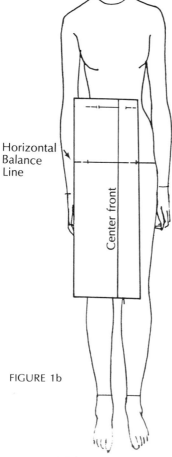

Horizontal Balance Line

Center front

FIGURE 1b

FIGURE 3
- At dart placement mark, fold first dart using one-half of the excess. (Fold excess toward center front.) Crossmark waist and dart leg.
- Pin dart to outermost bulge of the abdomen (approx. $3\frac{1}{2}$ inches).
- Mark space $1\frac{1}{4}$ inches.

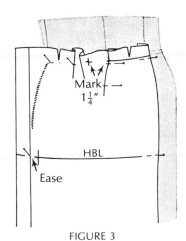

FIGURE 3

FIGURE 4
- Fold second dart and pin to equal length.
- Crossmark waist and dart leg at waist.
- Trim excess to within $\frac{1}{2}$ inch of waistline and 1 inch along hipline, blending cut line with seam allowance at HBL.

FIGURE 5
- Remove side seam pins. Fold back side drape and pin as shown.

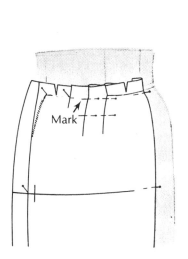

FIGURE 4

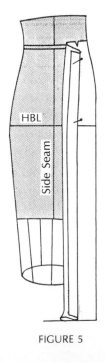

FIGURE 5

THE BACK SKIRT DRAPE

FIGURE 1a and 1b
- Place square line of muslin (HBL) on the HBL line of the form (Figure 1a) and figure (Figure 1b), aligning the center back of the muslin with the center back.
- Pin HBL at center back and side seam at crossmark of muslin.
- Pin center back at waistline.
- Pin at dart placement mark.

Personal fit: Pin excess to other side of figure to secure muslin while draping. Continue with the following instructions.

- With palm of the hand on hipbone, and fingertips touching side hip, move hand upward smoothing muslin along side seam to waistline.
- Crossmark waist and pin.

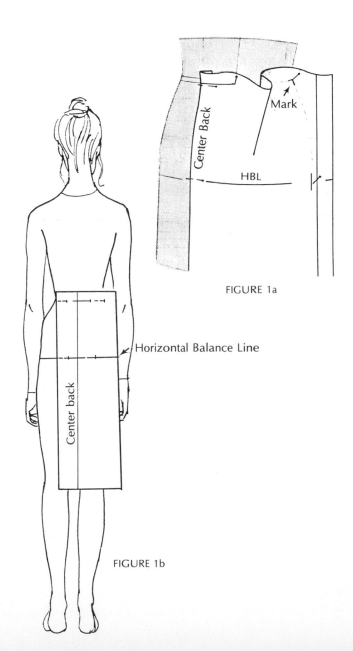

FIGURE 1a

FIGURE 1b

FIGURE 2

- From side waist, smooth muslin along waistline approximately 1 inch and pin $\frac{1}{4}$ inch tuck for ease (folds $\frac{1}{8}$ inch). Mark for waistline guide.
- Remove pin from HBL at side seam, and repin at second guideline mark on muslin (ease). Smooth upward from HBL to waist and pencil rub side seam so that hipline shape will show on muslin.

Personal fit: Place plastic ruler along hipline to side waist and draw hip shape.

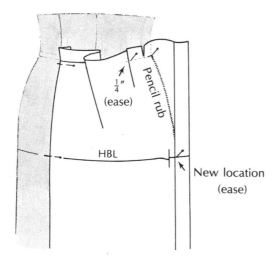

FIGURE 2

FIGURE 3

Dart information for skirt type 1:

- Divide excess into two equal darts.
- *Dart length:* $5\frac{1}{2}$ inches (or to the outermost bulge of hip).
- At dart placement mark, fold dart using one-half of the excess (excess folds toward center back). Crossmark waist at dart leg.
- Pin dart to end at the outermost bulge of the buttocks.
- Mark space $1\frac{1}{4}$ inches.
- Fold second dart and pin to equal length.
- Trim waist to within $\frac{1}{2}$ inch of waistline.
- Trim hip curve to within 1 inch of side, blending cut line at HBL.

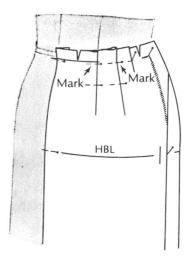

FIGURE 3

FIGURE 4

Dart information for skirt type 2:

- Divide excess into two parts.
- Long dart: Dart intake less $\frac{1}{2}$ inch. Length $= 5\frac{1}{2}$ inches (or to outermost bulge of buttocks). Pin dart.
- Space: $1\frac{1}{4}$ inches.
- Short dart: Dart intake $\frac{1}{2}$ inch. Length $= 3$ to $3\frac{1}{2}$ inches. Pin dart.
- Trim excess to within $\frac{1}{2}$ inch of waistline and 1 inch along hipline curve, blending line with seam allowance at HBL.

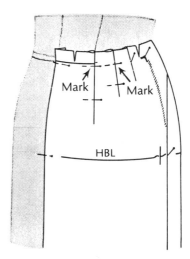

FIGURE 4

FIGURES 5 and 6
- Crease seam allowance along the hipline curve of the front skirt ending at the hemline.
- Place folded seam over the back seam, matching the HBL perfectly.
- Pin downward from the HBL to the hemline (Figure 5), and upward from the HBL to the side waist (Figure 6).

FIGURE 7

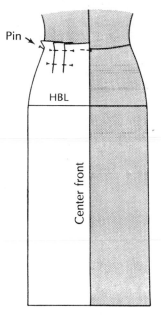

Perfect alignment

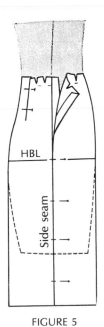

FIGURE 5

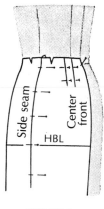

FIGURE 6

FIGURES 7, 8, 9, and 10

Skirt alignment. It is difficult to access the fit of the garment in the pinning stages; however, certain problems such as the alignment of the muslin with the center lines of the figure can be adjusted before transferring the muslin to paper. This will minimize fitting problems in the test fit.

To verify skirt alignment: Place a pin at the side waist to secure muslin to form or figure. Remove only pins from the center front and center back of the form at HBL and allow skirt to hang freely. A well-balanced skirt will fall in alignment with the center lines of the front and center back form or figure (Figure 7).

To correct alignment: If the skirt swings away from the center lines (Figure 8), lower the side waist. If the skirt overlaps centerline (Figure 9), raise the side waist. If only one of the sides overlaps or

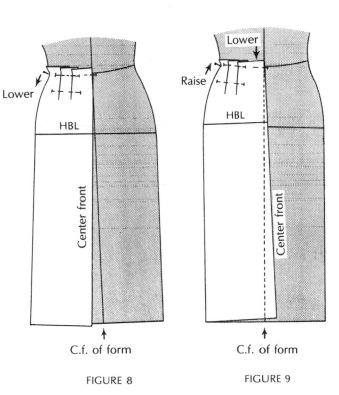

FIGURE 8   FIGURE 9

(Continued on next page)

swings away, release the entire side seam and raise or lower the side waist until the skirt does align with the center lines (Figure 10). Repin sides. Remark side waist, blend with waistline. Mark correct HBL at the side.

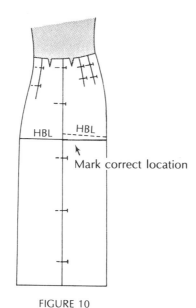

FIGURE 10

FIGURE 11

Pin bodice to skirt. Crease-fold waistline seam of the bodice and fold upward. Pin bodice to skirt, matching center lines sides and dart legs. (Note that pins may be placed parallel with waist.)

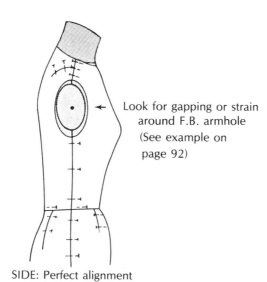

Look for gapping or strain around F.B. armhole (See example on page 92)

SIDE: Perfect alignment

FIGURE 11

FIGURES 12 and 13

Verifying fit. Remove holding pins at the center front and center back. Allow the drape to hang free. If the center lines stay at the center lines of the form, or figure, and the armhole falls away from the curve of the armhole evenly, it is a good drape (Figures 11, 12 and 13). The drape is imperfect when the garment falls out of alignment with the center lines of the figure, or form, and there is strain (insufficient fabric allowed), or gapping (misplaced excess) around armhole and other areas of the drape. If drape is imperfect, correct the muslin before continuing. If drape is perfect, remove drape from form or figure. Unpin and transfer to paper using the instructions that follow.

FRONT: Perfect alignment

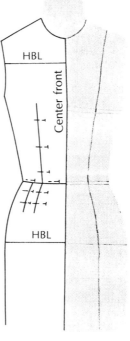

FIGURE 12

BACK: Perfect alignment

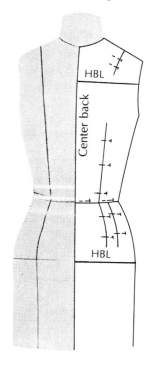

FIGURE 13

TRANSFERRING MUSLIN DRAPE TO PATTERN PAPER

The front and back bodice

With a warm iron (no steam), carefully press the front and back muslin bodice to flatten the surface. Using the dots and cross marks as a guide, draw lines around the pattern outline. Recheck *all* measurements and adjust lines where necessary. Important: After the skirt and bodice are transferred to paper, they should not be cut from paper until after the sleeve has been drafted (see page 73). The armhole and sleeve are adjusted before the test fit.

FIGURE 1

Transferring muslin to paper:

The pattern's outline may be transferred with the use of pushpins, as illustrated, or with a tracing wheel, by crossmarking dot marks at mid-armhole, armplate (armpit), dart points, and all corners.

- Cut paper 5 inches longer and wider than pattern.
- Draw vertical lines guideline through paper 1 inch from edge. Square a guideline across the paper 5 inches down from top.
- Place front and back muslin on paper, aligning the center front and back with the vertical guidelines, matching the HBL with the square guideline. Secure pattern with pushpins at neck, HBL, and waist.
- Place pushpins through each dot mark and through the centers of each crossmark as shown. *Caution:* Place pushpin through crossmark of plate (armpit) and not through seam allowance mark. Recheck and verify that all corners and other points are marked.
- Remove pins and muslin from paper.

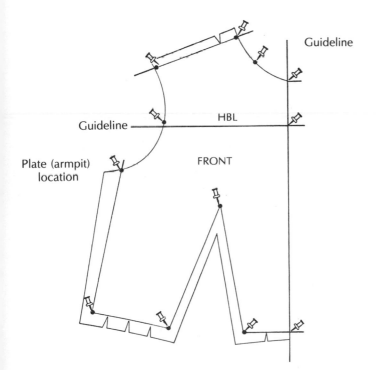

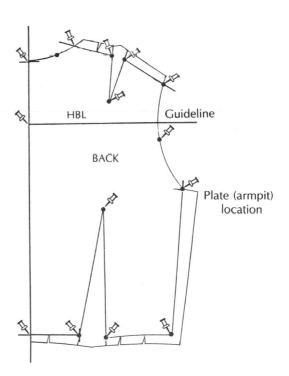

(Continued on next page)

FIGURE 2a and 2b

Outlining the front and back patterns:
- Draw connecting lines and square each corner.

Shoulder line: Measure up $\frac{1}{16}$ inch and draw line equal to shoulder length.

Armplate (armpit): Measure down $\frac{1}{2}$ inch (armhole depth) and out $\frac{1}{2}$ inch for ease ($\frac{5}{8}$ inch for size 18 and over). Draw side seam to side waist.

- *Darts:* Draw dart legs to dart points (back) and bust point (front). Center back dart point between dart legs.
- Redraw dart legs and true.

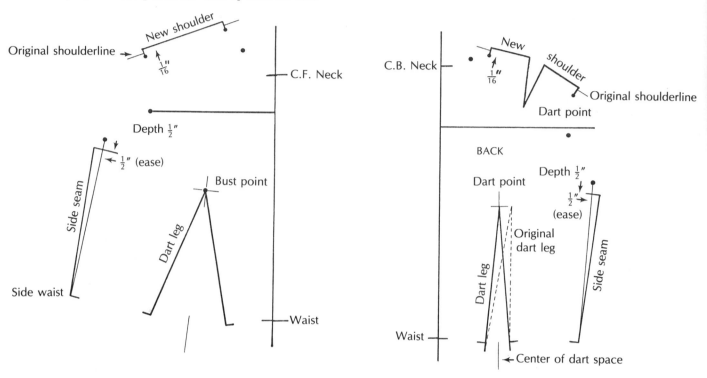

FIGURE 3a and 3b

Shaping the armhole, neckline, and waistline:
- *Armhole:* Curve ruler must touch shoulder tip, mid-armhole, and on, not below, square line at armhole depth. Draw curved line.

- *Neckline:* Curve ruler must touch shoulder at neck, mid-neck and front neck. Draw curved line.
- *Waistline:* Draw slightly curved lines from side waist to dart leg and dart leg to center front and back.

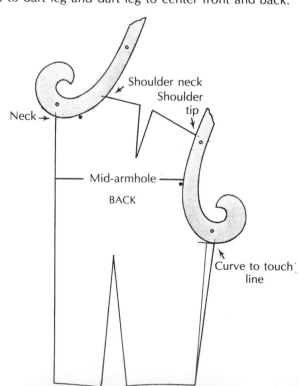

The skirt

Muslin preparation:
- Press muslin with a warm iron (no steam).
- Draw lines, connecting points.

FIGURE 4a and 4b

Paper preparation for front and back skirt:
- Draw vertical line through length of paper 1 inch from paper's edge.
- Square a line across paper 15 inches down from top of line equal to hip arc plus $\frac{1}{2}$ inch for ease (HBL).
- Place muslin on paper, matching center front and center back with vertical lines and hip line with square line. Pin center front and back and hip level at the side as shown.
- Transfer muslin to paper using either a tracing wheel along pencil lines (not illustrated) or the pushpin method as shown.
- Place pushpins through side waist, dart points, dart legs at crossmarks at waist and hemline.
- Remove pushpins and muslin from paper.

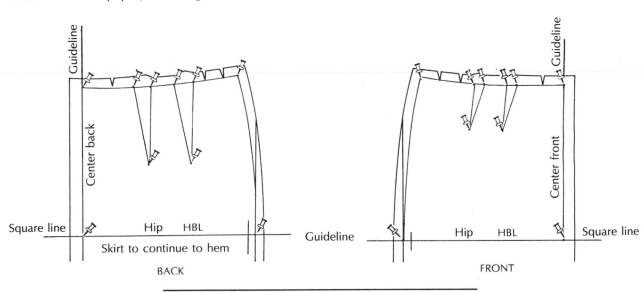

BACK

Skirt to continue to hem

FRONT

FIGURE 5

- Correct dart intake by adding to or subtracting from darts to equalize the intake. Darts can be adjusted by shifting dart points so that they are centered between the dart legs.
- Draw dart legs and true, adding to the shorter leg.
- Draw waistline using skirt ruler, French or vary form curve. Connect with dart legs.

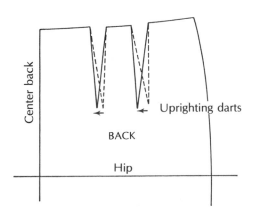

FIGURE 6

- Draw hipline curve using skirt curve for average hip lines, and diamond hips or French curve for heart, or square-shaped hips.
- True pattern using instructions on page 82.

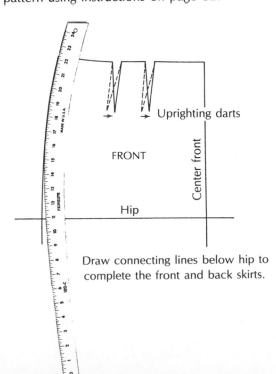

Draw connecting lines below hip to complete the front and back skirts.

The Commercial Basic Pattern Set is developed from the measurements of a composite figure whose proportions are perfect and symmetrical. These patterns come in a range of sizes and figure types. Several types of basic patterns are available, among them the Basic Try-On in a nonwoven fabric suitable for cutting, adjusting and stitching, and the tissue pattern that requires adjusting and cutting in muslin before being test fit.

FIGURE 1

   Pattern size. To determine which pattern is best suited to your figure type, compare your measurements and figure type (see Chapters 2 and 3 for figure analysis and measuring) with those of the commercial pattern company standards found in the back of each pattern book. Most pattern companies recommend that the bust size be used to determine the pattern size; however, for those whose bust cup is greater than a B-cup (standard for pattern companies), the above bust measurement should be substituted for bust circumference. See Figure 1 for taking above bust measurement.

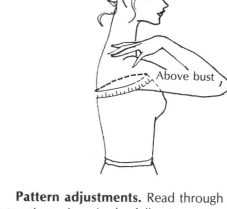

   Pattern adjustments. Read through all instructions given in the following series of possible fitting problems and adjust the pattern as needed. Omit those that are not applicable. Use your measurements from your Measurement Chart as a guide. After completing the following series of adjustments, use instructions for corrective fit contained in the pattern envelope and apply wherever appropriate.

   Test fit. After pattern adjustments have been completed, refer to instructions in Chapter 27 for test fitting. After the muslin has been perfected, the pattern should be traced onto paper for a seamless pattern by following the stitchlines. The seamless pattern will be used as a basis for developing patterns in the text. This will be illustrated later.

PREPARATION OF PATTERNS

- Press pattern with a warm iron. Pin front and back together along shoulder line and side seams.
- Place on figure and align center front and back of the pattern with the center lines of the figure. Pin pattern to figure and mark the true neckline of the figure on the pattern (not illustrated).
- Remove and unpin the pattern.

DART ADJUSTMENT FOR BRA CUP SIZES A, C, D, DD

Patterns are developed for persons who wear a bra cup size B. The garment will fit the figure too loosely or tightly for those with cup sizes A, C, D, and DD. The following adjustments should be made to the front bodice to minimize fitting problems later. First, locate bust cup size on the chart and use the measurements for spreading or overlapping bust point.

Locate bust point

FIGURE 2
- Draw a line through the center of the waist dart and side dart. Where lines intersect, mark bust point.
- Draw a line from bust point to mid-armhole.
- Slash through center of waist dart to bust point and from bust point to *stitch line* at mid-armhole.
- Slash from seam allowance at mid-armhole to, not through, stitch line (hinge effect). Label waist dart legs A and B. Use this pattern for the following adjustments.

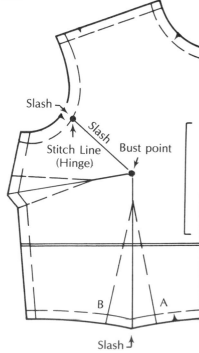

BRA CUP ADJUSTMENT CHART

Bra cup size

A	overlap 1/4 inch
C	spread 1/4 inch
D	spread 3/4 inch
DD	spread 1 inch

A-cup modification

FIGURE 3
- Overlap pattern $\frac{1}{4}$ inch at bust point to decrease dart intake. Secure with tape. Broken line indicates underlay.
- Center bust point. True dart leg A to equal B.
- Adjust waistline by trimming excess (shaded area).

C, D, DD cup modification

FIGURE 4
- Spread front pattern at bust point (using measurement for your bust cup size). Slip paper underneath and secure with tape (lined area).
- Center bust point.
- Add length to waistline by trueing dart leg A to equal B.
- If back bodice adjustment is needed it will be done at time of fitting.

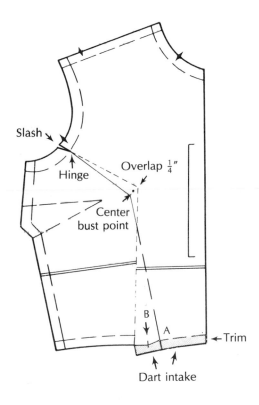

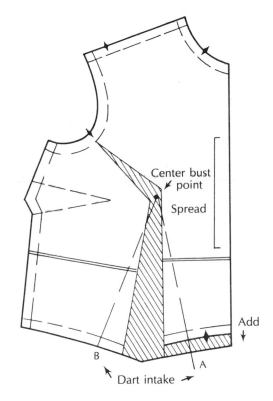

(Continued on next page)

ADJUSTMENTS FOR ASYMMETRY

Asymmetric shoulder (high and low shoulders)

FIGURE 5

> **Measurement needed**
> ▪ (8) Asymmetric shoulder difference _____

▪ Trace pattern on fold and open pattern.

▪ Draw slash lines on front and back bodice starting from high to low side (bold lines).
▪ Slash to, not through, other side and overlap for low side of figure on pattern using (8) measurement.
▪ Secure with tape and blend side-waist.

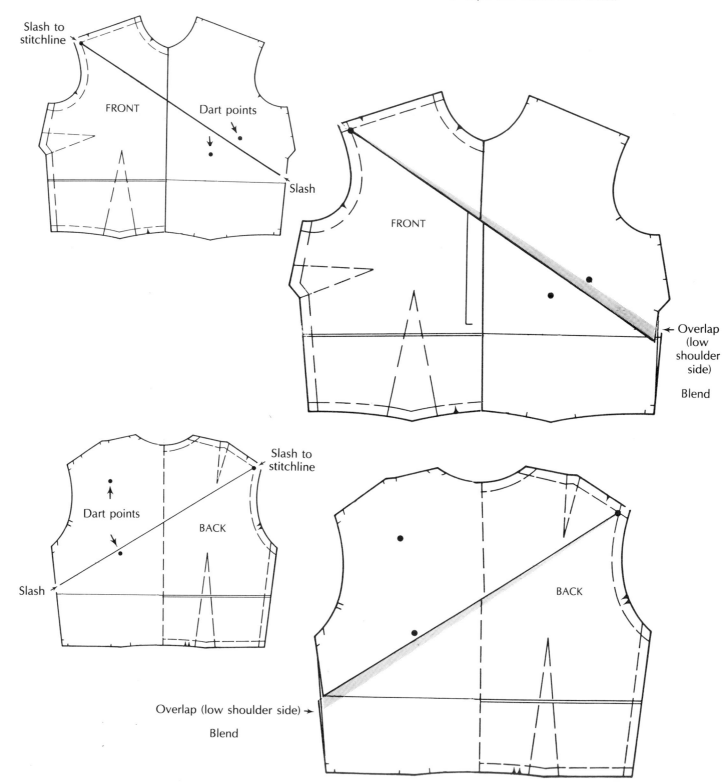

Asymmetric hip (high and low hiplines)

FIGURE 6

> **Measurement needed**
> ▪ (26) Asymmetric hip difference _____

▪ Trace pattern on fold and open.

▪ Draw slash lines on front and back bodice starting from high to low side (bold lines).
▪ Slash to, not through, other side and overlap for low side of figure on pattern using (26) measurement.
▪ Secure with tape, blend side and darts.

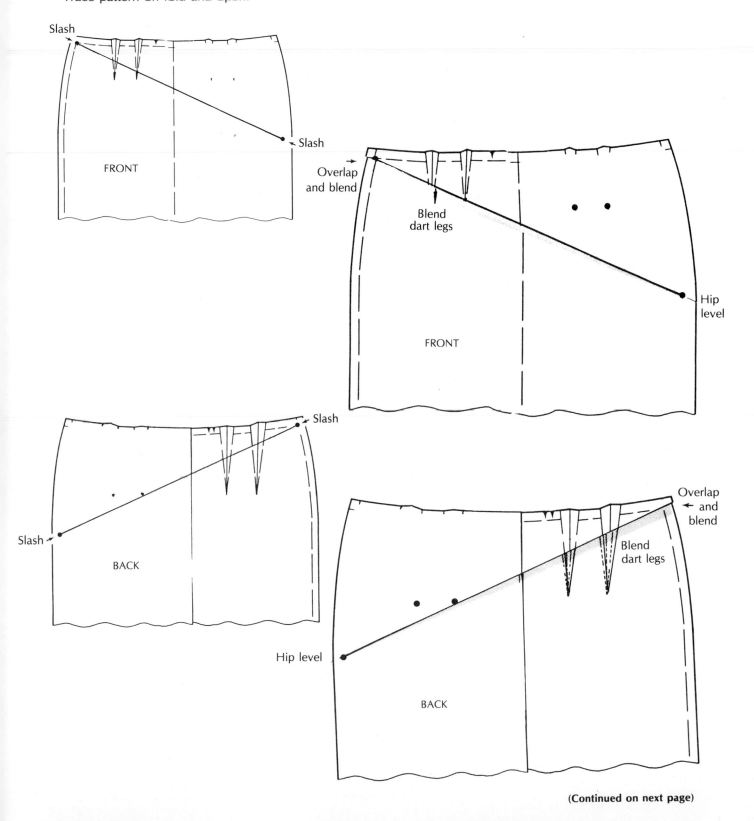

(Continued on next page)

Tilting waistline

FIGURE 7

Figures with tilting waist have more than a $\frac{3}{4}$ inch difference between the center front and center back lengths. (See page 56.) Adjust pattern using instructions given as a guide. The upward tilt of the front waist and backward tilt of the center back is the example given (Figure 7). The process is reversed for Figure 8.

Rule: What you remove from one joining section, you add to the other.

Measurements needed
- (5) Center front length _____
- (5) Center back length _____

Bodice:
- Measure down from center front and center back bodice neck marks, using center length measurement (5). Mark. (Tape paper to pattern if additional length is needed.)
- Square a short line indicating new waistlines. Using a skirt curve, draw slightly curved lines from new waist mark to side seam, as shown.
- Trim excess.

Skirt:
- Add an equal amount to front and subtract equal amount from back skirt sections. (Shaded areas = discarded areas, lined areas = added length.)
- Trim excess.

UPWARD TILTING WAISTLINE

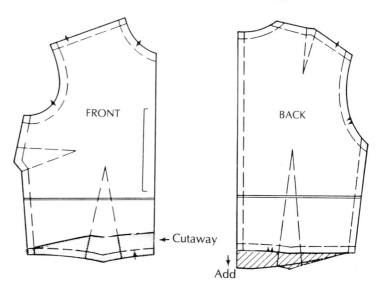

FIGURE 7

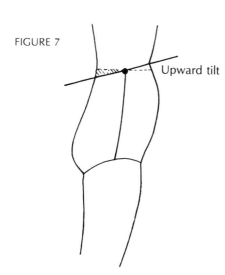

Upward tilt

FIGURE 8

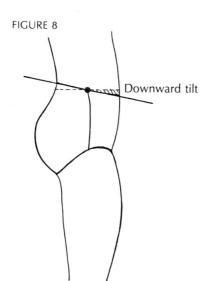

Downward tilt

Patterns not illustrated for figure with downward tilt.

Fold darts before trimming waistlines

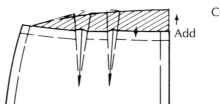

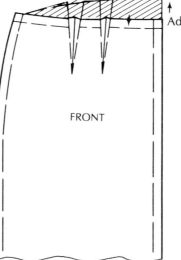

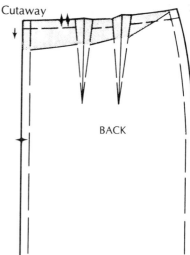

FRONT

BACK

OTHER ADJUSTMENTS

Instructions for corrections contained in the pattern envelope are clearly written and need not be repeated here. Apply wherever needed.

Special instructions

▪ To use the measurements from the Personal Measurement Chart for comparison with pattern measurements, divide the bust (1), waist (2) abdomen (3), and hip (4) in half. Add 1 inch ease to bust and hip and $\frac{1}{2}$ inch to waist. Place ruler or measuring tape on the stitchline of the pattern when taking measurements. Always measure from stitchline to stitchline. Do not include dart intake in measurement.

▪ Mark differences, and adjust pattern by drawing new stitch lines. To the new stitchlines add seam allowance. If necessary tape paper to pattern to add length and/or width. For guidance, see Chapter 27 of Part 7.

FIGURES 8 and 9

▪ Place stitchlines together at the sides of the bodice and skirt when taking bust and hip measurements.

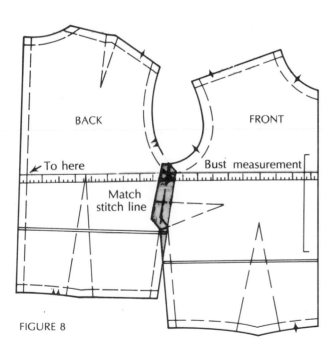

FIGURE 8

Skirt adjustment:

▪ To locate true waistline, use hip depth measurements (25 and 26). Measure up from hip level at center front and center back, mark and blend with waistline (Figure 9).

▪ *Personal dart intake:* Use dart intake recorded (21) or see dart chart, page 62.

▪ Draw new dart legs in red and blend with waist.

Recheck all measurements and joining seam lengths.

▪ *Waistline:* Verify waist after dart intake adjustment. If necessary, add to or subtract from side waist and blend to hipline. *Note:* Retrace patterns if necessary before preparing for test fit.

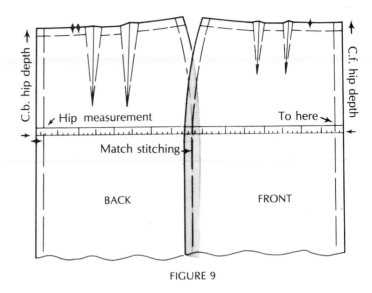

FIGURE 9

FIGURE 10

▪ *Sleeve cap:* If a shoulder pad is used to equalize an asymmetric shoulder, add an equal amount to the sleeve cap. Blend cap (indicated by broken line).

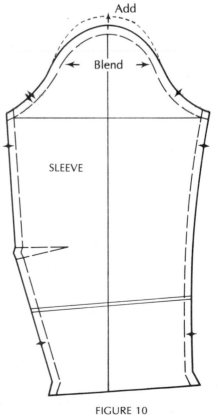

FIGURE 10

(**Continued on next page**)

MUSLIN PREPARATION FOR TEST FIT

▪ If using a try-on pattern, stitch as is; otherwise, pin pattern to fabric and cut, or place carbon under patterns, trace on muslin and remove.
▪ Cut patterns on unfolded muslin for patterns developed for asymmetric figure and for half-garment when fitting a form. (Add 1 inch extension to center front and center back).
▪ Stitch bodice to skirt. Stitch sleeve, do not attach to garment. See Chapter 27 for fitting problems and additional pattern corrections.

CONVERSION TO A ONE-DART BODICE AND SEAMLESS PATTERNS

After the fit of the garment has been perfected and the pattern corrected, convert the bodice front to a one-dart pattern as shown. Remove seam allowance for all patterns. Modifications are necessary because all pattern work in the text is developed from a seamless pattern and is based on a one-dart pattern.

The one-dart bodice front

FIGURE 11
▪ Slash through centers of waist and side darts *to,* not *through,* bust point (hinge effect).
▪ Bring side dart legs together at stitchline and secure with tape or pins. Continue with instructions.

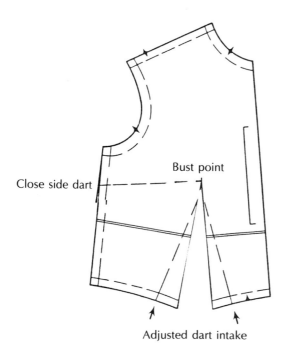

Close side dart

Bust point

Adjusted dart intake

Transferring patterns to paper

FIGURE 12
▪ Place all patterns on paper. Pin or staple to secure patterns.
▪ With a tracing wheel, carefully follow the stitchline around the pattern crossmarking each corner. Include grainlines, hip, biceps, and elbow lines. Mark notches, punches and circles.
▪ Remove patterns.
▪ Pencil in and true perforated lines. All lines must make smooth transitions, with corners clearly marked. Label patterns as shown.

    This completes the five-piece seamless pattern set for use when developing designs.

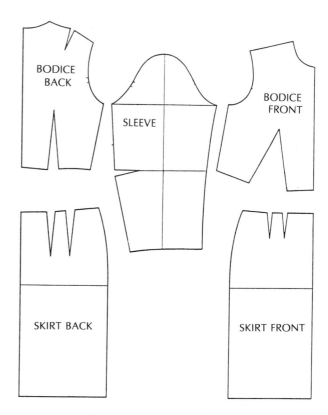

BODICE BACK

SLEEVE

BODICE FRONT

SKIRT BACK

SKIRT FRONT

Trace patterns on manila paper.

___ *part* *Two*

THREE MAJOR PATTERNMAKING PRINCIPLES

(INTRODUCTION TO FLAT PATTERNMAKING)

5

DART MANIPULATION
(PRINCIPLE #1)

Introduction 112
Working patterns 112
Patternmaking techniques 112
Design analysis and the three major patternmaking
  principles 112
Patternmaking terms 113
Test fit 113
DART MANIPULATION: PRINCIPLE #1 114
Design projects 114
Charting dart locations 115
SINGLE-DART SERIES—SLASH-SPREAD
  TECHNIQUE 116
Center front waist dart 116
Center front neck dart 118
Mid-shoulder dart 119
French dart 120
SINGLE DART SERIES—PIVOTAL-TRANSFER
  TECHNIQUE 121
Mid-neck dart 121
Side dart 123
Mid-armhole dart 124
Shoulder-tip dart 125
SELF-EVALUATION TEST 126
Consistency of dart angle 128
Proof of principle #1 128
TWO-DART SERIES—SLASH-SPREAD
  TECHNIQUE 129
The two-dart working pattern 129
Waist and side dart 129
Mid-shoulder and waist dart 131
Mid-armhole and waist dart 132
TWO-DART SERIES—PIVOTAL-TRANSFER
  TECHNIQUE 133
Mid-neck and waist dart 133
Shoulder-tip and waist dart 134
Center front neck and waist dart 135
SELF-EVALUATION TEST 136

INTRODUCTION

The flat patternmaking method is the fastest and most efficient method ever devised for developing patterns that will control the consistency of size and fit of mass-produced garments. This system depends upon patterns that have been previously developed and perfected. These patterns, called working patterns, are used as a base from which a variety of other pattern shapes are derived. The original working patterns are never altered and must remain in their original shapes to be used as a base for developing other pattern shapes. In this way, the original is retained as a master copy.

WORKING PATTERNS

Working patterns, as illustrated in this text, consist mainly of the basic back and front bodice, skirt, and sleeve, and other foundation patterns derived from them. The patternmaker may, however, choose a pattern that closely relates to a specific design detail without having to develop a complete new pattern from the basic pattern as patternmaking skill improves. This saves time, as part of the design detail has already been worked out. These working patterns should remain seamless, unless the patternmaker is experienced, as they are easier to manipulate and develop. (All technical illustrations in this text are based on seamless patterns for clarity.)

PATTERNMAKING TECHNIQUES

Patterns can be manipulated and changed into other shapes in two ways—through the slash-spread or pivotal-transfer techniques. The slash-spread technique is easy to understand as it clearly illustrates the changes taking place. The pivotal-transfer method is equally reliable, but more advanced, and may be preferred once the slash-spread technique has been mastered as it is less time consuming. Both methods will be illustrated in the beginning part of this text.

All pattern manipulation is done while the pattern lies flat on the table, hence the name flat patternmaking. While it is often difficult for the beginning patternmaker to visualize the three-dimensional form of a design with a flat pattern, this skill will improve with each exercise or practice pattern that is cut in cloth, sewn, and placed on a form for evaluation. This will take time and concentration, but it is worth the effort in terms of self-satisfaction and the monetary rewards that come to a skilled patternmaker.

DESIGN ANALYSIS AND THE THREE MAJOR PATTERNMAKING PRINCIPLES

Along with the manipulative skills needed in the Flat Patternmaking System, the patternmaker must also develop analytical skills. To do this the patternmaker must be able to analyze the creative detailing of each design by studying the differences between the basic garment and the design (Figure 1). This involves a knowledge of the three major patternmaking principles and their corollaries:

- Principle 1, Dart Manipulation
- Principle 2, Added Fullness
- Principle 3, Contouring

Designs are created generally without knowledge that certain principles are the basis for the creation. It is the patternmaker's responsibility to analyze designs and determine which principle(s) to apply to the developing pattern in order to assure that the exact replica of the design will emerge from the finished pattern shapes. The

FIGURE 1

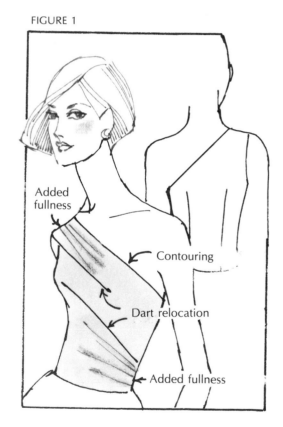

Added fullness

Contouring

Dart relocation

Added fullness

Design Analysis

beginning patternmaker should always study and compare the finished pattern shapes with the completed garment. This will help the patternmaker visualize the relationship between them. Eventually, the shape of the pattern will be visualized before the actual pattern is developed.

Designs introduced in this book contain a *design analysis* to help train the patternmaker to identify the design features and patternmaking principles involved. The design features are then *plotted* on the pattern as a guide for pattern *manipulation.* Through this process, the original shape of the pattern is changed to represent the design rather than the basic garment (Figure 2).

This is the essence of the flat patternmaking system.

PATTERNMAKING TERMS

Patternmaking terms and their definitions will be introduced wherever appropriate throughout the text, to help facilitate understanding the instructions.

Pattern plot. The act of placing lines on a traced copy of the working pattern that relate directly to the design features. They are used as guidelines for pattern development.

Pattern manipulation. The act of slashing and spreading, or pivoting the pattern sections to alter its original shape. The new pattern shapes represent the design features of the garment.

Design pattern. The finished pattern that contains all the features related to the design.

Pivotal point. A designated point on the pattern (for example, the bust point). The pattern is slashed to, or pivoted from, this point. This allows the pattern shape to be altered without changing its size or fit.

Template. A pattern that is drawn to scale equal to one-half or one-fourth the size of the original pattern. It can be used for practicing pattern manipulation and pattern development for projects in this text. Templates can be found at the back of this book.

TEST FIT

As each design project is completed, the design should be cut in a woven fabric and placed on a form or figure for a test fit (see chapter 27). One-half of the garment is needed when fitting the form (unless it is an asymmetrical design which requires a full garment). A full garment is required when fitting the figure. Seam allowances can be added in one of two ways for a test fit:

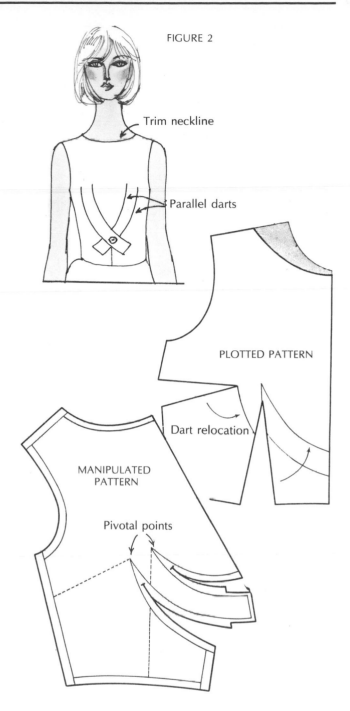

FIGURE 2

Trim neckline

Parallel darts

PLOTTED PATTERN

Dart relocation

MANIPULATED PATTERN

Pivotal points

1   The seamless pattern can be traced on cloth and the seam allowance drawn directly on the fabric.

2   Seam allowances can be added to the pattern before cutting in cloth.

The garment should then be stitched using a long stitch (6 to 10 stitches per inch), the seams pressed (without steam), and the garment placed on the form or figure for a test fitting. To complete the pattern, use the general pattern information on pages 20 through 28, Chapter 1, as a guide.

DART MANIPULATION—PRINCIPLE #1

Principle. A dart may be transferred to any location around the pattern's outline from a designated pivotal point without affecting the size or fit of the garment.

Corollary. The dart's excess can be in the form of gathers, pleats, tuck darts, stylelines, hidden ease in armhole, or flare. The dart's excess can be divided into multiple darts or style darts, or combined in other ways. These variations of the dart's excess are called *dart equivalents* and will be illustrated throughout the text.

DARTS AND DART EQUIVALENTS

| Style darts | Multiple darts | Stylelines | Gathers | Pleats | Tuck darts | Flare |

DESIGN PROJECTS

The design projects in the dart manipulation and dart equivalent series are all based on Principle #1. They illustrate universal concepts and principles that, once understood, become the model or prototype for all similar designs. Each project should be completed in the order given, as each will prepare the patternmaker for more advanced work later.

The front bodice is used to illustrate principles #1, #2, and #3, since most design detailing occurs on the bodice. Using the same methods illustrated for the bodice, darts on any of the five working patterns may be relocated. These will be illustrated under appropriate headings, such as sleeve, skirt, pant, and so on.

Dart manipulation introduces the slash-spread and pivotal-transfer patternmaking techniques to transfer the dart's excess from one location to another for design variations. It is the beginning of the pattern-manipulating process. It requires both artistic and technical skills to manage and control the pattern throughout the development process.

CHARTING DART LOCATIONS

A series of guidelines are drawn on a *traced* copy of the basic bodice front pattern. These guidelines establish common areas for dart relocation and design detailing. They are not, however, the only locations available, as a dart may be transferred to *any* location around the pattern's outline. When the dart excess is transferred to the center front bust, or to the shoulder, the space between the dart's legs will vary. This difference is due to the distance from bust point to the pattern's edge where the dart is placed. This does not change the fit of the garment, as the number of degrees contained between the legs of the dart remain the same. (This will be proven at the end of the dart series on page 128.)

The charted working pattern should be used for practicing the slash-spread and pivotal-transfer patternmaking techniques in the following series, and for design detailing later in the chapter. It is suggested that after charting and labelling the pattern the patternmaker cut a number of duplicate copies to expedite the projects.

Charting the front basic pattern

FIGURE 1
- Extend lines from bust point to each location illustrated. Note that a French dart can be placed at any location below straight or side dart. (The patternmaker should learn the names given to each location for clarity in communicating with others in the workroom.)
- Label the waist dart legs A and B as shown.

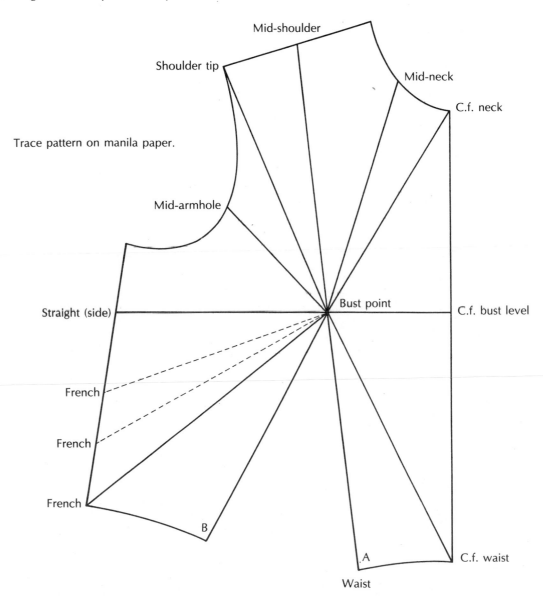

Mid-shoulder

Shoulder tip

Mid-neck

C.f. neck

Trace pattern on manila paper.

Mid-armhole

Bust point

C.f. bust level

Straight (side)

French

French

French

B

A

C.f. waist

Waist

SINGLE-DART SERIES—SLASH-SPREAD TECHNIQUE

The Slash-Spread technique, as the name implies, requires that a pattern be slashed, cut, and manipulated to form a new pattern shape. A *traced copy* of the original working pattern is used. The original is never altered. After the pattern is slashed and spread (manipulated), it is placed on another piece of marking paper or manila paper. It is retraced along the newly shaped lines and then discarded. The lines are blended, and seam allowance, grainline, and all other pertinent pattern information is added to complete the pattern after the test fit. For guidance refer to page 20, "Completing the Pattern." The seamless patterns from the single-dart series should be saved for use later in the text.

The bust has a round rather than pointed shape. To provide room for the bust mound, the dart should end approximately one-half inch from the bust point for single-dart control garment.

The hinge. To manipulate a pattern, all slash lines leading to a pivotal point or stitchline must be cut to, not through, it. The slight connecting part called the *hinge* keeps the pattern sections attached while the pattern is being spread or overlapped. If all slash lines are not cut to a pivotal point or stitchline, the pattern *cannot* be manipulated. (Caution: Patterns with seam allowances must also be slashed to *stitchline* from the pattern's edge to create the hinge effect.)

CENTER FRONT WAIST DART

Design Analysis: Design 1
The waist dart is relocated to the center front waist. Note the relationships that exist among the design, the plot, and the finished pattern shape.

Pattern plot and development

FIGURE 1
- Trace the charted pattern. Crossmark center front waist dart. Label dart legs A and B.
- Draw slash line from center front waist to bust point.

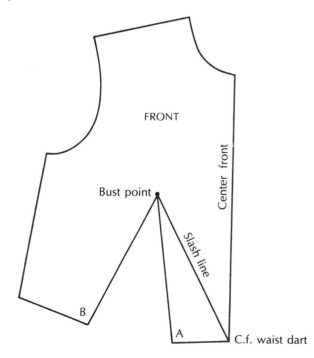

FIGURE 2
- Slash pattern from center front waist to, not through, bust point.

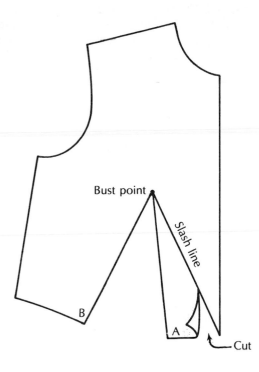

Bust point

Slash line

B

A

Cut

FIGURE 3
- Close dart legs A and B. Tape.
- Place pattern on paper and retrace. Discard pattern.
- Center dart point ½ inch from bust point.
- Draw dart legs to dart point.

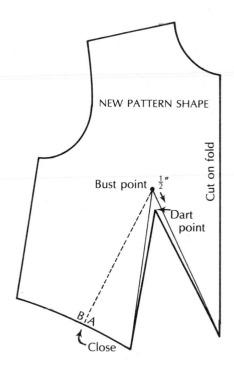

NEW PATTERN SHAPE

Cut on fold

Bust point ½"

Dart point

B A

Close

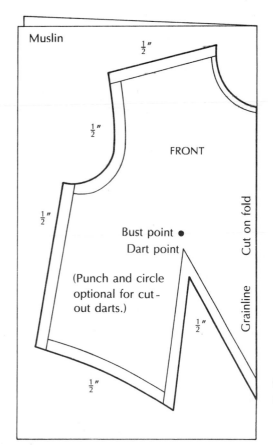

Muslin

½"

½"

FRONT

½"

Bust point •

Dart point

(Punch and circle optional for cut-out darts.)

½"

Cut on fold

Grainline

½"

½"

FIGURE 4
- For test fit, cut on fold for full front or for half-muslin, add 1 inch extension at front. Cut back pattern to complete design (not illustrated).
- Add seams to pattern or muslin.
- Complete pattern using general pattern information for guidance, if necessary (see page 20).
- Stitch, press front and back muslin (no steam). Place on form or figure for a test fit. (See Chapter 27 as a guide for correcting fit.)

Grainline can be drawn at center fold of pattern, or 1 inch in from fold (seen on patterns later).

CENTER FRONT NECK DART

Design Analysis: Design 2

Analyze the design, plot and manipulate the patterns for the next 3 designs.

Pattern plot and development

FIGURE 1
- Draw slash line to bust point.

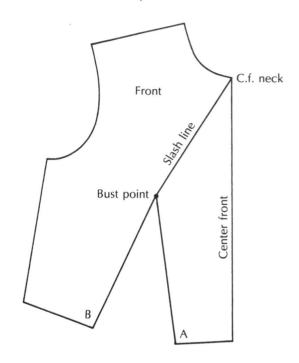

FIGURE 2
- Cut slash line to, not through, bust point.

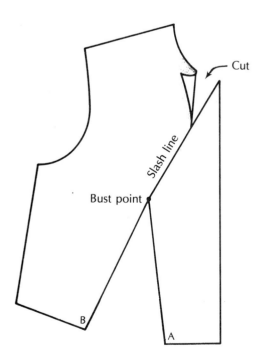

FIGURE 3
- Close dart legs A and B. Tape.
- Retrace and complete dart legs.

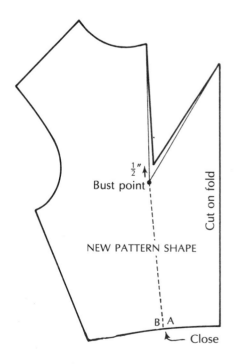

MID-SHOULDER DART

Design Analysis: Design 3

Pattern plot and development

FIGURE 1
• Draw slash line to bust point.

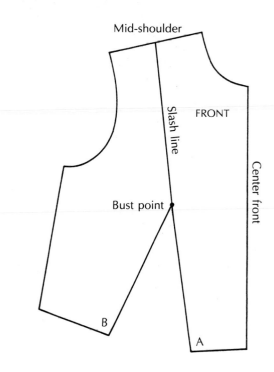

FIGURE 2
• Cut slash line to, not through, bust point.

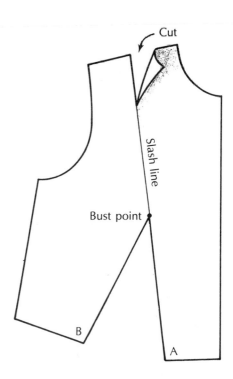

FIGURE 3
• Close dart legs A and B. Tape.
• Retrace and complete dart legs.

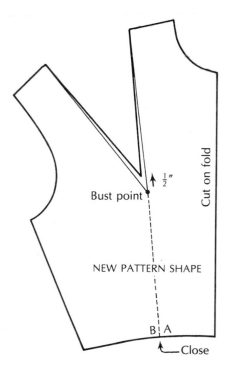

FRENCH DART

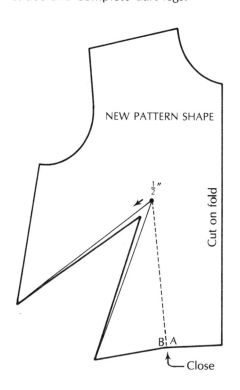

Design Analysis: Design 4

Pattern plot and development

FIGURE 1
- Draw slash line to bust point.

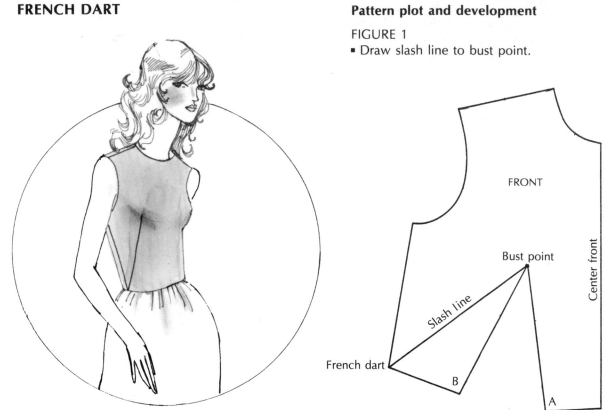

FRONT

Bust point

Slash line

French dart

B

A

Center front

FIGURE 2
- Cut slash line to, not through, bust point.

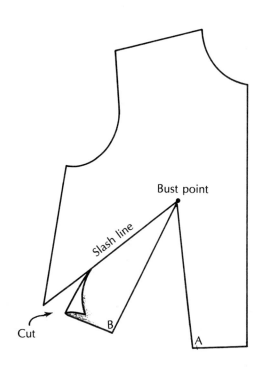

Bust point

Slash line

Cut

B

A

FIGURE 3
- Close dart legs A and B. Tape.
- Retrace and complete dart legs.

NEW PATTERN SHAPE

$\frac{1}{2}$"

Cut on fold

B A

Close

SINGLE-DART SERIES—PIVOTAL-TRANSFER TECHNIQUE

The pivotal-transfer technique involves manipulating the *original* working pattern into a new shape by pivoting, shifting and tracing, instead of cutting. The working pattern is placed on top of pattern paper with a pushpin placed through the pivotal point. For example, in transferring a dart, the new dart location is marked on paper underneath and then traced to an existing dart on the pattern. The pattern is then pivoted, closing original dart legs while opening space for the new dart. The remaining untraced pattern is traced to paper underneath. Once an area of the pattern has been traced, *it is not traced again.* This will be illustrated in the following design projects.

Pushpins are also used to transfer style lines within the pattern's frame. When the pattern is removed from the paper, these lines are trued with straight and/or curved rulers using the pin marks as a guide. The shaded area on the illustrations indicates the part of the pattern affected when traced. Complete the sequence of exercises and save the patterns for future use.

MID-NECK DART

Design Analysis: Design 5
The dart extends from mid-neck to bust point of Design 5. Note the relationships that exist among the design, the plot, and the finished pattern shape.

Pattern plot and development

FIGURE 1
- Place the working pattern on paper with pushpin through bust point (pivotal point).
- Mark mid-neck location (point C) and dart leg A on paper.
- Trace section of pattern from dart leg A to C (bold line and shaded area).

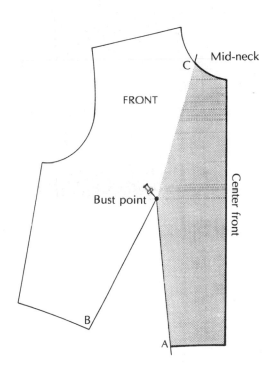

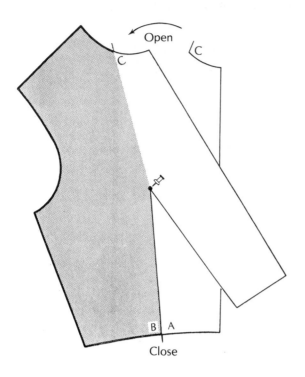

FIGURE 2
- Pivot pattern until dart leg B touches A on paper (closes waist dart, and opens space for mid-neck dart).
- Trace remaining section of the pattern from dart leg B to point C on pattern (bold line and shaded area). Note: Whenever the pattern is pivoted, it will overlay the previously traced pattern section. This is a natural occurrence. Remember, once a section of the pattern is traced, *it is not traced again.*

FIGURE 3
- Remove the working pattern from paper.
- Draw dart legs to bust point.
- Center dart point $\frac{1}{2}$ inch from bust point.
- Redraw dart legs to dart point.
- Cut in muslin for test fit.

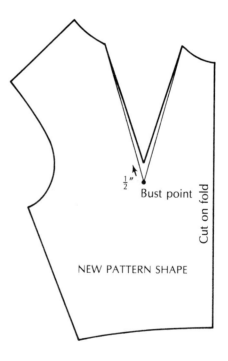

SIDE DART

Analyze the design, plot and develop patterns for the next three designs.

Design Analysis: Design 6

Pattern plot and development

FIGURE 1
- Mark new dart location and trace pattern from A to C.

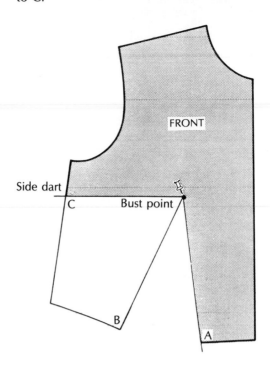

FIGURE 2
- Pivot pattern until dart leg B touches point A on paper (closes waist dart and opens space for side dart).
- Trace remaining pattern.

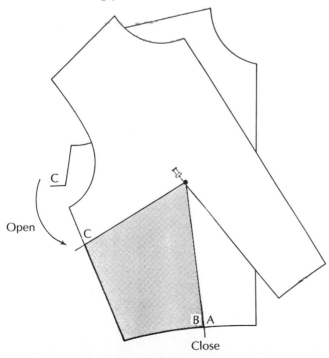

FIGURE 3
- Remove pattern, draw dart legs to bust, center dart point ½ inch from bust point and draw new dart legs.

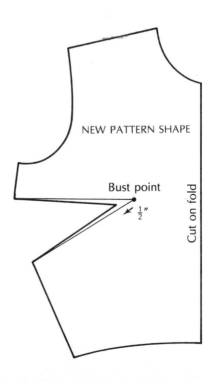

MID-ARMHOLE DART

Design Analysis: Design 7

Pattern plot and development

FIGURE 1
- Mark new dart location and trace pattern from A to C.

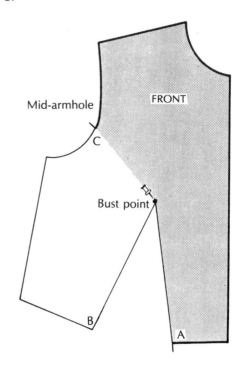

FIGURE 2
- Pivot pattern until dart leg B touches point A on paper (closes waist dart, and opens space for mid-armhole dart).
- Trace remaining pattern.

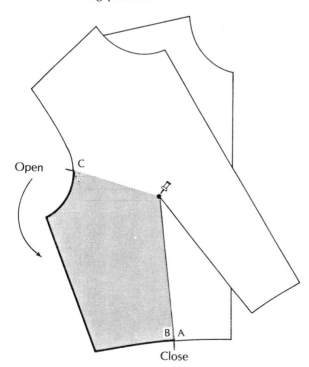

FIGURE 3
- Remove pattern, draw dart legs to bust, center dart point $\frac{1}{2}$ inch from bust point.
- Draw new dart legs.

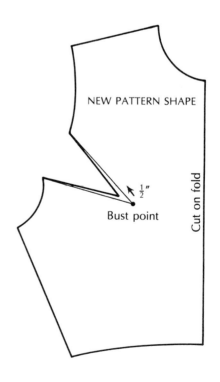

SHOULDER-TIP DART

Design Analysis: Design 8

Pattern plot and development

FIGURE 1
▪ Mark new dart location and trace pattern from A to C.

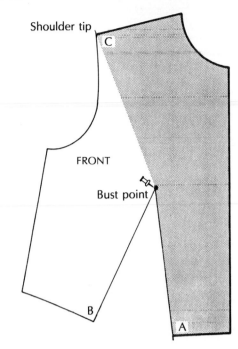

FIGURE 2
▪ Pivot pattern until dart leg B touches point A on paper (closes waist dart and opens space for shoulder tip dart).
▪ Trace remaining pattern.

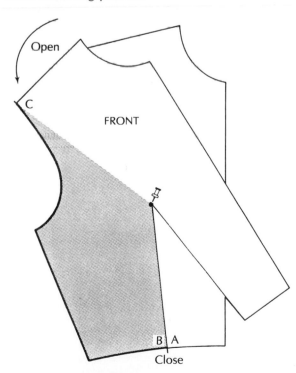

FIGURE 3
▪ Remove pattern, draw dart legs to bust, center dart point $\frac{1}{2}$ inch from bust point.
▪ Draw new dart legs.

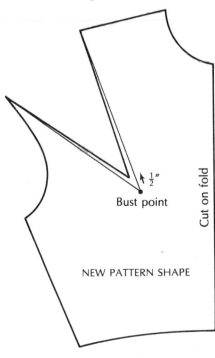

SELF-EVALUATION TEST

1 Develop patterns by transferring the waist dart to the locations listed below using the patternmaking techniques indicated: After each pattern is completed, fold darts using the three methods described on pages 24–26.

Slash-spread technique		Pivotal-transfer technique	
Location	*Corresponding pattern shapes for comparison*	*Location*	*Corresponding pattern shapes for comparison*
Shoulder-tip	Figure 3, page 125	Center front neck	Figure 3, page 118
Side dart	Figure 3, page 123	Mid-shoulder	Figure 3, page 119
Mid-armhole	Figure 3, page 124	French dart	Figure 3, page 120

2 The pattern for Design 1 has been developed (Figure 1). Develop the pattern for Design 2. Analyze the difference between Designs 1 and 2. How do they differ? (Answer can be found at the bottom of the page.)

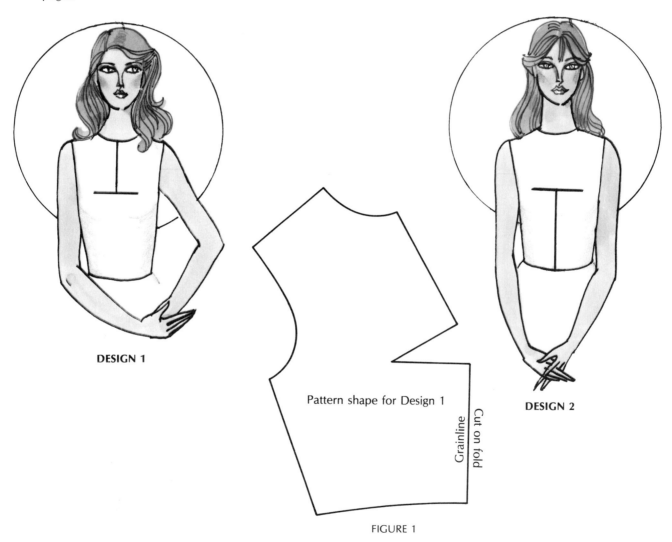

DESIGN 1

Pattern shape for Design 1

Grainline

Cut on fold

DESIGN 2

FIGURE 1

ANSWER: Design 1 is cut with center front on fold below the dart. Design 2 is cut with center front on fold above the dart.

3 The patterns for Designs 3 and 4 have been developed and labelled A and B. Match the design with the correct pattern shape. Write either A or B (below each sketch). Answers can be found at the bottom of the page.

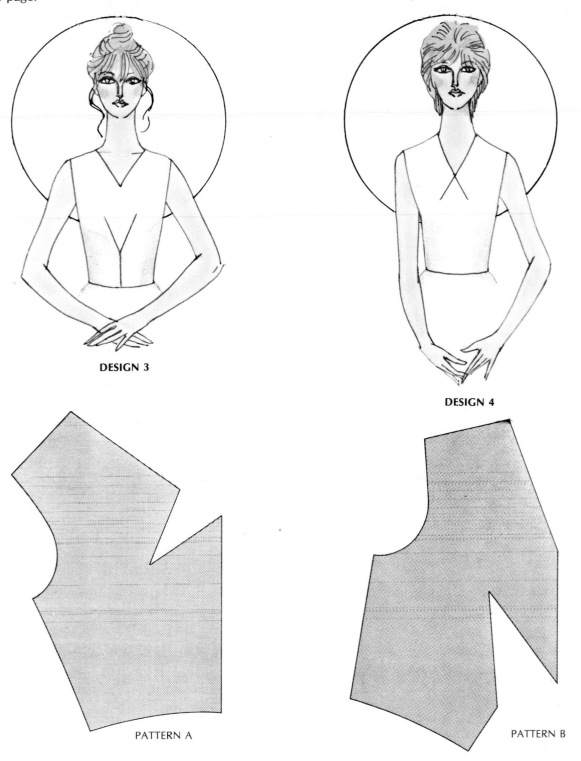

DESIGN 3

DESIGN 4

PATTERN A

PATTERN B

ANSWERS: Design 3 is based on pattern B. Design 4 is based on pattern A.

CONSISTENCY OF DART ANGLE

To prove that the dart angle remains constant without regard to its location around the pattern's outline, stack the following patterns in the sequence given: the shoulder dart (longest dart—bold line), the waist dart (lined pattern), and the center front bust dart (shortest dart—broken line). Place a pushpin through the bust points of all three patterns and align the dart legs. They all match, and have the same degree of angle, from the shortest to the longest dart. The spaces between the ends of the dart legs of each pattern varies. This difference is directly related to the distance from the bust point (or any pivotal point) to the edge of the pattern where the dart is located. The closer a dart is to a pivotal point, the narrower the space between the dart legs, and the further the distance the wider the space between the dart legs (Figure 1).

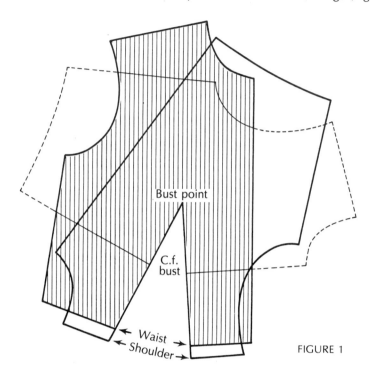

FIGURE 1

PROOF OF PRINCIPLE #1

In the preceding patternmaking exercises, the dart excess was transferred to many different locations around the outline of the front bodice pattern. The shapes of these patterns vary from the original working pattern. When the dart legs are closed and taped, the patterns are the original size and shape. This can be proven by using the patterns previously developed. Bring the dart legs together, cupping the pattern, and tape securely. Stack the patterns, aligning the center fronts. Observe that the patterns coincide exactly (Figure 2).

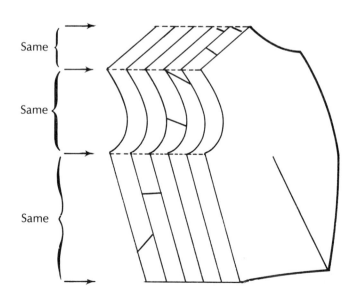

FIGURE 2

TWO-DART SERIES—SLASH-SPREAD TECHNIQUE

THE TWO-DART WORKING PATTERN

A two-dart working pattern (waist and side dart) will be developed for the series that follows.

The two-dart pattern is used in industry more often than the one-dart pattern. There are several advantages to dividing the dart excess into more than one location other than the creative aspects of the design:

- The pattern pieces fit the marker more economically.
- The natural bias of the fabric at side seam is less severe.
- The fit of a garment is improved by releasing ease around the bust mound from two dart points rather than from one dart point.

The dart points of a two-dart pattern generally end ¾ to 1 inch from the bust point, with the side dart from 1 to 2 inches from bust point. The variance depends on the size of the bust cup. For example: A cup, 1 inch; B cup, 1¼ inches (standard measurement); C cup, 1¾ inches; D cup and larger, 2 inches from bust point for the side dart.

The waist and side dart pattern should be completed on manila paper. It will be used as a base for other designs and foundations. For test-fitting, trace the front and back patterns and add seams on the muslin along with notches, and punch marks (working pattern to remain seamless). For guidance, refer to page 20, "Completing the Pattern," and for test fit refer to Chapter 27.

In the previous dart manipulation series only one slash line to bust point was required to transfer the dart to other locations. In this series transferring part of the dart excess requires two slash lines to bust point—one for the new dart location and the other from dart point to bust point. These slashes create a hinge that permits the manipulation of the dart.

WAIST AND SIDE DART

Pattern plot and development

FIGURE 1
- Trace front charted pattern. Crossmark side dart location and draw slash line to bust point.
- Label dart legs A and B and side waist X.
- Cut slash line to, not through, bust point (hinge).

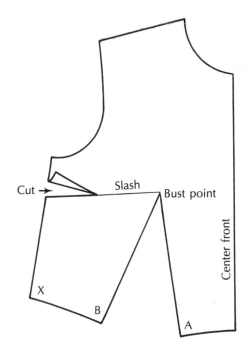

(Continued on next page)

FIGURE 2
- Draw a square line on paper.
- Place center front on square line with center front waist touching corner as shown. Secure.
- Close waist dart until point X touches square line as shown. (Broken line is original pattern.)
- Trace, mark bust point, and discard pattern.

FIGURE 3
- Center the point of waist dart 1 inch from bust and side dart $1\frac{1}{4}$ inches from bust point (note that dart point is not centered).
- Redraw dart legs to new dart point.
- Cut from paper

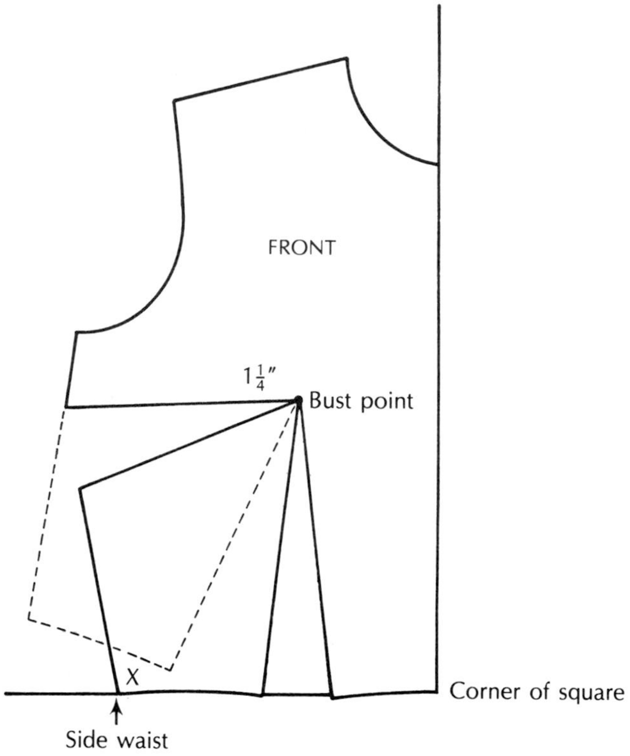

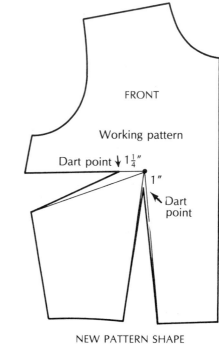

NEW PATTERN SHAPE

FIGURE 4
- Test fit: For a full front cut pattern on fold of muslin. For half of a garment add 1 inch extension for fold-back at center front/center back (not illustrated).
- Add seams as indicated.

Side dart: Center fold lies toward waist.

Waist dart: center fold lies toward center front (toward center back for back muslin). (Fold dart legs when cutting muslin.) (To shape darts on pattern see page 26.)
- Stitch, press and place on form for test fit. For corrective fit see chapter 27.
- Chart dart location on pattern for future use (not illustrated).

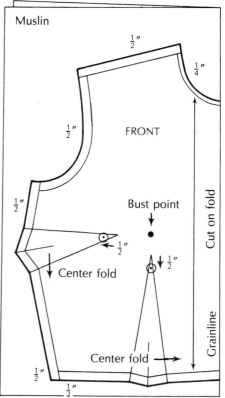

Punch and circles can be placed from $\frac{1}{4}$ to $\frac{1}{2}$ inch from dart points

MID-SHOULDER AND WAIST DART

Design Analysis: Design 1

Design 1 has a mid-shoulder and waist dart. The shoulder dart replaces the side dart. (This pattern can also be used as a seamless working pattern; however, it is not illustrated as such in this text.)

FIGURE 2
- Cut pattern from paper.
- Cut slash lines to, not through, bust point (hinge).

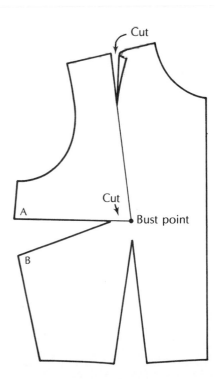

Pattern plot and development

FIGURE 1
- Trace pattern, mark bust point and mid-shoulder.
- Draw slash line to bust point from mid-shoulder and from dart point of side dart to bust point.

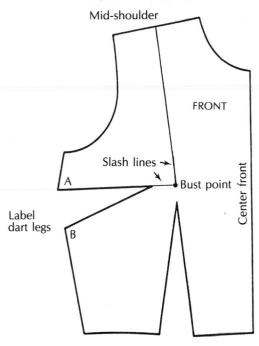

FIGURE 3
- Close dart legs A and B. Tape.
- Trace and discard pattern.
- Center dart point $1\frac{1}{4}$ inches from bust point.
- Draw dart legs to new dart point.

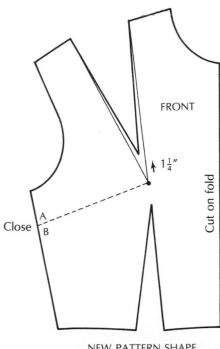

NEW PATTERN SHAPE

MID-ARMHOLE AND WAIST DART

Design Analysis: Design 2

Pattern plot and development

FIGURE 1

▪ Trace pattern. Mark bust point and mid-armhole. Cut from paper.
▪ Draw slash line to bust point from mid-armhole dart and from dart point of side dart to bust point.

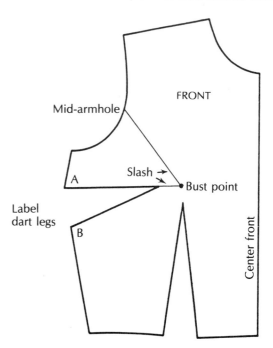

FIGURE 2

▪ Cut slash lines to, not through, bust point.
▪ Bring dart legs A and B together. Tape.

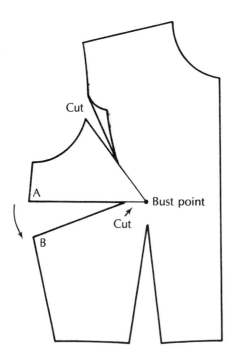

FIGURE 3

▪ Place on paper, trace, and discard pattern.
▪ Center dart point $1\frac{1}{4}$ inches from bust point.
▪ Redraw dart legs to dart point.

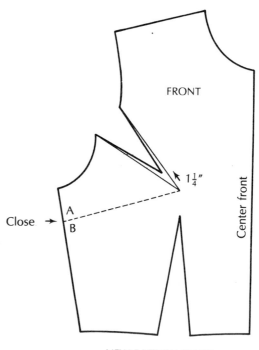

NEW PATTERN SHAPE

TWO-DART SERIES—PIVOTAL-TRANSFER TECHNIQUE

MID-NECK AND WAIST DART

Design Analysis: Design 3

FIGURE 2
- Pivot pattern downward until dart leg A touches B on paper.
- Mark point C at mid-neck and trace to dart leg A.

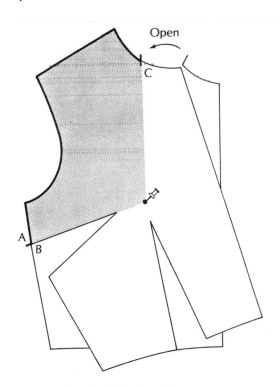

Pattern plot and development
FIGURE 1
- Place pattern on paper with pushpin through bust point. Mark mid-neck. Label C.
- Mark B and trace to point C.

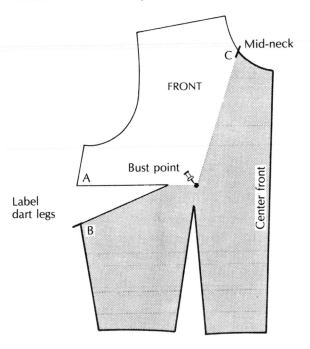

FIGURE 3
- Remove pattern and draw dart to bust point.
- Center dart point $1\frac{1}{4}$ inches from bust point.
- Redraw dart legs to dart point.

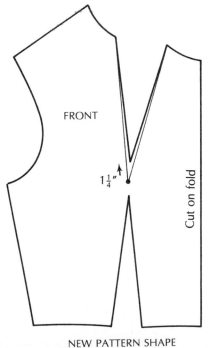

NEW PATTERN SHAPE

SHOULDER-TIP AND WAIST DART

Design Analysis: Design 4

Pattern plot and development

FIGURE 1
- Place pattern on paper with pushpin through bust point. Mark shoulder tip C.
- Mark at dart leg B and trace to point C.

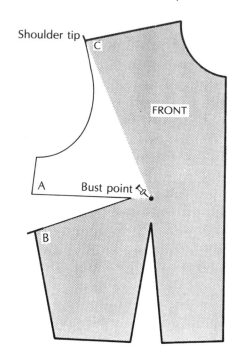

FIGURE 2
- Pivot pattern downward until dart leg A touches B on paper.
- Mark point C at shoulder tip and trace to dart leg A.

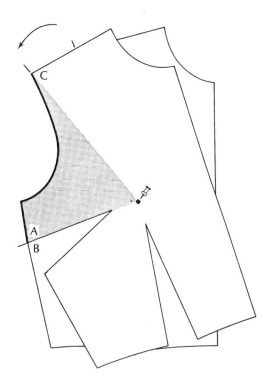

FIGURE 3
- Remove pattern. Draw dart legs to bust point.
- Center dart point $1\frac{1}{4}$ inches from bust point and redraw legs to dart point.

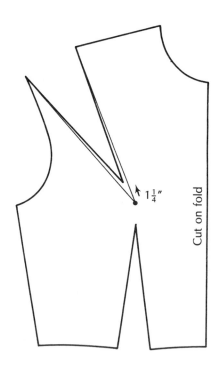

CENTER FRONT NECK AND WAIST DART

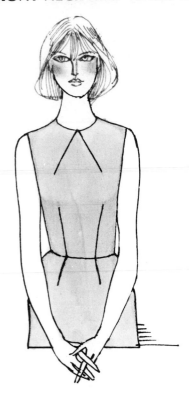

Design Analysis: Design 5

Pattern plot and development

FIGURE 1
- Place pattern on paper with pushpin through bust point. Mark center front neck C.
- Mark at dart leg B and trace to point C.

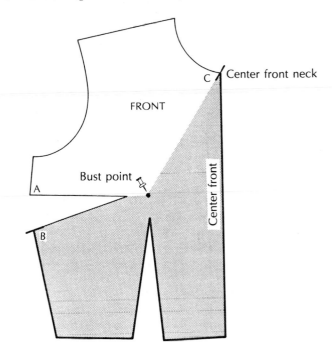

FIGURE 2
- Pivot pattern downward until dart leg A touches B on paper.
- Mark point C at neck and trace to dart leg A.

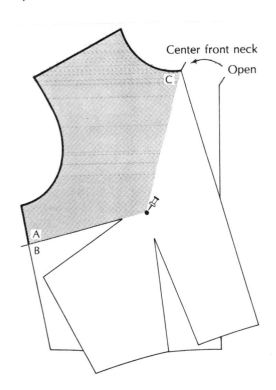

FIGURE 3
- Remove pattern, draw dart legs to bust point.
- Center dart point $1\frac{1}{4}$ inches from bust and redraw legs to dart point.

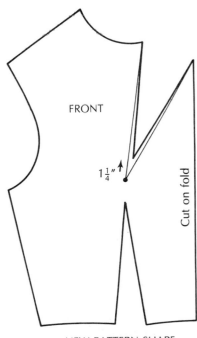

NEW PATTERN SHAPE

SELF-EVALUATION TEST

1 Develop patterns for the following dart locations using the patternmaking techniques indicated below: After patterns have been developed, fold in darts using the three methods described on pages 24–26.

Slash-spread technique		Pivotal-transfer technique	
Location	Corresponding pattern shapes for comparison	Location	Corresponding pattern shapes for comparison
Mid-neck and waist	Figure 3, page 133	Side dart and waist	Figure 4, page 130
Shoulder-tip and waist	Figure 3, page 134	Mid-shoulder and waist	Figure 3, page 131
Center front neck and waist	Figure 3, page 135	Mid-armhole and waist	Figure 3, page 132

2 Designs 1 and 2 differ from the two-dart series in which the waist dart remains and the side dart changes location. How do they differ? Analyze the two designs. Compare with that of the working pattern. Four pattern shapes are illustrated. Two patterns relate to the designs. Choose the correct pattern shape for each design. (Answer given at the bottom of the page.)

Using concepts given in the previous design projects, develop pattern shapes for designs 1 and 2. Use the slash-spread technique, then repeat the exercise using the pivotal-transfer method. Practice until the pattern shapes are identical to those illustrated. Have patience and perseverance.

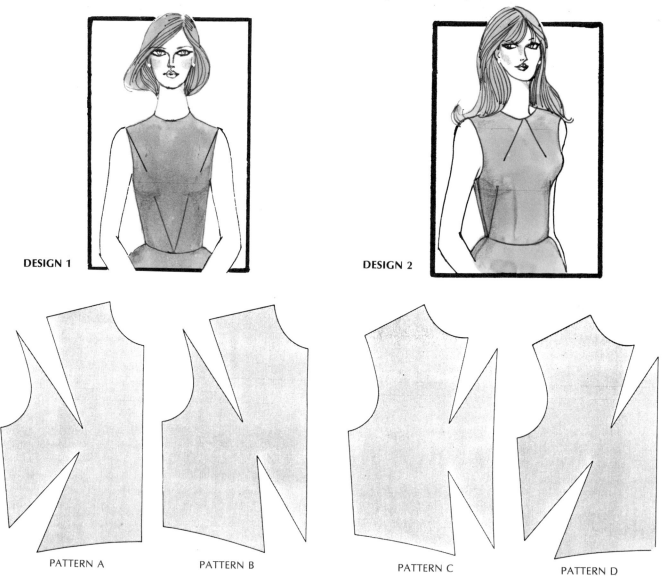

DESIGN 1

DESIGN 2

PATTERN A PATTERN B PATTERN C PATTERN D

ANSWERS: Pattern B relates to Design 1. Pattern D relates to Design 2.

6

TUCK-DARTS, PLEATS, FLARES, AND GATHERS

Introduction 138
Tuck-darts 138
Pleats 139
Flare 139
Gathers 140
CLUSTERS OF DARTS AND DART
    EQUIVALENTS 144
Waist cluster 144
Dart cluster 146
Tuck-dart cluster 146
Pleat cluster 146
Shoulder cluster 147
Center front bust cluster 148
GRADUATED AND RADIATING DARTS 149
Graduated darts 149
Radiating darts 150
PARALLEL DARTS 151
Parallel french darts 152
Parallel darts at neck 153
Parallel darts—cape effect 154
Parallel dart design variations 155
ASYMMETRIC DARTS 156
Asymmetric squared darts 156
Asymmetric radiating darts 157
Asymmetric curved darts 159
Asymmetric dart variations 160
INTERSECTING DARTS 161
Intersecting dart to shoulder 161
Intersecting dart to waist 162
Intersecting dart with gathers 163
INTERSECTING DART DESIGN VARIATIONS 164
THE SHOULDER DART 164
The multi-dispersion working pattern 165
Neck dart 165
Excess transferred to armhole 166
Shoulder dart variations 166

INTRODUCTION

The dart is one of the most flexible and creative parts of the pattern as illustrated by previous design projects. The space (excess) between the dart legs can be used in a variety of creative ways and is limited only by the creative imagination of the designer. When this space (excess) is used for design detailing other than stitched darts, it is referred to as a *dart equivalent*. Dart equivalents come in the form of tuck-darts, pleats, flare, and gathers. These dart equivalents replace the dart as the control. They will always end at the pivotal point of the pattern (Example: bust point). The only difference in development between the dart and the dart equivalent is the manner in which they are marked (and subsequently stitched). Darts are stitched end to end, tuck-darts are partially stitched, pleats are folded, and fullness is spread and gathered along the stitchline. (Other more advanced forms of darts and dart equivalents will follow this series.)

The following series illustrates these four common dart-equivalent design details, using the one-dart pattern for development. Gathers will be illustrated separately using the slash-spread and the pivotal-transfer techniques. It is suggested that a sample of each dart equivalent be cut in fabric. It is important to view the different effects created by varying the dart usage.

TUCK-DARTS

FIGURE 1a
▪ A tuck-dart is a partially stitched, inverted dart that must be marked by punch holes and circles along the centerfold and $\frac{1}{8}$ inch inside the stitchline, $\frac{1}{2}$ inch below the finished length.

FIGURE 1b
▪ The underside of the dart illustrates the stitched area. Note stitching $\frac{1}{2}$ inch beyond the punch holes.

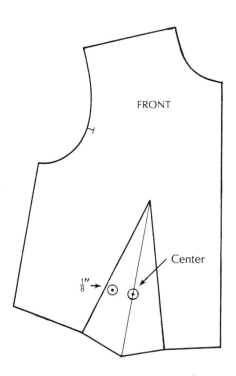

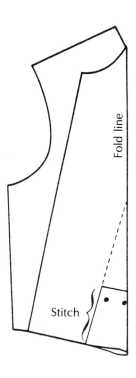

PLEATS

FIGURE 2

▪ A pleat is an unstitched, folded dart that is held securely along joining seamline. It is developed as a dart on the pattern but does not include punch and circle for dart point. Dart legs only are notched. (Broken lines indicate the original dart leg.)

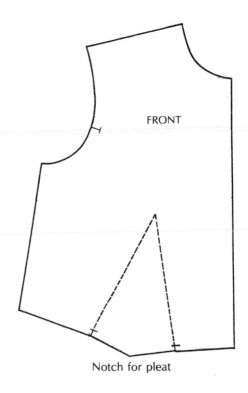

Notch for pleat

FLARE

FIGURE 3

▪ Flare is an open, unstitched dart. The open dart space is blended across the bottom. Punch holes, circles, and notches are unnecessary and not used. (Broken line indicates original dart.)

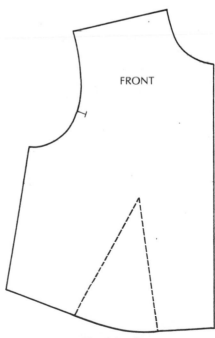

Blend for flare

GATHERS

▪ Gathers will be illustrated using the slash-spread and pivotal-transfer techniques. An example of shoulder gathers is illustrated. Although these gathers change the look of the basic garment, they will not affect the fit. The slash-spread technique illustrates *half* of the dart's excess used for gathers, and the pivotal-transfer technique illustrates how *all* of the dart's excess is transferred for gathers. Use the illustrations and instructions for Design 1 to develop patterns for Designs 2, 3, and 4.

DESIGN 1

DESIGN 2   DESIGN 3   DESIGN 4

Pattern plot and development: slash-spread technique

FIGURE 1

Gathers at neckline:

- Trace charted front pattern. Crossmark mid-shoulder. Label dart legs A and B.
- Draw slash lines 1 inch out from each side of mid-shoulder, ending at bust point (pivotal point).

FIGURE 2

- Cut slash lines to, not through, bust point.
- Place on pattern paper, and bring dart leg B halfway to A. Secure.
- Spread slashed sections equally and secure.
- Trace outline of pattern (bold line).
- Place notch marks ½ inch beyond first and last opening, for gather control.
- Draw blending line between openings touching center sections.

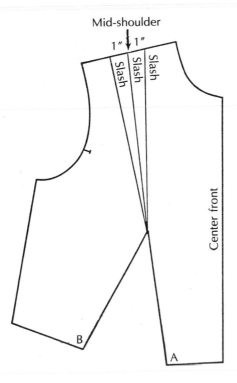

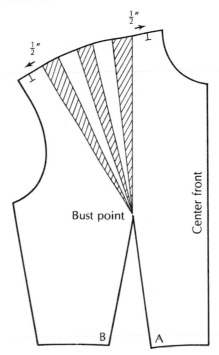

FIGURE 3

- Mark back shoulder same distance in from shoulder tip and shoulder at neck.

Pattern plot and development: pivotal-transfer technique

FIGURE 1
- Mark mid-shoulder and 1 inch on each side of mark. Label 1, 2, and 3.
- Label dart legs A and B.
- Place pattern on paper with pushpin through bust point.
- Divide waist dart into thirds on paper underneath. Label 4, 5, and 6.
- Trace from corner of dart leg A to shoulder mark 1, and crossmark.

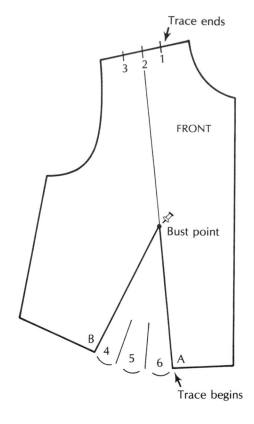

FIGURE 2
- Pivot dart leg B, covering space 4.
- Trace pattern from shoulder mark 1 to 2. (Broken line indicates section traced.)

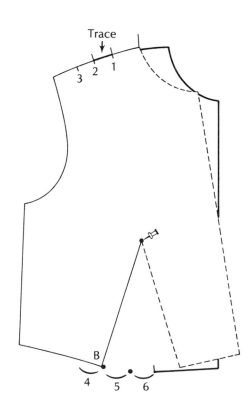

FIGURE 3
- Pivot dart leg B, covering space 5.
- Trace pattern from shoulder mark 2 to 3, and crossmark.

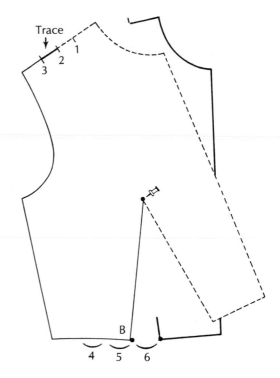

FIGURE 4
- Pivot dart leg B, covering space 6 (dart closes).
- Trace pattern from shoulder mark 3 to dart leg B.

FIGURE 5
- Blend shoulder line, touching centers of each section as shown. Crossmarks 1 and 3 should be notched for gather control.

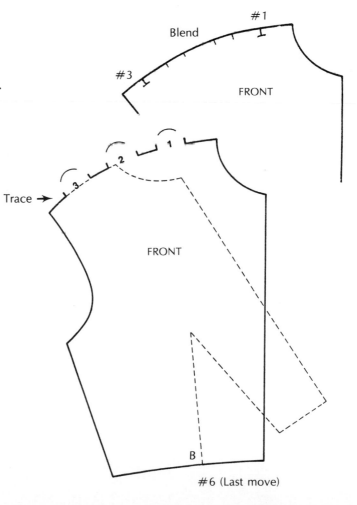

CLUSTERS OF DARTS AND DART EQUIVALENTS

The dart's excess may be divided among multiple openings that are spaced together and treated as a single design unit. When used as a single design feature, they may be identified as a group of basic or stylized darts, tuck-darts, pleats, or a variation in any combination desired.

The following instructions (Figures 1, 2, and 3) apply to the development of darts, tuck-darts, and pleat clusters. The method for *completing* each cluster differs and will be illustrated by Figure 4 (dart cluster), Figure 5 (tuck-dart cluster), and Figure 6 (pleat cluster). Seams are added in the beginning of pattern development.

WAIST CLUSTER

Tuck-Darts

Darts

Pleats

Pattern plot and development

FIGURE 1
- Trace basic bodice 1-dart pattern.
- Square a guideline out from each dart leg 1 inch below bust point.
- Draw parallel slash lines to guideline $1\frac{1}{2}$ inches away from dart legs.
- Connect to bust point.
- Cut pattern from paper.

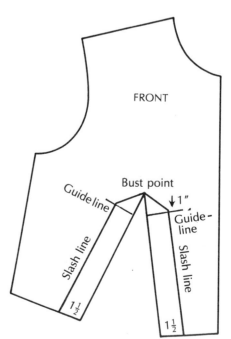

FIGURE 2

- Cut slash lines to, not through, bust point.
- Place on paper and spread equally (shaded area). Secure.
- Draw dart legs ending $\frac{1}{2}$ inch below guideline for dart points as shown.
- Trace pattern and discard.
- Add seams, and allow excess of paper below waistline for shaping darts.
- Cut from paper.

FIGURE 3

- Fold dart excess toward center front (allow pattern to cup).
- Draw blending line across waistline. Draw a seam allowance, $\frac{1}{2}$ inch line parallel with waistline.
- Cut away excess while darts are folded or trace (with tracing wheel) across seam allowance line.
- Unfold, pencil in perforated line.
- To complete the pattern, choose the dart equivalent desired (darts, tuck-darts or pleats, see Figures 4, 5, or 6).

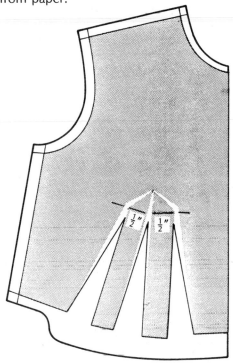

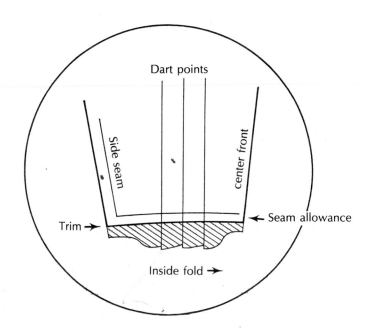

DART CLUSTER

FIGURE 4

- Center punch hole $\frac{1}{2}$ inch down from dart point.
- Circle punch hole mark.
- Notch pattern, including dart legs.
- Draw grainline. Cut basic back and complete for test fit.

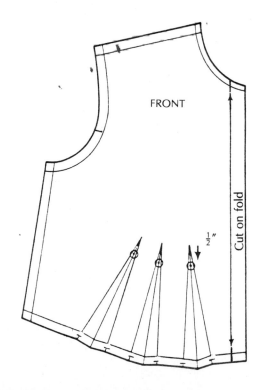

TUCK-DART CLUSTER

FIGURE 5
- Mark the center for punch holes one-half the distance to dart point (varies).
- Mark for punch holes $\frac{1}{8}$ inch from dart legs.
- Circle all punch marks as shown.
- Notch pattern and dart legs.
- Draw grainline. Cut basic back and complete for test fit.
- For stitching guide see instruction given on page 138, Figure 1b (unstitched dart indicated by broken lines).

PLEAT CLUSTER

FIGURE 6
- Notch each dart leg (broken lines indicate original dart legs). (Do not punch holes for dart points—not required for gathers.)
- Draw grainline. Cut basic back and complete for test fit.

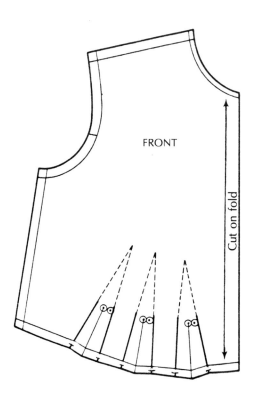

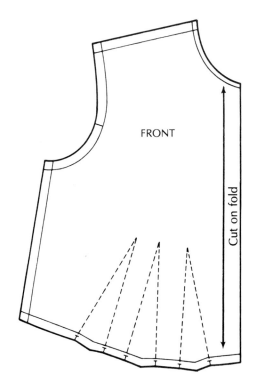

SHOULDER CLUSTER

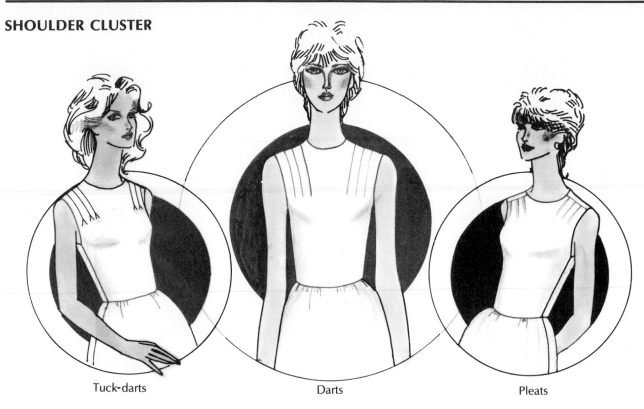

Tuck-darts   Darts   Pleats

Pattern plot and development

FIGURE 1

- Trace basic bodice 1-dart pattern.
- Mark mid-shoulder, and label dart legs A–B.
- Draw a slash line from mid-shoulder to bust point.
- Square a guideline $1\frac{1}{2}$ inches above bust point.
- Draw $1\frac{1}{4}$-inch parallel line out from each side of line to guideline. Connect to bust point.
- Cut pattern from paper.

FIGURE 2

- Cut slash lines to, not through, bust point.
- Close dart legs A and B. Tape.
- Place on paper and spread equally. Draw dart legs to guideline as shown.
- Add seams, allowing excess for shaping darts.
- To complete pattern for each design, see Figures 3, 4, 5, and 6, pages 145 and 146.

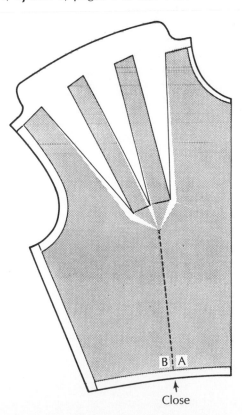

CENTER FRONT BUST CLUSTER

Tuck-darts

Darts

Pleats

Pattern plot and development

FIGURE 1

- Trace basic 1-dart bodice pattern. Label dart legs A and B. Square a line from center front to bust point.
- Draw guideline 1 inch from bust point, parallel with center front.
- Draw parallel line $1\frac{1}{4}$ inches out from each side of line to guideline (varies).
- Connect to bust point as shown.
- Cut pattern from paper.

FIGURE 2

- Cut slash lines to, not through, bust point.
- Close dart legs A and B. Tape.
- Place on paper and spread equally (shaded area). Secure.
- Draw dart legs to guideline as shown.
- Add seams, allowing excess for shaping darts (dart excess folds in the direction of the waist).
- To complete pattern for each design, see Figures 3, 4, 5 and 6, pages 145 and 146.

FRONT

Slash
Slash $1\frac{1}{4}''$
← C.f. bust
Slash $1\frac{1}{4}''$
↑
(Guide line)

B

A

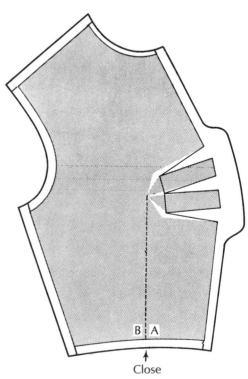

B A

↑
Close

GRADUATED AND RADIATING DARTS

Graduated darts are darts within a group whose lengths vary. Radiating darts spread out (radiate) in a balanced arrangement from a focal point and may be of the same or a graduated length. Each dart's intake varies with its placement or proximity to the bust mound—the closer it is, the greater its share of excess to prevent bulging at the tip of the dart farthest from the bust mound. The shorter dart's excess is generally $\frac{1}{2}$ inch at seam line, with all remaining excess being absorbed by the darts closer to the bust mound. Use back pattern to complete the design.

GRADUATED DARTS

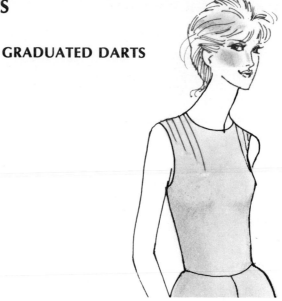

Pattern plot and development

FIGURE 1
- Trace basic 1-dart bodice pattern. Label dart legs A and B.
- Square a guideline from center front to side seam, passing through bust point.
- Divide the shoulderline into 5 equal parts as shown. Mark.
- Draw 4 parallel slash lines from shoulder marks to guideline so that the first line is spaced $1\frac{1}{4}$" from bust point. Label C.
- Draw an angle line from C to shoulder tip.
- Crossmark intersecting points (dart ends).
- Cut from paper.

Design Analysis: Design 1
Design I features graduating darts along the shoulderline. The longest dart ends at bust level.

FIGURE 2
- Cut across guideline from side seam to bust point.
- Cut slash lines from shoulder to, not through, guidelines. Slash from point C to, not through, bust point.
- Place pattern (shaded area) on paper and close dart legs A and B. Tape. Spread section $\frac{1}{2}$ inch, except for space above bust point. This dart absorbs the remaining excess. Secure pattern.
- Center dart points and draw legs.
- Trace pattern and discard.
- Complete pattern for test fit.

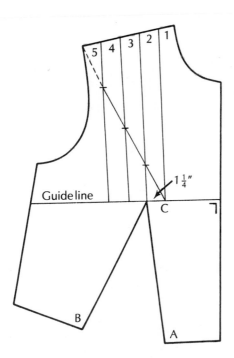

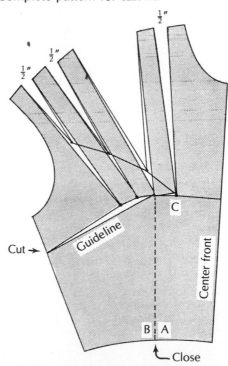

RADIATING DARTS

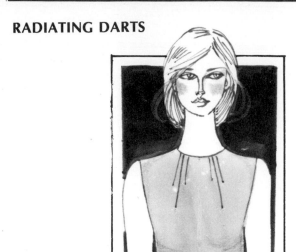

Design Analysis: Design 2

Design features radiating darts from neck, with the longest dart placed at mid-neckline.

Pattern plot and development

FIGURE 1

- Trace basic 1-dart pattern. Label dart legs A and B.
- Draw a slash line from bust point to mid-neck. Label C.
- Locate midpoint on C-line. Square out 1 inch each side. Label D and E.
- Measure out $\frac{1}{2}$ inch each side of C. Mark and draw slash lines to D and E, and bust point.

FIGURE 2

- Cut slash lines to, not through, bust point.
- Place on paper. Close dart legs A and B. Tape.
- Spread lines D and E $\frac{1}{2}$ inch at neck. Remaining excess is taken up by middle dart.
- Locate dart points between guidelines as shown with middle dart point 1 inch from bust point.
- Draw dart legs to dart point and true.
- Complete pattern for test fit.

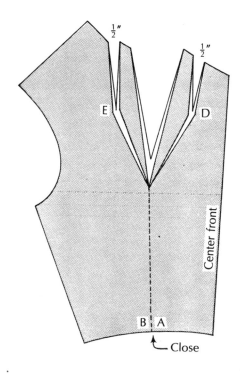

PARALLEL DARTS

The two-dart pattern is used to develop designs featuring parallel darts of varying shapes. To create parallel darts, example, curved French darts, the waist and side dart points (see Figure 1), or a combination of one dart point and bust point (see Figure 2) could be used. The distance between dart points, or bust point establishes the width of the parallel darts. To increase the width, shorten the length of the side dart (see Figure 3). This does not violate the principle of dart manipulation, since both darts originated at the bust point.

The following series can be used as a guide for developing parallel dart designs. Special instructions are given for specific design detailing where appropriate. Design 3 is given for the more advanced student. In this project instruction for developing the back pattern is not given. It is a thought problem to be worked out by the student without assistance from the instructor. Designs I and 2 require the basic back pattern. It is recommended that the patternmaker study the relationship between each design and the resulting pattern shapes in order to eventually be able to visualize the shape of a pattern by looking at the design. Seams are shown on the following illustration because of the darts' unique shapes or locations ($\frac{1}{4}$ inch at neck, $\frac{1}{2}$ inch along shoulder, armhole, waist, and $\frac{1}{2}$ inch to $\frac{3}{4}$ inch along side seam). Shaded section on illustration indicates part of pattern discarded. Facing instructions are given in Chapter 14. Pattern completion information is found on page 20 in Chapter 1.

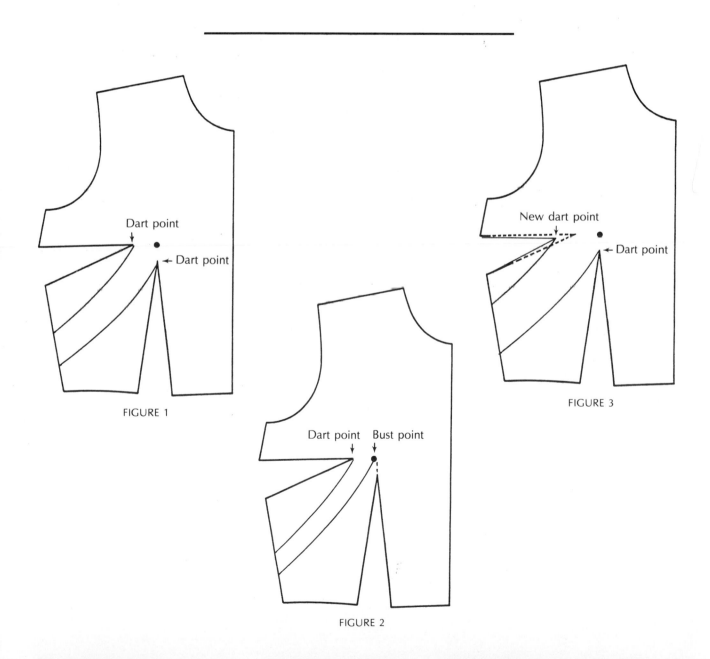

FIGURE 1

FIGURE 2

FIGURE 3

PARALLEL FRENCH DARTS

Design Analysis: Design 1

Design I features curved parallel French darts that are developed by transferring the waist and side dart excess to the curved dart lines using the dart points as the guide.

FIGURE 2

- Cut slash lines to, not through, dart points.
- Close side and waist darts. Tape.
- Trace pattern on fold. Discard.
- Add seams and grainline.

Method for finishing darts

- Add $\frac{1}{2}$-inch seam allowance to darts.
- Where seams come together, slash a line $\frac{1}{16}$ inch wide to within $\frac{1}{2}$ inch of dart point, following curve of dart.
- Use the basic back pattern to complete pattern for test fit.

Pattern plot and development

FIGURE 1

- Trace two-dart front bodice pattern.
- Draw curved parallel slash lines from dart points to side as shown.
- Cut pattern from paper.

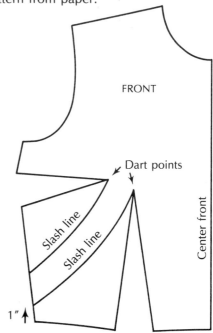

NEW PATTERN SHAPE

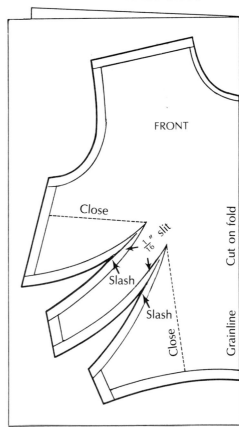

PARALLEL DARTS AT NECK

Design Analysis: Design 2

Parallel curved dart legs end at corner of neck and shoulder of Design 2. The neckline depth is placed 3 inches below the basic neck where it curves and intersects the dart legs.

NEW PATTERN SHAPE

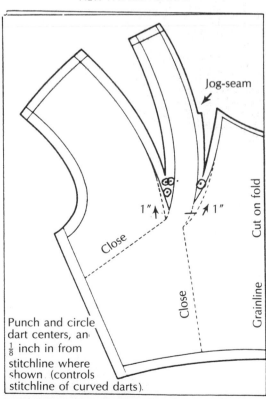

Jog-seam

Close

Close

1"

1"

Grainline

Cut on fold

Punch and circle dart centers, and $\frac{1}{8}$ inch in from stitchline where shown (controls stitchline of curved darts).

Pattern plot and development

FIGURE 1

- Trace two-dart front bodice.
- Draw curved slash line from dart point of waist dart to corner of neck. Crossmark at level with dart point of side dart.
- Draw parallel slash line from dart point of side dart to shoulderline.
- Draw curved neckline 3 inches down from center front neck.
- Cut from paper, discard unneeded neck section (shaded area).

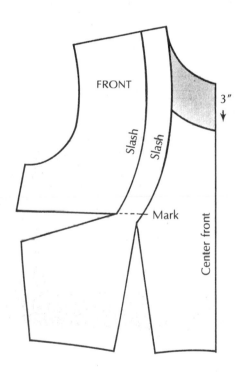

FRONT

Slash

Slash

3"

Mark

Center front

FIGURE 2

- Cut to, not through, dart points.
- Close side and waist darts. Tape.
- Place on paper and trace. Discard.
- Mark dart points 1 inch from original darts.
- Add seams and grain as shown.
- Jog-seam at dart and neckline require $\frac{1}{4}$ inch seam allowance for facing.

PARALLEL DARTS—CAPE EFFECT

Design Analysis: Design 3

Stylized darts form a cape effect on Design 3. The darts curve outward until they extend slightly beyond the shoulder tip. The neckline is a high scoop to complement the curved line of the darts. Advanced students can develop back pattern.

NEW PATTERN SHAPE

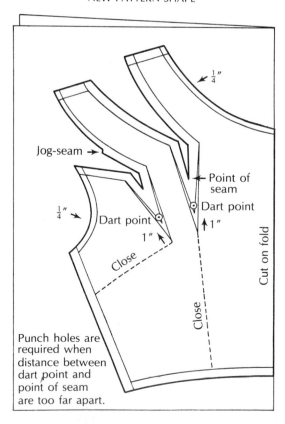

Punch holes are required when distance between dart point and point of seam are too far apart.

Pattern plot and development

FIGURE 1

- Trace two-dart basic bodice.
- Measure out approximately 1¼ inches from shoulder tip. (Broken line indicates original armhole.)
- Draw a vertical slash line up from dart point of side dart parallel with center front.
- Draw curve of cape from the extended shoulder point until line intersects with vertical line.
- Draw a parallel slash line up from bust point following a parallel curved line to shoulder.
- Draw parallel line for scooped neck.
- Draw slash line from dart point of waist dart to bust point.
- Cut from paper. Discard unneeded neckline (shaded area).

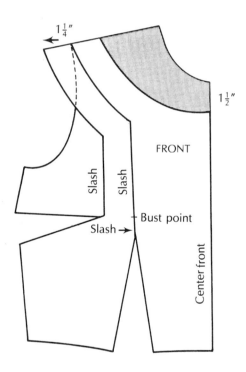

FIGURE 2

- Cut slash lines to, not through, dart point and bust point.
- Close side and waist darts. Tape.
- Place on paper. Trace and discard.
- Center dart point 1 inch from point of original dart. Draw dart leg. Mark punch and circles ½ inch from dart point.
- Add seams and grainline as shown.
- Jog-seam at armhole requires ¼-inch seam allowance.

PARALLEL DART DESIGN VARIATIONS

The following parallel dart designs are practice problems. The developed patterns are correct if they result in exact replicas of the designs.

ASYMMETRIC DARTS

Asymmetric darts are stylized darts that cross the center front of the garment. Pattern shapes will change radically from that of the working pattern. Asymmetric darts require special pattern handling and identification, as do all designs that differ from side to side. Compare pattern shapes with the creative features of each design. Cut basic back to complete the design for test fit.

- A full pattern is required for development.
- Right-side-up instructions are necessary.
- The existing dart of the working pattern may interfere with the placement of a stylized dart. If so, the darts should be transferred to another location before the pattern is plotted (example: mid-armhole).

Seam allowance is illustrated for each pattern because of the darts' unique shapes and locations ($\frac{1}{4}$ inch at neck, $\frac{1}{2}$ inch at shoulder, armhole and waist, and $\frac{1}{2}$ to $\frac{3}{4}$ inch at side seams).

ASYMMETRIC SQUARED DARTS

Design Analysis: Design 1

Design 1 features one squared dart that crosses to the opposite side of the garment, forming a point, and ends at mid-armhole. The other dart parallels the first dart, then squares ending at waist. Transfer waist darts to mid-armhole location where they will not interfere with plotting of the stylized darts.

Pattern plot and development

FIGURE 1
- Trace front pattern on fold, transferring waist dart to mid-armhole location.
- Cut from paper. Unfold.
- Draw slash lines for new dart locations from each bust point as shown.
- Cut pattern from paper.

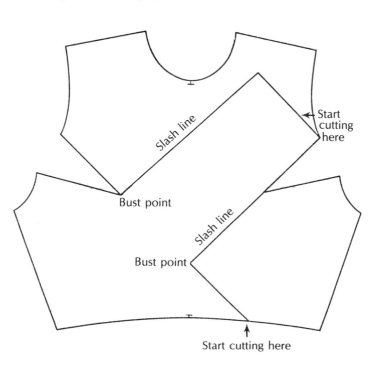

FIGURE 2

- Cut slash lines to, not through, bust points.
- Close side dart legs. Tape.
- Retrace and discard pattern.
- Center dart point 1 inch from bust and draw dart legs.
- Label right-side-up. Add seams and grainline.
- Complete pattern for test fit.

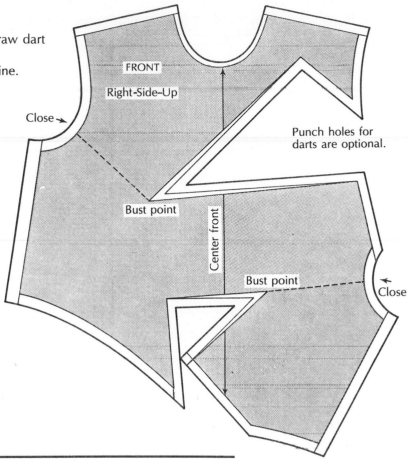

NEW PATTERN SHAPE

FRONT
Right-Side-Up

Close →

Bust point

Center front

Bust point

→ Close

Punch holes for darts are optional.

ASYMMETRIC RADIATING DARTS

Design Analysis: Design 2

Both darts end at the waist on the same side, forming tuck-darts on Design 2. Scoop neckline completes the design. Transfer waist darts to mid-armhole location where they will not interfere with plotting of the stylized darts. (Bow not illustrated.) Beginners may want to use a basic neckline.

(Continued on next page)

Pattern plot and development

FIGURE 1
- Trace pattern on fold, transferring waist dart to mid-armhole dart location. Draw neckline, as shown.
- Cut from paper. Unfold. Discard unneeded section (shaded area).
- Draw slash lines from bust points to side waist as shown.
- Measure up 3 inches from corner on slash lines and crossmark (indicates the length of the tuck dart).

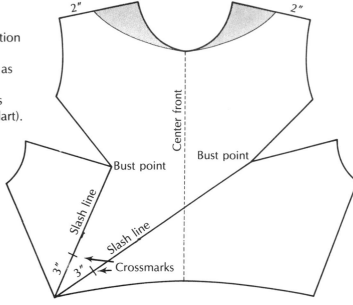

FIGURE 2
- Cut slash lines to, not through, bust point.
- Close dart legs. Tape.
- Retrace and discard pattern.
- Label right-side-up. Draw grainline and add seams.

Tuck-darts:
- Draw seams across open dart $\frac{1}{2}$ inch below each crossmark.
- Trim seam allowance to within $\frac{1}{2}$ inch of each dart leg opening. (Broken lines are the discarded part of dart legs.)

FIGURE 3
- To complete pattern, trace back, marking 2 inches in from shoulder tip ending at center back.
- Complete pattern for test fit.

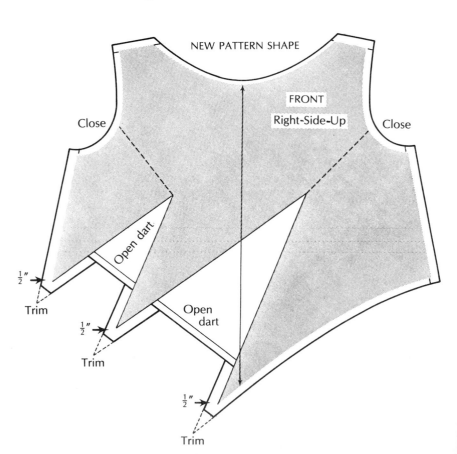

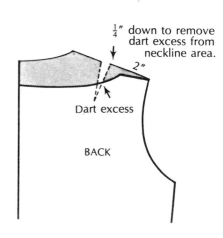

ASYMMETRIC CURVED DARTS

Pattern plot and development

FIGURE 1

- Trace front pattern on fold, transferring waist dart to mid-armhole location.
- Cut from paper. Unfold.
- Draw curved slash lines from bust point to mid-armhole and 1 inch above waist.

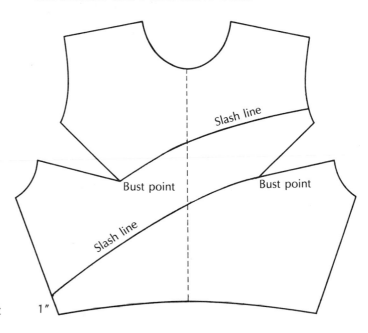

NEW PATTERN SHAPE

Design Analysis: Design 3

Design 3 features stylized curved darts that start at bust point and cross over the center front. One dart ends at mid-armhole and the other at a point just above the side waist. The waist dart interferes with the styleline location, and should be transferred to mid-armhole location before plotting the pattern.

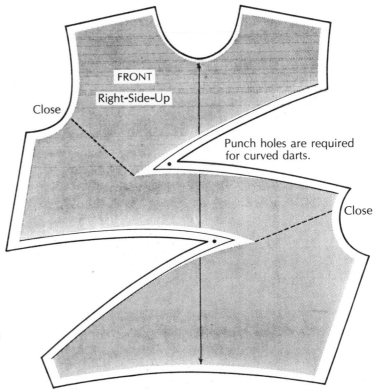

FIGURE 2

- Cut slash lines to, not through, bust points.
- Close dart legs. Tape.
- Retrace and discard pattern.
- Center dart points 1 inch from bust point. Draw dart legs as shown.
- Label right-side-up. Add seams and grainline.
- Complete pattern for test fit.

(Continued on next page)

ASYMMETRIC DART VARIATIONS

The following asymmetric dart designs are practice problems. The developed patterns are correct if they result in exact representations of the designs.

INTERSECTING DARTS

Intersecting darts resemble asymmetric darts and dart equivalents. They are also stylized darts that cross the center front of a garment but usually intersect each other along the dart leg. They require the same special pattern handling and identification as asymmetric darts. These designs are based on a one-dart pattern. To complete the design, use basic back pattern. See Chapter 14 for guidance in developing facings. See page 20 for instruction on completing the pattern.

INTERSECTING DART TO SHOULDER

Pattern plot and development

FIGURE 1
- Trace front pattern on fold.
- Cut from paper. Unfold.
- Draw slash lines as they appear on the design.

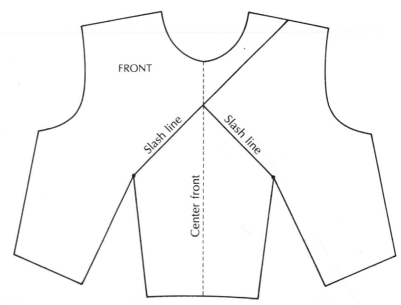

Design Analysis: Design 1

Design I features a stylized dart crossing the center front, ending at mid-shoulder on the opposite side. The second stylized dart intersects the first at center front.

NEW PATTERN SHAPE

Punch holes for darts are optional.

FIGURE 2
- Cut slash lines to, not through, bust point.
- Close dart legs. Tape.
- Retrace pattern and discard.
- Center dart point 1 inch from bust. Draw dart legs as shown.
- Label right-side-up. Draw grainline and add seams.
- Cut from paper.
- Complete pattern for test fit.

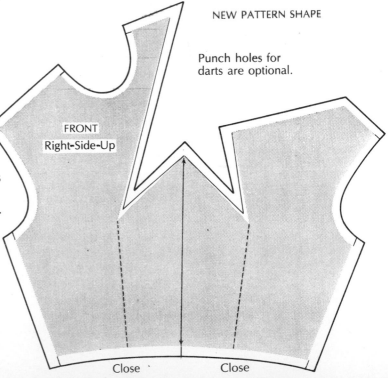

INTERSECTING DART TO WAIST

Design Analysis: Design 2

Design 2 features one dart crossing the center front, ending at the waistline on the opposite side. This dart intersects the other dart at center front. Darts are treated as pleats. The neckline is cut away.

FIGURE 2

- Cut slash lines to, not through, bust points.
- Close dart legs. Tape.
- *Pleats:* Form dart using the fold, ruler, or tissue method, pages 24–26.
- Add seams.
- Trim seam allowance (broken lines) from pointed section of dart leg.
- Notch pattern. (Notching for pleats has been emphasized.)
- Draw grain and label right-side-up.
- Cut from paper.

FIGURE 3

- To complete the design, trace back, marking 1 inch from shoulder at neck. Blend to center back neck.
- Complete the pattern for test fit.

Pattern plot and development

FIGURE 1

- Trace pattern on fold, transferring waist dart to mid-armhole.
- Draw neckline 1 inch out from neck at shoulder. Blend to center front neck.
- Cut from paper. Discard unneeded section (shaded area). Unfold.
- Draw slash lines as they appear on the design.

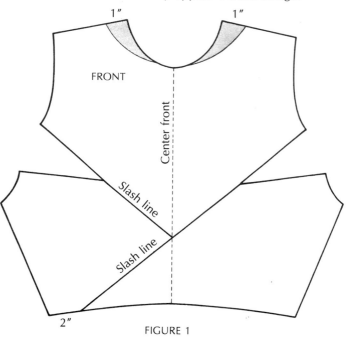

FIGURE 1

NEW PATTERN SHAPE

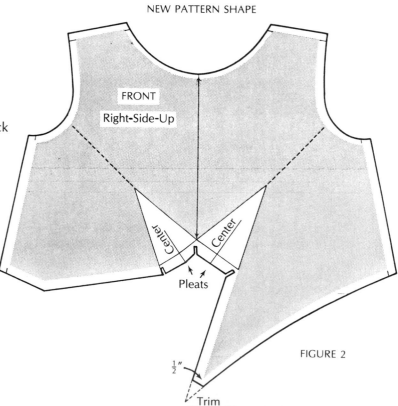

FIGURE 2

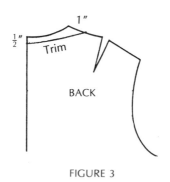

FIGURE 3

INTERSECTING DART WITH GATHERS

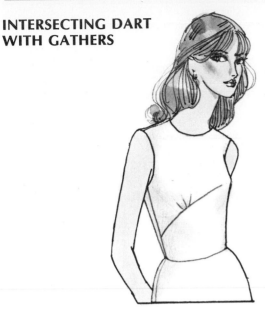

Design Analysis: Design 3

Design 3 features one stylized dart crossing the center front to the opposite side, ending above the side waist. Gathers (dart equivalents) form under the bust.

FIGURE 2

- Cut all slash lines to, not through, dart points.
- Close darts. Tape.
- Place on paper and spread section equally for gathers.
- Trace. Discard.
- Center dart point ½ inch from bust point.
- Add seams, blend gathered area, and draw dart legs to dart point as shown.
- Draw grainline, mark notches, and label right-side-up on pattern.
- Cut from paper.
- Trace basic back and complete pattern for test fit.

Pattern plot and development

FIGURE 1

- Trace pattern on fold, transferring waist darts to mid-armhole.
- Cut and unfold.
- Draw slash lines for dart and gathers.
- Mark notches ½ inch out from first and last slash line for gather control.

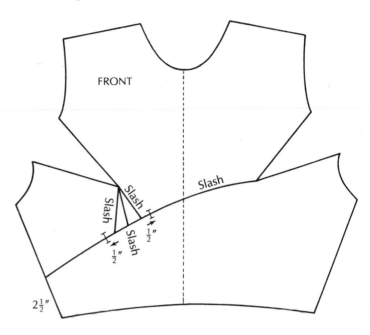

FRONT

Slash

Slash

Slash

Slash

½"

½"

2½"

NEW PATTERN SHAPE

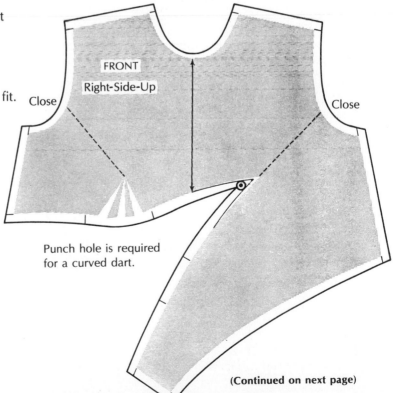

FRONT

Right-Side-Up

Close

Close

Punch hole is required for a curved dart.

(Continued on next page)

INTERSECTING DART DESIGN VARIATIONS

The following intersecting dart designs are practice problems. The developed patterns are correct if they result in exact representations of the designs.

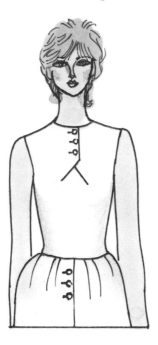
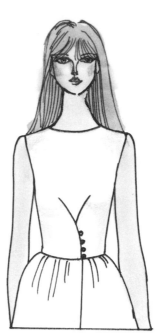

THE SHOULDER DART

The shoulder dart should be relocated whenever it interferes with a design detail or whenever the cost of sewing the dart is too expensive. The shoulder dart, like the bust dart, can be transferred to any location around the pattern's outline. It can be used creatively by changing its shape, or by transferring it to the waist dart when additional flare is desired at the waist or hemline of a top.

   The most common dart locations are illustrated. If preferred, other locations can be used. (*Note:* This information is placed after the front bodice series so there will be no interruption in information, not because it is less important.)

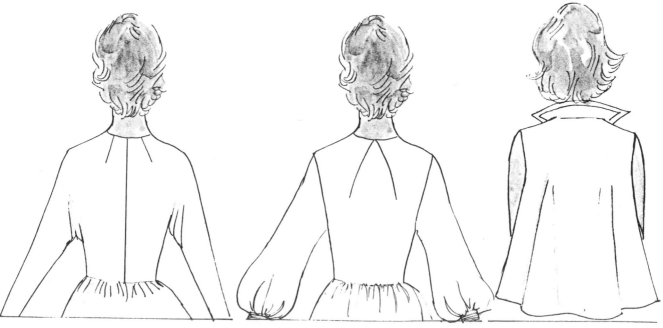

Neck darts   Curved darts   Flare

THE MULTI-DISPERSION WORKING PATTERN

(For use when shoulder dart not required)

Pattern plot and development

FIGURE 1a and 1b
- Trace back pattern, include the HBL line.
- Draw slash line from dart point and mid-neck to the guideline.
- Draw and cut facing from paper (broken line).

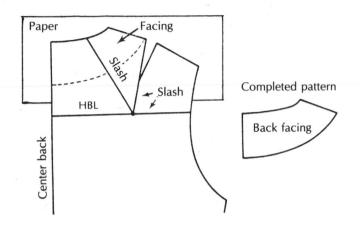

FIGURE 2
- Cut slash lines from neck, shoulder dart, and mid-armhole to, not through, pivotal point.
- Spread sections equally (indicated by broken lines).
- Place on paper. Secure.
- Trace and blend neck, shoulder and armholes.
- Mark ease control notches as shown. (Mark notches on front shoulder.)

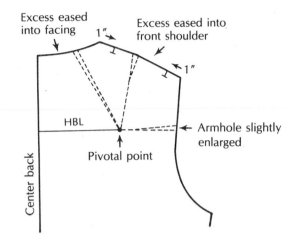

NECK DART

Pattern plot and development

FIGURE 1
- Trace back pattern and include all markings.
- Draw slash lines from mid-neck and shoulder dart point to dart point of waist dart.
- Crossmark a point 3 inches below neck on line.
- Cut from paper.

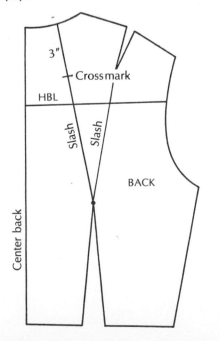

FIGURE 2
- Cut slash lines to, not through, dart point.
- Close shoulder dart. Tape.
- Trace pattern. (Be sure space between waist dart remains the same.) Discard.
- Center dart point at level with crossmark. Draw dart legs from neck to dart point.

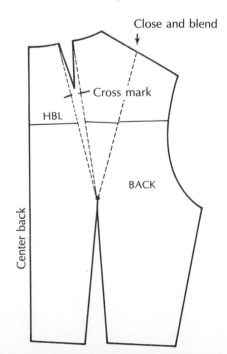

EXCESS TRANSFERRED TO ARMHOLE

▪ Dart excess is transferred to the armhole for the following reasons: (1) Cost of stitching dart is too expensive. (2) To enlarge the armhole when the sleeve cap excess puckers around the stitchline.

Pattern plot and development

FIGURE 1
▪ Trace back pattern and all markings.
▪ Draw line from dart point to HBL guideline.

▪ Slash from HBL at armhole to pivotal point and from dart point to, not through, pivotal point.

FIGURE 2
▪ Close shoulder dart. Tape. Retrace. Blend armhole.

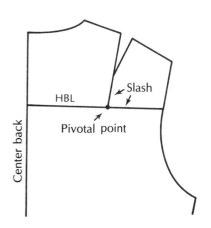

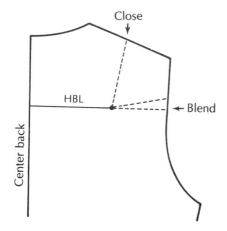

SHOULDER DART VARIATIONS

The following designs are practice problems and are examples of how shoulder–waist darts can be used creatively. Use previous instructions as a guide to develop patterns.

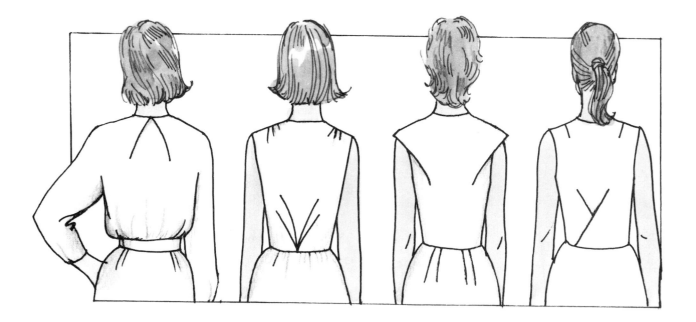

Introduction 168
THE CLASSIC PRINCESS STYLELINE 168
Classic princess styleline variations 171
ARMHOLE PRINCESS STYLELINE 172
Armhole princess styleline variations 174
OTHER STYLELINE VARIATIONS 175
THE PANEL STYLELINE 176
Panel styleline variations 178

7

STYLELINES

INTRODUCTION

Stylelines can be placed anywhere on a pattern and fall into two classifications, those that cross over bust points or dart points, and those that do not. The stylelines discussed in this chapter are those that *do* cross over bust points and dart points, replacing the dart legs with seams extending from one side of the pattern to the other. Stylelines that absorb dart excess within stitchlines control the fit of the garment and are called dart equivalents. This was discussed in the corollary for Principle #1, Dart Manipulation. The original size and fit of the garment have not been altered although the shapes of the pattern pieces have been changed and separated.

Stylelines that do *not* cross the bust point or dart points do not control the fit of the garment. The panel design included in this chapter represents this type and clarifies the difference between the two styleline types (see page 176). For facing instructions see Chapter 14, and for information on completing the pattern see page 20. Other variations are scattered throughout the text.

THE CLASSIC PRINCESS STYLELINE

The classic princess should be developed and perfected as a seamless working pattern as it is a popular base for other design variations. Seams are added as a guide for all stylelines:

- Neckline $\frac{1}{4}$ inch
- Armhole $\frac{1}{2}$ inch (with sleeve), $\frac{1}{4}$ inch (sleeveless)
- Side seam $\frac{1}{2}$ to $\frac{3}{4}$ inch (varies)
- All other seams $\frac{1}{2}$ inch unless otherwise stated.

Design Analysis

The classic princess is distinguished by a styleline that starts at the front and back waist darts. The styleline continues over bust point and shoulder blades, ending at mid-shoulder dart of the back (position of dart point can vary to improve styleline). These stylelines replace all darts. The design can be based on the one-, or two-dart pattern. (The two-dart pattern is illustrated.) The puff sleeve is illustrated in Chapter 13.

Pattern plot and development

FIGURE 1 *Front bodice:*

- Trace front two-dart pattern.
- Draw stylelines from mid-shoulder (in line with back shoulder darts) to bust point and from bust point to dart legs at waist.
- Crossmark for ease control notches, $1\frac{1}{2}$ inches above and below bust point (2 inches for bust cup sizes C and up).
- Draw slash line from bust point to dart point of side dart. Crossmark $\frac{3}{4}$ inch from bust point. Label X.

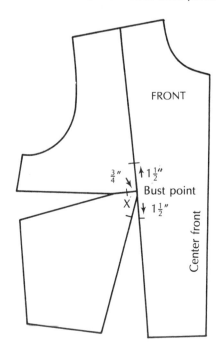

FIGURES 2 and 3   *Separate pattern:*
- Cut and separate pattern along styleline.

Side bust ease

FIGURE 4
- Cut slash line from bust point and dart point to, not through, point X.
- Close side dart legs. Tape. This provides ease for side of the bust.

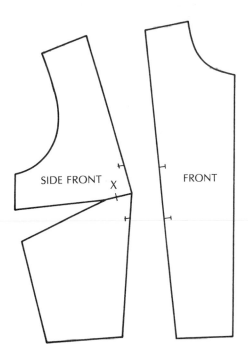

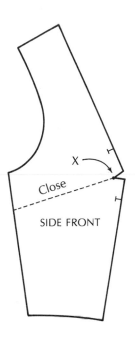

FIGURE 5   *Shaping styleline:*
- Retrace side front panel.
- Shape bust curve as shown. (Broken lines represent original shape of panel.)

FIGURE 6   *Adding more ease:*
- When developing designs from a one-dart pattern, or when more ease is needed, slash from bust point to side seam and spread $\frac{1}{4}$ inch or more. Retrace, blend and shape. See Figure 5.

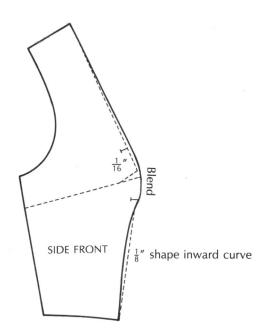

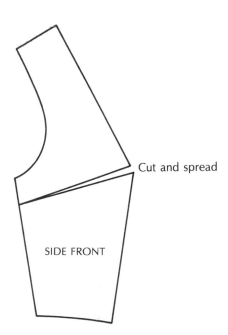

FIGURE 7   *Optional front panel shaping:*
- To shape front panel, place side panel pattern on top of front panel, matching waist and bust point.
- Trace shape of curve onto panel from waist to bust. Blend. (Broken line represents original shape of front panel and pattern underneath.)
- Adjust ease control notches on side front panel when trueing patterns.

FIGURE 8   *Back bodice:*
- Trace back pattern.
- Place skirt curve on shoulder dart leg X and waist dart point. Draw curve.
- Shift dart point of shoulder dart to styleline and redraw dart leg. (Broken line indicates original dart.)
- Crossmark dart points on styleline.

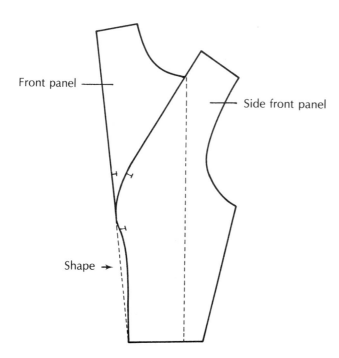

Front panel

Side front panel

Shape →

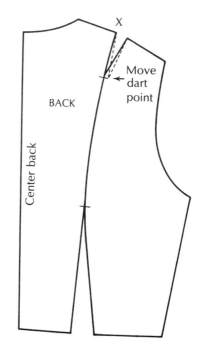

X

Move dart point

BACK

Center back

FIGURES 9 and 10
- Cut and separate pattern pieces.
- Front and back classic princess patterns are complete and remain seamless for use as a working pattern.

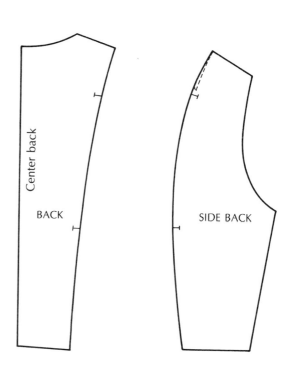

Center back

BACK

SIDE BACK

FIGURE 11 *Completed pattern:*
- Complete the pattern for a test fit as shown.

(*Note:* Grainlines for side panels are squared up from waistline.)

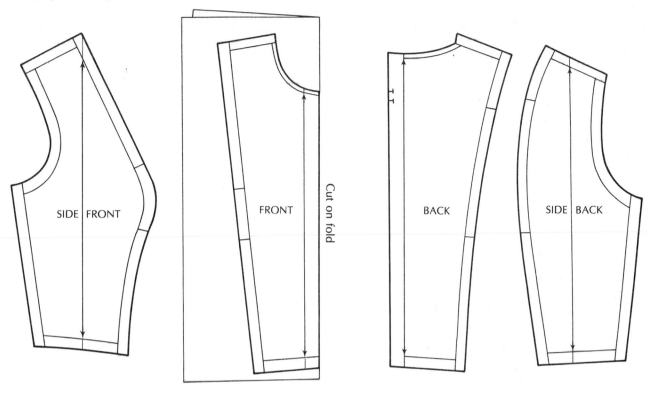

CLASSIC PRINCESS STYLELINE VARIATIONS

The following designs are based on the classic princess. Develop patterns for these designs or create other variations for practice. Use the classic princess if you are an advanced student, or develop the design from the basic pattern. Remember, draw stylelines on the pattern exactly as they appear on the design. The finished pattern shapes should result in perfect representations of each design. If not, locate the problem and try again.

ARMHOLE PRINCESS STYLELINE

Design Analysis

This design is a variation of the classic princess and features a styleline that curves from the bust point in front and the shoulder blades in back to mid-armhole. This design is developed from a two-dart pattern. When the design pattern is complete, you will notice that the side dart has been transferred to mid-armhole. Add seams, grainline, and notches for test fit. This pattern may be left seamless and used as a working pattern.

FIGURE 2 *Back:*
 • Trace and cut back pattern.
   Note: Transfer the shoulder dart excess into mid-armhole where it can be absorbed into the styleline.
 • Draw a line 2 inches up from dart point of waist dart and crossmark $1\frac{1}{2}$ inches up for notch.
 • Repeat styleline instructions, placing guideline from crossmark to mid-armhole.

Pattern plot and development

FIGURE 1 *Front:*
 • Trace and cut front pattern.
 • Draw slash line from waist and side dart points to bust point. Crossmark $\frac{3}{4}$ inch from bust point. Label X.
 • Draw a straight guideline from bust point to mid-armhole. (Position can vary along armhole.)
 • Mark $\frac{1}{2}$ inch up at midpoint of guideline.
 • Draw curved stylelines from mid-armhole to bust point. Draw dart legs to bust point as shown.
 • Crossmark for ease control notches, $1\frac{1}{2}$ inches above and below bust point (2 inches for bust cup C and larger).

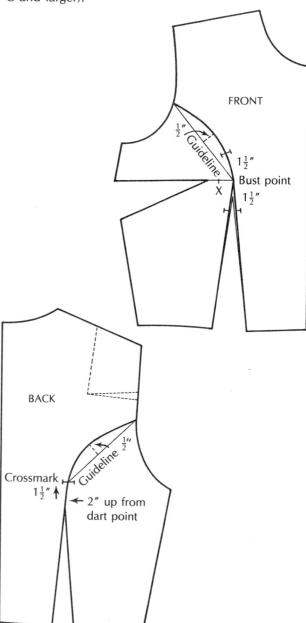

FIGURE 3   *Front:*
- Cut and separate pattern along styleline.

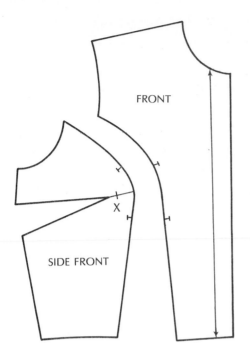

FIGURE 4
- Complete side panel using princess instruction for shaping styleline (see page 169, figure 5).

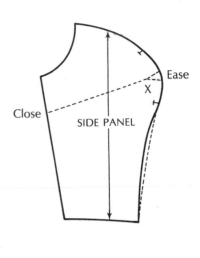

FIGURE 5   *Back:*
- Cut and separate pattern along styleline.
- To remove dart's excess from mid-armhole, draw the dart's length and width along styleline of back panel (shaded area), and trim excess from the pattern.

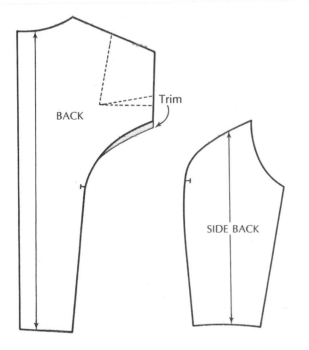

FIGURE 6   *Trueing and blending:*
- True pattern panels starting from styleline at waist and ending at armhole. If panels do not true at armhole, add paper to the shortened panel at armhole. Tape both sides securely.
- Blend armhole, adding to shorter side, and trim the longer side equally as shown.

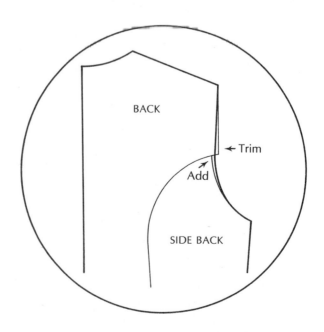

(Continued on next page)

ARMHOLE PRINCESS STYLELINE VARIATIONS

The following practice designs are based on the armhole princess. Develop patterns for these designs or create other variations. The finished pattern shapes should result in perfect representations of each design. If not, locate the problem and try again. When plotting the pattern, remember that lines are drawn on the working pattern exactly as they appear on the design. Develop these designs using the single dart pattern. (Advanced students may use the armhole princess pattern.)

OTHER STYLELINE VARIATIONS

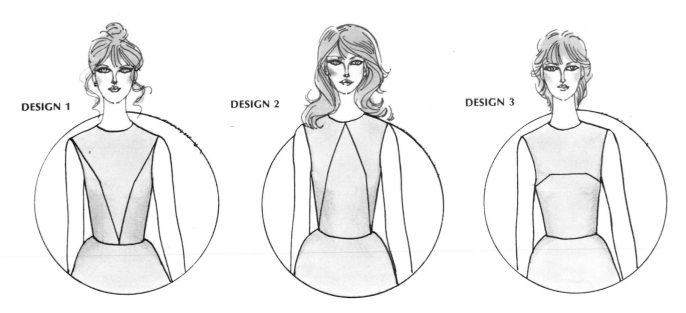

DESIGN 1   DESIGN 2   DESIGN 3

Design Analysis

Stylelines can be placed at *any* two locations around the pattern's outline as long as the two lines pass *at* or *within* 1 inch of bust point or dart point. Three designs are shown, with Design 1 being used as the example for the pattern development of Designs 2 and 3.

Pattern plot and development

FIGURE 1

- Trace pattern and square 1 inch out from bust point. Label X.
- Draw styleline as shown.
- Crossmark for ease control notches as shown.
- Cut from paper. Separate pattern along styleline.

FIGURES 2 and 3

- Cut from point X to bust point. Close dart legs.
- Blend bust area and shape dart legs if desired.
- Draw grainlines with side panel grain squared up from waistline. (When grainline is placed in this manner, dart angles of shoulder tip and center front dart can be seen.)

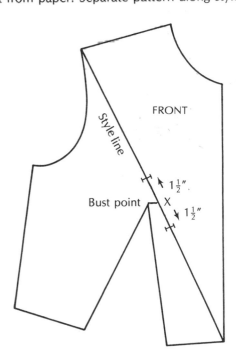

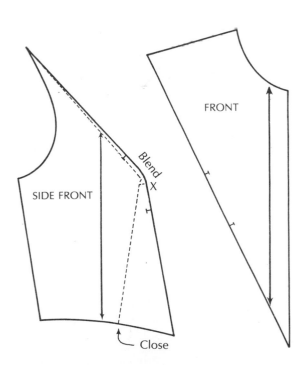

THE PANEL STYLELINE

The panel styleline is a styleline that is *not* a dart equivalent, because it does not pass through the bust point. The existing darts are still in control of the fit.

Pattern plot and development

FIGURES 1 and 2
- Trace front and back two-dart pattern and all markings.
Side panels:
- Measure in 3 inches from side seams and 3 inches up from armhole curves as shown. Mark.
- Draw straight line up from waist marks parallel with side seam. Blend into slightly curved lines to armhole marks.
- Draw slash lines from dart points to bust point.
- Cut patterns from paper.

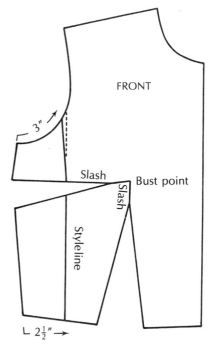

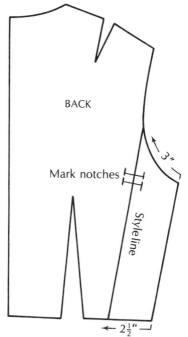

Design Analysis

The panel styleline does not cross over the bust or shoulder blades. It extends from the armhole curve to waist (front and back), forming a panel separating front and back of garment. The panel can be designed either with or without a side seam. It has a short, visible dart in front and a waist and shoulder dart in back.

Note: the back waist dart can be absorbed in the styleline if the panel styleline is placed close to it. In that case, the back panel styleline replaces the dart and partially controls the fit of the garment.

FIGURE 3
- Separate back pattern pieces along styleline.
- Draw 1-inch extension at center back.

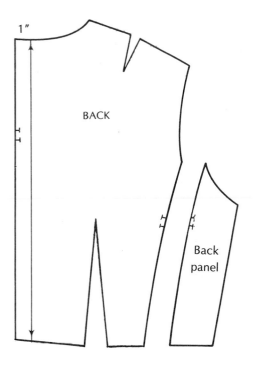

FIGURE 4
- Separate front pattern along styleline.
- Close dart legs on front side panel, and notch at this location.
- Close dart legs on front side panel. Complete dart leg as shown.

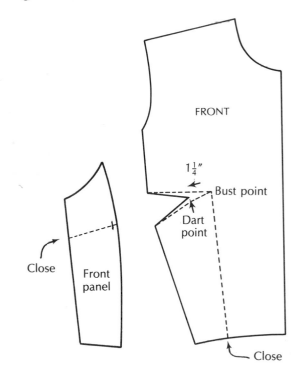

FIGURE 5
- To eliminate side seam, place front and back panels together and tape.
- Extend grainline through center of panels as shown.
- Mark notches on panel at waist and armhole.
- Complete pattern for test fit.

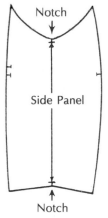

Side seams together

(Continued on next page)

ADDED FULLNESS: PRINCIPLE #2

Principle. To increase the fabric in a garment to an amount greater than that provided by the working pattern, the length and/or width within the pattern's outline must be increased.

Corollary. Adding to the outside of the pattern's outline increases the amount of fabric in a garment and can change the silhouette.

THREE TYPES OF ADDED FULLNESS

To add fullness to the garment, the working pattern is increased in one of three ways:

Equal fullness
Edges on opposite sides of the pattern are opened equally.

One-sided fullness
One edge of the pattern is opened forming an arc shape at each end.

Unequal fullness
One edge of the pattern is opened *more* than the other forming an arc shape at each end.

Study the differences between the design and the basic garment. Compare the effects of the three types of fullness on the design.

IDENTIFYING ADDED FULLNESS

A garment having added fullness appears fuller than the basic garment made from the working pattern (see figures on page 180). Fullness derived from the basic dart would end at bust level (Figure 1). Designs can be identified as having added fullness, if the fullness passes through the length, or width of the garment (Figure 2), when the fullness is directed away from the bust (Figure 3), and when the garment extends beyond the figure outline (Figures 1, 2, and 3). Fullness may appear in the form of gathers, pleats, drape, or flare. Fullness may be horizontal, vertical, or on an angle, and can be developed as equal, unequal,

or one-sided fullness. The dart may become a part of the added fullness when needed. Added fullness may be combined with Dart Relocation (Principle #1) and Contouring (Principle #3) in any design. (Examples of this will be illustrated throughout the text.)

The patternmaker must be able to determine which type of fullness is required from the way that fullness is rendered in the sketch of the design. When the patternmaker is unsure of the designer's intent, it is best to ask before developing the pattern.

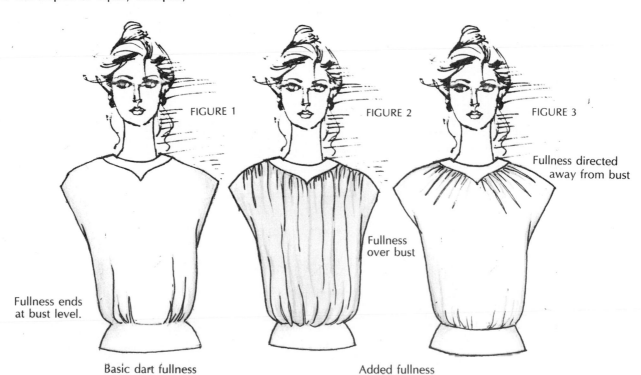

FIGURE 1

FIGURE 2

FIGURE 3

Fullness directed away from bust

Fullness over bust

Fullness ends at bust level.

Basic dart fullness

Added fullness

Method for plotting pattern for added fullness

Added fullness is plotted as a series of straight slash lines drawn across the pattern in the direction the fullness appears on the design (horizontally, vertically, or on an angle). Even though fullness may appear to end before reaching the outline of the garment, when preparing the pattern the slash lines must end at the bust point, dart point, or the pattern's outline. The designating points depend on where the fullness begins and ends on the design.

Formula for adding fullness

To determine the amount of added fullness desired, give consideration to the fabric type. Lightweight and loosely woven fabrics (cottons and chiffons, for

example) may require more fullness than bulky, closely woven fabrics. Using a 26-inch waist as an example, added fullness may equal:

• One and one-half times the distance covered (26" + 13" = 39")
• Two times the distance covered (26" + 26" = 52")
• Two and one-half times the distance covered (26" + 26" + 13" = 65).

To help train the eye to visualize different amounts of added fullness, it is suggested that examples of each type of fullness be stitched using 10 inches as the distance covered. Follow the formula above for each example (finished length of each sample should be 10 inches). Save these examples for use when determining amounts of fullness desired.

FULLNESS AT DART LEG

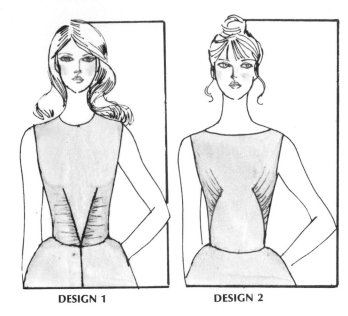

DESIGN 1 **DESIGN 2**

Design Analysis

Darts in Design I form a V-shape with gathers on one side of the dart leg, indicating one-side opening of the pattern. Design 2 is a practice problem. Design other variations placing dart in other locations.

Pattern plot and development

FIGURE 1

- Trace basic bodice, transferring dart to center front waist. (Dart legs can be shaped, see page 26.)
- Draw slash lines approximately 1 inch apart for gathers in the direction the folds lie.
- Cut pattern from paper.

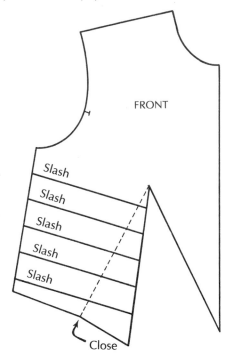

FIGURE 2

- Cut slash lines from dart leg to, not through, side seam.
- Place on paper.
- Spread section for gathers (lined area).

   Note: Spread should equal one-and-one-half to two times the length of the dart leg. (Example: dart leg of 7 inches, spread so that the line equals $10\frac{1}{2}$ inches or 14 inches.)
- Trace pattern's outline and discard.
- Draw blending lines along opened dart leg (bold line) and side seam.
- Draw grain and complete pattern for test fit using basic back pattern.

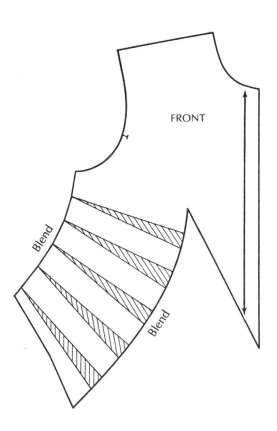

FULLNESS ABOVE BUST

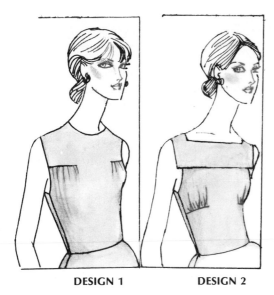

DESIGN 1   DESIGN 2

Design Analysis

A short styleline above the bust of Design I controls gathers ending at mid-armhole. Since there is no visible fullness at the waist, one-sided added fullness is indicated. Design 2 is given for practice. Design other variations using the bust area as a focal point.

Pattern plot and development

FIGURE 1

- Trace front basic bodice. Mark mid-armhole.
- Square a line from center front to mid-armhole.
- Square a slash line from styleline to bust point. Label X.
- Draw remaining slash line in the direction fullness lies.
- Cut pattern from paper.

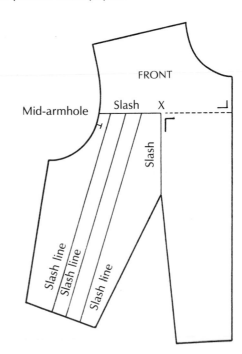

FRONT

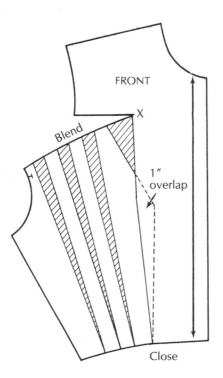

FIGURE 2

- Cut styleline from mid-armhole to point X.
- Cut slash line from bust point to point X, separating pattern.
- Close dart at waist, overlapping bust point 1 inch (to minimize excess over bust). Openings created by the spread areas next to bust compensate for any loss.
- Cut remaining slash lines to, not through, waist.
- Place on paper.
- Spread as desired. (Example: $\frac{1}{2}$ inch.)
- Trace pattern's outline and discard. Blend line as shown.
- Draw grain and complete for test fit using basic back pattern.

FULLNESS AROUND NECK BAND

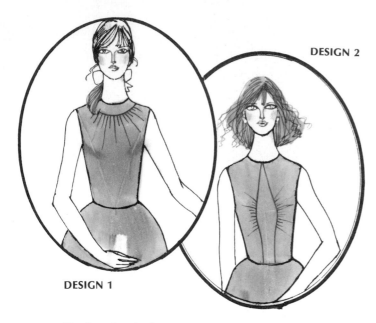

DESIGN 2

DESIGN 1

Design Analysis

Design I has gathers formed around an inset band that follows the shape of the neckline. Gathers above the bust end at bust level. Gathers at the side areas end along the outline of the garment at armhole and bust. This indicates one-sided fullness. Design 2 is for practice. Design other variations using the band as a theme.

Pattern plot and development

FIGURE 1

Front:
- Trace front basic pattern.
- Draw inset band $1\frac{1}{2}$ inches around front neckline.
- Draw slash line from bust point 2 inches in from center front. Draw slash lines $\frac{1}{8}$ inch on each side of center line to bust point.
- Draw remaining slash lines in the direction of the gathers.
- Mark for notch as shown.
- Cut patterns from paper.

FIGURE 2a and 2b
- Cut and separate inset band from pattern.
- Cut slash lines to, not through, pattern's outline and bust point.
- Close dart leg. Tape.
- Place pattern on paper.
- Spread sections as desired. (Example: $\frac{1}{2}$ inch except for fullness over bust area.)
- Trace and discard pattern.
- Blend styleline.

FIGURE 3

Back:
- Trace back pattern. Draw neckband $1\frac{1}{2}$ inches around neckline.

FIGURE 4a and 4b
- Add 1 inch extension at center back.
- Cut and separate patterns.
- Draw grainlines on patterns, mark for notches and complete for test fit.

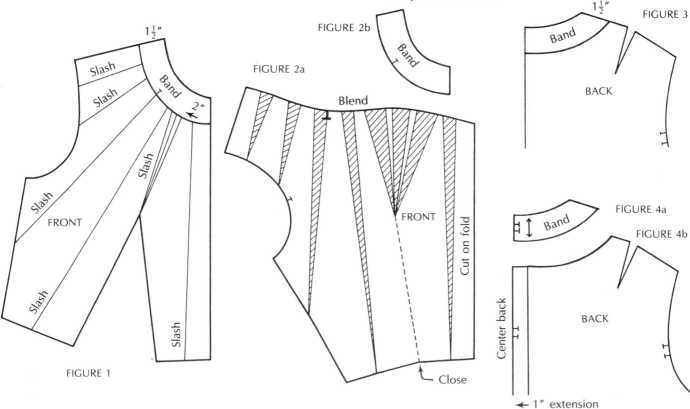

FIGURE 1

FIGURE 2a

FIGURE 2b

FIGURE 3

FIGURE 4a

FIGURE 4b

FULLNESS ALONG PRINCESS LINE

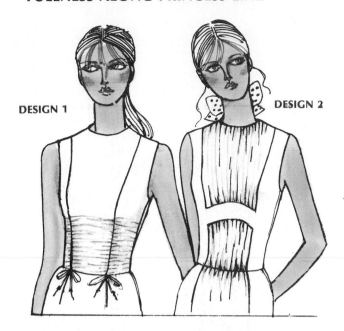

DESIGN 1   DESIGN 2

Design Analysis

The princess styleline of Design I is gathered on each side of styleline from waist to just under bust, with gathers at the front side seam. This indicates parallel fullness. Use front and back princess line pattern for design (see page 168). Back is not illustrated. A guideline is required to control the pattern parts whenever the pattern is cut through and spread for fullness. Design 2 is for practice. Design others using horizontal, vertical and diagonal fullness.

Pattern plot and development

FIGURE 1

- Trace front and side front princess panels. Include grainline.
- Draw slash lines in the direction folds lie.
- Number each section as shown.
- Cut from paper.

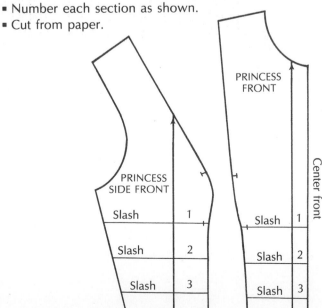

FIGURES 2 and 3

- Cut through slash line separating patterns.
- Draw guidelines on paper.
- Place slashed pattern parts on paper with center front pieces on fold. Match grainline of pattern with guideline. Spread equally using from $\frac{1}{2}$ to 1 inch for fullness (lined area). Secure pattern parts.
- Trace outline of pattern and discard.
- Blend styleline (bold line).
- Draw grain and complete for test fit.

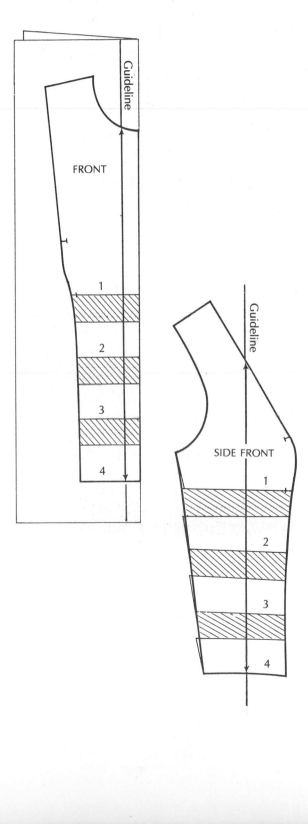

ADDED FULLNESS DESIGN VARIATIONS

The following practice designs are based on added fullness. Develop patterns for each design, or design other variations for practice. The finished garment should look like the design. If not, locate the problem and try again.

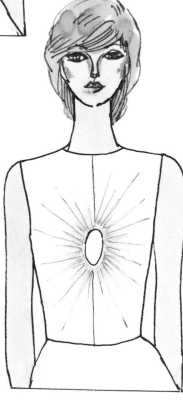

PIN TUCKS AND PLEAT TUCKS

A tuck is a stitched fold on the right side of the fabric resembling a pleat. Tucks as a design feature may be placed on any garment (top, skirt, dress, sleeves, pant, and so on). Tucks can be placed in any direction (vertical, horizontal, and diagonal). They may be of any width (finished to a width of $\frac{1}{16}$ inch to 1 inch, or more, and spaced close or far apart for varying effects. It is less expensive for a manufacturer to have tucking done by a trim house than in the factory. Tucking can be done by one of two methods: tucked on the running yard of fabric and then cut into individual pattern pieces, or individual cut pieces are sent to trim house for tucking. However, to test tuck placement and the "look" of the design before production, or to develop individual garments, use the following general instructions. Two designs are given which illustrate the development of tucking on individual garments. For additional information concerning skirt pleats see Chapter 12, button and buttonholes and facings see Chapter 14.

PLEAT TUCKS

Design Analysis: Design 1
Design 1 features pleat tucks from neck to waist with the stitchline of the tuck meeting fold line of preceding tuck, and extensions for button and buttonhole closure.

Pattern plot and development
The method shown for developing tucks does not involve slashing and spreading the pattern. The pattern is plotted for tuck locations, and pattern paper, or fabric is marked for the required tucks and tuck intake.

FIGURE 1
Pleat-tuck guidelines on working pattern:
- Draw first tuck placement $\frac{3}{4}$ inch in from center front (This placement is always the width of the extension if the stitch of the tuck is to meet the overlapped extension.) Place second tuck guideline $\frac{3}{4}$ inch from first line. If more tucks are desired, repeat the process.

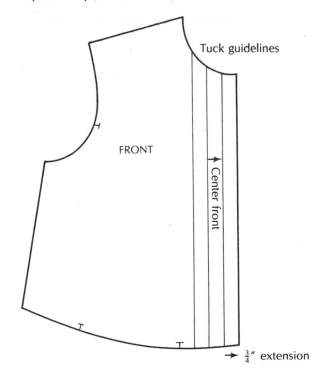

FIGURES 2, 3, and 4

Plotting for tuck placement and intake:
For industry, a paper pattern for tuck placement and intake is developed *before* a sample garment is cut. For individual garments, marking for tucks and intake can be done directly on the fabric. The garment is stitched without the need for a paper pattern. Because a tuck is a fold, tucks finishing $\frac{1}{2}$ inch wide require 1 inch for intake; tucks finishing $\frac{1}{16}$ inch require $\frac{1}{8}$ inch. In other words, allow twice the amount for intake than the finished width of the tuck. To develop a paper pattern mark tuck guidelines with pencil (Figures 2) and fabric with pins (Figure 3), or by slip stitching (Figure 4).
■ Draw two sets of parallel lines, 1 inch wide for tuck intake, and spaced $\frac{1}{2}$ inch apart (in this arrangement, fold of tuck is next to stitch of joining tuck). Start first line approximately 3 inches in from paper's edge (Figure 2).

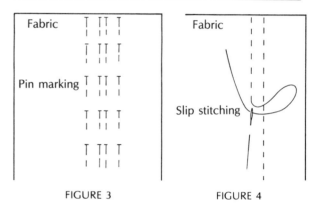

FIGURE 5
■ Fold paper, or fabric (on the right side) to form folded tucks. (Crease fold paper, or press fabric to control tucks.) Remember that the outside fold of the tuck lies toward the side of the garment.
■ Place pattern on paper (or fabric), aligning guidelines with the outside fold of the tucks. Trace pattern (add seams).

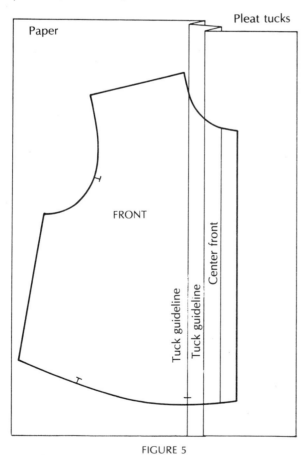

FIGURE 5

FIGURE 6
■ Cut pattern. Unfold, mark notches for tucks at top and bottom.
■ Complete patterns for test fit.
Suggestion: There is a method for controlling tucks without the need for stitching. Press tucks in position. Place fusible cloth on the back side of the garment covering all or part of the tucks and heat-press. Fusible cloth can be purchased at any fabric store, or through industry for mass-produced garments.

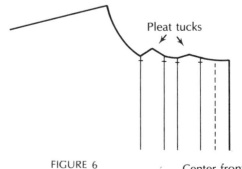

FIGURE 6   Center front

PIN TUCKS

Design Analysis: Design 2

Design 2 features pin tucks in a bibbed inset (cut on fold). In this example the pin tucks are placed with open spaces between them; however, they are developed in the same manner as pleat tucks.

Pattern plot and development

FIGURE 1

Plotting for tuck placement and intake:
- Trace pattern and draw bib styleline.
- Cut from paper and separate patterns.
- Draw first line $\frac{1}{16}$ inch in from center front. (Since pattern is cut on fold, this will equalize space on each side of front.) Draw additional parallel lines spaced $\frac{1}{4}$ inch apart.

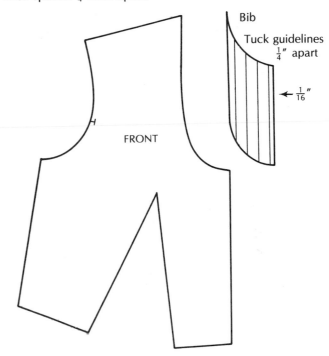

FIGURE 2
- Draw three sets of parallel lines, $\frac{1}{8}$ inch wide for tuck intake, and spaced $\frac{1}{4}$ inch apart. Draw first tuck line approximately 6 inches in from paper's edge. This will allow room to cut on fold (actual allowance will depend on the amount of tucks and the intake of a particular design).

Pin tuck intake

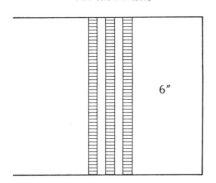

FIGURES 3 and 4
- Fold paper, place tuck guidelines of bib pattern on tuck folds of paper (Figure 3), cut, unfold (Figure 4). Fold paper and trace for other side (not illustrated).

Pin tucks

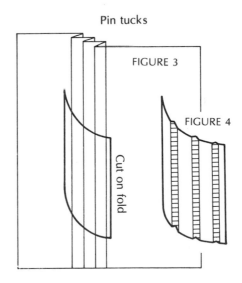

THE BLOUSON FOUNDATION

A blouson is a billowy-topped garment with an overhang anywhere from below the bust to the ankle. The blousing is controlled (held in place) by one of the following methods:

- Lining cut shorter than the finished length of the outer part.
- Elastic or drawstring inserted in the hemline of the top.
- Casing that accommodates elastic or drawstring (within the garment's frame).
- A yoke, band, or belt (either separate or attached below the section that blouses).

   The blouson foundation is developed by adding length and width to the pattern within its frame and at its outline. This is an application of Principle #2, combined with the existing dart's excess (Principle #1). To determine the amount of length to be added for the overhang, add twice the amount desired. For example, for a 1½-inch overhang, add 3 inches to the existing length.

   Blouson Designs 1, 2, and 3 are but a few examples of this type of style. Design 1 illustrates modified fullness. Included is a method for increasing fullness. Designs 2 and 3 are included as practice designs.

DESIGN 1   DESIGN 2   DESIGN 3

MODIFIED BLOUSON

Pattern plot and development

FIGURES 1 and 2
- Trace front and back two-dart pattern.
- Measure down $1\frac{1}{2}$ inches from front and back waistline. Draw a parallel line across hem for overhang, creating blouson effect.

- Measure out $1\frac{1}{2}$ inches at front and back side seams. Draw line from hem to armhole. To true side dart of front, fold dart and draw line from hem to armhole (not illustrated).
- Complete pattern for test fit.

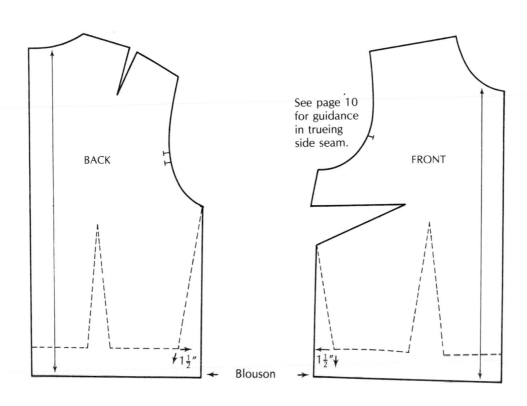

BACK

See page 10 for guidance in trueing side seam.

FRONT

$1\frac{1}{2}''$

$1\frac{1}{2}''$

← Blouson →

INCREASED FULLNESS

Pattern plot and development

FIGURES 1 AND 2

- Trace front and back patterns. Include the back horizontal balance line (HBL).
- Draw slash lines from front and back waist to approximately 3 inches up from armhole curve as shown.
- Draw slash line from dart points of waist and shoulder darts to a joining point at the HBL

FIGURES 3 and 4

- Cut slash lines to, not through, armhole and pivotal point (back).
- Close shoulder dart of back.
- Place patterns on paper and spread slash sections 1½ inches (varies). Secure pattern. Trace.
- Add 1 inch out from side seam of back to balance fullness between back and front. Draw line to armhole.
- Add length as desired. (Example: 1½ inches below waist for ¾-inch overlay.)
- Complete pattern for test fit.

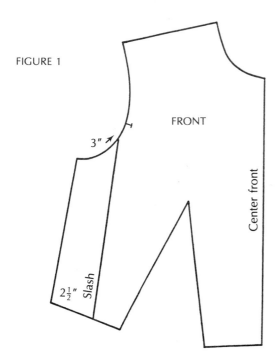

FIGURE 1

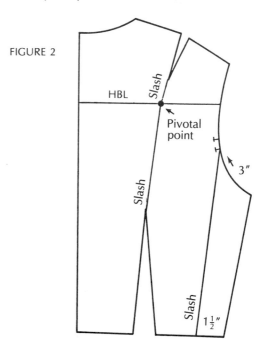

FIGURE 2

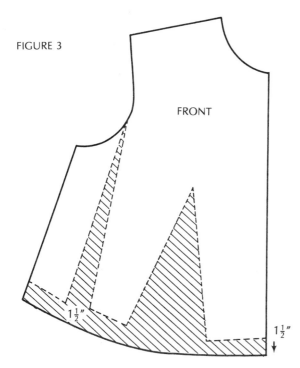

FIGURE 3

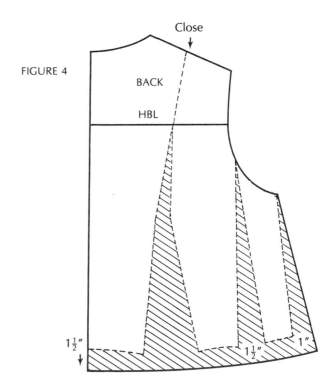

FIGURE 4

YOKES

A yoke is the upper part of a garment that fits the shoulder or hip area. It is attached to the lower section by a seam which may appear as a horizontal or stylized line. A yoke styleline can be placed anywhere above the bust level or on the back garment above, at, or below the shoulder blades. The yoke can control gathers, pleats, or a plain area to which it is attached. Yokes, as a design feature, are found on all types of garments.

The yoke series includes front collarless yoke (Design 1) and back designs with special emphasis on back design detailing. Designs 1 and 2 are used to illustrate basic yoke development by the slash/spread and pivotal/transfer techniques.

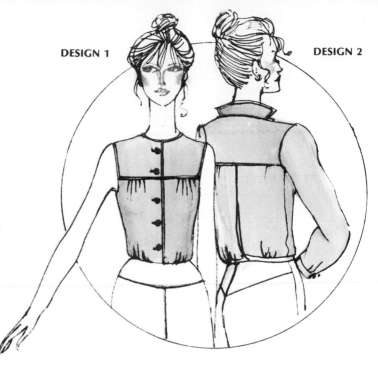

DESIGN 1   DESIGN 2

BASIC FRONT YOKE—SLASH/SPREAD

Pattern plot and development

FIGURE 1
- Trace front two-dart pattern.
- Square a line $2\frac{1}{2}$ inches down from center front neck to armhole (varies).
- Draw slash lines from bust point to yoke line parallel with center front, and from dart point of side dart to bust point.
- Mark notches as shown.
- Extend center front 1 inch for buttons and buttonholes.
- Mark notches $1\frac{1}{2}$ inches out from each side of slash line at yoke and dart legs at waist for gathers control.

FIGURE 2
- Cut and separate pattern sections.
- Cut slash lines to, not through, bust point.
- Close side dart and tape.
- Place on paper and retrace pattern. Discard.
- Blend areas for gathers (broken line sections).
- Draw grainlines. For instructions on button and buttonhole placement, see Chapter 14.
- Complete pattern for test fit.

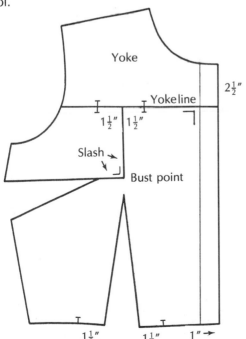

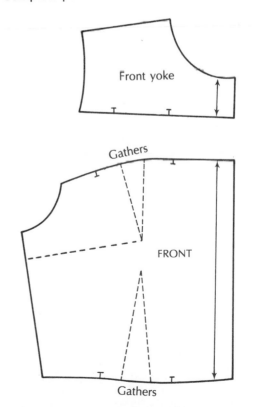

BASIC BACK YOKE—PIVOTAL/TRANSFER

Back yokes are developed without the shoulder dart. The excess from this dart is transferred to mid-armhole where it may remain (will gap slightly), or be eliminated at the yokeline of the armhole. This is illustrated in the project. Use this yoke to develop patterns for Designs 2, 3, and 4.

Pattern plot and development

FIGURE 1
▪ To establish the back yoke, square a line from the center back to mid-armhole, or at a point that is approximately one-fourth of the center back length. If the HBL is placed on the working pattern use this line.
▪ Draw a line down from dart point of the shoulder dart to yokeline for use as the pivotal point.

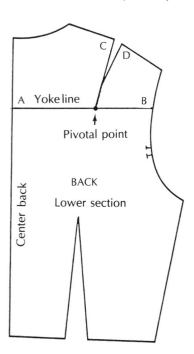

FIGURE 2
▪ Place pattern on paper with pushpin through pivotal point.
▪ Crossmark yokeline on paper at points A and B, and trace pattern from A to dart leg C. Crossmark (bold line of shaded area).

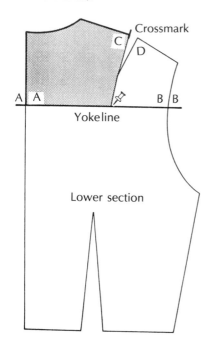

FIGURE 3
▪ Pivot pattern so that dart leg D touches crossmark on paper.
▪ Trace remaining pattern from dart leg D to B on pattern. Crossmark and label armhole E. Remove pattern.

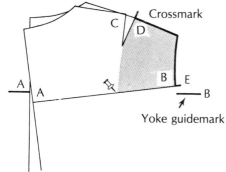

FIGURE 4
▪ Draw line connecting A to B. (The distance between E and B on paper represents darts' excess.) To remove excess, see Figure 5.

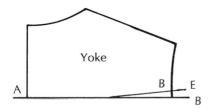

BACK YOKE WITH INVERTED BOX PLEAT

FIGURE 5

Lower back bodice:

- Trace lower pattern from yoke line (A–B). Mark pivotal point. Remove pattern.
- Draw a line connecting A to B as shown. The dart's excess can remain in the armhole for a casual fit or be removed from the lower section by measuring the distance from E to B of yoke (see Figure 4, page 194). Mark this amount down from B on lower section. Draw line to pivotal point and trim (shaded area). The yokeline of lower section will slope downward.
- Mark notches for gathers control at waist and blend.

Pleat:

- For a 1½-inch pleat, draw a 3-inch parallel line with the center back (lined area—inverted box pleat).
- Back may be cut on fold or with center back seam.

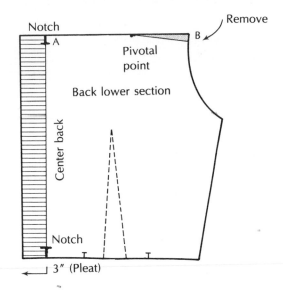

BACK YOKE WITH ADDED FULLNESS/GATHERS

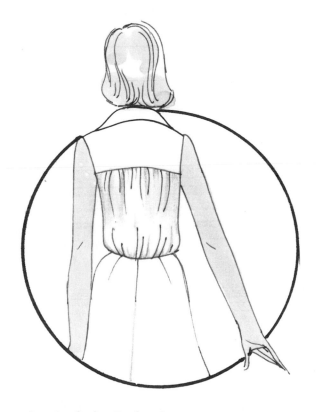

Design Analysis: Design 3

Gathers form across the back yoke of Design 3. To develop yoke line, refer to instructions given on page 194.

Pattern plot and development

FIGURE 1

- Trace lower back section, extending center back 3 or more inches for gathers. The excess from the waist dart (broken line) is absorbed into gathers.
- Mark notches for gathers and center back as shown.

Note: For yokes that are stylized, pointed, or curved, draw slash lines for spreading lower section (not illustrated).

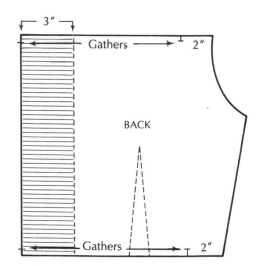

BACK YOKE WITH ACTION PLEAT

Pattern plot and development

FIGURE 1
- Crossmark B, 2½ inches from A (varies).
- Mark D, 3 inches from C.
- Draw line from B to D.
- Cut slash line from B to, not through, D and spread 3 inches for pleat intake (lined area).
- Mark gathers control notches 1 inch out from each side of dart leg. (Dart is indicated by broken lines.)

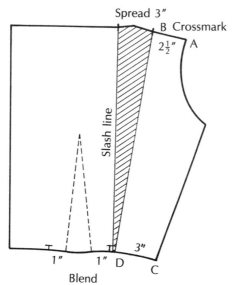

Design Analysis: Design 4

Design 4 features action pleats which are placed 1 inch in from armhole at yokeline. To develop yokeline, refer to instructions given on page 194.

YOKE DESIGN VARIATIONS

The following yoke design variations are practice problems. The developed patterns are correct if they result in exact representations of each design.

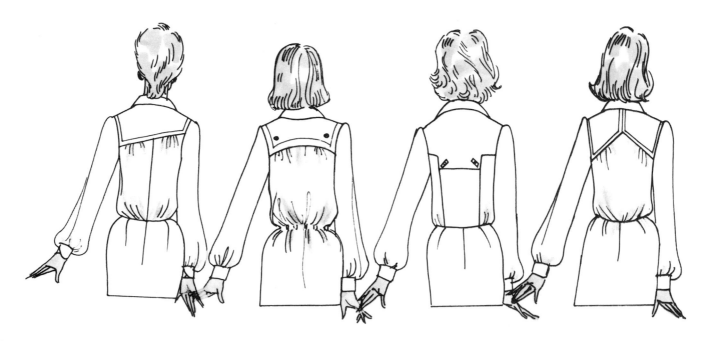

THE FLANGE

A flange is an extension or part of a pattern that forms a continuation of a garment. It may be part of the same garment or a separate, set-in piece (shaped as desired), and stitched within a styleline as a pattern addition. A flange may be developed anywhere along the shoulderline or at any location of any garment. When used at the shoulderline, it should not be placed where it will interfere with the actual armhole curve. That is, the armhole curve must *not* fall within the fold of the flange or the armhole of the garment will be distorted. The flange may extend to or beyond the armhole. It must remain free from the armhole curve. Flanges, when part of the same garment, are an application of added fullness (Principle #2).

DART FLANGE

Pattern plot and development

FIGURE 1
- Trace front bodice pattern, transferring dart to shoulder tip.
- Fold dart for pleat with inside fold toward center front.
- Mark notches at each dart leg.

Design Analysis: Design 1
The flange is placed at shoulder tip, using the dart's excess to create the effect of Design 1. The flange can be folded in as a pleat (Figure 1) or stitched partway (Figure 2) as a tuck-dart pleat when controlling the fullness is necessary (as indicated on sketch).

FIGURE 2 *Flange tuck pleat:*
- Trim excess within $1\frac{1}{2}$ inches of dart leg (shaded area).
- Mark dart legs and seam allowance notches.
- *Stitching Guide:* Stitch inside seams together. Fold dart legs. Top stitch 1 inch in from fold 4 inches down on dart legs on right side of garment.

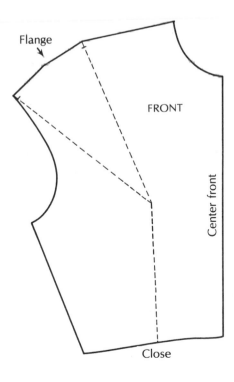

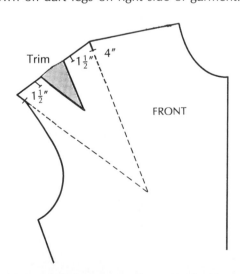

FLANGE TO WAIST

This type of flange is developed by adding fullness without the use of the dart.

Design Analysis

The front and back flanges of Design 2 are connected to each other and not to the shoulder seam. The flange extends slightly beyond shoulder tip.

Pattern plot and development

FIGURES 1 and 2

- Trace front and back patterns, transferring shoulder dart to mid-armhole.
- Mark A, 1 inch from front and back shoulder tip.
- Mark B, 3 inches in from waist.
- Draw slash line for flange from A to B. Cut patterns from paper.

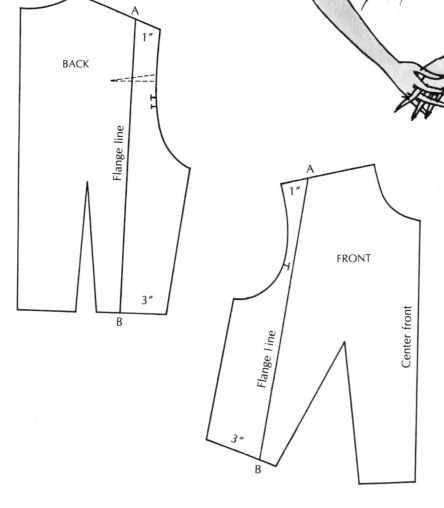

FIGURES 3 and 4
- Cut slash lines from A to, not through, B.
- Place on paper and spread A, 3 inches (for 1½-inch wide flange). (Lined area.)
- Trace and discard pattern.
- Draw a straight line across open space A.
- Mark punch and circles 3 inches down from center and ⅛ inch in from stitchline for stitching guide.
- Extend 1 inch at center front for button and buttonholes. See Chapter 14.
- Draw grainlines and complete for test fit.

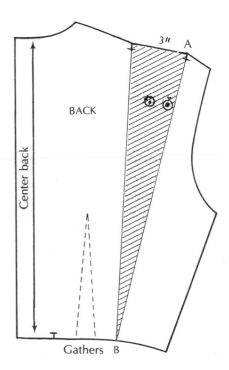

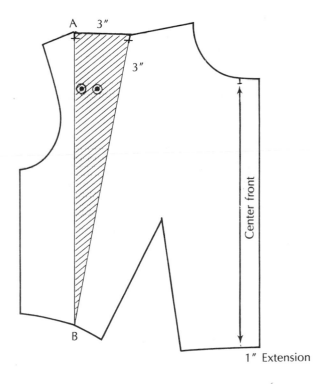

FLANGE INSET

Design Analysis
A flange effect is created by inserting a shaped section of fabric into the bodice.

Pattern plot and development

FIGURES 1 and 2
- Trace front and back patterns.
- Mark A, 1 inch from front and back dart legs at waist.
- Mark B, ½ inch in from front and back shoulder tips.
- Draw line to connect A and B (flange slash line).
- Measure A to B length for front and back flange. Record _____.
- Reshape armholes by blending to slash lines B, as shown. (Shaded area is discarded.)
- Mark notches where armhole touches flange line and for gathers control at waist as shown.
- Extend center back 1 inch for closure.
- Trim shaded area.

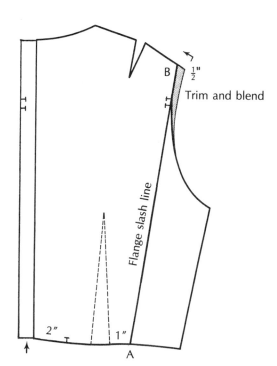

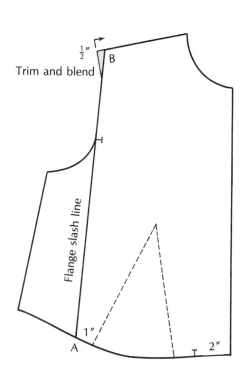

FIGURES 3 and 4
- Cut and separate pattern parts.
- Draw grainlines as shown.

FIGURE 5 *Flange:*
- Draw vertical line on paper equal to front and back flange length.
- Using A–B measurement of front bodice, crossmark shoulder tip location (label B). Fold paper.
- Square out from fold at B equal to desired flange width (example, 3 inches), and connect to flange points A using front and back A–B measurements as shown.
- Cut from paper. Complete pattern for test fit.

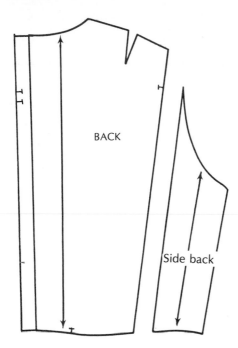

BACK

Side back

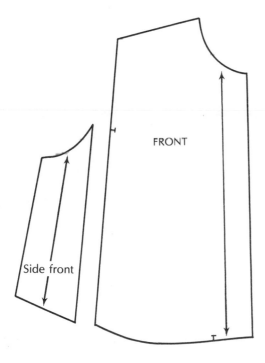

FRONT

Side front

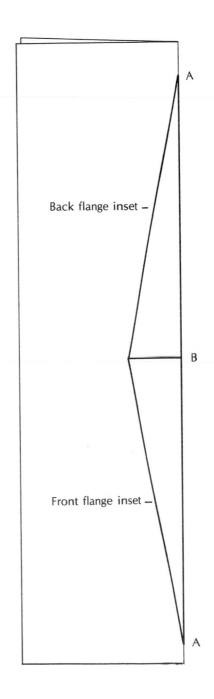

A

Back flange inset —

B

Front flange inset —

A

FLANGE DESIGN VARIATIONS

The following flange design variations are practice
problems. The developed patterns are correct if
they result in exact representations of the designs. If
they do not, locate the problems and try again.

Pocket

Pleat stitchline

CONTOURING: PRINCIPLE #3 204
Contour designs 204
Figure versus basic garment 205
Fitting problems 205
THE CONTOUR GUIDE PATTERNS 206
Preparing the contour guide patterns 206
How to use the contour guide pattern 210
THE CLASSIC EMPIRE 213
Empire with shirred midriff 215
STRAPLESS DESIGNS 217
Strapless princess 217
Princess with gathered panels 218
Strapless princess variations 219
SURPLICE (OR WRAP) DESIGNS 220
OFF-SHOULDER DESIGNS 222
Gathered shoulder 222
HALTERS 224
V-neck halter 224

9

CONTOURING
(PRINCIPLE #3)

CONTOURING: PRINCIPLE #3

Principle. To fit the hollow areas of the upper torso (its contours) closer than does the basic garment, the pattern is reduced *within* its frame to fit the dimensions of the body above, below, or in between the bust mounds and shoulder blades.

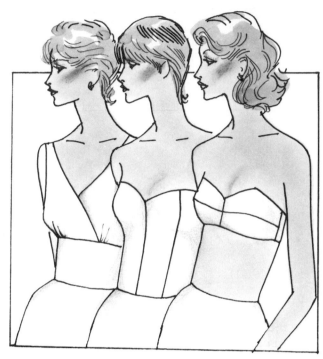

Corollary. To fit the upper torso closer than does the basic garment, the *outline* of the pattern is trimmed to fit the slope of the shoulder and side seam ease is eliminated.

CONTOUR DESIGNS

Contour designs are designs that follow the contour of the body rather than hang loosely over the hollow areas around the bust and shoulder blade. Contour designs include the empire styleline (contouring under the bust), strapless, bra top (contouring over, under, and at times between the bust), surplice (contouring over and under the bust), and cut-out armholes and necklines (contouring over the bust). Patterns that are developed for contour designs must be based on Principle #3 (Contouring) and its corollary, if fitting problems are to be avoided. Fitting problems occur if adjustments are not made to compensate for the differences between the pattern and the body's dimensions. The following information deals with the methods used to circumvent fitting problems through the use of the remarkable Contour Guide Pattern.

FIGURE VERSUS BASIC GARMENT

The contours of the figure are shown enclosed in a basic garment. (Visualize this as being a transparent garment.) The garment has straight lines touching only the outer limits of the figure and has added ease. It fits the figure loosely. Study the relationship between the contours of the figure (illustrated by broken lines) and the shape of the garment. The hollow areas above, below, and in between the bust mounds do not come in contact with the garment. The figure's dimensions measure less in those areas than does the garment or pattern in the same area. These differences are measurable, and compensation can be made for them by using the Contour Guide Pattern when developing patterns for designs that fit close to the figure.

View looking down

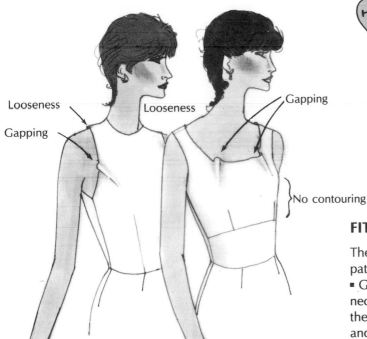

Looseness

Gapping

Looseness

Gapping

No contouring

FITTING PROBLEMS

The following fitting problems occur when the pattern has not been adjusted for contour designs.
- Gapping will appear wherever a portion of the neckline or armhole is cut out, as the garment loses the support of all or part of the shoulder and neck and falls to the hollow area over the bust.
- Looseness will appear along the shoulder, where the figure slopes inward, when the pattern is cut away in this area.
- Empire, strapless, or bra designs will have little or no bust definition. (That is, these designs will not fit close to the bust contour but hang loosely over the hollows of the figure.)
- The look is changed and a good design is ruined.

THE CONTOUR GUIDE PATTERNS

The Contour Guide Patterns were developed as tools to help the patternmaker circumvent fitting problems before they are incorporated into the design. These patterns are charted with guidelines indicating the actual amount of excess that will have to be removed from a styleline area or from a dart for a closer fit. These guidelines are labeled by design type and represent the maximum depth measurement between the garment and the hollow areas of the figure (above, below, and in between the bust mounds), decreasing in both directions to the bust point and to the pattern's outline. The back bodice is charted for designs featuring low cuts and for strapless garments. Illustrated below are the front and back Contour Guide Patterns. This is how the patterns should look after the guidelines have been charted. The development and use of these patterns will be illustrated in the pages that follow.

CONTOUR GUIDE PATTERNS

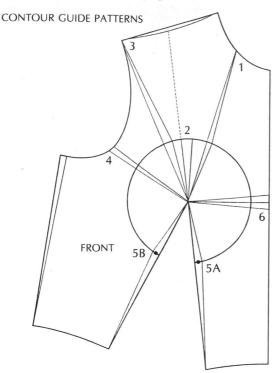

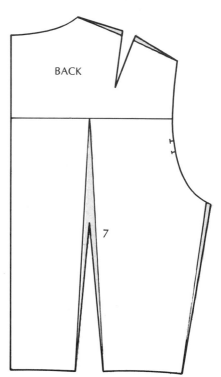

PREPARING THE CONTOUR GUIDE PATTERNS

Preparation for charting and measuring
Since the Contour Guide Patterns are used as working patterns for all contour designs, they should be traced on manila paper.

Measurement needed
- (9) Bust radius _____
(See Chapter 3 for measurement if needed.)

FIGURES 1 and 2
- Trace back, including horizontal balance line (HBL). (Equals one-fourth of center back length.)
- Trace basic front one-dart pattern, marking bust point.
- Using bust radius measurement, place compass point at bust point and draw circle referred to as the circumference of the bust. (Represents maximum depth of the hollow area between the figure and basic garment.)

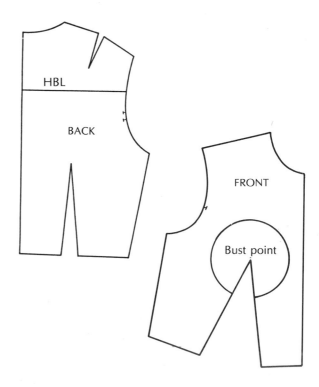

Measuring hollow areas and charting pattern
Patternmakers working with an industrial form having approximately an 11-inch difference between bust and waist should use standard measurements given in the following examples, or else measure form or figure as follows:

• Using bust radius measurement, pin mark above and below bust as a guide for measuring the depth of the hollow areas.

• Two rulers are required for depth measurement. One ruler is used to bridge the bust mound at each designated area. The other ruler is used to measure the depth at the ruler's edge to the hollow areas

marked by the pins (see examples given below). The measurement indicates the maximum amount of excess (gapping and looseness) that can be removed from the area for a closer fit.

Caution: When measuring the figure, do not press ruler into the flesh.

Suggestion: Color-code the spaces contained within the guidelines for emphasis.

Note: Single markings are illustrated for each guideline for clarity; however, all markings are to be placed on one pattern as indicated on example given on page 206. Measure, label, and chart each location as follows:

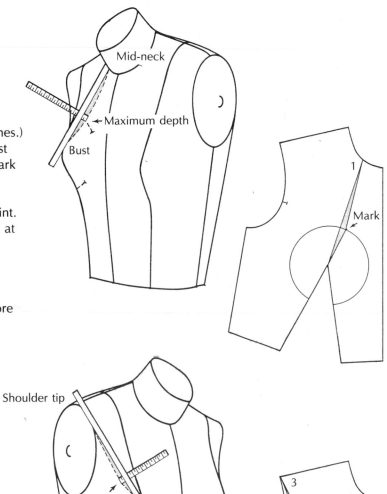

GUIDELINE 1
(Used for eliminating gapping of cut-out necklines.)
• *Form:* Place end of ruler at mid-neck and bust point. With other ruler measure depth at pinmark location. Record measurement on pattern as follows:
• *Pattern:* Draw line from mid-neck to bust point.
• Measure and mark distance from Guideline 1 at circumference line, as shown.
• Connect mark with bust point and mid-neck (shaded area).
• *(Standard intake $= \frac{1}{4}$ inch.)*
  Note: Guidelines 3 and 4 are charted before Guideline 2 (explanation follows later).

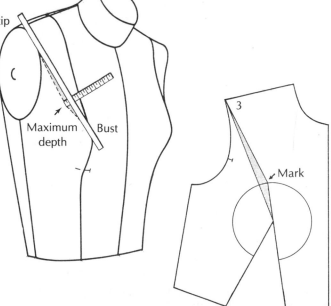

GUIDELINE 3
(Used for eliminating gapping for designs with cut-out armholes.)
• *Form:* Measure depth, add $\frac{1}{4}$ inch (includes armhole ease).
• *Pattern:* Draw line from shoulder tip to bust point.
• Measure and mark at circumference.
• Connect with bust point and shoulder tip (shaded area).
• *(Standard intake $= \frac{5}{8}$ inch.)*

GUIDELINE 4
(Used for eliminating ease in armhole for sleeveless garments.)
- *Pattern:* Draw line from curve of armhole to bust point.
- Measure out $\frac{1}{4}$ inch at armhole guideline. Mark.
- Draw line to bust point (shaded area).
- *(Standard intake = $\frac{1}{4}$ inch.)*

GUIDELINE 2
(Used for strapless tops, or those held up with narrow straps.)
- *Pattern:* Draw guideline from mid-shoulder to bust point.
- Combine the measurements of Guidelines 1, 3, and 4, and subtract $\frac{1}{8}$ inch. Using this measurement, measure out from guideline. Mark and connect with bust point (shaded area). Erase remaining guideline above circle (indicated by broken line).
- *(Standard intake = $\frac{5}{8}$ inch.)*

GUIDELINE 5
(Used for contouring under the bust.)
- *Form:* Measure depth under bust to pinmark.

- *Pattern:* Measure and mark one-half the depth measurement at circumference line of each dart leg label A and B as shown. Connect to bust point and waist (shaded area). Use for styleline crossing under the bust (for example, empire styleline).
- *(Standard intake = $\frac{3}{4}$-inch total—$\frac{3}{8}$ inch in from each side.)*

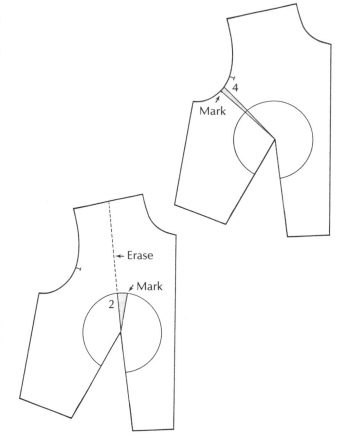

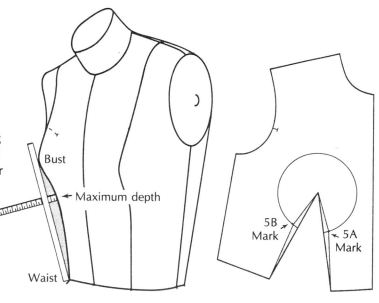

- For a semi-fit, use one-half the depth measurement when shaping darts or princess stylelines.
- *(Standard intake = For semi-fit, mark $\frac{3}{16}$ inches.)*

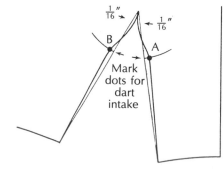

Example shows shape of semi-fit dart. Do not include shape on pattern.

GUIDELINE 6
(Used for contouring between the bust.)
- *Form:* Measure depth between bust.
- *Pattern:* Square a line from center front to bust point.
- Mark one-half the depth measurement on each side of Guideline 6. Connect to bust point (shaded area).
- *(Standard intake = $\frac{3}{4}$ inch ($\frac{3}{8}$ inch out from each side of guideline.)*

GUIDELINE: SHOULDER SLOPE
(Used with Guidelines 1 and 3 for cut-out necklines and armholes.)
- *Form:* Measure depth of shoulder slope at mid-shoulder.
- *Pattern:* Measure and mark pattern at mid-shoulder. Connect with neck and shoulder tip (shaded area).
- *(Standard intake = $\frac{3}{16}$ inch.)*

GUIDELINE: SIDE SEAM EASE
(Used for strapless and bra tops. Optional: sleeveless garments.)
- *Pattern:* Measure and mark corner of side armhole equal to ease added to pattern (front and back).
- Connect to side waistline (shaded area).
(Standard intake = $\frac{1}{2}$ inch [front and back].)

GUIDELINE 7
(Used for designs with low-cut and cut-out backs.)
- *Pattern: Back:* Point of Guideline #7 is in line with dart point. Draw line from this point to dart legs (shaded area).
- Mark shoulder slope and side ease guides as instructed for the front bodice.
This completes the guidemarking of the Contour Guide Pattern. See page 206 to verify that all marking are charted correctly.

   Important: Subtract $\frac{1}{8}$ inch from each guideline for garments cut in coarse or heavy weaves, or those with several plies of interconstruction. Add $\frac{1}{8}$ inch for garments cut in finely woven fabrics. Add $\frac{1}{8}$ inch to Guideline 1 for V-neck designs.

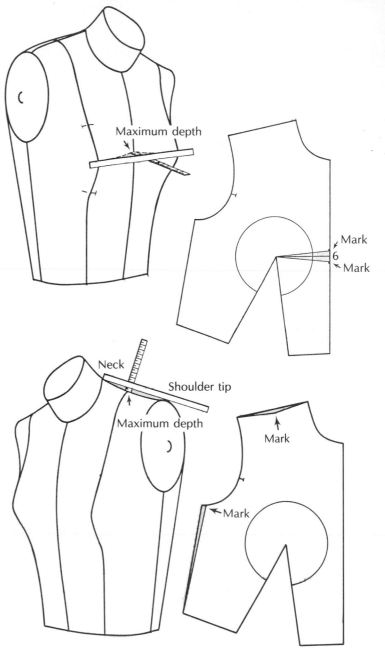

Maximum depth

Mark
6
Mark

Neck

Shoulder tip

Maximum depth

Mark

Mark

BACK

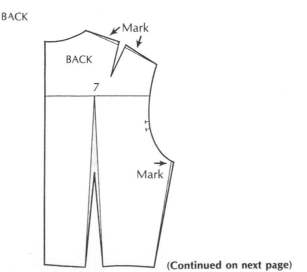

BACK

Mark

7

Mark

Mark

(Continued on next page)

HOW TO USE THE CONTOUR GUIDE PATTERN

The Contour Guide Pattern should be used for all designs that fit closer to the figure than does the basic garment. Designs may require more than one modification. This will be illustrated later.

Note: A styleline must cross a guideline before modification is required.

The amount of excess to be transferred, or absorbed for a closer fit, is indicated at *a point where the styleline crosses the guideline.* The closer a styleline is plotted to the circumference line on the pattern, the greater the intake. The further away, the lesser the amount.

The excess indicated between the guidelines (shaded areas on the pattern) can be transferred to an existing dart, or absorbed into design detailing (pleats, ease, or styleline). The excess can be trimmed from a styleline (example: princess stylelines) above or below the bust. The method chosen depends on the design features of the garment.

Designs 1, 2, and 3 feature cut-out necklines that are placed at, or varying distances from, the bust circumference line of the Contour Guide Pattern. Through design analysis determine which guidelines are required before plotting the pattern. For example, Designs 1, 2 and 3 require Guideline 1 (cut-out necklines), and front and back shoulder guide (always combined with cut-out necklines and armholes). Design 3 has a low back requiring Guideline 7 (illustrated in Figures 8 and 9).

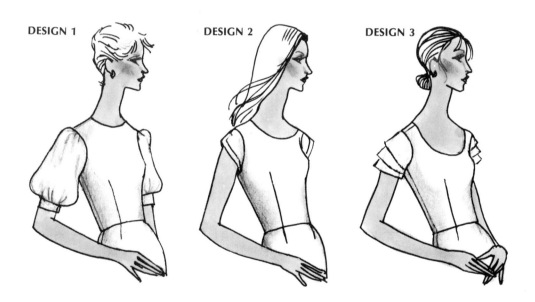

DESIGN 1   DESIGN 2   DESIGN 3

General procedure for pattern plot and development

FIGURES 1 and 2

▪ Trace front and back Contour Guide Patterns with a pushpin, transfer required guidelines to paper underneath (in the example, Guidelines 1 (front), 7 (back), and front and back shoulder guides).

Note: With a compass, draw bust circumference (all, or part), whenever needed as a reference for controlling placement of stylelines.

▪ Remove patterns and connect guidelines on traced copy. The straight guidelines are always the slash lines.

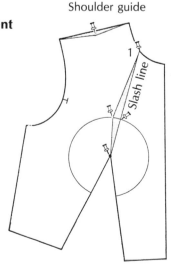

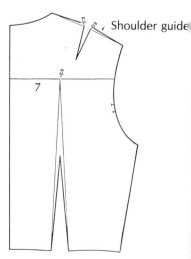

Shoulder guide

Shoulder guide

Slash line

FIGURE 1   FIGURE 2

Transferring excess from styleline

▪ Necklines for Designs 1, 2 and 3 are drawn to show the relationship of each neckline to the bust circumference and shoulderline. Remember, the amount of excess to be removed is indicated at the point where the styleline crosses the guideline. For clarity, label the styleline A and B at the guideline, as shown in each illustration.

▪ Cut pattern, discarding unneeded areas of neckline and shoulder.

▪ Cut slash line A to, not through, bust point.

▪ Bring slash line A to meet B—same procedure as transferring a dart. Tape, trace, and blend neckline.

FIGURE 3

▪ When stylelines cross a guideline indicating less than $\frac{1}{8}$ inch of excess, such as Design 1, modification of the pattern is not required.

FIGURES 4 and 5

▪ The neckline for Design 2 does not touch the circumference line; therefore, some of the excess (or looseness) will remain in the garment over the hollow area above the bust (indicated by the broken lines).

FIGURES 6 and 7

▪ *Front:* The neckline for Design 3 touches the circumference line of the bust. After the excess is removed, the neckline will fit the hollow area above the bust.

FIGURES 8 and 9

▪ *Back:* The low neckline crosses Guideline 7. After the neckline and shoulder are trimmed, slash the leg of one guideline and overlap to other guideline. Tape, trace, and blend.

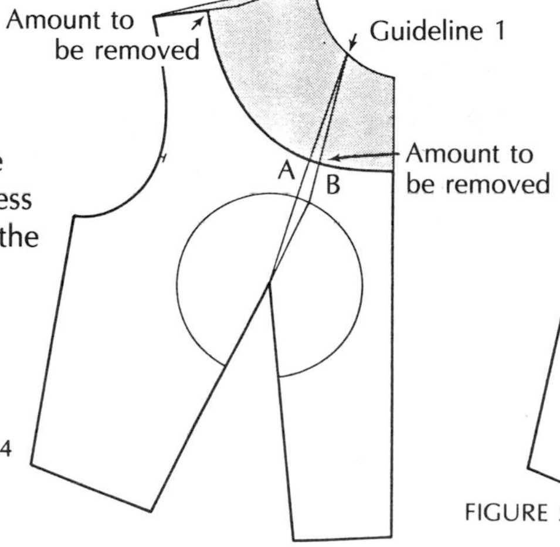

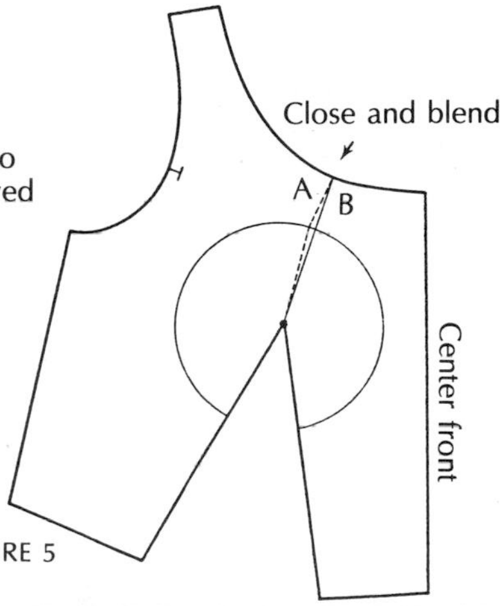

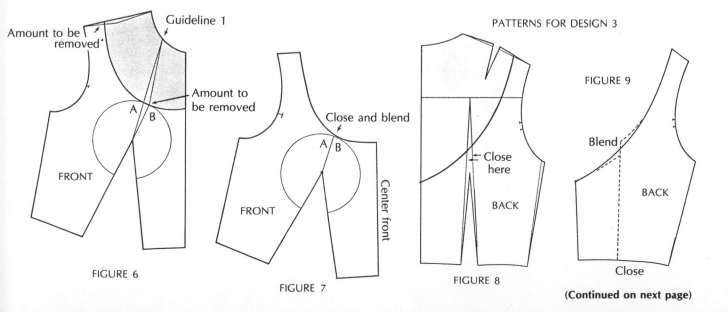

PATTERN FOR DESIGN 1

FIGURE 3

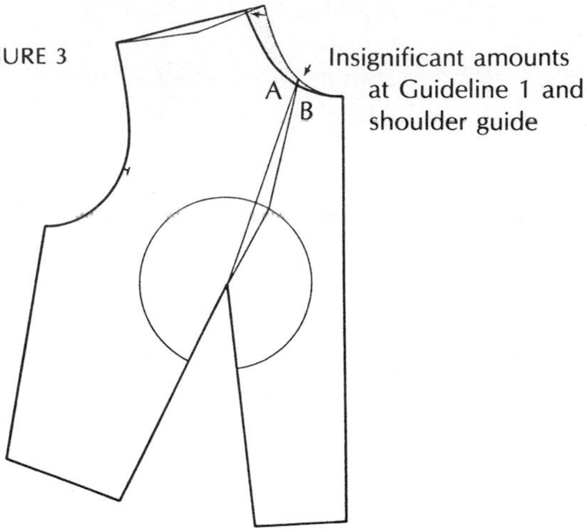

Insignificant amounts at Guideline 1 and shoulder guide

PATTERNS FOR DESIGN 2

Amount to be removed

Guideline 1

Amount to be removed

FIGURE 4

Close and blend

Center front

FIGURE 5

PATTERNS FOR DESIGN 3

FIGURE 9

Amount to be removed

Guideline 1

Amount to be removed

FRONT

FIGURE 6

Close and blend

FRONT

Center front

FIGURE 7

Close here

BACK

FIGURE 8

Blend

BACK

Close

FIGURE 9

(Continued on next page)

FIGURES 10 and 11 Additional information:
• *Modifying the facing:* The facing for cut-out necklines (scooped, square, V-neck) and armholes may be modified instead of the bodice. This is done by transferring the guidelines to facing pattern for slash and overlapping. The bodice and facings are notched to control the ease. Modifying the facing may be preferred if excess from several guideline areas are transferred to the dart. This can increase the space between the dart legs, causing looseness around bust point.

• *Stretch-gapping adjustment:* If a garment with a cut-out neckline and/or armhole is gapping or loose after pattern adjustment for contouring has been made, pin the excess on the garment and measure. Correct the pattern using instructions given.

FIGURE 12 *Sleeveless garments:*
▪ Slash across neckline and through mid-shoulder. Overlap the needed amount. Blend armhole and neckline. This will not decrease the armhole because the fabric will stretch to normal armhole when garment is cut.

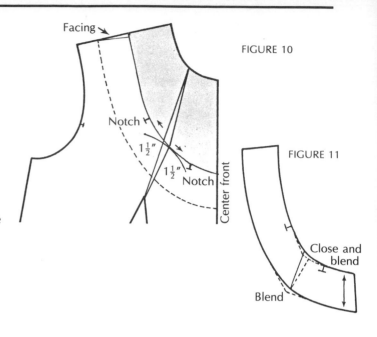

FIGURE 10

FIGURE 11

FIGURE 13 *Sleeved garments:*
▪ Slash from neck to, not through, mid-armhole, and overlap needed amount.

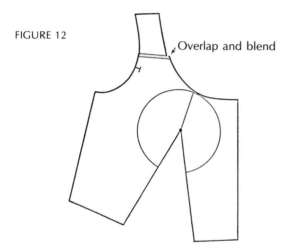

FIGURE 12

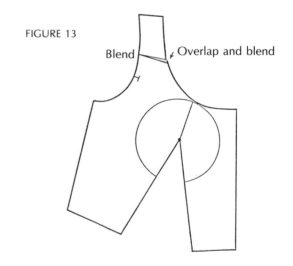

FIGURE 13

Designs with cut-out armholes
The following designs are practice problems. Use previous instructions and illustrations as a guide. Garments having cut-out armholes should include side seam guide markings for a tighter fit. More advanced designs requiring the Contour Guide Pattern follow.

Note: Use measurements from your guide pattern for future projects. Standard measurements will be given in the illustrations.

THE CLASSIC EMPIRE

The Classic Empire styleline can be found in many different types of garments. It is distinguishable by the styleline crossing below the bust. The midriff section (lower part) fits closely to the figure, emphasizing the bust contour. Bodice front variations can be developed from this pattern by placing the styleline above or below the original midriff line. The midriff can be fitted tightly or loosely, depending on the placement of the styleline and silhouette desired. It may or may not continue around the bodice back.

The Classic Empire is developed from the Contour Guide Pattern. Because of its popularity and its use in developing other design variations, it should be developed as a seamless working pattern. The pattern should include contour guidelines for convenience and future use. (Review Contouring—Principle #3.)

Pattern plot and development

FIGURE 1
For those not using the Contour Guide Pattern, follow plot and measurements given.
- Place side seams of the front and back contour guide patterns together. (Referred to as "banking" the patterns, and should be done whenever stylelines cross the seams of two joining patterns.)
- Trace patterns, and with pushpins transfer under bust Guidelines 5 a,b (front) and 7 (back). Include the back HBL line. Remove patterns.
- Draw bust circumference (standard measurement = 3 inches), and connect guidelines ($\frac{3}{8}$ inch in from each dart leg at circumference line, and $\frac{1}{4}$ inch from each dart leg of the back dart legs, at the time styleline is placed—shaded areas).
- Shape dart above the circumference line, blending together $\frac{1}{4}$ inch below bust point.
Empire styleline:
- Square a line from center front to dart legs at circumference line. Label C and D at center front.
- Mark side seam up from waist $\frac{3}{4}$ inch less than C–D measurement.
- Mark center back up from waist $1\frac{1}{4}$ inches less than C–D measurement. Square a short line.
- Draw remaining empire line touching mark at sides, ending at center back mark. Blend with square line.
- Cut and separate patterns, discarding unneeded sections (shaded areas).

Design Analysis
The midriff styleline of the Classic Empire crosses under the bust and slopes gently downward to the center back. The contour of the bustline is visible and the garment fits closer to the figure than does the basic garment. Darts control the fit above the midriff and shoulder.

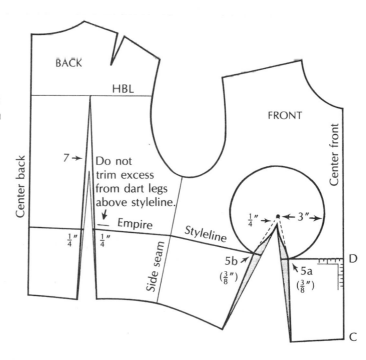

(Continued on next page)

FIGURE 2 *Front:*
- Retrace bodice. Include all contour guidelines for future reference (shaded areas).
- Extend dart legs ¼ inch and center front ⅛ inch for additional length (needed when fitting close to figure).
- Draw blending line across bottom. (Broken line indicates original shape.)
- Draw grainline.

FIGURE 3 *Back:*
- Trace back. Include the HBL line and Guideline 7.
- Extend center back 1 inch for closure as shown.
- Original dart is used; excess is removed from side seam when midriff is trued to bodice (broken line).
- Draw grainline.

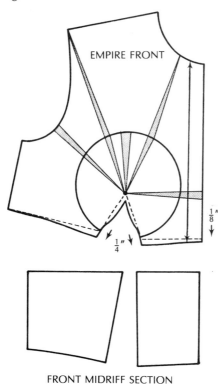

FRONT MIDRIFF SECTION

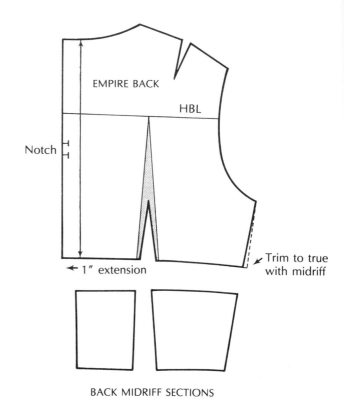

BACK MIDRIFF SECTIONS

FIGURE 4 *Midriff front:*
- Close dart legs. Tape.
- Trace on fold, and discard.
- Blend as shown.
- Draw grainline.
- Cut from paper.

FIGURE 5 *Midriff back:*
- Close dart legs. Tape.
- Retrace, and discard.
- Extend center back 1 inch for closure, as shown.
- Blend as shown.
- Draw grainline and true patterns.

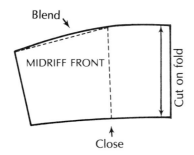

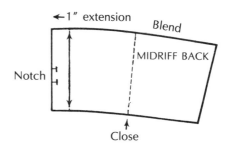

EMPIRE WITH SHIRRED MIDRIFF

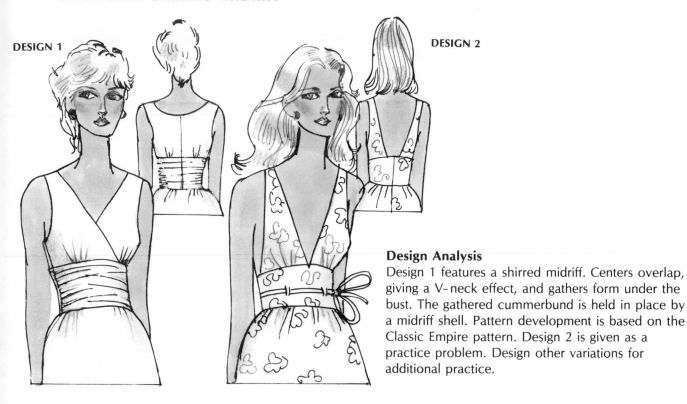

DESIGN 1

DESIGN 2

Design Analysis

Design 1 features a shirred midriff. Centers overlap, giving a V-neck effect, and gathers form under the bust. The gathered cummerbund is held in place by a midriff shell. Pattern development is based on the Classic Empire pattern. Design 2 is given as a practice problem. Design other variations for additional practice.

Pattern plot and development

FIGURES 1 and 2
For those not using the Contour Guide Pattern, follow plot and measurements given.
- Trace front and back Classic Empire patterns. (If not available, see page 213.)
- Transfer Guidelines 1 and 6. Mark shoulder guide.
- Remove patterns and connect guidelines.

Front:
- Extend center front $2\frac{1}{2}$ inches. Label A.
- Mark B, $1\frac{1}{2}$ inches from shoulder tips.
- Connect A and B.
- Extend Guideline 6 to styleline.

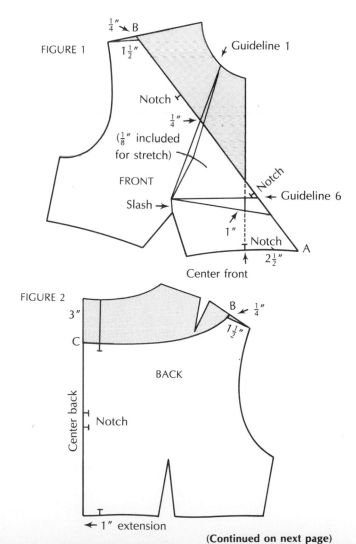

Back:
- Mark B, $1\frac{1}{2}$ inches from shoulder tips.
- Mark C, 3 inches below center back neck. Square a short line.
- Draw curved neckline from B to C, using guideline for shoulder.

(Continued on next page)

FIGURES 3 and 4
- Cut and separate patterns, discarding unneeded sections.

Front:
- Cut guidelines and dart point to, not through, bust point. Overlap Guideline 1 ($\frac{1}{4}$ inch), Guideline 6 (1 inch) and tape.
- Retrace patterns (broken line original pattern). Discard.
- Draw blending line from A to B and under bust.
- Mark $1\frac{1}{2}$ inches out from each dart leg for gather control notches.
- Draw center front grain, and notch.
- Back—Blend dart, notch for gathers, draw grain.

FIGURES 5 and 6
- Use original pattern as a base for developing and supporting the gathered midriff.

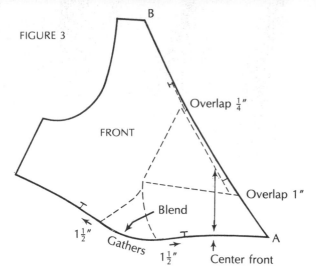

FIGURE 3

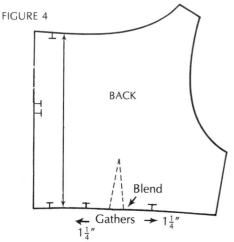

FIGURE 4

MIDRIFF BASE

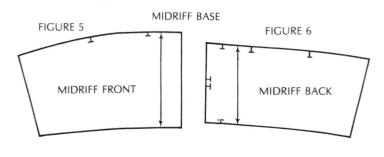

FIGURE 5

FIGURE 6

FIGURES 7 and 8
Cummerbund:
- Place center front of midriff on fold of paper and trace. Label A and B. (Broken line indicates waist of midriff.)
- Shift midriff downward until top of midriff touches B. Trace bottom and side of cummerbund.
- Using skirt curve, draw side seam. (Broken line outside of side seam is discarded.)

- Repeat for back (but do not place on fold).
- True side seams. (They must be of equal length.)
- Draw parallel or bias grainline. If bias, remove $\frac{1}{2}$ inch from side seam to compensate for stretch (not illustrated).
- True patterns and complete for test fit.

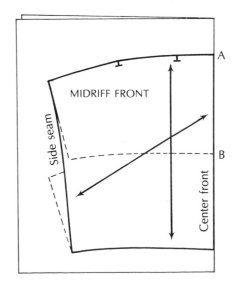

FIGURE 7

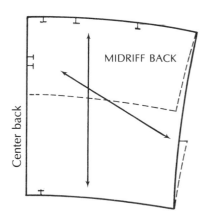

FIGURE 8

STRAPLESS DESIGNS

Strapless garments should have built-in support to keep them from slipping downward. This support is provided by interconstruction fabrics or by boning stitched to the seamlines from the waist over the bust, at center front and/or at the side seams. A holding ribbon can be slipped through the boning at center front just under the bust and hooked together in back. This will keep the garment close under and between the bust mounds. Spaghetti straps also hold strapless tops in place.

Pattern plot and development

FIGURES 1 and 2
For those not using the Contour Guide Pattern, follow plot and measurements given.
- Trace front and back patterns, and with pushpins transfer Guidelines 2, 5 (a, b), 6 (front), and 7 (back). Include the side seam guide and HBL line of back. Remove patterns.
- Draw arc above and below bust (standard measurement 3 inches, see broken lines).
- Connect reduction guidelines (shaded areas).
Strapless styleline:
- Draw curved line from center front bust to circumference line above bust. Continue styleline ending $\frac{1}{2}$ inch down and in from side. Connect to waist.
- Draw slash line from bust point to side.
- Draw curved lines to form bust contour along Guideline 5 a,b, of the princess line.
- Mark ease-control notches, $1\frac{1}{2}$ inches up and down from bust point (2 inches for bust cup C and larger).

STRAPLESS PRINCESS

Design Analysis: Design 1
The strapless design has a princess-style cut with the styleline ending at the center front bust level. The back is cut low and the garment fits above, below, and between the bust.

- *Back:* Use illustration as a guide for plotting low-cut back.
- Cut and separate patterns. Discard unneeded sections (shaded areas).

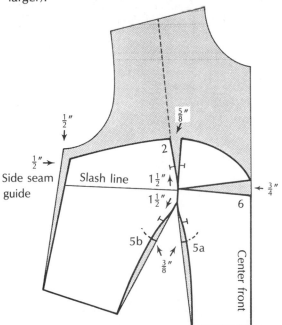

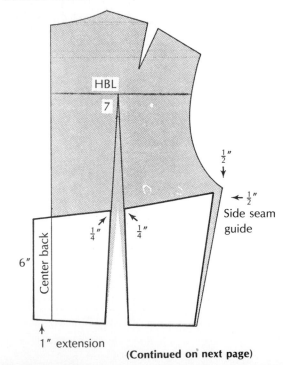

(Continued on next page)

FIGURES 3 and 4 *Front:*
- Cut slash line from bust to, not through, side front panel.
- Place on paper, spreading $\frac{1}{4}$ inches (ease). Tape.
- Close Guideline 6.
- Trace pattern and blend bust areas.

FIGURE 5 *Back:*
- Close dart legs. Tape.
- Place pattern on paper. Trace and blend.
- *Grainlines:* Draw grainlines straight as shown, or on bias.
Complete pattern for test fit.

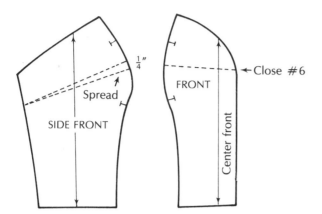

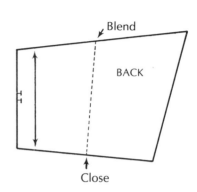

PRINCESS WITH GATHERED PANELS

Design Analysis: Design 2
This strapless design has a princess styleline, with gathered front panels shirred on an angle. This indicates added fullness (parallel openings) and is an application of Principle #2, combined with Principle #3. Use the strapless princess to develop this pattern (see page 217).

Pattern plot

FIGURE 1
- Trace back and front panels of the strapless princess patterns (include grainlines).
- Draw slash lines on an angle exactly as they appear on the design. Label each section for reference as shown.

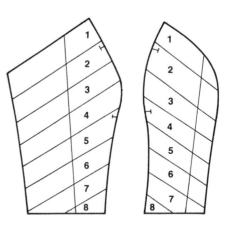

FIGURE 2
- Cut through the panels along each slash line.
- Draw vertical lines on paper as a guide.
- Place panel sections on paper, aligning each line with the vertical guideline on paper. Spread each section $\frac{1}{2}$ inch or more. Secure panel.
- Trace outline of pattern, marking corners of each section. Discard.
- Draw a blending line around the pattern sections.
- *Grainline:* Use vertical guideline as grain or draw bias grain (improves the look). If bias grain is used, trim $\frac{1}{4}$ inch from front along princess line and side panels (not illustrated).
- *Spaghetti straps:* 1 inch × 36 inches. Steam and stretch to eliminate give. Pin to garment while on figure for accurate placement and length.
- Trace basic back strapless, and complete patterns for test fit.

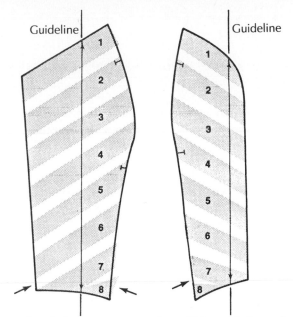

Trim $\frac{1}{4}$ inch from pattern seamlines if bias grain is used.

STRAPLESS PRINCESS VARIATIONS

Design Analysis: Designs 3 and 4
These designs both have princess stylelines and are developed from the same pattern. Design 3 has a princess styleline with the bodice continuing across the top of the bust. The garment contours the figure except between bust mounds. Design 3 is illustrated, and Design 4 is included as a practice design.

Pattern plot and development

FIGURE 1
- Develop patterns using instructions for Design 1 as a guide with the following exception:
The front panel does not include Guideline 6. The styleline is squared from center front to the circumference line above the bust.

FIGURES 2 and 3
- Completed patterns.

DESIGN 3   DESIGN 4

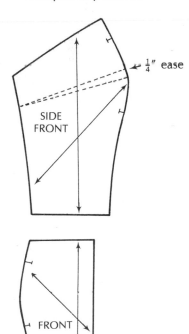

SURPLICE (OR WRAP) DESIGNS

Surplice designs are those whose right and left sides cross over each other. The underneath section of the lapped side can be the same as the other, or the underneath side can be controlled by a hidden dart. The top section may feature a design element such as gathers, tucks, or pleats. This type of style requires a full pattern for development and also special pattern instructions (Right-side-up). Design 1 is illustrated with controlled lapped section. Design 2 is for practice.

DESIGN 1

DESIGN 2

Pattern plot and development

FIGURE 1 *Front:*

For those not using the Contour Guide Pattern, follow plot and measurements given.
- Trace the front Contour Guide Pattern on fold. With a pushpin transfer Guideline 1 and the shoulder and side seam guides. Remove pattern. Connect guidelines, and cut pattern from paper. Unfold.
- Mark A, $1\frac{1}{2}$ inches from shoulder tip.
- Mark B, 2 inches up from side waist (opposite side).
- Draw slightly-inward curve line from A to B, touching bust point, as shown.
- Draw slash line to mid-armhole.
- Raise armhole $\frac{1}{2}$ inch from side guideline. Blend to armhole. (Broken line original armhole.)
- Cut pattern from paper, discard unneeded section (shaded area).

FIGURE 2 *Back:*

- Trace back Contour Guide Pattern, and with pushpin transfer shoulder and side seam guides.
- Mark C, $1\frac{1}{2}$ inches from shoulder tip and down $\frac{1}{4}$ inch to eliminate dart excess.
- Mark D, 1 inch down from center back neck. Square a short line and draw neckline.
- Raise armhole $\frac{1}{2}$ inch on side guide and blend.
- Draw 1 inch center back extension.
- Cut pattern from paper, discard unneeded sections (shaded areas).

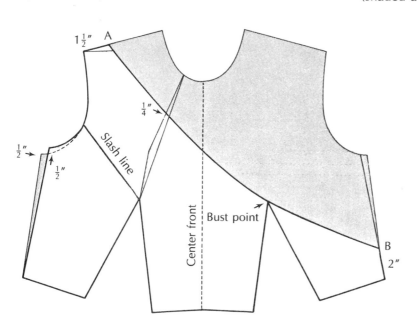

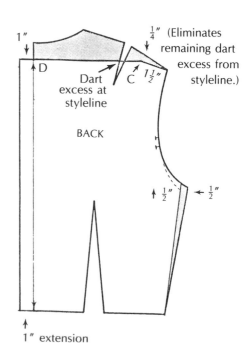

Preparing pattern for left side of garment

FIGURE 3
- Slash Guideline 1 to, not through, bust point.
- Overlap $\frac{1}{4}$ inch (includes $\frac{1}{8}$ inch for stretch). Tape.
- Turn pattern over, and trace, holding dart leg closed. Remove pattern and save to develop right front side.
- Blend line from A to B.
- Shape dart leg as shown.
- Label *Right-side-up.*

Preparing pattern for right side of garment

FIGURE 4
- Cut slash line from mid-armhole to, not through, bust point of the working pattern.
- Close waist dart. Tape.
- Draw slash line for gathers from bust to 1 inch below point B on other side.
- Draw a blending line from A to B, and trim pattern (shaded area).

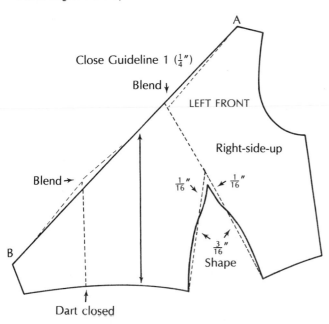

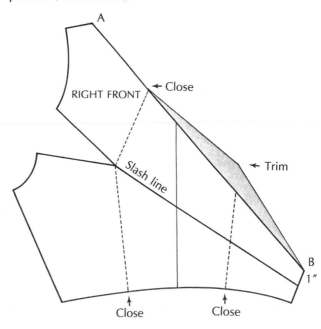

FIGURE 5
- Cut slash line for gathers to, not through, bust point.
- Close mid-armhole dart. Tape.
- Place on paper and trace. Discard pattern.
- Blend open space between dart legs at side.
- Label *Right-side-up.*

FIGURE 6
- To eliminate part of the fullness and to reduce the length of the A–B line (offset any additional bias stretch), reshape styleline using the suggested measurements given.

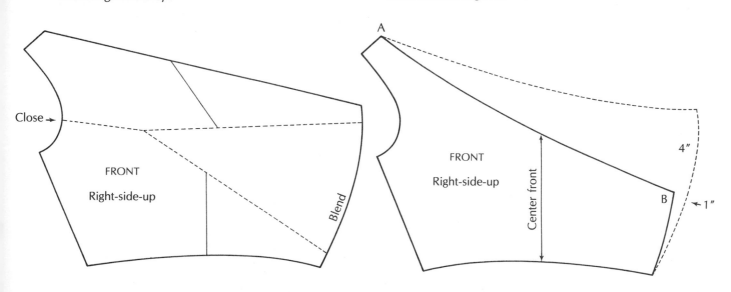

OFF-SHOULDER DESIGNS

GATHERED SHOULDER

Design Analysis: Designs 1 and 2

Design 1 features one shoulder gathered, with the other side fitted under the armhole. Part of the dart's excess is used for gathers; the remaining excess is used for waist dart control. Design 2 is for practice. Design other variations for additional challenge.

DESIGN 1   DESIGN 2

Pattern plot and development

FIGURE 1

For those not using the Contour Guide Pattern, follow plot and measurements given.

- Trace front pattern on fold and with pushpin transfer Guideline 2. Include side seam and shoulder guides. Remove pattern.
- Cut pattern from paper. Unfold.
- Connect guidelines, marking Guideline 2 on shoulderless side of the pattern only.
- Mark A, 2 inches from shoulder tip on guideline.
- Mark B and C, 1 inch below armholes on side seam guideline.
- Draw line from A to B.
- Blend armhole to point C.
- Draw slash lines from bust points to shoulder as shown.
- Cut pattern from paper, discarding unneeded section (shaded area).

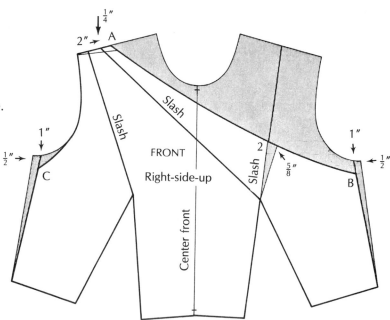

FIGURE 2
- Cut slash lines to, not through, bust points.
- Place on paper.
- Close dart legs $1\frac{1}{2}$ inches (broken lines indicate position of original darts). Secure.
- Close Guideline 2 (broken line). Tape.
- Trace pattern. Discard.
- Blend styleline and shoulder for gathers.
- Draw grainlines. Label *Right-side-up.*

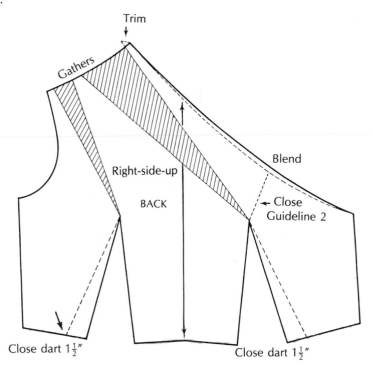

FIGURE 3   *Back:*
- Repeat instruction given for the front pattern for styleline and armhole shape. Label pattern *Right-side-up.* (Bold outline indicates the finished pattern. The broken lines pattern part is discarded.)
- Complete patterns for test fit.

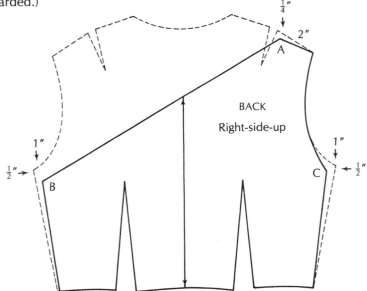

HALTERS

Halters are designs that feature bare shoulders created by cutting the armhole deeply into the shoulder line, thereby eliminating portions of the shoulderline (Design 1), or by cutting armhole to neckline with the garment held around the neck with a cord or band (Design 2). The back may be low-cut. Design 1 is illustrated, and Design 2 is included as a practice problem.

V-NECK HALTER

Pattern plot and development

FIGURE 1

For those not using the Contour Guide Pattern, follow plot and measurements given.

- Trace front pattern. With a pushpin, transfer Guidelines 3, 5 a, b (for modified fit), and 6. Include side seam guide. Remove patterns. Connect guidelines.

Neck:

- Mark neck A, and connect to Guideline 6.
- Draw an 8-inch line up from point A parallel with the center front line.
- Mark B $1\frac{1}{2}$ inches from point A.
- Draw a slightly inward-curved line from point B ending $\frac{1}{2}$ inch below armhole on side seam guide.
- Continue line from point B to tie point as shown.
- Cut pattern from paper. Discard unneeded sections (shaded areas).

DESIGN 1   DESIGN 2

FIGURE 2

- Slash Guidelines 3 and 6 to, not through, bust point.
- Overlap guidelines. Tape and trace. Blend stylelines.
- Draw grainlines.
- To develop low back use instructions on pages 217 and 218, Figures 2 and 5.

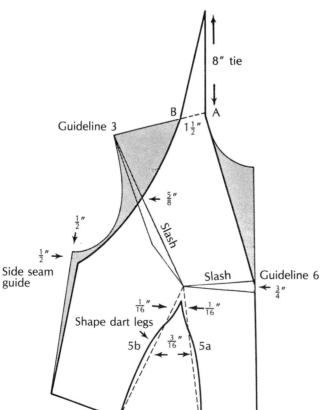

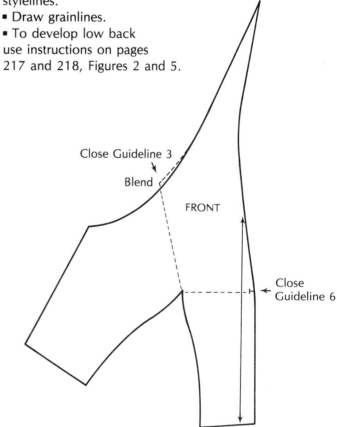

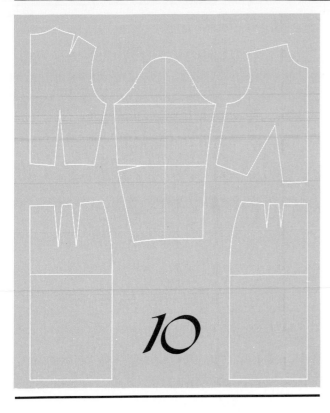

10

COWLS AND
BUILT-UP NECKLINES

BUILT-UP NECKLINES 226
Stovepipe neckline 226
Built-up bateau neckline 228
INSET BANDS 230
Rounded inset band 230
Inset band variations 231
COWLS 232
Pattern modification 232
High horizontal cowl 232
High relaxed cowl 234
Mid-depth cowl 236
Low cowl 238
Deep cowl 239
BACK COWLS 240
High-back cowl 240
Mid-back cowl 242
Low-back cowl 242
ARMHOLE COWLS 243
One-piece armhole cowl 243
PLEATED COWLS 244
Pleated shoulder cowl 244
EXAGGERATED COWLS 246
High exaggerated cowl 246
INSET COWLS 248
V-inset cowl 248

BUILT-UP NECKLINES

Built-up necklines extend above the base of the neck and must accommodate the position of the neck as it juts forward (Figure 1). There are two basic types of built-up necklines: all-in-one with the bodice (Figure 2) and set-in bands (Figure 3). Either type can be developed from any point along the shoulder and to any height. Added room is provided along the outer edge of the built-up neckline. This allows the neckline to rise up and away from the neck and shoulder of the garment to prevent strain from the neck's forward position. The development of this type of neckline is an application of Principle #1, Dart Manipulation (when transferring dart excess to the neckline) and/or Principle #2, Added Fullness (when adding to the pattern's outline). Because of the special features of this type of neckline, facings are included in the instructions. (More about facings can be found in Chapter 14.)

FIGURE 2

FIGURE 3

FIGURE 1

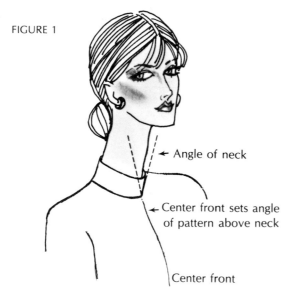

← Angle of neck

← Center front sets angle of pattern above neck

Center front

STOVEPIPE NECKLINE

Design Analysis: Designs 1 and 2
The neckline for Design 1 extends above the natural neckline in front and back, with seams at center front and center back. Design 2 is a practice problem.

DESIGN 1

DESIGN 2

Pattern plot and development

FIGURE 1 *Front:*
- Trace and cut front bodice pattern.
- Mark A, 2 inches down from center front.
- Mark B, $\frac{1}{2}$ inch in from neck at shoulder.
- Draw slash line from A to B.

FIGURE 2
- Cut slash line from A to, not through, point B.
- Place on paper and spread 2 inches. Secure.
- Trace and discard. Label center front neck C.

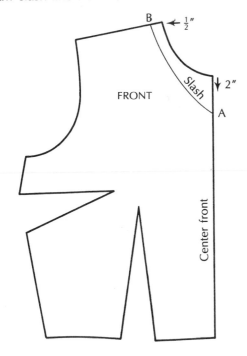

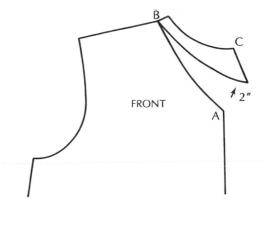

FIGURES 3 and 4
- Continue line up from point B to equal a total of $1\frac{1}{2}$ inches. From this point square a short line.
- Complete curved neckline to point C. Connect C with point A. Blend at A and B and notch.
- Cut from paper.

FIGURE 5 *Facings:*
- Place center front of pattern on fold of paper. Trace neckline from center front to 1 inch past B on shoulder.
- Remove pattern. Draw facing edge parallel with neckline edge. Notch center front neck.

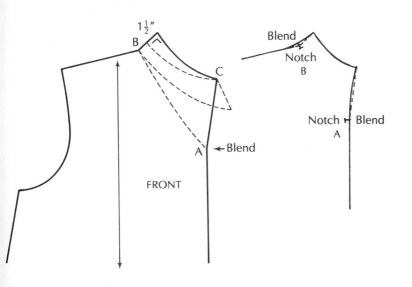

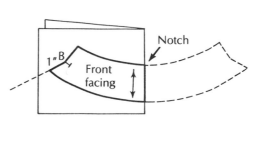

(Continued on next page)

FIGURE 6 *Back:*
▪ Trace back. Mark neck at shoulder A, and draw a guideline parallel with center back.
▪ Extend center back 1 inch. Label B and square a short line.
▪ Mark C, $\frac{1}{2}$ inch from A.
▪ From C draw line to guide that is $1\frac{1}{2}$ inches long. Label D.
▪ Blend curved neckline from D to B, and D to shoulderline.
▪ Add 1-inch extension at center back for closure and mark notches.

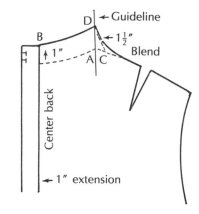

FIGURE 7 *Facing:*
▪ Trace back pattern 1 inch past point C, starting at *True center back.* Remove pattern. Draw facing's edge parallel with neckline edge. Notch at point C and center back. (Facing is lapped by fold-back of garment.)
▪ Draw grain and complete pattern for test fit.

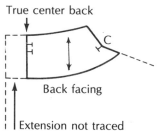

BUILT-UP BATEAU NECKLINE

Design Analysis: Designs 1 and 2
Design 1 extends upward from mid-shoulder and center front neck. Excess from dart is transferred to neckline to allow room for the neck which juts forward. Design 2 is included for practice. Design other variations for additional practice.

Pattern plot and development

FIGURE 1 *Front:*

- Trace one-dart front pattern, transferring $\frac{1}{2}$ inch of dart's excess to mid-neck.
- Extend center front $\frac{3}{4}$ inch up from neck and square a short line. Label A.
- Mark mid-shoulder. Label B.
- Draw line for built-up neck from point B (example: $1\frac{1}{2}$ inches long, ending $\frac{3}{4}$ inches up from shoulder). Label C.

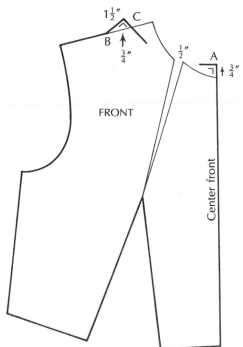

FIGURE 2

- Draw neckline, blending curved line with square lines A and C. Mark notch at point B. (Broken line indicates original pattern.)
- Cut pattern from paper.

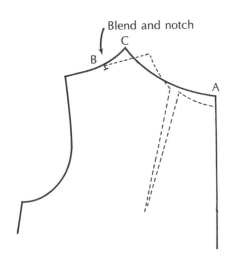

FIGURE 3 *Facing:*

- Trace neck area of pattern on fold for facing, ending 1 inch past B. Remove pattern. Draw facing edge parallel with neckline edge.

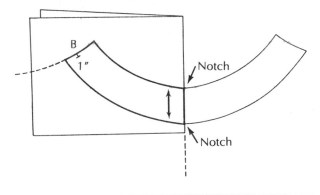

FIGURE 4 *Back:*

- Trace back pattern, transferring shoulder dart to neck (optional).
- Repeat front instructions for built-up neckline, ending neckline shape at *center back neck.*
- Draw 1-inch extension for closure. Mark notches.

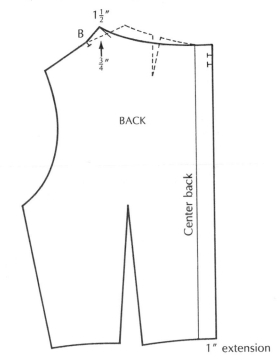

FIGURE 5

- Develop back facing (width same as front), ending at center back as shown.
- Draw grainlines and complete patterns for test fit.

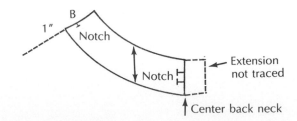

INSET BANDS

An inset band is developed from part of the front and back bodice sections located anywhere along the shoulder or neckline. The band is modified so that it will not lie flat on the model's neck. The following instructions apply to any type of inset neckline. The shoulder dart can be shifted to another location along the shoulderline, transferred to the neckline and become part of the band.

ROUNDED INSET BAND

Design Analysis: Design 1
The inset band is formed around the neck and out to mid-shoulder.

Pattern plot and development

FIGURE 1
- Trace front and back, transferring shoulder dart to neck where dart is closed.
- Place front and back shoulderlines together. Plan neckline and band using illustration as a guide. (Broken lines indicate original pattern.)
- Cut neck band from front and back patterns, discarding unneeded section (shaded area). (The lower part of the front and back bodice is used to complete the design.

FIGURE 2
- Draw three slash lines on each inset section starting in $1\frac{1}{2}$ to 2 inches from center front and center back as shown.

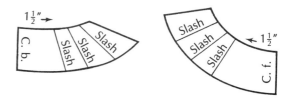

FIGURES 3 and 4
- Cut slash lines to, not through, neckline edge.
- Place patterns on paper with center front on fold.
- Spread each section $\frac{1}{4}$ inch and add $\frac{1}{2}$ inch at shoulder to zero at neckline edge as shown.
- Add a 1-inch extension at center back for closure.
- Draw grainlines, add seams, and complete for test fit.

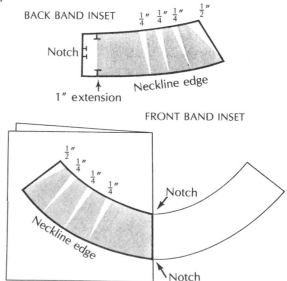

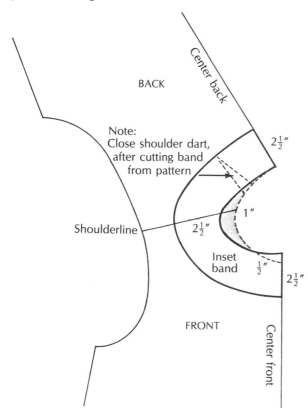

INSET BAND VARIATIONS

Design Analysis: Designs 2 and 3
Design 2 has an inset band that comes to a point at center front and curves around to center back.
Design 3 is given as a practice problem.

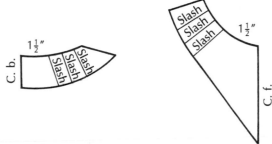

DESIGN 2   DESIGN 3

Pattern plot and development
• Use instructions for Design 1 and the illustrations as guides for developing the patterns.

FIGURE 1   *Plotted patterns:*

FIGURES 2 and 3   *Inset bands:*

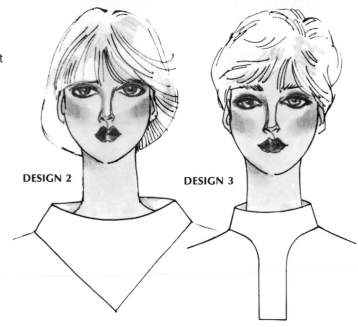

FIGURES 4 and 5
• Back bands, slashed and spread.
• Front inset, slashed and spread.
• Trace front on fold.
• Draw grainlines, add seams and notches.
Complete pattern for test fit.

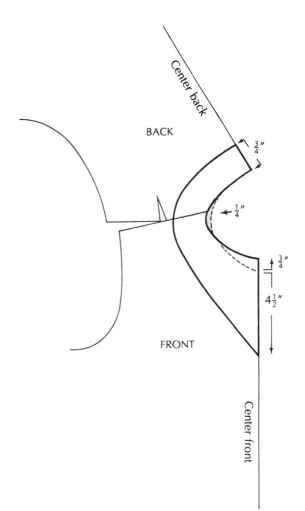

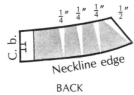

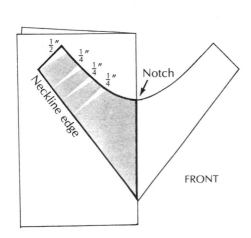

COWLS

A cowl is a fold or series of folds placed anywhere on any type of garment (bodice front and back, skirt, pants, or sleeves). The cowl can fall to a high, medium, or low depth. The depth of the cowl placed on a bodice front is controlled by the amount of dart excess transferred to the neckline area and is an application of Principle #1 (Dart Manipulation) and Principle #2 (Added Fullness). Deep, low cowls (below bust level) are usually stitched to a fitted shell. You will notice as the projects are worked out that all cowls are 90° at the centerlines.

Cowls drape best when cut on a true bias in soft fabrics such as crepes, chiffons, and certain knits. They may be either lined or unlined and have straight, pointed, or rounded facings (fold-back) that can be weighted at the tip to hold the cowl in place. Garments featuring cowls may be expensive due to a fabric loss when making a marker. Set-in cowls can be developed to help avoid this problem. The basic working pattern was developed for firm fabrics and is therefore less than ideal for garments cut in soft, stretchable fabrics. Manufacturers specializing in designs cut in crepes, chiffons, and knits usually develop patterns specifically for these fabrics. There are several ways of coping with the stretch factor, such as:

PATTERN MODIFICATION

1 After developing the cowl pattern, cut the garment in the chosen fabric, allowing excess in addition to the seam allowance. Mark center front with chalk or pins. Place cowl on the form, aligning center front of form with garment. Pin and mark the form's outline, starting at the cowl at shoulderline. When drape is complete, remove it from the form. True the new outline and trim the excess to within seam allowance. Place cowl on pattern, aligning garment at the top and at the center lines, and make final corrections.

2 Drape a basic front and back garment using the same fabric in which the garment will be cut. Follow draping instructions (found in Chapter 4, on page 86). Use this working pattern for all designs cut in fabric with same stretch factor. Develop other working patterns if the fabric is changed.

The following series of instructions and illustrations based on the single-dart bodice show the method used to develop the cowl. However, any pattern can be used to develop the cowl, using these general instructions and concepts.

HIGH HORIZONTAL COWL

Design Analysis: Design 1
Design 1 has a high horizontal cowl, indicating that excess has not been transferred into neckline. The basic back pattern is illustrated as a guide for developing a garment for a test fit. The shoulderline of front and back must be the same length.

Pattern plot and development

FIGURE 1

- Place center front of pattern on fold of paper.
- Trace and remove pattern.
- Mark B, $\frac{3}{4}$ inch from shoulder at neck.
- Square a line from fold, touching point B. Label center front A as shown.
- Draw a parallel line 1 inch above A–B line as a fold-back for facing.

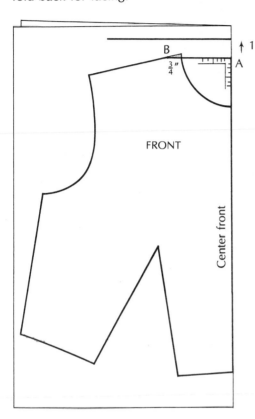

FIGURE 2

- Crease-fold paper across A–B line.
- Trace shoulder and unfold.

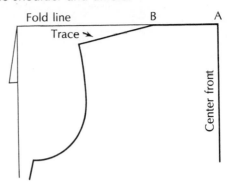

FIGURE 3   *Completed pattern:*

- Draw curved ends for fold-back facing, as shown.
- Cut pattern from paper. Unfold center front.
- Place triangle at center front and draw line for bias grain. (Straight grain is shown and is possible only for this type of cowl; however, bias is better.)

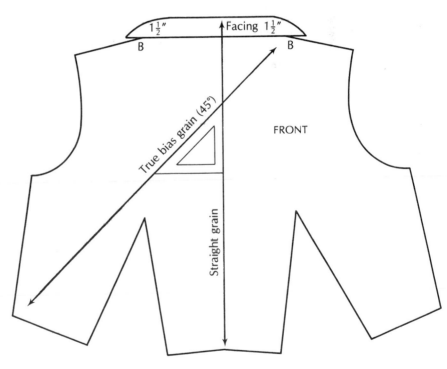

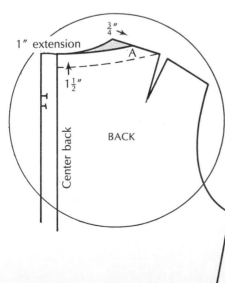

FIGURE 4

- Trace back.
- Mark A, $\frac{3}{4}$ inch in from shoulder at neck.
- Draw a blending curved line from point A, ending at center back neck. (Shaded area is discarded.)
- Extend center back 1 inch for closure.
- Mark facing $1\frac{1}{2}$ inches wide and parallel with neck ending at center back. Trace on paper.
- Draw grain. Complete pattern for test fit. For facing instruction, see Chapter 14.

HIGH RELAXED COWL

Design Analysis: Design 2

Design 2 has a relaxed cowl, indicating that part of the dart's excess was transferred to the neck area.

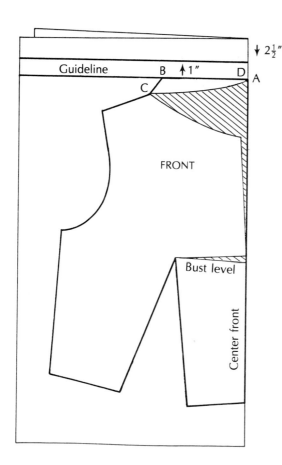

Pattern plot and development

FIGURE 1
- Trace front bodice pattern. Label center front neck A.
- Mark B, ¾ inch in from shoulder at neck.
- Mark C, ¾ inch from B.
- Draw slash lines from A to B and from A to C.
- Square a slash line from center front to bust point.
- Cut pattern from paper along A–B line, discarding unneeded section (shaded area). Broken line is original neckline.
- Cut slash lines to, not through, bust point and point C.

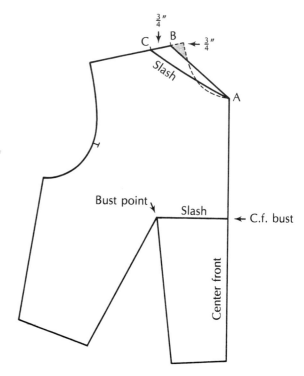

FIGURE 2
- Fold paper. Square a guideline 2½ inches down from paper's edge at fold. Label D as shown.
- Draw a parallel line 1 inch up from point D (for fold-back facing).
- Place pattern on paper so that point B touches guideline and point A touches point D, with center front aligned with fold of paper below bust level. (Part of waist dart excess is transferred to the center front.)
- Trace pattern from B to center front waist. Discard pattern.

FIGURE 3
- Crease-fold paper across A–B line.
- Trace shoulder.

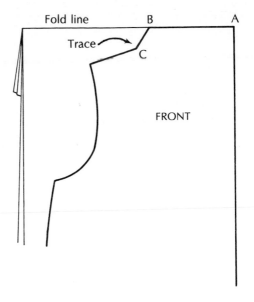

FIGURE 4
- Unfold and pencil in perforated lines. Blend shoulder (broken line original shoulder).
- Cut pattern from paper. Unfold.
- Draw bias grain.
- Develop back using instructions given on page 233, Figure 4.
- Complete pattern for test fit.

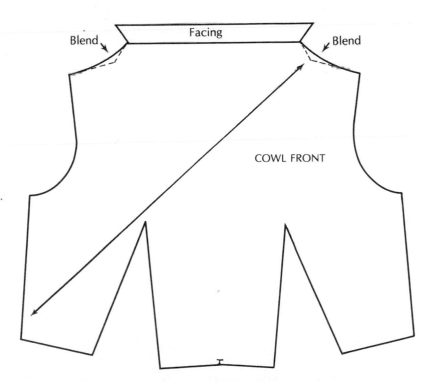

MID-DEPTH COWL

Pattern plot and development

FIGURE 1 *Front:*

- Trace front bodice and square a slash line from center front to bust point (bust level).
- Mark A between the center front neck and bust level.
- Mark B at mid-shoulder.
- Connect A with B.
- Draw slash lines from shoulder tip to bust level and another in between as shown.
- Cut pattern from paper, discarding unneeded section (shaded area).
- Cut slash lines to, not through, shoulder and bust point.

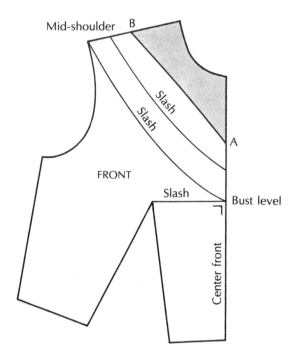

Design Analysis: Design 3

Design 3 features a cowl that drapes from mid-shoulder and falls between neck and bust level. (Half of the dart's excess is needed for the depth of this cowl.) The fold-back facing is rounded (sometimes pointed), illustrating another way to develop facings.

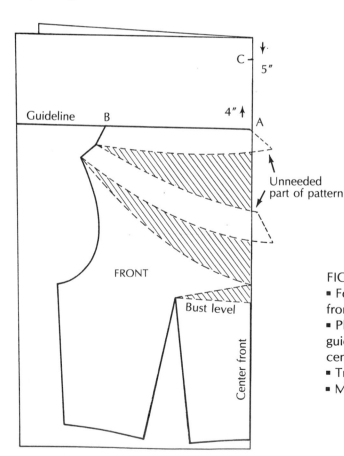

FIGURE 2

- Fold paper and square a guideline 5 inches down from paper's edge at fold.
- Place pattern on paper so that A–B line touches guide and point A touches fold of paper, with center front on the fold below bust level.
- Trace pattern from B to center front waist.
- Mark C, 4 inches up from A for fold-back.

FIGURE 3
- Crease-fold A–B line and trace shoulder.

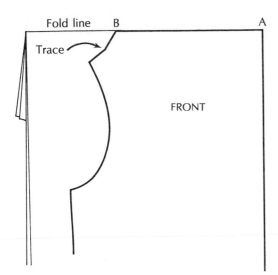

FIGURE 4
- Unfold and draw curved fold-back facing, as shown.
- Blend shoulder (broken line original shoulder).
- Draw bias grain.

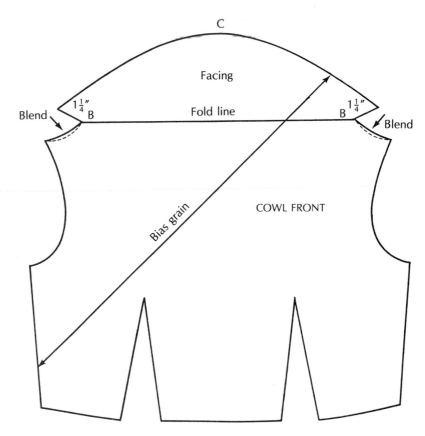

FIGURE 5 *Back:*
- To complete pattern for test fit, plan back neckline: Trace back pattern and mark A, $1\frac{1}{2}$ inches below center back. Square a short line. Mark B $\frac{1}{4}$ inch down from mid-shoulder as shown.
- Draw blending line from A to B.
- Draw facing (broken lines).
- Transfer facing to paper (not illustrated).
- Cut pattern from paper, discarding unneeded section (shaded area).
- Complete patterns for test fit.

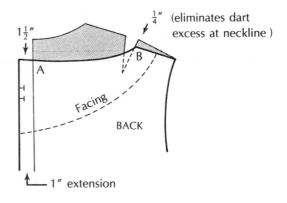

LOW COWL

Design Analysis: Design 4

The low cowl as featured in Design 4 drapes at or slightly below bust level. All of the dart's excess is needed for depth of this cowl.

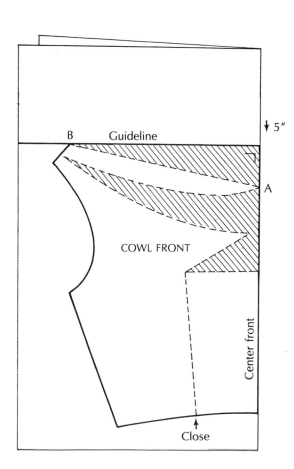

Pattern plot and development

FIGURE 1

- Trace front bodice.
- Square a line from center front to bust point. Label A (bust level).
- Mark B, 1½ inches from shoulder tip. Draw line from A to B.
- Draw slash line between shoulder tip and point B, ending at point A.
- Cut from paper, discard unneeded section (shaded area).
- Cut slash lines to, not through, shoulder and bust point.
- Close dart leg. Tape.

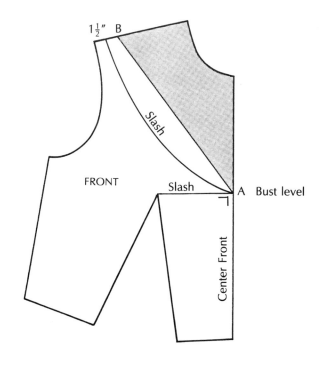

FIGURE 2

- Fold paper and square a guideline 5 inches down from paper's edge at fold.
- Place pattern with center front on fold and point B on guideline. Spread sections until point A touches somewhere on center front fold.
- Secure and trace from B to center front waist.
- Complete pattern for test fit.
- Develop back pattern using instructions on page 237, Figure 5 as a guide.

DEEP COWL

Design Analysis: Design 5

Deep cowls such as featured in Design 5 are
usually attached to a strapless fitted shell (illustrated
is a strapless princess style), where it is stitched into
the side seam when the front cowl is joined to the
back. The drape of the cowl falls below bust level,
indicating added fullness at the center front. Use
the Contour Guide Pattern to develop the fitted
shell for this design. (Refer to Chapter 9 for
contouring information.)

Pattern plot and development

FIGURE 1

For those not using the Contour Guide Pattern, use
plot and measurements given.

- Trace pattern, and with pushpins transfer
Guidelines 2, 5 a,b (semi-fit), and side seam guide
for development of the strapless shell pattern. Both
the shell and the cowl patterns are plotted on the
same traced copy. Each will be transferred to
another paper individually.
- Remove pattern and connect guidelines.

Shell styleline:

- Draw strapless styleline using measurements given
(indicated by broken line).

Cowl:

- Mark A at desired cowl depth down from bust
level at center front (example: 2 inches below bust
level).
- Mark B, $1\frac{1}{2}$ inches from shoulder tip. Connect A
to B.
- From A, draw slash line to bust point as shown.
- Cut pattern from paper.

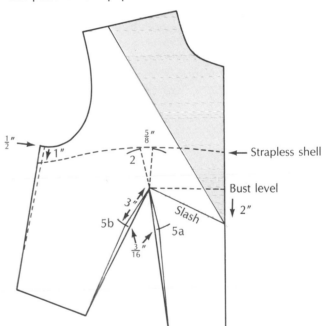

FIGURE 2 *Shell:*

- Trace strapless shell section of plotted pattern on
another paper. (Use pushpin marks across top of
strapless as a guide for shaping styleline.) With
pushpins transfer Guidelines 2, 5 a,b, and side seam
guideline. Remove paper and pencil in perforated
lines. Shape the dart legs and draw curved lines
slightly outward above bust.
- Cut and separate pattern. Discard unneeded
section (shaded area).
- Retrace princess panels for lining patterns (not
illustrated).
- Trim unneeded section from cowl pattern (shaded
area.)

Note: Mark notches $1\frac{1}{2}$" up from 5a and 5b.

FIGURE 3 *Cowl:*
▪ Cut slash line to, not through, bust point of the plotted pattern.
▪ Close dart legs. Tape.
▪ Fold paper.
▪ Place tip of center front waist at fold of paper near bottom. Secure with pushpin.
▪ Swing pattern away from fold until point A touches fold. Secure pattern and trace from B to center front waist. Discard pattern.
▪ Square a line from fold, touching point B.
▪ For fold-back and back pattern information, follow Design 3 on page 237 (Figures 3, 4 and 5).
▪ Complete pattern for test fit. (Stitching guide: The shell and lining are stitched together. Both the side seams of the shell and front cowl are stitched to side seams with back cowl.)

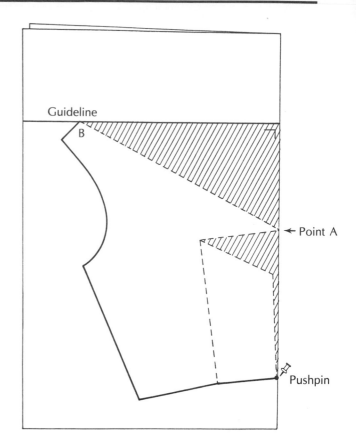

Guideline

B

← Point A

Pushpin

BACK COWLS

Back cowls are developed using a square ruler. Designs 1, 2, and 3 illustrate a method for developing high, medium (mid-center), and low cowls.

HIGH-BACK COWL

Pattern plot and development

FIGURE 1
▪ Trace back pattern in center of a 36-inch square sheet of paper.
▪ Mark A, 4 inches down from center back neck.
▪ Mark B at mid-shoulder. Measure A to B and record.
▪ Mark C from center back waist equal to width of waist dart.

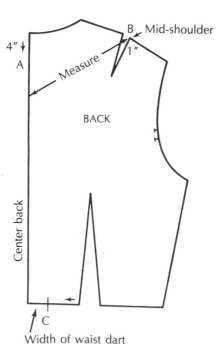

4" ↓
A
Measure
B Mid-shoulder
1"
BACK
Center back
C
Width of waist dart

DESIGN 1 **DESIGN 2** **DESIGN 3**

FIGURE 2

- Before folding paper, locate A–B measurement on one leg of ruler.
- Place this point on B and the other leg on C.
- Draw square line from A to B and A to C. (Broken line indicates original pattern showing ruler placement before paper is folded.)
- Measure down $\frac{1}{16}$ inch in between point B and shoulder tip. Draw curved line as shown. (Helps to control cowl folds.)
- Blend waistline.
- Fold paper on A–C line as shown. This is the new center back.
- Mark D, 3 inches up from A (fold-back).

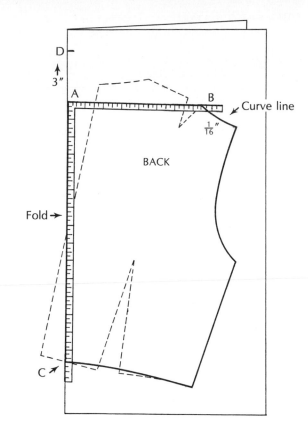

FIGURE 3

- Crease-fold paper on A–B line. Trace shoulder.

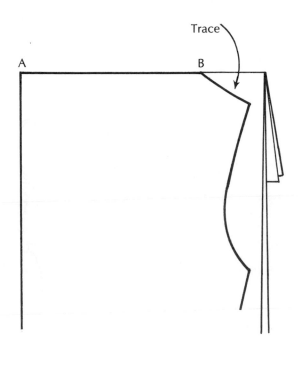

FIGURE 4

- Unfold. Pencil $1\frac{1}{4}$ inches of shoulder and shape to point D for fold-back.
- Cut pattern from paper. Unfold.
- Draw bias grain.
- Develop front pattern, trueing shoulder for test fit.

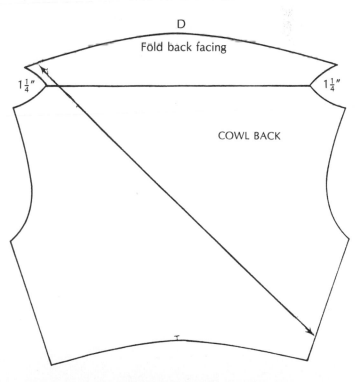

MID-BACK COWL

- Mark A midway between neck and waist.
- Mark B 2 inches from shoulder tip.
- Mark C equal to dart intake.
- Complete pattern using instructions given for Design 1, Figures 2, 3 and 4.

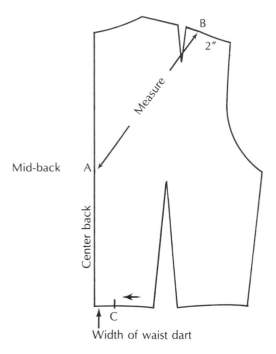

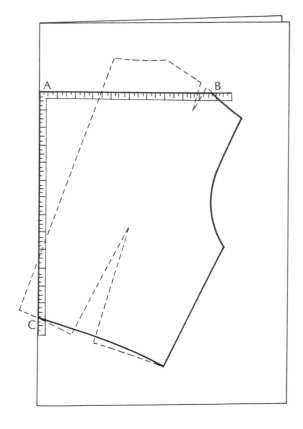

LOW-BACK COWL

- Mark A 4 inches up from center back waist.
- Mark B 1 inch in from shoulder tip.
- Mark C equal to dart intake.
- Complete pattern using instructions given for Design 1, Figures 2, 3 and 4.

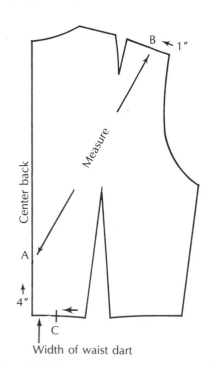

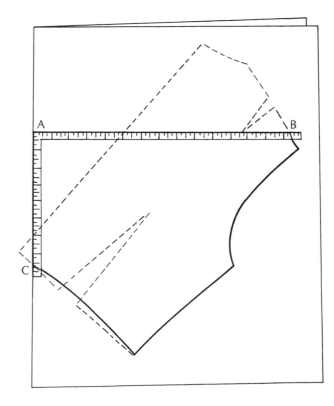

ARMHOLE COWLS

ONE-PIECE ARMHOLE COWL

Design Analysis: Design 1

Cowl drapes under armhole of Design 1, replacing side seams.

Pattern plot and development

FIGURE 1

• Use front and back basic bodice with shoulder dart of back transferred to armhole.

• Draw a square line on paper. Label A, B, and C.

• Place front bodice on A–B line. Place back bodice 1 inch in from B–C line (for extension) with 1-inch space between front and back side waists.

• Secure and trace front and back pattern, omitting sections indicated by broken lines. Remove patterns.

• Blend a curved line between front and back waist.

• Draw a line connecting front and back shoulder tips. Label D–E. (May be varied by drawing the connecting line at front and back mid-shoulders.

• Draw a 1-inch parallel line above D–E for fold-back facing.

• Fold D–E line. Trace shoulder. Unfold and pencil in perforated line.

• Draw grain parallel with center front. Add seams and notches as shown.

• Cut from paper and complete pattern for test fit. (Pattern may be cut with center front on fold or with center front seamed.)

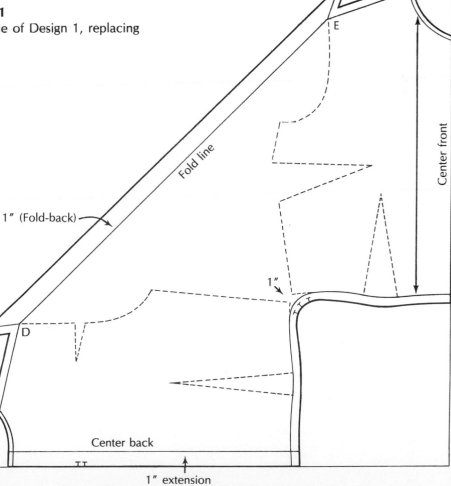

PLEATED COWLS

Pleats help to control the folds of the cowl. The instructions given below show how to develop a cowl with pleats along the shoulderline. The same procedure can be used for developing cowls with pleats along the armhole or side seams. The cowl designs show some of the possible cowl variations created with pleats with Design 1 being illustrated. For practice, develop patterns for Designs 2 and 3.

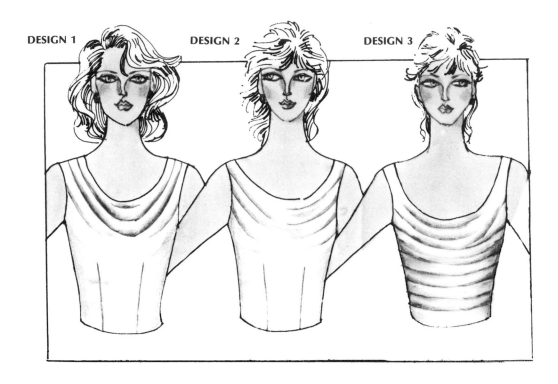

DESIGN 1   DESIGN 2   DESIGN 3

PLEATED SHOULDER COWL

Design Analysis
The cowl has two pleats at shoulderline with cowl depth above the bust level.

Pattern plot and development

FIGURE 1 *Front:*
- Trace and cut front pattern.
- Square a slash line from center front to bust point (bust level).
- Mark A between neck and bust level.
- Mark B at mid-shoulder.
- Connect A with B.
- Draw two lines between point B and shoulder tip and ending between point A and bust level.
- Cut pattern from paper. Discard unneeded section (shaded area).

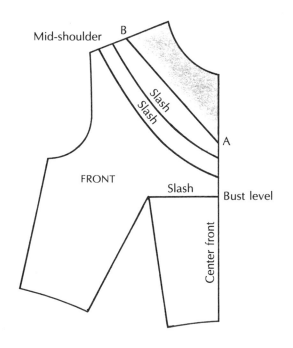

Mid-shoulder   B

Slash

Slash

A

FRONT

Slash

Center front

Bust level

FIGURE 2

- *Prepare paper:* Fold paper. Square a guideline 4 inches down from paper's edge at fold.
- *Pattern:* Cut slash lines to, not through, shoulder.
- Place section A–B on guideline with point A and center front of pattern touching fold line. (Part of waist dart will close and the slashed sections will spread.)
- Secure pattern sections.
- Draw a parallel line 2 inches in from center front, passing through pattern sections as shown.

FIGURE 3

- Release hinges at shoulderline.
- Spread each section 1 inch or more at shoulder, keeping each section on guideline. Secure.
- Trace outline of pattern and corner of each spread section along shoulder for pleats. Discard pattern.
- Locate and mark centers of each pleat. Draw connecting lines for pleats at shoulder by following the angle of the pattern sections as indicated by arrows, ending at center mark. Mark notches at each pleated section as shown.
- Draw a parallel line 1 inch above A–B line for fold-back (facing). Complete facing.

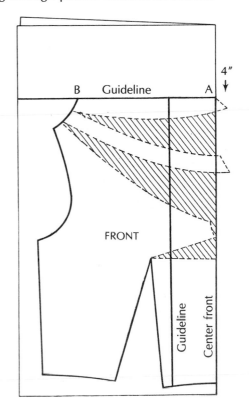

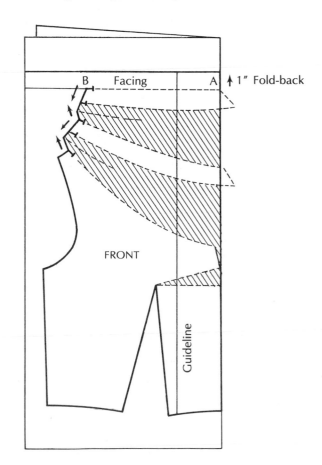

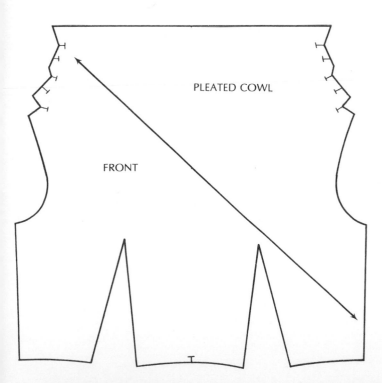

PLEATED COWL

FRONT

FIGURE 4

- Cut pattern from paper. Unfold.
- Draw bias grain.
- Complete pattern for test fit.
- To complete back pattern, follow instructions given on page 237, Figure 5.

EXAGGERATED COWLS

Fuller cowls can be achieved without pleats by spreading the pattern beyond the 90°-square line at center front. This type of pattern requires a seam at the centerline. The empire pattern was used to develop the design illustrated; however, any pattern can be used.

HIGH EXAGGERATED COWL

Design Analysis: Design 1
Design 1 features deep folds without pleats and a center front seam.

Pattern plot and development

Measurement needed
(12) _____ (or one-fourth of neck measurement).

FIGURE 1   *Front:*
- Trace basic front Empire bodice and midriff (pages 213-214).
- Extend a line up from center front neck and square a line 1 inch above shoulder at neck equal to one-fourth of neck measurement.
- Square down to shoulder. Blend with shoulder line. Label A and B as shown.
- Draw slash lines, squared from center front, with one slash line to bust point (bust level).
- Cut pattern from paper.

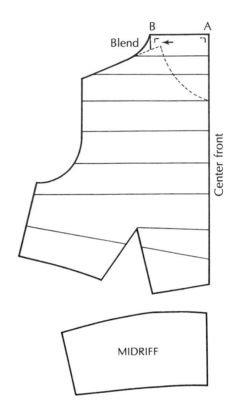

FIGURE 2

- Cut slash lines from center front to, not through, sides and bust point.
- Close dart legs. Tape.
- Place on paper and spread equally, or vary to control fullness as shown.
- Trace outline of pattern. Discard.

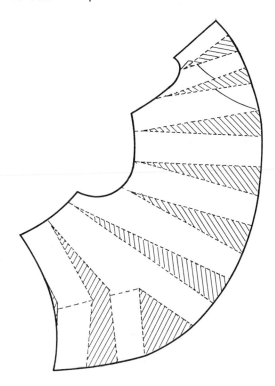

FIGURE 3

- Exaggerated pattern shapes should be labeled for identity.
- Draw grain.

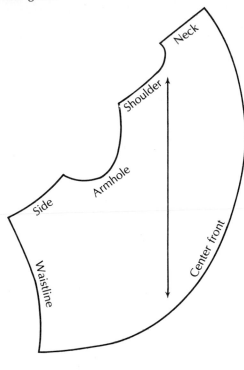

FIGURE 4 *Back:*

- Trace basic back empire bodice and midriff.
- Develop neckline, using front instructions.
- True front and back shoulderlines.
- Draw grain and complete pattern for test fit.

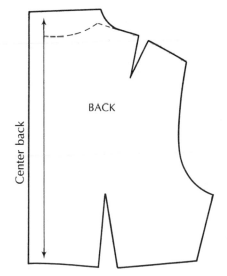

INSET COWLS

Inset cowls can be developed on any bodice, torso, or similar type of garment. Any styleline shape can be designed. For purposes of instruction, the cowl inset only is developed and does not represent a complete pattern. Back patterns are not illustrated. The second two designs are included as practice problems.

V-INSET COWL

DESIGN 1   DESIGN 2   DESIGN 3

Design Analysis
The V-inset cowl of Design 1 is placed away from neck at shoulder. The point of the V-styleline falls below bust level.

Pattern plot and development

FIGURE 1

- Trace front two-dart pattern. Square a guideline from center front to bust point (bust level).
- Mark A, 3 inches down from center front.
- Mark B, 2 inches from shoulder at neck.
- Connect A and B. Measure and record: _____.
- Mark C, 1½ inches from shoulder tip.
- Mark D, 1 inch below bust level guideline. Connect C with D.
- Measure down $\frac{1}{16}$ inch from shoulder between B and C and draw curved line as shown. (For controlling folds of the cowl when stitching to back shoulder.)
- Crossmark for notch between C and D.
- Cut pattern from paper. Discard unneeded section (shaded area).
- Cut inset from pattern (A, B, C, and D areas). (Lower section of pattern is used to complete the design.)

FIGURE 2

- Trace inset cowl section on center of paper.
- Locate A–B measurement on one leg of square ruler and place on draft with this point at B and the other leg of ruler touching D.
- Draw a line from A to B to D as shown.

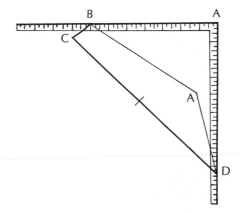

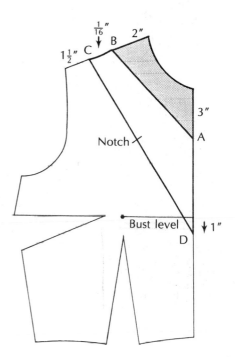

FIGURE 3

- Fold paper on A–D line. Trace pattern.
- Draw 1-inch line parallel with A–B line. Fold A–B line. Trace shoulder.
- Unfold and complete pattern.

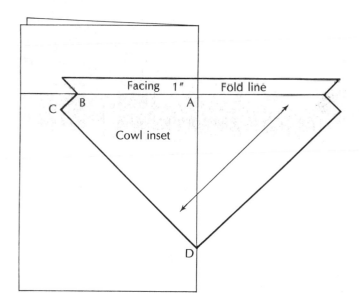

part Three

COLLARS, SKIRTS, SLEEVES, AND SLEEVE/BODICE COMBINATIONS

11

COLLARS

Introduction 254
Collar terms 254
Collar stand and roll types 255
Collar classifications 255
BASIC SHIRT COLLAR FOUNDATION 256
Straight collar 256
Undercollar 257
Folded basic collar 258
Collar corrections 259
PETER PAN COLLAR 260
Peter Pan with 1-inch stand 261
Peter Pan with 1/2-inch stand 262
Peter Pan with flat roll 263
SAILOR COLLAR 264
Basic sailor collar 264
Sailor with extension 265
Sailor with inset 266
COLLARS WITH DEEP OPEN NECKLINES 267
Collar for V-neck 267
Collar for square neck 267
MANDARIN COLLAR 268
Basic Mandarin 268
Mandarin collar variations 269
COLLAR WITH STAND 270
ALL-IN-ONE COLLAR AND STAND 271
ROLL COLLARS 272
Turtle neck 273
Roll collar with cutaway neck 273
COLLAR DESIGN VARIATIONS 274

INTRODUCTION

A collar is the part of a garment that encircles the neck and frames the face, offering great opportunities for design variations. Collars may be developed close to or away from the neckline. They may be wide, narrow, flat, or high, and with or without an attached stand. The collar edge may be stylized or may follow a basic shape—it may be round, curved, scalloped, square, or pointed (long or short) in any direction.

Other collar shapes such as the shawl or lapel collars are not included in this chapter, but will be discussed in Chapter 19 with jackets and coats.

COLLAR TERMS

Neckline edge. The edge of the collar that is stitched to the neckline of the garment.

Collar edge. The outer edge or styleline of the collar.

Collar stand. The underneath part of the collar that supports the folded-over section. It is described by its height (the distance from neckline edge of collar to roll line at center back). The neckline edge controls the collar by either allowing it to lie flat or forcing it upward to form a stand (Figures 1, 2 and 3). Collar and stand can be developed in either one or two pieces.

Roll line. The place where the collar folds over, dividing the collar into stand and outer-collar sections. Three types of collar rolls are illustrated:

COLLAR STAND AND ROLL TYPES

The broken lines indicate where the stand stops and the roll line begins.

FIGURE 1
1-inch stand (full roll)

FIGURE 2
½-inch stand (partial roll)

FIGURE 3
⅛-inch stand (flat roll)

COLLAR CLASSIFICATIONS

Within all possible variations, collars can generally be classified into two broad categories based on several specific characteristics:

Convertible collars. Those that can be worn open or closed (Figures 4 and 5). When unfastened, the collar springs open, lying flat across the chest (example: the basic collar).

Nonconvertible collars. Those that can be worn only closed (Figure 6). (Example: the Peter Pan collar.)

FIGURE 6

FIGURE 4   FIGURE 5

FIGURE 7

Neckline edge of the collar. (Broken line indicates neckline edge of garment.)
The nonconvertible collar is shaped to follow the general neckline curve of the garment to which it is stitched. This allows the collar to remain closed (Figure 7). The convertible collar has a straight and upward curve at the neckline edge in the opposite direction from the garment, causing the collar to be pulled back when unbuttoned. Collars with a straight neckline edge fit very loosely around the neck and are unappealing.

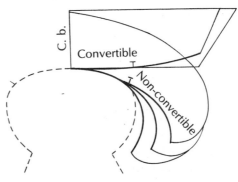

BASIC SHIRT COLLAR FOUNDATION

The basic collar is a convertible collar that may be worn open or closed at the neckline. The collar has a 1-inch stand at the center back, and its width may vary from 2½ inches to 3 inches. It can be developed with a seam along the collar edge, or folded and cut as either a one-piece or two-piece (center back seam) collar. The grainline may be either straight, crosswise, or bias, depending upon the design effects desired when cut in stripes, checks or plaids. The basic collar pattern may be used as is or modified for other designs.

Neckline measurements needed
Center back neck to shoulder: _____
Center front neck to shoulder: _____
Total: _____

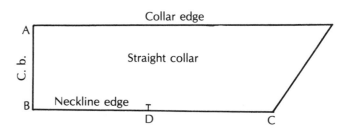

FIGURE 1
- Square a line in the center of the paper, mark and label the following locations:
A–B = 2½ inches (collar width).
B–C = Total neck measurement. Label C.
B–D = Mark center back to shoulder for notch.

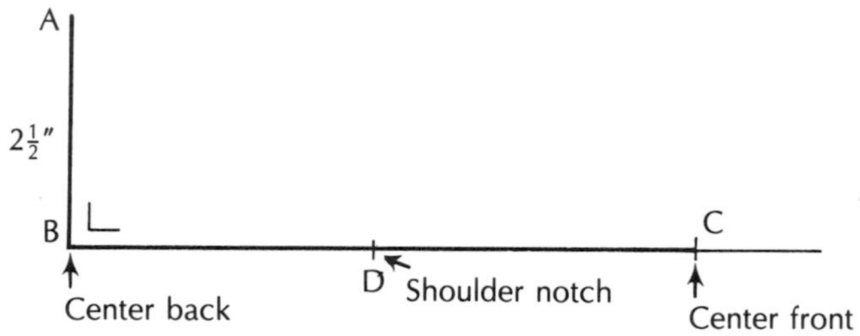

FIGURE 2
- Square a line up from C.
- Mark E, ½ inch from C.
- Draw a curved line from E blending with D. (The line B, D, and E establishes the neckline edge of collar.)
- Draw a diagonal guideline line out from C.

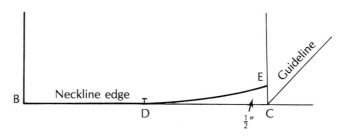

FIGURE 3
- Square a line out from A to guideline.
- Draw a line from E, parallel with guideline. (This completes the collar edge.) The broken lines indicate collar roll line, and the vertical line indicates the division between the front and back collar where the collar modification begins.
- Draw grain and cut collar from paper.

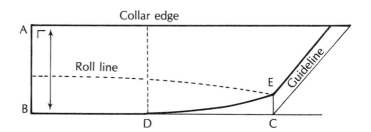

STRAIGHT COLLAR

FIGURE 4
- Develop collar using Figures 1, 2 and 3 of the basic collar, with the following exception:
The neckline edge is straight.

UNDERCOLLAR

The undercollar should be shorter in width than the uppercollar to prevent it from rolling out beyond the stitchline. The undercollar pattern is developed from the uppercollar. Two methods are given for its development. (The broken line indicates the original collar.) The undercollar should be notched $\frac{1}{4}$ inch out from each side of center. The following instructions apply to the development of all undercollars.

Method 1

FIGURE 5
- Trace uppercollar.
- Remove $\frac{1}{8}$ inch from center back to $\frac{1}{8}$ inch at point of collar edge (prevents point of collar from turning upward). Remove $\frac{1}{4}$ inch for bulky fabrics.

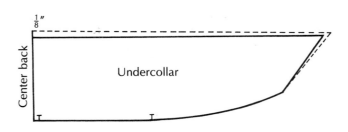

Method 2

FIGURE 6
- Trace uppercollar.
- Remove $\frac{1}{8}$ inch from center back to collar edge. Remove $\frac{1}{4}$ inch for bulky fabrics.

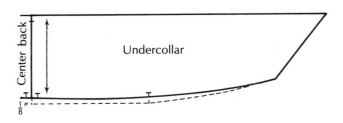

FIGURE 7
- Collar can be cut with seam at center back.
- Add seams and draw straight, crosswise, or bias grainlines as shown.

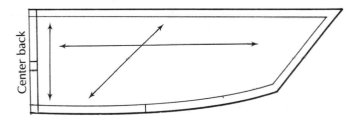

FIGURE 8
- Collar may also be cut on fold.

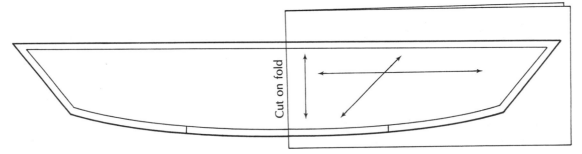

FOLDED BASIC COLLAR

FIGURE 1
- Fold paper lengthwise.
- Square a guideline down from the fold in center of paper.

- Place collar on paper with center back on guideline and collar edge along fold line.
- Trace collar. Discard. Cut out the collar, ending at center guideline.

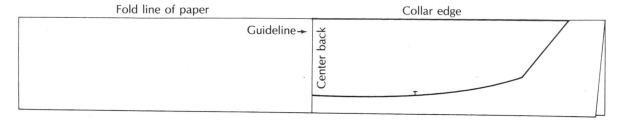

FIGURE 2
- Unfold paper. Refold collar and paper on guideline.

- Trace the collar. (Completed collar shown.)
- Cut from paper, notch, draw grainline as desired.

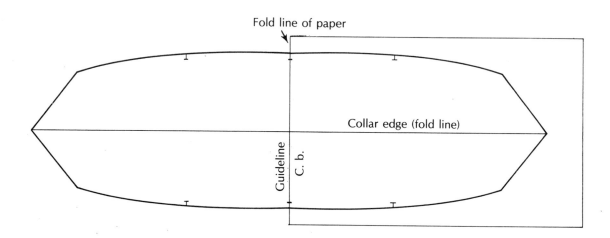

Increasing collar width

FIGURE 9
- Trace basic collar indicated by broken line.
- With pushpin at shoulder notch (point X), swing pattern downward $\frac{1}{2}$ inch.
- Retrace collar from point X to center back to establish new neckline edge. Remove pattern.
- Extend center back 1 inch as shown.
- Draw new collar's edge parallel with neckline. (Any collar shape may be designed.)

Collar variations

FIGURE 10
- Examples of collar designs that vary from the basic collar. Note that collar variations begin and blend approximately in line with shoulder notch.

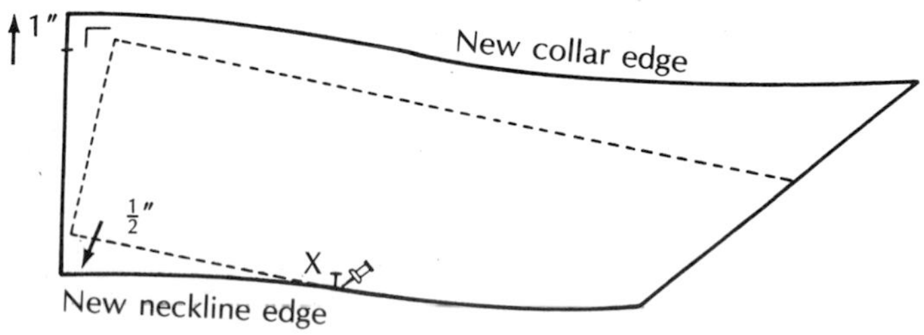

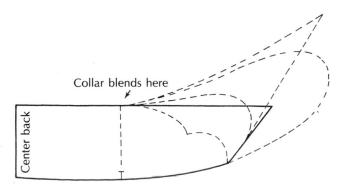

COLLAR CORRECTIONS

Collars with inadequate outer edge measurement

This problem is characterized by the collar riding up at the center back (showing the stitchline of the neck). This is caused by insufficient length at the collar's outer edge. To correct, cut three slash lines (indicated by broken lines on collar) between the shoulder and center back of the collar while it is on the form or model. Allow the collar edge to fall, and spread until the stitchline around neck is covered. (Pin center back of collar to center back of garment). Use masking tape to hold slashed sections at the desired location. Measure each slashed opening (not illustrated).

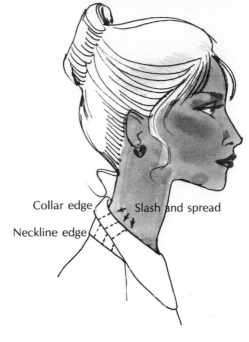

Collar edge / Slash and spread
Neckline edge

FIGURE 1

- Draw three slash lines on collar as shown.
- Cut slash line from collar edge to, not through, neckline edge. Use measurements of spread collar sections to spread pattern in equal amounts. (Broken line indicates original collar shape.)
- Retrace collar and cut for a test fit.

Note: This correction will change the neckline shape as well as the collar edge. It allows the collar to fall to its intended location.

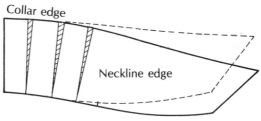

Collar edge

Neckline edge

Collars too loose or too flat around outer edge

- When the collar is too loose or has an insufficient stand, cut three slash lines on each side of collar between shoulder and center back. Overlap until the collar edge and stand are correct (not illustrated). Measure these amounts.

Slash and overlap / Collar edge

FIGURE 2

- Draw three slash lines on collar as shown.
- Cut slash lines from collar edge to, not through, neckline edge.
- Use measurements of overlapped collar sections to overlap pattern in equal amounts. Tape.
- Retrace and cut for a test fit. (Broken line indicates original pattern.)

Note: This correction will change the shape of the neckline edge as well as the collar edge, causing the collar to rise upward to its intended location.

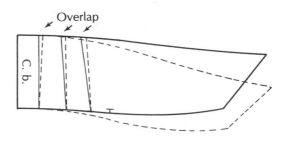

Overlap

C. b.

PETER PAN COLLAR

The Peter Pan is a rounded, nonconvertible collar developed in one or two pieces (open at front and back). It has a center-back stand ranging from a 1-inch stand to a flat roll. The Peter Pan, or any nonconvertible collar, is meant to be worn closed at the neckline and will not spring open when released. Any nonconvertible collar can be developed from the instructions given for the Peter Pan collar. When developed with a flat roll, this type of collar may be as wide as desired. The collar edge can be varied to develop other popular collars, such as the sailor, bertha, and pilgrim.

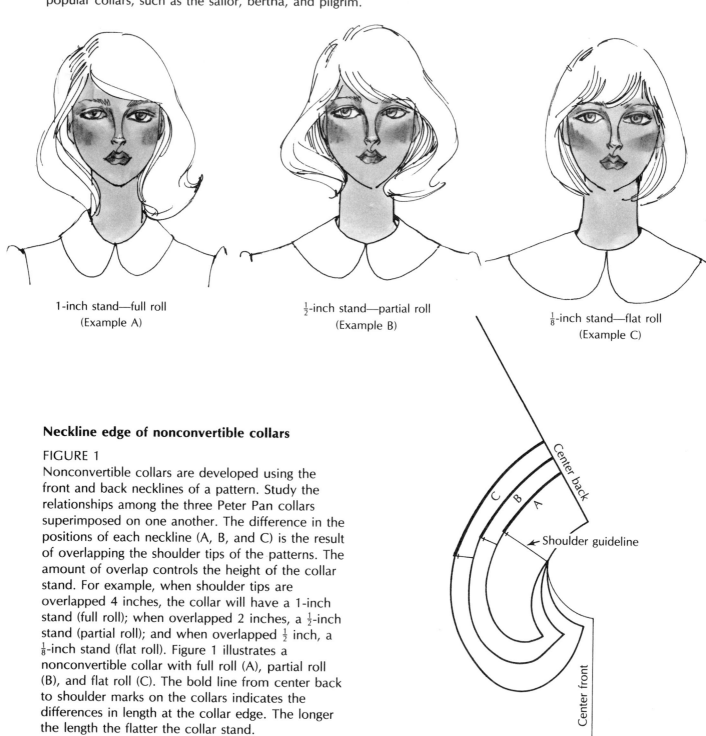

1-inch stand—full roll
(Example A)

$\frac{1}{2}$-inch stand—partial roll
(Example B)

$\frac{1}{8}$-inch stand—flat roll
(Example C)

Neckline edge of nonconvertible collars

FIGURE 1

Nonconvertible collars are developed using the front and back necklines of a pattern. Study the relationships among the three Peter Pan collars superimposed on one another. The difference in the positions of each neckline (A, B, and C) is the result of overlapping the shoulder tips of the patterns. The amount of overlap controls the height of the collar stand. For example, when shoulder tips are overlapped 4 inches, the collar will have a 1-inch stand (full roll); when overlapped 2 inches, a $\frac{1}{2}$-inch stand (partial roll); and when overlapped $\frac{1}{2}$ inch, a $\frac{1}{8}$-inch stand (flat roll). Figure 1 illustrates a nonconvertible collar with full roll (A), partial roll (B), and flat roll (C). The bold line from center back to shoulder marks on the collars indicates the differences in length at the collar edge. The longer the length the flatter the collar stand.

PETER PAN WITH 1-INCH STAND

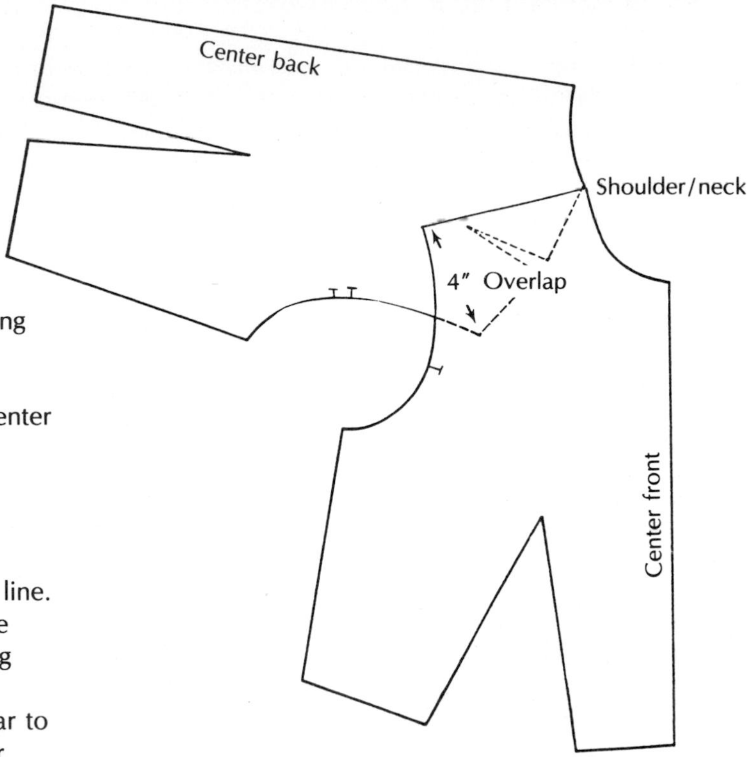

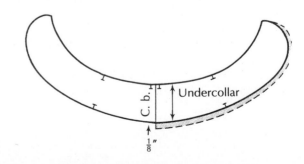

Pattern plot and development

FIGURE 1
- Place front and back patterns together matching neck at shoulder.
- Overlap shoulder tips 4 inches.
- Trace neckline and part of center front and center back. Remove patterns.

FIGURE 2 *Collar:*
- Extend center back $\frac{1}{8}$ inch and square a short line.
- Lower center front $\frac{1}{4}$ inch and redraw neckline curve from center front to center back, blending point where shoulder and neck intersect. (Modification of the collar's neckline helps collar to roll smoothly and prevents an overroll at center front.) Neckline should be a smooth continuous curve. (Broken line indicates original neckline.)
- Collar width = $2\frac{1}{2}$ inches.
- Draw collar edge parallel with new neckline, curving to center front as shown. (Any variation can be designed from shoulder to center front.)
- True neckline of collar and bodice. (Add to or subtract from center front of collar, if necessary for trueing.)
- Notch center back, shoulder and collar edge.
- Cut collar from pattern, discarding shaded area.

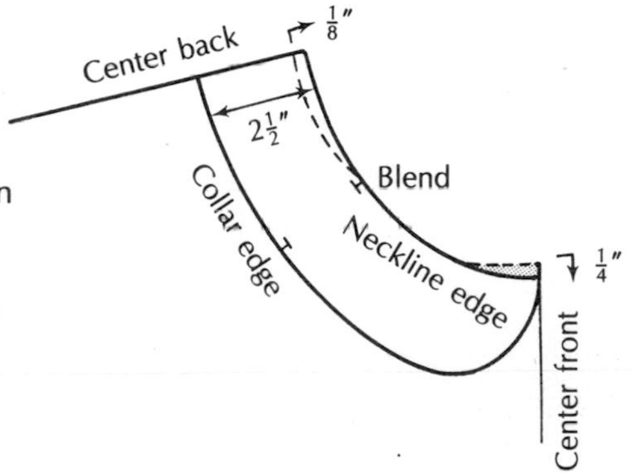

FIGURE 3 *Uppercollar:*
- Trace collar on fold of paper.
- Mark notches at center back.
- Cut from paper. Unfold.

FIGURE 4 *Undercollar:*
- Retrace collar to develop undercollar.
- Remove $\frac{1}{8}$ inch around collar edge. Blend to zero at center front of collar. (Shaded area is discarded.)
- Mark two notches at neckline edge to distinguish undercollar from uppercollar.
    Note: The center back can be seamed if desired (not illustrated).
- Draw grain and complete collar for test fit.

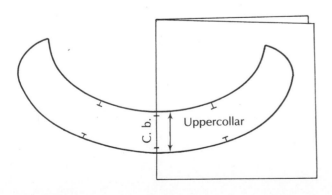

PETER PAN WITH $\frac{1}{2}$-INCH STAND

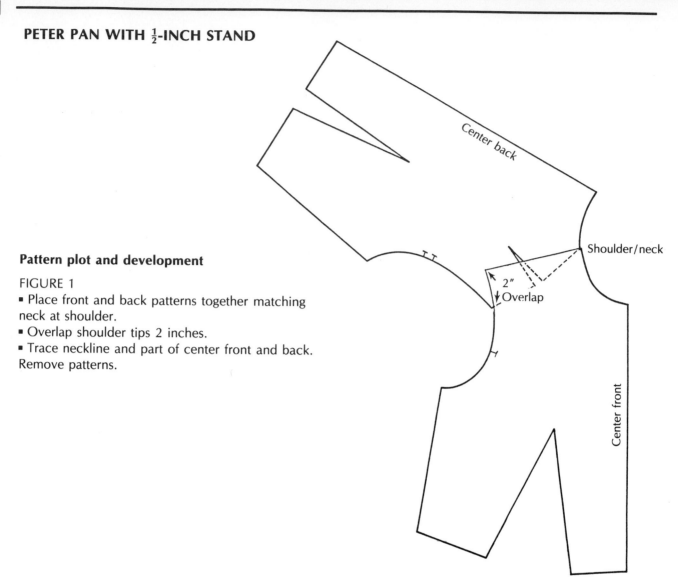

Pattern plot and development

FIGURE 1
- Place front and back patterns together matching neck at shoulder.
- Overlap shoulder tips 2 inches.
- Trace neckline and part of center front and back. Remove patterns.

FIGURE 2 *Collar:*
- Extend center back $\frac{1}{8}$ inch and square a short line.
- Lower center front neck $\frac{1}{4}$ inch (shaded area) and redraw neckline curve from center front to center back, blending point where shoulder and neck intersect. Neckline should be a smooth continuous line.
- Collar width = $3\frac{1}{2}$ inches.
- Draw collar parallel with new neckline, curving to center front as shown.
- True neckline of collar and bodice. (Add to or subtract from center front of collar, if necessary for trueing.)
- Mark notch at center back shoulder and collar edge.
- Cut collar from pattern, discarding shaded area.
- To develop undercollar, see Peter Pan with 1-inch stand (page 261, Figure 4).

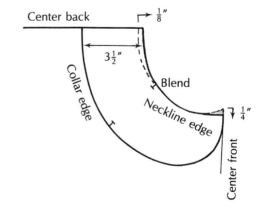

PETER PAN WITH FLAT ROLL

Pattern plot and development

FIGURE 1
- Place front and back patterns together matching neck at shoulder.
- Overlap shoulder tips $\frac{1}{2}$ inch.
- Trace neckline and part of center front and back. Remove patterns.

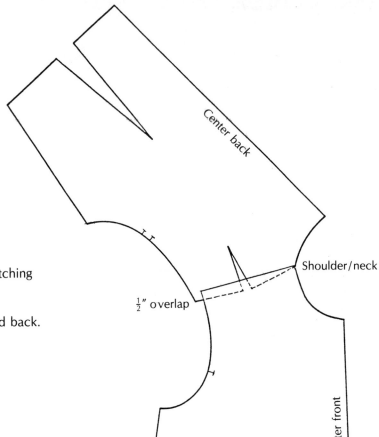

FIGURE 2 *Collar:*
- Extend center back $\frac{1}{8}$ inch and square short line.
- Lower center front $\frac{3}{8}$ inches (shaded area) and redraw neckline from center front to center back, blending point where shoulder and neck intersect. Neckline should be a smooth continuous line.
- Mark collar's width as desired (example: 5 inches).
- Draw collar parallel with new neckline, curving to center front as shown.
- True neckline of collar and bodice. (Add to or subtract from center front of collar, if necessary for trueing.)
- Mark notch at center back, shoulder, and collar edge as shown.
- Cut collar from pattern, discarding shaded area.
- To develop undercollar, see Peter Pan with 1-inch stand (page 261, Figure 4).

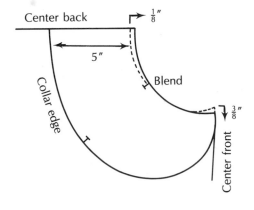

SAILOR COLLAR

The sailor collar was inspired by the sailor's uniform. The collar is developed low in the neckline and follows back neckline with collar edge long and wide. Designs 1, 2 and 3 show design variations based on the sailor collar.

   The sailor collar is based on instructions for a nonconvertible collar. The shape of the outer edge of the collar and the neckline of the bodice are altered.

BASIC SAILOR COLLAR

Design Analysis: Designs 1 and 2

Design 1 features a sailor collar that is long and squared in back, ending at a V-neck cut in front. The tie at front is detachable. Design 2 has an extension for button and buttonholes (see next page for pattern development).

Pattern plot and development

FIGURE 1

- With front and back necks touching, overlap shoulder tips $\frac{1}{2}$ inch.
- Trace center front, center back, and neckline. Remove patterns.
- A–B = Neckline depth (example: 6 inches).
- Draw line from neck to point B.
- C–D = Back collar length (example: 8 inches).
- D–E = Back width, squared from D (example: 7 inches).
- Square a line from E to shoulder, and from shoulder connect with B. Blend shoulder.
- Cut collar from paper and discard shaded area.

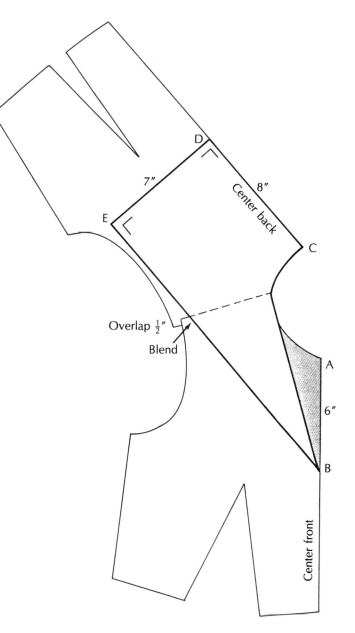

FIGURE 2 *Completed collar:*
- Retrace collar on fold, cut from paper, and unfold.
- Draw grain. (Broken line indicates shape of undercollar.)

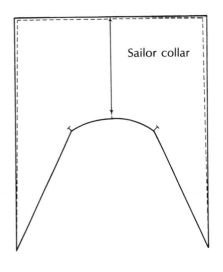

Sailor collar

FIGURE 3
- Establish sailor neckline on bodice. (Use A–B instruction.)
- Cut from paper, discarding shaded area. (Tie not illustrated.)

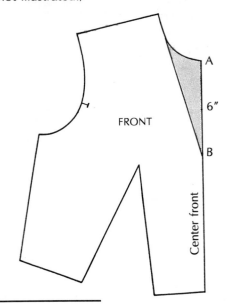

FRONT

A

6"

B

Center front

SAILOR WITH EXTENSION

FIGURE 1 *Collar:*
Repeat instructions for Design 1 with the following exceptions:
- Measure out 1 inch and draw line parallel with center front for extension. Draw line from shoulder through B to extension point C and complete collar as shown.

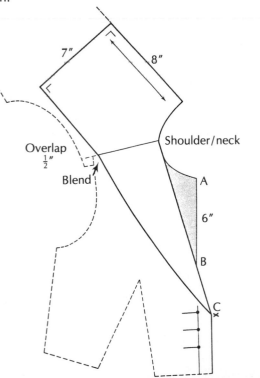

7"

8"

Overlap
$\frac{1}{2}$"

Blend

Shoulder/neck

A

6"

B

C
×

1" extension

FIGURE 2 *Bodice:*
- Establish sailor neckline on bodice using A–B instructions.
- Mark buttonhole placement. (See button and buttonholes, Chapter 14.)

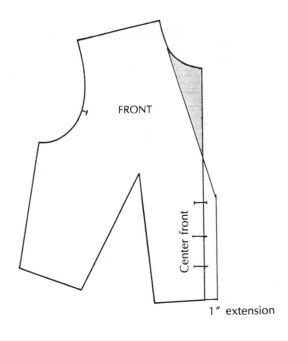

FRONT

Center front

1" extension

SAILOR WITH INSET

Design Analysis: Design 3

Design 3 is a stylized version of the sailor collar. The inset section in front controls the deep neckline. The sailor ends with a tie that is part of the collar.

Repeat instructions for Design 1 with following exceptions. (Broken line indicates original patterns.)

FIGURE 2

■ Trace wedge-shaped inset sections on fold (lined area).

Note: Draw 1-inch extension if one-sided opening for button or snaps is desired.

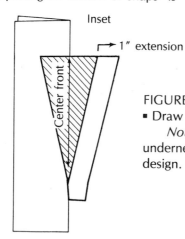

FIGURE 3 *Tie ring:*

■ Draw a 2-inch square.

Note: Tie ring can be attached to garment underneath tie. Pull tie through ring as shown in design.

Tie ring

FIGURE 1 *Collar:*

■ A–B = Depth desired (example: 12 inches).
■ Measure in ½ inch at shoulder/neck. Label C. Blend a curved line from C to center back neck. Draw line from C, touching B, extending line 6 inches beyond B (for tie).
■ D–E = Back length (example: 12 inches).
■ E–F = Back width (example: 7 inches), squared from E.
■ Square from F to shoulder. Continue line to tie level, passing a point 2 inches from B.
■ Draw tie curve as shown. Blend collar at shoulder.

Inset:

■ Square across from center front 6 inches below center front neck.
■ Cut collar from paper, discarding shaded area. Save wedge section for inset (lined area).

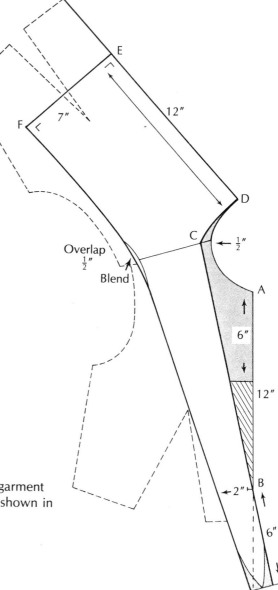

COLLARS WITH DEEP OPEN NECKLINES

Design Analysis: Designs 1 and 2

Designs 1 and 2 both illustrate collars on an open neckline. In Design 1, the collar with a flat roll passes shoulder at neck of the garment. In Design 2, the collar with a $\frac{1}{2}$-inch stand crosses shoulder.

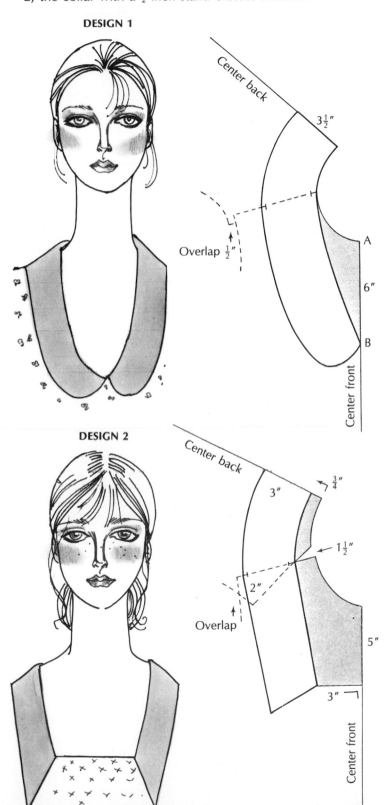

DESIGN 1

DESIGN 2

COLLAR FOR V-NECK

FIGURE 1

- Place front and back patterns together on paper, matching shoulder at neck.
- Overlap shoulder tips $\frac{1}{2}$ inch.
- Plan neckline (example: depth A–B = 6 inches).
- Draw line from B to neck. (Shaded area is discarded.)
- Develop collar: width $3\frac{1}{2}$ inches.
- Draw parallel line with new neck to establish collar.
- Shape curve for front collar. (Collar has a center back seam.)
- Cut collar from bodice and discard shaded area.
- To complete bodice pattern, trace using A–B instruction given for collar.

COLLAR FOR SQUARE NECK

FIGURE 2

- Plan neckline on front and back bodice as shown. Trim neckline (shaded area).
- Place front and back on paper, matching shoulder at new neckline. Overlap shoulder tips 2 inches and trace neckline, center back, and center front. Remove pattern.
- Develop collar: 3 inches wide, parallel to new neck as shown. Collar has a center back seam.
- Cut collar from paper.
- To complete pattern, use front and back pattern with trimmed neckline.

MANDARIN COLLAR

A Mandarin collar (also called military, Nehru, and Chinese collar) is a close-fitting, stand-up collar. It parts in front and varies in width from $1\frac{1}{4}$ to $1\frac{1}{2}$ inches on the average. This foundation is the base for the development of other collars, stands, and combination collar-and-stand variations. This type of collar may meet at the center front, be overlapped and buttoned, or be extended to any point along the neckline. The stand can be developed either close to or away from the neck. It can be curved, blunted, pointed, or extended for a partial folded-over collar effect. The neckline edge of the draft is the basis for all such collars.

BASIC MANDARIN

Measurements needed
Center back neck to shoulder: _____
Center front neck to shoulder: _____
Total: _____

Pattern plot and development

FIGURE 1
▪ Square a line in the center of the paper equal to the following measurements:
A–B = $1\frac{1}{2}$ inches (collar stand).
B–C = Total back and front neck. Label C.
B–D = Center back to shoulder measurement. Mark for shoulder notch.

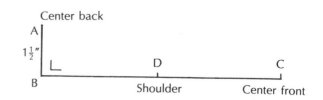

FIGURE 2
- Square up $\frac{1}{2}$ inch from C. Mark and label E.
- Draw a curved line from E to D, completing the neckline edge of collar.

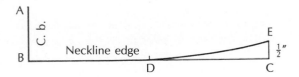

FIGURE 3
- Square a $1\frac{1}{2}$-inch line at right angles to E–D. Label F.
- Draw a line from A to F, parallel with B–D–E line.

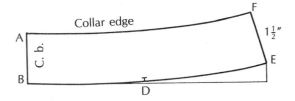

FIGURE 4
- Cut collar from paper.
- To complete pattern, trace on fold. Draw grainline and notch center back.
- Complete the pattern and trace to make a duplicate copy for the collar facing.

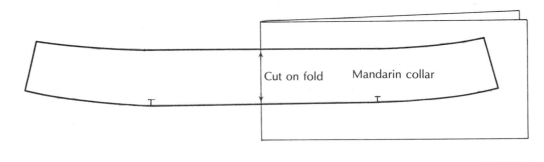

Cut on fold   Mandarin collar

MANDARIN COLLAR VARIATIONS

The following examples show variations of the Mandarin foundation. Trace pattern and modify as illustrated:

Curved neckline (Design 2)
- Draw curves as shown.

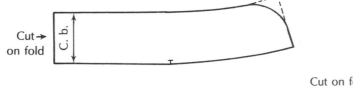

Cut on fold

Wing collar (Design 3)
- Extend line $1\frac{1}{4}$ inches at center front.
- Blend to collar band as shown.

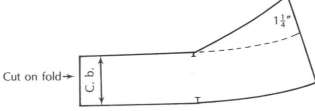

Cut on fold

COLLAR WITH STAND

Design Analysis
A collar is attached to the top edge of a Mandarin having an extension for button and buttonhole. (Also referred to as a shirt collar.)
To develop the Mandarin foundation see page 268.

Pattern plot and development

FIGURE 1
- Trace Mandarin stand.
- Square out 1-inch extension from A and B. Connect.
- Draw curved line (shaded area is discarded).
- Mark buttonhole placement as shown.

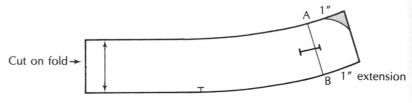

FIGURE 2
- Trace Mandarin stand. (Broken line indicates part of Mandarin not needed for collar.)
- Draw collar, using measurements given.
- Notch midpoint of upper edge of collar.

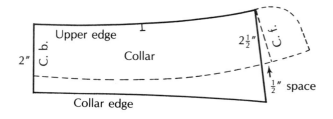

FIGURE 3
- Draw slash lines.
- Cut from paper.

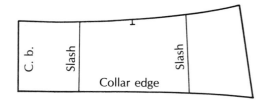

FIGURE 4
- Cut slash lines to, not through, collar's upper edge.
- Place center back on fold. Spread sections $\frac{1}{8}$ inch. Trace. (Spreading allows collar to lie on garment without riding upward at center back.)
- Cut from paper. For undercollar, trace and trim. (Refer to basic shirt collar instructions page 257, Figure 5 or 6.)

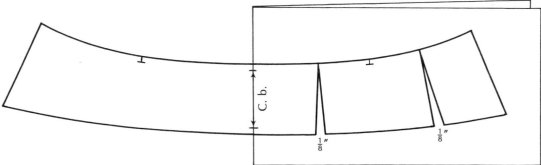

ALL-IN-ONE COLLAR AND STAND

FIGURE 1

- Trace Mandarin collar with extension. (See page 270, Figure 1.)
- Extend a line up from center front and center back equal to collar width plus $\frac{1}{4}$ inch.
- Draw a line parallel with bottom edge of Mandarin. Extend $1\frac{1}{4}$ inch beyond center front line to form point of collar. Connect with center front of stand.
- Draw slash lines.

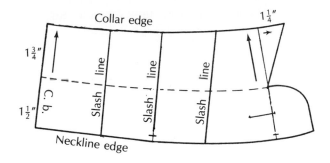

FIGURE 2

- Cut slash lines to, not through, neckline edge.
- Place center back on fold. Spread as shown (prevents collar from riding upward at center back).
- Trace. Discard pattern. Blend collar edge.

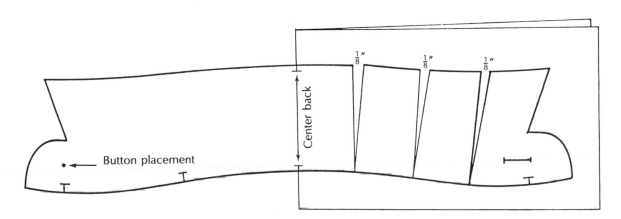

ROLL COLLARS

Bias-fold collar bands can be developed for any neckline (basic or cut-out). The finished length, however, should be slightly shorter than the area covered to compensate for the stretch of the bias fabric. The collar width may be planned for either a folded bias band or a band folded back on itself.

Both will be illustrated below. Cut the band equal to front and back neck measurement. Stretch collar slightly when stitching it to the neck of the garment. Trim the overhang and reduce the pattern by the same amount, or use the formula given in the instructions that follow.

TURTLE NECK

Design Analysis: Design 1

Design 1 has a folded bias band encircling the neck with an opening at the center back. The turtle neck can also be developed to fold back on itself.

Pattern plot and development

FIGURES 1 and 2   *Neckline modification:*
- Trace pattern and adjust neck as follows.
- Measure up $\frac{1}{4}$ inch at center front. Mark. Measure in $\frac{1}{8}$ inch at shoulder-neck of front and back patterns. Mark and label as shown.
- Blend new neckline as shown.
- Measure A–B, less $\frac{1}{4}$ inch (front neck). Record _____.
- Measure B–C, less $\frac{1}{4}$ inch (back neck). Record _____. (This is to offset stretch. More may be required.)

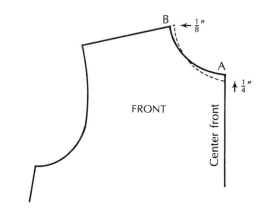

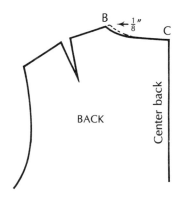

FIGURE 3 *Turtle band:*
- Fold paper.
- Square a line from fold to equal front and back measurement (A, B, C). Mark B for notch placement at shoulder.
- Draw parallel lines, spaced 3 inches apart for single fold (1½-inches finished width), or 6½ inches apart for double fold (3¼-inches finished width). (Indicated by broken line.)
- Connect ends.
- Draw bias grain and complete pattern for test fit.

FIGURE 4
- The center back can be closed with loops and buttons.

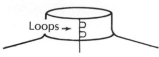

FIGURE 5
- The center back can also be left open when folded back on itself.

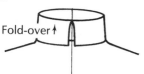

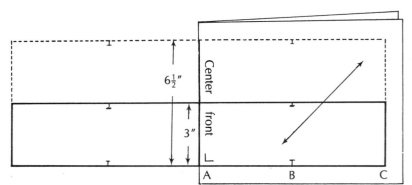

ROLL COLLAR WITH CUTAWAY NECK

FIGURE 1
- Plan new neckline by placing shoulderlines together, matching at neck. Use measurements given.
- Cut out new front and back necklines. Discard shaded area.

Design Analysis: Design 2
Design 2 has a bias band that encircles a cutaway shoulderline.

FIGURE 2 *Band:*
- Use instructions for the turtle neck as a guide for developing band using full front and back neckline measurements.

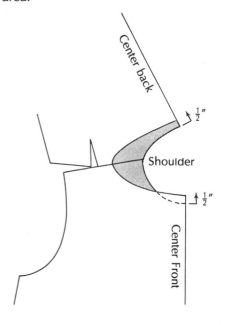

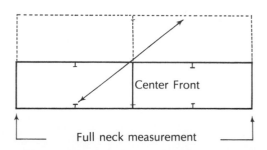

(Continued on next page)

COLLAR DESIGN VARIATIONS

The following collar designs are for practice. Use information previously given as a guide for pattern development.

12

SKIRTS

Introduction 276
Skirt lengths 276
The four major skirt silhouettes 277
Flexibility of skirt darts 278
LOW-WAISTED AND HIGH-WAISTED SKIRTS 279
Low-waisted skirt 279
High-waisted skirt 280
BASIC WAISTBAND 281
FLARED SKIRTS AND A-LINE SILHOUETTES 282
A-line skirt 282
Flared skirt based on basic pattern 284

One-dart skirt foundation 286
Flared skirt based on one-dart pattern 287
Added flare skirt 288
Clinging hipline with flare—the slinky 290
SKIRTS WITH GATHERED WAISTLINES 292
Gathered dirndl skirt 292
Flared skirt with gathered waist 293
GORED SKIRTS 294
4-gore flared skirt 294
6-gore flared skirt 296
8-gore flared skirt 299
10-gore skirt with pleats 300
12-gore foundation panel 303
12-gore graduated flare 304
Skirt variations using the 12-gore panel 306
PEGGED SKIRT SILHOUETTE 307
Pegged skirt with gathers 307
Pegged skirt with pleats 308
DRAPED SKIRT WITH A CASCADE WRAP 309
SKIRTS WITH YOKES 310
Yoke with gathered skirt 310
Diagonal yoke with flared skirt 312
TIERS 314
Terms 314
Attached tiers 314
Separated tiers 316
Peplums 319
PLEATS 320
Types of pleats 320
Pleat terminology 321
Kick pleats 321
All-around pleated skirt 323
Inverted box-pleated skirt 324
GODETS 327
Basic godet 327
Godet variations 328
WRAP SKIRT 330
Wrap skirt with side seam 330
All-in-one wrap skirt 331
CIRCLE/CASCADE RADIUS CHART 332
Terminology 332
Interpreting the chart 334
Use of the chart 335
The circle measuring tool 336
CIRCULAR SKIRTS 337
Full-circle skirt 338
Three-quarter-circle skirt 340
Half-circle skirt 342
Quarter-circle skirt 343
Two circles at waist 344
Gathered circular skirt 344
SKIRTS WITH UNEVEN HEMLINES 345
Circular skirt with handkerchief ends 345
Circular skirt with graduated-length hemline 346
SKIRT DESIGN VARIATIONS 348

INTRODUCTION

A skirt is a garment that covers the figure below the waist at varying lengths. The skirt silhouette (the outer lines, without regard to creative detailing within the skirt frame) is one of the major focal points used by designers who wish to change the look and direction of fashion. The silhouette may be radically altered by moving the skirt away from or closer to the figure, or by raising or lowering the hemline and/or waistline. For instruction on completing the pattern, see Chapter 1, pages 20–27.

SKIRT LENGTHS

Micromini

Mini
(mid-thigh)

Knee-length

Midi
(mid-calf)

Ballerina

Ankle-length

Floor-length

THE FOUR MAJOR SKIRT SILHOUETTES

The four major skirt silhouettes illustrated are the foundations used for developing all other skirt variations. The basic skirt, which is one of the four major silhouettes, is used to develop the A-Shape, Pegged, and Bell foundation patterns. It is the amount of deviation from the basic skirt that determines the new silhouette. Skirts are described in the following three areas:

- *The sweep:* The width of the skirt at hemline.
- *Movement:* The fullness of the skirt silhouette.
- *The break point:* The point from which the skirt breaks away from the body into fluid movement.

Straight or rectangular shape

The skirt hangs straight from hipline to hemline.

A-shape or triangular

The skirt hangs away from the hip, flaring out at the hemline, increasing the hemline sweep. (Circular and flared shapes are included in this category.)

Pegged or inverted triangle

The skirt falls inward from hip level to hemline. It may have increased waist and hip fullness or may be tapered from the hip to the hem.

Bell-shape

The skirt clings to the figure's curves at, above, or below the hip and breaks into fluid movement along the hemline.

Creative details, such as peplums, flounces, ruffles, and so on can be added onto the basic silhouettes.

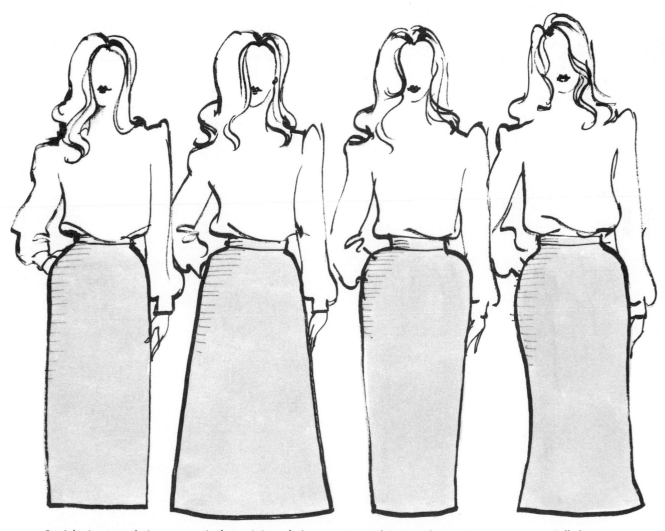

Straight (rectangular)   A-shape (triangular)   Pegged (inverted triangle)   Bell shape

FLEXIBILITY OF SKIRT DARTS

The following three groups of designs illustrate the flexibility of the waist dart when the major patternmaking principles are applied. (The second and third groups also show completed pattern shapes.) These are provided as a visual guide only, to encourage further exploration as many other design variations are possible.

Pleats

Tuck darts

Gathers

Curved darts

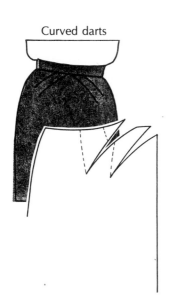

Radiating darts

Asymetric darts

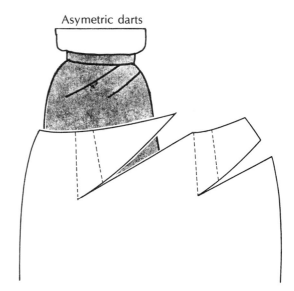

Waist darts–Added fullness

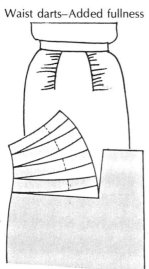

Side darts–Added fullness

Stylized darts–Added fullness

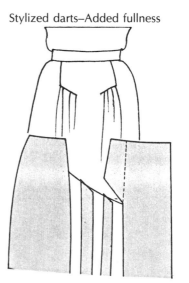

LOW-WAISTED AND HIGH-WAISTED SKIRTS

The waistline of any skirt can be changed so that it rises above or falls below the natural waistline, as illustrated by the low-waisted and high-waisted skirt developed from the basic skirt foundation.

LOW-WAISTED SKIRT

Design Analysis
The low-waisted skirt hugs the hipline below the waistline. The waistline can be lowered to any depth desired.

Pattern plot and development

FIGURE 1
- Trace front and back skirt patterns together at side for no seams, or separated for side seams (illustrated only to hip level).
- Measure down from waist desired amount (example: 3 inches), and draw line parallel to waist.
- *Front:* Remove $\frac{1}{4}$ inch at side seam for closer fit.
- *Back:* Remove leftover dart excess at side waist (shaded area).
- Cut patterns from paper, discarding shaded area.

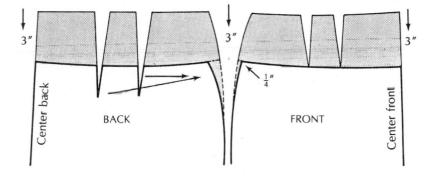

FIGURES 2 and 3 *Facing:*
- Trace the upper section of front and back skirt to $2\frac{1}{2}$ inches below new waist. (Center front should be cut on the fold.)
- Draw grain, notch, and complete for test fit.

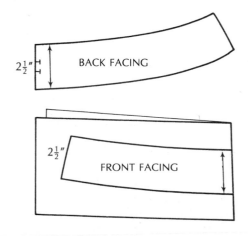

HIGH-WAISTED SKIRT

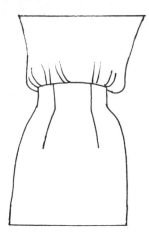

Design Analysis
To modify the waistline on any skirt so that it extends above the natural waistline, the darts on both the front and back are combined into a single dart which is then extended to the new waistline. The waistline can be extended any desired amount.

Pattern plot and development

FIGURE 1 *Extending waist:*
• Trace front and back skirt, crossmarking center line, dart points, and side waist. (Skirt is illustrated from waist to hip.) Remove pattern.
• Extend center lines upward $2\frac{1}{2}$ inches. Label A.
• Flip pattern over, aligning center lines and touching side seams. Draw 2 inches of pattern's side seam. Label B as shown. Remove pattern. (Broken lines indicate untraced pattern.)
• Draw new waistline connecting points A with B as shown. Blend side seams.
• Draw line in between dart legs at dart point level of skirt, keeping lines parallel with centerlines.

FIGURE 2 *Dart development:*
• Measure out from *each side* of line at high waist and at waistline as follows:
Back—$\frac{3}{4}$ inches. Mark. Front—$\frac{3}{8}$ inches. Mark.
• Connect lines to form waist darts.

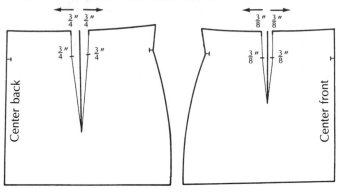

FIGURE 3
• To complete pattern for test fit, punch and circle darts as shown.

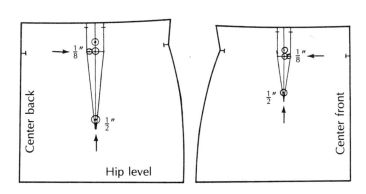

FIGURE 4 and 5 *Facings:*
• Trace top of skirt to 1 inch below waist, close darts, blend notch, add 1-inch extension in back. Cut front on fold.

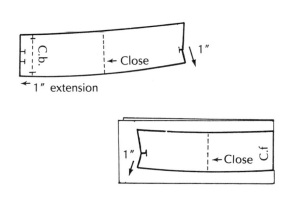

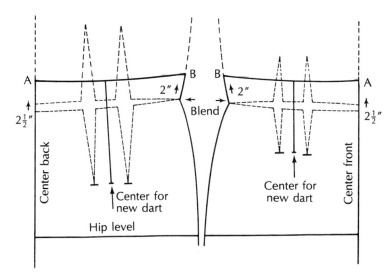

BASIC WAISTBAND

The waistline of a skirt (or pant) may be finished with an attached waistband, faced without a band, or with belting. An attached waistband should be larger than the true waistline measurement (without ease), to compensate for fabric bulk and thickness of the darts and seam allowances that are stitched into the band. The amount of ease allowance varies. A general average is $\frac{1}{2}$ inch. The waistline of the skirt has ease allowance that is greater than the waistband, with the difference eased into the waistband. Ease helps to eliminate possible abdominal stress and a rolling of the skirt just below the band. This difference varies with the amount of ease added to the original waistline of the skirt.

The extension (added to the waistband) is for a button (or buttonhole) and it can be placed on either end or on both ends of the band. Its shape can be blunted, pointed, or curved, and can extend 1 inch or more.

Example: 24-inch waist (without ease).
- Waistband length = 24 plus $\frac{1}{2}$ inch = $24\frac{1}{2}$ inches.
- Add 1-inch extension = $25\frac{1}{2}$ inches.
- Waistband width = $2\frac{1}{2}$ inches before folding.
- Finished width = $1\frac{1}{4}$ inches.

Pattern plot and development

> **Measurements needed**
> - (2) Waist _____
> - (19) Front waist arc _____

A–B = Finished width, squared from fold 1 inch in from paper's edge.
B–C = Waistband length, squared from B.
C–D = 1-inch extension (for button or buttonhole), squared to fold line.
B–E = One-half of B–C (location for center front).
- Locate side seam notches out from each side of E, using front waist arc measurement plus $\frac{1}{8}$ inch. Crossmark. (Indicated by broken lines.)

FIGURE 1
- Fold paper lengthwise as shown.
- Develop as follows using measurements above:

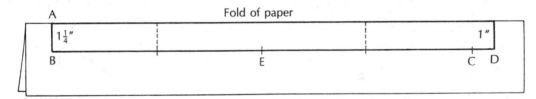

FIGURE 2
- Add $\frac{1}{2}$-inch seam allowance. Locate buttonhole and button placement (see Chapter 14). Cut from paper.

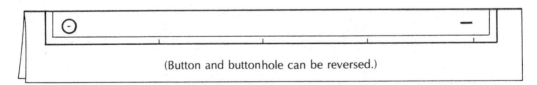

(Button and buttonhole can be reversed.)

FIGURE 3
- Completed waistband.
- Draw grainline for straight or crosswise grain.

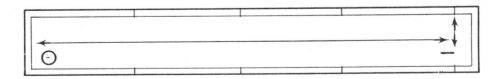

FLARED SKIRTS AND A-LINE SILHOUETTES

This series illustrates basic flared skirt foundations and other flared skirt variations developed from them. The flared silhouette is achieved by transferring part or all of the dart's excess to the hemline (Principle #1, Dart Manipulation). An additional amount is added to the sides of the pattern for an A-shaped flared effect (Principle #2, Added Fullness).

A-LINE SKIRT

Design Analysis: Design 1

The A-line silhouette (Design 1) is one in which the hemline measures greater than the hipline circumference and is achieved by transferring part of the dart's excess to the hemline and adding width to the side seam. This results in a more rounded effect along the hemline and provides additional stride room.

Pattern plot and development

FIGURES 1 and 2
- Trace front and back basic skirt.
- Draw slash lines from dart points (nearest side seams) to hemline, parallel with center lines.
- Label as shown.
- Cut from paper.
- Cut to, not through, dart points.
- Place on paper.

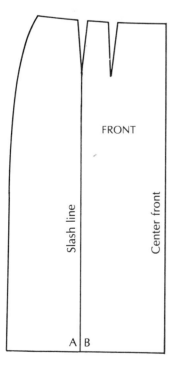

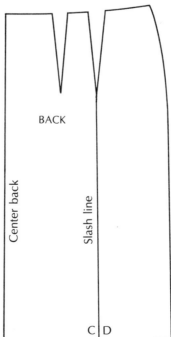

FRONT

BACK

Slash line

Center front

Center back

Slash line

A B

C D

FIGURE 3 *Front:*
- Close dart and trace pattern.
- Label openings at hem A and B.

A-line silhouette:
- Label side seam at hem X.
- X–Y = one-half of A–B space. Mark.
- Draw a line from Y to the outermost part of hipline.
- Where lines intersect, label Z.
- Z–Y = Z–X length. Square in from Y just past X.
- Draw blending line along hem. (Use these instructions when adding to the side seam of any skirt for A-shape.)

FIGURE 4 *Back:*
- Transfer just enough excess from waist dart to hemline so that space C–D equals A–B space of front skirt. The remaining dart excess is taken up by the next dart—divide this amount equally on each side of dart leg.
- Draw new dart legs to dart point (broken lines = original dart).
- Trace, add to side seam using X, Y, Z instructions (Figure 3).
- Draw grainline, cut from paper, and complete for test fit.

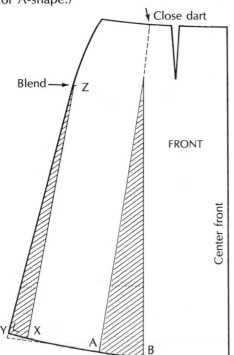

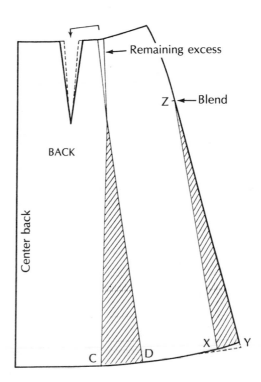

FIGURE 5
- Completed pattern shown with seam allowance.

  Note: For seamed front add 1 inch. Use seamless pattern as a foundation pattern and seams when used as a skirt design.

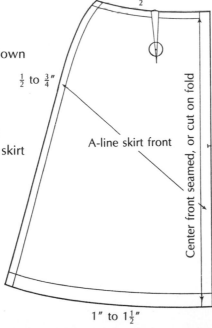

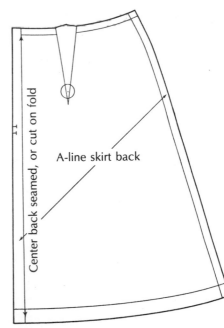

FLARED SKIRT BASED ON BASIC PATTERN

Design Analysis: Design 2

A flared skirt has more sweep along its hemline than does the basic A-line skirt because all of the dart excess has been transferred to the hemline as flare. The dart intake of the back skirt is greater than the front, causing the hemline sweep from front to back to differ. If this difference is not adjusted, the sides will hang unequally and the back will stretch more than the front due to a greater bias at the side seam. The longer length will be eased in by the operator. This will cause the seamline to twist and curl. To correct this problem, two methods are given for balancing the sides of the skirt.

For practice, it is recommended that the patternmaker try one by the slash-spread technique, using the basic pattern, and the other by pivotal-transfer, using the one-dart skirt foundation.

Pattern plot and development

FIGURES 1 and 2
- Trace front and back skirts.
- Draw lines from dart points to hemlines parallel with center lines.

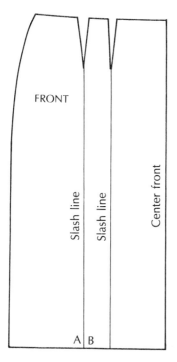

FRONT

Slash line   Slash line   Center front

A | B

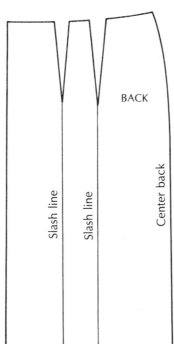

BACK

Slash line   Slash line   Center back

FIGURES 3 and 4
- Cut slash lines to, not through, dart points.
- Close darts. Tape.
- Trace patterns.
- Establish front and back A-shape at side, using

one-half of A–B space and instructions given for basic A-line skirt for blending hemline (see page 283, Figure 3).
- Blend across hemline as shown.
- Cut out back only.

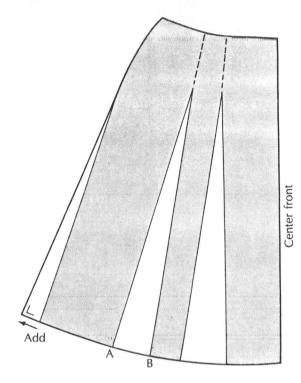

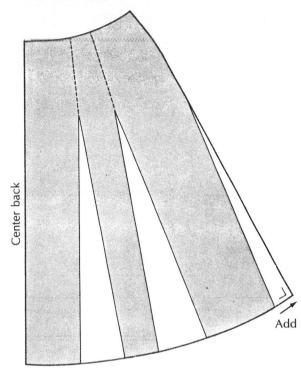

FIGURE 5   *Balancing the side seam:*
- Place back on top of front pattern, matching center lines.
- Measure and divide the difference between front and back skirt at the side hems.
- Add one-half this amount to the front and remove one-half from the back (lined section). Remove pattern.
- Blend side seams to hipline.
- Cut front skirt from paper. Draw grain and complete for test fit.

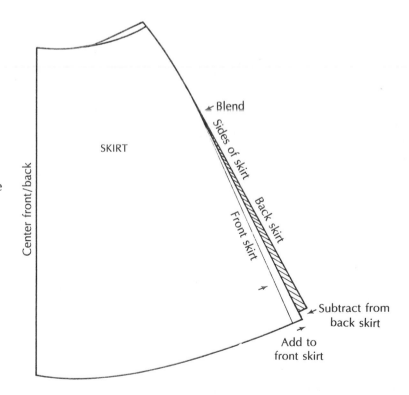

ONE-DART SKIRT FOUNDATION

A one-dart skirt pattern has darts of equal length and intake in front and back. This pattern may be used as the base for any flared skirt with a hemline sweep that is equal on the front and back. To develop the one-dart pattern, add the dart intake of the front and back patterns together. Record _____. Follow the example as a guide using your measurement instead of those given.

Example: Front dart intake: 1 inch

$$+$$

Back dart intake: <u>2 inches</u>

Total   3 inches

Divide total (3 inches) in half ($1\frac{1}{2}$ inches). Redraw darts on front and back using $1\frac{1}{2}$-inch intake for each dart as shown.

FIGURES 1 and 2

- Trace front and back patterns, disregarding dart legs (broken lines). Mark point in between darts at waist. Draw guidelines from marks to hemline, parallel with center lines.
- Measure down $4\frac{1}{2}$ inches from front and back waist on guideline and crossmark for dart point.
- Measure out $\frac{3}{4}$ inch from each side of guideline at waist. Mark and connect with dart point.
- Measure down on guideline from dart point, making a series of four marks spaced $1\frac{1}{2}$ inches apart. (Marks represent the future pivotal points used for developing clinging-type skirts—the slinky.)

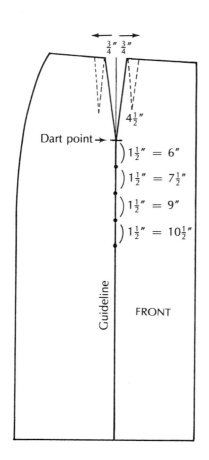

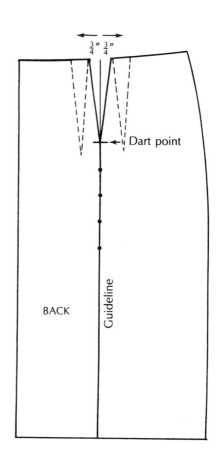

FLARED SKIRT BASED ON ONE-DART PATTERN

Pattern plot and development

FIGURE 1

- Trace front one-dart skirt pattern from A to C (shaded area).
- Crossmark at A and C on paper.

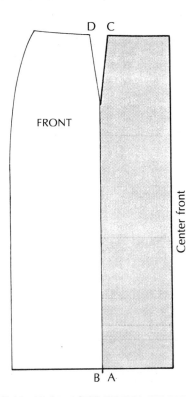

FIGURE 2

- With pushpin at dart point, bring dart leg D to C.
- Trace from D to B. Crossmark (shaded area). Remove pattern.

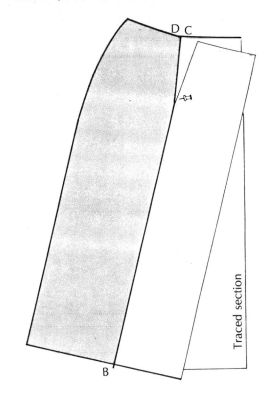

FIGURE 3

- Add to side seam using one-half of A–B space and follow A-line instructions for blending hemline (page 283, Figure 3). Mark grainline as shown. (Choice of grainline affects the hang of flared skirt: see page 338, Figure 1.)
- Repeat instructions to develop the back.

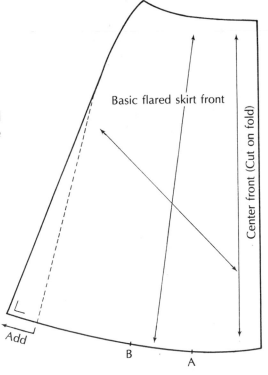

ADDED FLARE SKIRT

The hemline sweep of any skirt may be increased by adding additional flare within the pattern's frame and to the side seams for balance. This results in a skirt with more circularity than the basic flared skirt. Since skirts with great sweeping hemlines are often wider than the fabric, a separate pattern should be made for the section that extends beyond the fabric (Figure 3). Skirts with added flare may be developed from either the basic one-dart or two-dart skirt or from the circle chart (page 334). One-dart pattern is illustrated.

DESIGN 3

FIGURE 1
- Trace skirt pattern.
- Draw slash lines. Label A and B as shown.

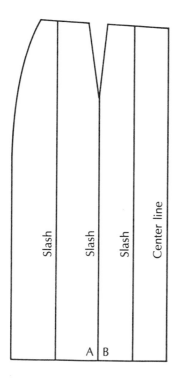

FIGURE 2   (opposite)
- Cut slash lines to, not through, waistline. Cut through dart point for spreading (as shown) if more flare is desired.
- Place on paper and spread each section 5 inches, or as desired.
- Trace outline and discard pattern.
- Add to side seams and blend hemline, using A-line skirt instructions as a guide (see page 283, Figure 3).
- For side seam, draw a straight line from hemline to waistline. (Broken line indicates the hipline curve no longer needed when sufficient fullness is added to skirt.)
- Draw grainline.
- Repeat instructions for skirt back.
- Complete pattern for test fit. Allow skirt to hang overnight before marking hemline of the skirt.

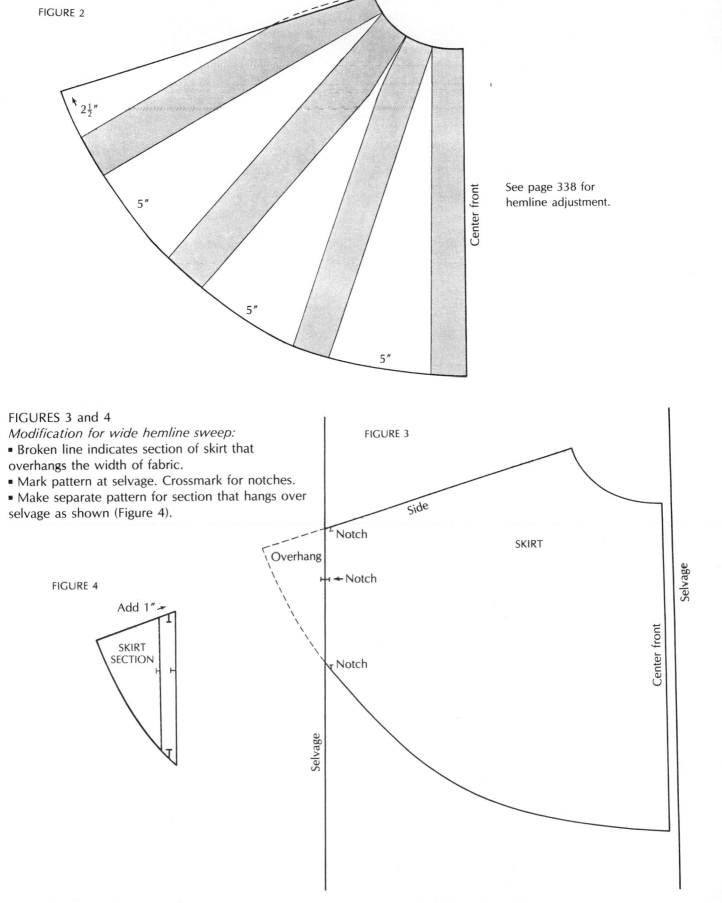

FIGURE 2

$2\frac{1}{2}''$

5"

5"

5"

5"

Center front

See page 338 for
hemline adjustment.

FIGURES 3 and 4
Modification for wide hemline sweep:
▪ Broken line indicates section of skirt that
overhangs the width of fabric.
▪ Mark pattern at selvage. Crossmark for notches.
▪ Make separate pattern for section that hangs over
selvage as shown (Figure 4).

FIGURE 3

Side

Notch

Overhang

Notch

Notch

SKIRT

Selvage

Center front

Selvage

FIGURE 4

Add 1"

SKIRT
SECTION

CLINGING HIPLINE WITH FLARE—THE SLINKY

To develop skirts that cling to the hipline, lower the pivotal point before closing out the darts. This will result in a loss of measurement around the hip circumference area, tightening the skirt slightly. This causes the skirt to cling to the hips and flare out from a point above, at, or below the hipline depending on the location of the pivotal point. Fabrics used for clinging skirts should be loosely woven, be cut on the bias, or be knit to allow the skirt to mold over the hipline.

DESIGN 4   DESIGN 5   DESIGN 6

Design Analysis

Designs 4, 5, and 6 show flared skirts using different pivotal points.
Each skirt clings to the hipline at varying locations.

FIGURE 1

▪ The illustration shows that when the pivotal point is lowered (B, C, and D), the hemline sweep is less flared (B', C', and D'). Also, the lower the pivotal point, the greater the cling around hipline.

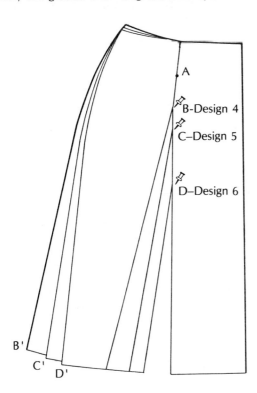

FIGURE 2

▪ The example shows pattern with dart closed at D point.

▪ Flare may be increased for a clinging skirt by adding approximately 1 inch to the side waistline and blending to hipline. The waist dart is increased by an equal amount (so the waistline measurement remains the same). The increased dart when transferred to hemline provides more flare.

▪ Add flare to side seam and at center front using one-half the flare of A–B space.

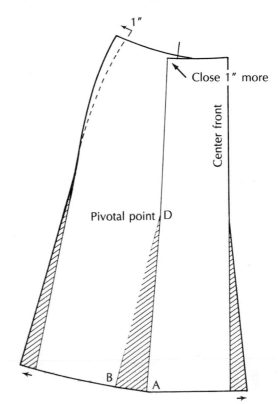

FIGURE 3

▪ Completed pattern for Design 6. Draw bias grainline. Repeat for back.

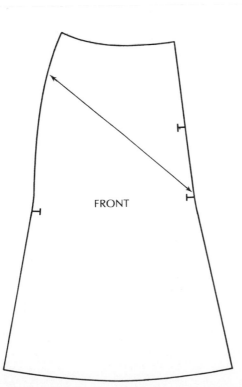

FRONT

SKIRTS WITH GATHERED WAISTLINES

Skirts featuring waistline gathers require an increase of the pattern's width within the pattern frame and at the side seams (Principle #2, Added Fullness). The amount of increase depends on the specific design features and the thickness of the fabric. Bulky fabrics limit the amount of gathering that can be stitched into the waistline, whereas lightweight fabrics can tolerate greater fullness.

Gathered skirts can be developed from either a flared skirt (creating an A-line silhouette) or a straight-line skirt (creating the dirndl or rectangular silhouette.) For flared skirts with hemlines exceeding the width of the fabric, a separate pattern section is made for that part of the skirt (page 289, Figure 4).

GATHERED DIRNDL SKIRT

Design Analysis: Design 1

The dirndl skirt for Design 1 is developed from a rectangular piece of goods that is gathered into the waistband. The amount of fullness depends upon the fabric width or the look desired. (Generally, two widths are used for 35-inch fabric, and one-and-a-half widths for 45-inch fabric, giving the skirt a 72-inch or $67\frac{1}{2}$-inch hemline sweep.)

Pattern plot and development

FIGURE 1
- Draw a vertical line on paper equal to desired length plus 3 inches (hem and seam allowance). *Example:* Finished length 26 inches plus 3 inches ($\frac{1}{2}$ inch at waist and $2\frac{1}{2}$ inches at hem); total 29 inches.
- Square a line out from the top and bottom of the vertical line each end equal to width of the fabric. Connect lines to complete the panel.
- Cut panel twice for 36-inch fabric, and $1\frac{1}{2}$ times for 45-inch fabric (not illustrated). Add more panels if desired.
- Lower center back panel $\frac{1}{2}$ inch (or use personal measurement for back hip depth). Blend to sides (shaded area).
- Notch center of panel's width for center front and center back. Notch hem and seams.
- Skirt can have either a side opening for entry or split panel at center back for seam and zipper (broken line).

Split here Front panel

Shape of back waistline

Back panel

Center back

FLARED SKIRT WITH GATHERED WAIST

Pattern plot and development

FIGURE 1
- Use the one-dart pattern to develop skirt. Follow illustration as a guide and instructions given on page 288. Modify skirt as follows:

Design Analysis: Design 2
The skirt for Design 2 has a gathered A-line silhouette achieved by adding uneven fullness within the pattern's frame and at the side.

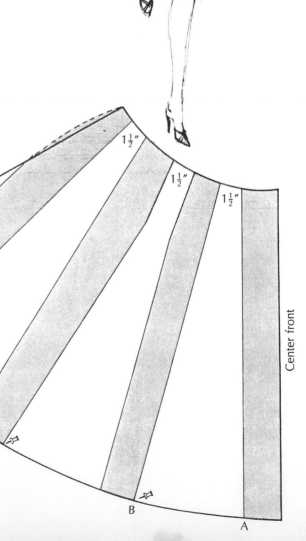

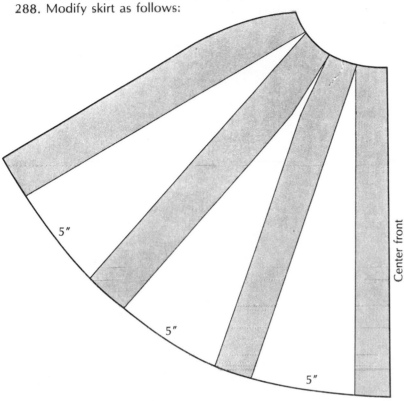

5″

5″

5″

Center front

FIGURE 2   *To add gathers:*
- Place pushpins in corners of hemline sections as shown.
- Separate and spread waistline 1½ inches or as desired.
- Trace outline and discard pattern. Measure out at side one-half of A–B space. Mark and draw a straight line from hem mark to side waist.

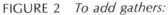

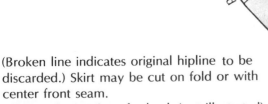

(Broken line indicates original hipline to be discarded.) Skirt may be cut on fold or with center front seam.
- Repeat instructions for back (not illustrated).
- Add 1-inch hem. Draw grainline and complete for test fit.

1½″

1½″

1½″

2½″

Add

Center front

B

A

GORED SKIRTS

A gore is a skirt panel that tapers toward the waistline. A gored skirt contains any number of gores—from 4 to 12 or more—equally spaced or in clusters, depending on the look desired. The gore may hang straight from hip level, or be angled, flared, or pleated, to break away at any point along the seamline of the gore. This results in a wide variety of silhouettes from the gored pattern. It is important to remember that each joining section (gore) must be notched appropriately to assure proper placement when stitched. Designs 1 through 8 are examples of gore variations.

4-GORE FLARED SKIRT

Design Analysis: Design 1

The basic 4-gore skirt of Design 1 is developed from the basic A-line skirt, and has an attached waistband. The belt shown is a separate belt and not part of the design.

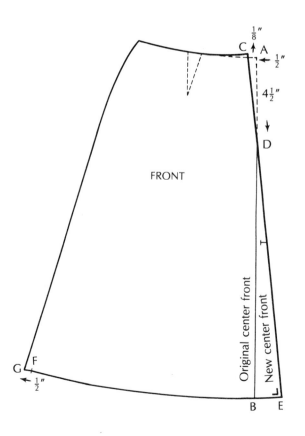

Pattern plot and development

FIGURE 1 *Front gore:*

- Trace basic A-line skirt (see page 282).

A–C $= \frac{1}{2}$ inch (or amount equal to one dart), and squared up $\frac{1}{8}$ inch.

A–D $= 4\frac{1}{2}$ inches.

Connect C to D to hemline equal to A–B measurement. Label hem E.
Blend C with waistline, and E with hemline.

F–G $= \frac{1}{2}$ inch. Draw line to outermost part of hipline curve. Blend with hemline.

FIGURE 2 *Back gore:*

H–I = $\frac{3}{4}$ inches (or one-half of one dart's excess), and squared up $\frac{1}{8}$ inch.

J–K = B–E of front skirt. Connect to point I. Blend with hemline.

L–M = $\frac{1}{2}$ inch. Connect with hip and blend hemline.

- Dart modification: Locate dart center $4\frac{1}{2}$ inches down from waist (new dart point).
- Measure in $\frac{3}{8}$ inch from each dart leg and connect to dart point. Blend with waistline.

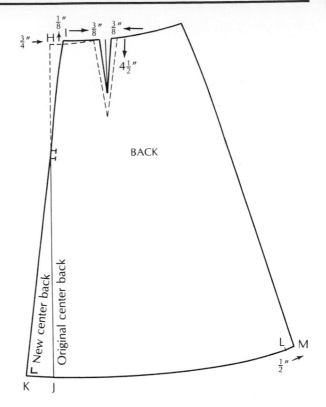

FIGURES 3 and 4

- Cut patterns from paper and draw straight, bias, and center grainlines (options for future reference).
- Complete pattern for test fit.

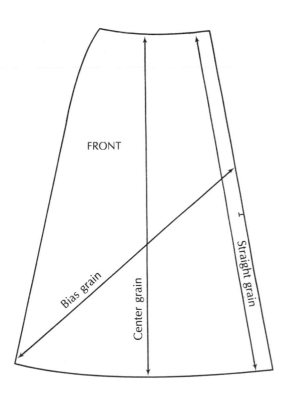

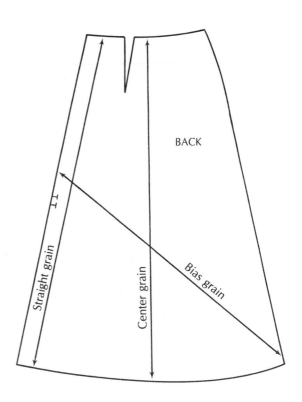

6-GORE FLARED SKIRT

To plot gore panels, draw gore guidelines on the working pattern, add flare to each side of the goreline, and adjust the hemline. This results in an overlapping of the flared section and the hemline. A piece of paper is placed under the plotted working pattern and each panel is traced separately.

Design Analysis: Design 2

The gore design of Design 2 has a full panel across the front and back and two panels joining each side for a total of six gores. The gore skirt is based on the basic front and back skirt.

Pattern plot and development

FIGURE 1 *Front gore:*
- Trace front basic skirt.
- Draw gore line from dart leg at waist to hem, parallel with center front. Label A–B. Crossmark a point level with dart point.

FIGURE 2 *Back gore:*
- Trace back basic skirt.
- C–D = A–B measurement on skirt front.
- Draw line from D to hem, parallel with center back. (Line may pass through open dart.)
- Crossmark at a point level with dart points.

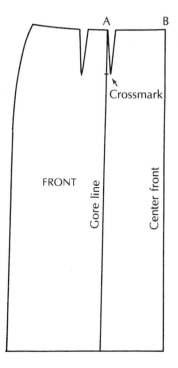

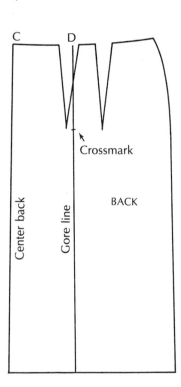

Dart modification:
- Darts will be absorbed through goreline.
- Standard dart intake is illustrated:
Two $\frac{1}{2}$-inch darts on front.
Two 1-inch darts on back.
Personal fit: Use your measurements.
Front dart:

FIGURE 3
- Measure dart intake out from each side of goreline (example: $\frac{1}{2}$ inch each side). Draw curve to crossmark (dart point).

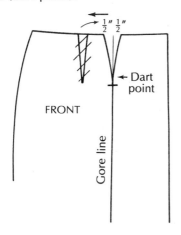

FIGURE 4 *Back:*
- Mark dart excess equally out from each side of goreline ($\frac{5}{8}$ inch each side), leaving $\frac{3}{4}$ inch for a small dart.
- Draw a curved line from marks to crossmark (dart point).
Small dart:
- Measure in $\frac{3}{8}$ inch on each side of original dart leg. Mark. (This dart to take up all remaining excess.)
- Measure up 1 inch from original dart point and connect dart legs to new dart point. Blend waist.

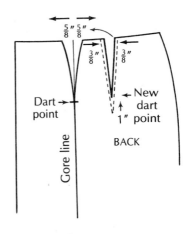

FIGURES 5 and 6
- Measure out from each side of goreline at hem to develop flare lines:
    Front—1$\frac{1}{2}$ inches. Mark.
    Back—2 inches (for better symmetry). Mark.
- Draw flare lines from each mark to dart point.

- Add 1$\frac{1}{2}$ inches to side seam at hem of front and back skirt for A-line (see page 283). Mark and draw line to outer hipline curve. Blend hemline.
- Notch joining sections as shown. (Lines with arrows indicate the width of each panel.)

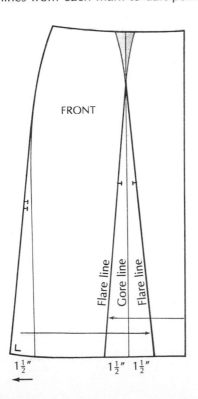

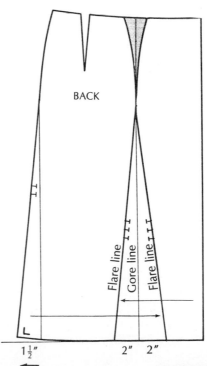

(Continued on next page)

FIGURES 7, 8, 9, and 10 *Separate gore panels:* To separate gore panels from the plotted pattern, slip pattern paper underneath the draft each time a section is traced. The paper is removed and the perforated marks are pencilled in. The side gore panels (Figures 7 and 9) have grainlines drawn through the centers of each panel. The front and back panels (Figures 8 and 10) are cut on the fold with grainlines drawn at, or parallel to, the center lines.

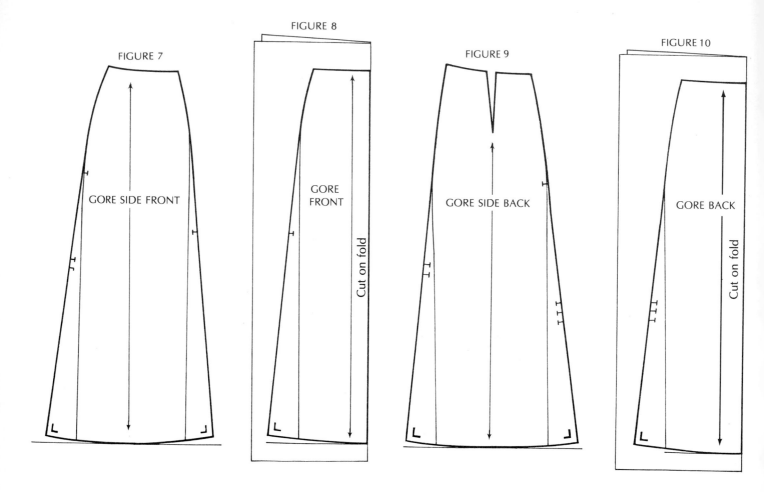

8-GORE FLARED SKIRT

Design Analysis: Design 3
Design 3 features an 8-gore skirt with 4 flared gores in front and back.

Pattern plot and development
Use the instructions for the 6-gore skirt to develop the 8-gore version, with the following variation. The center front and center back are seamed and notched, and modified as follows:

FIGURE 1 *Front gore:*
- Measure in $\frac{1}{2}$ inch from center front waist. Label A.
- Measure out $\frac{1}{2}$ inch at side of gore at waist. Label B.
- Measure out $1\frac{1}{2}$ inches at center front hem. Label C. Draw line from A to C (to equal original center front length).
- Square in from C to blend with hem. This establishes new center front line.
- Draw curved line from B, blending with goreline as shown.
- Cut pattern from paper, discarding unneeded section (shaded area).

FIGURE 2 *Back gore:*
- Repeat the instructions given for front panel, using measurements given on illustration.

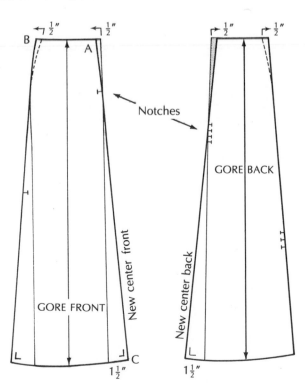

10-GORE SKIRT WITH PLEATS

Design Analysis: Design 4

The 10-gore panels or Design 4 are arranged so that the front panel is wider than the joining panels. All panels have pleats, except at side seam. This illustrates the flexibility of gores when used for design variations.

Pattern plot and development

FIGURE 1 *Front:*

- Trace basic skirt front.
- Measure the distance from dart point to center front.
- Mark hem from center front to equal this measurement, *plus* 1 inch. Label A.
- Draw goreline from mark to new dart mark.
- Redraw second dart $\frac{3}{4}$ inch toward side. (Broken line is original dart location.)
- Draw second goreline from new dart point to hem, parallel with first goreline. Label B.
- Add 2 inches to side seam at hem.
- Connect line to outermost part of hip. Blend hemline using A-line instructions (see page 283, Figure 3).

FIGURE 2 *Back:*

- Repeat process above.

   Note: Mark gore width (C–D) at hem equal to front gore width (A–B), and shift dart to goreline, as shown.

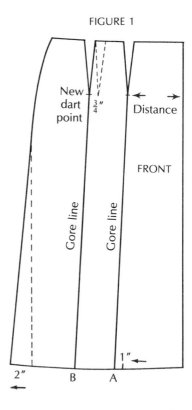

FIGURE 1

New dart point

$\frac{3}{4}''$

Distance

FRONT

Gore line

Gore line

2"

B

A

1"

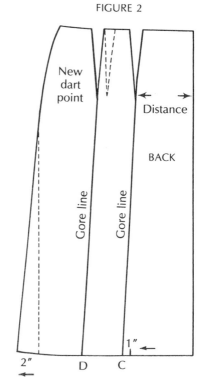

FIGURE 2

New dart point

Distance

BACK

Gore line

Gore line

2"

D

C

1"

FIGURES 3, 4, and 5   *Front:*
- Cut and separate gore sections.
- Trace gores, placing center front of gore on fold (Figure 5).
- Measure down from waist of gore panels to a location where pleats are to begin (example: 6 inches).
- Square out $\frac{1}{8}$ inch from each mark. Label X.
- With square held at this location, draw a line $1\frac{1}{2}$

inches out from point X for pleat depth. Mark.
- Square out $2\frac{1}{2}$ inches at hem. Mark and blend hem. Connect to complete pleats.
- Draw a blend line from X to gore panel as shown.
- Add $1\frac{1}{2}$ inches at side seam and connect to outermost hip curve. Blend A-line at hem (see page 283, Figure 3).
- Mark for notches and grain as shown.

FIGURE 3

FIGURE 4

FIGURE 5

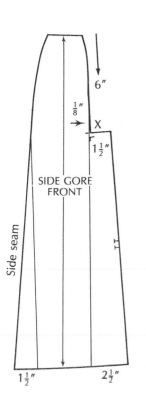

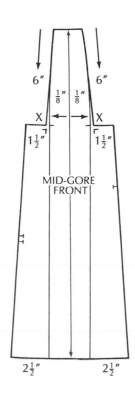

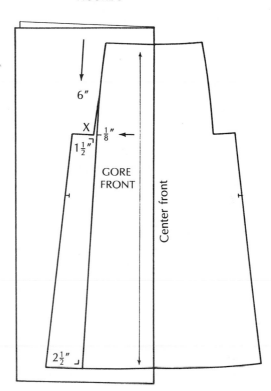

(Continued on next page)

FIGURES 6, 7, and 8 *Back:*
- Repeat instructions given for front gores.
- Mark notches as shown.

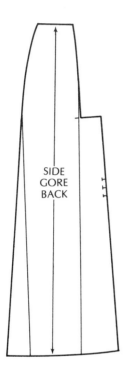

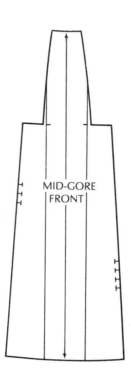

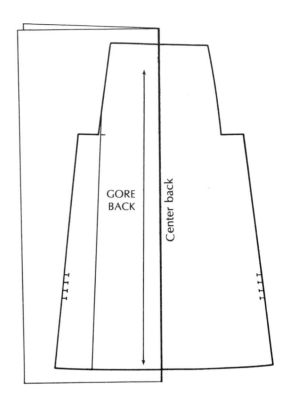

FIGURE 9 *Pleat support:*
- When adding seams (for gore panels with pleat), draw seamline from waist parallel to goreline, curving out to tip of pleat as shown.
- Place punch and circle $\frac{1}{8}$ inch in and up from point X.

   Note: Allow skirt to hang several hours (for bias to relax). Remark hemline if necessary.

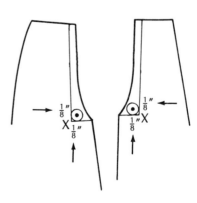

12-GORE FOUNDATION PANEL

A skirt with 12 gores (more or less as desired) is developed from a single panel that is drafted from the waist and hip measurements. The waist and hip measurements are divided by the number of panels desired. This foundation panel is duplicated for as many gores as it represents. The dart excess is absorbed among all panels at the waist. Flare or pleats may be developed at any point along the goreline of the panel and may be as wide as desired. Skirts such as the trumpet, flip, and tulip may be developed from this panel. For additional practice, it is recommended that a 10-gore skirt be developed using the general instructions given below.

Pattern plot and development
12-gore panel:

Measurements needed:
- (2) Waist _____ plus 1 inch ease.
- (4) Hip _____ plus 1½-inch ease.
- (25) Center front hip depth _____.

FIGURE 1
- Divide waist and hip measurements into twelfths.
- Divide these measurements in half and record:
    Waist _____, Hip _____.
- Draw A–B line on paper equal to skirt length.
- Locate center front hip depth down from A. Label C.
- Locate abdominal depth in between A and C. Label D.

FIGURE 2
- Square out from each side of points A, B, C, and D, using recorded measurement as follows:
    A = Waist.
    B and C = Hip
    D = Hip, less ⅛ inch.

FIGURE 3
- Connect points and blend a slightly outward curve from points above hip to waist as shown.
    Use the gore panel to develop the following designs. Design other variations for practice.

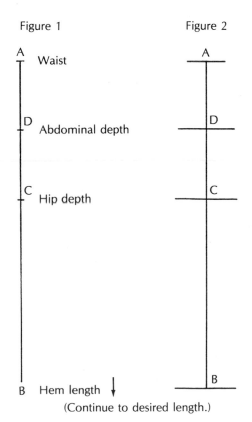

Figure 1

A — Waist

D — Abdominal depth

C — Hip depth

B — Hem length
(Continue to desired length.)

Figure 2

A

D

C

B

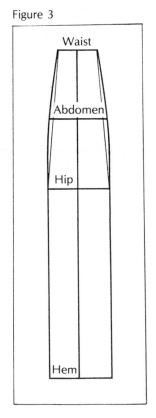

Figure 3

Waist

Abdomen

Hip

Hem

(Continued on next page)

12-GORE GRADUATED FLARE

Design Analysis: Design 1

The graduated flare can be developed from the 12-gore (or any gore) foundation panel by varying the hemline and the breakpoint for flare on each gore panel. The following example of a graduated flared skirt can be used as a guide for developing other design variations.

Pattern plot and development

FIGURE 1   (opposite)

■ Trace gore panel on paper. Label center front. Square line across panel and paper at hip level.
■ Retrace panel five times, matching hip level and side seam. (This represents one-half of skirt.)
■ Number each panel as shown.
■ Measure down $\frac{1}{2}$ inch from waist at center back (or use personal measurement for back hip depth). Draw corrected waistline to third panel (side seam).
■ Extend center front (Panel 1) and back (Panel 6) to desired length. Label A and B and draw line for new hemline.

Flare development:

■ Measure up from A at center front to a point where flare will start (example: 12 inches). Label C.
■ B–D = A–C. Mark. Draw line from C to D (break line for flare).

Panel 1:

■ Measure out from A to desired width of flare (example: 4 inches). Mark and connect with C. This line should equal A–C length. Blend gore panel to hem. Label Flare 1.
■ Repeat for other side of panel and continue marking flare on each side of each panel equal to length and width of Flare 1. (Bold lines indicate flare panels 1, 3, and 5. Broken lines indicate flare panels for Gores 2, 4, and 6.

Separate panels:

■ Place paper underneath pattern and transfer gores as follows: For Gore 1, trace bold line. For Gore 2 trace flare indicated by broken lines. Continue the process until all gores are transferred.

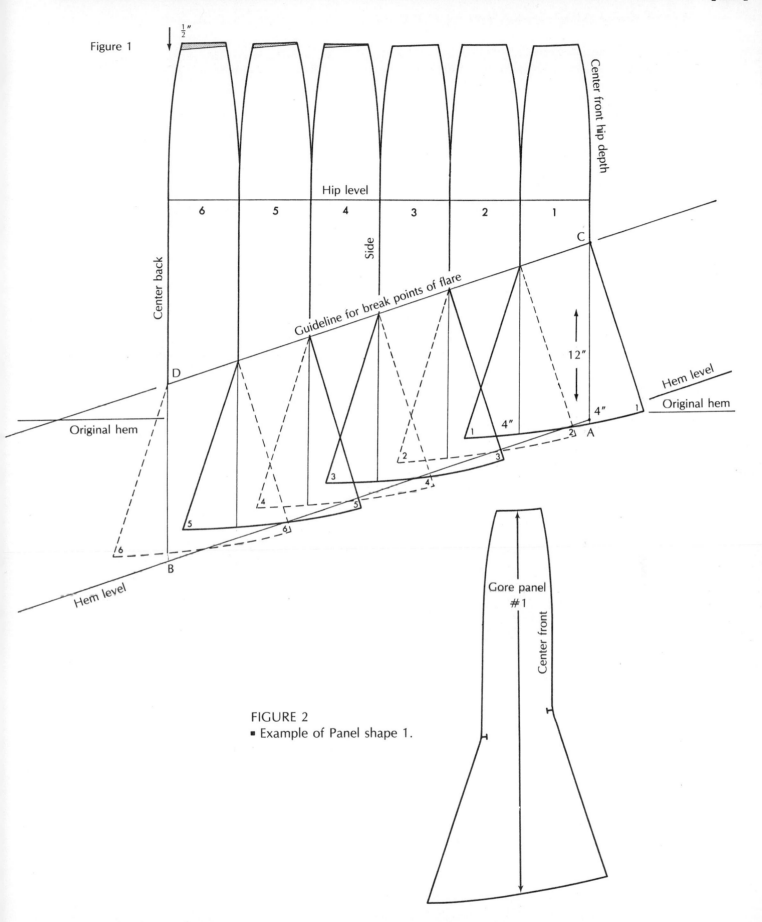

Figure 1

$\frac{1}{2}''$

Hip level

Center front hip depth

6 5 4 3 2 1

Side

Center back

C

Guideline for break points of flare

12"

D

Hem level

Original hem

1 4"

1 4" 1

Original hem

2 A

3

2

3

4

4

5

5

6

6

B

Hem level

FIGURE 2
▪ Example of Panel shape 1.

Gore panel
#1

Center front

SKIRT VARIATIONS USING THE 12-GORE PANEL

Design Analysis: Designs 2, 3, and 4
Cut 12 panels to desired lengths and complete Designs 2, 3, and 4.

DESIGN 2:
- Flared panel length (A–C) is equal to gore panel length (A–B). This results in an even hemline.

DESIGN 3:
- Flared panel is level with hemline of gore. This results in an uneven hemline.

DESIGN 4:
- Flare is added to only one side of each gore panel. The flared side of the panel is stitched to the straight side of each joining panel.

DESIGN 4

DESIGN 2

DESIGN 3

To knee level, or below.

9" to 14"

7"

A
Gore panel

A
Gore panel

A
Gore panel

C   5" ← B → 5"

10" ← B → 10"

B   → 12"

PEGGED SKIRT SILHOUETTE

The pegged silhouette is achieved by adding fullness at the waistline, either moderately or extremely, and/or tapering the side seams. The skirt may be gathered, pleated, or cowled into the waistband. For modified fullness at the waist, the basic back pattern may be used as is, or darts may be developed as gathers. For an exaggerated fullness at the waist, the back pattern should be spread the same as the front along the waistline.

PEGGED SKIRT WITH GATHERS

Design Analysis: Design 1

Design 1 has a skirt with a pegged silhouette, and gathers along the front and back waistline. Design 2 is a practice problem (see cowl drape pant for guidance).

Pattern plot and development

FIGURE 1
- Plot pattern, directing slash line from waist to hem and side seams for fullness.
- Repeat for back (not illustrated).

FIGURE 2
- Cut to, not through, hem and side seam.
- Place on paper and spread each section as shown (more or less as desired). Secure pattern pieces and trace outline. Discard pattern.
- Draw blending line across open spaces for gathers.
- Draw grain and complete pattern for test fit.
- Repeat for back (not illustrated).

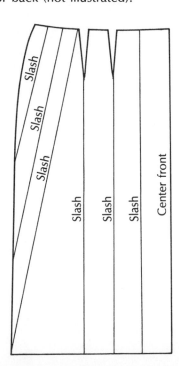

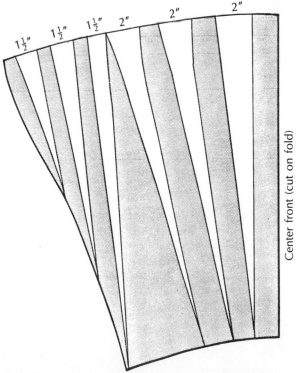

PEGGED SKIRT WITH PLEATS

Design Analysis: Design 2
The side seams are tapered for Design 2. Pleats form along waistline and radiate toward side seam. The stylized waistband points at center front. The basic back skirt is tapered with slit in back seam.

Pattern plot and development

FIGURE 1
- Trace front skirt.
- Draw a line from 1 inch below center front to within $\frac{1}{2}$ inch of dart leg at waist (shaded area).
- Mark 1 inch in at side hem and draw line to hip for pegged effect (shaded area).
- Draw slash lines for pleats as shown.
- Cut pattern from paper. Trim shaded areas and save wedge for belt development.

FIGURE 2
- Cut slash lines from waist to, not through, side and hem.
- Close darts (even broken line).
- Spread each section 2 inches or more. Secure.
- Trace around pattern, marking pleat opening.
Skirt pleats:
- For flat pleats, fold paper (between openings) to the end of skirt hem and side seams.
- For pleats to billow outward, fold pleats, ending the fold approximately half the distance of the spread opening. See uneven broken lines.
- With tracing wheel, cross over folded pleats at waistline. Open pattern and pencil in perforated marks at waist.
- Notch pleats as shown.
- Trace back, taper side seam, and notch for slit. (Example: 7 inches up from hem; not illustrated.)

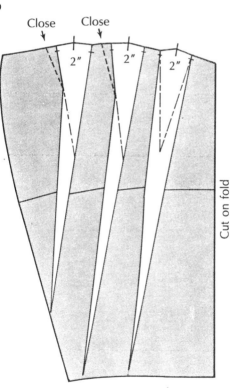

FIGURE 3 *Belt construction:*
- Trace basic belt (for center back opening) on fold of paper. (See page 281, for belt development, if needed.)
- Place wedge section to bottom of belt at center front and trace. Discard.
- Draw grain and complete pattern for test fit.

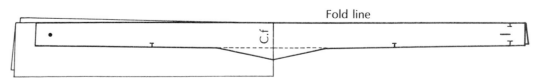

DRAPED SKIRT WITH A CASCADE WRAP

Pattern plot and development

FIGURE 1   *Skirt:*
- Trace full front skirt. Extend dart point A, 1½ inches. Draw slash lines as shown.
- B–C = 8 inches for cascade (varies). Draw curved lines. (Discard shaded area).

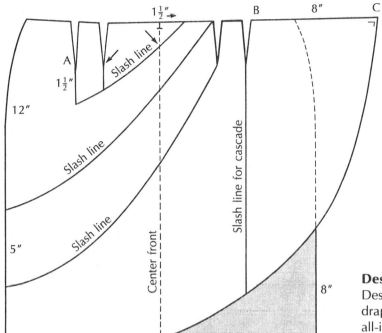

Design Analysis

Design 1 features an asymmetric drape with a flowing cascade, all-in-one with the wrap drape and attached to the side seams. The drape wraps a straight-line basic skirt.

FIGURE 2
- Cut slash lines and close darts.
- Place on paper and spread drape sections 4 inches (or more).
- Blend curved cascade hem, discarding overhang (broken lines).

Pleat underlay:
- Fold pleats and trace with tracing wheel.
- Unfold pleats and pencil in waistline.
- Mark notches for pleat and draw grainline.

Underneath skirt:
- Trace basic skirt front on fold and back with seam for entry (not illustrated).

SKIRTS WITH YOKES

YOKE WITH GATHERED SKIRT

Design Analysis: Design 1
The yoke for Design 1 begins $3\frac{1}{2}$ inches down from the waistline and is attached to a gathered dirndl skirt. The skirt is developed from a basic straight-line skirt and is spread for fullness.

Pattern plot and development

FIGURES 1 and 2
- Trace front and back patterns.
- Plan yoke (example: $3\frac{1}{2}$ inches below waist). Draw yoke line parallel with waistline.
- Draw slash lines spaced equally below yoke. Label as shown.
- Cut and separate patterns.

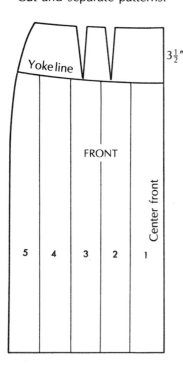

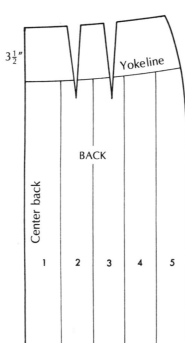

FIGURES 3 and 4   *Yoke:*
- Close darts and trace front yoke on fold. (Broken lines indicate closed darts.)
- Close back darts and trace. Add 1-inch extension to center back.
- Mark notches and grain as shown.
- Complete pattern for test fit.

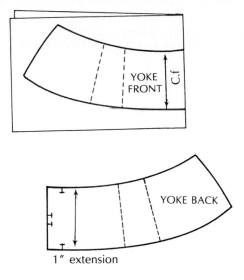

FIGURE 5   *Dirndl:*
- Fold paper. Square a horizontal guideline 3 inches up from bottom of paper at fold.
- Cut through slash lines of skirt. Place sections in sequence and spread equally across paper (example: 5 or more inches). Secure.
- Trace, blending across yoke line and hem.
- Repeat for back (not illustrated).
- Draw grainline. Complete pattern for test fit.

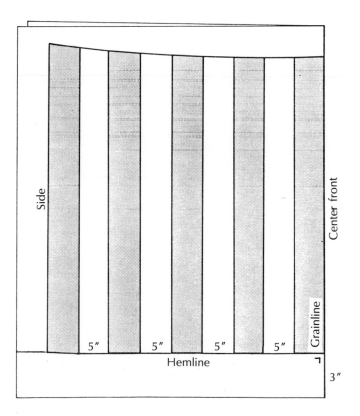

DIAGONAL YOKE WITH FLARED SKIRT

Design Analysis: Designs 2 and 3

The yoke for Design 2 is parallel with the waist to the point where it extends at a diagonal to the center front waist. Back yoke is parallel with waistline. The lower skirt sections are flared (one-sided fullness) with greater flare below point of yoke for a special effect. (Flare based on Principle #1—Dart Manipulation, and Principle #2—Added Fullness.)

Design 3 is a practice problem. Base design on one-dart pattern (see page 286). Front and back are the same.

DESIGN 2   DESIGN 3

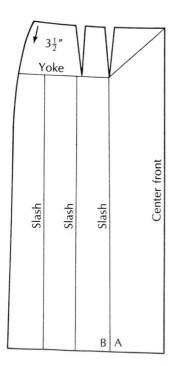

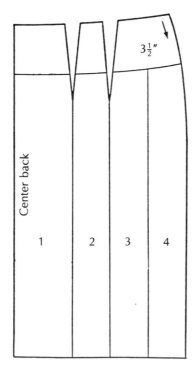

Pattern plot and development

FIGURES 1 and 2
- Trace basic front and back skirt.
- Plan stylelines or yoke (example: $3\frac{1}{2}$ inches below waist from side to dart point to center front waist on front). Continue yoke across back, parallel with waist.
- Draw slash lines. Label A and B as shown.
- Cut and separate patterns.

FIGURES 3 and 4
- Cut slash lines to, not through, waist.
- Place on paper. Spread A–B space 10 inches (more or less). Spread remaining spaces of front and back, as desired or to width of fabric (example: 3 inches).
- Trace patterns. Add to side seam as shown. Blend hemline (see page 283, Figure 3).

    Note: Close dart legs at waist of back skirt. Spread slash lines to equal front skirt.

FIGURES 5 and 6   *Yokes:*
- Close darts and trace. (Extend center back 1 inch for entry if side opening is not desired.)

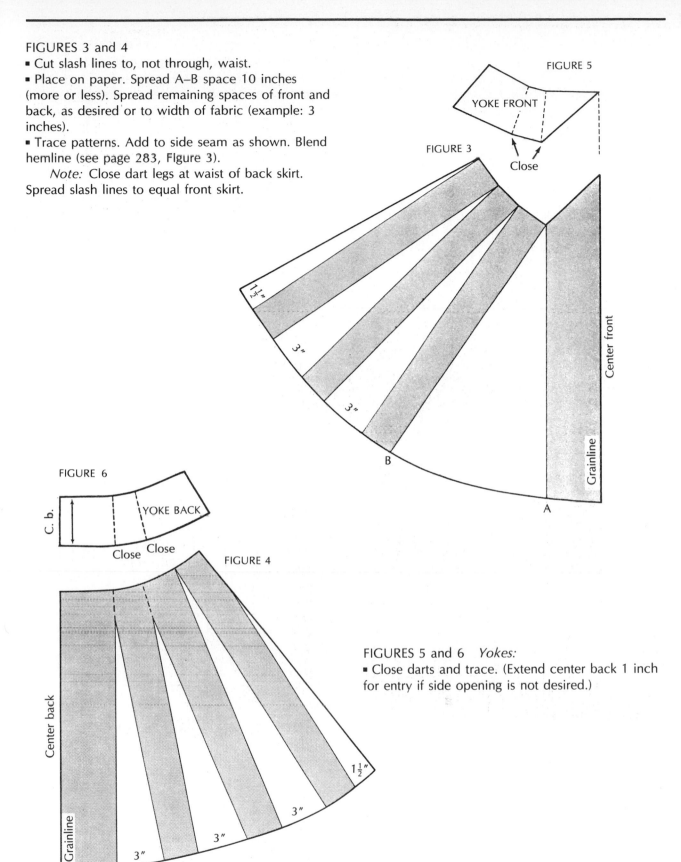

TIERS

Tiered designs are those featuring rows or layers of fabric attached to each other (as in Designs 1, 2, and 3) or separated and attached to a frame underneath (Designs 4, 5, and 6, page 316). Tiers may be of graduated or even lengths. The width of each tier can vary. When planning a tiered design, the first tier, which is attached to the waistline (or yoke), may be from 1 to $1\frac{1}{2}$ times the fabric width. Each subsequent tier may increase in width from $1\frac{1}{2}$ to 2 times the width of the previous tier depending on the amount of fullness desired.

DESIGN 1　　DESIGN 2　　DESIGN 3

TERMS

Fabric width. The distance from selvage to selvage.

One-half of fabric's width. The distance from the selvage to center of fabric's width.

Three-fourths of fabric's width. The distance from the selvage to a point three-quarters of the way across the fabric's width.

ATTACHED TIERS

Design 2 is illustrated and should be used as a general guide for developing patterns with attached tiers. For additional practice, develop Designs 1 and 3 (floor length) or create other variations based on these concepts. Use the skirt to proportionalize panels when developing tiers.

Pattern plot and development for Design 2

FIGURE 1 *Tiers:*
Plot skirt as shown.
- Length = 29 inches.
- Tier A = $6\frac{1}{4}$ inches.
- Tier B = $6\frac{3}{4}$ inches.
- Tier C = $7\frac{1}{4}$ inches.
- Tier D = $8\frac{3}{4}$ inches.

FIGURE 2 *Skirt panels:*
- Develop patterns for each tier (A, B, C, and D), using the tier length and fabric width as a guide.
- Tier A = Cut 1 width. Adjust back skirt by measuring down $\frac{1}{2}$ inch at center back, blending to side seam (or use personal measurement for back hip depth).
- Tier B = Cut $1\frac{1}{2}$ widths.
- Tier C = Cut $2\frac{1}{2}$ widths.
- Tier D = Cut $3\frac{3}{4}$ widths.
- If more fullness is desired, add an additional one-half width to each panel.

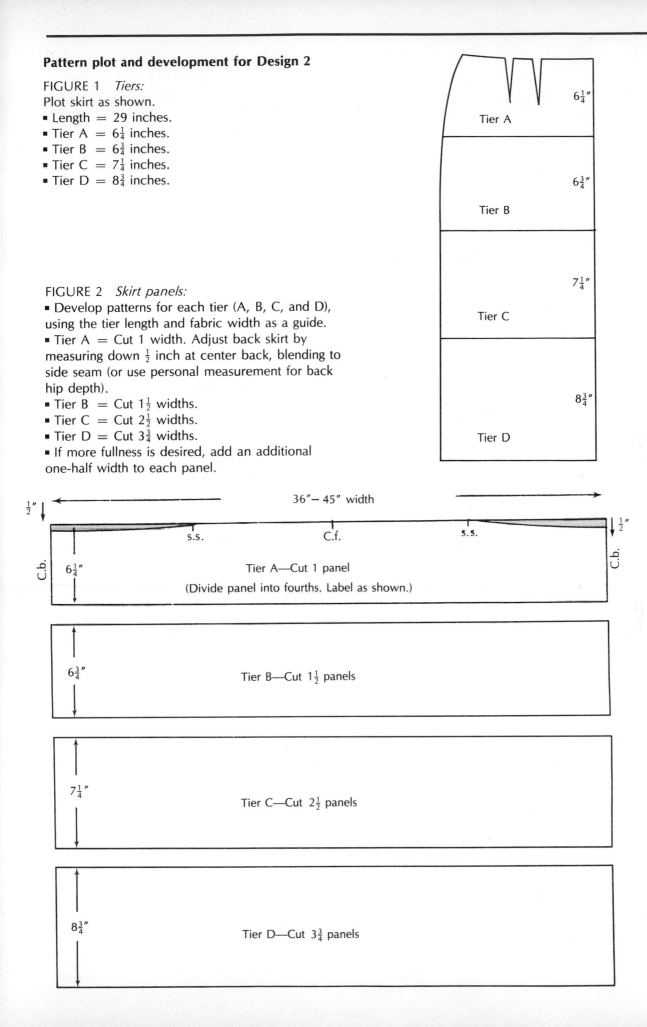

SEPARATED TIERS

Separated tiers may be attached to a basic skirt (guided by punch marks) or stitched in between seamlines of a divided basic skirt. The last section of the skirt is usually discarded. These tiers may also be attached to a basic flared skirt. Tiers overlay each other to conceal stitchline. Design 4 should be used as a guide for developing gathered tiers, and Design 5 for developing flared tiers. Design 6 has been provided as a practice problem.

The tiers are arranged on a traced copy of the front and back basic skirt. Use measurements given for tier placement (based on 26-inch length), or arrange tier proportions as desired. The plotted tiers are not cut from the pattern but used as a guide for developing tier patterns. However, the traced skirt is separated for use as a skirt frame when tiers are supported by seamlines rather than guided by punch marks. Plotting (Figures 1 and 2) applies to all three designs.

DESIGN 4   **DESIGN 5**   **DESIGN 6**

Pattern plot for Designs 4, 5, and 6

FIGURE 1
- Trace front basic skirt.
- Plot pattern for visual placement of tiers based on a 26-inch skirt length as follows:
    Tier A = 5 inches.
    Tier B = 8 inches.
    Tier C = 13 inches.

FIGURE 2 *Underlay:*
- Draw a parallel line $1\frac{1}{2}$ inches up from Tier A and Tier B (indicated by broken lines).
- The length of Tiers B and C should include the $1\frac{1}{2}$ inches for underlay when developing tier panels. (Use punch marks *only* if tier is to be attached to the basic skirt frame.)

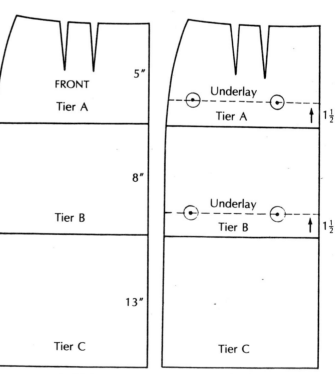

FIGURE 1   FIGURE 2

Gathered tiers for Design 4

FIGURE 3   *Tier panels:*
- Draw vertical lines equal to tier length plus 1 inch for hem for Panels A, B, and C. Remember, Tiers B and C include 1½ inch underlay.
- Square a line out from each end equal to fabric width, and connect to complete each panel.
- Draw grain and complete pattern for test fit.
- Cut panels (increase or decrease for fullness as desired).

(See page 315, Figure 2, for adjusting back waist.)

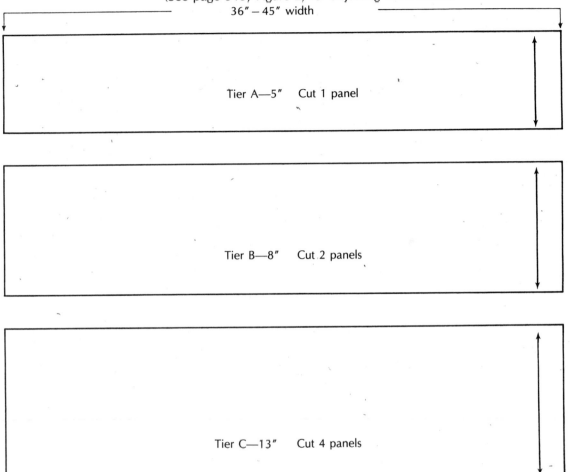

36" – 45" width

Tier A—5"   Cut 1 panel

Tier B—8"   Cut 2 panels

Tier C—13"   Cut 4 panels

FIGURE 4   *Skirt frame:*
- Tiers may be attached to skirt frame by using punch marks as a guide for stitching (see Figure 1), or tiers can be gathered and inserted into seams by separating panels at underlay lines, discarding lower section (broken lines). Tiers will overlay each other 1½ inches, hiding attaching seams.

Underlays A and B:
- Trace center front skirt parts on fold. Repeat instruction for back skirt (not illustrated).
- Draw grain and complete patterns for test fit.

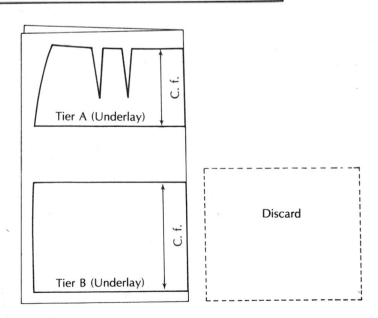

Tier A (Underlay)

C. f.

Tier B (Underlay)

C. f.

Discard

Flare tiers for Design 5
(Trace basic skirt and plot as instructed for
Design 4, Figures 1 and 2.)

FIGURE 1
- Trace and cut Tiers A, B, and C from tier underlay
to individual length lines.
- Draw slash lines from dart point to bottom of tier.
- Divide Tiers B and C into thirds and draw slash
lines.
- Label A–B as shown.
- Cut tier sections from paper.

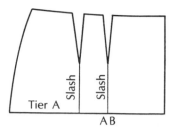

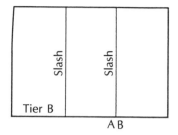

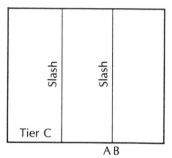

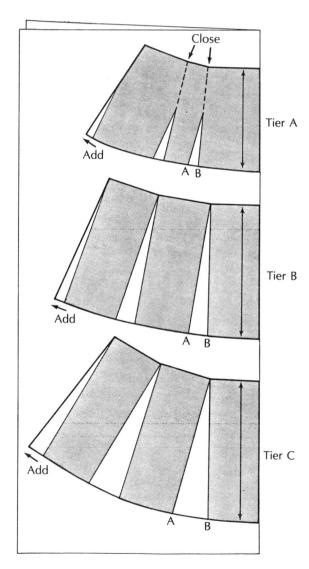

FIGURE 2
Cut slash line from hem to, not through, top of tiers.
Tier A:
- Close darts on Tier A. Retrace on fold. (If more
flare is desired, raise pivotal point of dart $\frac{1}{2}$ to 1
inch.)
Tier B:
- Spread slash sections twice as much as spaces in
Tier A. Retrace on fold.
Tier C:
- Spread slash section twice as much as spaces in
Tier B. Retrace on fold.
Side seams:
- Add one-half of A–B space to side seams.
- Draw line. Blend hemline (see page 283, Figure
3).
- Repeat for back. Spread panels and add to side
seam, so that hemline sweep equals $\frac{1}{2}$-inch more
than front tier panels.

PEPLUMS

A peplum is a flounce or short, flared tier that may
be added on to the waistline of any garment.
Peplums extend from the waist, down and
around the hips. They are developed in the same
manner as a tier. To develop patterns for peplums,
follow instructions given for tier designs.

PLEATS

A pleat is a fold in the fabric that releases fullness. Pleats are used to increase stride room (such as a single pleat on a straight skirt) or as a design, as with groups of pleats, or all over pleats. Pleats are found on skirts, bodices, sleeves, dresses, jackets, and so on. Pleats are formed in a variety of ways. They may be folded and left unpressed or pressed; stitched or left unstitched. They may be grouped together with either even or uneven spacing. The pleat depth may be single, double, or triple. For variation, they may be developed parallel with the fold line or at an angle to it.

TYPES OF PLEATS

Knife or side pleat
Pleats are grouped and all face in one direction.

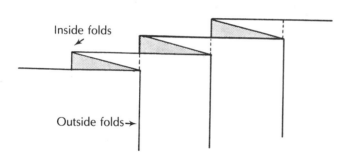

Box pleats
Pleats are folded away from each other on right side of garment.

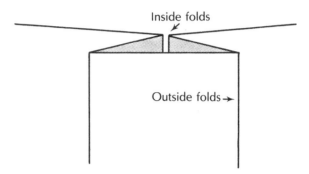

Inverted pleats
Pleats are folded to meet each other on right side of garment.

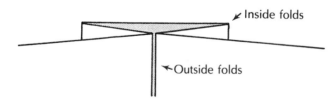

Accordion pleats
Pleats have folds resembling the bellows of an accordion. These pleats are close together and depth is equal from waist to hem.

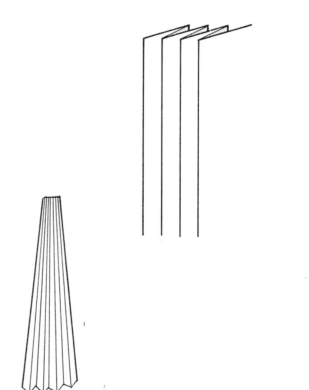

Sunburst pleats
Pleats fan out and graduate from the waist. They are used on circle skirts. To sustain pleating, the fabric used should be a synthetic or a blend with over 50% synthetic fibers.

PLEAT TERMINOLOGY

FIGURE 1

Pleat depth
Depth is the distance from the outside fold of the pleat (labelled X) to the inside fold (labelled Y). (See shaded area of first pleat.)

Pleat underlay (forms the pleat)
Pleat underlay is always twice the pleat depth (X to Y to Z). Example: 2-inch pleat depth = 4-inch underlay (lined area illustrated at second pleat).

Pleat spacing
Distance between pleats. Pleat markings on the pattern. (X–Y = Pleat depth; X–Z = pleat underlay; Z–X = space between pleats.)

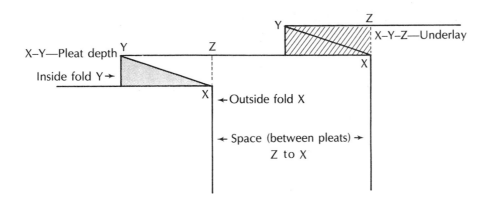

KICK PLEATS

Kick pleats are short pleats (side, inverted, or box pleats) placed at center front, center back, sides, or in a gore line.

Knife pleat at side

FIGURE 1
- Mark A for placement of pleat. (Example: 8 inches up from hem at center front.)
- Square out 2 inches from A for pleat depth. Label B.
- Repeat at hem and connect.
- When adding seams to skirt, add ½ inch along center line and curve outward to B for pleat control. Punch and circle ⅛ inch in and up from A.

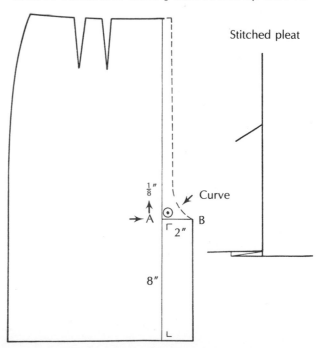

Inverted box pleat with backing

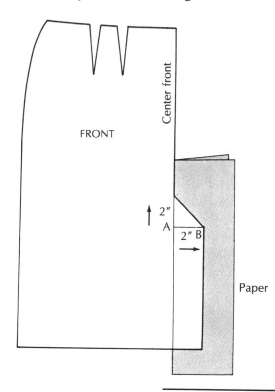

FRONT

Center front

2″
A
2″ B

Paper

FIGURE 1
- Mark A for pleat placement. (Example: 8 inches up from hem at center front.)
- Square out 2 inches from A. Label B. Repeat at hem and connect.
- Mark 2 inches up from A and connect with B.
- Cut pattern from paper.
- Place center line of pattern on fold of paper (shaded section) and trace pleat.

FIGURE 2
- Remove and cut pleat backing.

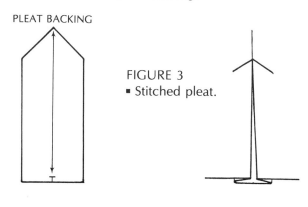

PLEAT BACKING

FIGURE 3
- Stitched pleat.

Inverted box pleat without backing

FIGURE 1
- Mark A for pleat depth. (Example: 8 inches up from hem at center front.)
- Extend a line out 3 inches from A (pleat depth $1\frac{1}{2}$ inches).
- Notch $1\frac{1}{2}$ inches from A.
- Repeat at hem.

FIGURE 2
- Stitched pleat.

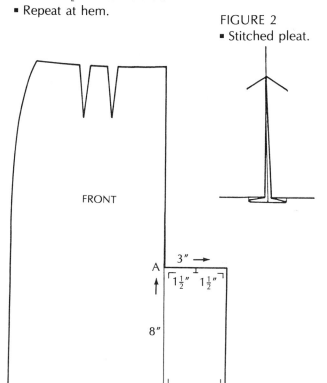

FRONT

A
3″
$1\frac{1}{2}$″ $1\frac{1}{2}$″
8″

Double inverted box pleat

FIGURE 1
- Mark A for pleat depth. (Example: 8 inches up from hem at center front.)
- Using 3 inches (pleat underlay) as a guide for each pleat, square a line out from A equal to the number of pleats desired. (Example: 6 inches for two pleats.)
- Notch every $1\frac{1}{2}$ inches for pleat fold.
- Repeat at hem, (notches optional).

FIGURE 2
- Stitched pleat.

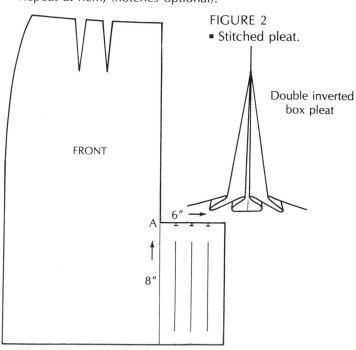

Double inverted box pleat

FRONT

A
6″
8″

ALL-AROUND PLEATED SKIRT

The all-around pleated skirt design can be developed by using the pleat formula as a guide, or the fabric may be pleated by professional pleaters. Generally, it is less expensive for a manufacturer to send out a skirt for pleating than to do it in the manufacturer's own factory. Professional pleaters will conform any pleating arrangement to the waist and hip measurements for all graded size ranges and to any skirt length desired. Some small firms will pleat fabric for those desiring a personal fit. (*Suggestion:* Contact yardage or notion departments for information on what services are available locally.)

Design Analysis: Design 1

Design 1 features 20 pleats that encircle the figure. Each pleat is stitched to approximately 7 inches below the waist and is developed using the pleat formula as a guide.

Pattern plot and development

Measurements needed
- (2) Waist _____
- (4) Hip _____
- Length _____

Example: 30 inch waist; 40 inch hip; length 26 inches plus 3 inches for hem and seams = 29 inches.

Pleat formula:
- Number of pleats (20 pleats).
- Depth of pleat ($1\frac{1}{2}$ inches $\times$ 2 = 3 inches—forms pleat).
- *Pleat spacing:* Divide the number of pleats (20) into the hip circumference (40) = 2-inch spacing.

FIGURE 1 *Planning pleats:*
Always start the pleat series with seam allowance (A), followed by pleat depth (A to B)—forms one-half of the pleat. Continue with pleat space (B to C) and pleat underlay (C to D). Repeat the process until the next to the last pleat is formed (E to F). Mark for space (F to G) and end with pleat depth (G to H)—this completes the other half of pleat number 1. Add to this seam allowance. (The seam is hidden in the center fold of the pleat.) If the pleat series is interrupted by a seam before completion, end with pleat depth and begin with seam allowance and pleat depth on the joining piece.

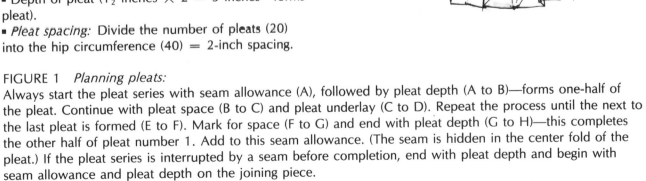

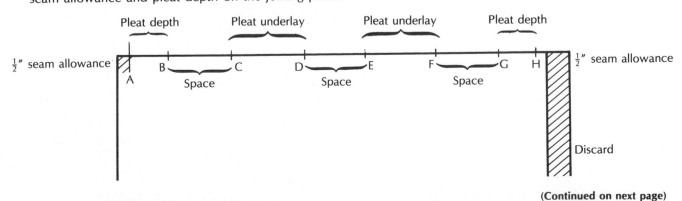

(Continued on next page)

FIGURE 2 *Adjusting pleats to waistline:*
Pleats are formed to fit the circumference of the
hip, making the skirt too wide for the waist. To
adjust the pattern, find the difference between waist
and hip measurements. (Example: 30-inch waist,
and 40-inch hip, the difference is 10 inches).
Divide: $\frac{10}{40} = \frac{1}{4}$ inch. This measurement represents
the amount each pleat will absorb in order to fit the
waist.

Use measurement as follows:
- Measure out $\frac{1}{4}$ inch from each side of pleat (X and
Z) at waist. Mark.
- Blend a curved line (new stitch line) from each
mark to approximately $4\frac{1}{2}$ inches below waist.
(Broken line indicates original fold line of pleat.
Shaded area indicates the amount taken up by the
pleats. Pleat may be top stitched at varying lengths
below the waist.)

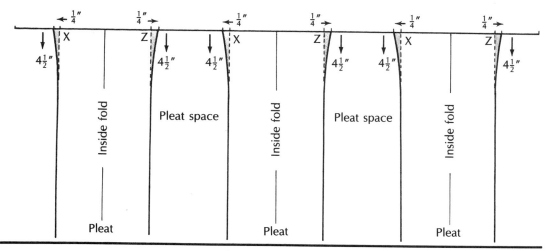

INVERTED BOX-PLEATED SKIRT

Design Analysis: Design 1
Design 1 features box pleats in front with slight
A-line flare at side seams. Back is basic with A-line
flare. Pleat can be either stitched (as shown) or
unstitched.

Pattern plot and development

FIGURE 1 (opposite)
- Trace basic skirt. (Back is developed the same as
the front; not illustrated.)
- Draw tentative line from dart point to hem,
parallel to center front (broken line).
- Measure over $1\frac{1}{2}$ inches from line at hem and
draw line to dart point. Label A–B as shown (pleat
placement guide).
- Measure out $1\frac{1}{2}$ inches at side seam for A-line.
Draw line to outermost part of hip. Blend hemline
(see page 283, Figure 3).
- Cut from paper.

Plotted skirt for Figure 1

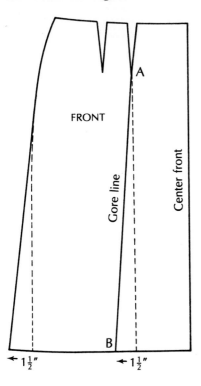

FRONT

Gore line

Center front

A

B

←1½"   ←1½"

FIGURE 2
- Place pattern on paper. Trace dart leg ending at point B (shaded area).
- Remove pattern.
- Measure over 3 inches from dart leg and 6 inches from point B. Connect. Label C–D.
- Repeat measurements for E and F. Connect.
- Extend line up from point A.

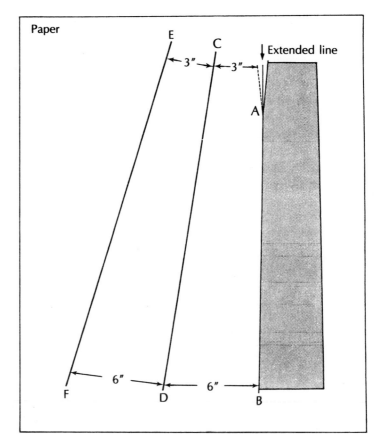

Paper

E

C

↓ Extended line

←3"→ ←3"→

A

F   6"   D   6"   B

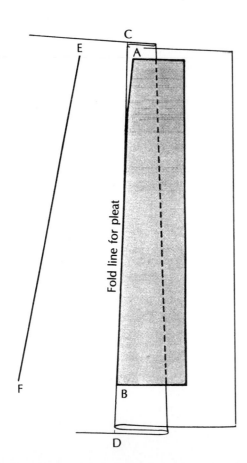

C
E
A

Fold line for pleat

F

B

D

FIGURE 3
- Fold A–B line to C–D line. Crease (broken line shows pleat underlay).

(Continued on next page)

FIGURE 4

• Fold E–F line to B–C line. Crease.

• *Working pattern modification:* Before replacing pattern for tracing, cut slash line from hemline to, not through, dart point. Close dart. Tape.

• Place pattern on draft, matching center front line. Trace remaining pattern (shaded area). Remove pattern.

• With tracing wheel, trace across pleats at waist and hemline to transfer shape to pattern underneath. Seams can be added at this time (not illustrated). Open pattern and pencil in perforated marks and blend hem.

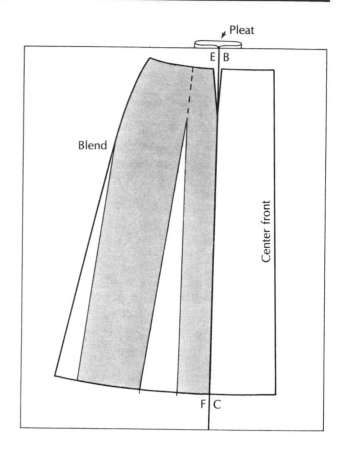

Methods for stitching darts

Method 1:

• Draw dart legs slightly curved and connect dart points.

• Notch dart legs and center in between dart legs.

• Place punch and circles in and up $\frac{1}{8}$ inch from corner, in $\frac{1}{8}$ inch along dart leg, and at center as shown.

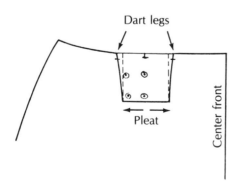

Method 2:

• Trim excess to within $\frac{1}{2}$ inch of dart legs (seam allowance).

• Notch corners and center fold as shown (lines indicate pleat).

• Cut from paper and retrace with center front on fold. Add grainlines and complete for test fit.

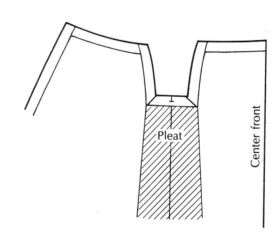

GODETS

Godets are generally triangular-shaped wedges of fabric placed between seams, into slits, or as a replacement for cut-out sections (of many shapes). Godets provide additional stride room or may be added simply as a design feature. They are used singularly or in a series around the skirt. They may extend evenly to the hemline or be graduated in length. Godets may be placed in a bodice, jacket, blouse, sleeve, and so on.

BASIC GODET

Design Analysis: Designs 1 and 2

Design 1 is an example of a single godet inserted in the center back or center front of the skirt for design effect or for additional stride room. This type of godet may be attached to the skirt or be in-one with the skirt (see Figure 1). Design 2 is a practice problem.

Pattern plot and development

FIGURE 1 *In-one with skirt:*
- Mark skirt pattern for godet placement. Measure this length (example: 10 inches) and label A–B.
- Extend hemline to desired width of godet (example: 4 inches). Label C. Connect A to C, marking a point on the line equal to A–B length.
- Blend with hemline.

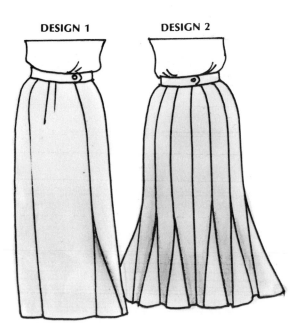

DESIGN 1   DESIGN 2

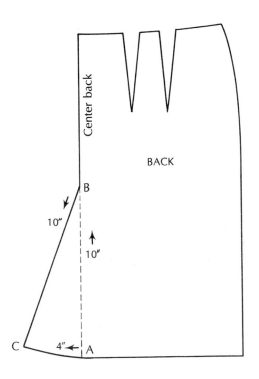

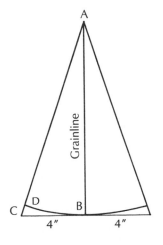

FIGURE 2 *Attached godet:*
- A–B = Godet length (also grainline).
- B–C = Godet width (example: 4 inches). Squared from B.
- Draw line from C to A.
- A–D = A–B length. Mark.
- Blend hemline.
- Repeat for other side.

GODET VARIATIONS

- Godets may be curved (Design 1), squared (Design 2), or pointed (Design 3); they may be a half circle, a three-quarter circle, or a full circle. Use general instructions and illustrations as a guide for developing godet variations.

Pattern plot and development

- Plot pattern for cut-out design.
- Cut from paper.
- Use cut-out section for spreading.
- Draw slash lines.
- Cut slash lines to, not through, top of section.
- Spread for flare as shown. Retrace.

- **Design 1:** see Figures 1, 2, and 3

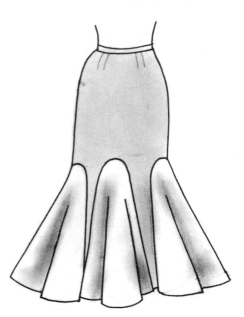

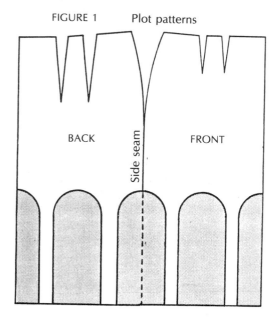

FIGURE 1 Plot patterns

BACK   Side seam   FRONT

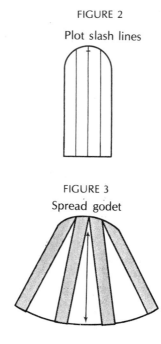

FIGURE 2
Plot slash lines

FIGURE 3
Spread godet

- **Design 2:** see Figures 1, 2, and 3

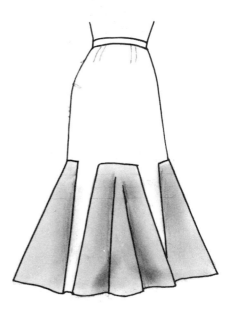

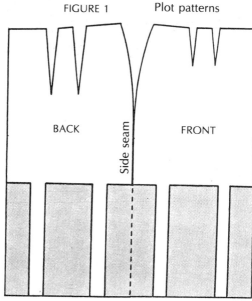

FIGURE 1 Plot patterns

BACK   Side seam   FRONT

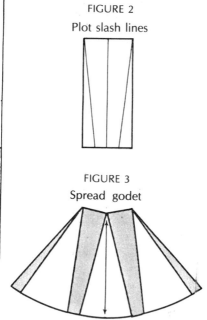

FIGURE 2
Plot slash lines

FIGURE 3
Spread godet

- **Design 3:** see Figures 1, 2, and 3

FIGURE 1   Plot patterns

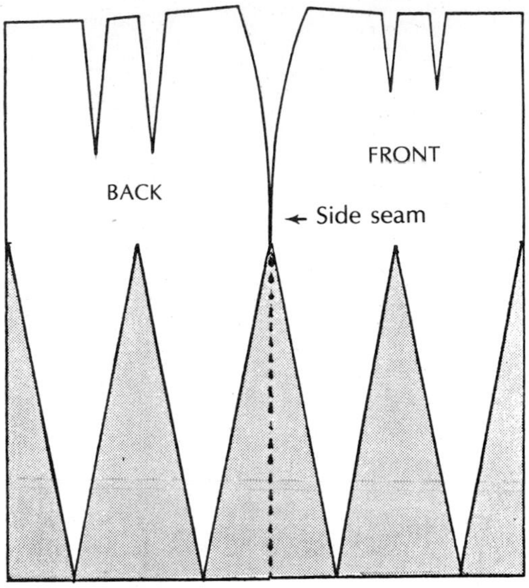

BACK

FRONT

← Side seam

FIGURE 2

Plot slash lines

FIGURE 3

Spread godet

Blend

Trim →

← Trim

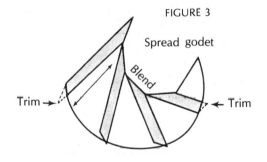

WRAP SKIRT

DESIGN 1 **DESIGN 2**

Any skirt (basic, A-line, flared, or gathered) can be developed into a wrap skirt by extending the center front. The hemline may be squared (Design 1), curved (Design 2), or of any other variation desired. Wrap skirts may have side seams or be developed all-in-one. Belts may be buttoned (Design 1) or tied (Design 2). Designs based on A-line flare skirt.

WRAP SKIRT WITH SIDE SEAM

Pattern plot and development

FIGURE 1
▪ Trace front skirt. Extend a 6-inch line out from center front at waist and hem (extension and fold-back for facing).
▪ Notch center front waist and 3 inches out from waist (indicates the fold line for facing). To develop oversized pocket and welt, see Chapter 15.

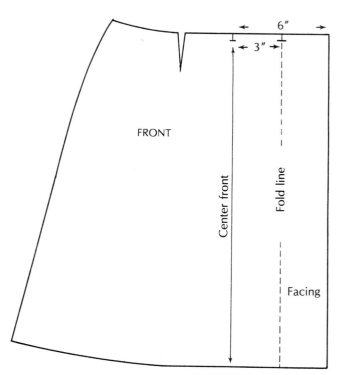

FRONT

Center front · Fold line · Facing

6" · 3"

FIGURE 2
▪ Trace back skirt on fold.

FIGURE 3 *Belt construction:*
▪ Belt extends to full length of waist. Mark for button and buttonhole. (Belt section underneath is buttoned so that it is not seen on right side of skirt.)

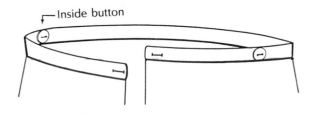

Inside button

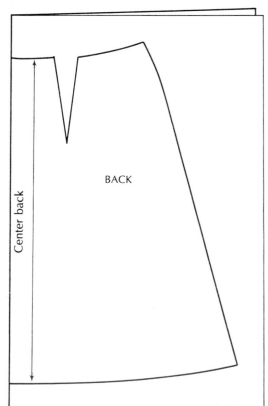

BACK

Center back

ALL-IN-ONE WRAP SKIRT

FIGURE 1
- Align side seams of the front and back skirt (straight, or A-line). Note that a dart is formed at the side waist.

- Add desired extension for wrap (example: equal to distance from center front to dart). Trace.
- Draw curve of hemline as shown.

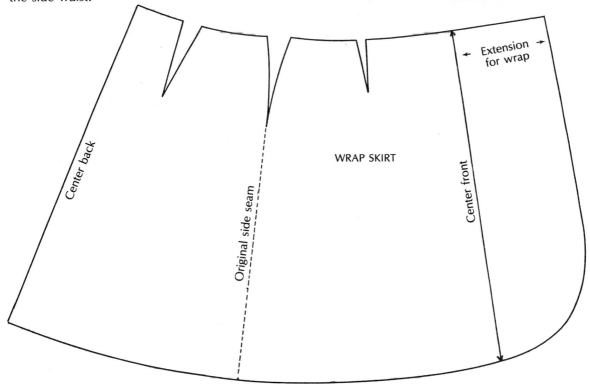

FIGURE 2 *Facing:*
- Trace skirt from waist to curve of hemline.
- Width = $1\frac{1}{2}$ inches to 3 inches.

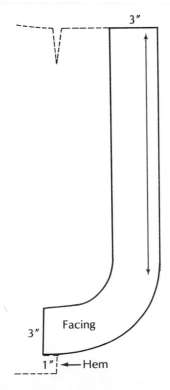

FIGURE 3 *Belt construction:*
- Belt extends 25 inches beyond length of waist at each end.
- Place buttonhole in waistband at right side of skirt for tie to pull through.

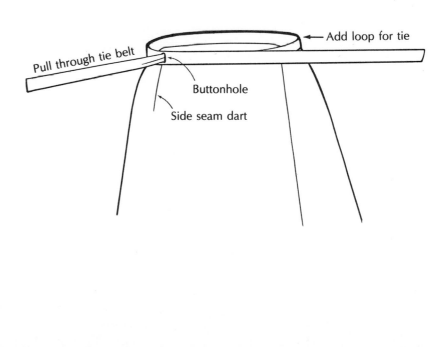

CIRCLE/CASCADE RADIUS CHART

TERMINOLOGY

Whole or partial circles are used to develop circular-type garments—skirts, sleeves, capes, and other design detailing such as cascades and flounces. Some explanation here of the terminology commonly used to describe circles as they relate to garments will help clarify the meaning.

Circle center. A point that is equidistant to all points around the outer edge of the circle (point A).

Radius. The distance or measurement from the center of a circle (point A) to its outer edge (point B). This measurement is used to draw the circle.

Diameter. The distance or measurement across the center of a circle. The diameter of a circle is always twice its radius (B to C).

Outer edge of a circle. The line drawn around the outer edge that encloses the circle, or the circle's circumference.

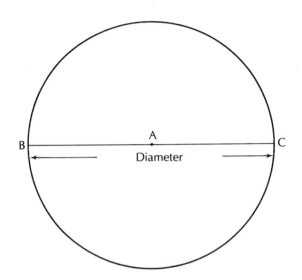

Inner edge of circle. The edge formed by drawing a smaller circle within the circle from the same center but with a shorter radius.

Inner edge as it relates to garments. The inner edge of the circle is attached to the garment. The length of the inner edge must equal the distance to be covered on the garment. The outer edge of the circle forms the hemline.

Off-centered circle. A circle drawn within another circle, using a different center. This creates an uneven distance from the inner edge of the small circle to the outer edge of the larger circle and results in an uneven hemline. (See page 347.)

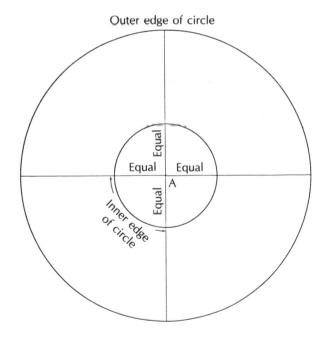

INTERPRETING THE CIRCLE/CASCADE RADIUS CHART

The following chart indicates the radius needed to develop a circle or part of a circle. It is easy to use and eliminates the need for complex mathematical formulas for developing patterns for circular-type garments or design details. One need know only the length required (the distance to be covered by the inside edge of the circle).

Column 1 represents the distance to be covered in whole numbers. For measurements in between whole numbers, use Column 1 as follows:

- $25\frac{1}{2}$ inches or less, use 25 inches.
- Over $25\frac{1}{2}$ inches, use 26 inches.

These measurements are close enough for test fitting.

Columns 2, 3, 4, and 5 represent the radius needed to develop a given circle or part of a circle that will cover the length (distance) given in Column 1.

CIRCLE/CASCADE RADIUS CHART

Column 1 Distance covered	Column 2 1/4 circle		Column 3 1/2 circle		Column 4 3/4 circle		Column 5 Full circle	
1	0	5/8	0	1/4	0	1/4	0	1/8
2	1	1/4	0	5/8	0	1/2	0	3/8
3	1	7/8	0	7/8	0	5/8	0	1/2
4	2	1/2	1	1/4	0	7/8	0	5/8
5	3	1/8	1	5/8	1	1/8	0	3/4
6	3	3/4	1	7/8	1	1/4	0	7/8
7	4	1/2	2	1/4	1	1/2	1	1/8
8	5	1/8	2	1/2	1	5/8	1	1/4
9	5	3/4	2	7/8	1	7/8	1	3/8
10	6	3/8	3	1/8	2	1/8	1	5/8
11	7		3	1/2	2	3/8	1	3/4
12	7	5/8	3	3/4	2	1/2	1	7/8
13	8	1/4	4	1/8	2	3/4	2	1/8
14	8	7/8	4	1/2	2	7/8	2	1/4
15	9	1/2	4	3/4	3	1/8	2	3/8
16	10	1/8	5	1/8	3	3/8	2	1/2
17	10	3/4	5	3/8	3	5/8	2	3/4
18	11	1/2	5	3/4	3	3/4	2	7/8
19	12	1/8	6	1/8	4	1/8	3	
20	12	3/4	6	3/8	4	1/4	3	1/8
21	13	3/8	6	5/8	4	1/2	3	3/8
22	14		7		4	5/8	3	1/2
23	14	5/8	7	1/4	4	7/8	3	5/8
24	15	1/4	7	5/8	5	1/8	3	3/4
25	15	7/8	7	7/8	5	1/4	3	7/8
26	16	1/2	8	1/4	5	1/2	4	1/8
27	17	1/8	8	5/8	5	3/4	4	3/8
28	17	3/4	8	7/8	5	7/8	4	1/2
29	18	1/2	9	1/4	6	1/8	4	5/8
30	19	1/8	9	1/2	6	3/8	4	3/4
31	19	3/4	9	7/8	6	5/8	4	7/8
32	20	3/8	10	7/8	6	3/4	5	1/8
33	21		10	1/2	7		5	1/4
34	21	5/8	10	3/4	7	1/4	5	3/8
35	22	1/4	11	1/8	7	1/2	5	1/2
36	22	7/8	11	1/2	7	5/8	5	3/4
37	23	1/2	11	3/4	7	7/8	5	7/8
38	24	1/8	12	1/8	8	1/8	6	1/8
39	24	7/8	12	3/8	8	1/4	6	1/4
40	25	1/2	12	3/4	8	1/2	6	3/8
41	26	1/8	13	1/8	8	5/8	6	1/2
42	26	3/4	13	3/8	8	7/8	6	5/8
43	27	3/8	13	5/8	9	1/8	6	7/8
44	28		14		9	3/8	7	
45	28	5/8	14	1/4	9	1/2	7	1/8
46	29	1/4	14	5/8	9	3/4	7	3/8
47	29	7/8	14	7/8	9	7/8	7	1/2
48	30	1/2	15	1/4	10	1/8	7	5/8
49	31	1/8	15	5/8	10	3/8	7	3/4
50	31	7/8	15	7/8	10	5/8	7	7/8

USE OF CIRCLE/CASCADE RADIUS CHART

General information

Follow the general outline for developing circle skirts, part of circles, cascades, and circle flounces.

Draft preparation:

Determine the following:

- Type and number of circles needed.
- Number of joining seams required (seam allowance is based on $\frac{1}{2}$ inch): add 1 inch for each seam.

1 inch for one joining seam;
2 inches for two joining seams;
4 inches for four joining seams.

Add the appropriate seam allowance to waist measurement.

- Stretch factor: Since the inside edge of the circle is on a bias, it will stretch, enlarging the waistline. To compensate for this stretch factor, *subtract 1 inch* from waist measurement. (Loosely woven fabrics may stretch more. When in doubt, cut a circle for a test fit approximately 5 inches in length. Place the edge of the inner circle flat along the ruler. The amount of stretch beyond the original measurement should be subtracted from the original measurement.)
- Measurement of distance covered by the inside edge of the circle. (Example: waistline.)
- Garment length, plus $1\frac{1}{2}$ inches (1 inch for hem, $\frac{1}{2}$ inch for seam allowance at waist.)

Locating the radius measurement:

The circle skirt will be used as the example.

- Waist measurement = 26 inches, plus 2 inches (two joining seams), less 1 Inch (for stretch) = 27 inches (adjusted waist).

Note: After radius has been determined, subtract $\frac{1}{2}$ inch (for seam allowance at waist) before drawing waist arc. Locate radius for a 27-inch waistline in Column 1. Use Columns 2, 3, 4, or 5 for the radius required for the circle desired. The following examples indicate that the inner circle of all four skirts will measure 27 inches. *The radius measurement represents a quarter section of the total skirt.*

Circle type	Radius (represents a quarter section of the skirt)
1/4 circle =	17 1/8 inches
1/2 circle =	8 5/8 inches
3/4 circle =	5 3/4 inches
Full circle =	4 3/8 inches

Segments of circles: The following illustrations show what quarter section(s) of the circle each of the circular skirts occupies (broken line-discarded section of circle).

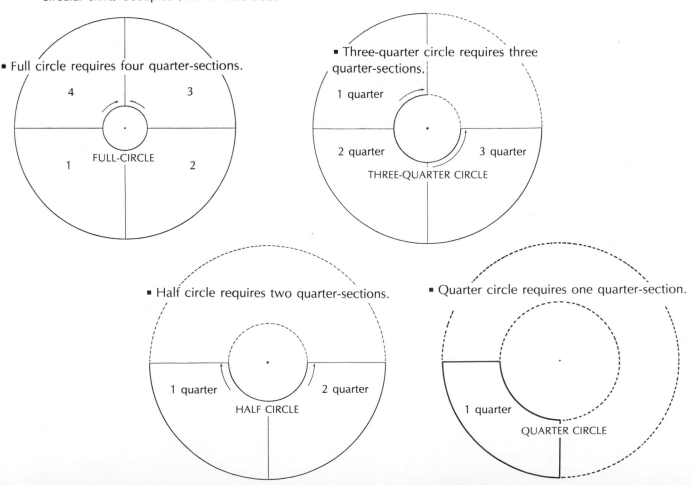

- Full circle requires four quarter-sections.

4 3
FULL-CIRCLE
1 2

- Three-quarter circle requires three quarter-sections.

1 quarter
2 quarter 3 quarter
THREE-QUARTER CIRCLE

- Half circle requires two quarter-sections.

1 quarter 2 quarter
HALF CIRCLE

- Quarter circle requires one quarter-section.

1 quarter
QUARTER CIRCLE

THE CIRCLE MEASURING TOOL

How to make the circle measuring tool
▪ Cut a strip of heavy weight pattern paper or cardboard 1 inch wide × 36 inches long (longer, if desired).
▪ Measure down 1 inch from the top edge and mark the center. Label X. Draw a guide line from X-point through the center of the strip.
▪ As each skirt is developed, complete the measuring tool by measuring down from X-point on the guideline to locate the radius for the waistline (labelled Y), and skirt's length (measured down from waistline point Y) labelled Z.
▪ Punch holes through marks Y and Z for pencil points to swing arc for waist and hemlines.

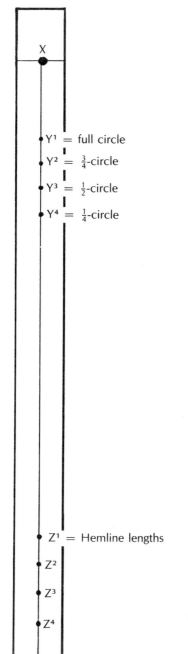

X

Y^1 = full circle
$Y^2 = \frac{3}{4}$-circle
$Y^3 = \frac{1}{2}$-circle
$Y^4 = \frac{1}{4}$-circle

Z^1 = Hemline lengths
Z^2
Z^3
Z^4

How to use the circle measuring tool
▪ To secure measuring tool to skirt draft, place pushpin through X-point at corner of paper (folded corner), positioning ruler at fold line of paper.
▪ Place pencil through desired Y hole; draw waistline arc. Place pencil through desired Z hole and draw hemline arc.

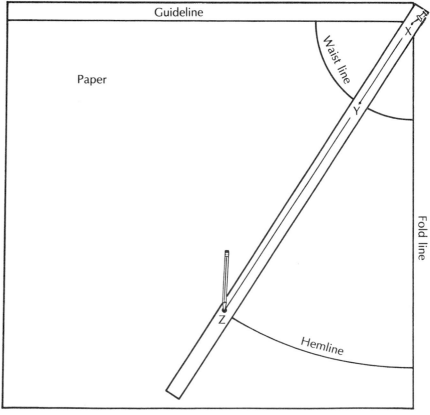

Guideline

Paper

Waist line

X

Y

Z

Hemline

Fold line

CIRCULAR SKIRTS

Circular skirt designs may be developed with varying hemline sweeps such as full, three-quarter, half, and quarter circle. These designs may be varied by changing the number of circles (single, double, triple, gathered, or tiered) or by changing the position of the grainline, thus affecting the placement of flare along the hemline sweep.

For purposes of this text, circular skirts are developed from the Circle/Cascade Radius Chart, eliminating the necessity for complex mathematical formulas. However, circular skirts may also be developed by the following methods that will not be illustrated:

(a) slashing and spreading the skirt pattern; and
(b) dividing the distance being covered to find the radius, as follows:

1/6—for full circle
1/5—for three-quarter circle
3/4—for half circle
2/3—for quarter circle

Seam allowances for waist, joining sections, and hem allowance are included in the circle formula.

(Continued on next page)

Grainline, bias, and flare relative to circular skirts

There is a direct relationship between the grainline and flare of skirts. Flare will develop along each side of the grainline, causing the skirt to flare out gracefully along its bias. By shifting the position of the grainline, the patternmaker can control the location of the flare along the skirt's hemline. For convenience, it is recommended that all three grainlines be indicated on each flared or circular working pattern. Choose appropriate grain for fabric and type of flared skirt desired.

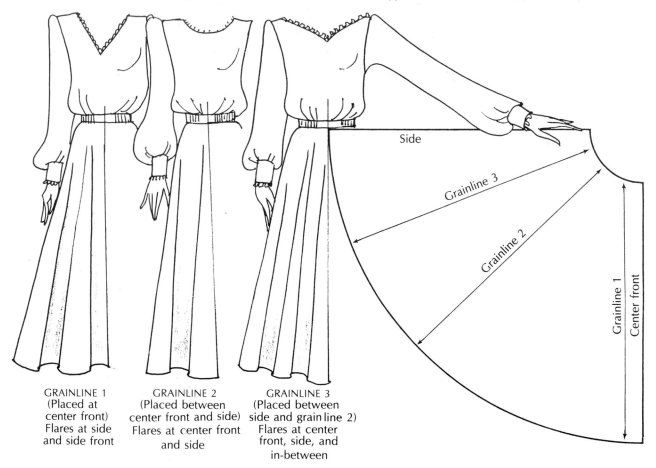

GRAINLINE 1
(Placed at center front)
Flares at side and side front

GRAINLINE 2
(Placed between center front and side)
Flares at center front and side

GRAINLINE 3
(Placed between side and grainline 2)
Flares at center front, side, and in-between

FULL-CIRCLE SKIRT

The information covering waistline adjustment, hemline modification, and grainline placement, applies to all circular type skirts. For easy reference, place tab on page 334 of the Circle/Cascade Radius Chart when developing circle skirts.

Note: Seam and hem allowances are included in the draft.

Hemline adjustments:

Some areas of circular type skirts will fall on the bias grain. The bias areas will grow in length and cause the hemline to be uneven. To make adjustments for the stretch factor after the skirt is cut in fabric do the following:

- Hang skirt on form, or pin waistline to the base of a hanger. Let skirt hang overnight (or longer for knits and chiffons), allowing time for the bias grain to relax and fall.
- Remark hemline on model or form, starting from center front, measuring up from the floor.

- Trim overhang and use for adjusting hemline by pinning pieces to pattern section where correction took place, or place the skirt flat on the pattern, and with a tracing wheel outline marked locations along hemline. Blend adjusted hemline.

Full-circle formula

- Waist measurement, *plus seam allowance:* 1 inch for one seam, 2 inches for two seams, and 4 inches for four seams. *Subtract* 1 inch for stretch or test fabric.
- Locate measurement in Column 1.
- Locate radius in Column 5 (full circle).
- Determine skirt length, add $1\frac{1}{2}$ inches (1 inch for hem, and $\frac{1}{2}$ inch for seam allowance at waistline). *Example:* 26-inch waist, plus 2 inches (two seams) less 1 inch for stretch = 27 inches.
- Radius = $4\frac{3}{8}$.
- Skirt length, plus $1\frac{1}{2}$ inches = 27 inches.

Pattern plot and development

Paper needed: 30 × 60 inches.

FIGURE 1

- Fold paper in half.
- Square a guideline from fold, 1 inch down from paper's edge.
- Label X on guideline at fold as shown.
- X–Y = Radius minus $\frac{1}{2}$ inch. Mark (Y).
- Y–Z = Skirt length. Mark (Z).

Circle measuring device:

- Mark and punch points Y and Z down from point X.
- Place pushpins through X points on ruler and pattern.
- Draw waist (Y point), and hem (Z point). (See page 336, for guidance, if necessary.)

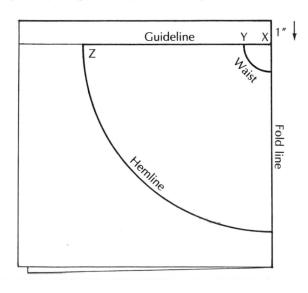

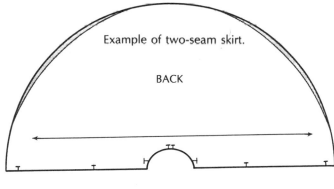

Example of two-seam skirt.

BACK

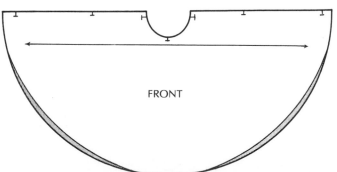

FRONT

FIGURE 2 *Waistline adjustment:*

(To compensate for slope at back skirt, and to flatten skirt over abdominal area.)

- Cut skirt from paper, except for waistline area. Trace waistline with tracing wheel. Unfold paper and adjust waist as follows:
- Square a line $\frac{3}{8}$ inch up from center front.
- Lower center back $\frac{3}{8}$ inch or use personal center back hip depth difference (shown as shaded area). (Broken line original waist.)

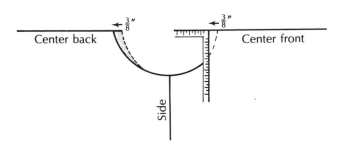

FIGURE 3

- Blend and trim waistline as shown.
- Separate panels at side seam. Cut center front and back on fold. Draw grainlines. Cut in fabric and hang for stretching.

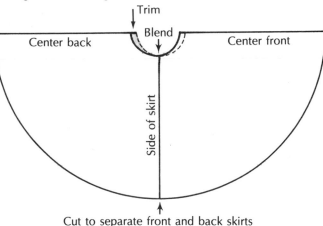

Cut to separate front and back skirts

FIGURE 4

- Shaded area shows needed hemline adjustment after hanging. Trim shaded area from pattern. Blend hemline. Notch, as shown.

Overhang: If skirt sweep overhangs fabric width, make a separate pattern for wedge section (overhang pattern) and piece garment. (See page 289.)

(Continued on next page)

FIGURE 5
Option: To divide circle into four or more parts, divide each section equally and notch sections for identification. Mark grainlines at center front and center back of each panel (or, as desired), and complete pattern for a test fit.

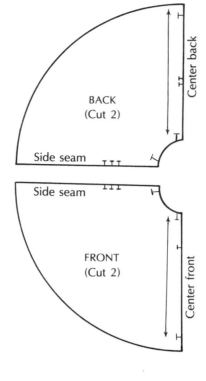

BACK
(Cut 2)

Center back

Side seam

Side seam

FRONT
(Cut 2)

Center front

Example of four-seam skirt.

THREE-QUARTER-CIRCLE SKIRT

Three-quarter-circle formula
- Waist measurement, *plus seam allowance:* 1 inch for one seam, 2 inches for two or three seams, and 3 inches for four seams. *Subtract* 1 inch for stretch or test fabric.
- Locate measurement in Column 1.
- Locate radius in Column 4 (three-quarter circle).
- Determine skirt length, add $1\frac{1}{2}$ inches (1 inch for hem, and $\frac{1}{2}$ inch for seam allowance at waistline). *Example:* 26-inch waist, plus 1 inch (one seam), less 1 inch for stretch = 26 inches.
- Radius = $5\frac{1}{2}$ inches.
- Skirt length, plus $1\frac{1}{2}$ inches = 27 inches.

Pattern plot and development
Paper needed: 64-inch square (tape together for length needed).

FIGURE 1
- Fold paper into fourths (fold evenly). Mark corner of fold X.
- X–Y = Radius minus $\frac{1}{2}$ inch. Mark (Y).
- Y–Z = Skirt length. Mark (Z).
Circle measuring tool:
Mark and punch points Y and Z down from point X. Place pushpins through X-points on ruler and pattern. Draw waist (Y-point), and hem (Z-point). (See page 336, for guidance, if necessary.)

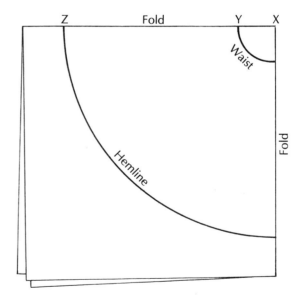

Z   Fold   Y   X

Waist

Hemline

Fold

FIGURE 2 *Waistline adjustment:*
▪ Cut skirt from paper, except for waistline area. Trace waistline with tracing wheel.
▪ Unfold paper and remove quarter section (broken lines). Adjust waistline and hemline using full-circle instructions as a guide. Shaded area is to be trimmed for hemline adjustment for bias overhang.

Example of one-seam skirt.

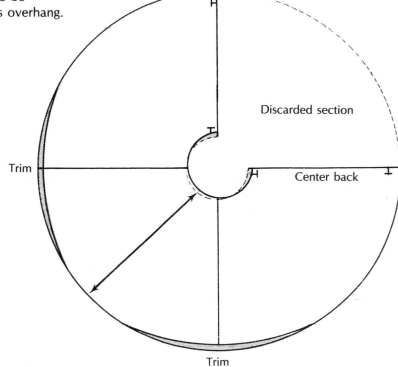

FIGURES 3 and 4
Option: If two or more seams are desired, divide panels into equal parts. Mark notches and center grainlines in each panel. Complete pattern for test fit.

Example of two-seam skirt.

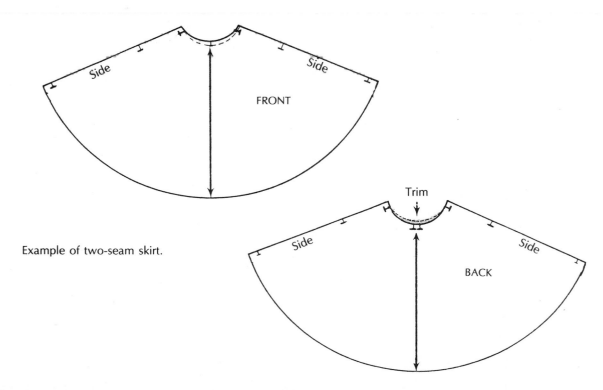

HALF-CIRCLE SKIRT

Half-circle formula

- Waist measurement, *plus seam allowance:* 1 inch for one seam, 2 inches for two or three seams, and 3 inches for four seams. *Subtract* 1 inch for stretch or test fabric.
- Locate measurement in Column 1 of Radius Chart.
- Locate radius in Column 3 (half-circle).
- Determine skirt length, add $1\frac{1}{2}$ inches (1 inch for hem, and $\frac{1}{2}$ inch for seam allowance at waistline). *Example:* 26-inch waist, plus 1 inch (one seam), less 1 inch for strech = 26 inches.
- Radius = $8\frac{1}{4}$ inches.
- Skirt length, plus $1\frac{1}{2}$ inches = 26 inches.

Pattern plot and development

Paper needed: 32 × 64 inches.

FIGURE 1

- Fold paper in half.
- Square a guideline from fold 1 inch down from paper's edge.
- Label X on guideline at fold as shown.
- X–Y = Radius minus $\frac{1}{2}$ inch. Mark (Y).
- Y–Z = Skirt length. Mark (Z).

Circle measuring tool:

- Mark and punch points Y and Z down from point X.
- Place pushpins through X-points on ruler and pattern.
- Draw waist (Y-point), and hem (Z-point). (See page 336 for guidance, if necessary.)

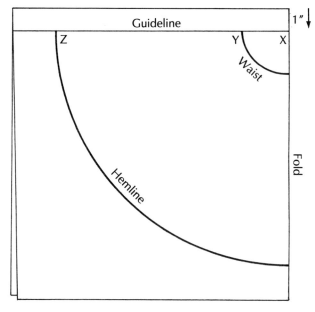

FIGURE 2   *Waistline adjustment:*
Cut skirt from paper, except at waistline. Trace waistline and unfold pattern. Refold matching the center backs. Adjust waistline and hemline using full-circle instructions as a guide. Unfold. Shaded area is to be trimmed for hemline adjustment for bias overhang.

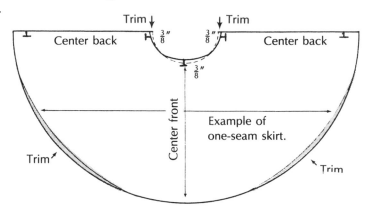

FIGURES 3 and 4
Option: If two or more seams are desired, divide panels into equal parts. Mark notches and center grainlines in each panel. Complete pattern for test fit.

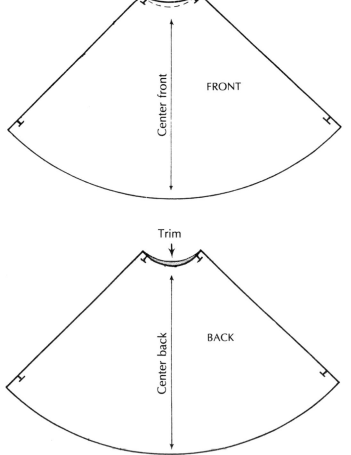

Example of two-seam skirt.

QUARTER-CIRCLE SKIRT

A quarter-circle skirt is one with a modified flare or sweep. When developed from a quarter circle, the pattern usually requires slight modification at the hip level to accommodate hipline circumference.

Quarter-circle formula

- Waist measurement, *plus seam allowance:* 1 inch for one seam, 2 inches for two or three seams, and 3 inches for four seams. (Do not subtract for stretch. The excess will be eased into waistband.)
- Locate measurement in Column 1 of Radius Chart.
- Locate radius in Column 2 (quarter-circle).
- Determine skirt length, add $1\frac{1}{2}$ inches (1 inch for hem and $\frac{1}{2}$ inch for seam allowance at waistline). *Example:* 26-inch waist, plus 1 inch (one seam) = 27 inches.
- Radius = $17\frac{1}{8}$ inches
- Skirt length, plus $1\frac{1}{2}$ inches = 27 inches.

Pattern plot and development

Measurement needed
- (4) Hip _____ .

- *Paper needed:* 45-inch square.

FIGURE 1
- Draw a square line on paper. Mark corner of square X.

FIGURE 2
- X–Y = Radius minus $\frac{1}{2}$ inch. Mark (Y).
- Y–Z = Skirt length. Mark (Z).
Circle measuring tool:
- Mark and punch points Y and Z down from point X.
- Place pushpins through X-points on ruler and pattern.
- Draw waist (Y-point), hem (Z-point). (See page 336 for guidance, if necessary.)
- Divide waist into four equal parts and crossmark. Label center A and other marks B and C. (Used for dividing skirt.) Draw line through center of skirt from point A (grainline).

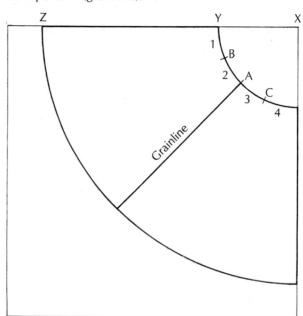

FIGURE 3
- Adjust waistline using full circle skirt instructions as a guide.
- Measure width of skirt at hip level (broken line). If less than hip measurement, add the difference equally on each side of hip level. Label C.
- Draw line from waist to hem touching C. Blend with hemline.

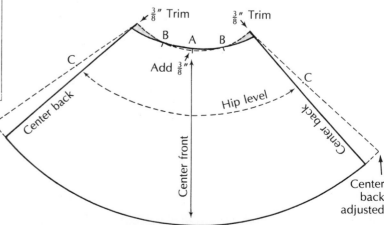

Example of one-seam skirt.

FIGURE 4
Option: If two or more seams are desired, divide panel into equal parts. Mark notches. Draw grain in center or bias. Complete pattern for test fit.

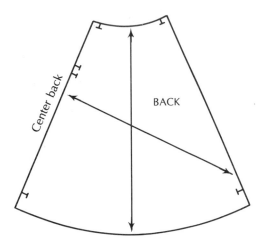 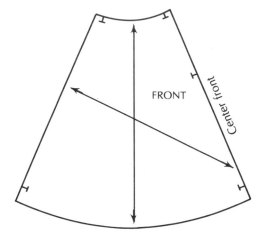

Example of two-seam skirt.

TWO CIRCLES AT WAIST
(Not Illustrated)

Pattern plot and development

> **Measurements needed:** Waist measurement plus seam allowance (two seams—add 2 inches, or four seams—add 3 inches).

- To develop circular skirt with two circles, divide the adjusted waistline measurement in half.
- Locate this measurement in Column 1 of the chart.
- Locate radius for full circle in Column 5.
- Cut two circles for area to be covered.
   Note: If more circles, or part of a circle, is desired at waist, always divide the number of circles desired into the waist measurement. Add for seams and subtract for stretch.

GATHERED CIRCULAR SKIRT
(Not Illustrated)

Pattern plot and development
- To add gathers to the waistline of a circular skirt, increase the waist measurement. (Example: waist measurement = 24 inches; add 8 inches for gathers = 32 inches at waistline.)
- Locate 32 inches on chart, and radius needed, in Column 2, 3, 4, or 5, depending on the sweep desired.

SKIRTS WITH UNEVEN HEMLINES

Design Analysis

Skirts with uneven hemlines are those whose hemlines are not parallel with the floor because of a difference in length at some point between the inner and outer edges. A number of hemline variations can be achieved by curving or pointing the outer circle, by placing the inner circle off-center, or by a combination of modifications to the inner and outer circles during pattern development.

The following examples of skirts may be used as a guide for developing uneven hemlines for any type of garment—skirts, peplums, sleeves, tiers, hoods, capes, and so on.

CIRCULAR SKIRT WITH HANDKERCHIEF ENDS

Design Analysis: Design 1

Design 1 features a circular skirt with a handkerchief hemline (squared or pointed hemline).

Pattern plot and development

Paper needed: Length, plus radius × 4 (2 pieces).

FIGURE 1

- Increase waistline measurement for gathers.
Suggestion: 8 inches more or less. Example: 24 inches + 8 inches = 32 inches.
- Locate 32 inches on chart.
- Locate radius for a full circle in Column 5 of chart.
- Fold paper in half. Label corner of fold X.
- X–Y = Radius measurement. Mark Y on fold.
- *Circle measuring tool:* Mark and punch point Y down from X. With pushpins through X-points and pencil through Y, draw waist from fold.
- Repeat for back skirt.
- Adjust front and back waist (see full-circle skirt directions for a guide).
- Cut waistline from pattern.

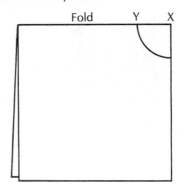

FIGURE 2

- Unfold patterns. Draw grain and complete for test fit.

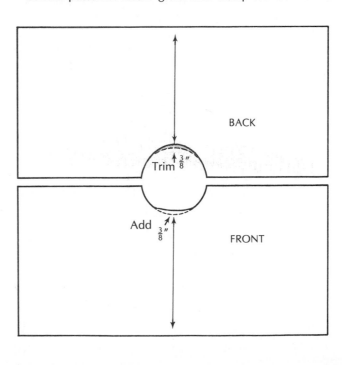

CIRCULAR SKIRT WITH GRADUATED-LENGTH HEMLINE

Design Analysis: Design 2

Design 2 features double circular skirts, one shorter than the other, with a cascade effect formed by the inner circle cut off-center. Waistband ties skirt together.

Formula:

- To find radius, follow full-circle instructions in Circle/Cascade Radius Chart (Columns 1 and 5).
- Determine shortest and longest lengths. Add both measurements together, plus 2 × radius, and record total measurement: _____.
- Divide this measurement in half and record: _____.

Example:

- 27-inch adjusted waistline = $4\frac{3}{8}$-inch radius (full circle).
- Shortest length = 20 inches
- Longest length = 36 inches
- 2 × radius = $8\frac{3}{4}$ inches

  Total = $64\frac{3}{4}$ inches
- One-half of total = $32\frac{3}{8}$ inches

Pattern plot and development

Paper needed: 65 × 45 inches.

FIGURE 1

- Fold paper into four equal parts (evenly). Mark corner A.
- Mark Z down from A, using one-half of total measurement recorded (example: $32\frac{3}{8}$ inches).
- Locate this measurement on the Circle Measuring Device down from point X. Place point X at point A on paper, and draw hemline. (See page 336, if necessary.)

Mark the following location:

- Z–Y = Short length of skirt. Mark on fold.
- Y–X = Radius measurement (example: $4\frac{3}{8}$ inches). Mark on fold.
- Cut circle from paper.

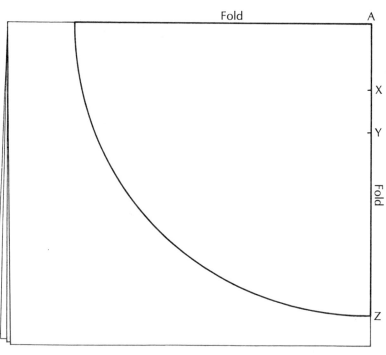

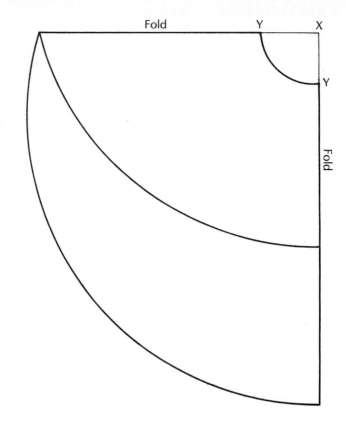

FIGURE 2
- Refold paper, using X-point for fold line.
- With measuring device, draw waist curve and cut waistline from paper.
- Adjust waistline and hemline.

FIGURE 3
- Open pattern.
- Draw styleline for curved hemline as shown and trim excess (broken lines). Separate front and back skirts.
- Retrace for top skirt. Trim $1\frac{1}{2}$ inches from length of skirt as shown by broken lines.
- Draw grain and complete pattern for test fit.

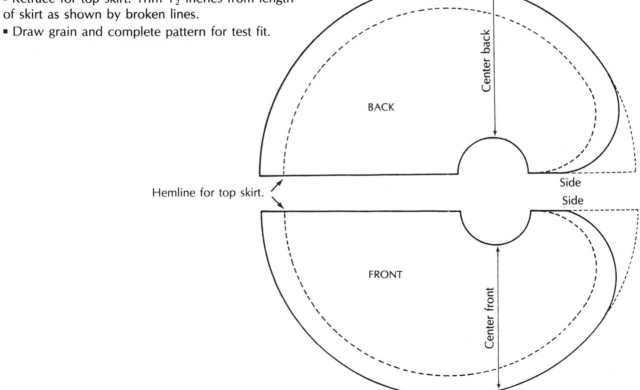

SKIRT DESIGN VARIATIONS

The following designs are based on circular and straightline skirts. Develop these designs for practice, or create new designs of your own, using concepts illustrated in this chapter and the three major patternmaking principles.

13

SLEEVES AND SLEEVE/BODICE COMBINATIONS

Introduction 350
Set-in sleeve 350
Terminology 351
Elbow darts 351
Shoulder pads 352
SLEEVE CUFFS 352
Basic shirt cuff 353
Self-faced cuff 353
French cuffs (used with cufflinks) 353
Contoured cuffs 354
Roll-up cuffs 355
CAP SLEEVES 356
Jutting cap 356
Close-fitting cap 356
DARTLESS SLEEVE PATTERN 357

SHIRTMAKER SLEEVE 358
Shirtmaker sleeve hemline options 359
BASIC BISHOP SLEEVE 360
EXAGGERATED BISHOP SLEEVE 362
BELL SLEEVES 363
PUFF SLEEVES 364
Fullness at hem 365
Fullness at cap 366
Fullness at hem and cap 366
CIRCULAR HEMLINE SLEEVES 367
Half-circle sleeve 367
Full-circle sleeve 368
PETAL SLEEVES 370
Plain petal 370
Gathered petal 371
Flared petal 371
LANTERN SLEEVES 372
Long lantern sleeve 372
Short lantern sleeve 374
SLEEVES WITH EXTENDED CAPS 375
Darted cap 375
Crescent-shaped, extended cap 376
Gathered crescent sleeve 377
LEG-OF-MUTTON SLEEVE 378
COWL SLEEVE 379
WEDDING SLEEVE 380
Traditional wedding sleeve 380
Sleeve variations with patterns 381
SLEEVE WITH LIFT 382
SLEEVE WITH LOWERED ARMHOLE 384

Sleeve/bodice combinations
BASIC KIMONO 387
Bodice modification 387
BASIC DOLMAN 390
ONE-PIECE COMBINATIONS 391
Kimono with shoulder dart 391
Full-sleeved kimono (without overarm seam) 392
Tapered sleeve (without overarm seam) 393
Kimono and dolman variations 393
KIMONO WITH GUSSET 394
BASIC RAGLAN 398
One-piece raglan 400
RAGLAN VARIATIONS 401
Armhole–princess raglan 401
Yoke raglan with bell sleeve 402
Other design variations based on raglan foundation 402
Deep raglan 403
EXAGGERATED ARMHOLES 404
Deep-cut square armhole 404
Square armhole with gathered three-quarter sleeve 406
DROP SHOULDER 408
Without lower sleeve 408

INTRODUCTION

Sleeves have always been in the forefront of fashion throughout history and have been used as a device for changing the silhouette of a garment. In the 1880s, the dominant silhouette was a leg-of-mutton sleeve—a sleeve that puffs out from the shoulder with the lower section tapered toward the wrist. For the next ten years, the sleeve puff varied from slim to voluminous and billowy. In the 1920s, a sleeve with a darted or extended cap became popular, and in the 1940s the sleeve became smooth and included padded shoulders ranging from a tailored square to oversized exaggeration. There was a return to a natural shoulder with minimal padding in the 1950s. This gave tailored garments a smooth look along the shoulder seam. From then until the present, these important sleeve silhouettes have appeared and disappeared, and will probably reappear again.

There are two major classifications of sleeves: the set-in sleeve cut separately and stitched into the armhole of the bodice and the sleeve combined with part or all of the bodice. The set-in sleeve is introduced here; the sleeve/bodice combination will be examined following the set-in sleeve series.

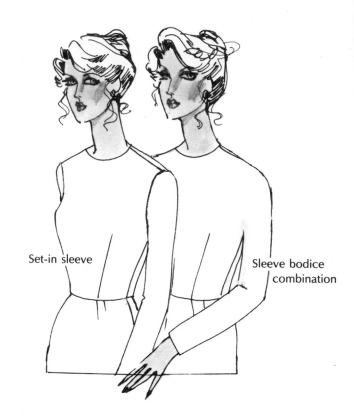

Set-in sleeve

Sleeve bodice combination

SLEEVE LENGTHS

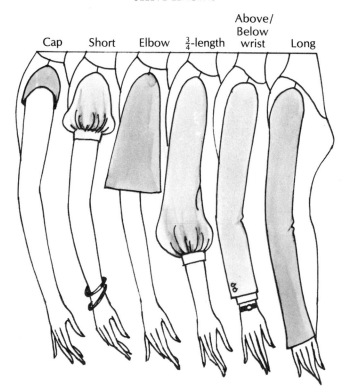

Cap Short Elbow 3/4-length Above/Below wrist Long

SET-IN SLEEVE

Set-in sleeves can be designed to fit the armhole smoothly or with gathers. They can be designed fitted or with exaggerated fullness, and can be cut to any length.

The hemline of the sleeve can be finished in a number of ways. A straight or full sleeve can be confined by an attached cuff, band, elastic, or casing (for elastic or tie). If not confined, the sleeve may have a self-hem (either folded-back or rolled-up), or may be faced or edged with trim. The opening for hand entry can also be treated in a variety of ways, from slits with plackets, facing, or fold-back, to zipper-type closures.

TERMINOLOGY

Terms relating to sleeve development

Sleeve cap. The curved top of the sleeve from front to back.

Cap height. The distance from biceps to cap at center.

Biceps. The widest part of the sleeve dividing cap from lower sleeve.

Sleeve ease. Additional allowance at biceps, elbow, and wrist to accommodate the circumference of the arm. Allows ease for freedom of movement. Ease ranges from 1½ to inches.

Cap ease. Difference between cap and armhole measurement (ranging from 1½ to 2 inches).

Elbow level. The location of the dart, level with elbow of arm.

Wrist level. The bottom (hemline) of the sleeve, level with wrist of arm.

Grainline. Center of sleeve from top of cap to wrist level—straight grain of sleeve.

Quartering sleeve. Sleeve divided into four equal parts from cap to wrist. Used as guidelines for spreading the sleeve. Quarter sections are labelled X (see illustration).

Notches. One notch indicates front sleeve, two notches indicates back sleeve. Cap notch indicates where shoulder seam will meet (its position can vary).

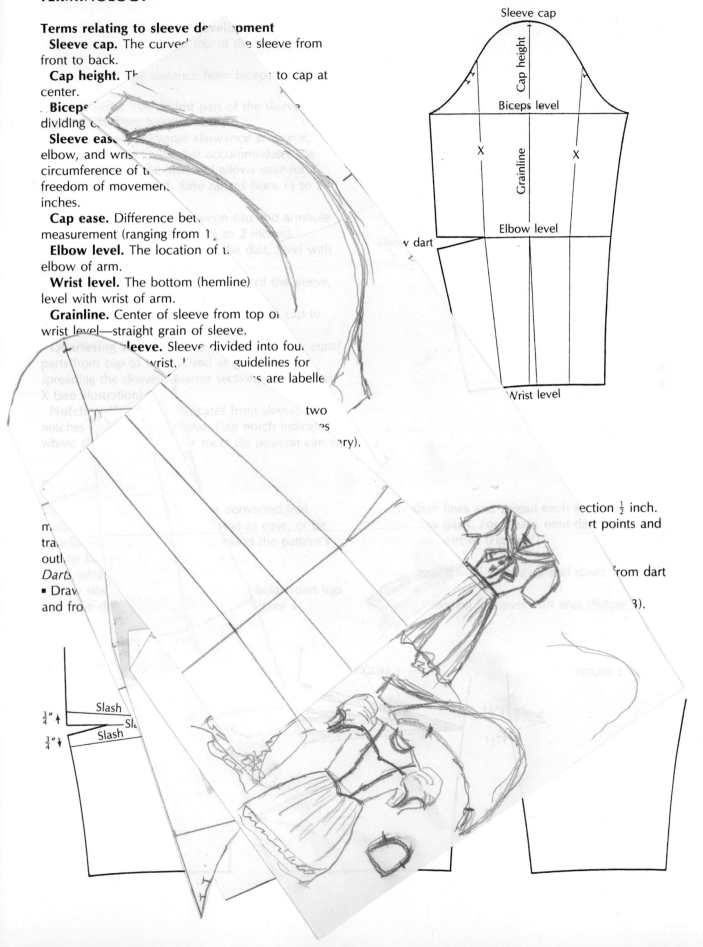

SHOULDER PADS

The shoulderline of the bodice and the cap of the
sleeve must both be modified when shoulder pads
are used by adding the height of the shoulder pad
to the shoulder tips of the bodice and the sleeve
cap. For example, when using a $\frac{1}{4}$-inch-thick
shoulder pad, extend the front and back shoulder
tips and sleeve cap $\frac{1}{4}$ inch as shown. Add an
additional $\frac{1}{4}$ inch to shoulder tips for thicker
shoulder pads.

SHOULDER PAD

Measure thickness

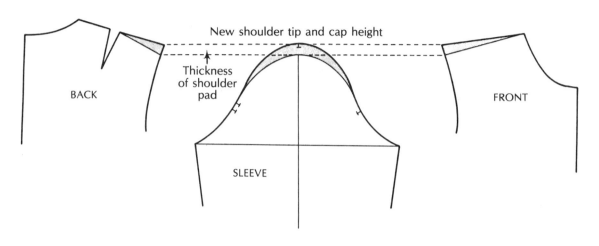

New shoulder tip and cap height

Thickness
of shoulder
pad

BACK

FRONT

SLEEVE

SLEEVE CUFFS

Sleeve cuffs can be developed in a variety of
widths and styled in a number of ways (curved,
pointed, and so on). The most common are the
basic shirt cuff, the French cuff, the closed cuff, the
roll-up cuff, and the wide, contoured cuff. Other
design variations are easily developed using these
general instructions as a guide. The grainline can be
varied for straight, bias, or crossgrain to
accommodate the marker or fabric design (plaids
and stripes).

Measurements needed
(39) Around hand _____, plus $\frac{1}{2}$-inch ease.
Cuff width as desired.
Example: 8-inch wrist (including ease) for a
basic cuff 2 inches wide.

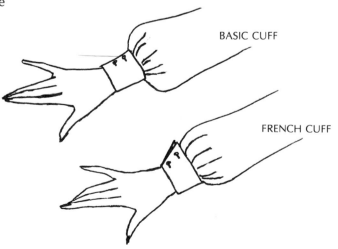

BASIC CUFF

FRENCH CUFF

BASIC SHIRT CUFF

FIGURE 1
- Fold paper lengthwise. Cuff will be developed on fold.
- Square a 2-inch line from fold. Draw parallel line 8 inches long. Mark.
- Add 1 inch for extension.

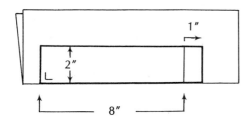

FIGURE 2
- Add $\frac{1}{2}$-inch seams.
- Mark button placement in center of extension.
- Center buttonhole $\frac{3}{4}$ inches from edge (see Chapter 14 on button placement).
- Cut from paper.

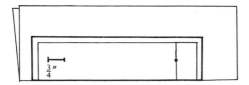

FIGURE 3
- Unfold cuff pattern. Add grain, straight or crosswise.

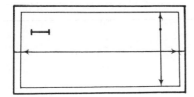

SELF-FACED CUFF

FIGURE 4
- Develop cuff using general instructions above.
- Cuff can be designed with square corners or curves (broken lines).
- Cut four pieces to complete the set.

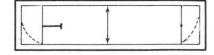

FRENCH CUFFS (USED WITH CUFFLINKS)

One-piece cuff

FIGURE 5
- Fold paper lengthwise.
- Square a 4-inch line from fold equal to twice the cuff's width.
- Draw parallel line 8 inches long. Mark for notch and add 1-inch extension to both ends of cuff. Connect ends.
- Mark for buttonholes (see Chapter 14).
- Add seams and grainline.
- Cut from paper.

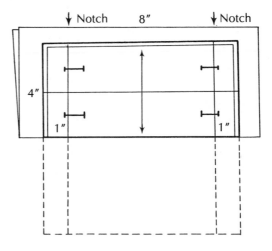

Two-piece cuff

FIGURE 6
(Straight or pointed ends. See broken lines.)
- Develop cuff on open paper, using instructions for folded French cuff.
- Add seams to all sides of pattern.
- Draw grainline.
- Cut from paper.

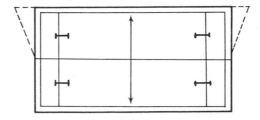

CONTOURED CUFFS

Design Analysis

Contoured sleeve cuffs follow the shape of the arm and can be as wide as desired, ranging anywhere from the wrist to the elbow. They may be straight, pointed, curved, or varied in some way (see broken lines, Figures 1 and 3).

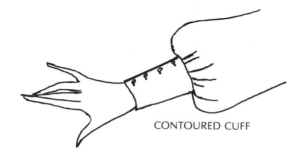

CONTOURED CUFF

Cuff based on basic sleeve

FIGURE 1

- Trace sleeve from wrist to desired cuff width (example: 6 inches).
- Draw parallel line 6 inches above wrist.
- Notch 1 inch in from underseam on right side for extension (tightens cuff).
- Mark for buttons and buttonholes (see Chapter 14).
- Cut cuff from pattern.

   Note: If cuff is pointed or curved, the sleeve joining cuff should also be pointed or curved. (See broken lines on Figures 1 and 3 for design variations.)

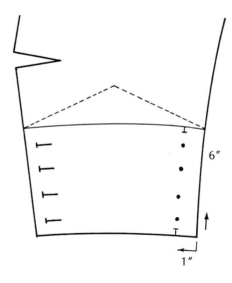

Cuff based on dartless pattern

FIGURE 2

Develop cuff as follows:

- Draw line equal to wrist measurement (example: 8 inches).
- Square up from both ends equal to cuff width (example: 6 inches). Draw line across.
- Divide into four equal parts.

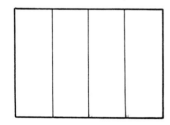

FIGURE 3

- Slash and spread each section $\frac{1}{4}$ inch.
- Add 1-inch extension.
- Mark for buttons and buttonholes.

   Note: Remember to subtract cuff length from pattern before developing sleeve pattern (not illustrated).

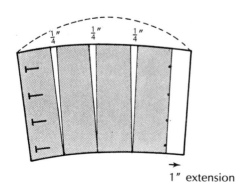

1" extension

ROLL-UP CUFFS

Design Analysis

Roll-up cuffs are developed all-in-one with the sleeve, or as a separate cuff stitched to the sleeve and then turned up. To develop this type of cuff, determine the finished length of sleeve (biceps level to hem) and add cuff width. Example: Sleeve length below biceps = 4 inches; cuff $1\frac{1}{2}$ inches (amount rolled up). Use these measurements or personal measurements.

All-in-one cuff with sleeve

FIGURE 1
- Trace sleeve to finished length desired. Label A–B.
- Draw three parallel lines spaced $1\frac{1}{2}$ inches apart below hem (A–B line). Label sections 1, 2, and 3.

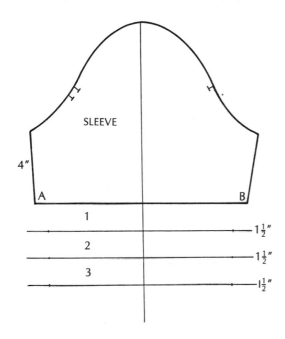

FIGURE 2
- Fold so that section 1 is up, section 2 down, and section 3 underneath.
- Draw underseams with ruler on both sides of fold as guides and cut from paper. Unfold.

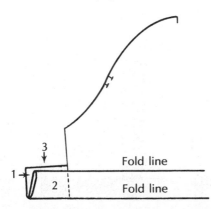

FIGURE 3
- The completed sleeve.

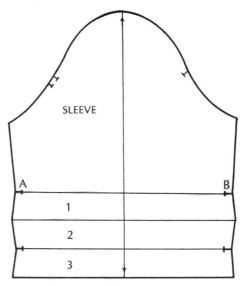

Separated cuff

FIGURE 4
Follow instructions above for all-in-one cuff, with exceptions:
- Omit third section.
- Cut along A–B line, separating cuff from sleeve.
- Add seams.

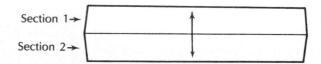

CAP SLEEVES

Cap sleeves may either jut away from the arm (Design 1) or fit the arm snugly (Design 2). This type of sleeve can be shaped in a variety of ways and is usually designed for a bodice, dress, or blouse.

JUTTING CAP

Pattern plot and development

FIGURE 1   *Sleeve cap:*
- Trim approximately 1 inch from cap height (causes hemline to swing away from arm).
- Hemline may be straight (Figure 1) or curved (Figure 2) to vary design (see broken lines).
- Use illustrations as guide for development.
- Use fold-back technique for sleeve with straight hem. (See page 355.)

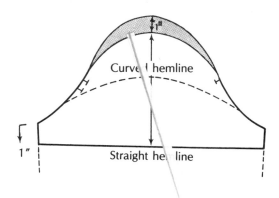

FIGURE 2
- Example of short curved sleeve (self-faced).

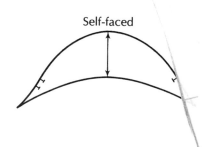

CLOSE-FITTING CAP

FIGURE 1
- Trace sleeve 1 inch below biceps line. Divide into fourths and label slash lines X.

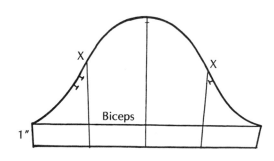

FIGURE 2
- Slash and overlap X guidelines.
- Trim underseams, blend cap and shape hem (self-faced).

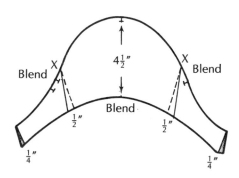

DARTLESS SLEEVE PATTERN

Sleeves are developed from two types of working patterns—the basic foundation and a straight dartless pattern. The basic pattern can be used for all sleeve designs, but patternmaking for full sweeping hemlines and other types are more easily developed from a dartless sleeve or half of a dartless sleeve.

A dartless working pattern is used to develop sleeves with added fullness (bell, flare, bishop, and so on) and sleeves not requiring an elbow dart (shirtmaker types). Generally, the back half (from center grainline to underseam only) is used. It is placed on the fold for pattern development. The front armhole curve is transferred to the paper underneath as a reference for modifying the pattern when open. (This will be illustrated throughout this chapter.) The dartless sleeve foundation is based on the basic sleeve as follows:

Pattern plot

FIGURE 1
- Trace basic sleeve, include all markings. Label as shown. (Broken line indicates original pattern not needed.)
- Continue line from elbow so that C–D equals A–B length.
- Connect D with B.
- Label grainline E, as shown.
- E–F = D–E (adjusted wrist level). Connect with A.
- Crossmark one-half of desired wrist measurement on each side of E.
- Cut from paper, discard unneeded section.

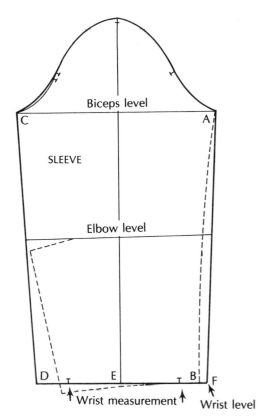

FIGURE 2   *Full sleeve:*
- Draw lines equally on both sides of grain to quarter the sleeve. Label X as shown.

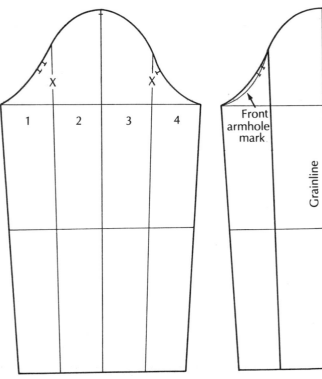

FIGURE 3   *Half sleeve:*
- For convenience, make a separate copy of back sleeve from grain to underarm seam. Trace front armhole curve on top of back armhole. (Used for developing front and back sleeve at one time— illustrated where appropriate.)

SHIRTMAKER SLEEVE

Design Analysis

The shirtmaker sleeve is developed from the dartless sleeve. The wrist level is modified to provide sufficient elbow room for the arm when bent, and a slit is provided for hand entry. The hemline of the sleeve may be gathered, pleated, or tapered into a cuff of any desired width, or it may be developed using a combination of these treatments. The shirtmaker sleeve is used for casual or active garments. It's best when attached to a casual top, shirt, or dress, with a modified (enlarged) armhole that offsets the sleeve cap ease. (See dartless pattern development, page 357, and cuff instructions, page 353.)

Sleeve may be further modified for a higher lift (see page 382), or a lowered armhole (see page 384).

Pattern plot and development

FIGURE 1

- Trace dartless sleeve and all markings.
- Draw parallel line 2 inches up from wrist level and subtract for cuff width. Label A as shown.
- Measure down $\frac{3}{4}$ inches from A (elbow bending room).
- Draw new hemline with a French curve. Crossmark slit line $2\frac{1}{2}$ inches up from A (opening for hand entry).
- Cut from paper. Discard unneeded section (shaded area).

FIGURE 2

- Cut $\frac{1}{16}$-inch-wide slit along slit line, folding pattern to notch at crossmark. (Confirms the limits of the slit if pattern is torn through use.)
- Draw grain and add seams after hemline is developed. Option 1 hemline is illustrated on completed sleeve. (See other options on next page.)

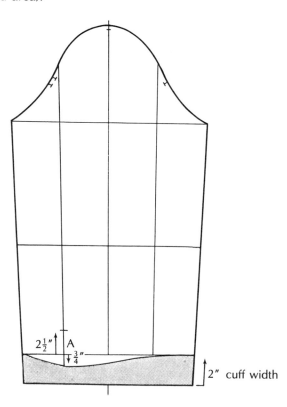

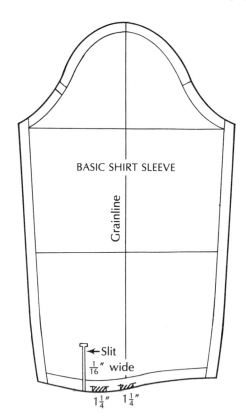

BASIC SHIRT SLEEVE

Grainline

←Slit

$\frac{1}{16}$" wide

$1\frac{1}{4}$" $1\frac{1}{4}$"

$2\frac{1}{2}$"   A

$\frac{3}{4}$"

2" cuff width

SHIRTMAKER SLEEVE HEMLINE OPTIONS

Subtract around hand measurement from hemline measurement to determine excess. Example: 7 inches around hand; 11-inch hemline allows 4 inches of excess to be absorbed by darts, pleats, gathers, and/or tapering underarm seam.

Measurements needed
- (39) around hand _____

Option 1: Two pleats

FIGURE 1
- Mark two $1\frac{1}{4}$-inch darts $\frac{3}{4}$ inches away from right side of slit. Dart space = $\frac{3}{4}$ inch.
- Remove $\frac{1}{2}$ inch from underarm seam at wrist (broken line), allowing $\frac{1}{2}$ inch for ease. Blend a curved line to elbow.

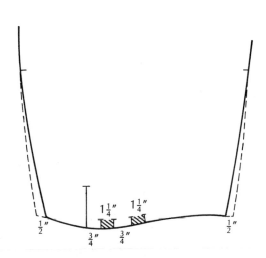

Option 3: Gathers

FIGURE 3
- For a gathered sleeve, notch hemline $1\frac{1}{2}$ inches in from underseams.

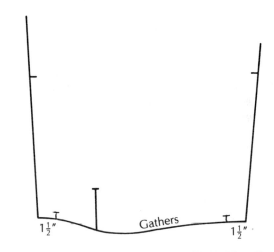

Option 2: One pleat

FIGURE 2
- Shift slit $\frac{1}{2}$ inch, as shown.
- Mark $1\frac{1}{4}$-inch pleat $\frac{3}{4}$ inch from slit. Allow $\frac{1}{2}$-inch ease on left side of slit.
- Remove $1\frac{1}{4}$ inches from underarm seam at wrist, blending to elbow.

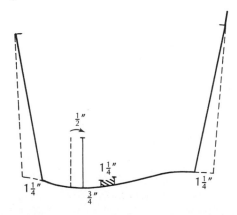

Option 4: Plain

FIGURE 4
- Allow $\frac{1}{2}$ inch for ease. Remove $1\frac{3}{4}$ inches from underseam at wrist, blending a slightly curved line to elbow.

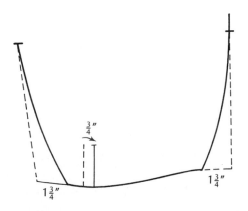

BASIC BISHOP SLEEVE

Design Analysis

The bishop is a long (or three-quarter length) full sleeve that hangs gracefully over the arm from a smooth cap below which it flares out, and is contained in a cuff, giving it a blouson effect. It is developed from the shirtmaker sleeve, using Principle #2, Added Fullness. It has greater excess in back than in front and additional length at the hemline for blousing. Once developed, this pattern can also be used for an exaggerated bishop sleeve. The pivotal-transfer technique is used for this illustration.

Pattern plot and development

FIGURE 1
- Trace sleeve and all markings.
- Label panels. Mark each side of cap $\frac{1}{2}$ inch from grainline (reference for eliminating part of cap ease), and label A and B. Label C at grainline of hem. Mark X at quarter sections.

   Note: When spreading hemline of sleeve, the sleeve widens up to the cap, making it unnecessary to include cap ease.

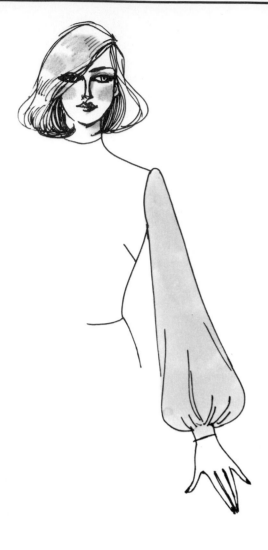

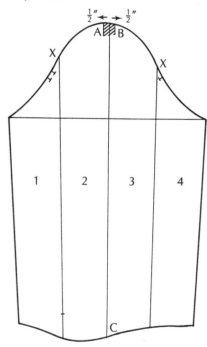

FIGURE 2
- Draw vertical guideline on paper (new grainline).
- Place pattern on guideline with A–C of sleeve on guideline.
- Trace back cap and wrist of Panel 2 (shaded area). Label D at hem.
- Measure out 3 inches from D on paper and mark.

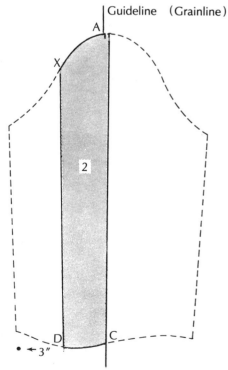

FIGURE 3
- With pushpin at X, pivot pattern until D is in line with mark on paper.
- Trace Panel 1 (shaded area) and crossmark at point D.

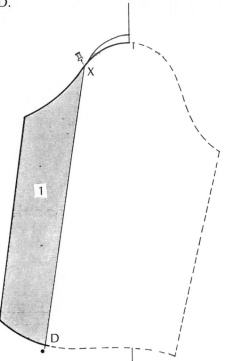

FIGURE 5
- With pushpin at X, pivot pattern until E is in line with mark on paper.
- Trace Panel 4 (shaded area) and crossmark. Remove pattern.

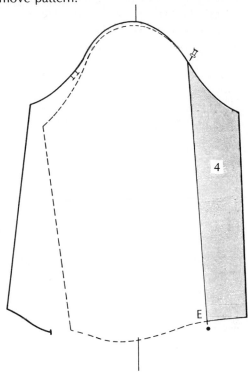

FIGURE 4
- Return pattern to guideline with B and C of sleeve on guideline.
- Trace cap and wrist of Panel 3 (shaded area) and crossmark point E.
- Measure out $1\frac{1}{2}$ inches from E and mark on paper.

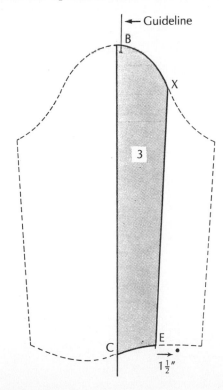

FIGURE 6
- Draw blending curved line across hemline of sleeve. (Lined area indicates fullness added to sleeve.) For blousing, add $\frac{3}{4}$ inch to length of sleeve at hemline.
- *Slit:* Draw $2\frac{1}{2}$-inch line between open space of back sleeve. Draw parallel line $\frac{1}{16}$ inch wide. Cut slit open and fold notching at end of slit.
- Draw grain and complete for test fit.

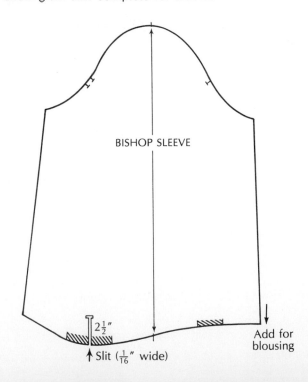

EXAGGERATED BISHOP SLEEVE

Design Analysis
The exaggerated bishop sleeve is based on the basic bishop pattern but has greater fullness at the wrist and may be longer, for greater blousing, than the basic bishop sleeve. For cuff development, see page 353.

Pattern plot and development

FIGURE 1
- Trace basic bishop sleeve. Mark quarter sections X, as shown.
- *Draw slash lines:* Divide each quarter section in half (eight panels).
- Cut from paper.

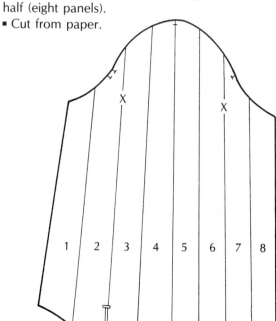

FIGURE 2
- Cut up from hem to, not through, sleeve cap.
- Spread as desired or follow illustration.
- Draw pattern outline. Discard.
- Draw curved hemline 1 inch or more below original length (for blousing), tapering to underseams (Panels 1 and 8), as shown.
- *Slit:* Draw slit 2 inches long, $\frac{1}{16}$ inch wide.
- Draw grain; cut and notch slit.
Complete pattern for test fit.

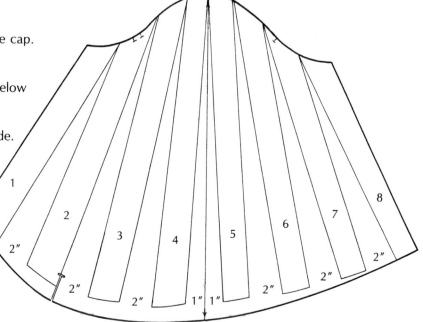

BELL SLEEVES

Design Analysis

Bell sleeves are full sleeves with a smooth cap and an unconfined hemline flaring out in the shape of a bell. They may be developed to any length desired. Depending upon the amount of flare desired, the bell can be based on either the dartless sleeve back, the bishop, or the exaggerated bishop sleeve (with the hemline trimmed). The dartless sleeve is illustrated, showing three sleeve lengths.

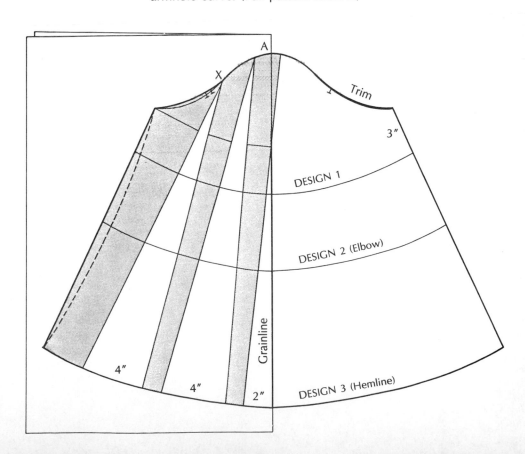

Pattern plot and development

FIGURE 1

- Trace dartless sleeve back. Include quarter line. Label X.
- Mark length of bell sleeve as desired. (Example: 3 inches below biceps for Design 1, elbow level for Design 2, and full length for Design 3.)
- Draw slash line between X-line and grainline.
- Mark A, ½ inch from cap to eliminate ease.
- Cut slash lines to, not through, cap.

FIGURE 2

- Fold paper.
- Place point A of sleeve on fold of paper and spread for desired hemline sweep or use measurements given.
- Trace pattern outline. Trace front curve of sleeve.
- Draw an inward curve to taper underseam (broken lines).
- Cut from paper, unfold, draw grain and trim front armhole curve. (Full pattern shown.)

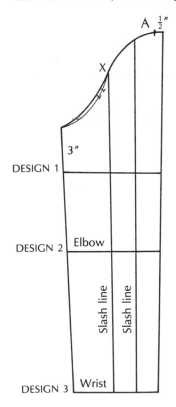

PUFF SLEEVES

DESIGN 1

DESIGN 2

DESIGN 3

Design Analysis

Puff sleeves are developed by adding fullness to the sleeve's width. This is an application of Principle #2, Added Fullness. There are three types of basic puff sleeves, those with fullness at the hem (Design 1), fullness at the cap (Design 2), and fullness at both cap and hem (Design 3).

Puff sleeves can be of any length desired. (Two lengths are illustrated for each style.) The illustrations show a sleeve length 2 inches below biceps line. Each sleeve was developed from the back half of the dartless sleeve pattern, page 357. Use the general instructions below to prepare the pattern for each of the puff sleeves. Individual instructions are given for each puff type where appropriate. *Note:* The amount of spread and length can be increased or decreased according to the fabric and design.

Pattern plot and development

FIGURE 1

■ Trace back half of dartless sleeve pattern, 2 inches below biceps. Include all markings. Remove pattern and connect hemline.
■ Mark A, $\frac{1}{2}$ inch in from cap to remove ease.
■ Draw slash line between X-point and grain.
■ Cut from paper.
■ Cut slash lines from hem to, not through, sleeve cap.

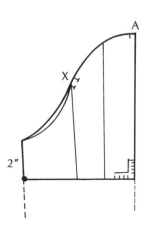

FULLNESS AT HEM

FIGURE 2
- Fold paper.
- Place sleeve on p̶a̶̶
- Slash and spr̶̶
- Trace sle̶̶ notches ar̶̶

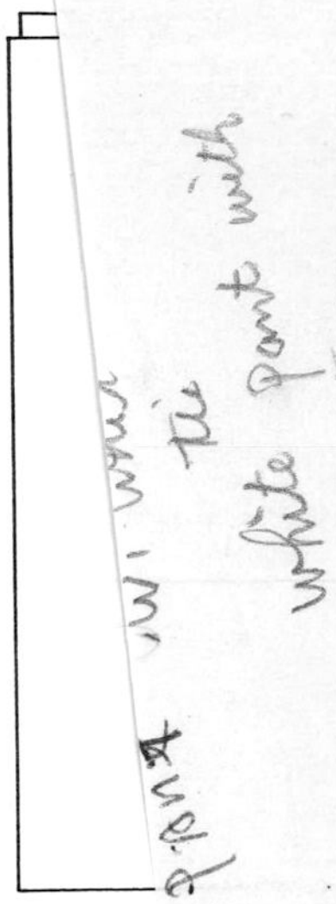

FIGURE 3
- Extend hemline 2 inches at center front and blend curve line to underseam.
- Add $\frac{1}{2}$-inch seams.
- Extend underarm seam for notch placement guide.
- Mark notches as shown.
- C̶̶ ̶̶ ̶̶paper.

2"   2"   1"   2"

her
notch

No̶̶ Seams are il̶̶trated as a guide. Seams s̶̶ ̶̶ be ad̶̶ before ̶̶tting pattern from paper.

FIGURE 4
- Unfold pattern, ̶̶
- Trim front sleev̶̶

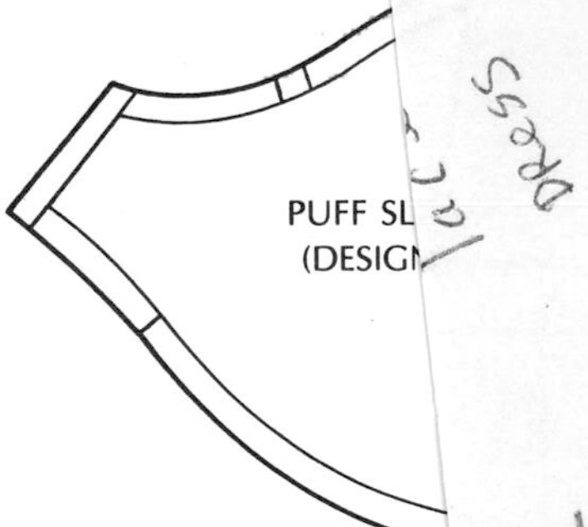

PUFF SL̶̶
(DESIGN̶̶

FIGURE 5 ̶̶ sleeve band̶̶
Sleeve bands are used for ̶̶ s̶̶eves. For
sleeves ending above elbow, use ̶̶
measurement (15). For those endin̶̶ ̶̶ow elbow,
̶̶ easure the arm at the level of ̶̶ sleeve length.
̶̶yd = 27 inches̶̶ inches
̶̶̶̶ 2 inches finished band equal̶̶ ̶̶nch).

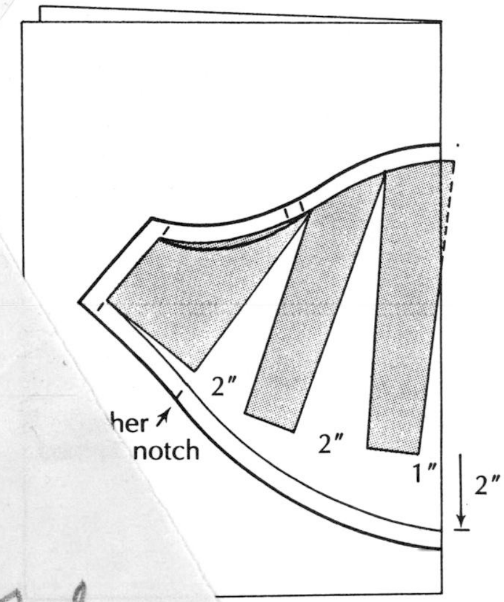

Handwritten notes (overlaid):

Fabric

Plant wi̶̶ tie to
white paint with
white tace.

3.½ lace ort

width
3 in

1.5 yards

pieces

Dress

yds.

¾ yd = 27 inches

½ yd = 18 inches

FULLNESS AT CAP

FIGURE 1
- Use sleeve preparation on page 364 for Design 2.
- Place sleeve on paper with hem touching fold and place hem ½ inch over fold line to tighten hemline if desired.
- Slash and spread as shown.
- Trace sleeve and front sleeve curve. Discard.
- Measure up 2 inches from cap. Mark and draw curve line for cap as shown.
- Cut from paper.

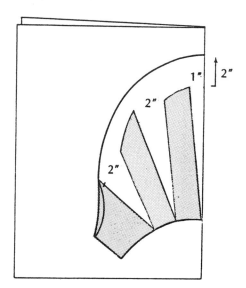

FULLNESS AT HEM AND CAP

FIGURE 1
- Use sleeve preparation on page 364 for Design 3.
- Square a guideline 3 inches up from fold.
- Place pattern on fold with hemline on guideline (indicated by broken lines). Label A and B.
- Measure up 2 inches from cap and 2 inches down from hem. Mark.
- B–C = One-half of A–B. Mark on guideline.
- Shift pattern along guideline until point B touches C mark.
- Trace sleeve to X-guideline, including front sleeve curve (shaded area). Discard pattern.
- Blend curve line at cap and hem as shown.
- Cut from paper.

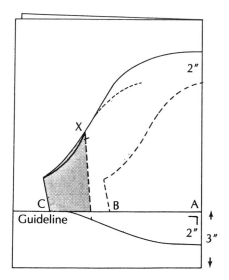

FIGURE 2
- Unfold pattern.
- Draw grain and notch.
- *Facing:* Trace hemline of sleeve 1¼ inches wide.

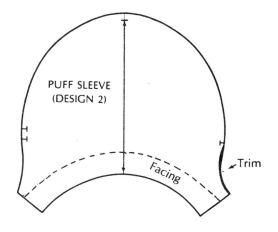

FIGURE 2
- Unfold pattern, draw grain. Notch. Trim front sleeve curve.

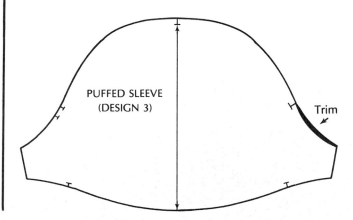

CIRCULAR HEMLINE SLEEVES

HALF-CIRCLE SLEEVE

Design Analysis

The dartless sleeve pattern is used as a basis for increasing sleeve hemline fullness to a half circle. The sleeve can be developed to any length desired; see Designs 1, 2, and 3. The short sleeve (Design 1) is illustrated and should be used as a guide for longer lengths. (See Chapter 12 for the Circle/Cascade Radius Chart as another way to develop this type of sleeve.

Pattern plot and development

FIGURE 1

- Trace dartless sleeve back 2 inches below biceps. Remove pattern. Square a line across sleeve hem.
- Draw slash lines in between X-guideline as shown.
- Cut slash lines to, not through, cap.

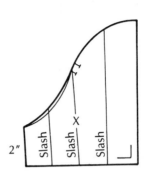

FIGURE 2

- Fold paper.
- Square a guideline 2 inches down from fold.
- Place sleeve on paper with cap $\frac{1}{2}$ inch over fold line to remove cap ease.
- Spread each section until underseam touches or is parallel with guideline.
- Trace sleeve and front sleeve curve. Remove pattern.
- Cut from paper.

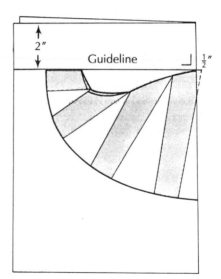

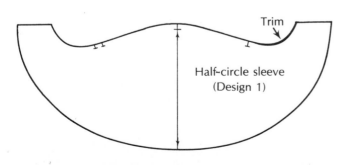

Half-circle sleeve
(Design 1)

FIGURE 3

- Unfold pattern.
- Draw grain. Notch. Trim front sleeve curve.

FULL-CIRCLE SLEEVE

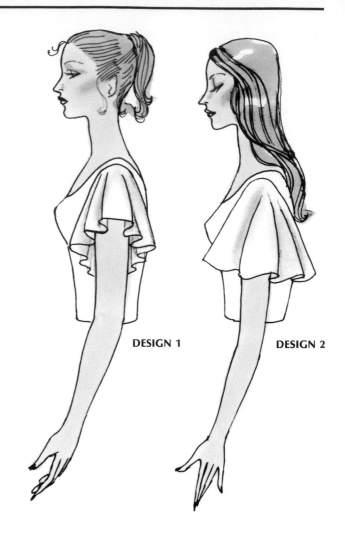

DESIGN 1   **DESIGN 2**

Design Analysis
The full-circle sleeve for Designs 1 and 2 is developed using the Circle/Cascade Radius Chart (found in Chapter 12, Circle Skirts). To draw circle, see measuring device. Design 1 is illustrated showing an uneven hemline, while Design 2 is provided as a thought problem. (*Question:* Is the pattern the same for both designs? Analyze both designs and pattern for the answer.)

Pattern plot and development

> **Measurements needed**
> - Sleeve length as desired (example: 8 inches).
> - Measure front and back armholes (example: 16 inches).
> - Locate measurement in Column 1 of the Circle/Cascade Radius Chart and find the circle's radius in Column 5.

Paper needed: Sleeve length (measured from cap) × 2, plus 5 inches. (Example: Sleeve length 8 inches = 16 + 5 inches, or a total of 21 inches.) Cut a 21-inch square of paper.

FIGURE 1
- Fold paper into four equal parts. Label corner of fold A.
- Draw outer circle with measuring device using sleeve length plus radius from chart.
- Label hem of circle B at fold as shown.

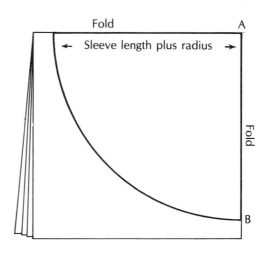

FIGURE 2
- Cut circle from paper and unfold. (Broken line represents original fold line.)
- A–C = Radius less $\frac{1}{2}$ inch (for seam). Mark.
- Draw inner circle using C as center.
- Label D above C as shown (notch placement).
- Cut inner circle by slashing through pattern from B to A. (B to A should be notched for seam allowance, $\frac{1}{2}$ inch on each side. Seam allowance eliminates stretch factor.) If inner circle does not stretch to equal armhole, trim $\frac{1}{16}$ inch or more from inner circle until it does.

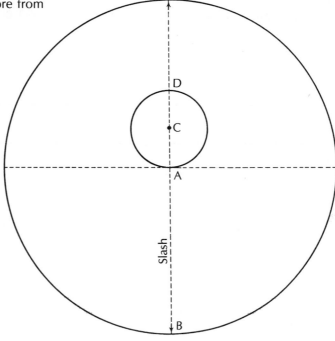

FIGURE 3   *Position of sleeve to armhole of Design 1:*
- Circle is placed in armhole with point D at shoulder tip seam and point A (underseam) at side seam of armhole. (Broken line indicates inner circle under the overlapping sleeve.)

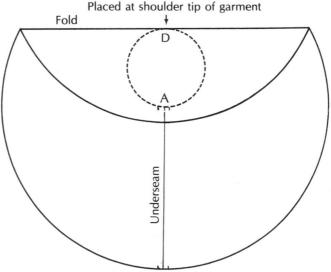

PETAL SLEEVES

Design Analysis

Petal sleeve is a term used to describe a shaped sleeve that resembles a petal as the sleeve sections cross over each other at the cap. These sleeves are developed in a number of ways and at varying lengths. Several petal sleeves are illustrated as a guide for development of this type sleeve. The full dartless sleeve is used to develop the petal. The front sleeve curve is modified. All three variations illustrated are developed from the same frame.

Note: Sleeve may be self-faced or include separate facing.

DESIGN 1   **DESIGN 2**   **DESIGN 3**

PLAIN PETAL

Pattern plot and development

FIGURE 1
- Trace dartless sleeve to $1\frac{1}{2}$ inches below biceps line for Design 1. Include all markings.
- Measure in $\frac{1}{2}$ inch from underseam. Draw line to corner of sleeve.

    A–B = 5 inches. Mark.
    A–C = $3\frac{1}{2}$ inches. Mark.

- Draw petal styleline as shown.
- Cut back petal from paper.

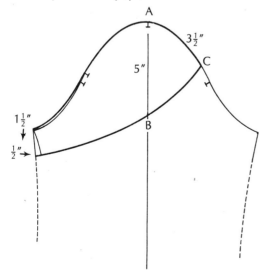

FIGURE 2   *Two-piece petal:*
- Retrace back pattern, transferring front sleeve curve for front panel.
- Cut front, trim excess from front armhole curve (shaded area). Draw grain.

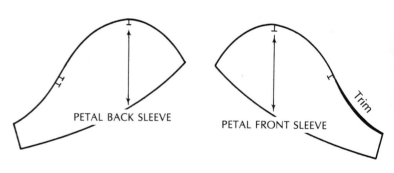

PETAL BACK SLEEVE   PETAL FRONT SLEEVE

FIGURE 3   *All-in-one petal:*
- Align underseams and retrace pattern.
- Draw grain and cut from paper and trim sleeve curve (shaded area).

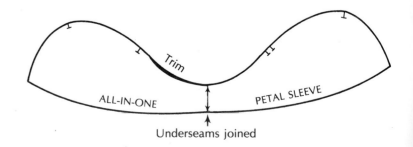

ALL-IN-ONE   PETAL SLEEVE

Underseams joined

GATHERED PETAL

FIGURE 4
- Trace back petal frame for Design 2. Extend underseam length 3 inches. Blend as shown (broken line is original petal sleeve).
- Draw slash lines.

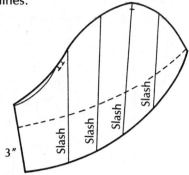

FIGURE 5 *Back sleeve:*
- Cut and slash lines to, not through, hemline. Place on paper and spread for gathers.

(Example: 1 inch each section; $\frac{1}{2}$ inch on each side of center.)
- Trace and remove pattern.
- Add 1 inch to cap height. Blend and cut from paper.

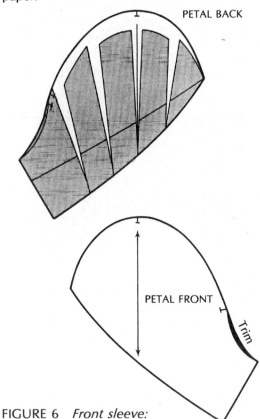

FIGURE 6 *Front sleeve:*
- Retrace for front sleeve.
- Cut and trim excess from sleeve curve.

(If all-in-one petal is desired, align underseams. See Figure 3.)

FLARED PETAL

FIGURE 7
- Trace back petal sleeve for Design 3.
- Draw slash lines equally across pattern as shown.

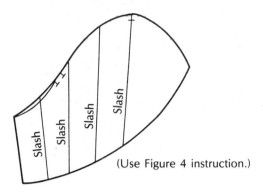

(Use Figure 4 instruction.)

FIGURE 8
- Cut slash lines to, not through, cap.
- Draw squared guidelines on paper. Square out from each side of vertical line for horizontal guideline.
- Align cap with vertical line and corner of underseam with horizontal guidelines. Spread pattern sections as shown.
- Trace and discard pattern.
- Shape petal to within 2 inches of notch point as shown (lined area discarded). Cut from paper.

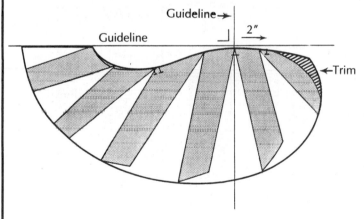

FIGURE 9
- Retrace for front sleeve.
- Draw grain. Cut and trim front sleeve curve.

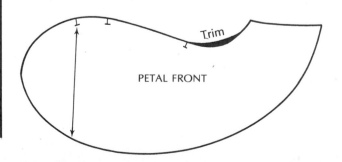

LANTERN SLEEVES

Design Analysis

A lantern sleeve is a two-section sleeve that flares out from the cap (upper section) and hemline to a styleline within the sleeve. These sleeves can be developed at varying lengths and fullness. The three designs illustrated show the flexibility of the lantern sleeve silhouette. Design 3 is given as a practice problem.

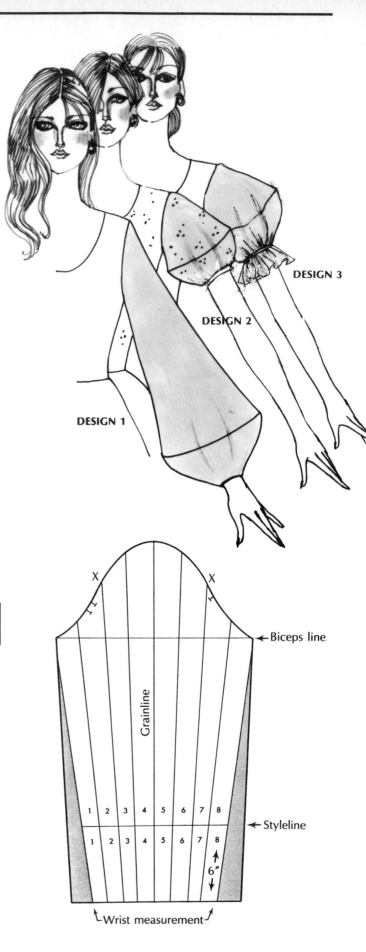

DESIGN 3

DESIGN 2

DESIGN 1

LONG LANTERN SLEEVE

Measurement needed
- (39) Around hand _____

Pattern plot and development

FIGURE 1
- Trace dartless sleeve pattern and all markings for Design 1.
- Label quarter sections X.
- Mark one-half of desired wrist measurement out from each side of grain at hemline.
- Draw lines from wrist marks to biceps.
- Draw lantern styleline 6 inches up from hem (varies).
- Divide sleeve into eight parts and number as shown.
- Cut and discard unneeded section (shaded area).

X   X

← Biceps line

Grainline

1 2 3 4 5 6 7 8

1 2 3 4 5 6 7 8   ← Styleline

↑ 6" ↓

⌐Wrist measurement⌐

FIGURES 2 and 3
- Cut and separate upper from lower section.

UPPER SLEEVE

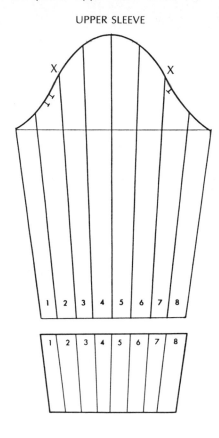

FIGURE 4   *Upper sleeve:*
- Cut slash line to, not through, cap.
- Mark $\frac{1}{2}$ inch out from each side of cap. Separate center sleeve at cap.
- Place on paper, overlapping center cap matching $\frac{1}{2}$-inch marks on each side of cap (eliminates cap ease). (Broken line indicates underlay of back sleeve cap.)
- Spread desired amount (or follow illustration).
- Trace and discard.
- Measure down 1 inch from bottom of Panel 2.
- Blend curved line to underseams.
- Notch center line of sleeve.
- Cut from paper.

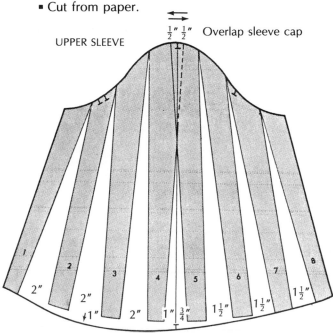

UPPER SLEEVE

$\frac{1}{2}$" $\frac{1}{2}$"   Overlap sleeve cap

FIGURE 5   *Lower sleeve:*
- Develop lower section using same spread as upper sleeve.

   Note: Lantern styleline must measure equally to true to upper section.

LOWER SLEEVE

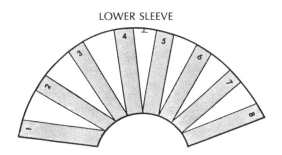

SHORT LANTERN SLEEVE

Pattern plot and development

FIGURE 1
- Trace back half of dartless pattern to 5 inches below biceps for Design 2. Include front armhole curve.
- Draw line from biceps to $\frac{1}{2}$ inch in from hemline. (Broken line indicates original underseam.)
- Mark A, $\frac{1}{2}$ inch in from cap.
- Draw lantern styleline, dividing upper and lower sections equally.
- Draw slash lines and label as shown.

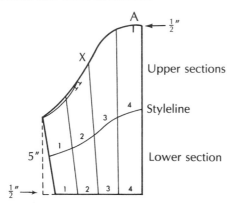

FIGURES 2 and 3
- Cut sleeve from paper.
- Cut and separate upper from lower section.

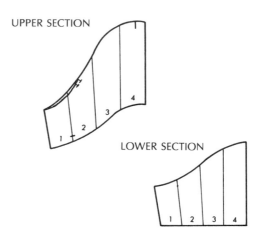

FIGURE 4
- Cut slash lines to, not through, cap and hem of both sections.
- Place sleeve sections on fold of paper (point A of upper section touches fold line to eliminate ease).
- Spread upper and lower sections. (Example: $1\frac{1}{2}$ inches; $\frac{3}{4}$ inch each side of center line.)
- Trace patterns and front armhole curve.
- Extend center line of sleeve sections 1 inch at styleline, blending curved line as shown. (Upper and lower stylelines must measure equally.)
- Notch where shown and cut from paper. Unfold and trim front sleeve curve (shaded area).

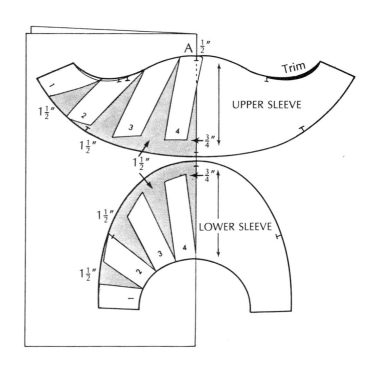

SLEEVES WITH EXTENDED CAPS

DARTED CAP

Design Analysis
Sleeve projects out from the ball of the arm and is controlled by three darts for Design 1. Design 2 is based on the same pattern except that the cap is blended for gathers.

Pattern plot and development

FIGURE 1
- Trace basic sleeve.
- Draw slash lines 2 inches away from center grain.
- Draw $\frac{1}{8}$-inch wedge *along* each slash line at cap ($\frac{1}{16}$ inch out from each side of notch) to zero at grain and biceps line. (This eliminates some of the cap ease.)
- Cut sleeve from paper. Discard unneeded sections (shaded area).

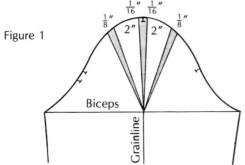

Figure 1

FIGURE 2
- Slash from cap to, not through, corners of biceps line.
- Raise biceps $1\frac{1}{4}$ inches as shown. Spread sections equally.
- Trace and discard pattern.
- Center and mark dart points $1\frac{1}{4}$ inches down each opening as shown. Draw legs as shown.

FIGURES 3 and 4
- Fold dart legs, cupping pattern while blending cap.
- Unfold and mark notches and punch circles.

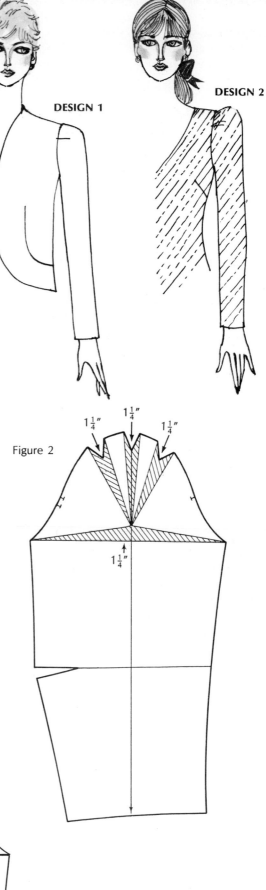

Figure 2

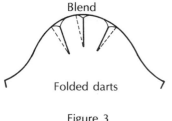

Blend

Folded darts

Figure 3

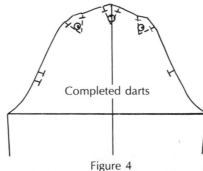

Completed darts

Figure 4

DESIGN 1

DESIGN 2

CRESCENT-SHAPED, EXTENDED CAP

Design Analysis

The sleeve cap for Design 3 is extended forming a crescent-shaped styleline parallel with armhole. Instruction for Design 4 follows this project.

DESIGN 3   **DESIGN 4**

Pattern plot and development

FIGURE 1

▪ Trace basic sleeve and all markings.
▪ Label center grain A. Mark E, $1\frac{1}{4}$ inches down from A.
▪ Mark B and C, 4 inches from A.
▪ Square in $1\frac{1}{4}$-inch lines from B and C, and in between A–B and A–C as shown.
▪ Draw curved line from D to E to F parallel with sleeve cap.

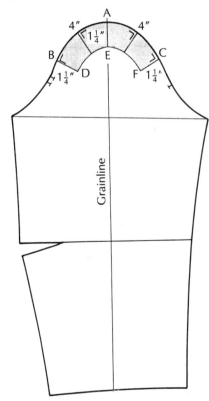

FIGURE 2 (opposite page)

▪ Cut sleeve from paper.
▪ Cut slash lines *carefully* from A to E, E to D, and E to F.
▪ Cut out capline from A to B and A to C.
▪ Cut to, not through, remaining slash lines (from inner to outer cap). Place paper underneath and secure.
▪ Spread until sections D and F touch curve of sleeve as shown.
▪ Measure the opened space and use as spread amount for next section.
▪ Secure by pinning spread sections to paper underneath.

- Square lines from A equal to panel width (1¼ inches). From this point, draw straight lines to D and F. (*Note:* D and F lines should both equal 4 inches. If not, adjust by increasing or decreasing spread.)
- Cut from paper.

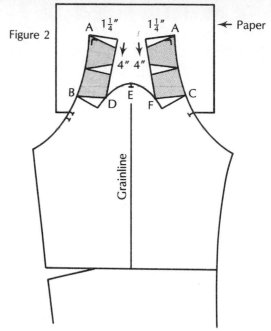

Figure 2

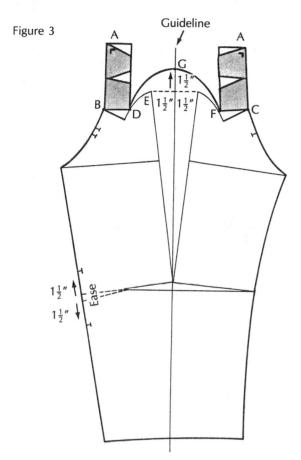

Figure 3

FIGURE 3
- Draw vertical guideline (grainline) on another paper.
- Slash sleeve from E to elbow level and across elbow level to, not through, underseam and dart.
- Place on paper. Spread E, 1½ inches out from each side of guideline. Secure. (Part or all of elbow dart may close.)
- Measure up 1½ inches from guideline. Mark and label G.
- Draw curve from G to D, and from G to F. Curved line must measure 4 inches. If not, adjust spread. Trace sleeve and remove.
- Notch 1½ inches each side of dart legs. Blend for remaining ease.

GATHERED CRESCENT SLEEVE

Design Analysis
Sleeve extends beyond the ball of the arm with gathers forming around cresent styleline.

FIGURE 1
- Follow instructions given for crescent-shaped, extended cap, with the following exceptions:
- Spread point E a total of 6 inches.
- Measure up 3 inches to form gathered section ending at D and F as shown.

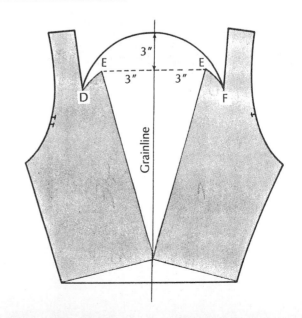

LEG-OF-MUTTON SLEEVE

Design Analysis

Design 1 is developed by enlarging the biceps and cap area, tapering the fullness toward the elbow level.

Design 2 is developed by doubling or tripling the measurements given.

Pattern plot and development.

FIGURE 1

• Trace basic sleeve and all markings. Label cap A and B.

• Mark 4 inches down from cap on grainline. Label C.

• Draw slash lines from C as shown.

• Cut from paper.

DESIGN 1   DESIGN 2

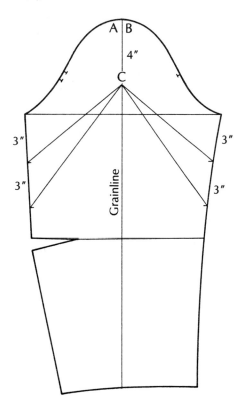

FIGURE 2

• Cut slash line to C and to, not through, underseams.

• Draw vertical guideline in center of paper.

• Place pattern on paper, matching sleeve grain with guideline.

• Spread A and B sections 2 inches, spacing remaining sections equally apart. Secure.

• Trace and discard.

• Measure up 1½ inches from cap and blend to sleeve notches as shown.

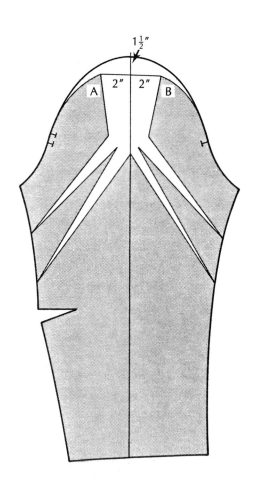

COWL SLEEVE

Design Analysis

The cowl sleeve drapes from the center of the sleeve cap to any desired depth (example: 5 inches). It is developed from the dartless back sleeve to any sleeve length desired. Design 2 is a practice problem—Clue: there is a seamline separating front and back sleeve.

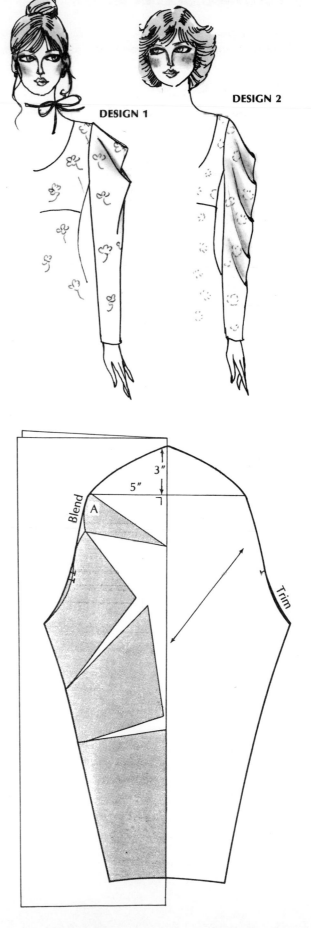

DESIGN 1

DESIGN 2

Pattern plot and development

FIGURE 1

- Trace dartless back sleeve.
- Mark A, ½ inch from cap (eliminates cap ease).
- Mark B, 5 inches down from cap. Connect A and B.
- Mark C, 2 inches from A.
- Mark D, between biceps and elbow.
- Draw slash lines from C and D to B.
- Cut from paper. Discard wedge (shaded area).
- Slash from B to, not through, C at cap, D at underseam, and from elbow level to underseam.

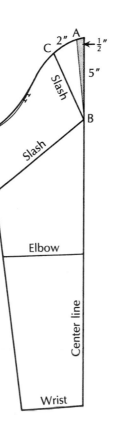

FIGURE 2

- Place pattern on fold, spreading sections until point A is 5 inches from fold.
- Trace pattern outline and front sleeve curve to paper underneath. Discard.
- Square a line from fold to point A.

Fold-back facing:

- Measure up 3 inches from square line at fold and draw curve line to A.
- Cut from paper, unfold, trim front sleeve curve (shaded area). Draw bias grain.

WEDDING SLEEVE

The traditional long, buttoned wedding sleeve is based on the basic sleeve with the elbow dart transferred to hemline. Other variations are also possible, see Designs 2 and 3.

TRADITIONAL WEDDING SLEEVE

Pattern plot and development

FIGURE 1
- Trace basic sleeve.
- Draw slash line from dart point to wrist 2 inches in from underseam. Label A.
- Label B at corner of front underseam as shown.
- Draw guideline 1 inch over from grain and $1\frac{1}{4}$ inches down from hem. Label C.
- Draw styleline from C to A and B.
- Cut from paper.

DESIGN 1

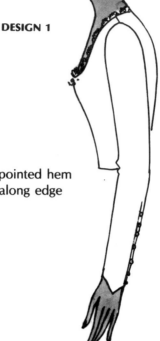

Design Analysis
Sleeve of Design 1 has pointed hem with loops and buttons along edge of opening.

FIGURE 2
- Cut slash line to, not through, dart point.
- Close elbow dart. Tape.
- Trace pattern and mark grainline.
- Mark placement for loops. Space as desired (see Chapter 14).

FIGURE 3   *Facing:*
- Trace sleeve section for facing (indicated by broken line in Figure 2).
- Separate facing at dart point.
- Add seams and grain.

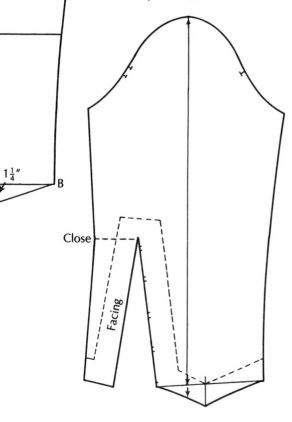

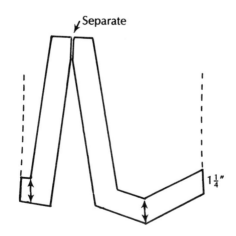

SLEEVE VARIATIONS WITH PATTERNS

Designs 2 and 3 show possible sleeve variations with the elbow dart transferred to hemline (Principle #1, Dart Manipulation). In Design 3, the dart is transferred to the cap area. (Remember, the dart can be transferred to *any* location around the pattern's outline.) Designs include added fullness (Principle #2).

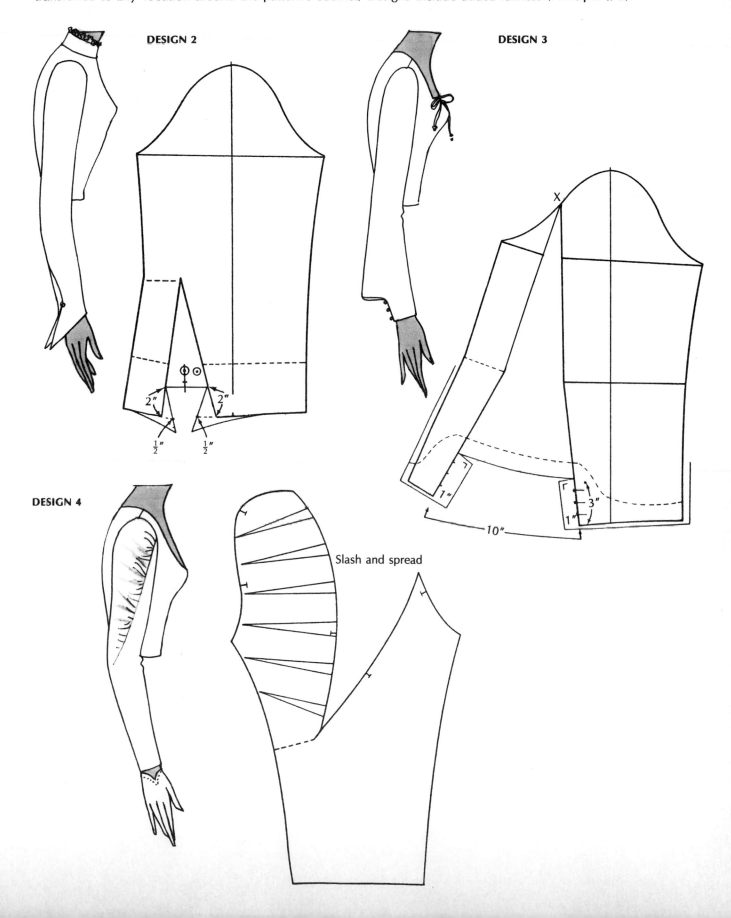

DESIGN 2

DESIGN 3

DESIGN 4

Slash and spread

SLEEVE WITH LIFT

The underarm sleeve length can be increased to provide a greater range of movement for the arm in actionwear garments. Lengthening the underarm seam tends to flatten the cap height and add width to the biceps. This does not affect the overall cap measurement or sleeve length, but allows diagonal fold lines to form under the arm.

Pattern plot and development

FIGURE 1   *1-inch lift:*
• Draw vertical line in center of paper. Square a guideline out from each side of vertical line 8 inches down.
• Draw a parallel line 1 inch up from guideline (for lift).

FIGURE 2
• Place sleeve pattern on paper, matching grain with vertical line and biceps with lower horizontal guideline. Label A and B as shown.
• Trace sleeve, omitting section indicated by broken lines (A to X, B to X).

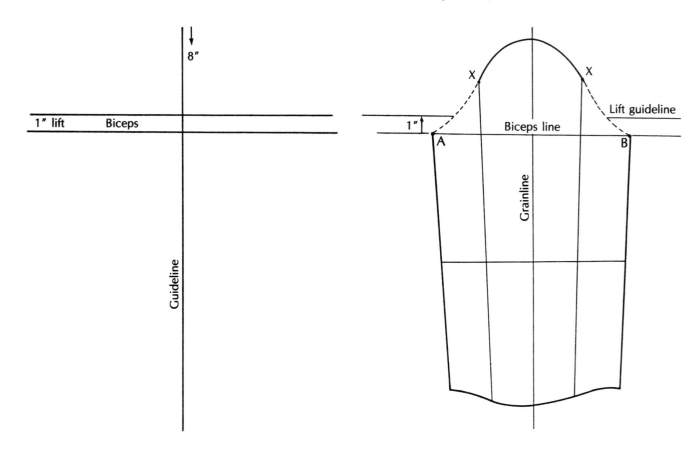

FIGURE 3   *1-inch lift:*
- Swing pattern upward until A touches lift guideline. Trace armhole curve from A to X (shaded area). (Sleeve is illustrated from cap to elbow.)

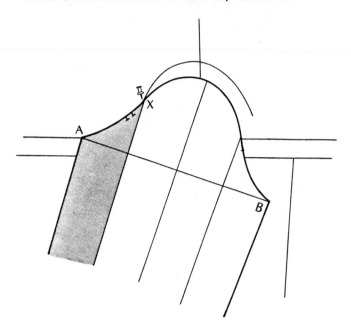

FIGURE 5
- Draw a curved line from A and B to elbow. Blend cap.

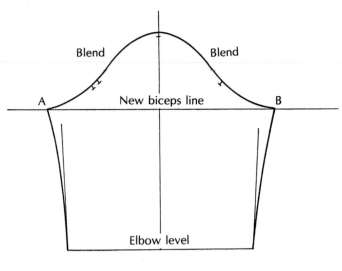

FIGURE 4
- Repeat for opposite side.
- Remove pattern.

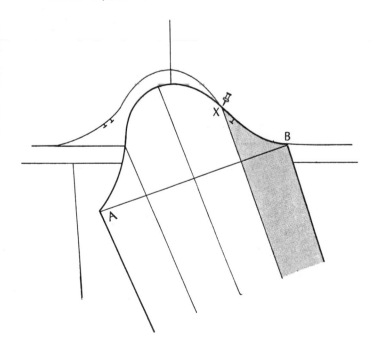

FIGURE 6   *2-inch lift:*
- Repeat process. *Exception:* Draw a 2-inch parallel lift line up from biceps guideline.

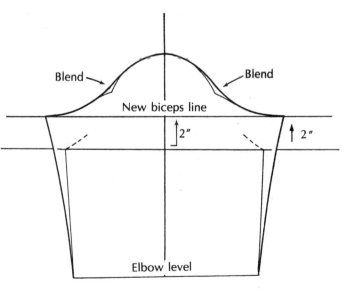

SLEEVE WITH LOWERED ARMHOLE

Design Analysis
Designs with deep-cut armholes require a sleeve and bodice modification. The underarm seam of the sleeve must be increased equal to the lowered bodice armhole depth; otherwise, the arm cannot be raised without strain on the upper garment. A diagonal fold will appear on the sleeve from the ball of the arm, draping slightly under the armhole. *Exception:* A very full garment with sufficient flare will allow the arm to move freely and will *not* require modification to the *lowered* armhole. There are two methods for modifying the sleeve, and both are illustrated. Method 1 requires that the sleeve be slashed and spread; Method 2 does not.

Pattern plot and development
Method 1: Slash and lift

FIGURE 1 *Sleeve and bodice:*
▪ Measure down 2 or more inches on sleeve and bodice. Mark.
▪ Draw curved line from marks to notches.
▪ Draw another curved line 2 inches below first line of sleeve.

    Note: Shaded area is cut from bodice and sleeve.

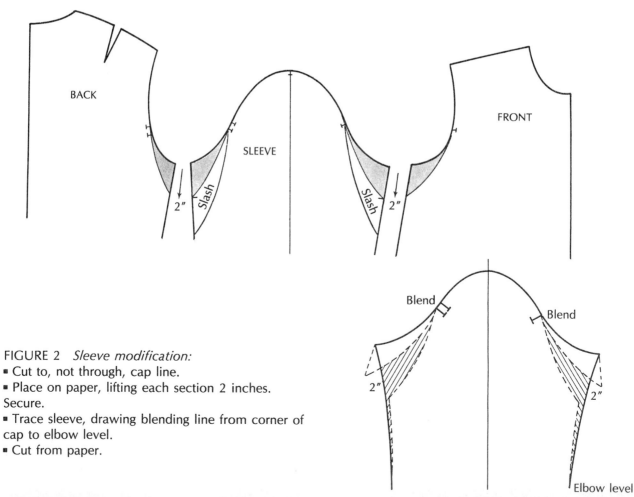

FIGURE 2 *Sleeve modification:*
▪ Cut to, not through, cap line.
▪ Place on paper, lifting each section 2 inches. Secure.
▪ Trace sleeve, drawing blending line from corner of cap to elbow level.
▪ Cut from paper.

Method 2: Extending biceps

FIGURES 3 and 4   *Lowering armhole:*
- Lower bodice armholes 2 or more inches and blend to notch locations.
- Measure original armhole and subtract from lowered armhole. Use these measurements when extending biceps line.

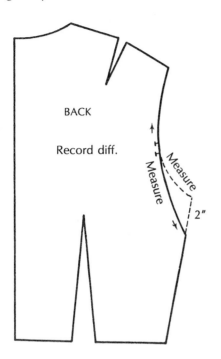

BACK

Record diff.

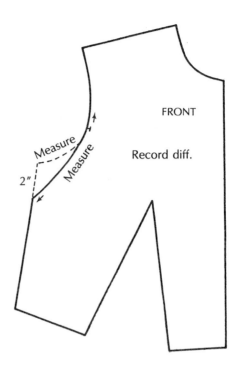

FRONT

Record diff.

FIGURE 5   *Modifying sleeve:*
- Extend biceps line equal to measurements recorded from front and back armholes. Modify back sleeve, then front sleeve. (Broken line indicates original sleeve.)
- Blend line from biceps to elbow level. True sleeve to armhole and cut from paper.

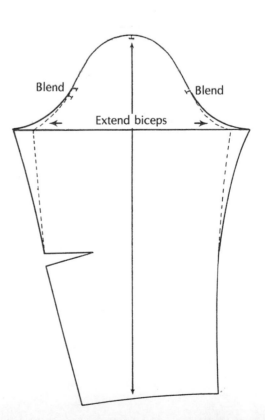

Blend   Blend

Extend biceps

Sleeve/bodice combinations

The sleeve and bodice of any type garment (blouse, dress, jacket, or coat) can be combined in a variety of ways during pattern development. These designs are categorized as follows:

Kimono designs. The sleeve is combined with the full bodice pattern.

Raglan designs. The sleeve is combined with part of the bodice armhole and shoulder area.

Deep-cut armhole designs. The armhole section of the bodice is combined with the sleeve.

Drop-shoulder designs. Part of the sleeve cap is combined with the bodice. (The garment can be developed with or without the lower sleeve attached to the styleline of the drop shoulder.)

Each of the basic combination patterns can be used to develop other design variations by exaggerating one of their special characteristics or by changing the styleline position.

Deep-cut armhole

Drop-shoulder

Raglan

Kimono

BASIC KIMONO

The Western-style kimono is developed by combining the sleeve and bodice. The basic kimono, once developed, is the basis for developing the dolman sleeve. Both of these sleeves can be adapted or modified for a variety of other designs, several of which are illustrated. With part or all of the armhole absorbed into design details, compensation must be made to the front bodice armhole to avoid strain on the garment when the arm is in a forward position. This is corrected by transferring part of the dart's excess to the mid-armhole before the patterns are combined. The back shoulder dart can remain where it is or be transferred to mid-armhole.

BODICE MODIFICATION

Pattern plot and development

FIGURE 1 *Back bodice:*
- Trace back, transferring shoulder dart to mid-armhole. Label A and B.
- Square guidelines from center back crossing shoulder tip and corner of armhole.

FIGURE 2 *Front bodice:*
- Slash traced bodice from curve of armhole to bust point.
- Place pattern on paper with shoulder tip (C) and corner of armhole touching guidelines. Trace pattern and discard. Label C and D.
- Blend armhole (broken line is the original pattern shape).
- Cut patterns from paper and use as working patterns for kimono and other similar design combinations.

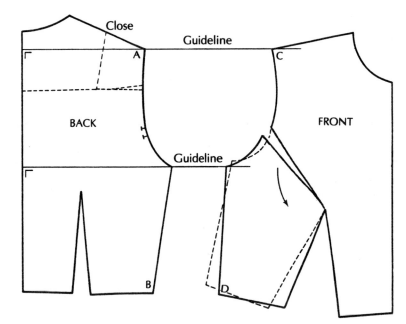

FIGURE 3
- Draw vertical guideline on paper.
- Place sleeve grain on guideline. Trace only the sleeve cap, marking both sides at elbow level. Mark wrist level as shown (broken lines are untraced sleeve). Remove sleeve.
- Mark $\frac{1}{4}$ inch above cap on guideline and square lines out from each side.
- Draw guidelines through biceps and across paper. Draw line across elbow level.
- Label biceps E and F.

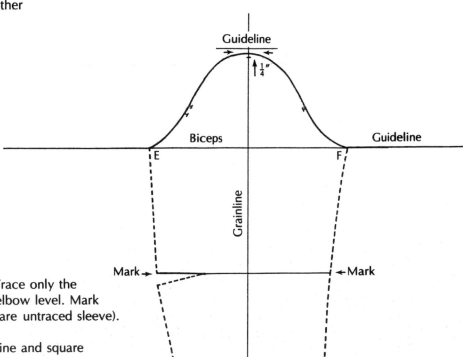

(Continued on next page)

FIGURE 4 *Back:*
- Mark $\frac{3}{4}$ inch out on guideline.
- Place pattern on draft with shoulder tip (A) at mark on guideline and B on biceps guideline.
- Trace pattern, except for armhole (broken lines). Label X at corner of armhole.

Front:
- Mark G from F on guideline equal to B–E distance.
- Place bodice on draft with D touching G and point C on guideline.
- Trace pattern, except for armhole (broken lines). Label X at corner of armhole.

FIGURE 5 *Adjustments:*
Shoulders:
If points A and C are not equally spaced between cap guideline, measure the distance (between A and C) and divide in half. Using this measurement, measure out from each side of guide, mark, and draw new shoulder to necklines (broken lines original shoulders).

Side seams:
Measure from biceps guide to point X (front and back). Add together and divide in half. Using this measurement, measure out biceps to mark new location for points X. Draw new side seams (broken lines original side seams).

Personal fit: If point X of front overlaps biceps guideline, subtract amount of overlap from back measurement and adjust both side seams.

Personal fit: Necklines may overlap. Continue with draft and mend necklines after patterns are separated.

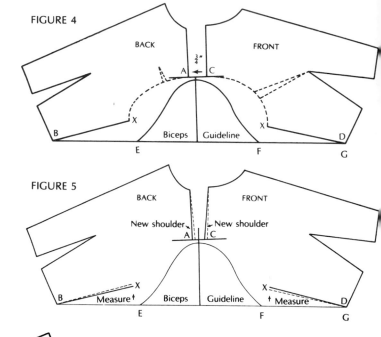

FIGURE 6
Overarm seam:
- Mark $\frac{1}{4}$ inch up from A and C (new shoulder tips). From these marks draw straight lines to wrist, and curved lines to mid-shoulder. Blend curve line.

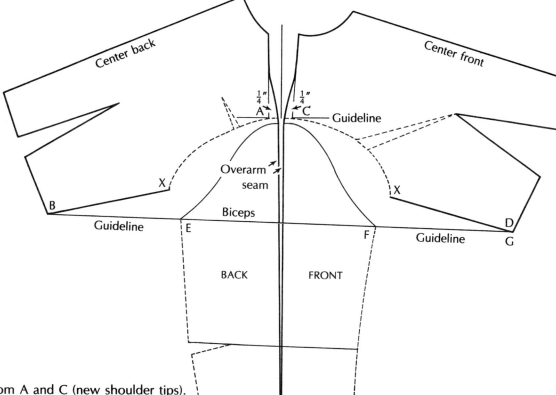

FIGURE 7

Underarm seam:

- Back: Square a line from overarm seam at wrist equal to one-half of desired wrist measurement.
- Draw line from wrist ending 1 or more inches below X, and draw a 2-inch diagonal line.
- Crossmark midpoint between X and B and X and D. For a lower underseam, place a crossmark lower.

- Draw curve line from crossmark to elbow level and notch as shown.
- Front: Repeat instructions given for back, or cut out back pattern and place on top of front draft, matching side seam and overseam to trace shape for front underarm.
- Cut and separate patterns, discarding unneeded section (shaded area).

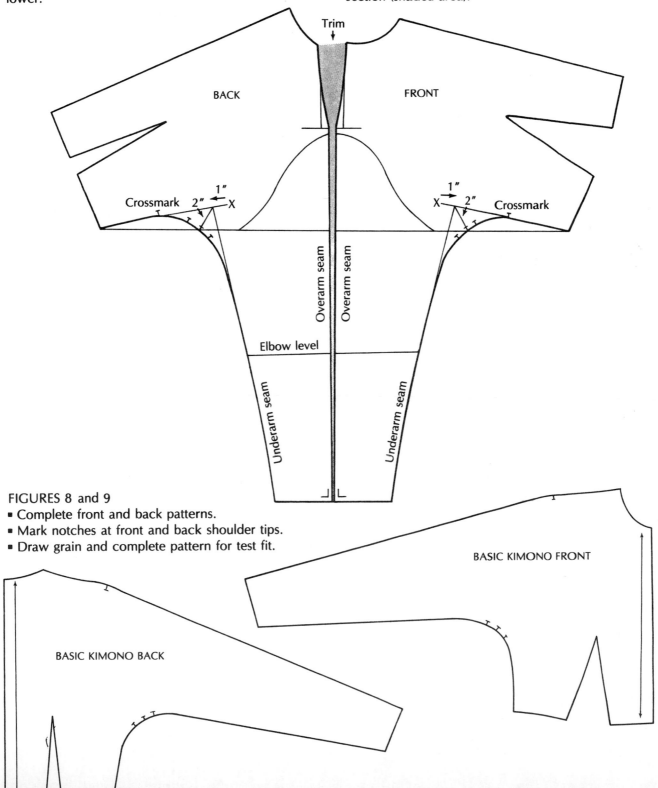

FIGURES 8 and 9

- Complete front and back patterns.
- Mark notches at front and back shoulder tips.
- Draw grain and complete pattern for test fit.

BASIC KIMONO BACK

BASIC KIMONO FRONT

BASIC DOLMAN

Design Analysis

The dolman has deep underseams with exaggerated folds under arms, providing for a high arm lift. It is developed from the basic kimono.

Pattern plot and development

FIGURES 1 and 2
- Trace front and back Kimono foundation.
- Draw slash lines from shoulder tips, ending 3 to 4 inches up from side waist.

FIGURE 3   *Front:*
- Slash or pivot, spreading underarm sleeve to give as much lift as desired. Blend underseam.
- Repeat for back and true underseams.
    Note: Bold and uneven broken lines indicate possible dolman-sleeve stylelines. For practice, explore other design variations.

ONE-PIECE COMBINATIONS

One-piece combination designs are developed by aligning the front and back patterns either along the sleeve (Design 1) or the shoulder (Designs 2 and 3 on following pages). The instructions given for the basic kimono apply also to the dolman, raglan, or kimono with gusset.

   Use the following illustrations as a guide for developing this type of design, noting the special instructions given below.
Grainline options:
- Parallel with center front.
- Bias.
- Along original overarm seam (see Figure 1 for guidance).

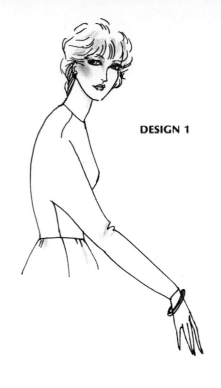

DESIGN 1

KIMONO WITH SHOULDER DART

FIGURE 1
- To prevent a pucker at dart point, space 1 inch between shoulder tip.
- Blend shoulders to meet $1\frac{1}{2}$ inches below shoulder notch.

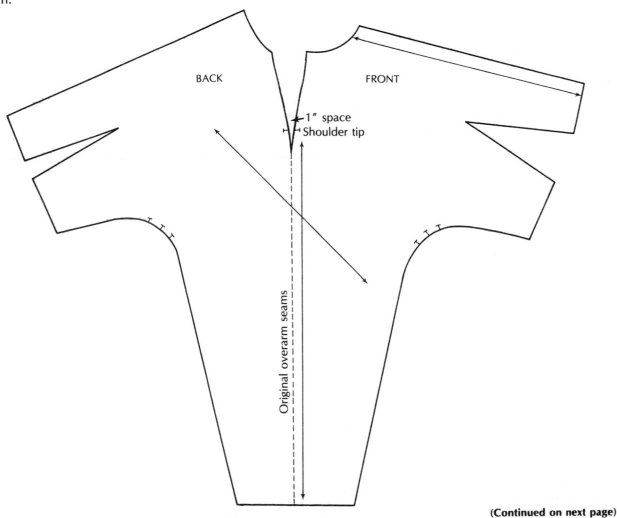

(Continued on next page)

FULL-SLEEVED KIMONO
(WITHOUT OVERARM SEAM)

(Sleeve is gathered when stitched, forms a bell when left unstitched.)

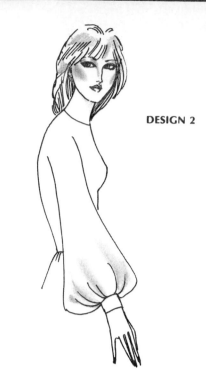

DESIGN 2

FIGURE 2
▪ Place shoulder at neck and shoulder tips together. Trace. (Broken lines indicate sleeve position.)
▪ Blend curved area across open space at wrist.
▪ For additional fullness, add to underseam of sleeve. This sleeve has no overarm or shoulder seam.

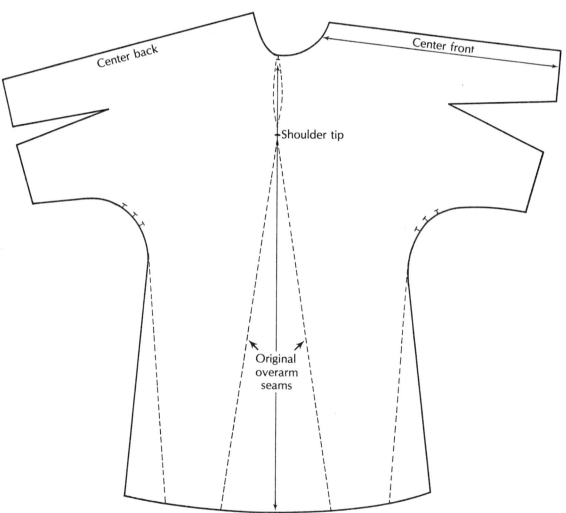

TAPERED SLEEVE
(WITHOUT OVERARM SEAM)

FIGURE 3
- Place shoulder at neck and shoulder tips together. Trace. (Broken lines indicate sleeve position.)
- Mark center point between sleeves at wrist.
- Draw line to shoulder tip. Square out one-half of wrist measurement on each side of line and blend underseam. Taper sleeve as desired.

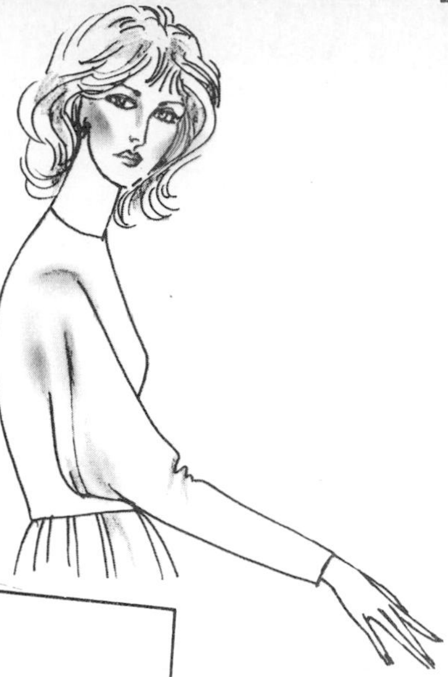

DESIGN 3

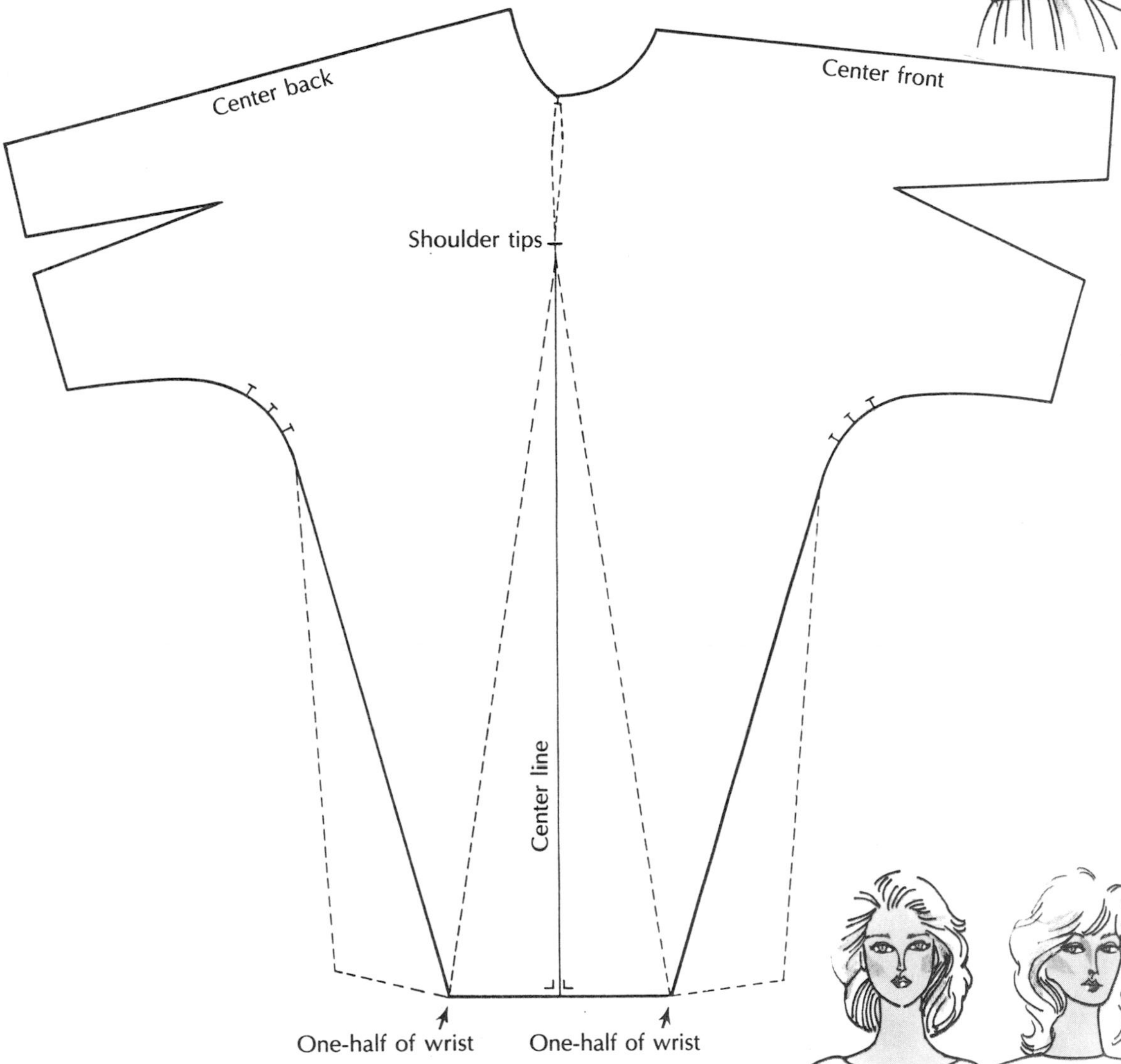

Center back

Center front

Shoulder tips

Center line

One-half of wrist   One-half of wrist

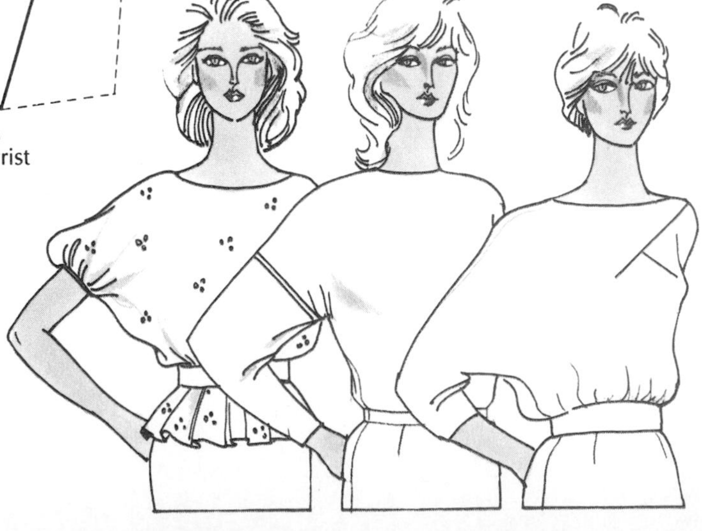

KIMONO AND DOLMAN VARIATIONS

The following practice problems are design variations based on the kimono and dolman patterns.

KIMONO WITH GUSSET

The basic kimono is developed to fit the arm loosely, allowing the arm to lift and move in any direction. When the arm hangs at the side of the figure, folds (or drapes) will appear under the arm. To eliminate these folds and develop a smooth, close fit, the sleeve must have a gusset to provide room for arm movement and lift; otherwise, strain lines will appear and the arm will be constricted.

Gussets are triangular or diamond-shaped wedges inserted in slits in the underarm sleeve section (as either one or two pieces). Two types are illustrated—those providing a maximum lift (180°) and those providing a minimum lift (90°). The choice depends on the use and the appropriateness for a specific design, and is controlled by the pitch (or angle) of the sleeve when attached to the bodice at the time the pattern is developed.

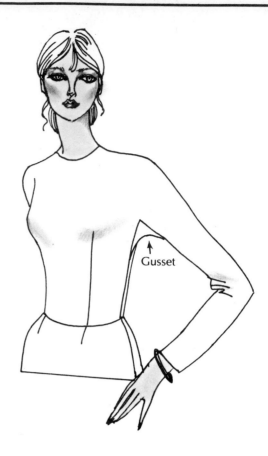

Pattern plot and development

FIGURE 1   *Back sleeve:*
▪ Trace back half of sleeve to midpoint of wrist (placement for overarm seam), include all markings. (Broken lines indicate part of sleeve not traced.) Remove pattern.
▪ Connect cap grainline with wrist mark. Extend grain $\frac{1}{4}$ inch up from cap and square a short guideline.
▪ Crossmark $1\frac{1}{2}$ inches below biceps at underseam. Label X.

FIGURE 2   *Front sleeve:*
▪ Repeat instructions given for back.
▪ Draw a straight line from biceps to wrist at front underseam.

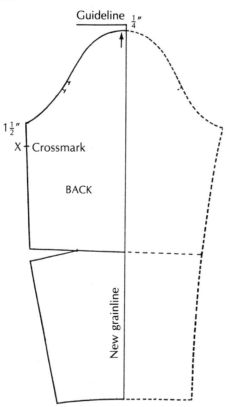

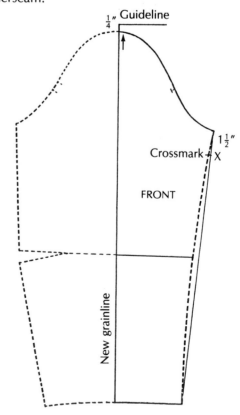

FIGURE 3 *Back bodice and sleeve combined:*
- Place back bodice on sleeve matching X-points. Shoulder tip (label A) must touch somewhere on guideline. (Curve of sleeve cap may overlap armhole.)
- Trace and remove.
- Measure up $\frac{1}{4}$ inch from A. Mark.
- Measure down 3 inches from guideline and out $\frac{1}{2}$ inch. Mark.
- Draw a straight line from mark to wrist. (Line can be drawn parallel, enlarging sleeve for a more casual fit.) This line establishes the overarm seam.
- Draw a curved line from mark, ending at mid-shoulder.
- Draw a $3\frac{1}{2}$-inch line from X-point in direction of sleeve/bodice intersection. Label B.

FIGURE 4 *Front bodice and sleeve combined:*
- Trace bodice, transferring $\frac{1}{2}$ inch to mid-armhole. Cut from paper.
- Repeat instructions given for back.

Elbow dart options:
(Options are noted on illustrations.)
1—Use elbow dart (seldom used for this type of sleeve unless sleeve is tapered from above elbow to wrist).
2—Excess from elbow dart used as ease. Mark ease control notches $1\frac{1}{2}$ inches up and down from dart legs. Front: Mark notches $1\frac{1}{2}$ inches up and down from elbow level as shown.
3—Eliminate dart at wrist level by squaring a line from the overarm seam (shaded area).
4—Use half of dart's excess as ease, removing the other half at wrist level.

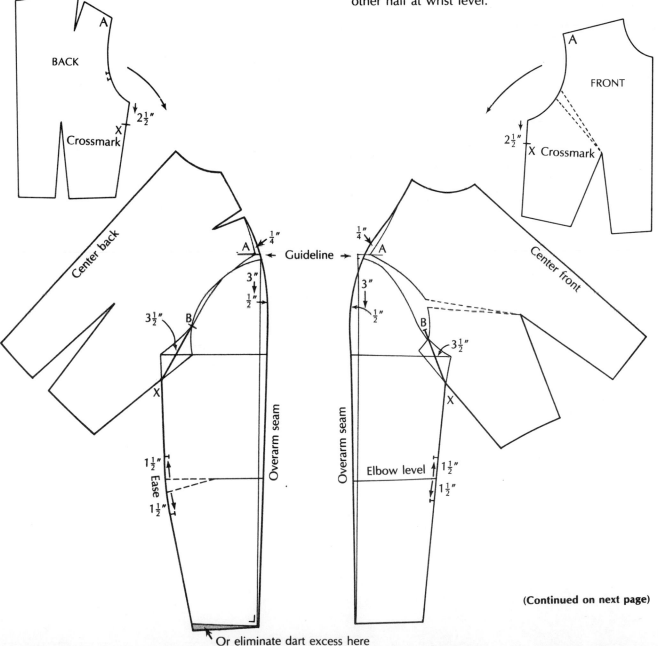

(Continued on next page)

FIGURE 5   *Slit for gusset:*
Front:
▪ Mark $\frac{1}{4}$ inch out from each side of X (seam allowance).
▪ Draw a line from point B through mark to side seam of front bodice. Label C.
▪ Draw a line from point B through mark equal to B–C measurement. Label D. Connect C with D.
▪ Connect D with elbow level for new underseam.
Back:
▪ Repeat instructions for back using B–C measurements. Blend.

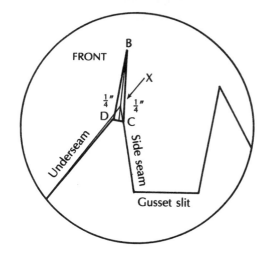

FIGURE 6
Gusset with maximum lift:
▪ Fold paper. Square a 2-inch line from fold at center of paper. Label B.
▪ From B, draw two lines to fold of paper equal to B–C measurement. Cut and unfold.
Option 1:
▪ One-piece gusset stitched in as is.

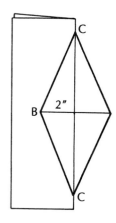

FIGURES 7 and 8
Options 2 and 3:
▪ Separated gusset (vertical or horizontal) trimmed $\frac{1}{4}$ inch at center to zero at ends. (Broken line indicates original shape.)

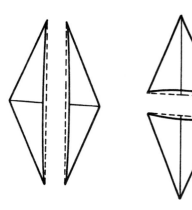

FIGURE 9
Gusset with moderate lift:
▪ Draw 90° angle equal to B–C measurement.
▪ Draw a 2-inch diagonal line out from corner. Draw blending curve as shown.

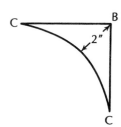

FIGURES 10 and 11
- Cut front and back patterns and gussets from paper. (Front and back patterns are shown with elbow dart removed.)

Gusset slit:
- Cut $\frac{1}{16}$-inch-wide opening through X–B line. Fold slit line and notch across end (crossbar). (This prevents pattern from tearing when making marker.)
- Draw grains and complete pattern for test fit.

Trueing patterns:
- True over- and underarm seams. Blend curved lines at shoulders and adjust length difference at hem of sleeve if necessary.

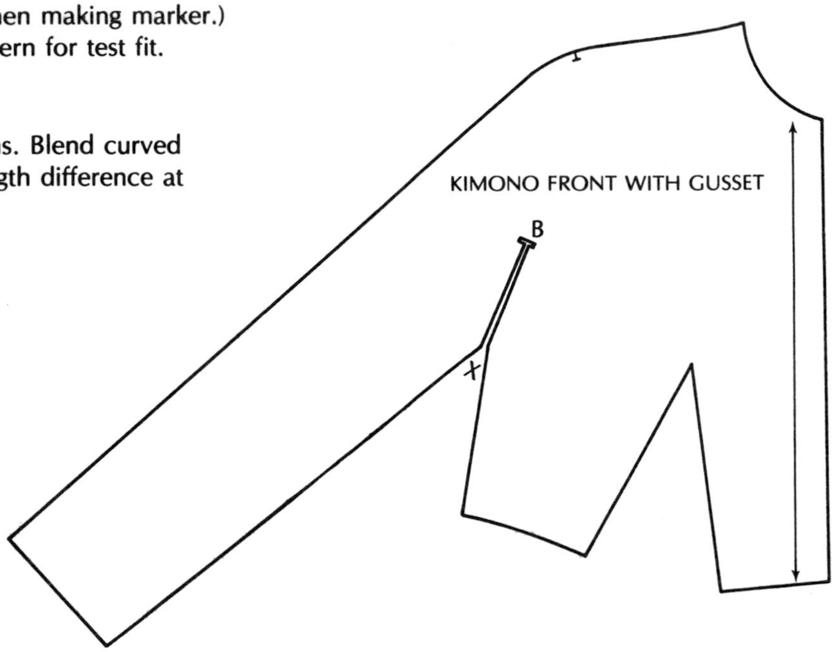

KIMONO FRONT WITH GUSSET

B

X

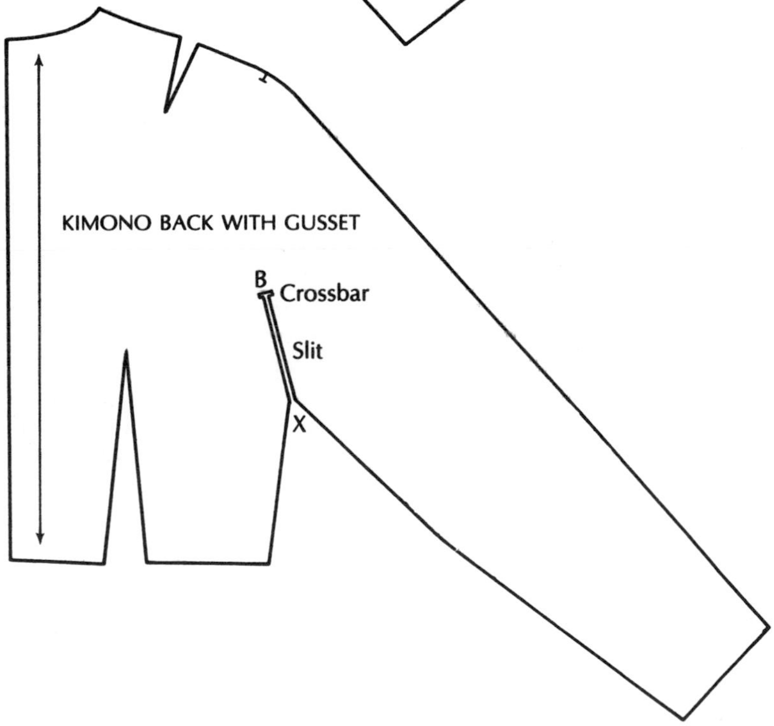

KIMONO BACK WITH GUSSET

B Crossbar

Slit

X

BASIC RAGLAN

A raglan styleline is developed using part of the neckline and armhole attached to the sleeve. The armhole can be lowered for silhouette change (see page 403).

Pattern plot and development

FIGURES 1 and 2   *Preparation of bodice patterns:*

▪ Trace patterns, transferring back shoulder dart and $\frac{1}{2}$-inch excess of front dart to mid-armholes. Blend armhole as shown.

▪ Measure front and back armholes, subtract to find difference. Adjust shoulder tips so that both armholes measure the same (see below).

▪ Label back armhole A–E and front armhole B–F.

Back:

▪ A–X equals one-half of armhole less 1 inch.

▪ Draw straight guideline from X, ending $1\frac{1}{4}$ inches down from shoulder at neck.

▪ Mark $\frac{1}{2}$ inch up from midpoint of guideline.

▪ Draw raglan curve (shaded area).

Front:

▪ Repeat instructions given for back. (B–X = A–X distance.) Mark and label.

▪ Separate patterns along raglan styleline. Upper yoke sections attach to sleeves, and lower sections used to complete patterns.

ADJUSTED SHOULDERLINE

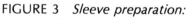

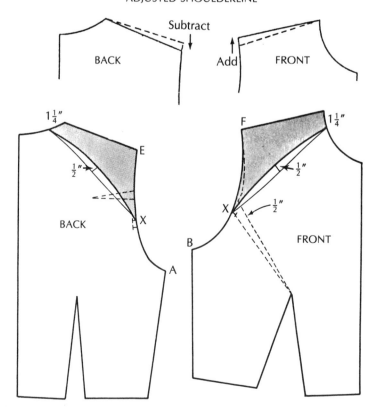

FIGURE 3   *Sleeve preparation:*

▪ Trace full sleeve (upper part illustrated). Label biceps C and D. Measure and mark as follows:

   C–X = A–X of bodice, plus $\frac{1}{4}$-inch for ease.
   D–X = B–X of bodice, plus $\frac{1}{4}$-inch for ease.

▪ Draw curved slash lines from C and D to cap grain.

▪ Divide wrist in half. Mark and draw new grainline.

▪ Separate sleeve along new grainline.

▪ Cut slash lines to, not through, cap.

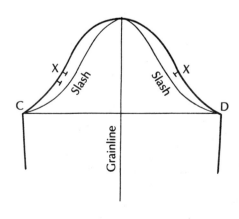

FIGURES 4 and 5 *Adding lift:*
- Place sleeve sections on paper. Raise points C and D 1 inch to increase underarm length for arm lift (lined area).
- Trace sleeve indicated by bold lines. (Broken-line section of sleeve cap not traced.) Include notches.
- Discard patterns.
- Blend underseams from C and D to elbow level.
- Extend grain $\frac{1}{4}$ inch and square a short guideline.

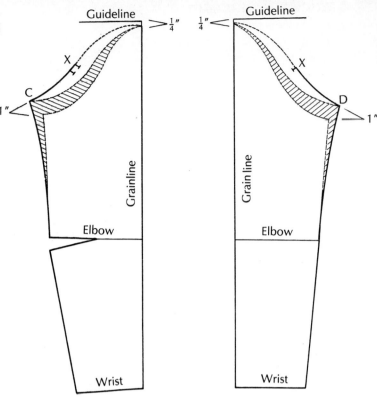

FIGURES 6 and 7 *Attaching yokes:*
- Place raglan yoke sections (shaded area) on sleeves with X-points touching, and E and F touching somewhere on short guideline. Secure.
- Trace and discard.

Sleeve back:
- Square a line from sleeve grain to point C. Label G (biceps line).

Sleeve front:
- Square a line from grain to point D.
- Extend D line to equal biceps line C–G. Mark and label H.

Sleeve back and front:
- Draw new overarm seam from wrist through and beyond point H.
- Mark $\frac{1}{4}$ inch out from E and F (shoulder tips) and blend curve to mid-shoulder and to overarm seams as shown.
- Mark notches and shoulder tips.

Elbow dart:
- See page 395 (kimono with gusset) for elbow dart instructions. Option 3, eliminating dart, is illustrated.
- Cut patterns from paper. True overarm seams and shoulder curve lines. Blend where needed.

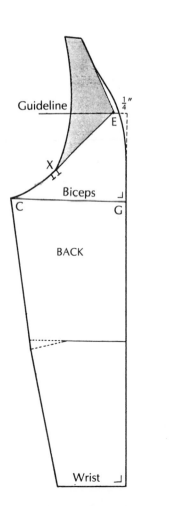

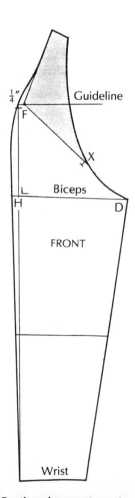

(Continued on next page)

FIGURES 8, 9, 10, and 11
- Complete raglan patterns.
- Draw grain and complete for test fit.

Trueing patterns:
- True over- and underarm seams. Blend curved line over shoulder. Adjust length at hem of sleeve if necessary.

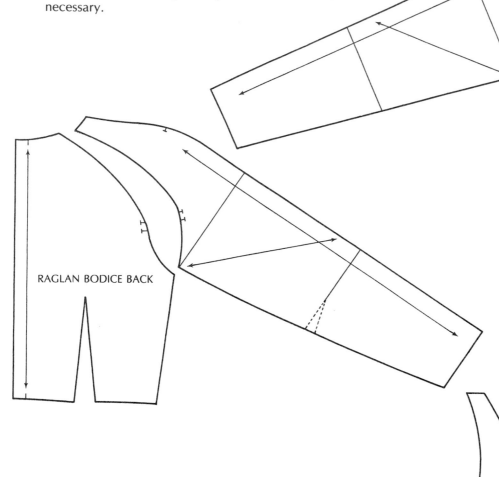

RAGLAN BODICE FRONT

RAGLAN BODICE BACK

ONE-PIECE RAGLAN

FIGURE 12
- Draw a vertical guideline on paper.
- Place overarm seams on guideline, spreading biceps $\frac{1}{2}$ inch and keeping wrist levels together.
- Trace front and back sleeves and all markings. Remove.
- Draw a guideline connecting shoulder tips.
- Mark a point 3 inches down on guideline. Label X.
- Draw curved line from X to shoulder tips. From this point, measure down 1 inch for punch hole and circle placements. Mark for dart point guide 1 inch below.
- Blend hemline. (Shoulder should be stitched along a curved line, not a straight line, for better fit.)

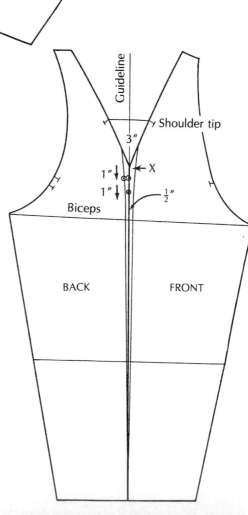

RAGLAN VARIATIONS

General instructions

To simplify pattern development, use the basic raglan sleeve with the basic front and back patterns. Plot and separate patterns. Use illustrations shown below as a visual guide to develop the armhole princess raglan, the yoke raglan, or any other similar raglan design. (The broken lines on the pattern plot indicate the original raglan shape.)
Note: Lower notches on front and back armhole and sleeve if styleline is placed at or near them. See page 398 to determine styleline placement on basic pattern (A-X and B-X).

ARMHOLE-PRINCESS RAGLAN

Pattern plot and development

FIGURES 1 and 2
- Draw princess line from X-points to dart points for Design 1.
- Separate patterns. (Broken lines indicate raglan yoke.)

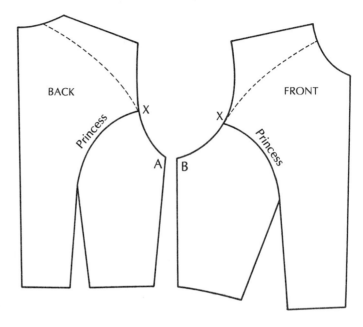

FIGURES 3, 4, 5, and 6
- Place raglan sleeves on pattern sections 1 (back) and 4 (front) matching neck and X-points. (Broken line indicates original raglan sleeve.) Place on paper and trace.
- Mark for length and fullness. To make cuff pattern, see pages 356 and 365.

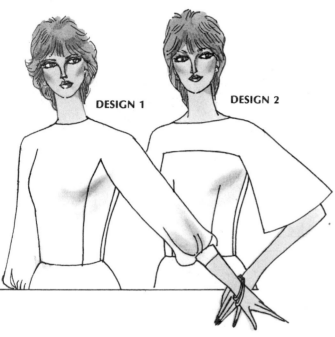

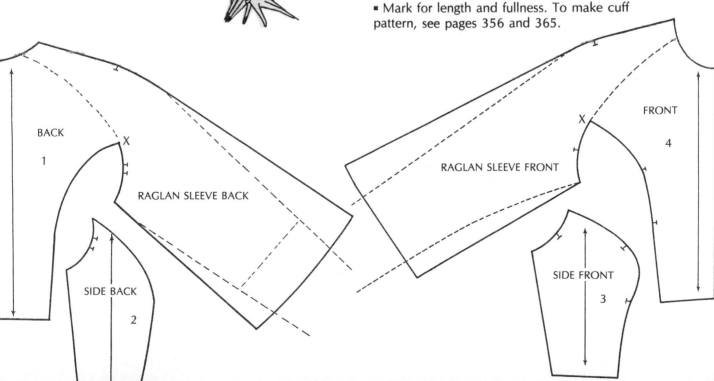

YOKE RAGLAN WITH BELL SLEEVE

Pattern plot and development

FIGURES 1 and 2   *Yokeline:*

• Square line from center front and center back to armhole (X-points).

• Separate pattern.

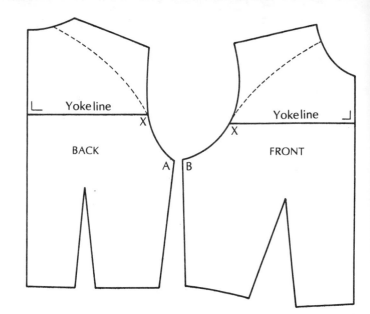

FIGURES 3, 4, 5, and 6

• Place front and back raglan sleeve on sections 1 (back) and 4 (front), matching neck and X-points. Place on paper and trace.

• Mark for bell length and flare.

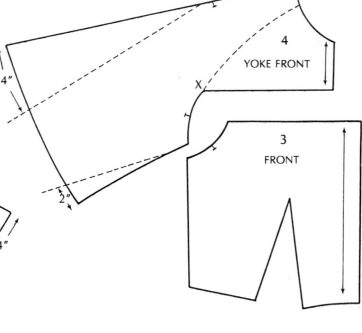

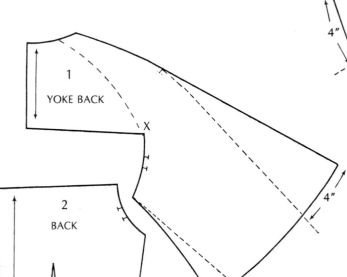

OTHER DESIGN VARIATIONS BASED ON RAGLAN FOUNDATION

The following additional designs based on the raglan foundation are developed by changing the direction of the styleline from X-points. Develop these for practice or design other variations.

DEEP RAGLAN

Many design variations are possible using the deep raglan armhole. Design is based on basic raglan.

Pattern plot and development

FIGURES 1 and 2
- Plan armhole depth (example: 2 inches).
- Label as shown. Draw curved lines from A and B to X and blend with raglan styleline. (Broken lines indicate section of pattern to be removed.)

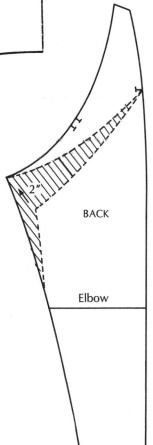

FIGURE 3
- Lower armholes 2 inches, and blend to notches. Draw slash lines to shoulder tips.

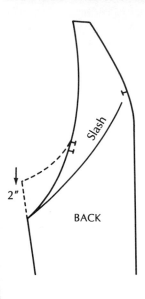
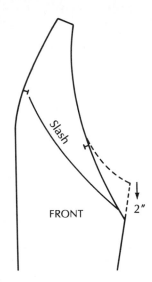

FIGURE 4
- Slash and lift 2 inches. Retrace sleeve. Blend to elbow.

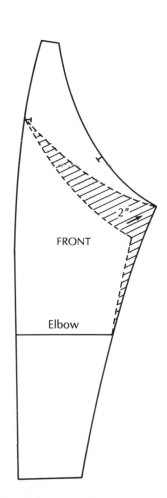

EXAGGERATED ARMHOLES

Armholes can be exaggerated by cutting deeply and widely into the garment. A pattern for this type of design is developed by attaching that portion cut from the bodice to the sleeve, as illustrated by the squared armhole designs. The instructions for these patterns should be used as a guide for developing similar designs where the total armhole area of the bodice is attached to the sleeve.

DEEP-CUT SQUARE ARMHOLE

Design Analysis
Sleeve is set deeply into a square armhole of the bodice and tapers to wrist level.

Pattern plot and development

FIGURES 1 and 2   *Bodice modification:*
- Trace front and back bodice. Transfer back shoulder dart to mid-armhole.
- Mark A, $\frac{1}{2}$ inch out from front and back shoulder tips.
- Mark B, 3 inches down from front and back armholes.
- Mark C, 2 inches squared from B.
- Connect C with A using a slightly curved line. (Broken lines of front and back bodice indicate original armhole.)
- Cut from paper. Discard unneeded portion (shaded area). This completes the front and back patterns.

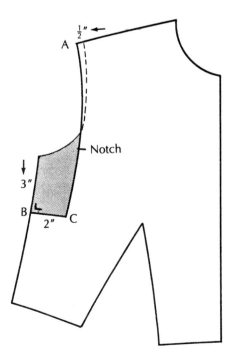

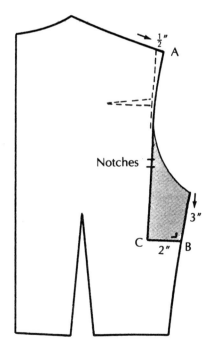

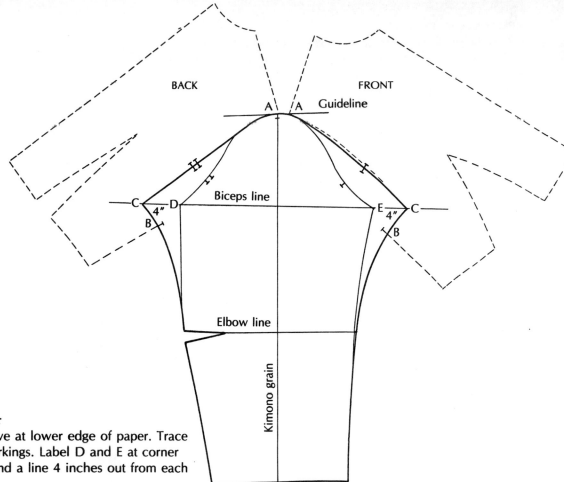

FIGURE 3 *Sleeve:*
▪ Center basic sleeve at lower edge of paper. Trace and include all markings. Label D and E at corner of biceps and extend a line 4 inches out from each end for guide.
▪ Square a short guideline out from each side of grain at cap level.
▪ Place back and front patterns on draft with C on biceps guideline mark and A touching somewhere on cap guideline.
▪ Draw bodice armhole, including notches, and remove pattern. (Broken lines indicate untraced pattern.) Crossmark points B on sleeve. Remove pattern.
▪ Redraw front armhole curve, flattening slightly.
▪ Draw curved lines from B to elbow level on front and back.

    Note: The space on the front cap between A-points is cap ease. If this measures more than $\frac{1}{2}$ inch, slash grainline from grain at cap to, not through, wrist and overlap to remove unneeded excess. Tape pattern (not illustrated).

FIGURE 4
▪ Draw curved slash line from B to midpoint of cap line.
▪ Divide area into 3 sections and draw slash line as shown.
▪ Cut sleeve from paper.
▪ Starting at points B, cut slash lines to, not through, cap line.

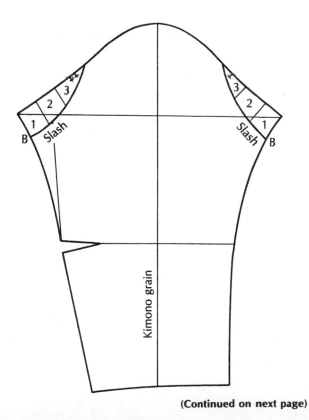

(Continued on next page)

FIGURE 5
- Place sleeve on paper
- Raise points B 3 inches, spreading sections evenly as shown.
- Trace pattern (bold lines) and discard.
- Draw curved lines from points B to elbow.
(Underarm seam can be drawn straight. See elbow dart options, page 395.)
- Draw grain and complete for a test fit.

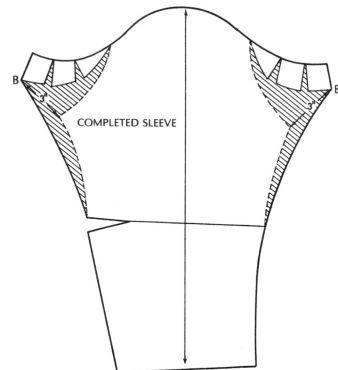

SQUARE ARMHOLE WITH GATHERED THREE-QUARTER SLEEVE

To develop the pattern for this and similar designs, follow the general instructions given for the deep-cut square armhole, page 404.

Pattern plot and development

FIGURES 1 and 2
- Mark styleline for armhole as shown.
- Cut and separate bodice. Discard unneeded section (shaded area).

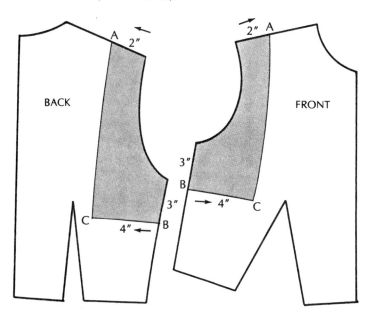

Design Analysis
Design 2 has a three-quarter-length gathered sleeve set deeply into a squared armhole. Sleeve is cuffed.

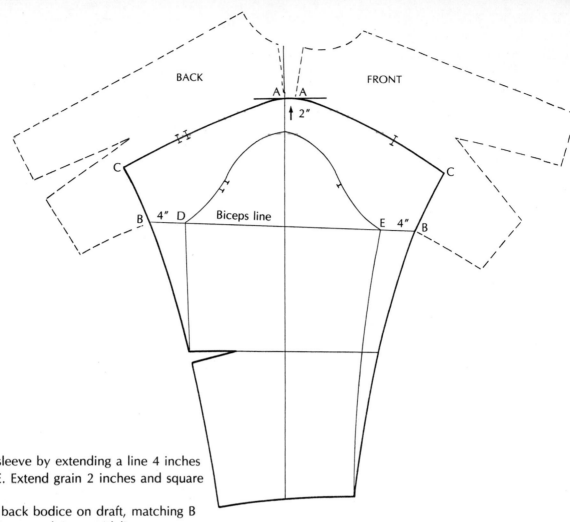

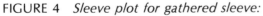

FIGURE 3
▪ Prepare traced sleeve by extending a line 4 inches out from D and E. Extend grain 2 inches and square guideline.
▪ Place front and back bodice on draft, matching B to guidelines at biceps and A to guideline at cap. Trace and remove pattern. (Broken line section of pattern not traced.)

FIGURE 4 *Sleeve plot for gathered sleeve:*
▪ Mark length 4 inches below elbow level. Blend dart.
▪ Cut sleeve from paper.
▪ Discard section below sleeve length.

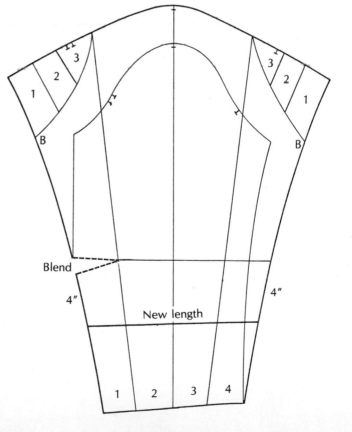

FIGURE 5
- Spread sleeve on paper as shown. Trace.
- Discard pattern.
- Measure down 1 inch from sleeve hemline (between space 1 and 2). Mark slit $2\frac{1}{2}$ inches up from this point. Blend hemline and dart area.
- Cut from paper for test fit.
- To develop cuff, see page 353.

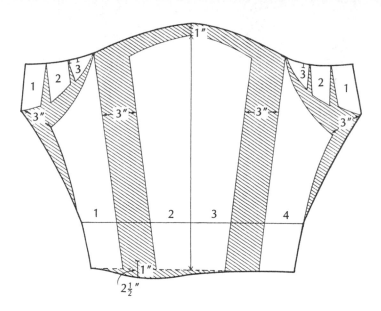

DROP SHOULDER

Drop-shoulder designs are developed by attaching a portion of the upper sleeve cap to the bodice. The dropped shoulder extends beyond the shoulder tip and covers part of the upper arm at varying lengths. It may be developed without the lower sleeve (Design 1) or with the lower sleeve (Design 2). Instructions given can be used for all similar designs.

WITHOUT LOWER SLEEVE

Pattern plot and development

FIGURES 1 and 2
- Trace front and back bodice, transferring back shoulder dart to back armhole.
- A–X = One-half of back armhole.
- B–X = One-half of front armhole.
- Mark and label as shown.

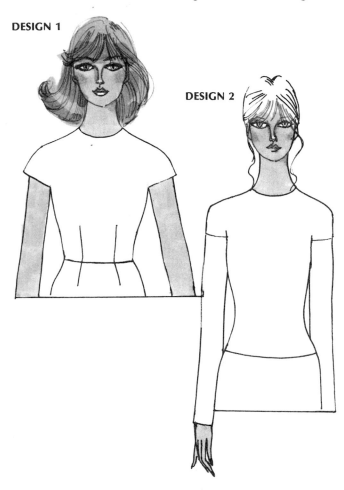

DESIGN 1

DESIGN 2

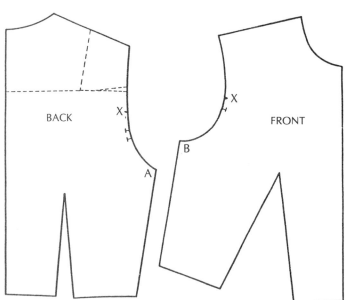

BACK

FRONT

FIGURE 3 *Sleeve:*
- Trace basic sleeve.
- Measure and mark as follows:
C–X = A–X distance plus $\frac{1}{4}$ inch for ease. Mark.
D–X = B–X distance plus $\frac{1}{4}$ inch for ease. Mark.
- Draw straight guideline connecting X-points. At grain, mark $\frac{1}{2}$ inch below guideline.
- Draw blended curved line from X-points to guidemark.
- Separate cap from lower sleeve (shaded area).
- Cut cap apart along grainline.

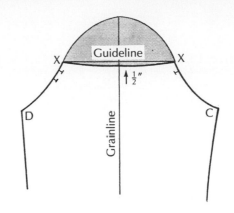

FIGURE 4 and 5 *Sleeve cap to bodice:*
- Place cap sections on front and back bodice with X-points touching and curve of cap $\frac{1}{4}$ inch away from shoulder tips.
- Mark $\frac{1}{4}$ inch up from shoulder tips and draw blending curve over cap, ending at mid-shoulder as shown.

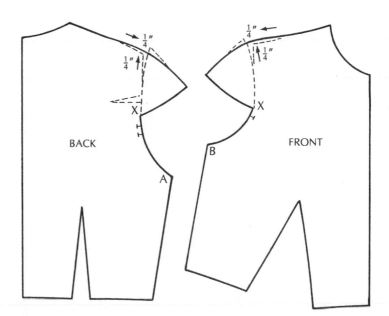

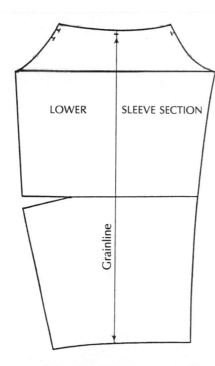

LOWER   SLEEVE SECTION

Grainline

FIGURE 6
Design 2: Use bottom of sleeve section.
   Note: For a more casual fit, add $\frac{1}{2}$ inch to width of cap. Split sleeve along grainline and spread 1 inch. True to cap.

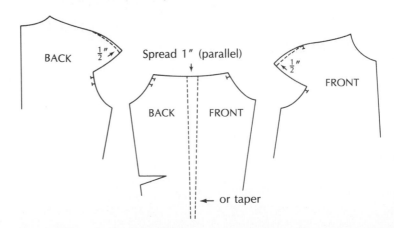

_part *Four*

PATTERNMAKING DETAILS

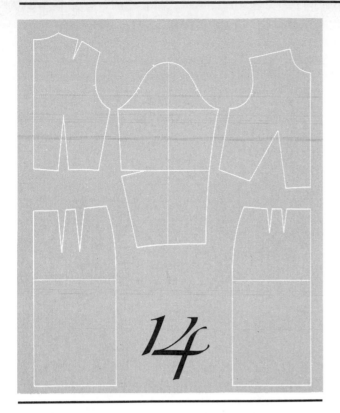

BUTTONS AND BUTTONHOLES 414
Basic types of buttons 415
Types of buttonholes 415
Closure 415
Button/buttonhole placement guide 416
FACINGS 418
Types of facings 418
Facings for cut-out necklines 420

14

BUTTONS/BUTTONHOLES
AND FACINGS

BUTTONS AND BUTTONHOLES

Buttons and buttonholes are both functional and decorative, but their primary purpose is to hold two sides of a garment together by having the button slipped through an opening or loop on the corresponding side of the garment. (Other types of closures used are Velcro, snaps, hooks and eyes, and grippers.)

Buttons range in size from small to large and come detailed or flat in a wide range of geometric shapes, such as circles, squares, rectangles, quarter-balls, half balls, and full balls (see illustration). They are commonly designated by "line" (ligne), inches or centimeters representing the diameter of the button (see chart).

Buttons can be made of plastic, metal, or natural substances (wood, bone, mother-of-pearl), or covered in fabric or leather. They can be plain or decorative—jeweled, corded, carved, or saddle-stitched. There are buttons for every type of garment from sportswear to formal, making the button an important fashion statement.

Buttonholes are openings or loops wide enough to accommodate the size of the button, placed in an overlapping section of the garment or as a loop (where the centerlines meet). Women's-wear garments button right over left, through vertical, horizontal, or angled slits.

Flat

Quarter ball

Half ball

Full ball

BUTTON SIZES

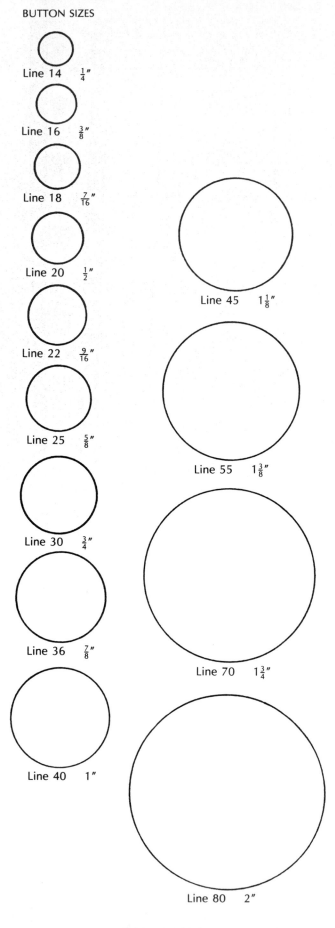

Line 14 $\frac{1}{4}''$

Line 16 $\frac{3}{8}''$

Line 18 $\frac{7}{16}''$

Line 20 $\frac{1}{2}''$

Line 22 $\frac{9}{16}''$

Line 25 $\frac{5}{8}''$

Line 30 $\frac{3}{4}''$

Line 36 $\frac{7}{8}''$

Line 40 $1''$

Line 45 $1\frac{1}{8}''$

Line 55 $1\frac{3}{8}''$

Line 70 $1\frac{3}{4}''$

Line 80 $2''$

BASIC TYPES OF BUTTONS

Sew through. Sew-through buttons have two or four holes for attachment.

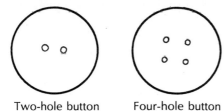

Two-hole button   Four-hole button

Shank buttons. Shank buttons have a solid top and some type of shank (wire, fabric, loop, metal, or plastic) attached to the underside. (This type raises the button away from the fabric surface, allowing room for layers of fabric to fit smoothly under the button when closed.)

Metal shank   Cloth shank

TYPES OF BUTTONHOLES

Machine-stitched. Buttonholes can be stitched for straight or keyhole openings.

Straight   Keyhole

Bound buttonholes. Folded fabric covers the raw edge openings in the garment. This type of buttonhole can be made by a seamstress or sent to a trim house for stitching.

Bound

Loops. Loops are narrow strips of turned bias with or without a filler. For mass-produced garments loops are generally made by a trim house. Loops are stitched at centerline. The joined side can be developed with or without an extension.

Slits. Slits can be cut in leather, plastic, or fabric that will not ravel (not illustrated).

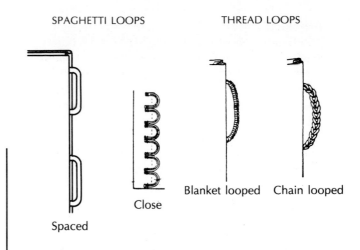

SPAGHETTI LOOPS   THREAD LOOPS

Spaced   Close   Blanket looped   Chain looped

CLOSURE

Overlap. Button closures require an overlap extending beyond the centerline. This overlap should be equal to the diameter of the button (or one-half the diameter plus $\frac{1}{4}$ inch, on inexpensive garments). On asymmetric garments, this extension is parallel with the asymmetric line. The center of the button rests along the centerline with equal amounts on the garment and the extension.

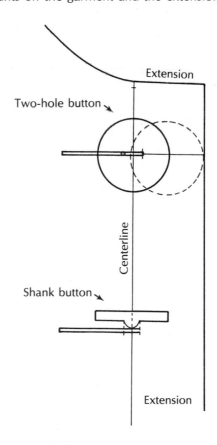

Extension

Two-hole button

Centerline

Shank button

Extension

Buttonhole length. The length of the buttonhole is determined by the diameter of the button plus $\frac{1}{8}$ inch for a flat button. For stylistic buttons (odd shapes), it is best to cut a slit in the fabric and slip the button through the opening to determine the length. Use this measurement to mark pattern.

Placement. The buttonhole placement generally starts $\frac{1}{8}$ inch out from the center front toward the extension. However, consideration must be given to the distance between the holes of the button or to the width of the button shank. Placement of the buttonhole out from the center line is always one-half the distance between the holes of the button and one-half the width of the shank. Otherwise, the buttonhole will not be centered with the button.

BUTTON/BUTTONHOLE PLACEMENT GUIDE

Necklines. Mark buttonhole at a distance down from neckline equal to one-half the diameter of the button, plus $\frac{1}{4}$ inch.

Belted garment. Mark position so that buttonhole is at least $1\frac{1}{2}$ inches up and down from belt or buckle. Waist can be secured with Velcro or hook and eye, if needed (see following examples). For waistband on buttonhole side, apply same rule.

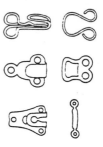

Unbelted garment. Mark buttonhole placement at waistline to secure waist.

Buttonhole spacing. Mark first and last buttonhole. Divide the remaining space among the remaining buttonholes needed. When spacing buttonholes, consider placing buttonhole as near to bust level as possible to avoid gapping. This may require closer or wider placement than desired.

Button placement. Mark for buttons on left side corresponding to buttonholes, centering space between holes of button or center of shank on centerline of garment.

Diagonal buttonholes. Rules stated above apply.

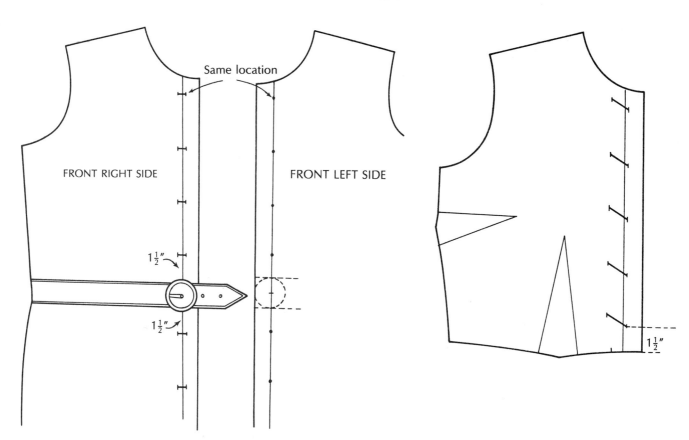

Same location

FRONT RIGHT SIDE   FRONT LEFT SIDE

$1\frac{1}{2}''$

$1\frac{1}{2}''$

$1\frac{1}{2}''$

Vertical buttonholes. For inset bands or used with tiny buttons. Button placement can be centered or placed at the top of the buttonhole.

Lapels. Mark button and buttonhole at a point where the lapel folds over from the extension to the body of the jacket (breakpoint). Place remaining buttons and buttonholes using previous information.

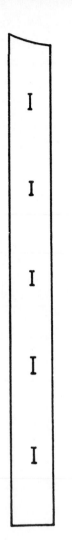

←Fold-over (breakpoint)

Waistbands and cuffs. Same instructions for button and buttonholes apply.

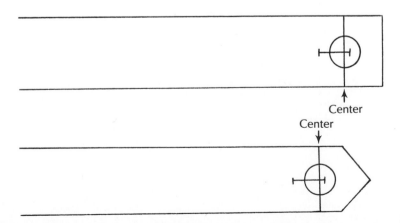

Center

Center

FACINGS

A facing is a shaped piece of fabric stitched to the outside edge of a garment and folded over to conceal the raw edges. Facings can control the fit of the outer section of the garment when the cut edge is bias (stretches) or crosses the hollow areas above the bust. Fold-back facings are facings developed as part of the main pattern piece and are then folded back over the area being faced, rather than being stitched on to it.

The following instructions apply only to neckline, shoulder, and armhole facings. Fold-back facings requiring buttons and buttonholes are discussed with shirts. Fold-back facings for hemlines of shirts, jackets, sleeves, pockets, collars, cuffs, yokes, inset hemlines, and other self-faced sections are covered under these titles where appropriate.

Facings are usually planned as part of the pattern plotting. They are generally traced from the pattern before or after the design pattern is developed. Facings for deeply cut-out necklines and/or armholes may be modifed with the cut edge

of the neck and armhole of the garment eased into the facing, offsetting stretch or causing the garment to fit closer to the figure. Both methods will be illustrated.

TYPES OF FACINGS

Two types of facings are featured:
Separate facings: Individual facings for armhole and/or neck.
Combined facing: All-in-one armhole and neckline facing.

Facings vary in width and shape but are generally from $1\frac{1}{2}$ to 2 inches around the neck and armhole. Combined facings have a blended line, connecting facing of neck with the armhole facing. Facing width at center back is generally planned to exceed the depth of the front neckline for a better look and hanger appeal.

Note: Facings that differ are illustrated with the specific design pattern in the text.

Separate facings

FIGURES 1 and 2

▪ Facings are traced from the front and back design pattern. The outer edge of the facing is trimmed $\frac{1}{16}$ inch at the shoulder to zero at shoulder tip and $\frac{1}{8}$ inch in from side to zero at armhole. (This eliminates the looseness and stretch.) Broken line indicates original pattern from which the facing is traced.

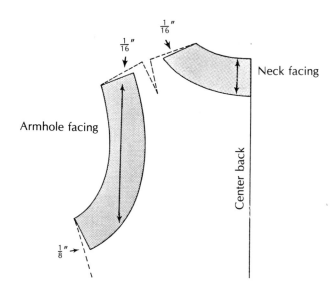

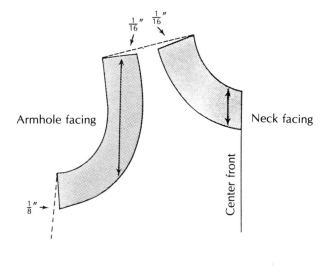

Combined facings

FIGURES 1 and 2
- Combined facings are traced from front/back patterns and trimmed $\frac{1}{8}$ inch at shoulder, neck, and sides, with line blended to zero as shown.
- To complete back facing, the shoulder dart is closed (broken line); otherwise, it would be too bulky.
- Facing length at center back varies according to depth of front neck. Measurements given may be used for basic neckline.

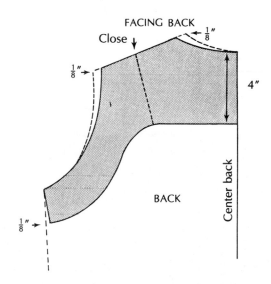

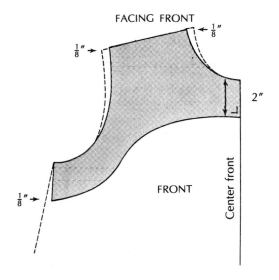

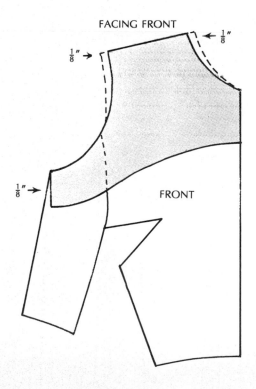

FIGURE 3
- Facings for garments with stylelines should be developed before the bodice pattern is separated. However, if the pattern has been separated before facing is developed, place style seamlines together and trace section being faced.
- Trim $\frac{1}{8}$ inch at shoulder, neck, and side, with line blended to zero as shown.
- Repeat for back (not illustrated). (Broken lines indicate original pattern.)

FACINGS FOR CUT-OUT NECKLINES

Cut-out neckline designs are featured here because of the special features of the facings. In this series, facings are illustrated modified and unmodified. Facings are modified for stretch, or so that the edge of the garment can be eased into the facing for a closer fit. Use contour facing to correct a fitting problem if neckline or armhole gap (looseness). (Review contouring for guidance as to when facing rather than bodice is modified.) Cut-out necklines with sleeves or cut-out armholes with collars have a separate facing. Cut-out neck and armholes have all-in-one facings.

V-neck facing

Two types of V-neck facings are illustrated, modified for stretch and modified for contouring.

FIGURES 1 and 2

- Draw necklines on front and back patterns as shown. (Broken line area discarded from pattern.)
- Draw front and back facings (shaded areas). Center back facing should be deeper than depth of V-neck on front (example: 10 inches).
- Mark shoulder line $\frac{1}{16}$ inch down from shoulder of front and back bodice.

V-NECK   SQUARE NECK   SCOOP NECK

- Draw slash line across facing, one-third the distance up from center front on V-line.
- Measure $\frac{3}{8}$ inch for overlap. This measurement varies according to stretch of fabric. Mark. (Lined area.)
- Mark ease control notches as shown.
- Cut front and back patterns from paper.
- Trace facings from pattern. Cut from paper.

FIGURE 3 *Modify for stretch:*
- Cut through slash line. Overlap and tape.
- Trace and blend.

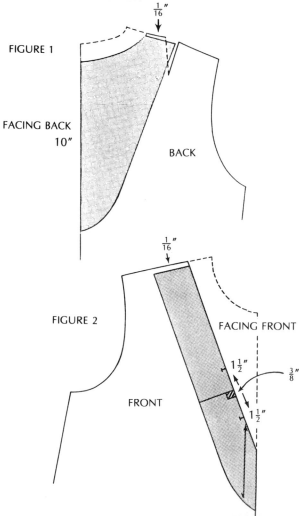

FIGURE 1

FACING BACK
10"

BACK

$\frac{1}{16}$"

FIGURE 2

FACING FRONT

FRONT

$1\frac{1}{2}$"

$1\frac{1}{2}$"

$\frac{3}{8}$"

$\frac{1}{16}$"

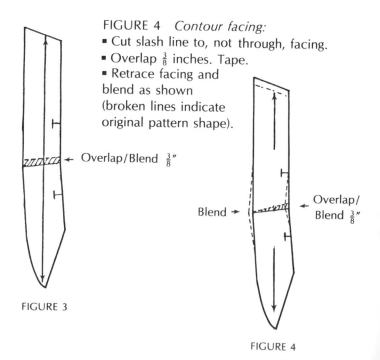

FIGURE 4 *Contour facing:*
- Cut slash line to, not through, facing.
- Overlap $\frac{3}{8}$ inches. Tape.
- Retrace facing and blend as shown (broken lines indicate original pattern shape).

← Overlap/Blend $\frac{3}{8}$"

Blend →

Overlap/ Blend $\frac{3}{8}$"

FIGURE 3

FIGURE 4

Scoop-neckline facing

FIGURE 1
- Plan facing using illustrations as a guide. (For back facing see V-neckline, Figure 1.)
- This facing can be used as is, modified for stretch, or for contour fit.

FIGURES 2 and 3
- Modify facing for bodice if required. Follow illustrations for pattern development.

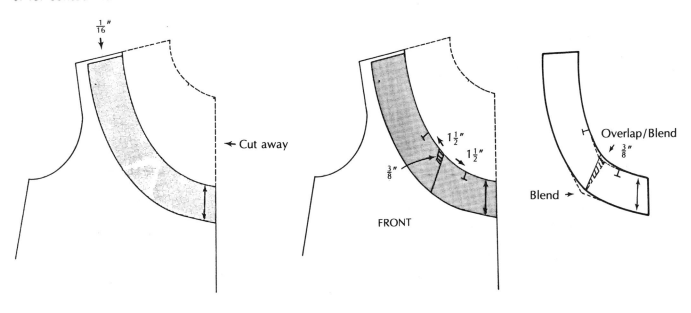

Square-neckline facing

FIGURE 1
- Repeat instructions given for scoop-neckline facing.

FIGURE 2
- Draw slash for overlap.

FIGURE 3 *Contour facing*

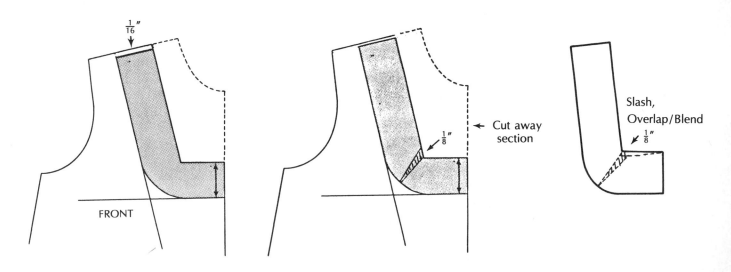

(Continued on next page)

Cut-out armhole facing

FIGURE 1

• Draw cut-out armhole on front and back patterns (back not illustrated).

• Draw facing (shaded area). (Facing may be used as is, or modified for stretch or closer fit.)

FIGURE 2

• Draw slash line and ease control notches.

FIGURE 3   *Contour facing*

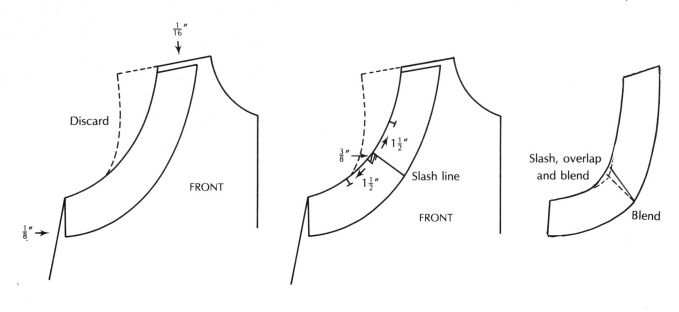

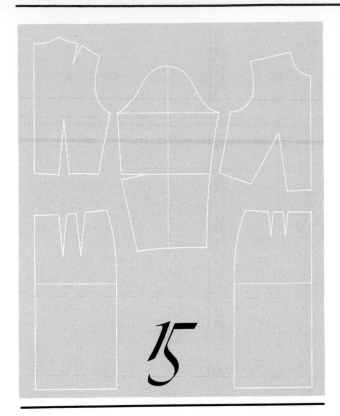

15

PLACKETS AND POCKETS

PLACKETS 424
Pointed placket and facing-in-one 424
Wing collar and placket 426
Slit opening with placket 428
POCKETS 429
Pocket classification 429
OUTSIDE POCKETS 429
Patch pocket 429
Patch pocket variations 430
Stylized outside pocket 430
INSERTED POCKET 431
Stylized opening 431
Variation of an inserted pocket 432
POCKET IN-ONE WITH SEAM 432
Pocket in-one with side seam 432
Stylized yoke pocket 433
Bodice pocket 434
Welt pocket 435
INSERT POCKETS—SIDE-SEAM POCKET 436
Pocket with gathered front 436
Pocket with control lining 437

PLACKETS

Plackets are finished slits or faced openings designed on all types of garments—bodice, sleeve, skirt, dress, jacket, pant, and so forth. Plackets can be of any length and width, with blunt, pointed, rounded, or stylized ends. Some plackets have buttons and buttonholes, others do not. When designed for neckline openings, the placket can end at the neck edge or be extended beyond the neck and become part of the collar. The measurement can vary to create different effects.

POINTED PLACKET AND FACING-IN-ONE

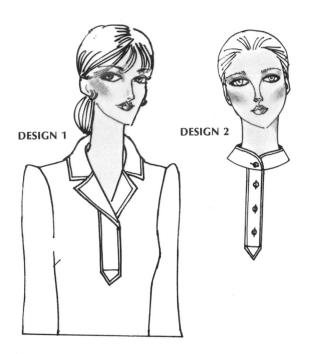

DESIGN 1   DESIGN 2

Design Analysis
The pointed placket of Design 1 is set into a cut-out section of the bodice with collar attached. (Collar not illustrated in pattern plot.) Top stitching finishes the placket. Design 2 is included for practice.

Pattern plot and development

FIGURE 1
- Fold paper.
- Place center front of pattern on fold and trace.
Plan placket:
A–B = placket length (example: 8 inches).
B–C = 1 inch.
C–D = 1 inch.
- Square lines $\frac{3}{4}$ inches in from B and C. Label E and F.
- From F, draw a line to neck, parallel with center front.
- Connect point F with D.
Plan facing for placket:
- Start facing 2 inches from shoulder at neck, ending $\frac{3}{4}$ inches from E. Connect facing with E as shown. (Indicated by broken line.)
- Trace placket and facing to underneath side.

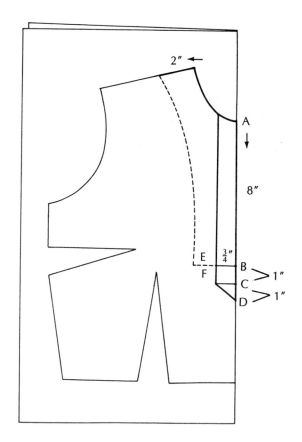

FIGURE 2
- Unfold and pencil in perforated line (broken line).
- Place paper underneath pattern and trace placket and facing for *right side* of garment (lined area). Remove paper and pencil in perforated line.

FIGURE 3
- Repeat for other side, tracing placket across at level with point B as shown (lined area). Note that point of placket is not included.
- Remove paper and pencil in perforated line.

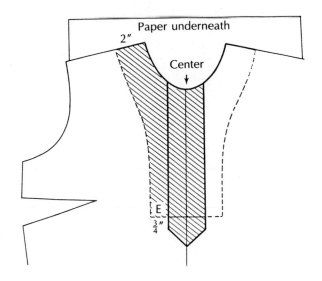

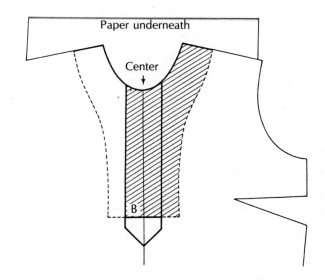

FIGURE 4   *Placket for right side:*
- Fold paper along placket edge. Square from fold at neck touching centerline. (Broken line indicates original neck.) Trace placket only (lined area). Omit facing section. Unfold and pencil in perforated line. (Finished pattern shape shown.)

FIGURE 5   *Placket for left side:*
- Repeat for other side.

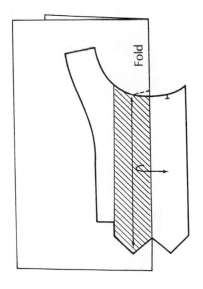

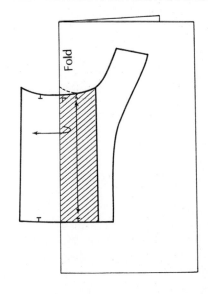

(Continued on next page)

FIGURES 6 and 7 *Placket:*
▪ Add seams and label *Right-side-up* (RSUP). Lined area indicates facing side of placket.

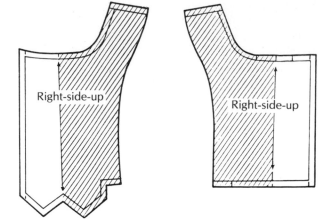

FIGURE 8 *Bodice section:*
▪ Add seams and notches and grainline.
▪ Cut from paper, trimming excess from placket inset area, and unfold.
▪ Cut basic back to complete design.

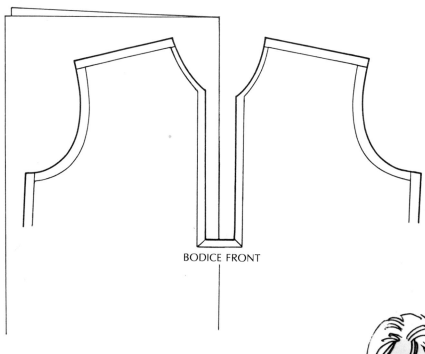

BODICE FRONT

WING COLLAR AND PLACKET

Design Analysis

Design 1 features an all-in-one placket and collar set into a cut-out opening in front. The placket is connected halfway up, ending at shoulder-neck location. Seam allowance is indicated because of its unique feature. Design 2 is included for practice.

DESIGN 1

DESIGN 2

Pattern plot and development

FIGURE 1

- Trace front pattern on left side of paper.
- A–B = placket length (example: 10 inches).
- A–C = Depth of opening (example: 6 inches). Mark.
- A–E = $1\frac{1}{2}$ inches or more.
- Draw curved line from E to F and E to C. Blend.
- B–D = $1\frac{1}{2}$ inches, squared from B. Connect D with F.
- Place paper underneath (indicated by broken line), and trace placket (B, D, F, E, to B). Remove paper and pencil in perforated line.

FIGURE 2

- Finish placket with $\frac{1}{4}$-inch seam allowance. Notch. Cut 4 pieces—self-faced. (Placket joined from C to B.)

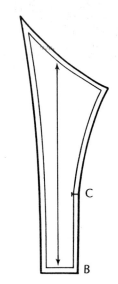

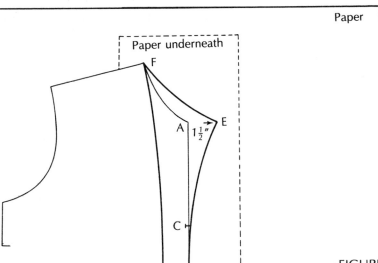

FIGURE 3 *Bodice:*

- Fold paper at center front. Add seam allowance ($\frac{1}{4}$ inch where placket is attached). Cut from paper, triming excess from placket insert area.
- Cut basic back to complete design.

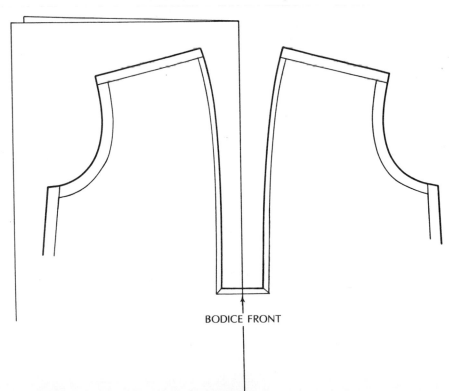

BODICE FRONT

SLIT OPENING WITH PLACKET

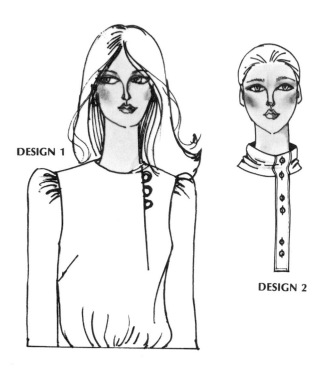

DESIGN 1

DESIGN 2

Design Analysis
Placket band of Design 1 is attached to a slit on one side of the garment and three spaghetti loops and buttons are used for closure. Design 2 is included for practice.

Pattern plot and development

FIGURE 1
- Trace and cut a full front.
- Draw 8-inch (varies) parallel line for slit, 2 inches from center line.
- Draw another line $\frac{1}{16}$ inch from slit line. (Space is needed for width of pencil lead when tracing pattern on paper, fabric, or when making a marker.) Cut slit line and crossnotch end. Label A and B.
- Mark for loops.
- Draw facing 1½ inches wide at shoulder following neckline and slit as shown (indicated by broken lines).
- Mark for loop placement.
- Draw transfer facing by placing paper under pattern and trace (broken line area).
- Remove pattern. Pencil in facing.

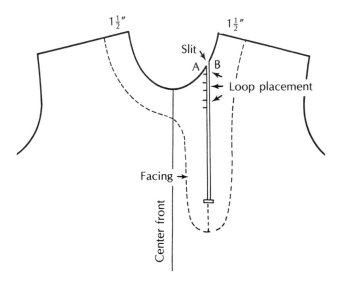

FIGURE 2
- Completed facings.

   Note: Facing can be separated, as illustrated, or developed as a one-piece facing cut on the fold and slit (not illustrated).

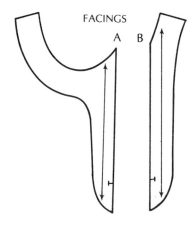

FACINGS

FIGURE 3 *Placket extension band:*
- Draw a line twice the length of slit (example: 16 inches).
- Draw a parallel line equal to desired width (example: 1¼ inches).
- Label C and D and midpoint E. Band is self-faced. To stitch, fold band at point E with points C and D touching. Stitch across top and on one side at band. The raw edge of the band stitches to B side of slit on garment. (Band is the underlay to conceal opening and for button attachment.) Facing is then attached to garment, concealing all raw edges around neck and slit.
- Draw grain.

Fold up for facing side

POCKETS

A pocket is a cavity or pouch that has a closed end and is usually sewn into or onto a garment. It can be a decorative or functional feature, or both. Its primary use is as a depository or temporary holding place for items and/or hands. The pocket opening should be wide enough for hands, and deep enough to keep objects from falling out. Pockets may be designed for all types of garments. Type of pocket, size, shape, and placement should complement the design.

POCKET CLASSIFICATION

Outside pockets. Pockets, such as the patch pocket, attached to the outside of a garment. This type of pocket can be designed in a number of sizes and shapes, with or without a flap as shown.

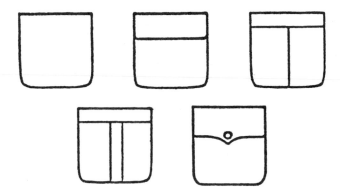

Inserted pockets. Pockets inserted into a straight or stylized seam, with the cavity or pouch on the inside of the garment. Inserted pockets can also be stitched to the inside of a garment, giving the appearance of a patch pocket on the right side of the garment. (To be illustrated later.)

Welt pockets. Any pockets characterized by a separate strip or flap stitched to the pocket opening with the pouch falling to the inside of the garment. These pockets can have a double welt or single welt, or can be stylized with or without flaps as shown.

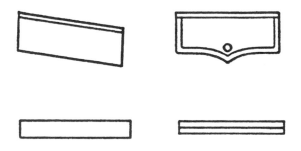

OUTSIDE POCKETS

PATCH POCKET

The patch pocket should be planned and drawn on the working pattern for placement. The pocket is indicated by punch and circles marked $\frac{1}{4}$ to $\frac{1}{2}$ inches inside the finished length and width as shown. The pocket is developed on the fold of the paper, with or without a flap, using one-half of the desired width of the pocket plus length. (See possible variation on next page.) Generally, seams of $\frac{1}{2}$ inch or more are given for fold-back seams, with $\frac{1}{4}$-inch seam allowance for faced sections to complete the pocket.

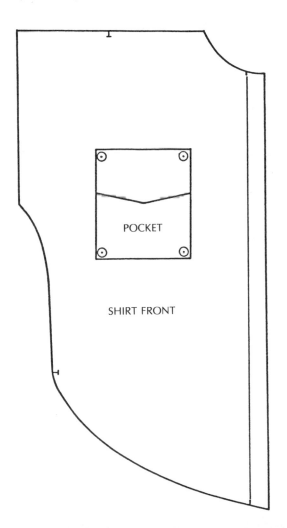

POCKET

SHIRT FRONT

PATCH POCKET VARIATIONS

FIGURE 1
• Patch without a flap, and fold-under hem.

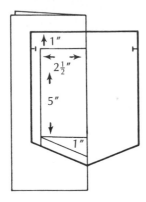

FIGURE 2
• Patch without a flap is folded and stitched to finish pocket.

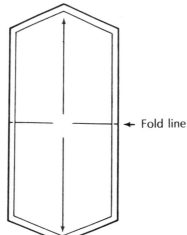

← Fold line

FIGURE 3
• Patch with fold-over flap in-one with pocket. (*Options:* Pocket flap may be faced by tracing flap end and adding $\frac{1}{2}$ inch at bottom; see flap in Figure 4. Pocket can also be cut twice and self-faced.)

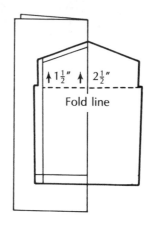

FIGURE 4
• Patch with separate flap and fold-over hem.

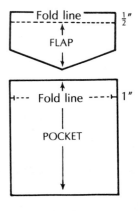

STYLIZED OUTSIDE POCKET

Two designs are given to illustrate outside pockets. Figure 5 shows pattern development for Design 1 (pant). Figure 6 shows pattern development for Design 2 (skirt). Use instructions and illustrations as a guide. (Broken lines indicate the design pattern shape.)

DESIGN 1

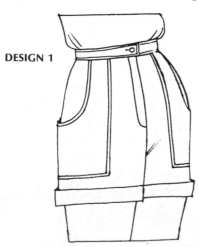

FIGURE 5
• Plot pocket design using measurements given.
• Plan facing on entry side of pocket (broken line).
• Trace pocket by placing a paper underneath.
• Remove paper and pencil in pocket outline.

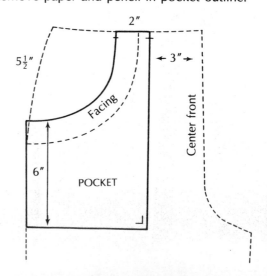

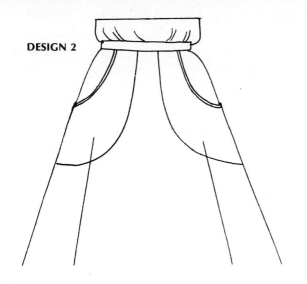

DESIGN 2

FIGURE 6
• Follow illustration and instruction given for Design 1, Figure 5.

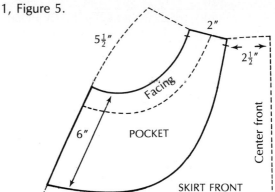

5½"

2"

2½"

Facing

6"

POCKET

Center front

SKIRT FRONT

INSERTED POCKET

STYLIZED OPENING

Design Analysis
Pocket opening curves from waistline to side seam of Design 3.

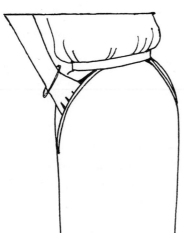

FIGURE 2
• Trace two copies of pocket, including pocket's curved opening.
• Label one copy *Backing*.

FIGURE 3
• Trim to curved opening on other traced pocket. Label *Facing*.

Pattern plot and development

FIGURE 1
• Trace pattern and draw pocket shape by using illustrations and measurements as a guide. (Broken line indicates outer edge of pocket pouch.)

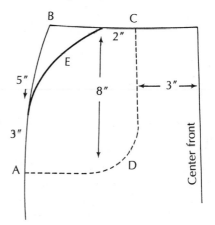

B

C

2"

E

5"

8"

3"

3"

A

D

Center front

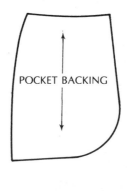

POCKET BACKING

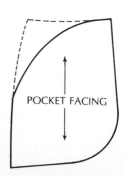

POCKET FACING

VARIATION OF AN INSERTED POCKET

Design Analysis

Design 4 features a pocket that extends out $\frac{1}{2}$ inch from the side, providing additional room for entry.

FIGURE 2 *Pocket facing:*
▪ Trace pocket sections C, D, E, and F. Label *Facing.*

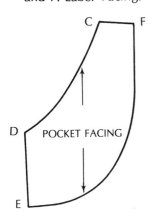

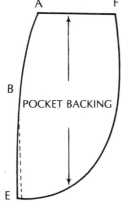

Pattern plot and development

FIGURE 1 *Plan pocket:*
▪ Use illustration and measurements given.
▪ Draw line from D to zero at hem.
▪ Draw curved pocket pouch from F to E as shown.
▪ Draw line from E, blending with B (broken line).

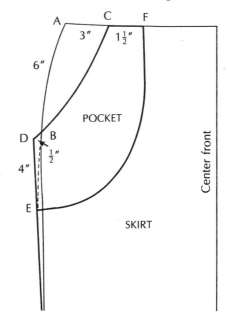

FIGURE 3 *Pocket backing:*
▪ Trace pocket section A, B, E, and F. (Broken line indicates original hipline.) Label *Backing.*

POCKET IN-ONE WITH SEAM

POCKET IN-ONE WITH SIDE SEAM

Pattern plot and development

FIGURE 1
▪ Plan pocket along side seam of the front pattern. (Repeat for back; not illustrated.)
▪ Place punch mark $1\frac{1}{2}$ inches down from waist at side seam and $\frac{1}{8}$ inch out on pocket side. Repeat 6 inches below for hand entry. Circle punch marks.
▪ *Stitching guide:* Stitch down from waist and up from hem to just beyond punch mark. (The unstitched space forms pocket opening.) Stitch around pocket. Pocket is placed on front side of garment.

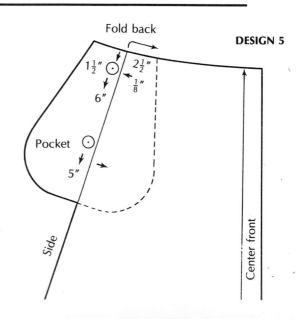

STYLIZED YOKE POCKET

Design Analysis
Pocket of Design 6 is shaped in-one with part of the yoke seam. The pouch is stitched to the inside, securing the pouch facing. Stitching outlines pocket shape on the outside of the garment. Button holds pocket in place.

FIGURE 2 *Yoke section:*
- Trace yoke and pocket extension (pocket backing), omitting curved line of pocket.
- Draw grain.

FIGURE 3 *Skirt section:*
- Cut skirt section from paper, including curved line of pocket section.
- Mark facing and buttonhole placement on curved section as shown.
- Draw grain.

FIGURE 4 *Pocket facing:*
- Trace facing for curved section of pocket.
- Draw grain in either direction as shown.

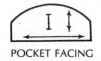

POCKET FACING

Pattern plot and development
FIGURE 1
- Draw yokeline 3 inches down from waist.
- Mark center on yokeline and shift point $\frac{1}{2}$ inch toward side seam. Draw guideline 5 inches below and 1 inch above yoke, between center front and side seam (broken line).
- Develop one-half the pocket shape on each side of guideline as shown. Mark button placement at center.

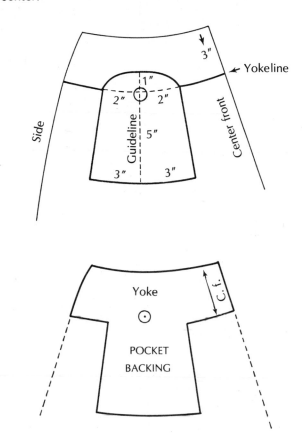

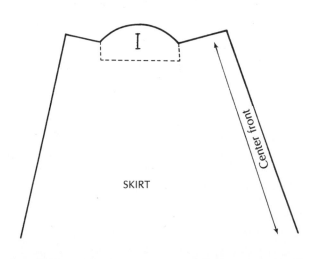

SKIRT

BODICE POCKET

Design Analysis

Pocket of Design 7 is formed in-one with part of yokeline on bodice.

Pattern plot and development

FIGURE 1   *Plan pocket:*
- Square yokeline from center front.
- Locate center on yokeline and move point $\frac{3}{4}$ inches toward side. Pocket width: 4 inches. Length: 3 inches.
- Mark for button and buttonhole placement. Label sections A and B.

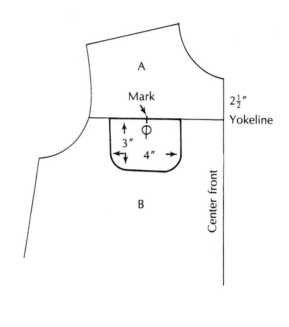

FIGURE 2   *Section A:*
- Trace section A, including pocket shape. Mark button placement.

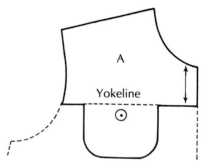

FIGURE 3   *Section B:*
- Fold pattern on yokeline. Trace pocket.
- Unfold, pencil in pocket.
- Cut section B, including traced pocket (bold line).
- Discard section indicated by broken lines.

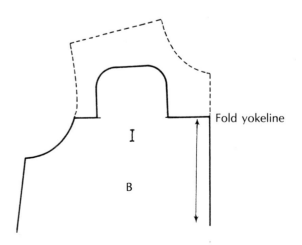

WELT POCKET

Design Analysis

Design 8 combines a welt with an insert pocket detail. Welt pocket with inside pocket pouch is stitched to inside of skirt for backing. Outline of pocket appears on the outside of skirt.

FIGURE 1

• Plan welt opening on skirt at a pleasing location. (Example: welt width $\frac{1}{2}$ inch; length 5 inches.)
• Draw cutting line in between welt, ending $\frac{1}{2}$ inch from each end. Connect with corners. Label A, B, C, and D as shown.

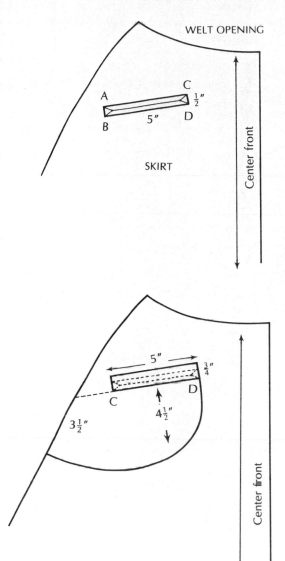

FIGURE 2

• Plan pocket and welt band on pattern, starting at C–D of welt. (Welt band finishes $\frac{3}{4}$ inch wide and will extend beyond welt opening. Broken line indicates original opening.)
• Continue C–D line to side seam (broken line).
• Draw curve of pocket as shown.

FIGURE 3   *Pocket/welt backing:*

• Trace pocket and welt band.
• Trim $\frac{1}{4}$ inch of band (broken line). Label E and F.

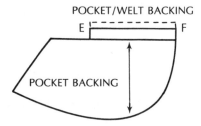

FIGURE 4   *Welt band:*

• Develop band, $1\frac{1}{2} \times 5$ inches. (Finished width: $\frac{3}{4}$ inch.)
• Add $\frac{1}{4}$-inch seams to pocket and welt bands.

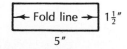

Stitching guide:

• Welt opening on garment is cut along lines indicated on pattern (broken lines).
• Pocket backing E–F is stitched to A–B of welt opening on skirt and pulled through. Pointed ends of opening are folded under and stitched on backing.
• Welt band is folded lengthwise, stitched across each end, and turned. This is stitched to C–D of welt opening.
• Pocket backing is double-stitched to inside of skirt (see design). Top of each corner of the welt is tacked to skirt.

INSERT POCKETS—SIDE-SEAM POCKET

POCKET WITH GATHERED FRONT

Design Analysis
Side seam of Design 9 is straight from the hip level to the waistline, with fullness absorbed in the waistband as gathers. Part of the side seam pocket is developed on the skirt section. (Same technique can also be used for pants.)

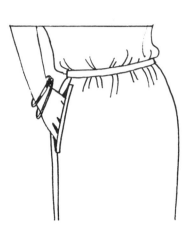

FIGURE 1   *Front pocket:*
• Draw a curved line $\frac{1}{2}$ inch out from side waist, ending 6 inches down from side seam. Mark and label X (end of opening).
• Draw pocket, using illustrations and measurements as a guide. (*Note:* Pocket shape ends 1 inch below point X.) Mark notch 1 inch down from waist.
• Trace two copies of pocket section.

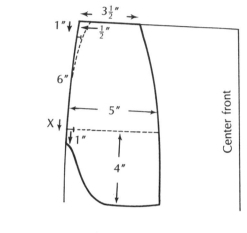

FIGURE 2   *Pocket facing:*
• Label one copy of traced pocket *Facing.*

FIGURE 3   *Pocket backing:*
• Separate second copy of traced pocket, using measurements given. Mark notches. Label backing and sections A and B.

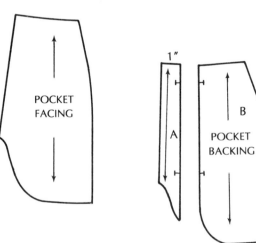

FIGURE 4   *Back skirt:*
• Adjust side seam, using front skirt instructions. Excess from side waist is taken up equally by the darts. (Broken lines indicate dart intake.)
• Align pocket section A to side seam and waist. Section B is pocket backing. Tape to pattern, or trace (eliminates seamline at pocket entry).

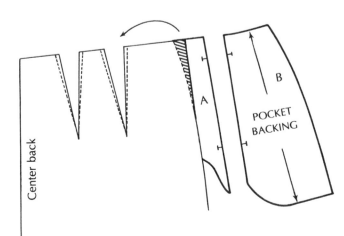

POCKET WITH CONTROL LINING

Design Analysis

The inserted pocket at side seam of Design 10 has a facing combined with lining that extends from side opening to center front. This type of inserted pocket with extended lining is used to hold the garment in place and allow the pleats and pocket to lie flat.

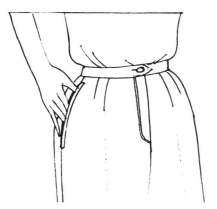

Stitching guide:
- Pocket facing is stitched to garment (front pocket opening).
- Pocket backing is stitched flat on top of lining and stitched with lining to back pant seam.
- Facing is stitched to lining to complete the pocket. The center front secures the lining.

FIGURE 2

- Slash to, not through, pattern and overlap both dart legs (broken lines). Tape. Retrace and label as shown.

FIGURE 3 *Pocket facing:*

- Trace lining sections A, E, F, and C. Include notches. Label pocket facing.

FIGURE 4 *Pocket backing:*

- Trace lining sections A, B, C, and D. Include notches. Label pocket backing.

FIGURE 1

Note: Use illustration and measurements as a guide.
- Trace section of upper pattern.
- Plan lining. Draw dart points to lining depth (shaded areas). Mark notches as shown.
- Cut pattern from paper.

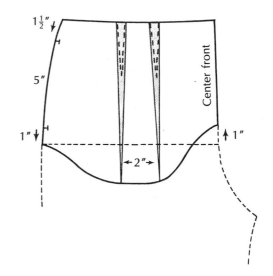

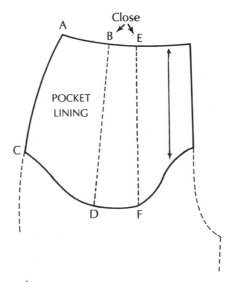

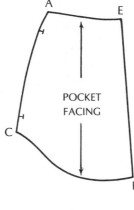

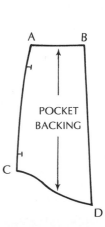

 _part_ _Five_

DRESSES, TOPS, JACKETS, COATS, CAPES, AND HOODS

(PATTERNMAKING BASED ON TORSO FOUNDATION)

THE TORSO DRAFT 442

16

THE TORSO DRAFT

THE TORSO DRAFT

The torso foundation, as a garment, fits the figure like a bodice and skirt, except that around the waistline (which has no seam), it fits somewhat more loosely. A closely fitted waistline would cause strain in the garment and displace the horizontal balance line at hip and hemline. The fit of the garment is controlled by two sets of double-ended darts at front and back, with side darts controlling the crosswise grain so that it lies parallel with the floor (see sketch).

The torso foundation, as a pattern, is developed from the basic one-dart bodice front and back with the lower section developed to the hipline of the figure (broken line on the sketch). When the upper and lower torso is combined, the waistline seam is omitted. This important and versatile pattern is the basis for the other foundation patterns:

- Tops (dartless knit and shirts)
- Dresses (without waistline seams)
- Jackets and coats
- Active wear (jumpsuits, body suits, leotards, swimsuits)

For figures with asymmetric hips, the torso pattern should be developed on a fold, using the high hip side measurement. The low hip side is adjusted after the draft has been completed. (For guidance, see Chapter 4.) The draft for figures with tilting forward or backward waistlines will look different from the standard draft.

Measurements needed
- (25) Hip depth: CF _____
      CB _____
- (26) Side hip depth: _____ (for personal fit only)
- (23) Hip arc: F _____ B _____.
- (21) Dart intake: F _____ B _____.

Bodice preparation for draft

FIGURE 1 *Front bodice:*
- Trace one-dart basic front pattern.
- Place square at center front with leg of ruler touching bust point and draw slash line from bust point to side seam as shown.

FIGURE 2
- Trace back pattern.
- Draw slash line from 2 inches in from side to armhole notch of back pattern.
- Label front and back side waists X.
- Cut patterns from paper and slash to, not through, armhole (back) and bust point (front).

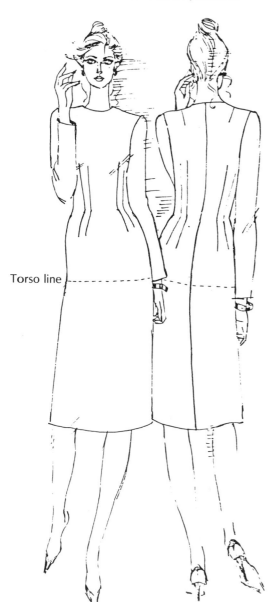

Torso line

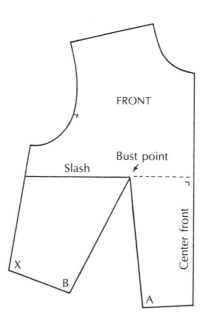

FRONT

Bust point

Slash

Center front

X

B

A

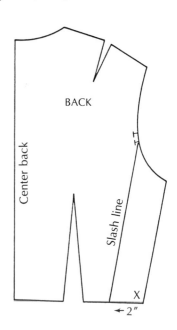

BACK

Center back

Slash line

X

← 2″

Torso front draft

FIGURE 3

- Square a line on paper. Label A at corner of square and mark the following:

A–B = Center front hip depth (example: 8 inches).

A–C = Front hip plus $\frac{1}{2}$-inch ease.

C–D = A–B, squared from C.

- Connect D to B. Crossmark $\frac{3}{4}$ inch in from D.

Personal fit: C–D = Side hip depth, squared from C. Square a line 3 inches in from D. Crossmark a point $\frac{3}{4}$ inch in from D.

- Place front bodice on draft so that the center front aligns with the vertical line and the center front waist touches point B exactly.
- Close part of waist dart until side waist (point X) touches somewhere on B–D guideline at waist. Secure and trace. Omit sections indicated by broken lines. Discard pattern.

Torso back draft

FIGURE 4

- Square a line on paper. Label E at corner of square and mark the following:

E–F = Center back hip depth (example: $7\frac{3}{4}$ inches). Square a short line.

E–G = Back hip plus $\frac{1}{2}$-inch ease.

G–H = C–D (from front draft) squared from G.

- Square in $\frac{3}{4}$ inches from H. Crossmark.
- Draw a curved waistline from crossmark blending with square at point F.
- Extend a 5-inch guideline out from H.
- Place back bodice on draft with center back aligned with vertical line and center back waist touching point F exactly.
- Spread slashed section until side waist (X-point) touches somewhere on waist guideline. Secure pattern.
- Trace pattern from neck, shoulder, and armhole. Omit section indicated by broken lines.
- Remove pattern. Blend armhole curve.
- Square a line across back that is one-fourth the center back neck to waist length (horizontal balance line).

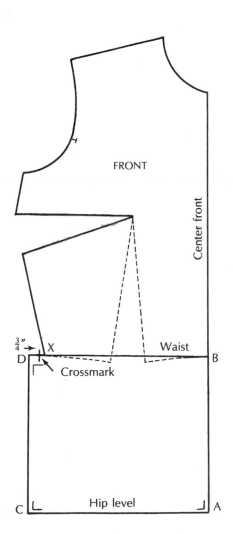

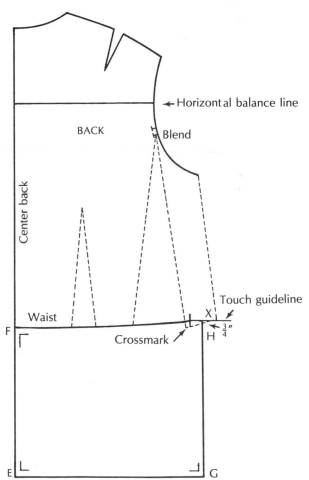

Side seam and hip shape

FIGURE 5 *Front torso draft:*
- Draw hipline curve starting approximately 2 inches up from hip and ending at crossmark at waist.
- From crossmark draw line to side dart of front. (*Note:* this is a temporary line.)
- Side dart: Mark dart point $1\frac{1}{2}$ inches from bust point and connect to dart leg as shown.

Double-ended darts:
From center front, square guidelines $1\frac{1}{2}$ inches below bust point and 3 inches below waist.
- Square a line to bust point, and from bust point square a line to guideline below waist, for center of first dart.
- Draw a parallel line $1\frac{3}{4}$ inches from first line for center of second dart.
- Use measurements given for dart intake (or use personal measurements). Connect dart legs to guidelines establishing double-ended dart points.

FIGURE 6 *Back torso draft:*
- Draw hipline curve to crossmark at waist and continue line to armhole.

Double-ended darts:
- From center back, square guidelines 1 inch below armhole level and $5\frac{1}{2}$ inches below waist.
- Mark $3\frac{1}{4}$ inches in from center back at waist.
- From this mark, draw a line parallel with center back ending at guideline for center of first dart.
- Draw a line $2\frac{1}{4}$ inches from first line for center of second dart.
- Use measurements given for dart intake (or use personal measurements). Connect dart legs to guidelines establishing double-ended dart points.

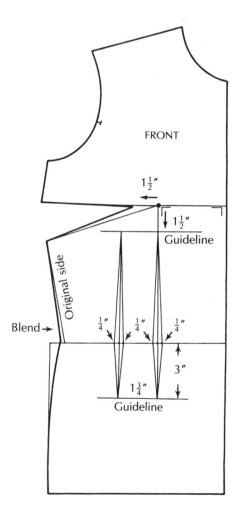

FRONT

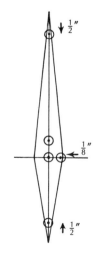

Marking for double-ended dart.
Punch and circle as shown.

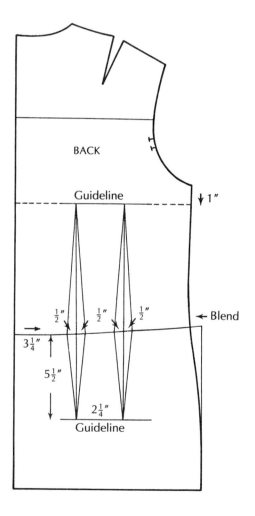

BACK

Trueing the pattern

▪ Cut back torso from paper. True side seams by placing back pattern on top of front pattern starting at hip level and ending at armhole. If front and back patterns do not true, adjust the side dart by increasing or decreasing the dart intake by the amount needed to lengthen or shorten the front side seam. Redraw the dart legs to dart point (not illustrated). Cut front pattern from paper, allowing paper around side dart. Fold dart and draw straight line from armhole to waist. Trim side seam line with dart folded. (See page 10 for trueing.)
▪ To test fit, cut in muslin, stitch, press seams open (no steam), and place on form or figure.

Correction information

▪ The hipline (horizontal balance line) *must* remain at hip level location when adjusting fit. There is a tendency to want to fit close to the waistline at side seam. The sides may be taken in, providing that the hipline (HBL) does not change location in the process. Darts may be adjusted by taking them in for a closer fit or let out if strain develops. (See Chapter 27 for correcting fit.)

Contour guidelines

FIGURES 7 and 8
▪ After pattern has been corrected, include front and back contour guidelines for reference when developing patterns for contour fitted designs (shaded areas). (See contouring, Chapter 9, for guide.)

▪ Both back darts are extended from waist to the horizontal balance line. (Used when developing low-cut back designs—close darts to new dart points for a tighter fit.)

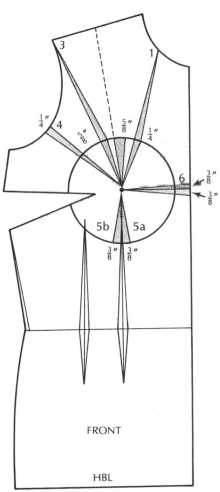

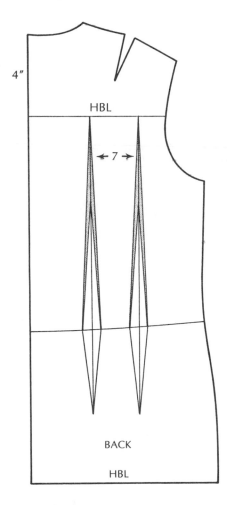

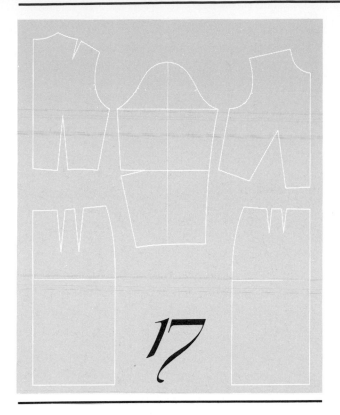

DRESS CATEGORIES 448
THE THREE BASIC DRESS FOUNDATIONS 448
PRINCESS-LINE FOUNDATION 450
A-LINE PRINCESS 451
STYLIZED PRINCESS WITH CAP SLEEVES 452
PANEL DRESS FOUNDATION 454
EMPIRE FOUNDATION 456
EMPIRE WITH SLINKY SKIRT 458
TENT FOUNDATION 460
OVERSIZED DRESS 462
JUMPER 463
SPECIAL PATTERNMAKING PROBLEMS 464
Gathers crossing dart areas 464
Stylelines crossing dart areas 465
Stylized one-piece front 466
CAFTAN 467
DRESS DESIGN VARIATIONS 468

17

DRESSES WITHOUT WAISTLINE SEAMS

DRESS CATEGORIES

Dresses may be grouped into two major categories —those with a waistline seam (combining a bodice with a skirt), and those without a waistline seam. Dresses designed without the waistline seam are based on the torso foundation pattern. Other important dress foundations such as the fitted sheath, the semi-fitted shift, the straight-line and A-line silhouettes, the princess, the panel, the empire, the tent, and the oversized dress are also based on the torso pattern. Dresses without waistline seams are featured in this chapter.

Knit dress designs
Garments designed for knits should be based on the dartless knit patterns 1 and 2 (see Chapter 18). Other patterns may be used as a base for knit designs; however, these patterns as well as the dartless knit patterns should be modified to compensate for the stretch and/or shrinkage factor of knits (see Chapter 25). Knit designs are not illustrated.

Shirtmaker dresses
To develop patterns for shirtmaker dresses, see Chapter 18 for shirt with yoke, without yoke, and the oversized shirt. To these patterns add desired dress length.

THE THREE BASIC DRESS FOUNDATIONS

The following three basic dress foundations (sheath or fitted, shift or semi-fitted, and straightline or box-fitted silhouettes) can be developed with either a straight- or A-line effect below the waist and hip. To use these foundation patterns for design variations, extend for length parallel with hip level. For A-line hems, add approximately $1\frac{1}{2}$ inches at side seam and connect to outermost part of hip. Blend with hemline (see A-line skirt for guidance, Chapter 12). Include contour guidelines, for future reference. (See Contour Guide Pattern, Chapter 9.)

The sheath (fitted silhouette). Both darts of the front and back torso patterns are marked for stitching.

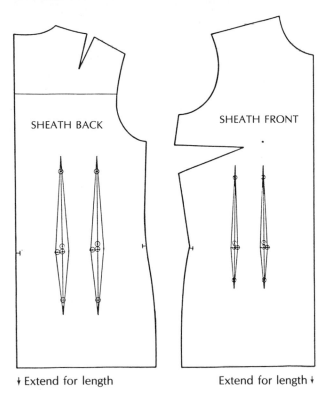

The shift (semi-fitted silhouette). One waist dart is marked for stitching and the other dart is left unmarked (broken lines) as ease around the waistline.

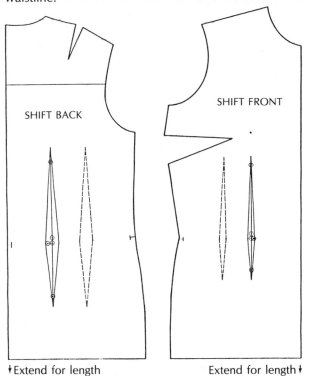

The straightline (box-fitted silhouette). Waist darts are left unmarked (broken lines) and unstitched as ease around the waistline.

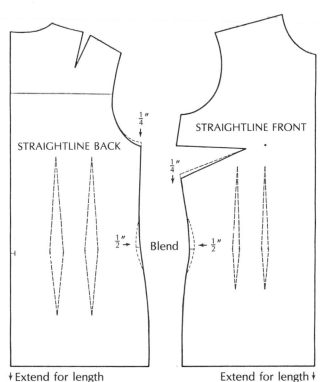

To modify the torso pattern for a box fit:
- Increase the side dart intake by measuring down $\frac{1}{4}$ inch on the lower dart leg and connecting to dart point as shown. Lower the back armhole by $\frac{1}{4}$ inch, blending back armhole. This shortens the side-seam length, holding the garment away from the figure for the box-fit effect. This does not affect the hipline placement on the figure since the shorter length represents the true length when garment does not follow contour of the figure. (Broken lines indicate original pattern shape.)
- Measure out $\frac{1}{2}$ inch at waistline and blend for new side seam.
- Before cutting pattern from paper, true dart legs and blend with side seam. After cutting, true front and back side seams (up from hip level), adjusting back armhole if needed.

PRINCESS-LINE FOUNDATION

The princess-line foundation is used to develop all designs with similar styleline features.

Pattern plot and development

FIGURES 1 and 2

▪ Trace front and back torso foundations. With pushpins, transfer darts to pattern underneath.
Back styleline placement:
▪ With skirt curve, draw line from leg of shoulder dart to dart point of first dart and from bottom of dart point to hip level, parallel with center back.
▪ Move shoulder dart point (broken line) to styleline and connect with dart leg.
Front styleline placement:
▪ Draw styleline from mid-shoulder (in line with back dart) to bust point and from bottom of dart point to hip level, parallel with center front.
▪ Draw slash line from bust point to dart point. Crossmark $\frac{3}{4}$ inch from bust point on slash line.
▪ Mark notches $1\frac{1}{2}$ inches (or 2 inches for bust cup size C and over) up and down from bust point on styleline, at side waistline and darts, as shown.

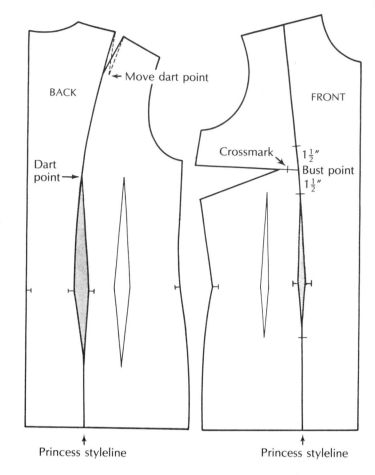

Princess styleline   Princess styleline

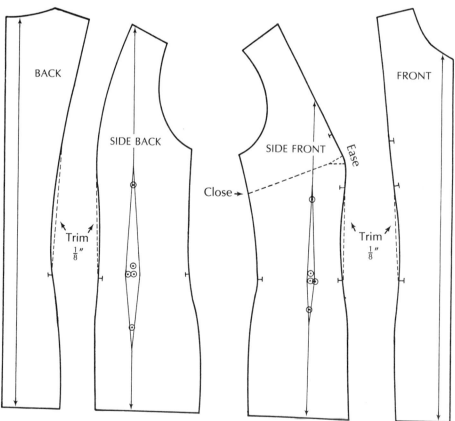

FIGURES 3, 4, 5, and 6
▪ Cut and separate styleline on each side of the dart legs. Trim shaded area between darts in Figures 1 and 2.
▪ Cut slash line from bust point and dart point to, not through, the crossmark.
▪ Close side dart legs. Tape.
▪ Retrace princess panels.
▪ Shape and blend styleline as shown. (Broken line indicates original pattern.)
▪ Draw grain. Punch and circle darts using examples given for basic torso.

This completes the princess-line dress foundation. To use as a base for design variations, extend length parallel with hip level. Several designs are given using the princess line as a foundation pattern.

A-LINE PRINCESS

Design Analysis

Design 1 features a fitted princess-line dress with an A-line silhouette. The pattern is based on the princess-foundation pattern. Design 2 is a practice problem based on the same foundation pattern.

Pattern plot and development

FIGURES 1 and 2

- Draw a horizontal guideline on paper.
- Place the back panels together with hipline on guideline and trace. Transfer darts and grainline with pushpin to paper underneath.
- Repeat for the front.
- Square down from hipline to length desired.
- Square across for hemline.
- Draw a line down from dart points parallel with center front and back (broken lines). Label A and B as shown.
- Measure out $1\frac{1}{2}$ inches at A and B and connect to dart points from A, and to outermost part of hip from B.
- Square in from side at hemline and blend to styleline.

DESIGN 1   DESIGN 2

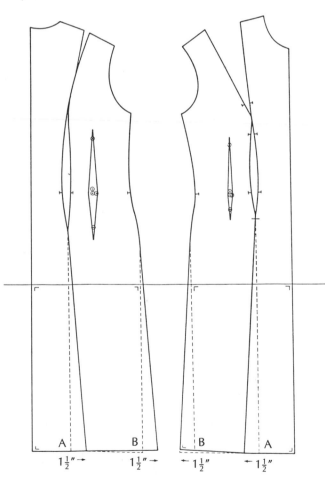

A   B   B   A

$1\frac{1}{2}''\rightarrow$ $1\frac{1}{2}''\rightarrow$ $\leftarrow 1\frac{1}{2}''$ $\leftarrow 1\frac{1}{2}''$

(Continued on next page)

FIGURE 3
- Cut and separate patterns along styleline.
- Draw grain, punch and circle darts.

Option:
- To add flare at princess styleline, measure out 1½ inches from points X. Draw line to hip. Blend hemline at flare.

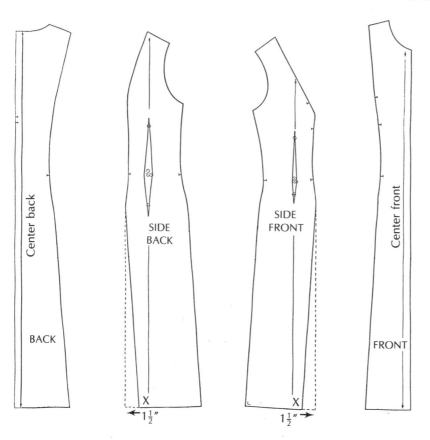

STYLIZED PRINCESS WITH CAP SLEEVES

Design Analysis

The princess-line effect has a one-piece front with tuck darts forming a box pleat. Cap sleeves and a cut-out neckline complete the design. The styleline takes up excess from second dart. Pattern is based on princess front torso combined with basic back torso. See opposite page for pattern development.

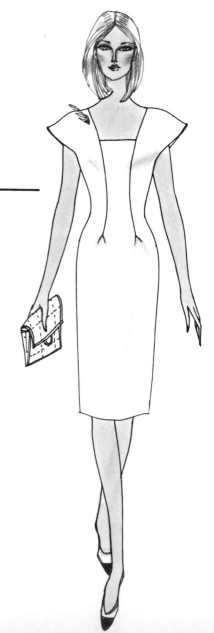

Pattern plot and development

FIGURE 1 *Front:*

- Trace the front princess panel. Remove pattern. Continue hip level across paper (broken lines).
- Extend line down from hip level at center front to desired length.
- Square across for hemline to equal hip measurement.
- Draw neckline 4 inches down from center front neck and square across pattern.
- Measure in $\frac{1}{2}$ inch and blend with bust (contour fit). (Broken line indicates original pattern to be discarded.)

Side panel preparation:

- Trace panel and cut from paper. Slash from mid-armhole to, not through, bust point.
- Place side panel on hip guideline. Space 2 inches from front panel.
- Spread slash line $\frac{3}{4}$ inch at armhole. Secure and trace pattern. Discard.
- Measure in $\frac{1}{4}$ inch on each side of waist at styleline and blend as shown (broken line is original pattern).
- Crossmark 3 inches below waist on both panels. Label A and B.
- Draw line from A to B and notch center for box-pleat control.
- Mark $\frac{1}{8}$ inch down from shoulder at styleline. Label C.
- Mark $\frac{1}{4}$ inch up from shoulder tip. Label D.
- Draw line 6 inches long from C through D.
- Mark 3 inches below armhole and out 1 inch.
- Connect with shoulder to form cap sleeve and blend line with waist. Connect hip with hemline.

FIGURE 2 *Back:*

- Trace back torso pattern.
- Plan neckline in from shoulder tip equal to side front panel. Mark 2 inches down from center back neck. Square a short line. Draw neckline.
- To develop shoulderline of sleeve cap and hemline, follow instructions given for front.

FIGURES 3 and 4 *To complete pattern:*

- Add 1-inch extension at center back, and regular seam allowances except for the following: Add $1\frac{1}{4}$ inches fold-back for self-facing on front and back sleeve and at front neck. (Facing is indicated by broken lines.)
- Add $1\frac{1}{2}$ inches for hem. Mark notch placement and punch and circle darts as shown.

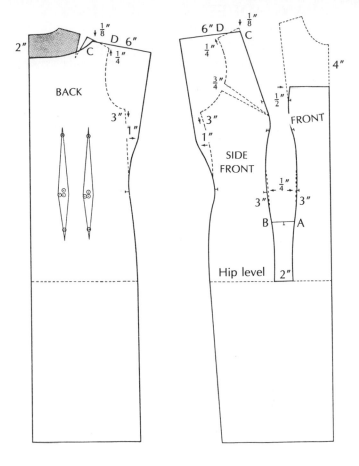

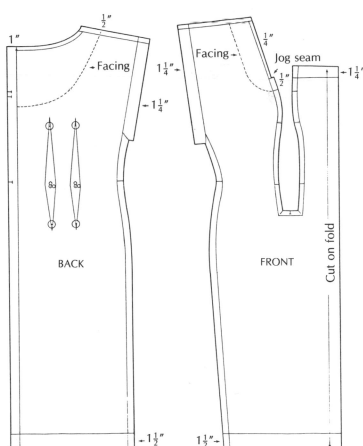

PANEL DRESS FOUNDATION

The panel-torso foundation has a semi-fit and is developed without a side seam. This foundation can be used as is (see Design 1) or as a base for all similar designs (see Design 2). Develop patterns for both designs for practice. Extend for length parallel with hip level.

Pattern plot and development

FIGURES 1 and 2

- Trace front and back torso. Mark waistline level.
- Mark 3 inches in from side seam at hip of front and back patterns and square up to armholes.
- Mark $\frac{1}{2}$ inch down from styleline at armhole and draw a blended curve to styleline. (Broken line indicates original lines and darts.)
- Reposition dart to stylelines. Use intake from one dart, plus one-half of the other. Divide equally on each side of styleline at front and back waist.
- Draw new dart legs as shown. Shape darts slightly outward above waist and slightly inward below waist for a better fit (shaded area).
- Draw slash line for side dart 1 inch below original location ending at dart point.
- Cut and separate pattern panels along styleline, discarding unneeded section (shaded area between dart legs).

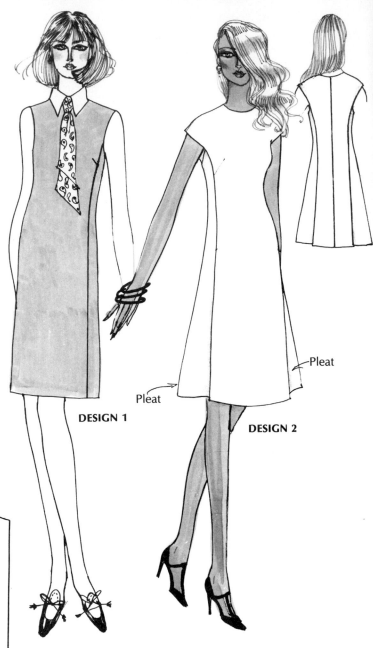

DESIGN 1

DESIGN 2

Pleat

Pleat

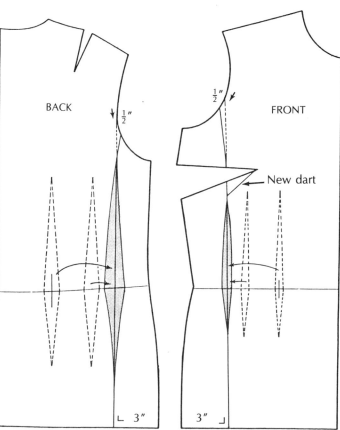

BACK

$\frac{1}{2}''$

$\frac{1}{2}''$

FRONT

New dart

3"

3"

FIGURES 3 and 4   *Front and back panels:*
- Cut slash line for new dart. Close dart. Tape.
- Add 1-inch extension at center back (for test fit).
- Draw grain and mark notch as shown.

FIGURE 5   *Joining side panel:*
- Close side dart of front panel. Tape.
- Draw a horizontal guideline on paper and square a vertical line in center.
- Place front and back side panels (indicated by shaded area) on squared guideline with hip level of front and back directly on horizontal guideline, and corners of armhole touching vertical guideline. If armhole of front and back are not at same level, blend the lower armhole so that both armholes meet.
- Label A, B, and C as shown. (*Note:* Position of panels may vary from illustration, but this will not affect instruction.)

FIGURE 6   *Shaping panels:*
- Measure space B–C. Using one-half of this measurement, measure in from each side of front and back panels at hip level. Mark and square up from marks approximately 3 inches. (If B and C meet, disregard instruction.)
- Mark $\frac{1}{4}$ inch in from back waist and $\frac{1}{2}$ inch from front waist. Blend to square lines (or hipline if B and C meet) and above to side seam.
- Cut pattern from paper, discarding unneeded section (indicated by broken lines).

FIGURE 7   *Finished panel*

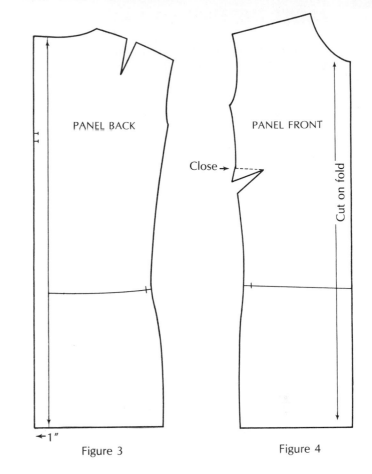

Figure 3   Figure 4

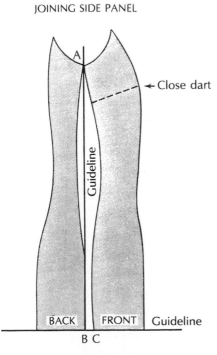

JOINING SIDE PANEL

Figure 5

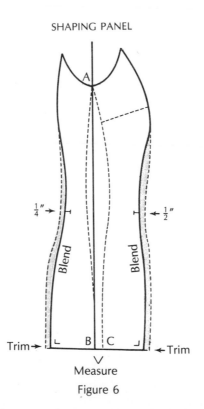

SHAPING PANEL

Figure 6

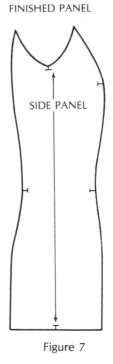

FINISHED PANEL

SIDE PANEL

Figure 7

EMPIRE FOUNDATION

The empire dress, like the empire bodice, has a styleline crossing under the bust and across the back with a single dart above the styleline and a pair of darts below the styleline to control the contour fit. By extending length it may be used as is (Design 1), or used as a base for design variations (Design 2).

The empire foundation is developed from the basic torso and should include all contour guidelines shown on the basic torso for reference. The measurements and instructions given below are standard. Use personal measurements where appropriate.

DESIGN 1   DESIGN 2

Pattern plot and development

FIGURE 1   *Front torso:*
- Trace front torso. With pushpin, transfer darts, bust point, and Guideline 5—contour guide marks. Remove pattern.
- With compass, draw bust circumference (example: 3-inch radius).
- Draw slash line from dart points of side and underbust dart to bust point.
- Crossmark 1 inch below bust point.

Empire styleline:
- Square line across pattern from center front, touching guidemarks under bust at circle. Label A at side (broken line).
- Mark B, $\frac{3}{4}$ inches down from A.
- Draw curved line from B to guidemarks under bust. Excess of second dart above styleline is left for ease.
- Label C at side waist.

Lower section:
- So that patterns true along empire styleline, measure out $\frac{3}{16}$ inch from each side of dart leg at styleline and connect to waist (shaded area).

Personal fit: Use measurement equal to one-fourth of total dart intake given for Guideline 5.

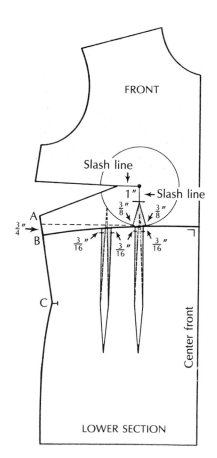

FIGURE 2 *Back torso:*
- Trace back torso. Include horizontal balance line (HBL) and back darts. Label side waist D.

Empire styleline:
- D to E equals C to B (on front).
- F to G = D to E, less $\frac{1}{2}$ inch. Square a short line.
- Draw curved styleline from E, blending with G.
- Develop one dart above styleline. Mark center for new dart between existing darts.
- Draw line from mark to the HBL, parallel with center back. Crossmark at level with dart points.
- Draw dart legs equal to dart intake on each side of line. Connect with dart point.

Lower section:
- Mark $\frac{1}{8}$ inch out from each dart leg at styleline (shaded area).
- Draw new dart legs, ending dart at waist as shown.

FIGURES 3 and 4
- Separate patterns along stylelines.

Front:
- Cut slash line from dart point to, not through, bust point.
- Close side dart. Tape. Retrace pattern and discard.
- Extend dart legs $\frac{1}{4}$ inch below bust and $\frac{1}{8}$ inch at center front (square a short line). Blend lines and shape dart legs as shown. (For gathering under bust and back, draw blending lines across darts—broken lines.)

Trueing:
- True upper and lower torso patterns along joining empire stylelines. If front does not true (excluding $\frac{1}{4}$-inch ease) adjust pattern by increasing or decreasing bust dart intake. Adjust the dart leg nearest to the side. If the back does not true, subtract from side seam of back upper torso. Blend to zero at armhole (broken line).

Contour guidelines:
After empire foundation pattern is developed, include all contour guidelines from basic torso for future reference. For designs, trace pattern. Extend pattern to desired length, parallel with hip level. Complete pattern for test fit (Figures 3 and 4).

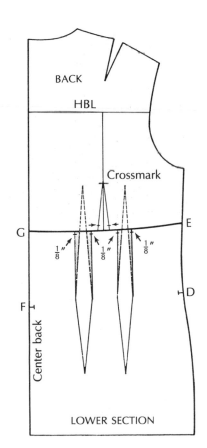

Figure 2

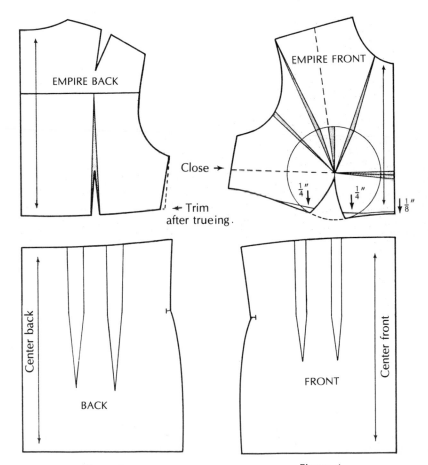

Figure 3

Figure 4

EMPIRE WITH SLINKY SKIRT

The empire slinky (named for its sinuous and graceful movement) is developed from the empire foundation. The front and back darts of the lower section are equalized to control the hemline sweep. By lowering the pivotal point, the skirt will cling around the hipline area. This type of garment molds the hipline best when cut on the bias. The lower the pivotal point, the greater is the cling of the garment. The basic empire is illustrated with the slinky to demonstrate their differences and similarities.

Other similar designs, some of which are illustrated at the end of this chapter, can be developed using the empire foundation along with the instructions for the slinky. (See Chapter 12, section on slinky skirt, for more information.)

Pattern plot and development

▪ The lower section of the empire torso is illustrated. The bodice of the upper torso remains the same for this foundation.

General information:

▪ One front and back dart replaces the two darts of the pattern. The dart's excess is equalized to control hemline sweep. Measure front and back dart intake at empire styleline (not at waist). Add front and back dart intakes together, then divide equally between one new front and back dart as illustrated. Example: Front darts = 1 inch. Back darts = 2 inches. Combined front and back darts = 3 inches. Divide in half (1½ inches). Front and back dart intake to equal 1½ inches each.

FIGURES 1 and 2 *New darts intake and locations:*

▪ Draw line between existing darts on front and back parallel with center front and center back.
▪ Mark one-half of dart intake on each side of line. (Example: Using computations above, the measurement equals ¾ inch.)

Note: For bias, crepe, knit, or chiffon, add an additional ¼ inch to each side of the dart. This section is smaller than the upper section along the styleline to offset bias stretch.

▪ Crossmark for dart point 5 inches down from waist (crossmark can be up to 12 inches below waist for variation; the lower the pivotal point, the greater the cling.)
▪ Draw dart legs by connecting with dart point. Label A and B as shown.
▪ Cut pattern from paper.

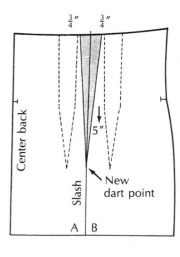

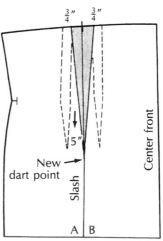

FIGURES 3 and 4

- Cut slash line from hem and waist to, not through, dart points.
- Close darts. Tape.
- Place on paper. Trace, marking hip level (broken line).
- Extend from hip level to desired length.
- Add to side seam one-half the distance of space A–B. Mark.

- Draw a line from mark to outermost part of hip.
- Blend hem and waistline at side.

For crepe, knit, or chiffon, add additional sweep at side seam (bias relaxes differently than firm wovens; example: 5 inches). Cut garment, do not stitch, and allow to hang overnight on form or hanger. Remark the side seam and hemline. Correct pattern.

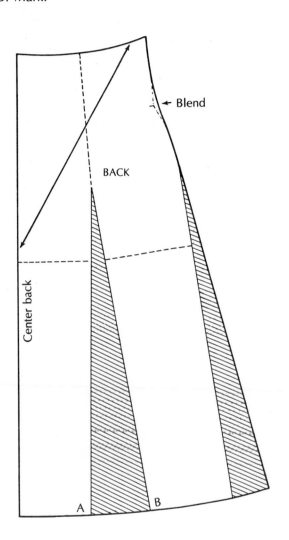

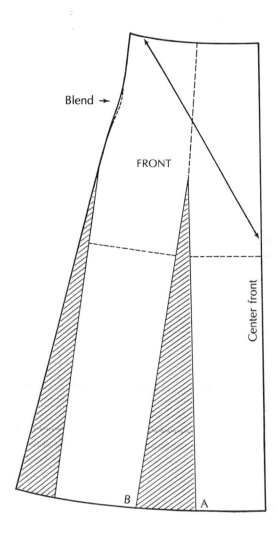

TENT FOUNDATION

The tent silhouette may be developed with exaggerated fullness at the hemline, or the amount of fullness at hem can be controlled by transferring the side dart to hemline and adding flare to side seam. The tent foundation may be used as is (Design 1), or used as a base for design variations (Designs 2 and 3).

DESIGN 1 **DESIGN 2** **DESIGN 3**

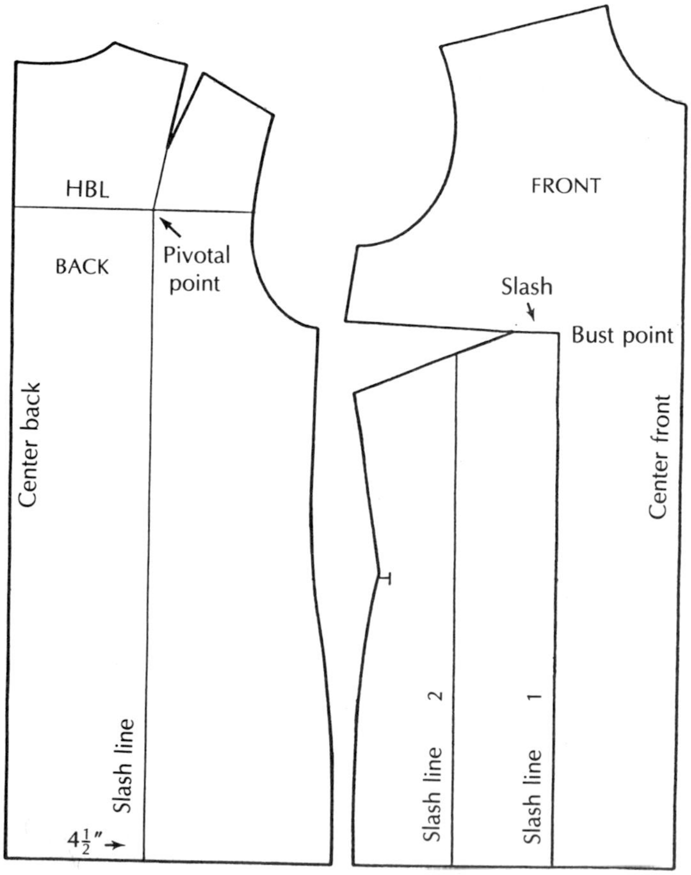

FIGURE 1

FIGURE 2

Pattern plot and development

FIGURE 1 *Back:*
- Trace back torso, include horizontal balance line (HBL),omit waist darts.
- Square slash line $4\frac{1}{2}$ inches in front center back, ending at horizontal balance line. Draw slash line from dart point of shoulder dart as shown.
- Cut patterns from paper.

FIGURE 2 *Front:*
- Trace front torso. Omit waist darts.
- Draw slash line from dart point to bust point. Draw first slash line from bust point to hip level, parallel with center front. Draw second slash line in between first slash line and side seam as shown.

FIGURE 3 *Back:*
- Cut slash lines to, not through, point on HBL.
- Close shoulder dart. Tape. Place pattern on paper and trace.
- Label A, B, and C as shown.
- Mark ½ inch *out* from side waist. Label E.
- C–D equals one-half of A–B. Mark.
- Draw line from E to D, continuing line to desired length.
- To complete hem, square down from hip at center back and blend hemline parallel with hip.

FIGURE 4 *Front:*
- Cut slash lines from hip level to bust point, cutting through bust point to, not through, dart point of side dart.
- Cut second slash line to, not through, dart leg.
- Place pattern on paper. Close side dart, spreading sections equally. (Dart legs may not meet at side.)
- Tape. Trace outline of pattern. Discard.
- Blend side seam.
- Extend length from hip level equal to back (even broken lines—uneven broken line discussed later). (Keep hem parallel with hip level.)
- Mark ½ inch in at side waist. Connect with hem and blend with side as indicated by bold line.

Equalizing hemline sweep:
- To equalize hem, cut back pattern and place on top of front, matching side seam from armhole to waist. Divide sweep overhang in half, adding one-half the difference to the back and subtracting one-half from the front. (Uneven broken line is adjusted side seam.) Blend side seam.

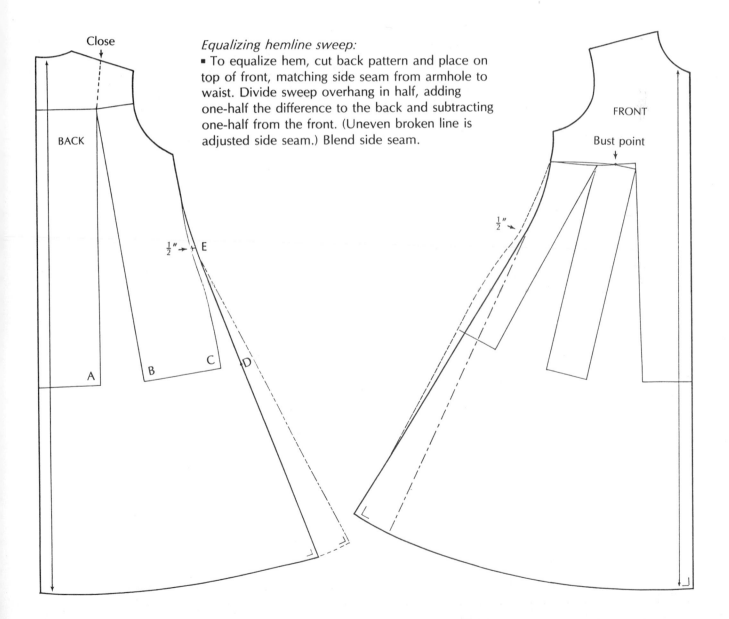

OVERSIZED DRESS

Design Analysis

Oversized garments are developed from the torso by adding to the width of the pattern as illustrated by pattern development for Design 1. This results in the side dart excess being held automatically in the armhole area. (Color blocking is not included.) Design 2 is a practice problem.

Pattern plot and development

FIGURES 1 and 2

- Trace front and back torso, transferring back shoulder dart to mid-armhole. (Patterns are indicated by broken line within the frame of the design patterns.)
- (Use measurements given or increase to vary this silhouette.)
- Extend length at center front and center back as desired.

Hemline:

- Square across hem from center front and back to equal 1 inch more than front and back hip measurements.
- Plan neckline as shown.
- Draw necklines.

DESIGN 1   DESIGN 2

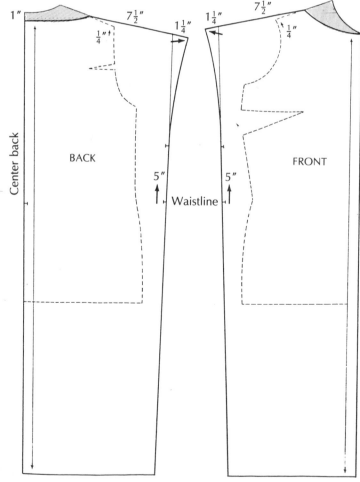

Shoulderline:

- Mark $\frac{1}{4}$ inch up from front and back shoulder tips.
- If shoulder pads are used, raise the shoulder equal to width of shoulder pads plus $\frac{1}{4}$ inch.
- Extend line from mid-shoulder, touching shoulder marks, to desired length of new shoulderline (example: $7\frac{1}{2}$ inches).
- Draw new side seam from hem to new shoulder length.
- Mark notches 5 inches up from side waist to establish the beginning of the armhole.
- Extend shoulderline another $1\frac{1}{4}$ inches and draw inward curve to notch.
- Draw grain and complete pattern for test fit.
- Adjust shape of cap over shoulder at time of fitting.

JUMPER

Design Analysis

Design 1 has deeply cut-out armholes and a scoop neck, with buttons down the center front. A jumper is a garment generally worn over another garment, and therefore, not fitted close to the figure. Design 2 is a practice problem.

DESIGN 1   DESIGN 2

Pattern plot and development

FIGURES 1 and 2

• Trace front and back torso foundation, transferring shoulder dart to mid-armhole. With a push pin transfer first dart of front and back patterns, omitting the second dart.

• Extend to length desired. Add flare. Blend hemline.

• Plan armhole and neckline as shown.

• Crossmark 4 inches below front and back armholes at sides (depth of new armhole).

• Styleline on front passes through an open dart. To control shape of the styleline, A–C must equal A–B length. Continue the styleline from C to crossmark at side (or fold dart and draw styleline).

• Draw a 1-inch extension at center front, plus 2 inches for fold-back. (When pattern is cut, fold paper along extension and trace neckline shape onto fold-back. Completed shape is shown.)

• Draw grain. Mark button and buttonholes. (See Chapter 14 for closure information.) Mark punch and circles for dart intake.

• Plan facing on pattern approximately $1\frac{1}{2}$ inches around deep armhole (see broken line).

• Front facing ends 1 inch from center front. It is stitched to fold-back (eliminates bulk).

• Trace and cut facing.

FIGURES 3 and 4   Facing:

• Connect front facing at dart legs. Tape.
• Trim $\frac{1}{8}$ inch from each side of facing to zero at center front and center back. (Broken line indicates original facing.)

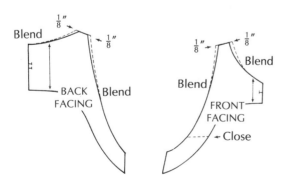

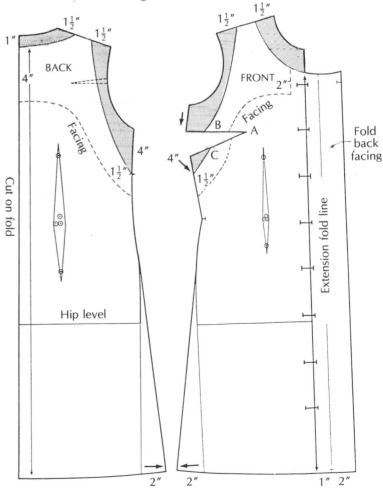

SPECIAL PATTERNMAKING PROBLEMS

The following examples illustrate the methods used for plotting and pattern development for designs that feature creative detailing that cross through darted areas of the pattern. Design 1 shows gathers, and Design 2 shows stylelines in the darted areas. Designs 3 and 4 (page 466) feature stylelines that require a one-piece front. The examples do not represent completed patterns, but should be used as a guide for plotting patterns with similar features. To complete the designs, and for practice, plot the back patterns with appropriate stylelines for each of the designs.

GATHERS CROSSING DART AREAS

DESIGN 1

FIGURE 1 *Plot the working pattern as follows:*
- Remove $\frac{1}{2}$ inch from the center front to compensate for bias stretch. (If garment is too loose at time of fitting, remove more from the gathered area.)
- Eliminate the dart's excess at the center front by drawing the width and length of both darts as shown (shaded area).
- For under-bust contouring, remove an additional $\frac{3}{4}$ inch at the center front (at level with the bust circumference).
- When pattern is cut from paper, the unneeded section is trimmed from the pattern (shaded areas).

FIGURES 2 and 3 *Completed pattern:*
- The pattern is slashed, spread, retraced, and blended.

STYLELINES CROSSING DART AREAS

FIGURE 1 *Plot the working pattern as follows:*
- Draw stylelines across the open darts (use placements indicated by the design).
- Number each section for placement.
- For bust contouring, increase dart intake under bust.

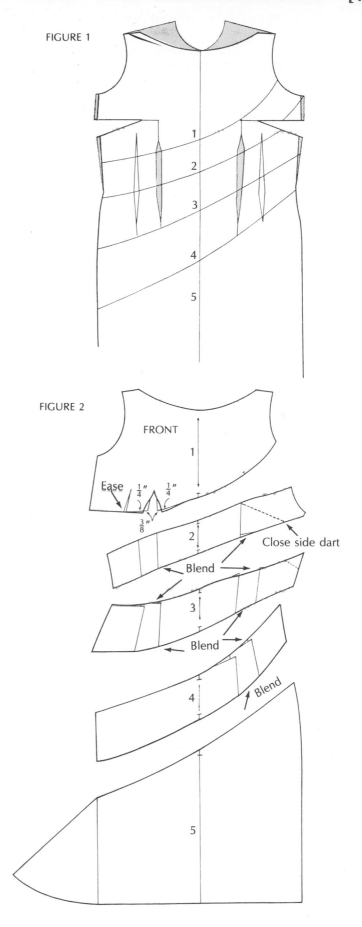

FIGURE 1

1
2
3
4
5

FIGURE 2

FRONT

1

Ease   ¼"   ¼"

⅜"

2

Close side dart

Blend

3

Blend

4

Blend

5

FIGURE 2 *Completed pattern:*
- Separate patterns along the stylelines.
- Close all darts.

   Note: Stylelines that cross open darts at an angle will not true when darts are closed. This is adjusted when the panels are traced and blended.

STYLIZED ONE-PIECE FRONT

Designs 3 and 4 illustrate garments created as one-piece fronts without side darts. To plot working patterns for such designs, the styleline must end at bust point or the dart point of the side dart. After the styleline is cut and the side dart is closed, the pattern opens, allowing space between the stylelines to complete the details of the design (such as flare—Design 3, and pleats—Design 4). This would not be possible if the side dart remained as a dart. Develop the pattern for Design 4 for practice. Design other variations using this concept.

FIGURE 1 *Plot the working pattern as follows:*
- Draw styleline to bust point.
- Draw all other stylelines. (Relocate waist darts if indicated by the design.)

DESIGN 3   DESIGN 4

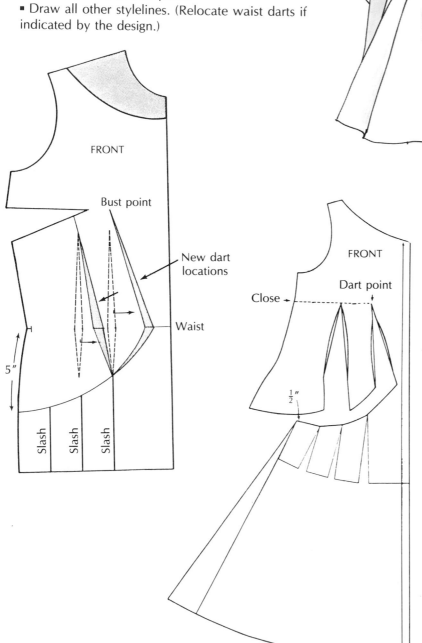

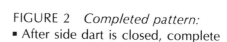

FIGURE 2 *Completed pattern:*
- After side dart is closed, complete the remaining pattern.

  Note: Allow space for seam allowances where needed.

CAFTAN

A caftan (also known as *kaftan*) is a long, wide-sleeved robe, usually fastened by a belt or sash, worn in Eastern Mediterranean countries. The following two caftans are stylized versions of this great robe and are based on the torso foundation pattern.

Design Analysis

Design 1 features a caftan that is gathered below the shoulder tips, tied at the neck, or snapped for closure. The sleeve hem is tacked to hold the front and back together. (When the arm is relaxed, a flare appears under the arm.) Design has a slit at side seam. Design 2 is a practice problem based on the same concepts as Design 1. Note that cowl under the arm is on the fold.

Pattern plot and development

FIGURE 1

- Front and back are drafted together.
- Fold paper in half lengthwise.
- Place back torso on paper edge with shoulder at neck touching fold of paper. Trace neck and remove pattern. Label A.
- Place shoulder at neck of front pattern at point A, keeping center front parallel with paper edge. Trace pattern and remove. Extend curve of neckline to paper edge. (Use as the extension for closure.)

DESIGN 1   DESIGN 2

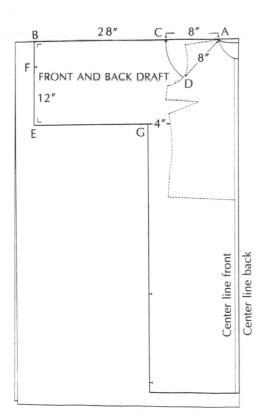

- Extend length at centerline. Include $1\frac{1}{2}$ inches for hem, and square line across paper (use center neck to floor length).
- A–B = shoulder and sleeve length plus 1-inch fold-back for facing (example: 28 inches).
- A–C = 8 inches.
- A–D = 8 inches (to touch curve of armhole).
- Draw curved line from C to D (gathers control line).
- B–E = 12 inches, squared from B.
- B–F = One-half of wrist measurement, plus $\frac{1}{4}$ inch. Mark. (Attach point when stitched.)
- E–G ends 4 inches from side, squared from E.
- Square down from G to hem.
- Cut from paper, except for neckline.
- Trace curve of back neckline to paper underneath.
- Unfold and trim to front and back neck (not illustrated).
- Notch for side slit as desired.

Stitching guide: Thread line curve for guide. Place on model, shirr to a comfortable point over arm area. Top stitch on twill tape placed on underside of curve. Curved line is gathered. Garment may be finished with a self- or contrast binding or facing made for neckline and center front.

DRESS DESIGN VARIATIONS

The following dress designs are for practice and design inspiration. Develop patterns for these designs or create your own using information from previous lessons. The patterns are correct if they result in garments that are exact representations of the designs.

DARTLESS KNIT FOUNDATION 470
Dartless stretchy knit—draft 1 470
Dartless firm knit—draft 2 472
BASIC SHIRT WITH YOKE 473
Shirt facing and band variations 474
BASIC SHIRT WITHOUT YOKE 476
Basic shirt—oversized 478
LARGE SHIRT 479
PEASANT BLOUSE 482
Blouse design variations 484

18

TOPS

DARTLESS KNIT FOUNDATION

Two dartless knit drafts are given, one for tops cut in two-way stretch and tubular knits, and the other for tops and dresses cut in firm knits (example: double knits). Both are based on the torso foundation pattern.

Design patterns are not illustrated with these foundations. Use previous information to develop patterns for the designs shown below (or design others) using one of the knit foundation patterns. *Note:* Knit garments stitched on an overlock machine require $\frac{3}{8}$-inch seam allowances; otherwise use $\frac{1}{2}$ inch. There are a number of textbooks devoted to handling knits. Read them for instruction on stitching and ribbing attachment. To use these foundations as a base for dresses, extend length to patterns.

DARTLESS STRETCHY KNIT—DRAFT 1

The front and back pattern pieces are drafted together, with the only difference being in the shape of the front and back necklines. They are separated after the draft is complete.

Pattern development

FIGURE 1
- Trace back torso as indicated by bold lines. Omit sections indicated by broken lines.
- Move pattern upward on centerline $\frac{1}{2}$ inch and draw approximately 3 inches of armhole as shown. Remove pattern.
- Label shoulder at neck A, shoulder tip B. For closer fit, measure in $\frac{1}{2}$ inch at waist from side seam and draw new side seam.

FIGURE 2
- Place front torso on top of back draft, matching *hip* and *centerlines.*
- Trace corner of center front neck, shoulder at neck, shoulder tip, and bust point. Omit sections indicated by broken lines.
- Remove pattern, draw bust circumference for reference when developing stylelines and necklines. Label shoulder/neck C and shoulder tip D. (Line up of patterns may appear different from illustration.)

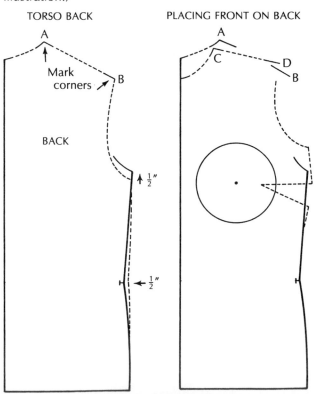

TORSO BACK   PLACING FRONT ON BACK

FIGURE 3

- Draw guideline through A and C. Mark midpoint between A and C. Label E.
- Locate midpoint between D and B. Label F.
- Draw a straight line from E to or through F equal to front shoulder length. From E, draw a blending curve to center back neck and center front neck (establishing new neckline).
- With French curve, draw armhole, blending curve with lower armhole as shown.

Personal fit: Narrow shoulders and large bust pose a problem when blending the armhole. Extend shoulder $\frac{1}{4}$ inch to $\frac{1}{2}$ inch and blend armhole.

- Cut pattern from paper.

Separating front and back patterns

FIGURE 4

- Trace a copy of this pattern and label *Knit back*.
- Measure armhole and record.

FIGURE 5

Trim front neck from original pattern. Label *Knit front*.

- Trim $\frac{1}{8}$ inch from curve of armhole and blend as shown.
- Cut patterns from paper.

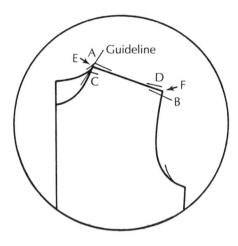

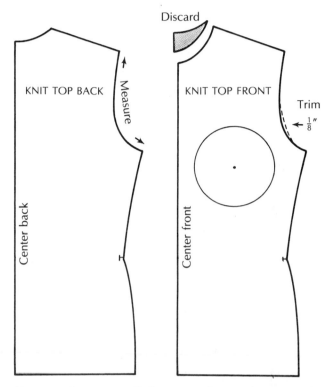

(*Note:* When using rib knit, straighten side seam of front and back patterns to avoid runs in the knit.)

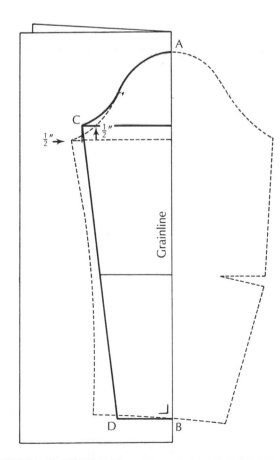

FIGURE 6   *Knit sleeve:*

- Fold paper. Place sleeve front on paper with center grain on fold line and trace.
- Mark biceps, elbow, and cap notch. Remove. Label grainline A–B as shown. (Broken line indicates original sleeve.)
- Measure in $\frac{1}{2}$ inch on biceps line. Mark. Square up $\frac{1}{2}$ inch from mark and label C. Square new biceps line from fold to point C. Erase original line.
- Blend new armhole curve with cap.
- Square a line from B equal to one-half of wrist (plus $\frac{1}{4}$ inch) measurement. Label D.
- Draw a slightly inward curved line from D to C.

FIGURES 7 and 8   *Sleeve adjustment:*
▪ Sleeve cap should measure up to $\frac{1}{4}$ inch more than armhole. Measure sleeve cap and compare with armhole measurement.
▪ If cap measurement is less than armhole, extend biceps and blend with cap. Draw line from biceps to elbow.
▪ If cap measurement is more than needed, measure in from biceps and blend new cap. Draw line to elbow or wrist level.
▪ Mark for center cap notch.

FIGURE 9
▪ Cut sleeve from paper. Unfold.
▪ Complete sleeve. Label *Knit sleeve.* The sleeve is shaped equally on both sides.
▪ Add seams to all patterns ($\frac{1}{2}$ inch, or $\frac{3}{8}$ inch for overlock stitch).

ADDING MEASUREMENT

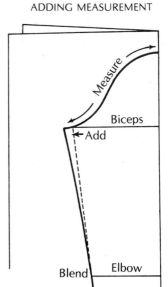

SUBTRACTING MEASUREMENT

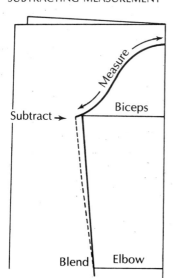

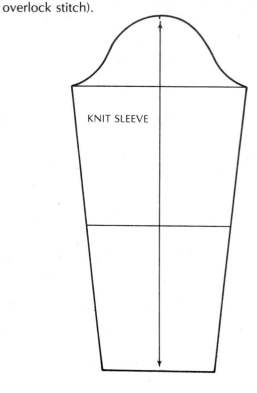

KNIT SLEEVE

DARTLESS FIRM KNIT—DRAFT 2

FIGURES 1 and 2
▪ Trace torso foundation pattern, transferring shoulder dart (back), and side dart (front) to armhole as shown. *Realign side seam and shoulders as follows:*
▪ Add $\frac{1}{2}$ inch to side seam of back at armhole and draw new side seam to waist (broken line is original side seam).
▪ Add $\frac{1}{4}$ inch to back shoulder and draw new shoulderline.
▪ Subtract $\frac{1}{2}$ inch from front side seam at armhole and draw new side seam to waist (broken line is original pattern).
▪ Subtract $\frac{1}{4}$ inch from shoulder and draw new shoulderline (trim shaded area).
▪ Cut patterns from paper. Label as shown.
Note: Use basic sleeve for this armhole. Sleeve should measure at least $\frac{1}{2}$ inch more than total armhole. If not, adjust sleeve using instructions given above.

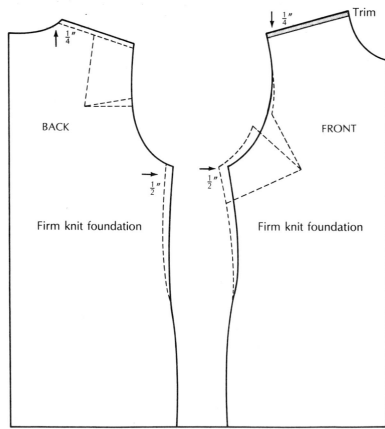

BASIC SHIRT WITH YOKE

The shirt foundation #1 is developed from the torso foundation. One-half inch of the side dart excess is transferred to the armhole, with the remaining dart's excess being transferred to mid-shoulder for gathering into a yoke. (See shirt sleeve and cuff—Chapter 13; and basic collar—Chapter 11.) The shirt dress is based on this foundation. Extend pattern to length desired.

Pattern plot and development

FIGURE 1 *Back:*
- Trace back torso, transferring shoulder dart to mid-armhole and blend. Mark waist notches.
- Square a line across pattern 4 inches down from center back neck to form yokeline.
- To bring the back shoulderline forward for a yoke effect on front garment, align shoulder of front torso pattern with back shoulder line on draft (broken line). Trace 1 inch of front neckline (A) and armhole (B). Remove pattern and connect A to B.
- Mark notches at neck and shoulder tip of original shoulder (broken line) and 1 inch in from each end of forward yoke as shown.
- Add ½ inch along side seam for looser fit.
- Draw curved hemline of shirt using measurements given. (Shaded area to be discarded.)

FIGURE 2
- Cut and separate pattern along back yokeline.

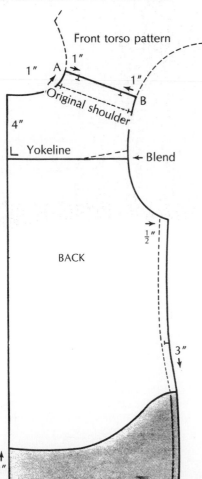

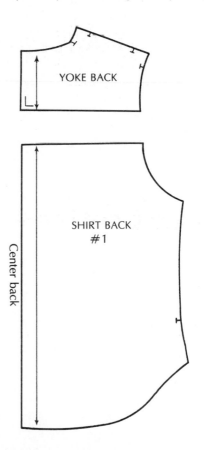

FIGURE 3 *Front:*
• Trace front torso, transferring $\frac{1}{2}$ inch of side dart to mid-armhole and remaining excess to mid-shoulder as shown (indicated by broken lines).
• Blend armhole and across shoulder.
• Add $\frac{1}{2}$ inch along side seam for looser fit.
• Draw curved hemline using measurements given. (Shaded area to be discarded.)
• Notch waistline.
• To eliminate that part of front shoulder traced onto back yoke, draw a parallel line 1 inch down from shoulderline (shaded area to be discarded). Notch 1 inch from each end to control gathers.
• Add $\frac{3}{4}$-inch extension to center front (varies).
• Mark for button and buttonholes (see Chapter 14). This completes the basic shirt foundation. (Continue for instruction on facing variations.)

• Five variations for facings are given with two versions (Types 1 and 2) illustrated in Figure 4. Choose the one most appropriate for the design being developed. Note that Types 4 and 5 include instruction for band with facing. Facing widths can vary from those given.

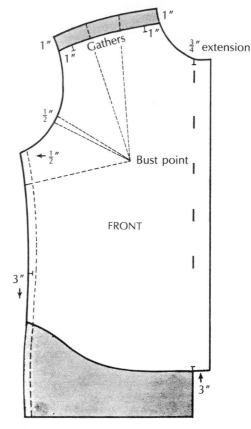

FIGURE 3

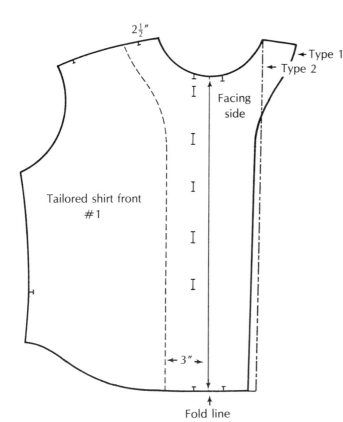

FIGURE 4

SHIRT FACING AND BAND VARIATIONS

Type 1: Shaped fold-back facing

FIGURE 4
• Mark facing on pattern, $2\frac{1}{2}$ inches wide at shoulder and 3 inches in from extension line. Follow neckline curve and continue parallel with center front (broken line).
• Fold pattern on extension line. With tracing wheel trace facing outline.
• Notch center front top and bottom.
• Unfold and pencil in neckline and shoulderline (bold line).

Type 2: Straight fold-back facing

FIGURE 4
• Fold pattern on extension line. With tracing wheel trace neckline. Notch center front, top and bottom. Unfold and pencil in.
• Width of facing is parallel with extension line so that fold-back ends at corner of shoulder neck (uneven broken lines). (This type edge is often placed on the selvage of the goods.)

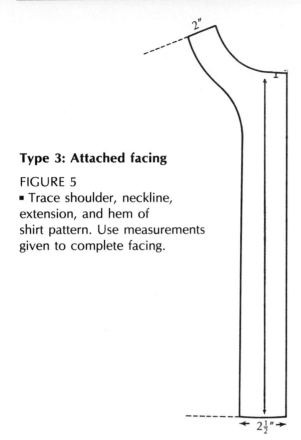

Type 3: Attached facing

FIGURE 5
- Trace shoulder, neckline, extension, and hem of shirt pattern. Use measurements given to complete facing.

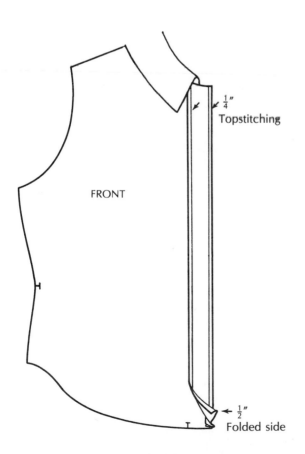

Type 4: Self-faced band

FIGURE 6 *Trace band:*
- Band is same width on each side of center front notch (example: extension is $\frac{3}{4}$ inches wide.)
- Develop band by tracing $1\frac{1}{2}$ inches of neck and hem of shirt pattern (broken line is untraced pattern).
- Mark notches at center front, top and bottom.
- Remove pattern.
- Draw line to connect top and bottom to complete band.

FIGURE 7 *Completed band:*
- Draw grain and mark buttonholes.
- Add $\frac{1}{4}$-inch seams with $\frac{1}{2}$ inch on side folded under as shown.

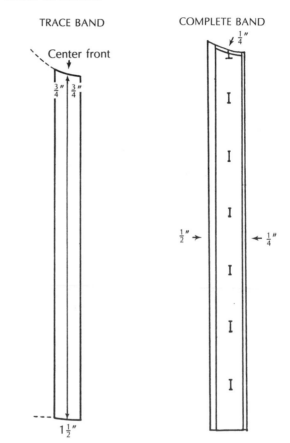

TRACE BAND   COMPLETE BAND

FIGURE 8 *Stitching guide:*
- To stitch band to shirt, place underside of band to the underside of the garment and fold back $\frac{1}{2}$ inch seam allowance. Stitch band up the extension, ending at the center front notch at neck. Turn banding to right side of shirt and top stitch $\frac{1}{4}$ inch in from fold line and at extension side as shown.
- Upper collar is stitched to neckline. Under collar is folded over raw seam and stitched in the ditch (not illustrated).

Type 5: Set-in band with attached facing

FIGURE 9   *Facing:*
▪ Trace pattern for facing using instructions given in Figure 5 (broken lines), or reduce width to equal width of set-in band (bold lines).

FIGURES 10 and 11   *Band and garment:*
▪ Measure in from center front equal to width of extension.
▪ Draw line parallel with extension line.
▪ Separate pattern along this line.
▪ Trace patterns and add seams.

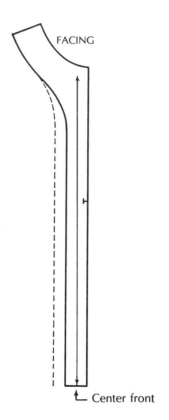

FACING

Center front

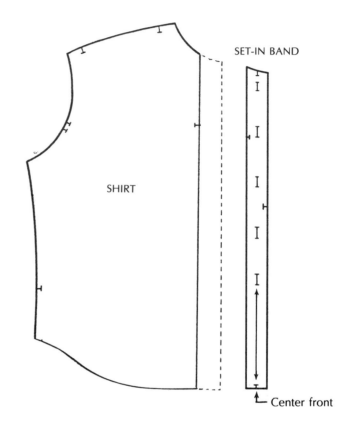

SHIRT

SET-IN BAND

Center front

BASIC SHIRT WITHOUT YOKE

Shirt foundation 2 fits more loosely around the armhole than does foundation 1 in that all of the excess from the side dart is transferred to mid-armhole. The enlarged front and back armholes vary in measurement and should be equalized to balance the sleeve. This foundation is used for shirt designs that fit more casually than those based on foundation 1. Design 1 is illustrated and Design 2 is given as a practice problem. To use this foundation for a dress, extend pattern to desired length.

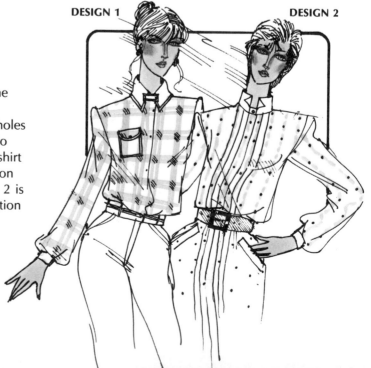

DESIGN 1   DESIGN 2

Pattern plot and development

FIGURES 1 and 2
- Trace front and back torso patterns, transferring shoulder and side dart excess to mid-armhole as shown (indicated by broken lines).

Equalize front and back armholes:
- Measure enlarged front and back armholes. Subtract and record difference _____. (Example: front armhole = 10 inches, back armhole = 9 inches. Difference 1 inch.)
- *Front armhole:* Measure down from shoulder tip one-half of difference. Mark and draw a line to neck parallel with shoulder (example: ½ inch).
- *Back armhole:* Measure up one-half the difference (example: ½ inch). Mark and draw a line to neck parallel with shoulder.
- Extend front and back shoulderlines ½ inch from shoulder tips. (Note that back is extended ¼ inch at mid-armhole.) Blend armholes as shown.
- Add ½ inch to front and back side seams and blend with armhole and hipline.

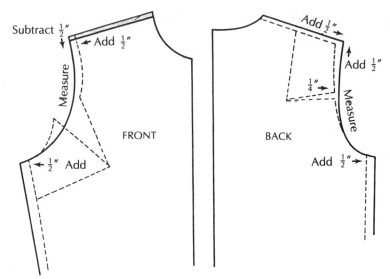

FIGURES 3 and 4
- Add ¾ inch extension to center front. Square in at neck and hemline.
- Mark for buttons and buttonholes (see Chapter 14).

Facings:
- Complete pattern using facings (or banding and facings) given on pages 474–476.
- Draw curved hemline using measurements given.
- Cut patterns from paper and discard unneeded section (shaded areas).

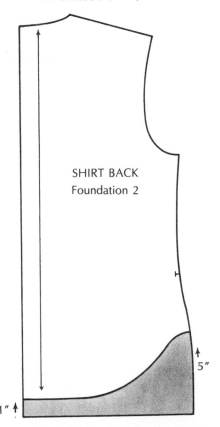

(Continued on next page)

FIGURE 5 *Sleeve:*
▪ Measure down $\frac{1}{2}$ inch at cap and blend to front and back notches (shaded area) of sleeve. This adjustment compensates for shoulder extension.
▪ True sleeve to armhole. If sleeve does not measure at least $\frac{1}{2}$ inch more than front and back armhole, add equally to both sides at biceps line and blend to wrist. (Broken line indicates adjusted sleeve.) If deeper armhole and/or lift is desired, refer to Chapter 13 for instructions.

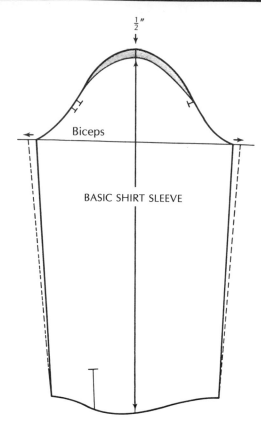

BASIC SHIRT—OVERSIZED

FIGURES 1 and 2 *Without shoulder pads:*
▪ Slash through front and back shirt patterns and spread for oversize (example: $\frac{1}{2}$ or more inches—lined areas).

FIGURE 3 *Sleeve modification:*
▪ Trim length of sleeve at hem.
▪ Redraw slit to equal length.

FIGURES 4, 5, and 6 *With shoulder pads:*
▪ For shoulder pads, add to height of shoulder and to sleeve cap (indicated by lined areas).

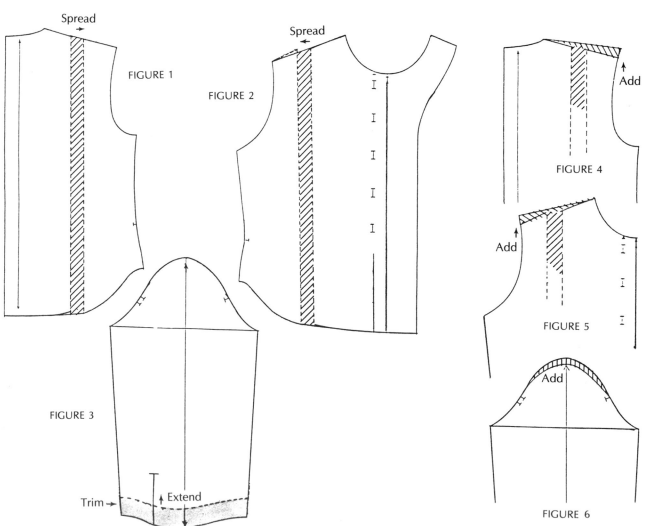

LARGE SHIRT

Design Analysis

The oversized shirt, influenced by fashion and mens wear, can be worn with or without shoulder pads depending on the trends of fashion. The sleeve is attached far beyond the natural shoulder of the figure and hangs loosely around the body. Featured are large patch pockets, traditional banding and yoke. To develop collar with band, see Chapter 11 as a guide. Use this as a foundation pattern for design variations. To use as a base for a shirt dress, extend pattern to length desired. The measurements given are for all sizes.

Pattern plot and development

FIGURE 1 *Equalizing the neckline:*
- The front and back will be developed together and then separated.
- Trace back torso indicated by bold line, omitting armhole and shoulder (even broken-lined area).
- Draw a vertical guideline at corner of shoulder at neck, parallel with center back.
- Place front torso on top of back draft, matching hip level and corner of shoulder at neck, touching guideline. (Center front must be parallel with center back.)
- Trace center front and neckline to corner of shoulder, omitting part of front pattern indicated by uneven broken lines.
- Remove pattern.
- Mark center between front and back neck on guideline. Label A and draw a blending line to front and back neck to form new neckline (bold line).

Note: For a wide and looser neck, trim $\frac{1}{8}$ inch around front and back neckline.

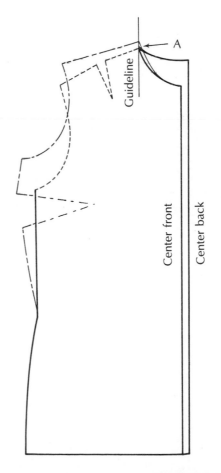

(Continued on next page)

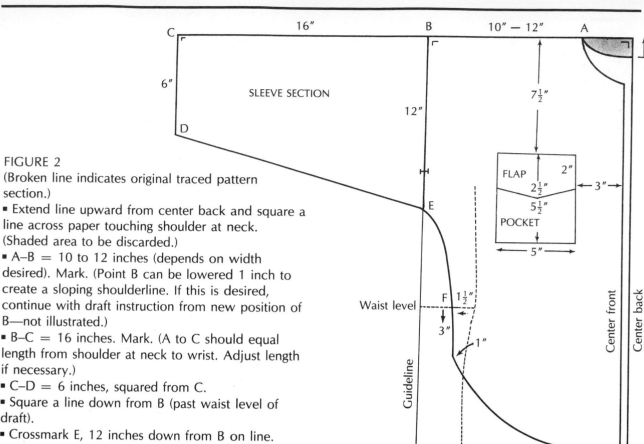

FIGURE 2

(Broken line indicates original traced pattern section.)

- Extend line upward from center back and square a line across paper touching shoulder at neck. (Shaded area to be discarded.)
- A–B = 10 to 12 inches (depends on width desired). Mark. (Point B can be lowered 1 inch to create a sloping shoulderline. If this is desired, continue with draft instruction from new position of B—not illustrated.)
- B–C = 16 inches. Mark. (A to C should equal length from shoulder at neck to wrist. Adjust length if necessary.)
- C–D = 6 inches, squared from C.
- Square a line down from B (past waist level of draft).
- Crossmark E, 12 inches down from B on line. Connect E with D.
- Mark notches on B–E line to indicate front sleeve.
- Mark F, $1\frac{1}{2}$ inches out from side waist.
- From E, draw curve line to point F. Continue line 3 inches below waist, ending 1 inch out from hip. Crossmark. Draw curved hemline as shown.
- Draw square pocket and flap on pattern, using measurements given.
- Cut pattern from paper using center back and back neckline. Discard unneeded section (shaded area).
- Cut and separate sleeve section along B–E line.
- Trace pattern for back copy and trim neckline to center front of original pattern for front copy.

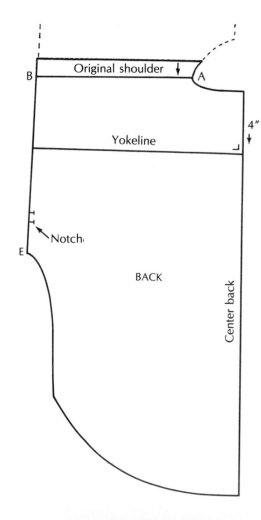

FIGURE 3 *Back:*

- Square a line across pattern 4 inches down from center back neck for yokeline.
- To create yoke effect on front shirt, place front shoulder A–B to back shoulderline. Trace 1 inch of shoulder and neckline. Remove pattern and connect lines.
- Mark second notch $\frac{1}{2}$ inch below first notch to indicate back.

FIGURE 4 *Yoke section:*

▪ Cut yoke section from back pattern. (Lower back not illustrated.)

▪ Notch at each end of original shoulderline and center of yokeline.

▪ Draw grain.

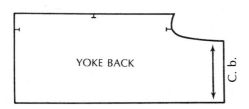

YOKE BACK

C. b.

FIGURE 5 *Front:*

▪ Trace front (or use pattern and mend for extension).

▪ Draw a parallel line 1 inch down from shoulder. Cut this section from pattern. Discard broken-line section.

▪ Mark notch at center of shoulderline.

▪ Punch and circle for pocket and flap placement, $\frac{1}{2}$ inch in from each corner.

▪ Draw a parallel line $\frac{3}{4}$ inch out from center front for extension. Square a line in at neck and hem.

FIGURE 6

▪ For self-faced band, see Figures 6 and 7 (page 445).

FIGURE 7 *Pocket:*

▪ Slip paper underneath pattern and trace a separate pattern for pocket and flap.

▪ Add 1-inch fold-back to pocket. (Flap is self-faced.)

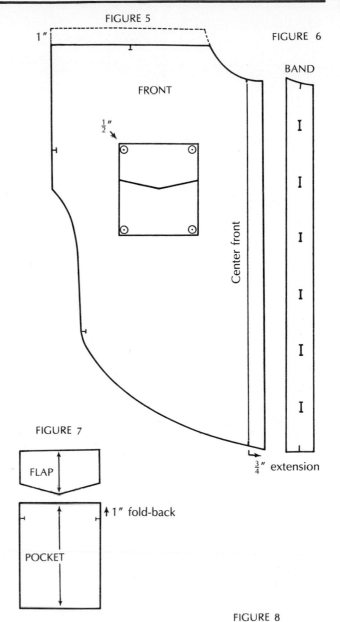

FIGURE 5

FIGURE 6

BAND

FRONT

$\frac{1}{2}''$

Center front

$\frac{3}{4}''$ extension

1"

FIGURE 7

FLAP

POCKET

1" fold-back

FIGURE 8 *Sleeve:*

▪ Place B–C line of the front and back sleeves together (broken line). Tape. Retrace and discard.

▪ Pleats: Mark as shown. (Lined area indicates pleat intake.)

▪ Notch is placed $2\frac{1}{2}$ inches up from wrist at underseam for entry opening.

▪ Mark center and back notches to match back shirt.

FIGURE 9 *Cuff:*

▪ Cut cuff 4 inches × 10 inches, on fold.

▪ Mark for buttons and buttonholes. (See Chapter 13.)

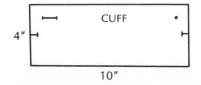

CUFF

4"

10"

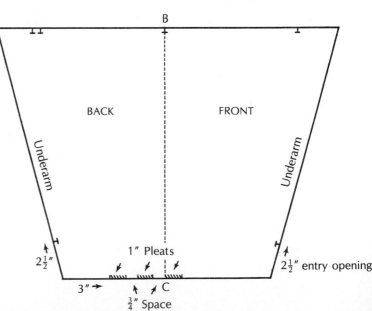

FIGURE 8

B

BACK

FRONT

Underarm

Underarm

$2\frac{1}{2}''$

1" Pleats

$2\frac{1}{2}''$ entry opening

3"

C

$\frac{3}{4}''$ Space

PEASANT BLOUSE

Design Analysis

The peasant blouse is a loose-fitting garment, which makes it possible to develop the front and back together. For designs in which the front neckline differs from the back, develop the front and back separately. Two variations are illustrated. Design 1 is illustrated, and Design 2 is included as a practice problem. To develop as a dress, extend pattern to desired length.

Pattern plot and development

FIGURE 1 *Front:*
- Trace front torso.
- Plan neckline depth in between neck and bust level.
- Mark point A, 1½ inches in from shoulder tip. Draw curved neckline.
- Mark B, ¼ inch above shoulder tip. Draw a line from A through B, extending line to sleeve length desired. Label C. (Example: B–C = 10 inches.)
- Mark D, 1 inch below armhole at side.
- Draw styleline, separating sleeve from blouse from mid-neck through D and beyond.
- Mark notch 1½ inches down from D. Label E.
- Mark F, 1 inch from E on guideline.
- Draw curve of sleeve hemline from C to F.
- Notch styleline as shown.
- Draw slash line from bust point to new neckline and from side dart to bust point as shown.
- Cut pattern from paper. Discard unneeded section (shaded area of neck).
- Cut and separate sleeve from bodice.

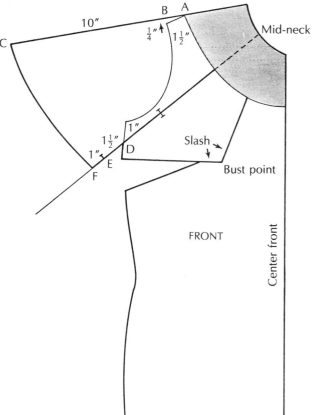

FIGURE 2 *Bodice section:*
- Cut slash line from neck and dart point to, not through, bust point.
- Close side dart. Tape.
- Draw slash lines from neck to hem as shown.
- Extend line from D, $1\frac{1}{2}$ inches. Label E.
- Square up from hem, touching E. (Broken line indicates original pattern.)

FIGURE 3
- Cut bodice from paper.
- Cut through slash lines on pattern.
- Fold paper and square a guideline on paper.
- Place patterns on paper with hemline on guideline and center front on fold.
- Spread as shown (or as desired). Secure.
- Trace outline of pattern and discard.
- Blend neckline area as shown.

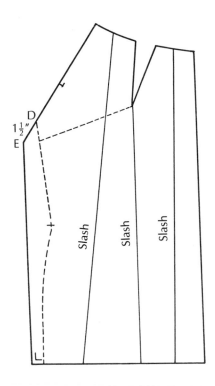

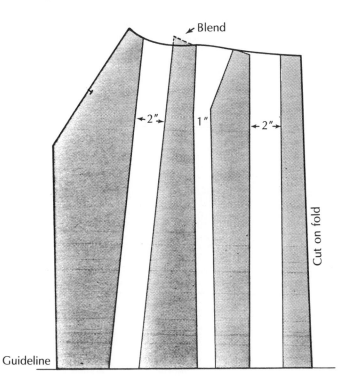

FIGURE 4 *Back:*
- Trace front pattern on fold for bodice back.
- Adjust back pattern by drawing a blending line across curved line. (Curved line on front is needed for bust mound.)
- Notch for sleeve.
- Cut patterns from paper.
- Mark for back sleeve notches and draw grain.

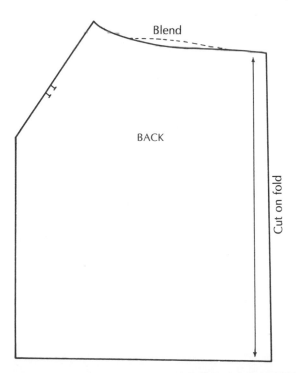

(Continued on next page)

FIGURE 5   *Sleeve section:*
- Draw slash lines as shown.

FIGURE 6
- Cut slash lines from neck to, not through, hem.
- Place on fold and spread as shown.
- Trace and discard.
- Notch where indicated. Mark two notches indicating back sleeve (full pattern shown).
- Draw grain and complete for test fit.

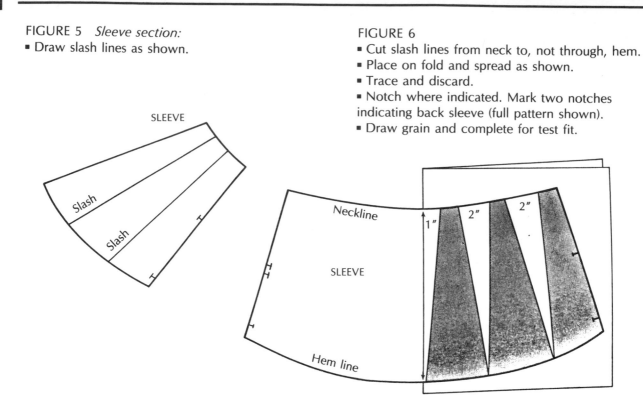

BLOUSE DESIGN VARIATIONS

Develop patterns for the following designs. If you observe that the designs are based on part of a circle, see the Circle/Cascade Radius Chart, Chapter 12.

19

JACKETS AND COATS

Introduction 486
Terms and definitions 486
Jacket and coat foundations 486
Sleeve draft for jacket and coat 488
Two-piece sleeve 490
LAPEL DESIGNS 492
Basic notched lapel 492
Low-notch lapel 496
Portrait lapel 498
DOUBLE-BREASTED JACKET WITH LAPEL 500
DESIGN VARIATIONS 501
SHAWL FOUNDATION 502
Shawl draft 502
Shawl collar variations 503
Wide shawl collars 504
*Shawl collar with separated undercollar and
    facing 505*
INTERCONSTRUCTION FOR JACKETS AND
    COATS 506
Terms and definitions 506
Guide for interconstruction placements 507
STYLE JACKET WITH FACING, LINING, AND
    INTERCONSTRUCTION 508
Facing 509
Lining 510
Outer garment 512

INTRODUCTION

Jackets and coats are outer garments designed to be worn over other garments. Therefore, patterns developed for these garments should be larger than the figure's dimensions. They may be designed in a variety of ways featuring collars, lapels, and revers, or they may be collarless (cardigan style). Collars may follow the basic neckline, a V-shaped or scooped neckline, or a neckline of any other shape. Use previously given instructions for dress stylelines (princess, armhole princess, and panel—Chapter 17), bodice/sleeve combinations (kimono, raglan, drop shoulder), and lowered armhole (see Chapter 13), when designing jackets and coats.

This chapter features the development of jacket and coat foundation patterns based on the torso foundation. It features the development of various lapels that may be used on any one of these garments (jacket lapel is illustrated). Also included are instructions on how to develop linings, facings, shoulder pads, and interconstructions for either the jacket or coat.

TERMS AND DEFINITIONS

Following are some common terms and definitions as used in this chapter (see examples):

Lapel. The part of a coat or jacket that folds back on the chest, forming a continuation of the collar (or the collar plus revers).

Revers (revere). The collarless part of the lapel which turns back to show the reverse side (or facing). When combined with a collar it becomes a lapel.

Breakpoint. The point at the front extension where the lapel ends and folds back (where roll line begins).

Roll line. The fold line where the lapel turns outward. (On a collar, it is the edge of the stand where the collar turns downward.)

Collar stand. The height at the center back of the collar where collar rolls over.

Center front depth. The point where the lapels overlap at the center front. (This point may be placed at any depth desired.)

Notched collar. A lapel design featuring a collar attached to revers, forming a wedge between the collar and the revers.

Shawl collar. A one-piece lapel (collar and revers in one).

SHAWL COLLAR
NOTCHED COLLAR
Collar
Depth
Notch collar
Lapel (Revere without collar)
Roll line
Breakpoint

JACKET AND COAT FOUNDATIONS

The jacket foundation (opposite page) is developed from the torso foundation. After the jacket foundation has been developed, it may be used as a base for developing the coat foundation, using the same instructions. (Or the coat foundation may be developed directly from the torso using the instructions below and doubling the measurements given.) Other design variations and silhouette changes are developed from a traced copy of either of these two foundations after they have been test fit and corrected.

Special notation: Ease has been added to the front armhole, neckline, and side seams to compensate for the interconstruction and thickness of the fabric layers. Very bulky and/or heavy weaves may require an additional $\frac{1}{4}$ inch to be added to each measurement given.

FIGURE 1 *Back draft:*
- Trace back torso pattern.
- Measure in $\frac{1}{8}$ inch around neck.
- Measure up $\frac{1}{8}$ inch from shoulder at neck and $\frac{1}{4}$ inch up from shoulder tip. Draw a connecting line across shoulder.
- True shoulder dart legs, adding to the shorter leg and blend with shoulder.
- Measure out $\frac{1}{4}$ inch from shoulder tip and at mid-armhole. Measure down $\frac{1}{2}$ inch at armhole and out $\frac{1}{4}$ inch at side seam. Blend armhole.
- Draw line parallel with side seam.

FIGURE 2 *Front draft:*
- Trace front torso, transferring $\frac{3}{8}$ inch to armhole and $\frac{1}{4}$ inch to mid-neck from the side dart (indicated by broken lines).
- Shift bust point $\frac{1}{4}$ inch toward side seam.
- Measure in $\frac{1}{8}$ inch around neckline.
- Measure up $\frac{1}{8}$ inch from shoulder at neck, and $\frac{1}{4}$ inch up from shoulder tip. Draw a connecting line across shoulder.
- Measure out $\frac{1}{4}$ inch from shoulder tip and down $\frac{1}{2}$ inch from armhole and out $\frac{1}{4}$ inch at side seam. Blend armhole and draw line parallel with side seam, as shown.
- Cut patterns from paper. Discard shaded areas around neckline and armholes. True patterns and test fit.

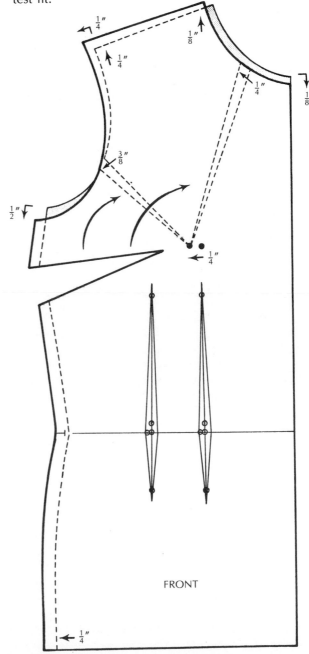

BACK

FRONT

SLEEVE DRAFT FOR JACKET AND COAT

The basic sleeve is used to develop the jacket and coat sleeves. (For coat sleeve, double the measurements given.) The sleeve may be developed by one of three methods, two of which are illustrated. The third method for enlarging the basic sleeve involves grading by following guidelines where growth occurs, or use company standards (not illustrated).

Folded-paper method

FIGURE 1   *Sleeve preparation:*
- Trace basic sleeve.
- Divide sleeve in half on each side of grain at biceps level. Mark.
- Square guidelines up and down from each mark. Label X and Y.
- Draw a guideline across cap connecting guidelines X, and Y. Label Z at grainline.
- Place sleeve on paper and extend guidelines X, Y, and Z. Remove sleeve. Connect lines across paper.

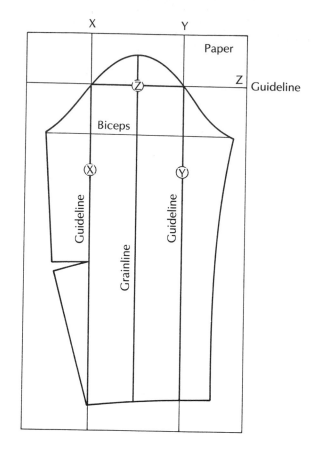

FIGURE 2
- Fold paper $\frac{1}{4}$ inch (folds to $\frac{1}{8}$ inch) along X, Y, and Z guidelines.

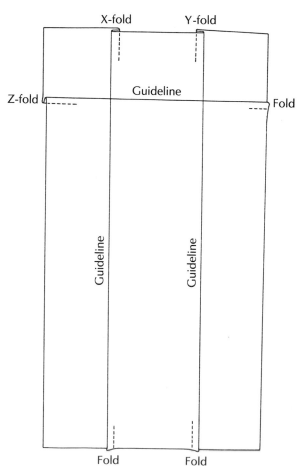

FIGURE 3
- Replace sleeve on paper matching X, Y, and Z guidelines with folds on paper. Trace sleeve. Remove.
- Unfold paper, blend across open spaces, and add $\frac{1}{4}$ inch at biceps to zero at wrist (see Figure 4).
- Cut pattern from paper.

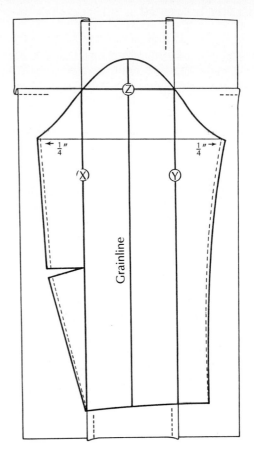

Cut-and-separate method

FIGURE 4
- Cut and separate sleeve along X, Y, and Z guidelines.
- Draw a vertical line through the center of the paper (sleeve grainline).
- Square a line out from each side of line, 8 inches down from top of paper (biceps line).
- Place pattern sections on paper matching grainline and biceps line with guidelines. Spread each section $\frac{1}{4}$ inch (shaded area). Secure pattern parts and trace.
- Remove pattern, blend across open spaces, and add $\frac{1}{4}$ inch at biceps to zero at wrist.
- Cut pattern from paper.

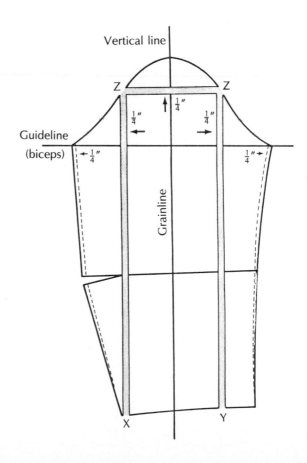

TWO-PIECE SLEEVE

The two-piece tailored sleeve has an upper- and undersection, with the elbow dart being replaced as ease. Both sections are drafted together from the basic sleeve pattern and then separated.

Uppersleeve (unshaded area)

FIGURE 1

▪ Trace the basic sleeve and all markings.

▪ Divide sleeve in half on each side of grainline at biceps and elbow, and into fourths at wrist level. Mark and connect points. Label X guidelines as shown.

▪ Measure in and out from X guidelines, and mark as follows:

$1\frac{1}{4}$ inches at biceps.

1 inch at elbow.

$\frac{3}{4}$ inch at wrist.

▪ To complete uppersleeve, connect marks outside of X guidelines (unshaded area).

▪ Mark ease notches $1\frac{1}{2}$ inches up and down from each dart leg, and square in $2\frac{1}{2}$ inches. (For convenience, erase part of sleeve shown as shaded area.)

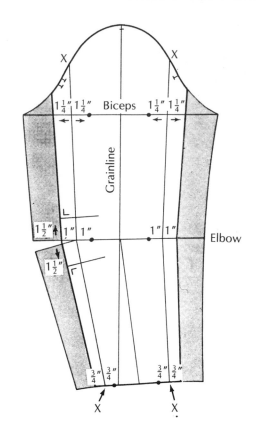

Undersleeve (shaded area)

FIGURE 2

▪ Connect marks inside X guidelines.

▪ *Armhole curve:* Basic sleeve is used to draw underarm curves of sleeve. (Broken lines indicate basic sleeve placement, matching X guidelines and biceps line.) Use back sleeve to draw back underarm curve. Use front sleeve to draw front underarm curve.

▪ Place paper under draft.

▪ Trace the undersleeve, grain, and notches (shaded area). Crossmark corners. Remove paper and pencil in outline of undersleeve (not illustrated).

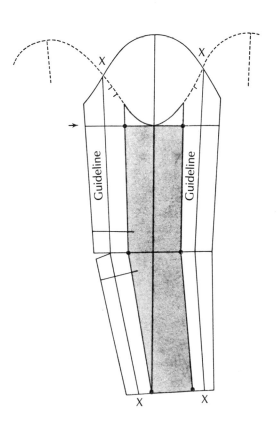

FIGURES 3 and 4
- The completed sleeve is shown. *Note:* To true sleeve, start from top of sleeve to first notch point, slip pattern to hem and true from bottom up to notch point. Adjust undersleeve notches, if necessary. Blend hemline.

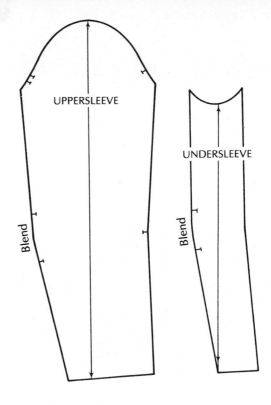

FIGURES 5 and 6
- If it is necessary to increase elbow ease or to give more angle to the sleeve, trace the upper- and undersleeve, slash along elbow level to, not through, other side, and spread (example: $\frac{1}{4}$ to $\frac{1}{2}$ inch).
- Retrace patterns.

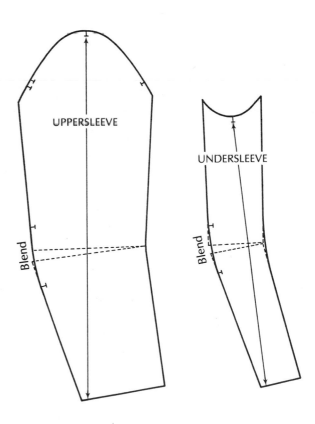

LAPEL DESIGNS

Each of the lapel designs shown are popular lapel variations and can be developed by modifying the basic notched lapel pattern—by lowering or raising the notch, changing the depth at center front, and by modifying the width and stand of the collar. Any number of variations can be developed using the same general instructions as a guide.

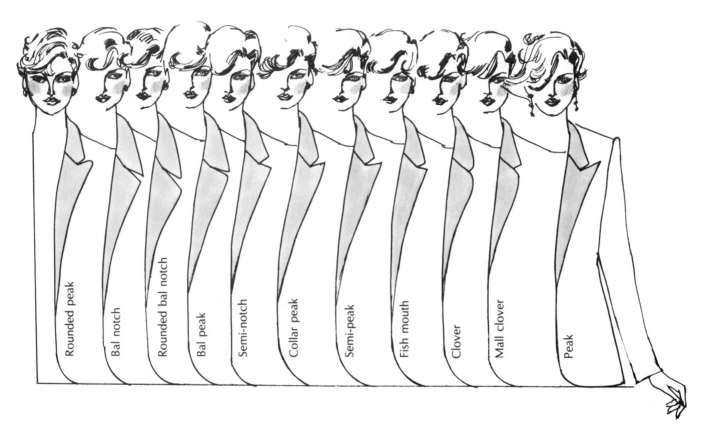

Rounded peak   Bal notch   Rounded bal notch   Bal peak   Semi-notch   Collar peak   Semi-peak   Fish mouth   Clover   Mall clover   Peak

BASIC NOTCHED LAPEL

Design Analysis

The basic notched lapel is developed with the wedge (notch) level with the base of the neck. Other variations may be developed using these instructions. (Jacket design not included.)

Note: The shape of the lapel, and measurements given can vary to change the look of the design. If a wider collar is desired, follow basic collar instructions first. Design desired collar over basic pattern. Basic collar is needed for slash and spreading formula. (See page 495, Figures 9, 10, and 11.)

Pattern plot and development

FIGURE 1

- Trace front and back jacket patterns (back not illustrated).
- Label shoulder neck A.
- Label center front depth B. (Example: 1 inch above bust level—point where lapels overlap.)
- *Extension:* Draw a parallel line 1 inch from center front, ending at level with B. (Extension should equal diameter of button.)
- A–C = 1 inch (collar stand). Draw line from C through B, ending at extension (roll line). Label D (breakpoint of lapel).

FIGURE 2

- Fold paper along roll line and trace neckline and A–C line. Unfold paper.

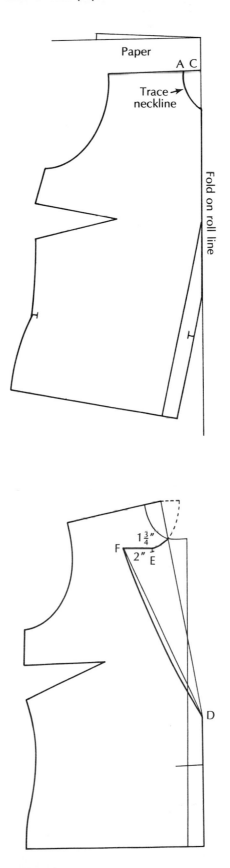

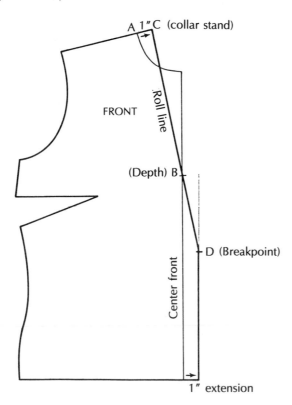

FIGURE 3 *Lapel development:*

- Following the curve of the traced neckline (broken line), extend curve 1¾ inches into frame of jacket. Label E and mark for notch.
- *E–F = 2 inches.* (*Guide:* Place square rule at center front to draw line.) Draw straight line from F to D. Redraw line, curving slightly outward as shown (shaded area).

FIGURE 4
- Refold paper along roll line, tracing complete outline of lapel (shaded area).
- Crossmark points E and D (notch placements). Unfold and pencil in lapel.

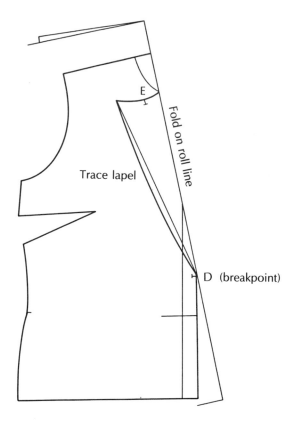

FIGURE 5 *Collar development:*

A–G = $\frac{1}{4}$ inch.

G–H = Width of collar (example: $2\frac{3}{4}$ inches for basic collar). Square from G and mid-neck.

G–I = Back neck measurement of pattern. Locate measurement on ruler and place at point G with ruler touching mid-neckline. Draw line.

G–J = One-half of G–I. Mark.

I–K = $\frac{1}{2}$ inch.
       Draw line from J to K. Blend back neckline.

K–L = $2\frac{3}{4}$ inches, squared from K–J line. Draw collar edge from L to H parallel with back neckline.

E–M = $1\frac{3}{4}$ inches ending approximately $\frac{3}{4}$ inch from lapel.
       This completes the basic collar.

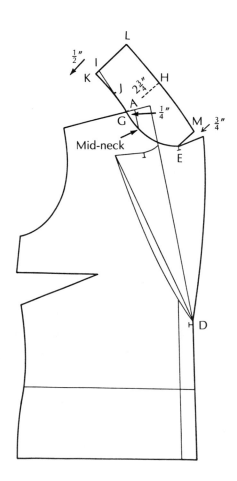

FIGURE 6
- Place paper underneath draft and trace collar (shaded area). Broken line is part of jacket draft not traced. Crossmark G (notch placement).

FIGURE 7 *Completed collar:*
- Remove paper and pencil in collar. Roll line starts 1 inch up from center back of collar and blends to roll line of lapel. (Broken lines indicate roll line of collar when attached to jacket.)

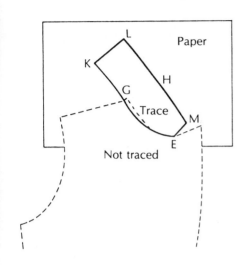

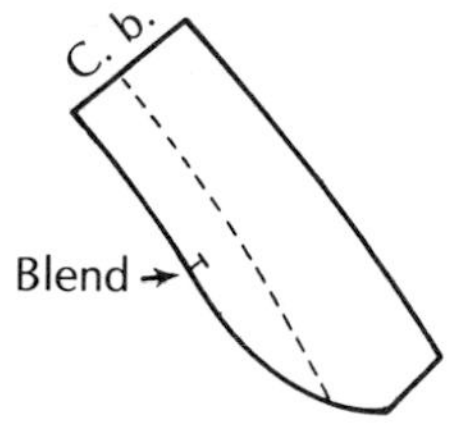

FIGURE 8
- Cut jacket section from paper following original neckline curve (E to A, not E to G). (Broken line indicates collar which is not traced.)

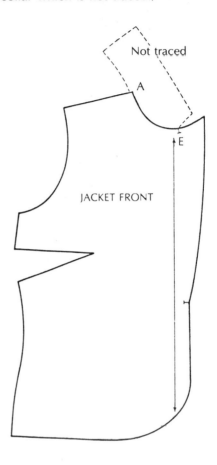

Collar modifications
Follow instructions if a lower stand and wider collar are desired. Broken lines on illustrations show possible design variations.

Note: Spread may be increased for very bulky fabrics. Test fit collar before stitching complete garment. To develop undercollar, see page 513.

FIGURE 9
- To modify collar, divide the back collar into four equal parts.
- Cut slash lines from collar edge to, not through, neckline edge. Spread as shown.

FIGURE 10 *½-inch stand:*
- Spread each section $\frac{3}{8}$ inch. Collar width—$3\frac{1}{2}$ inches. (Collar design should blend with back collar level with shoulder notch.)

FIGURE 11 *Flat roll:*
- Spread each section $\frac{1}{2}$ inch. Collar width—may be of any width and design.

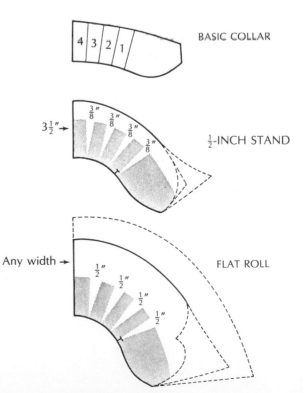

LOW-NOTCH LAPEL

Design Analysis

The only difference between the low-notch design and the basic notch is that the center front neckline and notch are lowered, requiring an adjustment to the basic neckline. When planning neckline, consider location of depth placement. If neckline is too close to depth mark, lapel will be short and unflattering. Designs 1, 2 and 3 show varying depths of the low notch.

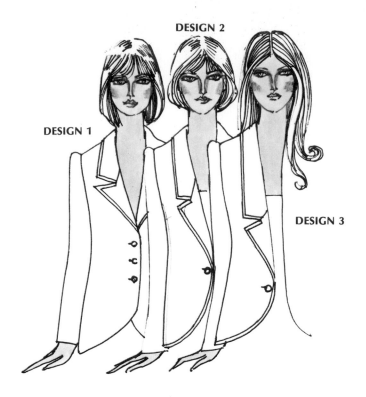

Pattern plot and development

FIGURE 1

- Trace front and back jacket patterns. (Back not illustrated.)
- Label shoulder at neck A and center front depth B (example: At bust level—point where lapels overlap).
- *Extension:* Draw a parallel line 1 inch from center front, ending at level with B. (Extension should equal diameter of button.)
- A–C = 1 inch (collar stand). Draw line from C through B, ending at extension (roll line). Label D (breakpoint of lapel).

FIGURE 2   *New neckline shape:*
- Fold paper along roll line. Draw curved line for new neck from point A to fold line. Bold line (between neck and bust level) is chosen for draft. (Broken lines indicate other variations.)
- Trace new neckline and A–C line. Unfold paper.

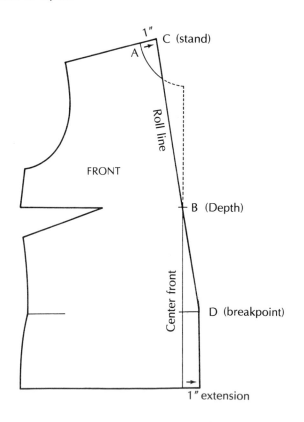

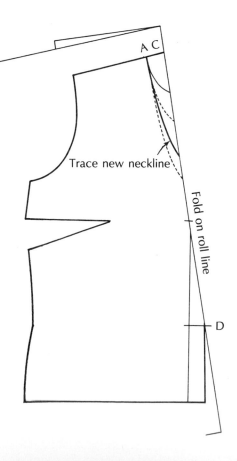

FIGURE 3 *Lapel Development:*
- Following curve of traced neckline (broken line), extend curve 1 inch (or more) into frame of jacket. Label E and mark for notch.
- E–F $= 2\frac{1}{2}$ inches (more or less). Connect F with D.
- Redraw line, curving slightly outward as shown.

FIGURE 4
- Refold paper along roll line, tracing complete outline of lapel.
- Crossmark E and D (notch placement). Unfold and pencil in lapel.

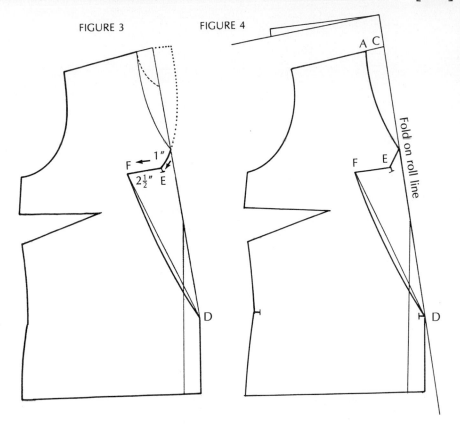

FIGURE 3   FIGURE 4

FIGURE 5 *Collar development:*
A–G $= \frac{1}{4}$ inch.
G–H $=$ Width of collar (example: $2\frac{3}{4}$ inches).
G–I $=$ Back neck measurement of pattern. Locate measurement on ruler and place at point G with ruler touching mid-neckline. Draw line.
G–J $=$ One-half of G–I. Mark.
I–K $= \frac{1}{2}$ inch.
Draw line from J to K. Blend back neckline
K–L $= 2\frac{3}{4}$ inches, squared from K–J line.
Draw collar edge from L to H, parallel with back neckline.
E–M $= 2$ inches, ending approximately $\frac{3}{4}$ inch from lapel.
This completes the collar.

FIGURES 6 and 7
- To transfer collar from draft and to modify collar, refer to instructions given for the basic notch (Figures 6 through 11, page 495).

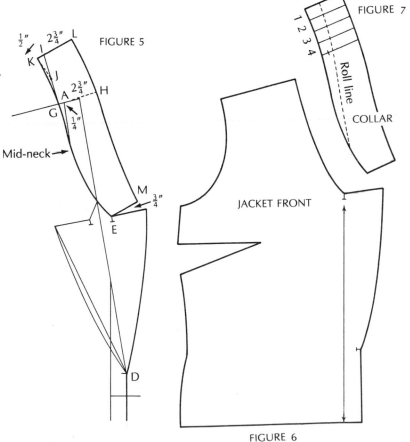

FIGURE 5   FIGURE 7

COLLAR

JACKET FRONT

FIGURE 6

PORTRAIT LAPEL

Design Analysis
A portrait lapel frames the face around an open neckline much like a picture in a frame. This draft is based on the basic notch with the difference being in the placement of collar at shoulder and the development of a new neckline. The jacket design is not included with the lapel development.

Pattern plot and development

FIGURES 1 and 2
- Trace the front and back jacket patterns.
- Label A, 2 inches from front/back shoulder at neck.
- Draw back neck, ending $\frac{3}{4}$ inch down from center back. Measure and record for collar development.
- Label center front depth B (example: Bust level—point where lapels overlap).
- *Extension:* Draw a parallel line 1 inch from center front, ending at level with B. (Extension should equal diameter of button.)
- A–C = 1 inch (collar stand). Draw line from C through B, ending at extension (roll line). Label D (breakpoint of lapel).
Neckline:
- C–X = 3 inches (varies—personal choice as to depth).
- Connect A to X and draw a curved line for neck approximately $\frac{1}{16}$ inch out from midpoint, as shown.

FIGURE 3
- Fold paper along roll line and trace new neckline and A–C line.

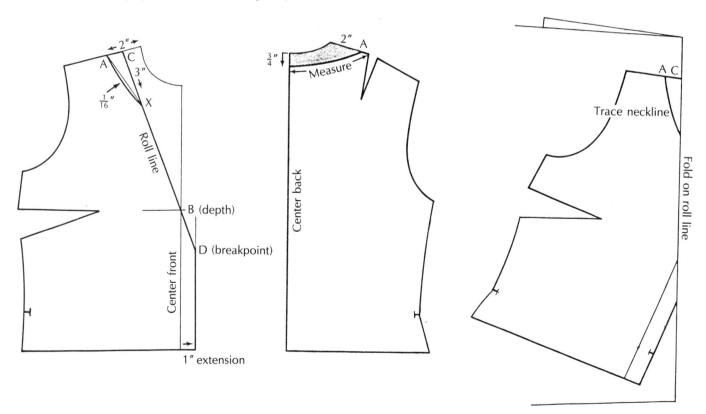

FIGURE 4
- Unfold paper.
- Following the curve of the traced neckline (broken line), extend curve 3 inches into frame of jacket. Label E and mark for notch.
- E–F = 2 inches (more or less). Connect F with D. Redraw line, curving slightly outward as shown.

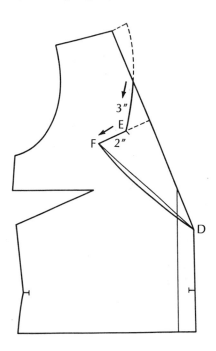

FIGURE 5
- Refold paper along roll line, tracing complete outline of lapel.
- Crossmark E and D (notch placement). Unfold and pencil in lapel.

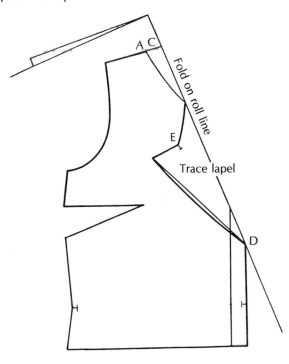

FIGURE 6 *Collar development:*

A–G = $\frac{1}{4}$ inch.

G–H = Width of collar (example: $2\frac{3}{4}$ inches).

G–I = Back neck measurement. Locate measurement on ruler and place at point G with ruler touching mid-neckline. Draw line.

G–J = One-half of G–I. Mark.

I–K = $\frac{1}{2}$ inch.
Draw line from J to K. Blend back neckline.

K–L = $2\frac{3}{4}$ inches, squared from K–J line.
Draw collar edge from L to H, parallel with back neckline.

E–M = 2 inches ending approximately $\frac{3}{4}$ inch from lapel.
This completes the collar.

FIGURES 7 and 8 *Finished pattern pieces:*
- To transfer collar from draft and to modify collar, refer to basic notch instructions (Figures 6 through 11).

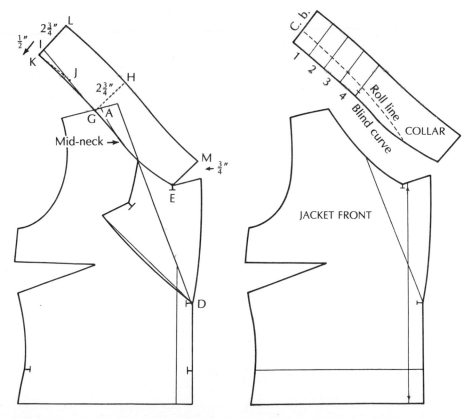

DOUBLE-BREASTED JACKET WITH LAPEL

Design Analysis
A double-breasted jacket has an extension wider than that of a basic jacket. Follow the general instructions for lapel development with the following modifications:

- The front extension should equal at least three times the diameter of the button (or more, if desired), and the breakpoint should be established before the roll line is drawn.
- The higher the breakpoint, the higher the point of overlap at the center front.

   Note: These same instructions apply to double-breasted coats. (The sleeve and design details are not included.)

Pattern plot and development

FIGURE 1
- Trace the front and back torso patterns. (Back not illustrated.)
- Follow instructions for basic notched lapel.
- Establish center front extension: Draw a parallel line equal to three times the diameter of the button (example: $2\frac{1}{4}$ inches).
- Establish the desired breakpoint on the extension line (example: at waist level). Connect with C (roll line). Label D (breakpoint).

FIGURE 2
- Complete the draft.

   Note: Buttons are spaced at an equal distance from the center front as shown. Refer to Buttons and Buttonholes, Chapter 14, for more information, if necessary. (For convenience, facing is indicated by broken lines that follow the shape of the jacket.)

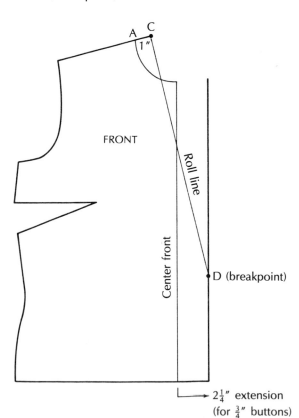

FRONT

A C
1"

Roll line

Center front

D (breakpoint)

$2\frac{1}{4}$" extension
(for $\frac{3}{4}$" buttons)

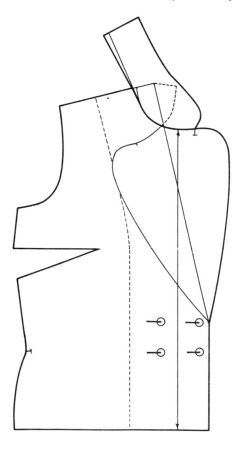

DESIGN VARIATIONS

Other jacket and/or coat designs may feature collars or be collarless. The following designs are included for inspiration and as practice problems. Instructions provided in previous chapters for collars, built-up necklines, cut-out necklines, sleeves, and so on, should be used as a guide for developing these patterns.

▪ Designs 1 and 2 feature cut-out necklines with collars.

▪ Design 3 shows a built-up neckline and extended sleeves.

▪ Design 4 illustrates the classic collarless cardigan.

▪ Design 5 illustrates the asymmetric overlap.

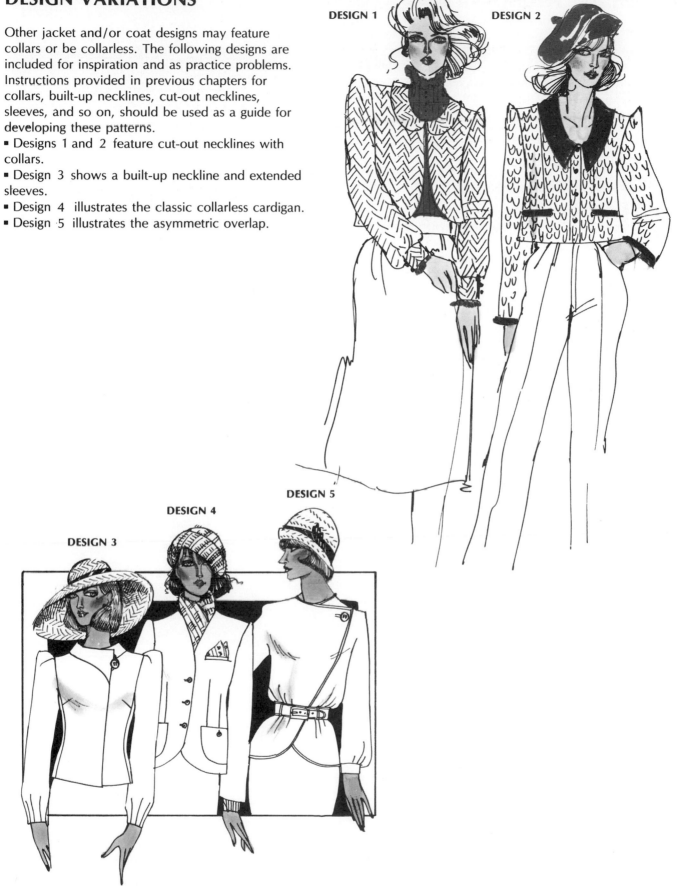

DESIGN 1 DESIGN 2

DESIGN 5

DESIGN 4

DESIGN 3

SHAWL FOUNDATION

The basic shawl foundation is developed in-one with the front jacket. The collar extends beyond the shoulderline, and attaches to the back neckline of the jacket. A hidden dart stitched under the lapel removes excess when original neckline is not used. Any number of lapel shapes can be developed from this draft by varying the shape between points H and D on the draft. Some of them are illustrated in the series that follows. Apply the instructions to the coat foundation for shawl designs. *Note:* The same instructions apply to shawl collars featured on blouses and dresses.

SHAWL DRAFT

Pattern plot and development

FIGURES 1 and 2   *Neckline modification:*
- Trace front jacket foundation including all markings.
- Trace basic back transferring shoulder dart to neck.

Realign shoulders:
- *Front:* Measure down $\frac{1}{4}$ inch from shoulder at neck (label A). Connect to shoulder tip. Cut away shaded area.
- *Back:* Measure up $\frac{1}{4}$ inch from shoulder at neck and connect with shoulder tip (broken line indicates original pattern).
- Blend neckline.

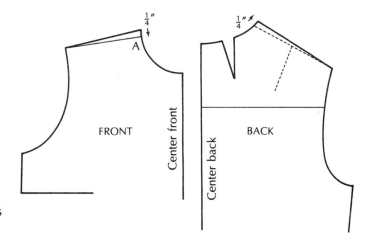

FIGURE 3
- Label shoulder at neck A and center front depth B (example: 1 inch above bust level—point where lapels overlap).
- *Extension:* Draw a parallel line 1 inch from center front, ending at level with B. (Extension should equal diameter of button.)

A–C = Back neck measurement of pattern. Locate measurement on ruler and place at point A with ruler touching point B. Draw line, ending at extension. Label D (breakpoint).

A–E = One-half of A–C. Mark.

C–F = $\frac{1}{2}$ inch.
Draw line from F to E. Blend for back neckline.

F–G = $2\frac{3}{4}$ inches, squared from F–E line.
Extend line from shoulder $2\frac{3}{4}$ inches past A. Label H.
Draw collar edge from G to H parallel with back neckline.

Hidden dart:
- Measure down 6 inches from A. Crossmark midpoint and measure out $\frac{1}{8}$ inch each side of crossmark. Draw curved line as shown. (Punch and circle dart in center only when $\frac{1}{4}$ inch wide as shown. Dart may be shortened when needed. This completes the shawl foundation draft. Shawl designs are developed from point H as illustrated in the following series. *Note:* Hidden dart is not used if draft is developed for blouses or dresses.

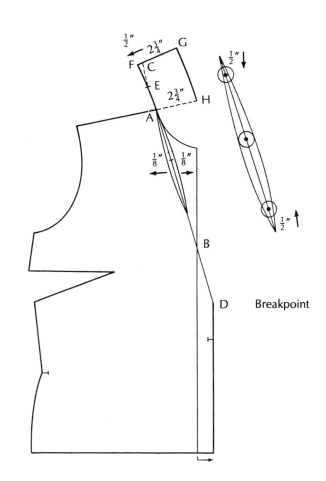

SHAWL COLLAR VARIATIONS

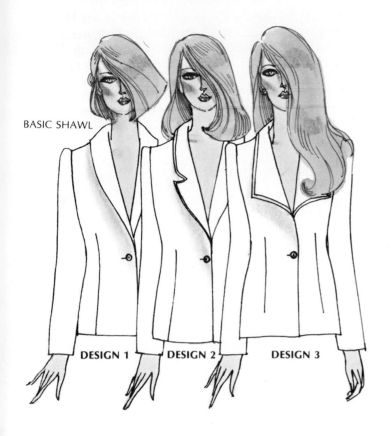

BASIC SHAWL

DESIGN 1   DESIGN 2   DESIGN 3

Design 1: Basic shawl lapel

FIGURE 1
- Draw curve outward from H to D as shown.

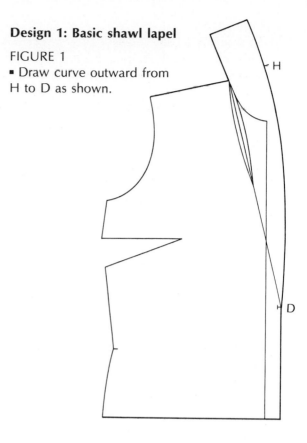

Design 2: Shawl with notch

FIGURE 2
- Draw curve from H to D and notch where desired, or as shown.

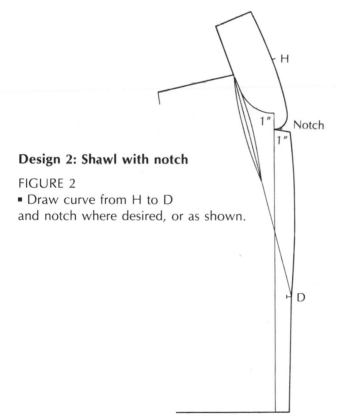

Design 3: Winged shawl

FIGURE 3
- Draw line outward from H, curving inward to D, for width desired. (Use depth level point B as a guide.)

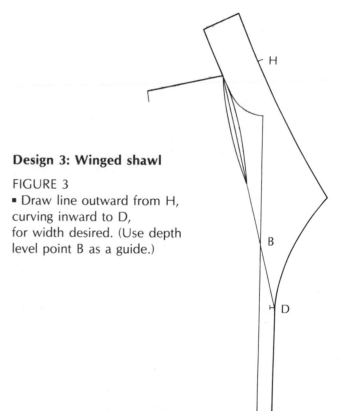

WIDE SHAWL COLLARS

Design Analysis
The technique for developing wide shawl collars requires modifying the back collar of the shawl draft. The collar may be developed with a ½-inch stand with widths up to 3½ inches along the back (below H, it may be of any width), or as a flat-roll collar of any width desired. A variety of lapel shapes can be designed from them, as suggested in the illustration (indicated by bold and broken lines). For practice, develop lapels for Designs 1, 2, and 3.

FIGURE 1   *Pattern preparation:*
- Trace back collar of shawl. (Broken lines untraced section.)
- Divide into four equal parts.
- Cut from paper, and slash from collar edge to, not through, neckline edge.
- Trace shawl pattern and place slashed collar on draft as shown.

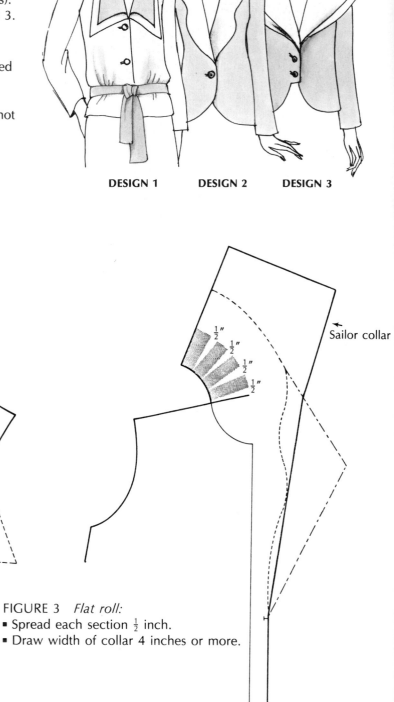

DESIGN 1   **DESIGN 2**   **DESIGN 3**

Extend

Various shawl designs

FIGURE 2   *½-inch stand:*
- Spread each section ⅜ inch.
- Draw width of collar 3½ inches.

FIGURE 3   *Flat roll:*
- Spread each section ½ inch.
- Draw width of collar 4 inches or more.

Sailor collar

SHAWL COLLAR WITH SEPARATED UNDERCOLLAR AND FACING

Instructions apply to any shawl lapel design. The basic shawl with notch is illustrated.

Pattern plot and development

FIGURE 1
- Trace basic shawl pattern. Include hidden dart.
- Draw notch placement anywhere along shawl line. Curve the lapel below notch as shown. (Broken line is original shawl.)
- Draw a curved line from shoulder at neck to notch at lapel. (This is the pattern for the undercollar.)
- Draw facing, starting 2 inches from shoulder at neck and ending $2\frac{1}{2}$ to 3 inches from center front at hemline.

FIGURE 2 *Facing:*
- Trace facing section from pattern.
- Extend center back collar $\frac{1}{8}$ inch and blend to zero at collar point.
- Add $\frac{1}{8}$ inch at midpoint of lapel. Blend to notch and breakpoint as shown. (Broken line indicates original pattern.)
- *Hidden dart:* The hidden dart may be removed between the facing and the lining by shifting the dart to stitchline and trimming from pattern (shaded area). It may be stitched at its original location, or it may be left unstitched (not ideal).

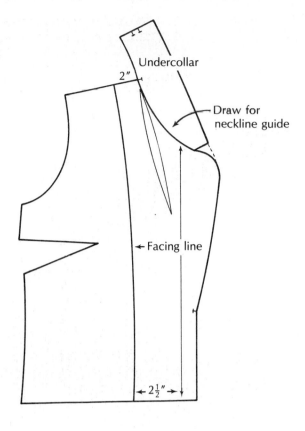

FIGURES 3 and 4
- Cut and separate collar from jacket (becomes under collar). Place punch and circles as shown. (See page 513.)

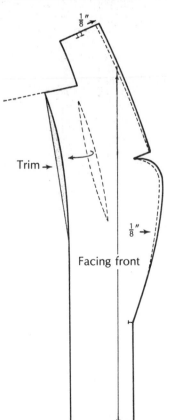

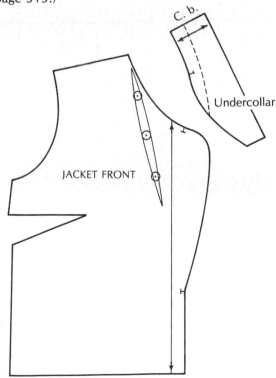

INTERCONSTRUCTION FOR JACKET AND COATS

Interconstructions of woven or nonwoven fusible materials are placed in jackets and coats to give them shape and form, and also for insulation. As many as four layers of interconstructions can be found in a garment depending upon the style and type of garment, the fabric, and the cost of the garment. Softly tailored garments require little interconstruction, whereas man-tailored garments require the maximum layers. Following is a description of the four basic types as illustrated:

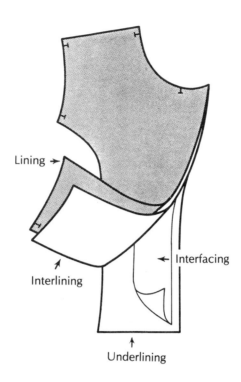

TERMS AND DEFINITIONS

Interfacing. Interfacing is the layer placed between the outer fabric and the facing. Its functions are to shape and stabilize detail areas, such as collars, cuffs, flaps, lapels, waistbands. It prevents stretching and supports the garment at strategic stress points—necklines, sharply angled points, gussets, diamond-shaped inserts. *The pattern for interfacings is developed from the garment pattern and facing patterns.* Seam allowance is used on patterns for woven materials and seamless for fusible nonwovens.

Underlining. (Also called backing or mounting.) Underlining reinforces the outer fabric and provides body to the cloth. *Patterns for underlinings are cut from the same pattern piece as the outer garment*

and on identical grain. When sewn together with the outer fabric, it acts as one layer of fabric.

Interlining. Interlining is the layer between the lining and underlining. Its purpose is to add insulation between the lining and underlining for warmth. It is omitted in pleats and sleeves (too bulky). *The pattern for interlining is the same as the lining pattern.* The interlining is stitched to the lining sections individually, then to the garment as a single layer.

Lining. A lining is a finishing layer that is a cover-up for inside construction. It is developed from the jacket pattern, and will be illustrated on a suit with interconstruction.

GUIDE FOR INTERCONSTRUCTION PLACEMENTS

Use the following guides (examples by Facemate and by the Pellon Corp.) for the placement of fusible woven and nonwoven interconstruction parts on each of the jacket (or coat) sections. (Remove part of seam allowances of patterns cut for fusing.)

FACEMATE

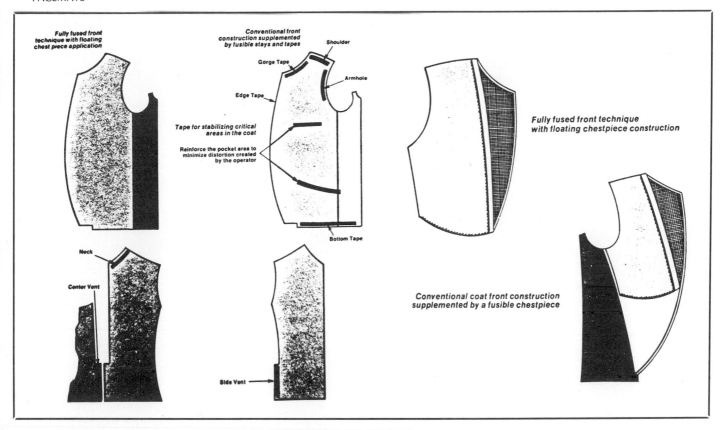

PELLON ®

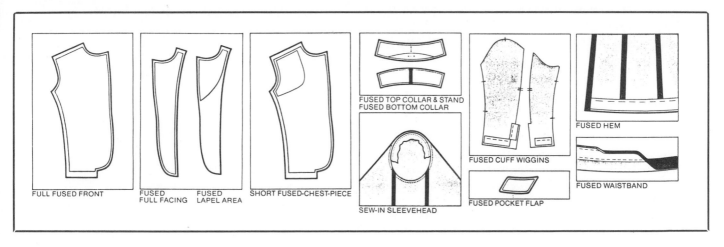

STYLE JACKET WITH FACING, LINING, AND INTERCONSTRUCTION

The basic notched lapel pattern with armhole princess styleline is used as an example of how to develop a jacket with a lining, facing, shoulder pads, and interlinings. This information is appropriate for all styles of lined jackets and coats.

Design Analysis

A semi-fitted jacket shows a curved styleline from mid-armhole (over bust) to waist (armhole princess). The design features a basic notched lapel, pocket flaps, and a curved opening.

Pattern plot and development

FIGURES 1 and 2

- Draft a basic notched collar and lapel on basic jacket foundation (see page 493). Modify jacket as follows:
- Mark for length 5 inches below front waistline and draw line parallel with front and back hip level.
- Draw a styleline from the front at mid-armhole to bust point. Continue line to hem parallel with the center front. Draw slash line from bust point to side dart. (Second dart is omitted.)
- Crossmark 2 inches up and down from bust point.
- Draw curve of hem from center front to styleline as shown.
- Draw styleline for back touching dart point of dart nearest center back. (Second dart is omitted.) Crossmark dart point.

Dart development:

- At waistline, measure out $\frac{3}{8}$ inch from each side of styleline in front and $\frac{5}{8}$ inch in back. (Shaded areas to be discarded.)
- Connect marks to bust notch on front and crossmark in back to form dart above waist.
- Connect dart legs $3\frac{1}{2}$ inches below waist in front and $4\frac{1}{2}$ inches in back, forming double-ended darts. (Shape dart for better fit.) Mark for notches at waistline and sides at waist level.
- Mark notch $\frac{1}{2}$ inch up from front styleline of jacket for lining placement later. Label X.
- Add $1\frac{1}{2}$-inch hem allowance, starting at side panel in front and across back.
- Draw pocket flap placement (5-inch width and $2\frac{1}{2}$-inch length). Mark punch and circle $\frac{1}{2}$ inch in from corners to guide positioning flap on jacket when sewing.

Facing

- Draw location for facing on pattern for later reference. *Note:* Facing can be cut to follow the styleline of a jacket or it can bypass the styleline as the illustration will show. The facing continues upward from the bust as indicated by broken lines.

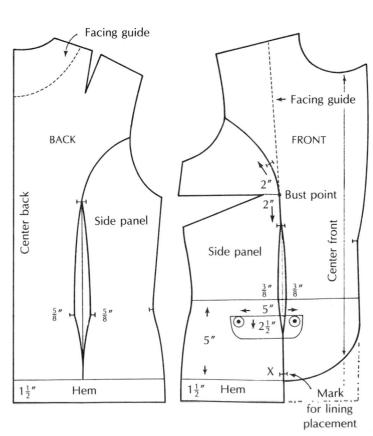

Shoulder adjustment for shoulder pads (if required)

FIGURES 3 and 4
- Garments with shoulder pads require an adjustment to the shoulderline and the sleeve cap as follows: Raise the shoulder tips and height of sleeve cap equal to the thickness of the shoulder pad. Blend cap and shoulderline as shown (shaded area). If thickness of shoulder pad is more than $\frac{1}{4}$ inch, add an additional $\frac{3}{8}$ inch to shoulder tips.
- Cut pattern from paper. *Do not separate along styleline yet.*

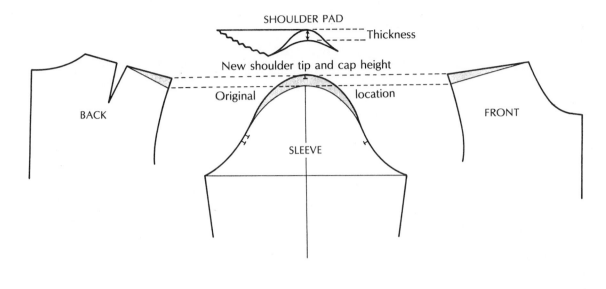

FACING

FIGURE 5
- Trace front facing from pattern and all notch markings. Use a pushpin or tracing wheel to transfer the facing lines within the pattern (indicated by bold lines).
- Add $\frac{1}{8}$ inch to lapel at midpoint ($\frac{1}{4}$ inch for bulky fabrics), blending as shown. (Broken line indicates original shape.)
- *Use facing to establish interconstruction pattern.*

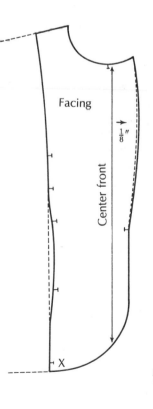

FIGURE 6
- Place fold of paper at center back and trace facing.

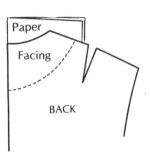

FIGURE 7
- Remove paper. Pencil in facing and draw grain.

(Continued on next page)

LINING

The lining is usually lighter in weight than the outer garment fabric and should be cut larger than the garment to avoid stress and to compensate for shrinkage. The lining may be developed to follow the styleline of the jacket or coat, but is more often modified to avoid placing seamlines in the same place as on the outer garment. This will help avoid excessive bulk. (The facing can be modified for the same reason.) Hemlines are developed in a number of ways, depending on how the lining is to be attached. The lining illustrated is meant to be machine stitched to the hemline.

Lining pattern development

FIGURES 1 and 2
- Trace front and back patterns to establish the lining.
- Mark all notches including point X.
- Omit stylelines and sections used for facings (bold line indicates lining pattern, and broken lines unneeded sections).
- Remove pattern.
- Extend front and back shoulders ½ inch.
- Add ¼ inch to side seam at armhole, blending to original side seams at hip as shown (or ¼ inch parallel to side seam).
- Extend side seam ½ inch above armhole. (This will raise the lining over the edge of the seamline of the outer garment to prevent puckering and stress under the arm of the garment.)
- Blend front and back armholes as shown.

Hemline of lining
- The lining should end above the bottom of the jacket. The amount varies.
- Hemline in this example is ½ inch less than hem allowance of jacket (example: 1 inch). From point X, measure down 1 inch for hem of lining. Draw hemline parallel with jacket hem. (Figure 1)
- Repeat hem allowance for back as shown. (The fold line of the hem is placed at notch (point X) of the facing when stitching.)

Action pleat at center back
- Add 1½ inches to 2 inches at center back. Pleat may be parallel with center back or tapered to waist level (uneven broken lines). (Figure 2)

Shoulder dart
- To remove dart, measure in from facing line equal to width of dart.
- Draw blending line as shown. (Shaded area to be trimmed from pattern.)

Waist darts
- Back dart can be developed as a dart or tuck dart.
- Front waist dart is removed through seamline of lining as shown.

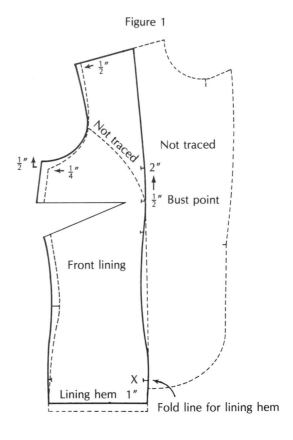

Figure 1

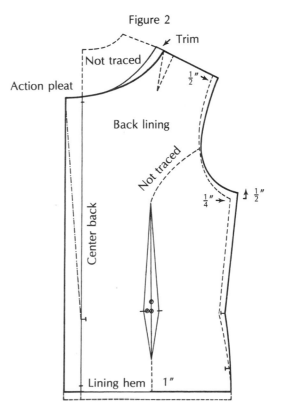

Figure 2

Side dart of front lining

FIGURES 3, 4, and 5

▪ The side dart of the lining may be left in its original location and stitched, or transferred to mid-shoulder. It can be either folded or stitched as a tuck dart and used as an action pleat, or trimmed to seamline of lining. (Broken line indicates original dart.)

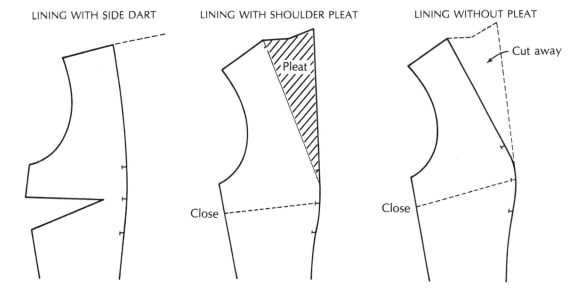

LINING WITH SIDE DART   LINING WITH SHOULDER PLEAT   LINING WITHOUT PLEAT

Basic sleeve modifications

FIGURE 6

(Instructions apply to any style of sleeve used with jacket or coat designs.)

▪ Trace basic sleeve. Add $1\frac{1}{2}$ inches for hem allowance.

▪ Fold hem and trace both sides of sleeve at hem. Unfold and remove $\frac{1}{8}$ to $\frac{1}{4}$ inch from sides of hem to avoid bulk when lining is attached. Label fold line X.

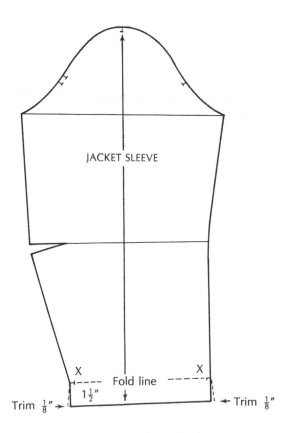

(Continued on next page)

Sleeve lining

FIGURE 7

- Trace sleeve. Remove.
- Subtract $\frac{1}{2}$ inch from sleeve cap height. Blend. (Shaded area to be trimmed from pattern.)
- Raise front and back armholes $\frac{1}{2}$ inch. Blend.
- Add $\frac{1}{4}$ inch to underseam to zero at hemline as shown (or $\frac{1}{4}$ inch parallel with underseams).
- Hemline of lining is $\frac{1}{2}$ inch less than hem allowance of sleeve (example: 1 inch).
- Notch $\frac{1}{2}$ inch up from points X to establish fold line for hem. (Broken line indicates original sleeve.) *Note:* Elbow dart may be stitched as a dart, folded as a pleat, or eased in. If eased in, mark notches $1\frac{1}{2}$ inches up and down from dart legs and other side 1 inch up and down from elbow level. Blend dart (not illustrated).
- True hem of lining with hem of jacket, trimming equally on each side.

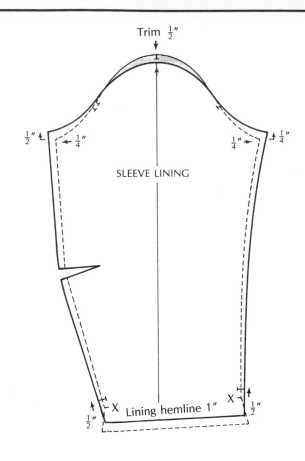

OUTER GARMENT

FIGURES 1, 2, 3, 4

After the lining and facings have been traced from the pattern, the outer pattern is separated along the stylelines. Pattern is cut apart through waist darts and mid-armhole in front and back, with the center back on the fold as shown. Add grainline to each pattern.

Side front panel

- Slash from bust point to, not through, dart point of side dart. Close dart. Retrace, blending bust line.
- *Use these patterns to develop interlining (if desired) and other interconstruction parts.*

FIGURE 5

- Trace pocket flap.

POCKET FLAP

Note: Label patterns with felt-tip pens using the following colors:
- Black—Outer garment patterns
- Red—Lining patterns
- Green—Interconstruction patterns.

(Colors help to group patterns for markers.)

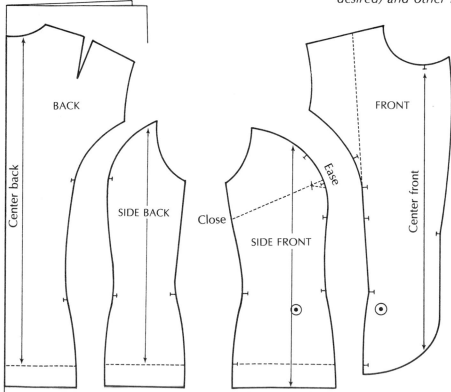

Collar

FIGURE 1   *Uppercollar:*
- Trace collar on fold, include all marking.
- Measure up $\frac{1}{8}$ inch at center back of collar. Draw blending curve to tip of front collar and cut from paper.

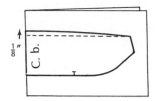

FIGURE 2
- Unfold and label *Uppercollar.* Mark center back notch.
- Draw straight grainline.
- *Trace this pattern or undercollar for interconstruction parts.*

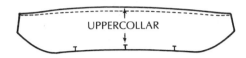

FIGURE 3   *Undercollar:*
- Trace collar on fold, include all markings.
- Mark notch for top of collar at center back and notch $\frac{1}{8}$ inch away from center back collar at neckline edge. (Two notches indicate undercollar.) Cut from paper.

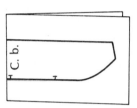

FIGURE 4
- Unfold and label *Undercollar.*
- Draw straight grainline.

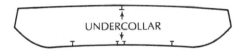

FIGURE 5   *Two-piece bias undercollar:*
- Cut undercollar in two pieces. Draw grain—straight or bias (collar will roll more smoothly). To develop interconstruction patterns for fusables, remove some or all of seam allowances. Label *Interconstruction patterns* with a red or green felt-tip pen.

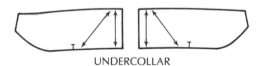

CAPES 516
A-line cape foundation 516
Flared cape foundation 518
HOODS 520
How to measure for hood draft 520
Contoured hood foundation 520
Contoured hood design 523
Loose hood foundation 524
Design variations 525

20

CAPES AND HOODS

CAPES

A cape is a sleeveless garment that fastens at the neck and hangs over the back and shoulders. It can be worn separately over coats, jackets, dresses or sportswear, or attached to a dress or cloak. Two basic cape foundations developed from the torso are illustrated. The straight A-line cape and the circular cape, once developed, can be used to develop any number of variations, depending on current fashion trends.

A-LINE CAPE FOUNDATION

Design Analysis

Cape has A-line silhouette with slits for arm entry. Three buttons secure cape. Design illustrates how this foundation can be used.

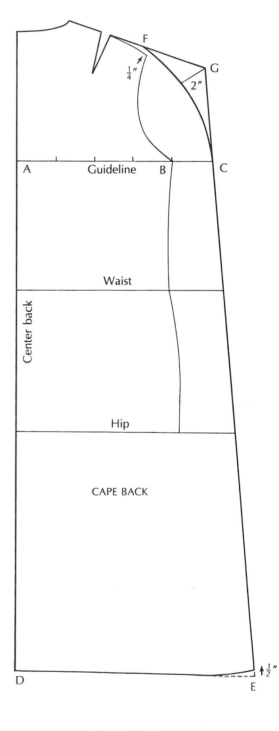

Pattern plot and development

FIGURE 1 *Back:*

- Trace back torso.
- Square a guideline from the center back touching armhole. Label A and B. Divide A–B line into fourths.
- B–C = One-fourth of A–B. Extend line.
- Extend center back to length desired. Label D.
- D–E = A–C plus $2\frac{1}{2}$ inches, squared from D.
- Draw a line from E. Extend line through C.
- Blend hem $\frac{1}{2}$ inch up at side seam.
- Mark $\frac{1}{4}$ inch above shoulder tip. Label F.
- Extend line from mid-shoulder through F, intersecting E–C line. Label G.
- Draw a 2-inch diagonal line from G, and draw shoulder curve from C to F to mid-shoulder.
- Cut pattern from paper.

FIGURE 2
- Trace front torso, transferring side dart to mid-shoulder in line with back dart (broken line).
- Square a line from center front touching armhole. Label H.
- H–I = B–C of back cape.
- Add length to center front below hip equal to back. Label J.
- J–K = D–E of back cape, squared from J. Connect K with I.
- Blend hemline $\frac{1}{2}$ inch up from side seam.
- Draw 1-inch extension parallel with center front.

Armhole slit:
- Mark 1 inch in from side waist. Label L. Square 5 inches up and down from L. (Placement and length can vary.) Slit should be cut $\frac{1}{16}$ inch wide and notched across top and bottom.
- Cut welt strip 10 inches × 3 inches (not illustrated). *Note:* slit is faced with lining.

FIGURE 3.
- Place back on top of front cape, matching guidelines with C and I touching. (Back indicated by broken line.)
- Trace curve of back cape, ending at the *back* shoulder dart leg (will cross front dart leg). Mark. Remove pattern. (If back shoulder is higher or lower than front, balance the difference at shoulder tip and blend curve line.) Adjust shoulder curve on figure.

    Note: To add shoulder pads extend shoulders equal to thickness of pad.
- Center dart point $1\frac{1}{2}$ inches up from bust point and draw adjusted dart legs to dart point.
- Complete pattern for test fit. (See Figure 2.)

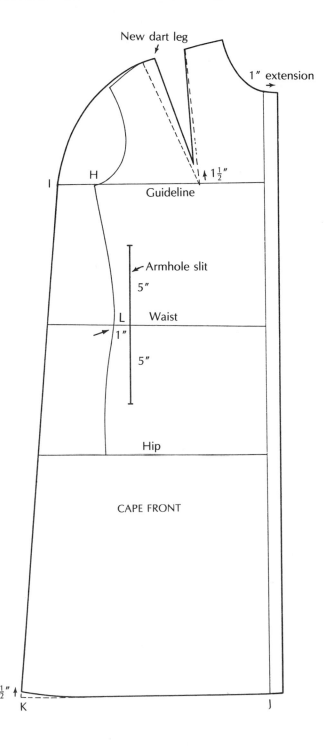

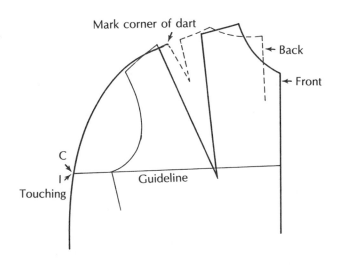

FLARED CAPE FOUNDATION

Design Analysis
Flared cape with tied neck and turned up Peter Pan
flat roll illustrates how this foundation can be used.
(Collar and tie not included.) Develop the flared
cape foundation from the front and back torso.

Pattern plot and development (opposite page)
■ Trace front and back patterns, transferring
shoulder and side darts to hip level and cut from
paper.

FIGURE 1
■ Square a line on paper. Place back and front on
square line with shoulder tips 1 inch apart. Trace
and discard patterns. Label sidehips A and B.
■ Mark center between shoulder tips and points A
and B. Draw separating line.
■ Mark C, after letter A $1\frac{1}{2}$ inches down on line
from shoulder tips.
■ Draw curved shoulder from C to front/back
mid-shoulders, passing $\frac{1}{4}$ inch above shoulder tips.
■ Mark notch for shoulder tips.
■ Shape hemline between front and back patterns.
■ Extend hemline to desired length. New hemline is
parallel with hip level.
■ Draw 1-inch extension at center front for button
and buttonholes, if desired.

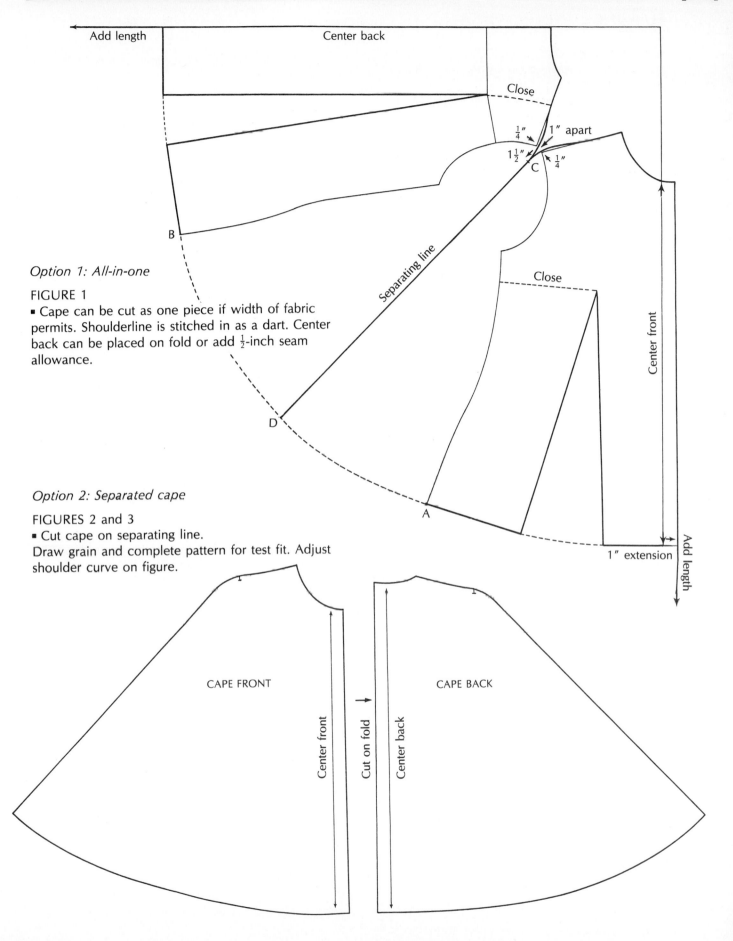

Add length

Center back

Close

$\frac{1}{4}''$ 1" apart

$1\frac{1}{2}''$ $\frac{1}{4}''$

C

B

Separating line

Close

Center front

D

A

1" extension

Add length

Option 1: All-in-one

FIGURE 1

- Cape can be cut as one piece if width of fabric permits. Shoulderline is stitched in as a dart. Center back can be placed on fold or add $\frac{1}{2}$-inch seam allowance.

Option 2: Separated cape

FIGURES 2 and 3

- Cut cape on separating line.
Draw grain and complete pattern for test fit. Adjust shoulder curve on figure.

CAPE FRONT

CAPE BACK

Center front

Cut on fold

Center back

HOODS

Hoods cover the head and neck, and sometimes part of the face. They can be worn separately, or as part of a garment; for protection from the weather, or as a design feature. Hoods, like all garments, come in endless styles and varied shapes.

Two hood foundations are illustrated—the contour hood and the loose-fitting hood. From these two foundations, other variations can be developed, such as the design and practice problems shown. (Hoods illustrated are attached to the garments.) The front and back neckline of the pattern to which the hood is attached is used in the draft.

HOW TO MEASURE FOR HOOD DRAFT

FIGURE 1   *Overhead measurement:*
▪ Place measuring tape at center front neck (between clavicles) and hold end of tape while measuring around the head, starting at center front neck.
▪ Record one-third of this measurement and add $\frac{3}{4}$ inch.

FIGURE 2   *Horizontal measurement:*
▪ Place tape at hairline at eye level and measure to other side. Record one-half of measurement.

Center front neck

Overhead measurement record:

Horizontal measurement record:

CONTOURED HOOD FOUNDATION

Design Analysis
The contoured hood fits the shape of the head, with control darts at the crown and neck area. The hood is attached to the neckline of the garment, starting at the center front.

Pattern plot and development

FIGURE 1

- A–B = Overhead measurement
  (example: 10 inches).
- B–C = A–B, less 1 inch. Square from B.
- C–D = 1½ inches. Square from C.
- A–E = One-half of A–B. Mark.
- E–F = ¾ inch, squared from E.
- F–G = Horizontal measurement squared from E
  (example: 8 inches).
- B–H = 1 inch. Mark.
- B–I = One-half of B–C. Mark.

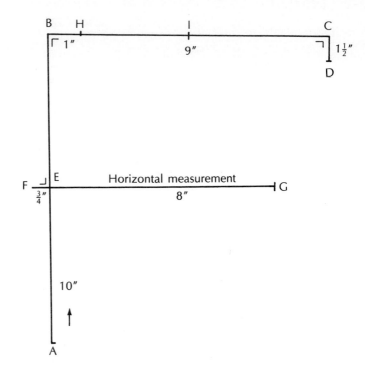

FIGURE 2

- Place back pattern on draft with center back on A–B line and neck at A.
- Trace back neck to corner of shoulder. Label J.
- Shift pattern ¾ inch, keeping center back parallel with A–B line.
- Trace shoulderline from corner of neck to dart leg. Label K. (Broken lines indicate untraced pattern.)
- Remove pattern.

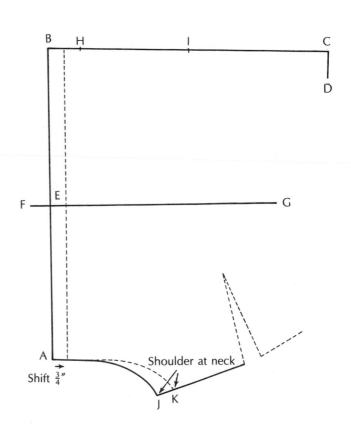

(Continued on next page)

FIGURE 3
- Extend shoulderline (for guideline).
- Place shoulderline of front pattern on guideline with corner of neck touching point K.
- Trace front neck. Label center front neck X. (Broken lines represent untraced pattern.)
- Remove pattern.
- K–L = 3 inches. Mark.
- L–M = $\frac{3}{8}$ inch. Mark and draw line from H to M.
- H–N = $\frac{3}{4}$ inch. Mark.
- Square out from both sides of N, $1\frac{1}{8}$ inches. Label O and P.
- N–Q = One-third of H–M. Mark and connect Q with O and P.

FIGURE 4   *Shaping hood:*
- Draw outward curved line of hood, connecting points A, F, and O, and P, I, and D.
- Draw inward curves from D, G, L, to X. Blend at point G, for continuous inward curve if necessary.
Neck dart:
- Locate center in between points J and K. Draw a 3-inch line parallel with A–B line. Label R.
- Connect J and K with R.
Crown dart:
- Locate midpoint between points O–Q and Q–P and measure out $\frac{1}{8}$ inch. Mark and draw curved lines connecting points Q with O and P.
- Draw grainline parallel with A–B line. Complete pattern for test fit.

   Note: When adding seam allowance, fold neck dart with excess in direction of A–B line. Trace to shape dart across stitch line.

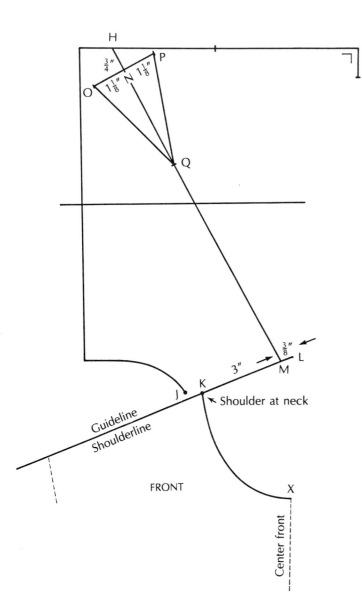

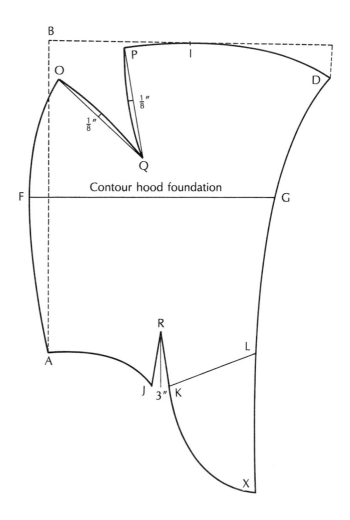

Contour hood foundation

CONTOURED HOOD DESIGN

Design Analysis

The contoured hood encircles the face, buttoning from the chin down the center front of the neck and garment to which it is attached. The hood gathers along the neckline and the styleline ends at the side of the face. Design 2 is included for practice.

FIGURE 1

- Trace contour hood foundation, including F–G line and K–L line. (See hood draft, page 520.)
- Draw styleline from dart point of crown dart ending 4 inches below G–line.
- Square down from point F (for fullness), and blend neckline across dart (dart excess is part of gathers).

Extension at neck:

- X–Y = 3 inches. Mark.
- Locate 1½ inches on square rule and place at point Y, with other leg at point X. Draw square line connecting X with Y. Label point Z. Blend from Z to point L.
- Draw 1-inch extension parallel with X–Z line.
- Connect ends.

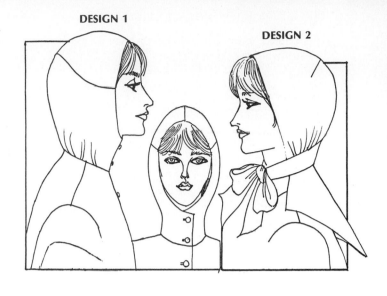

DESIGN 1

DESIGN 2

FIGURES 2 and 3

- Cut pattern from paper and separate.
- Mark for button and buttonholes (see Chapter 14).
- Draw grain and complete pattern for test fit.

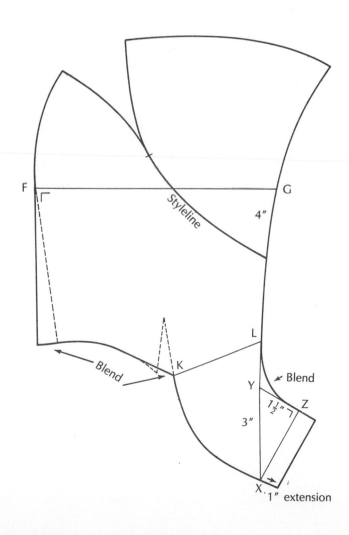

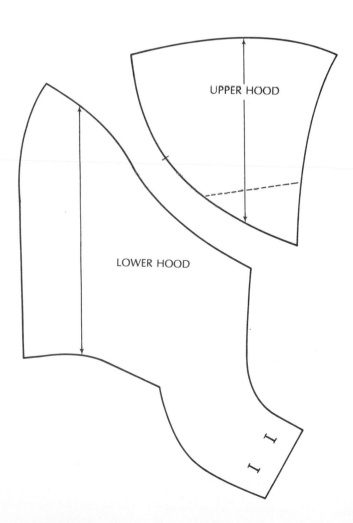

LOOSE HOOD FOUNDATION

This type of hood is used most often on coats and capes. The hood may be pointed or squared in back, with the front hood folded back.

Design Analysis

The foundation is drafted with a fold-back and fits to the height of the crown of the head, with either a point or a square across the back eliminating the point. Instructions are given for both Design 1 and Design 2.

DESIGN 1   **DESIGN 2**

Pattern plot and development

(For greater looseness, add 2 inches or more to A–B measurement. See Design 2.)

FIGURE 1

- A–B = Overhead measurement (example: 10 inches).
- B–C = $2\frac{1}{2}$ inches.
- C–D = A–B, squared from C.
- Square down from D, as shown.
- Place center back on A–C line with corner of neck touching A.
- Draw neck to corner of shoulder. Label E.
- Shift pattern $\frac{3}{4}$ inch, keeping center back parallel with A–C line.
- Draw shoulder, starting at corner of neck, to dart leg. Label F.
- Remove pattern and extend shoulderline (guideline). (Broken line untraced pattern.)

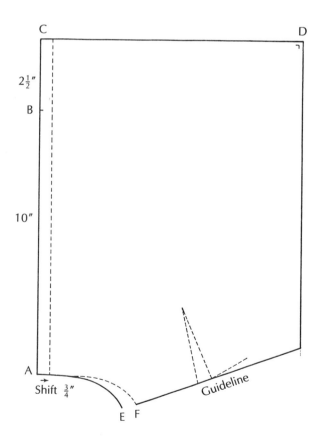

FIGURE 2
- Place front shoulder on shoulder guideline of draft with corner of neck touching point F.
- Dot mark center front neck (indicated by broken line).
- With pushpin at point F of front pattern, swing front pattern 2 inches away from dot mark.
- Trace neckline. Remove pattern and label center front H.
- Draw curve of hood from point H, blending with square line at shoulder guide as shown.

FIGURE 3
- Locate center of dart between E–F. Draw 3-inch line parallel with A–C line. Label I.
- Draw connecting line from E and F to I.
- To remove point from hood, square out $2\frac{1}{2}$ inches from B. Label J.
- Square up from J to C–D line.
- Cut section from pattern.
  Note: Center back of hood is cut on fold.
- Draw grain and complete for test fit.

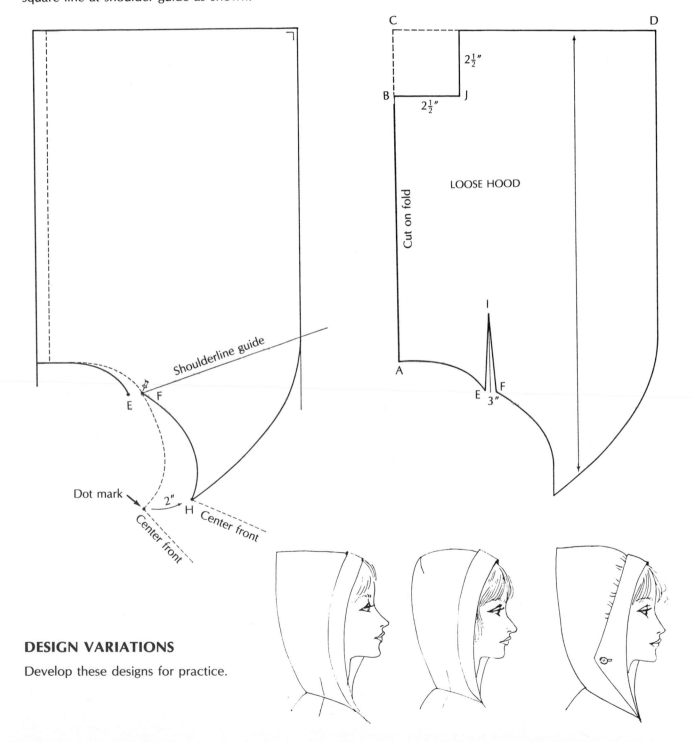

DESIGN VARIATIONS
Develop these designs for practice.

___ *part* *Six*

PATTERNMAKING FOR BIFURCATED GARMENTS

21

PANTS

BIFURCATED—WHAT'S THAT? 530
THE LEG RELATIVE TO THE PANT 531
PANTS 531
Terminology 531
Analysis of pant foundations 532
Summary of the pant foundations 533
Culotte—foundation 1 534
Trouser—foundation 2 536
Slack—foundation 3 540
Jean—foundation 4 541
Dartless jean pant 544
COMPLETING THE PANT PATTERN 545
How to true the pant pattern 545
Seam allowance 546
PANT DESIGNS 547
Box-pleated culotte 547
Gaucho pant 548
Culotte with wide-sweeping hemline 550
Tiered culotte 551
Pleated trouser 552
Baggy pant 554
Pull-on pant with self-casing 555
High-waisted pant 556
Hip-hugger 557
Jean with back yoke 558
Contour pant with creaseline flare 560
Pant with flared leg 561
Pant with curved hemline 562
Knickers 563
Pleated cowl-draped pant 564
Clown pant 566
Geometric-draped pant 567
PANT DERIVATIVES 568
Shorty-shorts 569
Shorts 570
Jamaicas 570
Bermudas 571
Pedal pushers 571
Toreador 572
Capri 572
Design variations 573
JUMPSUIT FOUNDATIONS 574
Trouser/slack jumpsuit foundation 574
Jean/jumpsuit foundation 575
Culotte jumpsuit foundation 576
Great coverall 577
Jumpsuit design variations 579

BIFURCATED—WHAT'S THAT?

Thank heavens, Mrs. Bloomer knew! She was immortalized for the bloomer, the first divided (bifurcated) pant for ladies.

We have come a long way since Mrs. Bloomer's bloomers in embracing not only pants but jumpsuits, swimsuits, and bodysuits as well—as though our very lives depended upon them. No matter what shape, what length, what color, or even how outlandish the bifurcates, they have found their way into our hearts, our wardrobes, and our lives.

New concepts in the way pants should fit the female figure have become the focal point for designers and patternmakers. The grand old standby, the trouser, has not always resulted in the look desired, nor has it responded well to the uniqueness of the female form. Designers and patternmakers have been forced to rethink the philosophy of fit and the utility of pants and their derivatives.

The basic principles underlying pant development are not being challenged here. These principles are being utilized in a special way, always keeping in mind the distinct characteristics of the female figure.

THE LEG RELATIVE TO THE PANT

The leg performs a variety of functions, such as walking, running, bending, squatting, and sitting. Whenever the leg socket moves or the knee bends, the muscles and skin of the lower torso increase and decrease in length. The illustrations show where and when the body increases and decreases in length due to this movement. If a garment is to fit comfortably and hang well on the figure, the pant must not hinder the actions of the leg.

To insure that the pant will fit well when the leg is in motion, measurements must be taken with care and accuracy (Chapter 3). For a personalized fit, review Figure Analysis (Chapter 2). All draft instructions must be followed, and sufficient ease must be added to the pattern for comfort. Instructions are provided in the standard draft for modifying patterns for figures that deviate from the symmetrical, well-proportioned figure. After drafting, each pant foundation should be cut in a firm fabric, not a knit, and test-fitted on the figure. The foundation pattern should be corrected and perfected before it is used for other designs; otherwise, fitting errors will be passed on to all designs based on it.

PANTS

TERMINOLOGY

Terms relate to the pant draft, the human figure, and the pant garment. See figure below which cross-references terms and locations.

Bifurcated. Divided into two parts (right and left sides).

Crotch. Base of torso where legs join the body.

Crotch depth. The distance from waist to crotch base of the figure. This measurement (plus ease) is used in the pant draft.

The rise. A tailor's term referring to the crotch depth.

Crotch length. A measurable distance from the center front waist, around crotch base, to the center back waist.

Crotch extension. An extension of crotch line at center front and back that provides covering for the inside part of the leg.

Crotch point. End of crotch extension.

Crotch level. Dividing line separating torso from legline of the pant. (The total width across the pant from the front crotch point to back crotch point.)

Outseam. Side seam joining front and back pant.

Inseam. Seam between the legs joining front and back pant.

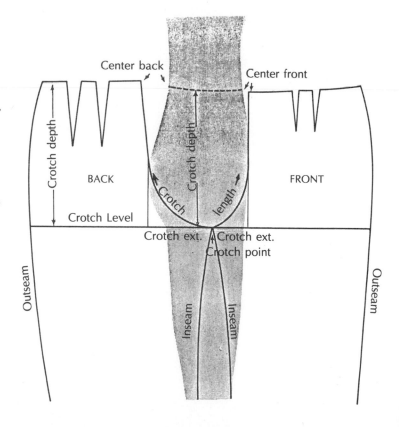

ANALYSIS OF PANT FOUNDATIONS

The principle. The length of the crotch extension *controls* the pant foundation. The longer the crotch extension, the looser the fit around the crotch. The shorter the crotch extension, the closer the fit.

The foundation of a pant covers the area from the waist to the crotch, while the style is determined by the shape of the legline. The foundation is separated from the pant style at crotch level (illustrated as broken lines on the following four pant foundations). The portion of the pant that covers the inside part of the leg is the crotch extension. The length of this extension is determined by the foundation desired, a percentage of the hip measurement, and the upper thigh measurement.

Analyze and compare the four pant foundations illustrated below. Each pant foundation fits the abdomen and buttocks in a special way. Aside from their legline styles, how do they differ?

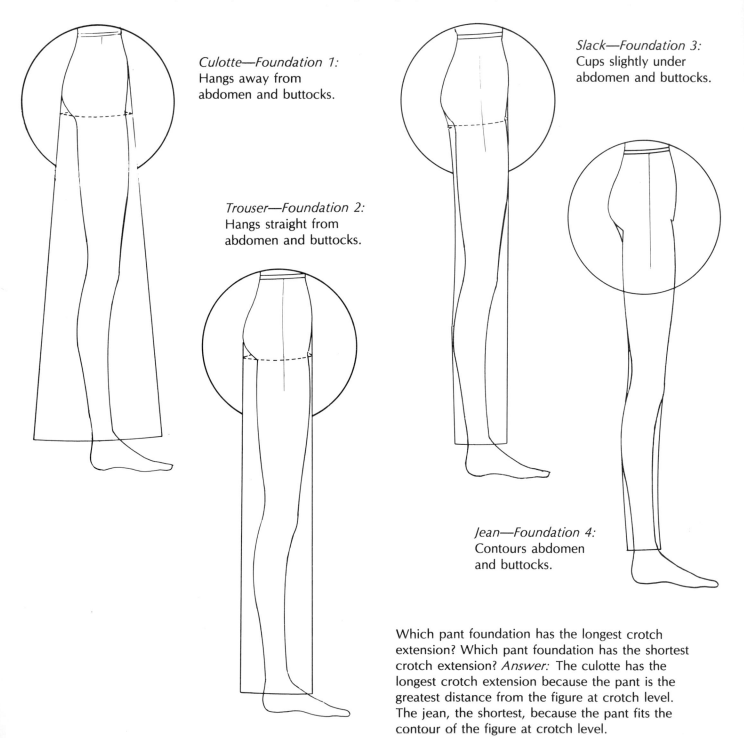

Culotte—Foundation 1:
Hangs away from
abdomen and buttocks.

Trouser—Foundation 2:
Hangs straight from
abdomen and buttocks.

Slack—Foundation 3:
Cups slightly under
abdomen and buttocks.

Jean—Foundation 4:
Contours abdomen
and buttocks.

Which pant foundation has the longest crotch extension? Which pant foundation has the shortest crotch extension? *Answer:* The culotte has the longest crotch extension because the pant is the greatest distance from the figure at crotch level. The jean, the shortest, because the pant fits the contour of the figure at crotch level.

SUMMARY OF THE PANT FOUNDATIONS

A pant is divided into its *foundation* (that part above crotch level) and *legline,* its style (below the crotch level). There are four major pant foundations characterized by the hang of the pant from abdomen and buttocks: The culotte hangs away, the trouser hangs straight, the slack cups, and the jean contours the abdomen and buttocks area.

The foundation of a pant is controlled by the lengths of the front and back crotch extensions. These extensions are based on a percentage of the hipline measurement, with consideration of the upper thigh measurement and shape.

Formula for crotch extension:

Culotte: Back—One-half of back hip, plus $\frac{3}{4}$ inch.
Front—One-half of front hip, minus $\frac{3}{4}$ inch.

Trouser: Back—One-half of back hip.
Front—One-fourth of front hip.

Slack: Back—One-half of back hip, minus $\frac{3}{4}$ inch.
Front—One-fourth of front hip.

Jean: Back—One-half of back hip, minus $\frac{3}{4}$ inch.
Front—2 inches. (Subtract $\frac{1}{8}$ inch for sizes under 10 and add $\frac{1}{8}$ inch for each size over 14.)

The *crotch level* measurement (the distance from crotch point to crotch point) should measure greater than the upper thigh measurement, as follows:

- *Trouser:* $3\frac{1}{2}$ inches more.
- *Slack:* $2\frac{1}{4}$ inches more.
- *Jean:* $1\frac{1}{2}$ inches more.

The *crotch length* of the pant should measure *at least* the same as that of the form or figure. When it does not, length should be added in one of three ways:

- By pitching the back pant of the jean foundation.
- By pitching the back pant and extending back crotch point of the slack equally.
- By extending front and back and crotch points of the trouser equally.

To test the fit of a foundation pant, cut the pant in firm fabric. To test the fit of styled pants, cut them in the fabric being used for the specific design.

The pant is drafted to accommodate the increased length of the legs when walking, sitting, and bending. If the pant shows strain, pulling, or looseness, due to insufficient or excessive fabric in any area on the figure, the pant will be uncomfortable and will not hang well. The pattern must be corrected and the garment refitted until it fits perfectly.

CULOTTE—FOUNDATION 1

When it first became fashionable for women to ride bicycles, it was unfashionable (even improper) for them to wear pants. A garment was needed that was both functional and ladylike. This led to the development of the culotte (then known as the divided skirt), a pantlike skirt providing the wearer with maximum mobility and yet acceptable for the mores of that period. So successful and practical was the culotte that it was accepted as a style for both casual and dressy garments, and continues to be an important fashion item from time to time.

The culotte foundation is developed from a basic A-line skirt; however, any skirt design can be adapted into a pantlike skirt by following the instructions given. This foundation is used not only as a base for the traditional box-pleated culotte but also for designs with varying lengths and wide-sweeping hemlines. Culotte designs are given on pages 547–551.

Culotte draft preparation

The draft instructions are for one-half of the front and back pant. For a personal fit, follow the standard draft instructions, using *Personal Fit* instructions where applicable. (Refer to Chapter 3 for measurement taking.)
Use measurements from:
- Measurement Chart or
- Company specifications, if available.

Culotte draft

Measurements needed
(refer to Personal Measurement Chart):
- (24) Crotch depth _____ plus $\frac{3}{4}$ inch
(varies up to $1\frac{1}{4}$ inches.)

- *Pattern needed:* Front and back A-line skirt and belt construction, see Chapter 12.

FIGURE 1 *Front:*

Place patterns at least 8 inches from paper's edge to allow for crotch extensions. Trace front and back skirt. Include all markings.

A–B = Crotch depth.

A–X = One-half of A–B. Mark.

B–C = One-half of front hip, less ¾ inch, squared from B.

D–E = B–C, squared from D.
Connect C with E.

B–b = 1½-inch diagonal line.
Draw crotch with curve touching C, b, and ending at or near X-point as shown.

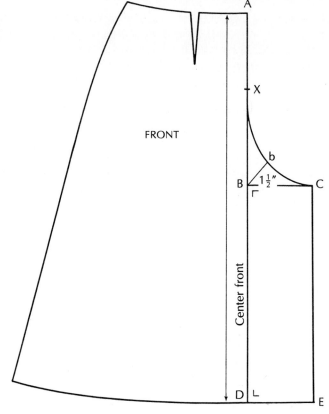

FIGURE 2 · *Back:*

F–G = D–B (of front pattern).

G–H = One-half of back hip plus ¾ inch, squared from G.

F–J = G–H, squared from F.
Connect J with H.

G–X = B–X (of front pattern). Mark.

G–g = 1¾-inch diagonal line.
Draw crotch with curve touching H–G line, g and ending at or near X-point as shown.

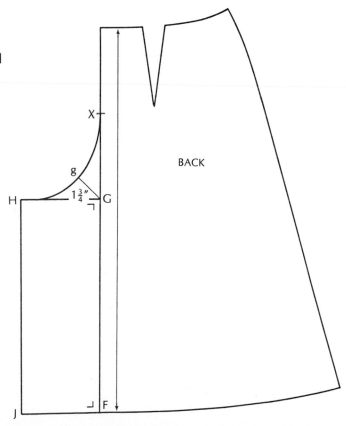

TROUSER—FOUNDATION 2

The trouser is a pant that hangs straight downward from the outermost part of the abdomen and buttocks. It fits closer to the body than does a culotte because the front crotch extension is shorter. This pant may be worn in its present form or modified for other pant designs, such as the mannish waist-pleated trouser, the baggy, the clown, and the gaucho (see Pant Designs). It is also used as a base for pant derivatives such as the short, the Jamaica, the Bermuda, and the pedal pusher, to name a few.

Trouser draft preparation

The draft instructions are for one-half of the front and back pant. For a personal fit, follow the standard draft instructions, using *Personal Fit* instructions where applicable. (Refer to Chapter 3 for measurement taking.) *Note:* The draft for figures with tilting waistlines will look different than the standard draft; see page 630 to acquaint yourself with possible waistline shapes. Place a tab at Chapter 26 for modification of pant for personal fit. *Use measurements from:*

- Measurement Chart or
- Company specifications, if available.

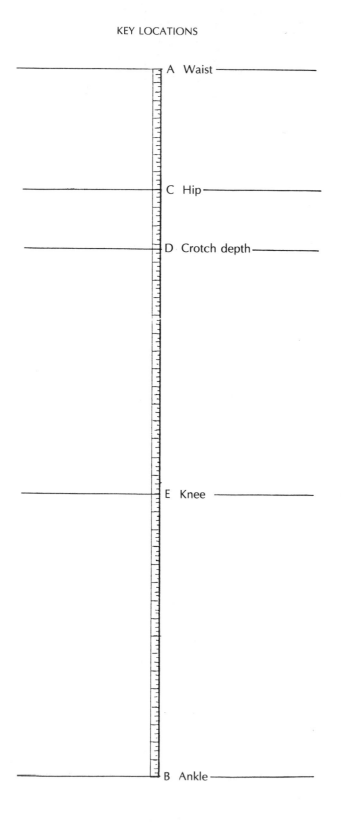

KEY LOCATIONS

A Waist

C Hip

D Crotch depth

E Knee

B Ankle

Measurements needed

- (27) Pant length to ankle _____.
- (24) Crotch depth _____.
- (23) Front hip _____. Back hip _____.
- (19) Front waist _____. Back waist _____.

Additional personal fit measurements

- (25) Hip depth CF _____, CB _____.
- (27) Knee depth _____.
- (21) Dart intake: Front _____. Back _____.
- (22) Abdomen (record if greater than hip) Front _____. Back _____.

Trouser draft

Key locations:

Personal fit: Locate hip and knee depth down from A (when marking key locations).

FIGURE 1

A–B = Pant length.

A–D = Crotch depth plus $\frac{3}{4}$-inch ease (varies up to $1\frac{1}{4}$ inches).

D–C = Hip depth, one-third of D–A. (Half-sizes: one-fourth of D–A; petites: one-half of D–A.)

B–E = Knee depth, one-half of B–D plus 1 inch (toward crotch level).
Square out from both sides of A, B, C, D, and E.

FIGURE 2

Personal fit: Use abdominal measurement if greater than hip.

Back:
C–F = Back hip plus $\frac{1}{4}$ inch.
D–G = Same as C–F.
A–H = Same as C–F.
    Connect G with H.
G–X = One-half of G–H.
G–I = One-half of G–D.

Front:
C–J = Front hip plus $\frac{1}{4}$ inch.
D–K = Same as C–J.
A–L = Same as C–J.
    Connect K with L.
K–X = One-half of K–L.
K–M = One-fourth of K–D.

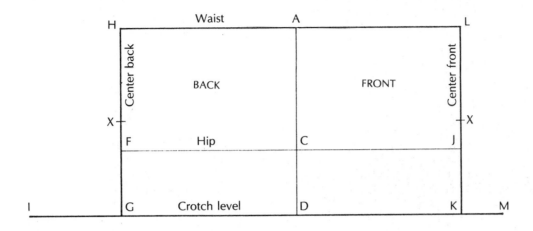

FIGURE 3

Personal fit: Use Personal Dart Intake, plus $\frac{1}{4}$-inch ease. Divide dart intake in half when marking darts.

Back dart intake:
H–N = Back waist plus 3 inches for dart intake and ease.
H–O = 4 inches (first dart placement). Mark.
• Dart intake: Mark 1 inch from O, space $1\frac{1}{4}$ inches and mark 1 inch for second dart.
• Locate dart centers and square down 5 inches.
• Square up and down from dart marks.

Front dart intake:
L–P = Front waist plus $1\frac{1}{4}$ inches for dart intake and ease.
L–R = 3 inches (first dart placement).
• Dart intake: Mark $\frac{1}{2}$ inch from R, space $1\frac{1}{4}$ inches and mark $\frac{1}{2}$ inch for second dart.
• Locate dart centers and square down 3 inches.
• Square up and down from dart marks.

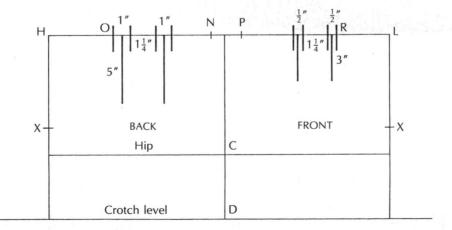

FIGURE 4

Back:

H–S = $\frac{3}{4}$ inch in from H and squared up $\frac{1}{4}$ inch.
       Draw straight line from S to crotch level
       touching point X.

G–g = 2-inch diagonal line.

• Draw curve with ruler touching points X, g, and
somewhere near I.

Front:

K–k = $1\frac{1}{2}$-inch diagonal line.

• Draw curve with rule touching points X, k, and M.

*For all Personal Fits, see Chapter 26 for further
adjustments before continuing.*

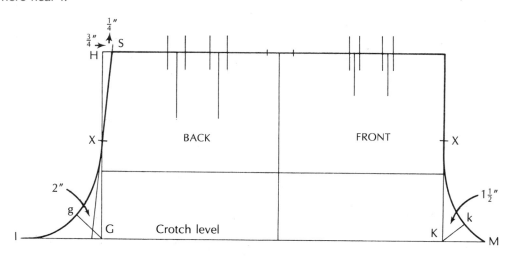

FIGURE 5 *Back and front:*

• Draw an inward curved line from S to N (back).

• Draw an inward curved line from $\frac{1}{4}$ inch below L
to P (front).

• Draw dart legs from waistline curve to dart points
from guidelines.

• True dart legs by adding to shorter leg. Blend with
waistline.

• Draw hip curves *just above* C to N (back) and to
P (front).

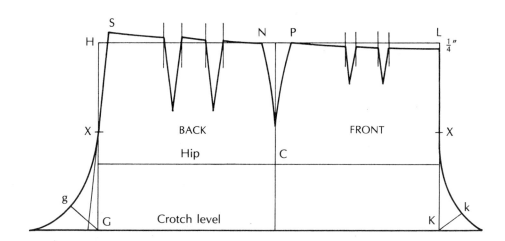

FIGURE 6

Back:

D–U = One-half of D–I plus $\frac{1}{4}$ inch (toward I). Mark.

- Square up and down from U.

Front:

D–W = One-half of D–M plus $\frac{1}{4}$ inch (toward M).

- Square up and down from W.

This completes the foundation part of the pant. A basic legline is attached to the foundation for the test fit and becomes part of the foundation when developing pant designs.

Legline for test fit:

- Measure out from both sides of ankle using measurements given. (Petites: subtract $\frac{1}{2}$ inch from each measurement.)

- *Outseams:* Draw straight lines from ankle marks to point C. Blend with hip.

- *Inseams:* Mark $\frac{1}{2}$ inch in from I and M. Draw straight lines from ankle marks to these marks.

- Draw slightly inward curved lines from I and M, blending with line above knee.

- *Note:* Crotch level (I to M) should measure *at least* 4 inches more than upper thigh. If not, adjust by extending points I and M equally.

Personal fit: Bottom-heavy, knock-knees, or full-thigh figures will correct leglines at time of fitting.

- For trueing and seam allowance instructions, see pages 545–546.

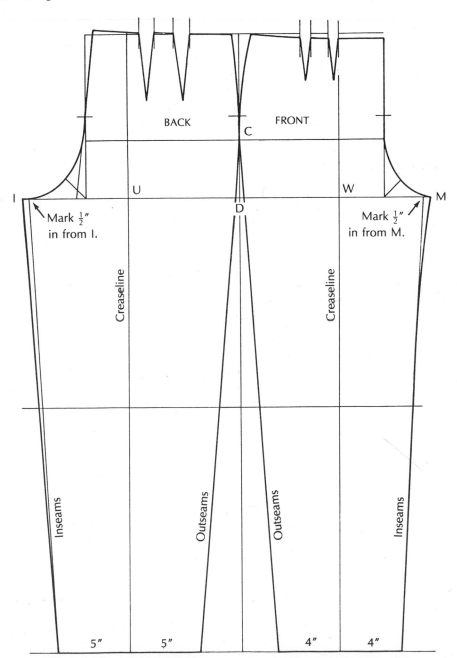

SLACK—FOUNDATION 3

This pant is closely related to the trouser and is based on its foundation. The slack fits closer to the figure than does the trouser because of shorter crotch extensions. The shortened extension causes the slight cupping under the buttocks that creates the slack's unique fit. Pant designs based on the slack have a classic appeal for most women, especially those who are uncomfortable in the loose trouser or the contour-fitted jean. The slack foundation is very versatile as it may be worn in its present form or adapted to countless other pant designs (see Pant Designs). It is a popular base for pant derivatives, such as the short, the Jamaica, and the pedal pusher, to name a few.

Slack draft

FIGURES 1 and 2
- Trace front and back trouser, omitting darts closest to side seam. Modify pattern using illustration and measurements as a guide.
- Shaded area indicates parts of the pattern that are cut away.
- Broken lines indicate original pattern shape.

- Bold lines indicate slack foundation.

Personal fit: Bottom-heavies, do not indent $\frac{1}{4}$ inch at crotch level. Knee level should measure at least 1 to $1\frac{1}{2}$ inches more than bent knee. Adjust measurement equally.

- For trueing and seam allowance instruction see pages 545–546.

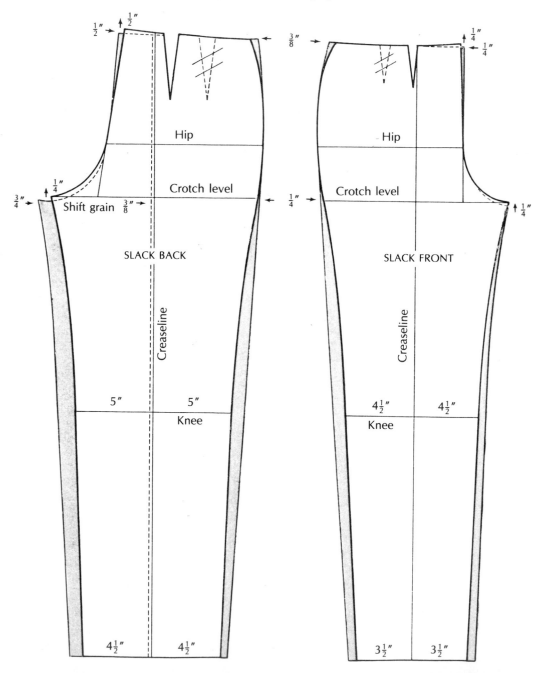

JEAN–FOUNDATION 4

Pant designs based on the jean are overwhelmingly popular. The continued success of this pant lies in the fact that the pant completely contours the abdomen and buttocks. Regardless of age or shape, most women like wearing jeans.

The jean foundation is drafted with a very short front and back crotch extension, resulting in a pant that contours the figure. The shortened extension causes a loss in crotch length, therefore the center back waist is extended (pitched) far beyond the waistline of the draft in order to gain back the crotch length measurement that Is required for a good fit.

The jean foundation is as versatile as the other pant foundations. It may be used in its basic form or modified for an endless variety of designs, such as the bell-bottom, the flare, the Wrangler, and the saddle pant, to name a few (see Pant Designs). It is also a common base for the short, the Jamaica, and other pant derivatives.

Jean draft preparation

The draft instructions are for one-half of the front and back pant. For a personal fit, follow the standard draft instructions, using *Personal Fit* instructions where applicable. Refer to Chapter 3 for measurement taking. The draft for figures with tilting waistlines will look different from the standard draft. Place a tab at Chapter 26 for pant adjustment.

Use measurements from:
- Measurement Chart or
- Company specifications, if available.

Measurements needed
- (27) Pant length to ankle _____.
- (24) Crotch depth _____.
- (23) Front hip _____. Back hip _____.
- (19) Front waist _____. Back waist _____.

Additional personal measurements

- (25) Hip depth: CF _____. CB _____.
- (27) Knee depth _____.
- (22) Abdomen (record if greater than hip): Front _____. Back _____.

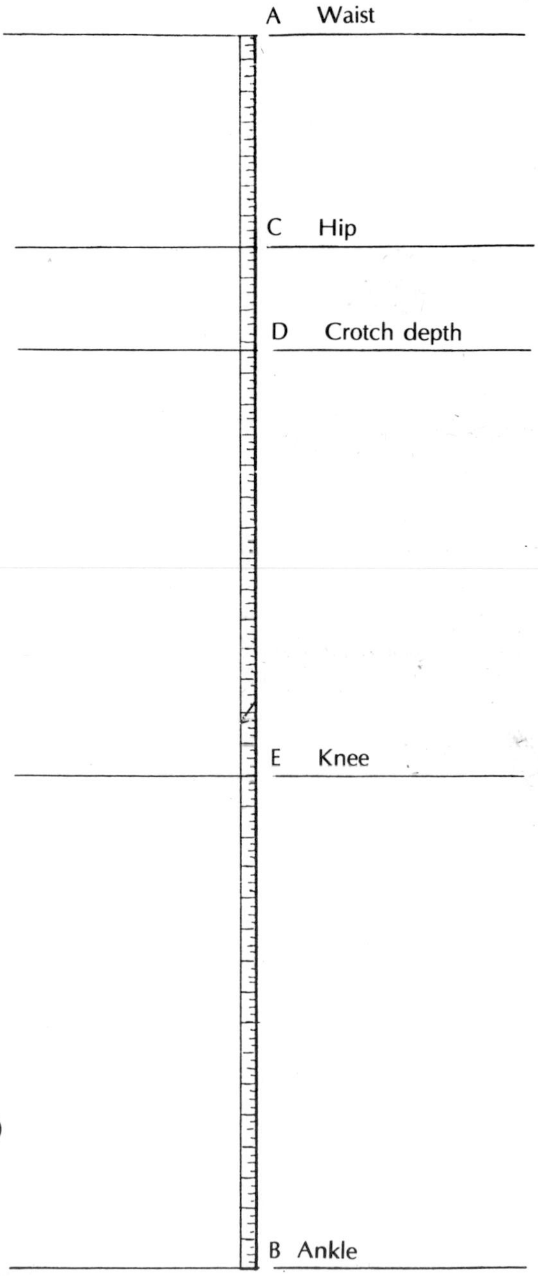

Jean draft

Key locations:

Personal fit: Locate hip and knee depth down from A when marking key locations.

FIGURE 1
A–B = Pant length.
A–D = Crotch depth. (Subtract $\frac{1}{4}$ to $\frac{1}{2}$ inch for higher crotch.)
D–C = Hip depth: One-third of D–A. (Half-sizes: one-fourth of D–A; petites: one-half of D–A.)
B–E = Knee depth: one-half of B–D plus 1 inch. Square out from both sides of A, B, C, D, and E.

A Waist
C Hip
D Crotch depth
E Knee
B Ankle

Personal fit: Use abdominal measurement if greater than hip.

FIGURE 2

Back:

C–F = Back hip plus $\frac{1}{8}$ inch.

D–G = Same as C–F.

A–H = Same as C–F.
Connect G with H.

G–X = One-half of G–H, less $\frac{1}{2}$ inch.

G–I = One-half of G–D less $\frac{3}{4}$ inch. (Add $\frac{1}{4}$ inch
for sizes over 14; subtract $\frac{1}{8}$ inch for sizes
under 10.)

Front:

C–J = Front hip plus $\frac{1}{8}$ inch.

D–K = Same as C–J.

A–L = Same as C–J.
Connect K with L.

K–X = One-half of K–L plus $\frac{1}{4}$ inch.

K–M = 2 inches. (Add $\frac{1}{4}$ inch for sizes over 14;
subtract $\frac{1}{4}$ inch for sizes under 10.)

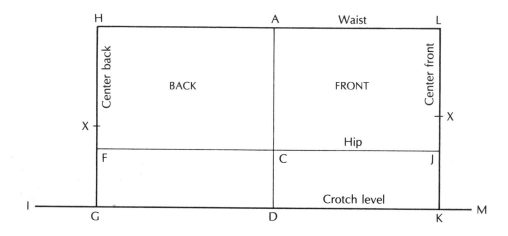

Waist and dart intake:

Dart intake instructions apply to standard and personal drafts. (If points N and P meet or overlap point A, don't be alarmed. Adjustment will be made later.)

FIGURE 3

Back:

H–N = Back waist plus $2\frac{5}{8}$ inches.

H–O = One-half of H–N.
Square down $4\frac{1}{2}$ inches.
Measure out $\frac{1}{2}$ inch each side of O. Mark.
Square up and down from dart marks.

Front:

L–P = Front waist plus $1\frac{5}{8}$ inches.

L–R = $3\frac{1}{4}$ inches.
Square down $2\frac{1}{2}$ inches.
Measure out $\frac{1}{4}$ inch each side of R. Mark.
Square up and down from dart marks.

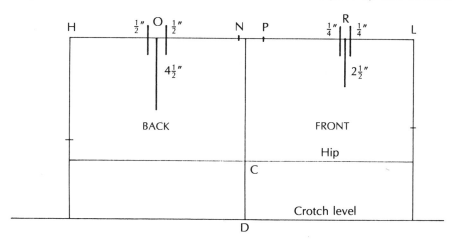

FIGURE 4

Back:

H–S = In 1¾ inches and square up 1 inch.
    Draw straight line from S to crossmark to crotch level.

G–g = 1¾-inch diagonal line.

▪ Draw curve with rule touching X, g, and at or near I, as shown.

Front:

L–T = In ½ inch and square up ¼ inch.
    Draw straight line from T to crossmark to crotch level.

K–k = 1¼-inch diagonal line.
    Draw curve with rule touching X, k, and M as shown.

For all Personal fits: See Chapter 26 for further adjustments before continuing. Place tab to find page quickly.

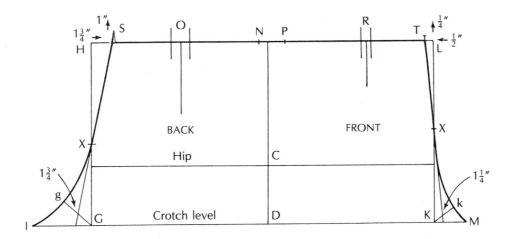

FIGURE 5

Back and front:

▪ Draw slightly curved line from S to N and T to P as shown.

▪ Draw dart legs from waistline curve to dart points from guidelines.

▪ True dart legs by adding to shorter leg. Blend with waist.

▪ Draw hip curves *just above* C to N and to P.

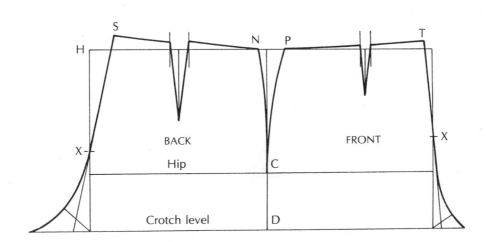

(Continued on next page)

FIGURE 6

Back:
D–U = $\frac{3}{8}$ inch.
I–V = One-half of I–U.
　　　Square up and down from V.

Front:
D–W = $\frac{3}{8}$ inch.
M–X = One-half of M–W.
　　　Square up and down from X

This completes the foundation part of the pant. A basic legline is attached to the foundation for the test fit and becomes part of the foundation when developing other pants.

Legline for test fit:
▪ Measure out from both sides of ankle and knee using measurements given. Mark. (Petites: Subtract $\frac{1}{4}$ inch from each measurement. Hips 44 and over: Add an additional $\frac{3}{4}$ inch to each side of back knee only.)

▪ *Outseams:* Draw straight line from ankle marks and knee marks to crotch level. Use flattest inward curve of skirt rule to draw legline from *just above knee* to *just past U* and W and blend outward curves to C.
▪ Blend hip, if necessary.

Note:
▪ For trueing and seam allowance instruction, see next page.

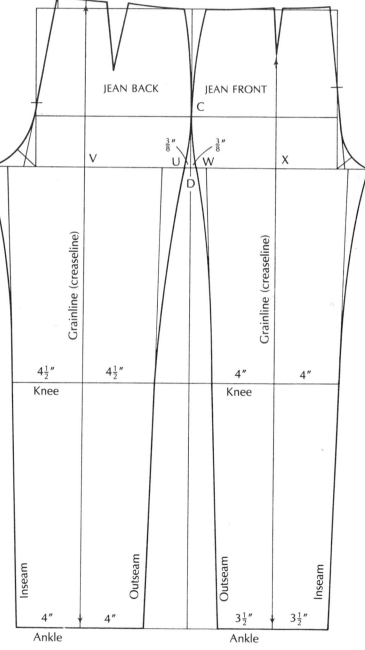

DARTLESS JEAN PANT

Use the following illustration as a guide.

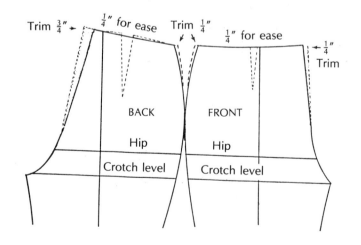

COMPLETING THE PANT PATTERN

All patterns should be trued before cutting a garment for test fitting. Use the following information for all pant foundations and pant design patterns. Adjustments for patterns with asymmetric hiplines can be found under pattern corrections, Chapter 27.

HOW TO TRUE THE PANT PATTERN

Always true the pant by beginning at hemline and working upward, in order to keep the pant garment balanced.

FIGURE 1

FIGURE 1
- Cut pant front from paper.
- Place on top of pant back, matching inseams at hem.
- Walk the pattern along inseams (using pushpin to control pattern), ending at crotch point of front pant. Mark and remove pattern. (Because of the difference of angle between front and back legline, back will be somewhat longer than front.)

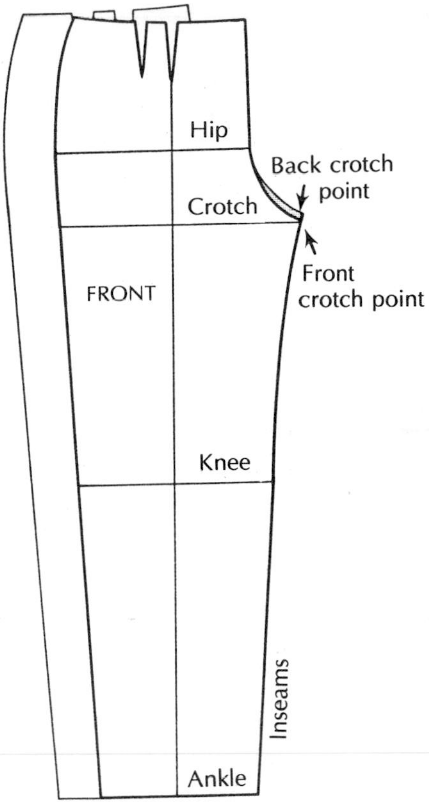

FIGURE 2
- From mark, draw new crotch curve and blend. (Shaded area is discarded from the back pant.)

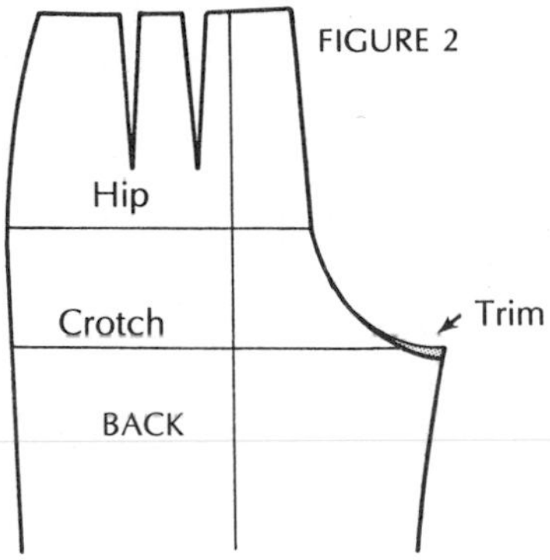

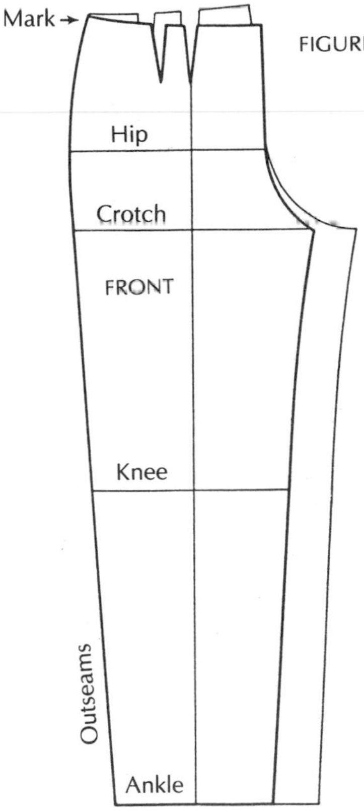

FIGURE 3
- Place front on top of back pattern, matching outseams at hemline. Walk pattern along outseam (using pushpin to help control pattern) ending at side waist. Mark and remove pattern.

FIGURE 4
- *Option 1:* Notch the hip level and ease excess in between waist and hip notch.
- *Option 2:* Trim excess above mark at side waist, and blend waistline to dart leg.
  Note: The waistband for the pant should fit tighter than a skirt waistband. The pant is eased into the waistband. Example:
- Waistline = $24\frac{1}{2}$ inches.
- Waistband length = $24\frac{1}{4}$ inches plus 1-inch extension.
- Width = $2\frac{1}{2}$ inches (to finish $1\frac{1}{4}$ inches when folded).
  For guidance see Chapter 12.

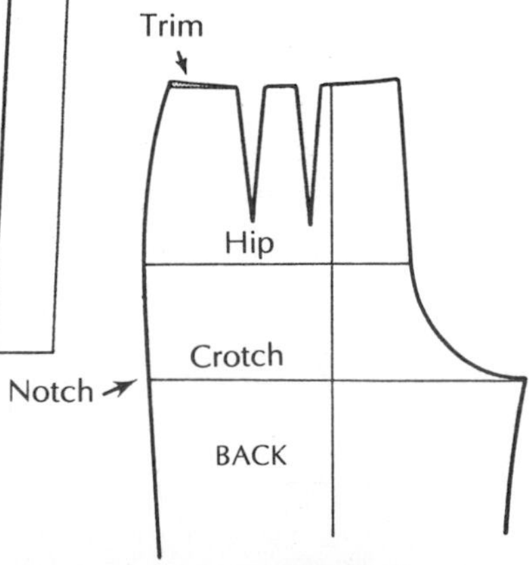

(Continued on next page)

SEAM ALLOWANCE

The pant foundations should remain seamless when used as a working pattern to develop pant designs; however, experienced patternmakers generally work with seams. If seams are to be added to pant design patterns, extend lines out from each corner of the pattern as a guide for notching. Use the following seam allowances for test fitting and for pant design patterns. When test fitting the basic foundations, add seams directly on the muslin.

FIGURE 1
- Waistline $= \frac{1}{2}$ inch.
- Inseams $= \frac{1}{2}$ inch.
- Outseams (side seams) $= \frac{1}{2}, \frac{3}{4}$ to 1 inch.

- Hemline (fold-back) = 1 inch. Fold hem and cut to inseams and outseams.
- Around crotch $= \frac{1}{2}$ inch.
- Zipper $= \frac{1}{2}, \frac{3}{4}$ to 1 inch. (Length = 1 inch longer than zipper.)
- Zipper notch $= \frac{1}{2}$ inch longer than zipper length.
- *General stitching guide for test fitting:* Stitch inseams and outseams together. Press seams open (no steam). Stitch around crotch, joining front and back pant. Allow a 7-inch opening at center back. (Zipper is not required unless desired.) Fold waistband and stitch around waist with one seam folded under and the other lying flat. (This allows the pant to be pinned together for the fitting.) Press and crease pant (no steam). Place on figure for a test fit. Refer to Chapter 27 for guidance on fitting and pattern corrections.

Note: For test fit mark grainline, hip, crotch, and knee guidelines on muslin.

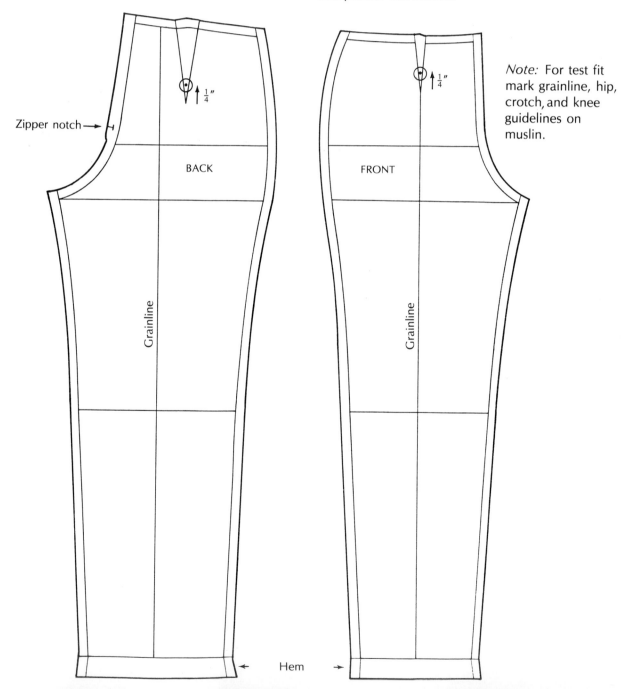

PANT DESIGNS

BOX-PLEATED CULOTTE

Design Analysis
The pant has center-front box pleat, stitched approximately 5 inches below the waist. The culotte back foundation completes the design. Additional flare is added to the center-front extension to improve the hang of the pleat.

Pattern plot and development

FIGURE 1
- Place center-front culotte foundation on paper. Secure, and square a guideline across pattern from center front as shown.
- Trace center front, crotch extension, hem, and $2\frac{1}{2}$ inches of waistline. (Broken lines indicate part of pattern not traced.) Label A and B as shown.

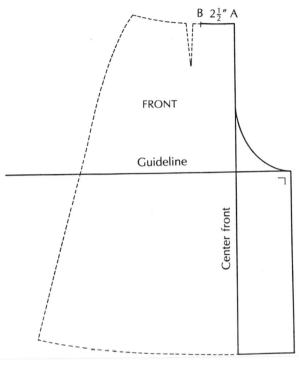

FIGURE 2
- Shift pattern 5 inches along guideline for pleat (pleat intake varies).
- Trace remaining pattern starting at the center front, as shown. Label C.
- Draw parallel lines from points A and C to hem. Connect C with B at waist and blend hem.

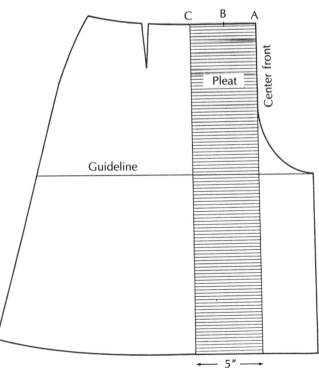

(Continued on next page)

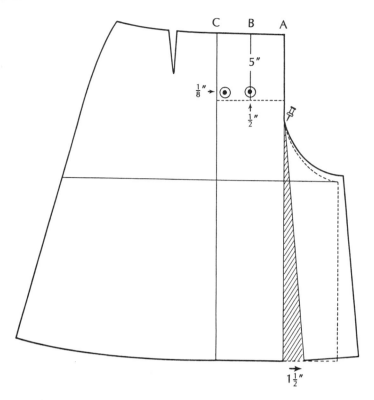

FIGURE 3

- *Pleat guidemarks:* Draw a 5-inch line down from B parallel with center front. Punch and circle $\frac{1}{2}$ inch up on line, and $\frac{1}{8}$ inch in from C line as shown.
- For additional flare at center front/center back, place culotte foundation on top of traceoff. With a pushpin at crotch curve, swing pattern $1\frac{1}{2}$ inches away from center front at hem. Trace crotch extension. Blend hemline. (Broken line indicates original extension, lined section is added fullness for flare.)
- Trace culotte back foundation to complete the design. (If back pleat is desired, follow instruction given for front.)
- Draw grain and complete pattern for test fit.

GAUCHO PANT

The American designers' version of the gaucho, originally inspired by the South American gauchos from the Pampas region, has become a classic. Variations can be developed from the basic gaucho pant silhouette.

Design Analysis

The gaucho design's length falls to just below knee level, but may vary. The pant has additional flare at the center front and back of the crotch extension. Deep-cut pockets are part of the front design detail. The gaucho can also be developed from the slack foundation.

Pattern plot and development

FIGURES 1 and 2
- Trace front and back patterns and all markings.
- Lengthen pant to 2 inches below knee level.

- Shift waist dart ½ inch toward side.
- Plot pocket section. Draw pocket style using measurements given. (See pockets, Chapter 15.)

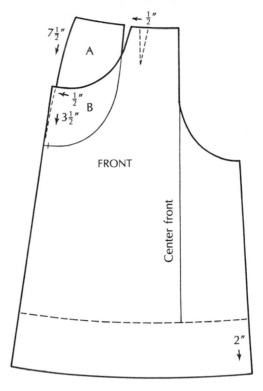

FIGURE 3
- Slip two papers underneath pocket section.
- Trace back side of pocket, section A, using original hipline shape (broken lines).
- Trace underside of pocket, section B.
- Remove paper and pencil in perforated line.

FIGURES 4 and 5
- Cut backside of pocket (section A) from paper.
- Cut underside of pocket (section B) from paper. Discard unneeded section above pocket curve (broken lines).

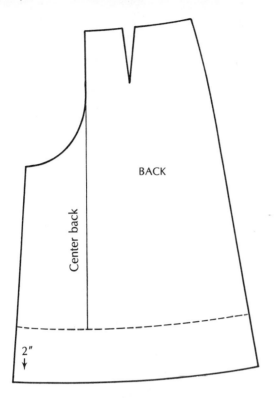

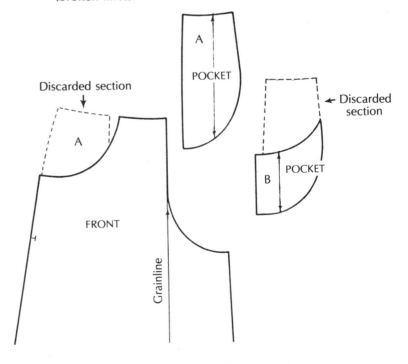

FIGURE 6 *Gaucho front:*
- Discard section A (broken line).
- Draw grain and complete pattern for test fit.

CULOTTE WITH WIDE-SWEEPING HEMLINE

To develop culottes for evening wear with wide-sweeping hemlines, use the suggested skirt silhouettes as a base. (See Chapter 12 for pattern development if needed.) Add length and crotch extensions, using instructions given for the culotte foundation, page 534.

- The slinky skirt. (Page 291.)
- Gathered waist with flare skirt. (Page 293.)
- Dirndl skirt. (Page 292.)

Pattern for culottes with full-sweeping hemlines may not fit the width of the fabric. In this instance, the overhang is separated from the pattern and placed elsewhere on the fabric. Use illustration (Figures 1 and 2) as a guide for modifying culotte for this problem. (See page 289.)

SLINKY

GATHERED FLARE

DIRNDL

Selvage

BACK

Selvage

Guide notch →

Section A

Section B

Width of fabric

Notch ½"

Section B

← 1"

TIERED CULOTTE

Design Analysis

The design features a three-tiered pant without side seams. Each tier is gathered slightly, with the bottom tier having the greatest amount of fullness.

Pattern plot and development

FIGURE 1

- Trace culotte front and back with side seams joined. Include all markings. Draw line to connect waistline at side waists. Extend length, keeping line parallel with original hemline.
- Draw tiers parallel with hemline as follows:
    Top tier hemline at mid-thigh location.
    Middle tier hemline at mid-calf location.
    Bottom tier extends to hemline.
- Draw slash lines on second and third tiers for spreading, as shown.

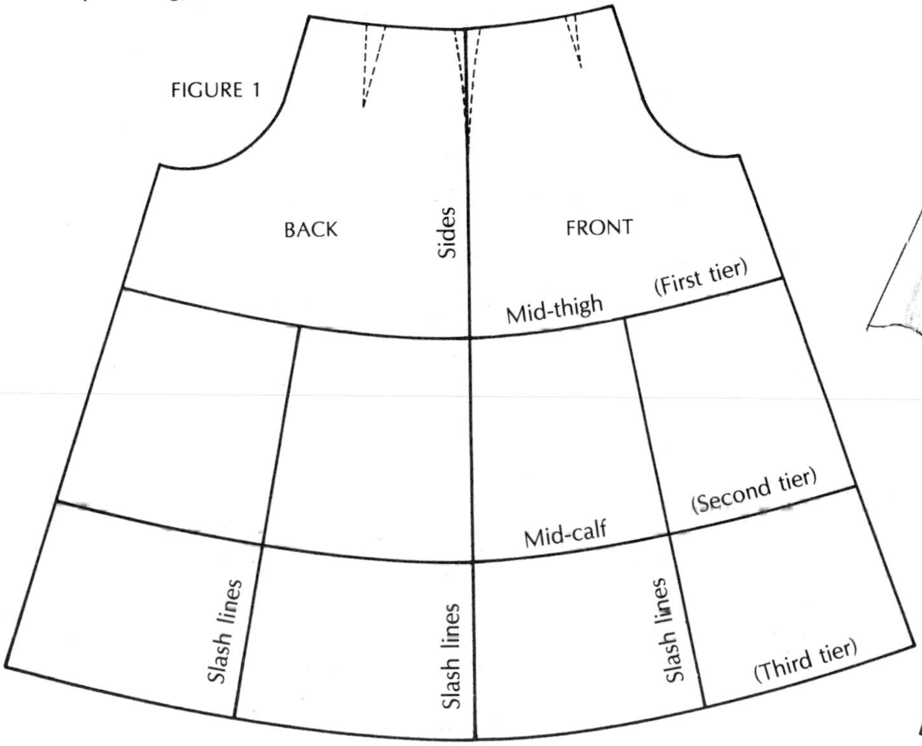

FIGURE 1

BACK · Sides · FRONT

Mid-thigh · (First tier)

(Second tier)

Mid-calf

Slash lines · Slash lines · Slash lines · (Third tier)

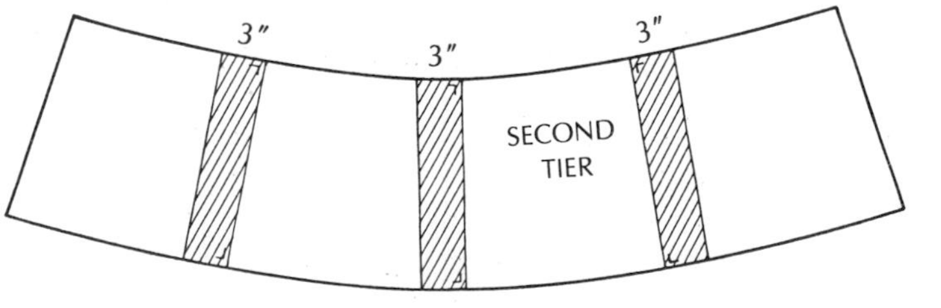

3" · 3" · 3"

SECOND TIER

FIGURE 3

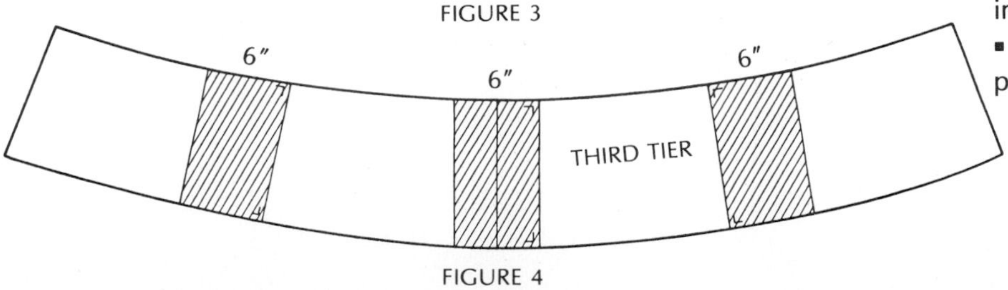

6" · 6" · 6"

6"

THIRD TIER

FIGURE 4

FIGURES 2, 3, and 4

- Cut and separate tiers. Cut through slash lines.

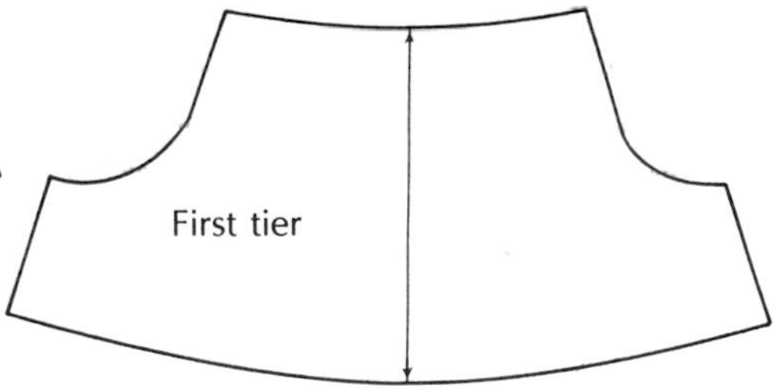

First tier

FIGURE 2

- *Second tier:* As a guide for adding fullness, square out 3 inches from top and bottom of each section as it is traced. *Third tier:* Repeat, adding 6 inches between spaces.
- Draw grainlines and complete pattern for test fit.

PLEATED TROUSER

Design Analysis
The pant design resembles a traditional trouser with a full front pleat (added fullness) and a smaller companion pleat (dart equivalent), seam pockets, and a basic waistline belt. The decorative belt is not part of the design. The pant back has no design detailing. This design is based on the trouser foundation.

Pattern plot and development

FIGURE 1
- Trace trouser front from grainline at hem to first dart leg (bold line). Omit section indicated by broken lines. Trace trouser back pattern to complete design (not illustrated).

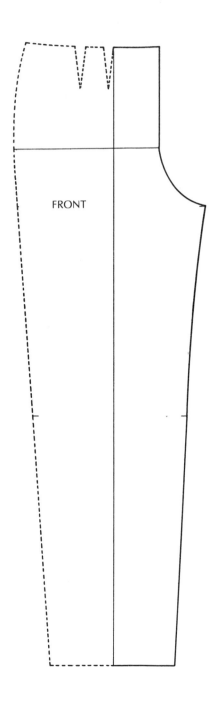

FRONT

FIGURE 2

- With pushpin on grainline at hem, swing pattern out 2 inches (or more for deeper pleat) from tracing. Trace remaining pattern to dart leg as shown. Remove pattern.
- Notch each side of opening for pleat control (lined area). Transfer dart excess to other dart by placing notch $\frac{1}{2}$ inch out from dart leg as shown. This is the second pleat (shaded area).
- Blend hemline.

FIGURE 3

- Draw pocket details using measurements given. (See instructions for pockets, Chapter 15, for more information.)
- Slip two papers under pocket section and trace two copies (for back side and underside).

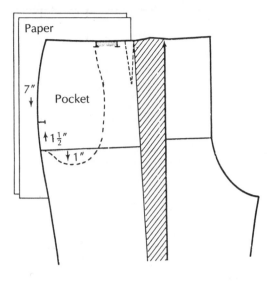

FIGURES 4 and 5

- Remove paper. Trace pockets and label as shown.
- Draw grainline. Cut patterns from paper and complete pattern for test fit.

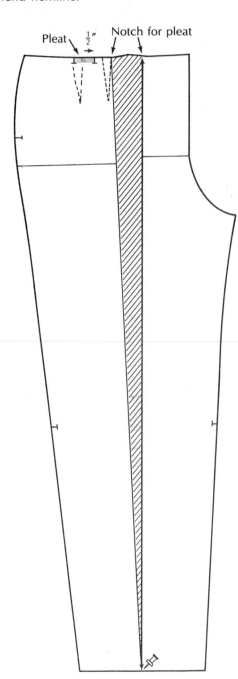

BACK SIDE

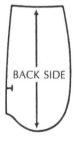

UNDER SIDE

BAGGY PANT

Design Analysis

Baggy is a full, wide, step-in pant, lengthened and cuffed without side seams. A rope drawstring is pulled through a buttonhole at waist. An envelope pocket with an attached fold-over flap is placed between knee level of front and back pant. This design is based on the trouser foundation.

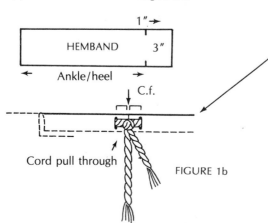

FIGURE 2 *Hemband:*
▪ Length = at least ankle/heel measurement. Width = 3 inches (finished width = $1\frac{1}{2}$ inches). If button and buttonhole are desired, add 1-inch extension; otherwise, the band is seamed together.

Pattern plot and development

FIGURE 1a and 1b
▪ Draw a horizontal guideline across the paper, 15 inches below paper edge.
▪ Place front and back patterns on the paper, matching crotch levels with guideline. Space patterns at crotch 1 to 3 inches (or more) for added fullness.
▪ Trace patterns (indicated by broken lines for clarity of design detailing).

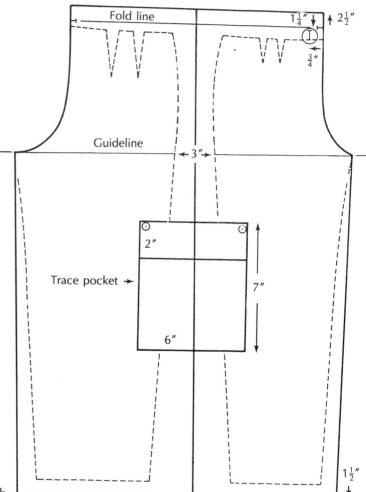

Modify as follows:
▪ Add $1\frac{1}{2}$ inch to length of pant for overhang.
▪ Extend center front $2\frac{1}{2}$ inches and square across pattern. Draw a line to connect with center back. (When folded it becomes a casing for cord pull through. Figure 1b.)
▪ Mark notch for fold-over $1\frac{1}{4}$ inches down from top.
▪ Mark buttonhole placement $\frac{3}{4}$ inch in from center front on extension, as shown.
▪ Square down from crotch points to hem.
▪ Draw pocket using measurements given.
▪ Mark punch and circles $\frac{1}{2}$ inch down and in from corners.

PULL-ON PANT WITH SELF-CASING

Design Analysis
A pull-on pant has elastic inserted in self-casing that causes slight gathering at the waistline, replacing darts. Pant should be cut in a firm knit and modified to offset stretch. The pull-on pant can be developed on any pant foundation. The slack pant is illustrated.

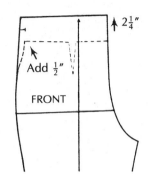

FIGURE 5 *Casing:*
• Should be $\frac{1}{4}$ inch greater than elastic to facilitate insertion. Use safety pin or bodkin to insert elastic.

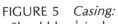

Elastic → Casing

Pattern plot and development

Measurement needed
• (2) Waistline circumference _____.

FIGURES 1 and 2
• Trace front and back of slack foundation.
• Extend waist $2\frac{1}{4}$ inches (for 1-inch wide elastic).
• *Elastic:* Width = 1 inch. Length = waist measurement less $1\frac{1}{2}$ inches. Use $\frac{1}{2}$ inch for overlap.

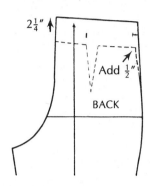

$2\frac{1}{4}''$ Add $\frac{1}{2}''$ BACK   Add $\frac{1}{2}''$ FRONT $2\frac{1}{4}''$

FIGURES 3 and 4
• When cut in a firm knit, modify pattern (shaded areas) by following illustrations.
(For more information concerning knits, see Chapter 25.)
• Draw grainline and complete pattern for test fit.

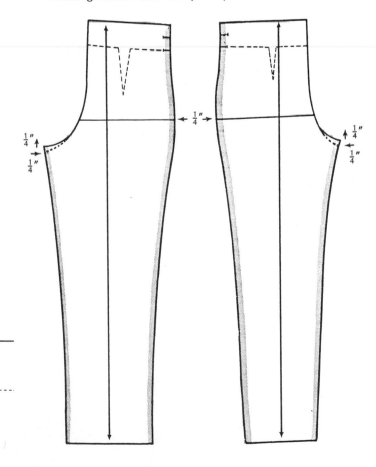

HIGH-WAISTED PANT

Pattern plot and development

FIGURES 1 and 2
- Trace front and back pant and all markings.
- Flip patterns upward touching center front, center back, and sides at waistline. (Waistline is shown as broken lines.)
- Trace $2\frac{1}{2}$ inches up from waist of flipped pattern; include darts. (Broken lines are untraced part of pattern.)
- Remove pattern and draw line across top, parallel with waist.
- *Darts:* Extend line from dart points through center of darts ending at high waist. Measure out $\frac{1}{4}$ inch on each side of darts for back, and $\frac{1}{8}$ inch on each side of dart for front at high waistline. Draw new dart legs to waist, as shown.

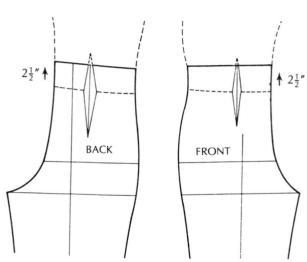

FIGURE 3
- Punch and circle darts as shown. Notch dart legs at high waist.

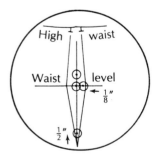

FIGURE 4   *Facing:*
- Trace 3 inches of front and back waist section.

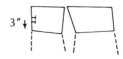

Design Analysis

Waistline extends above the natural waist. Pant has cuffed hem, zipper back, and separate suspenders. The high-waisted effect can be developed on any pant foundation. The jean pant is illustrated. (Cuff not included.)

FIGURES 5 and 6
- Close dart legs and trace with front facing cut on fold. Blend as shown.
- Draw grainline and complete pattern for test fit.

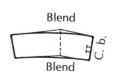

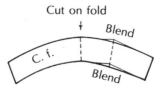

HIP-HUGGER

Design Analysis

The pant waistline falls 3 inches below the normal waist. A $1\frac{1}{2}$-inches-wide band simulates a belt. Fly front zipper opening. The hip-hugger effect can be developed on any pant foundation. The jean pant is illustrated.

Pattern plot and development

FIGURES 1 and 2

- Trace jean front and back and all markings.
- Draw a parallel line 3 inches below front and back waist (varies). (Broken line indicates unneeded sections.)
- Draw a parallel line $1\frac{1}{2}$ inches wide for belt (varies). Belt is indicated by angle lines.
- Cut and discard unneeded sections.

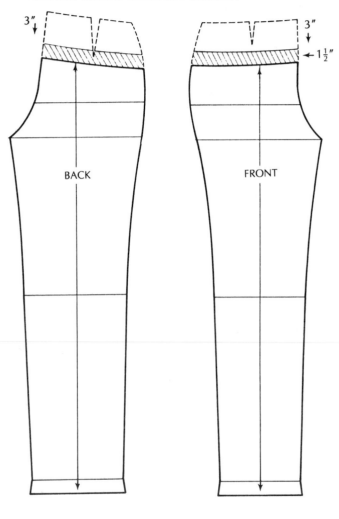

FIGURES 3 and 4 *Band:*

- Cut band section from pant. Place front and back bands together at the side and trace two copies. On one copy, extend front band 1 inch on the left side for button, with the other copy ending at center front for buttonhole. Blend.
- Notch side seams, center front and back as shown.

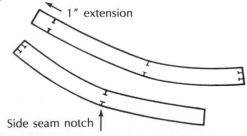

1″ extension

Side seam notch ↑

FIGURE 5 *Fly front:*

- Length = $6\frac{1}{2}$ inches (for a 5-inch zipper), width = $1\frac{1}{2}$ inches.
- Draw grainline and complete pattern for test fit.

Fly

$1\frac{1}{2}$″

$6\frac{1}{2}$″

JEAN WITH BACK YOKE

Design Analysis

Design 1 features a dropped waist, contoured band with belt loops and a V-shaped yoke and patch pockets in back. Legline is tapered. Design 2 has all the same features except that the hemline is widened to fit over a boot. The yoke effect can be developed on any pant foundation. The jean pant is illustrated.

DESIGN 1   DESIGN 2

Measurements needed
- (32) Ankle/heel _____,
- (30) Knee bent measurement _____.

Pattern plot and development

FIGURES 1 and 2

- Trace jean front and back and all markings.
- Draw a parallel line 1½ inches (or more) below waist for the belt section (lined area).
- Reduce legline to equal ankle/heel and knee bent measurements. (Divide measurements into fourths and measure out equally from both sides of grainline at hem and knee level.)
- *Back yoke:* Center back length = 3 inches. Side length = 1½ inches. Draw connecting line.
- *Pocket:* Draw a rectangular pocket (5 inches × 7 (or larger) inches) curving the bottom side as shown. Place approximately 1 inch below yoke.
- Cut and separate patterns. Save sections indicated by lined area for contour belt.

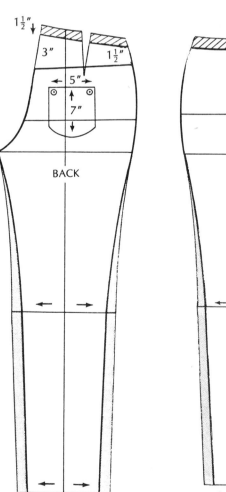

BACK   FRONT

FIGURES 3 and 4

- Trim remaining dart excess from both sides of the front waist, and at the center back waist. (Broken lines indicate original pattern.)

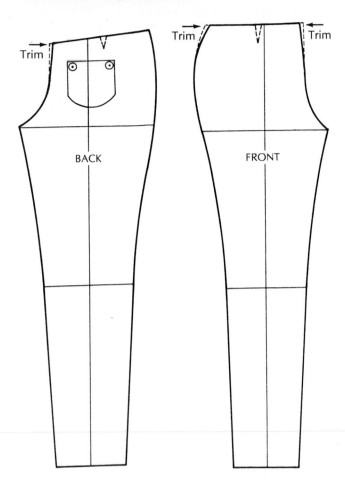

BACK

FRONT

Trim

Trim

Trim

FIGURES 7 and 8

- *Contour belt:* Close dart legs. Tape. Place front and back sides together and tape. Trace four copies (two copies each for right and left side). The center back belt will be seamed. Draw 1-inch extension on left side belt for button attachment (Figure 7). Belt for right side will end at the center front (Figure 8). Notch between the center front and center back for belt loop placement. Notch side seam.
- *Belt loop:* Cut four strips 1 inch $\times$ $1\frac{3}{4}$ inches, plus seams (not illustrated).

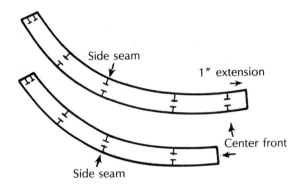

Side seam

1" extension

Center front

Side seam

FIGURE 5 *Back yoke:*

- Close dart and trace.

YOKE

FIGURE 6 *Pocket:*

- Slip paper underneath pocket section and trace, or draft pocket using measurements given. On pant pattern, punch and circle pocket placement $\frac{1}{4}$ inch from corners as shown in Figure 3.

POCKET

FIGURE 9 *Design 2:*

- Measure in $\frac{1}{2}$ inch at knee level and out 1 inch at each side of hemline. Draw curved legline as shown.
- Draw grainlines and complete pattern for test fit.

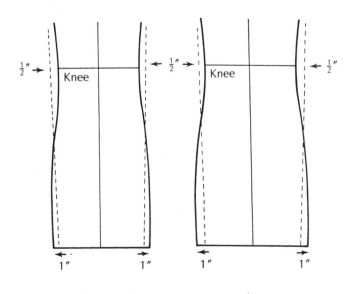

$\frac{1}{2}"$

Knee

$\frac{1}{2}"$

$\frac{1}{2}"$

Knee

$\frac{1}{2}"$

1"

1"

1"

1"

CONTOUR PANT WITH CREASELINE FLARE

Design Analysis

Contouring for this pant design is achieved by removing excess from under buttocks via a seam replacing the back creaseline. Pant hemline flares out at side and back seamlines, dropping low at center back and rising at center front. This design is based on the slack foundation.

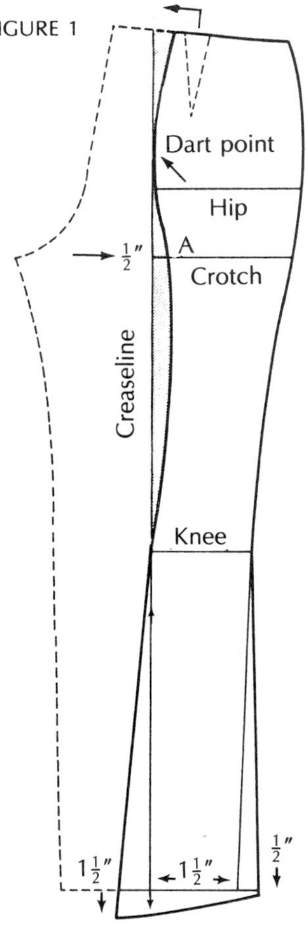

Pattern plot and development

FIGURE 1

- Trace pant back from side seam to creaseline (broken line indicates untraced section). Shift dart to creaseline so that it can be removed through the styleline.
- Measure in $\frac{1}{2}$ inch from creaseline at crotch level. Label A.
- *Buttocks contour:* From point A, draw a slightly inward curve blending with an outward curve to dart point. Continue curve from A to knee level.
- *Hemline flare:* Extend hemline $1\frac{1}{2}$ inches (more or less). Measure down $1\frac{1}{2}$ inches from creaseline. Mark. Measure down $\frac{1}{2}$ inch at side seam. Mark. Draw straight lines from marks to knee levels. Draw curved hemline.

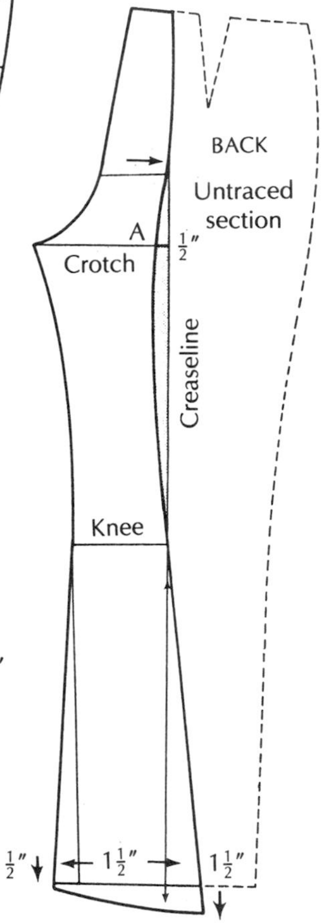

FIGURE 1

FIGURE 2

- Trace pant back from inseam to grainline (broken line indicates untraced section). Repeat the process for shaping pant.

FIGURE 3

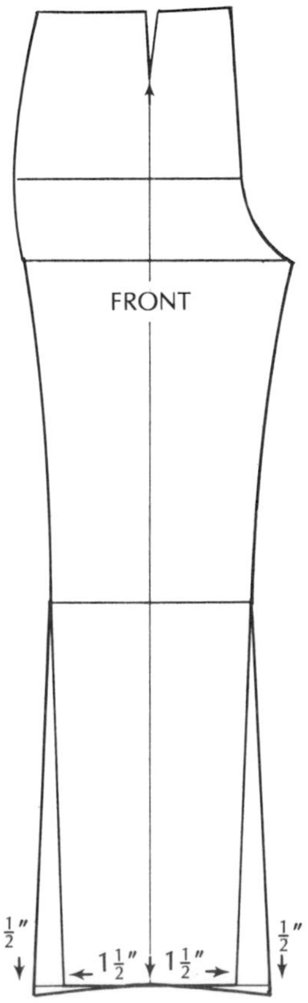

FIGURE 3

- Trace pant front. Extend hemline $1\frac{1}{2}$ inches at side and inseam. Measure down $\frac{1}{2}$ inch at each end. Draw straight lines from each mark to knee level. Blend inward curve at hemline as shown.
- Cut pant patterns from paper, discarding unneeded sections (shaded areas). Draw grainlines and complete pattern for test fit.

PANT WITH FLARED LEG

Design Analysis

The hemlines of the three designs have a flared or bell-shaped effect, starting at varying locations along the legline. Flared leglines can be developed on trouser, slack, or jean foundations.

Pattern plot and development

The width or flare of a pant is usually determined by the fashion silhouette or personal preference. Following is one method for adding width to the hemline:

FIGURES 1 and 2

- Add length to pant (approximately 1 inch).
- Measure the *back* crotch level, divide in half, and record _____. Using this amount, measure out from each side of creaseline at hem. Mark.
- Draw line from marks at hem to any location along legline, using illustration as a guide.
- Square in from legline, blending to grainline at hem of pant as shown.
- Repeat instructions for front, subtracting $\frac{1}{2}$ inch from measurement.
- Draw grainline and complete pattern for test fit.

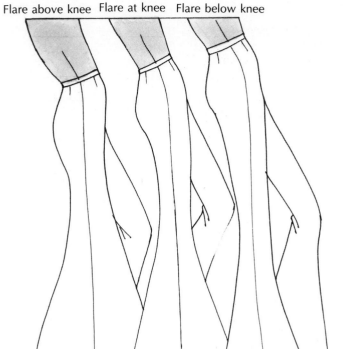

Flare above knee Flare at knee Flare below knee

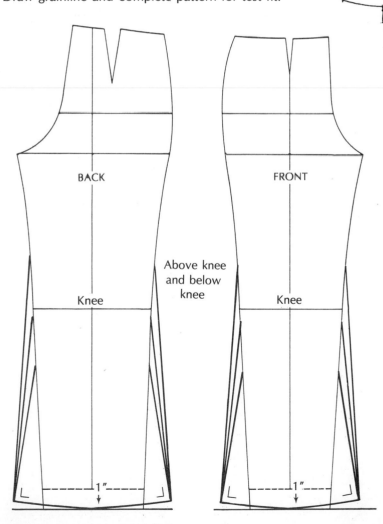

BACK

Knee

FRONT

Above knee and below knee

Knee

1"

1"

PANT WITH CURVED HEMLINE

Design Analysis

Hemline curves upward in front and downward toward center back. This legline can be developed on the trouser, slack, or jean foundations.

Pattern modification

FIGURES 1 and 2
- The following are approximate measurements. Extend grainline at hem $1\frac{1}{4}$ inches on pant front and back. Square lines across paper from the creaseline (broken line).
- *Front:* Measure up $\frac{1}{2}$ inch from creaseline.
- *Back:* Measure down $\frac{3}{4}$ inch from creaseline.
- Shape hemline with a curved rule, as shown. Hemline requires a facing $1\frac{1}{2}$ inches wide (not illustrated).

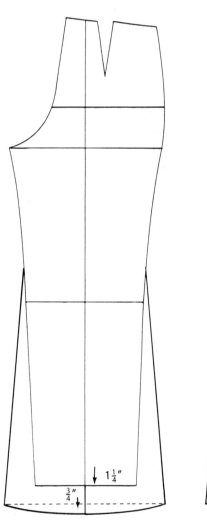

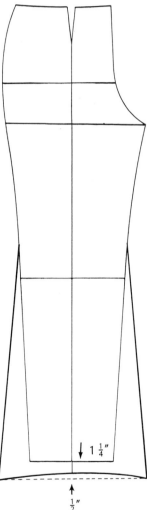

KNICKERS

Design Analysis

Pant length ends below the knee where it is gathered slightly into a wide band buttoning at the side. Short pants can be developed on any pant foundation. The slack is illustrated.

Pattern plot and development

FIGURES 1 and 2
▪ Trace pant front and back to $1\frac{1}{2}$ inches below knee level. Include all markings. (Add to sides if fuller leg is desired.)

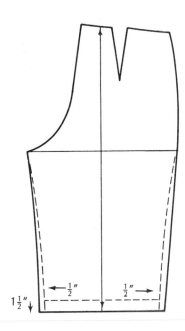 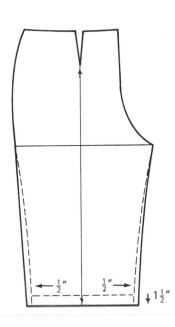

FIGURE 3 *Band:*
▪ Knee measurement plus 2 inches (1 inch for ease, and 1 inch for button extension).
▪ Complete pattern for test fit.

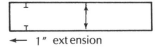

← 1" extension

PLEATED COWL-DRAPED PANT

Design Analysis

Three deep-pleated cowls form along the front and back of each leg. The elongated legline is pushed up and held by the ankle. The pleated cowl effect can be developed on the trouser or slack foundation. The trouser pant is illustrated.

Measurement needed
- (32) Ankle/heel _____.

Pattern plot and development

FIGURES 1 and 2
- Trace pant front and back. Crossmark crotch level and midpoint between crotch and knee. Draw knee and grainline.
- Extend length 5 inches.
- Equalize front and back dart intake. Add front and back dart excess together and divide into fourths. Adjust each dart to equal this amount and redraw dart leg ending $4\frac{1}{2}$ inches below waist. (Broken lines indicate original darts.)
- Draw slash lines from each dart point to crotch mark and midpoint mark.
- Taper hemlines to equal ankle/heel measurement. Mark.
- Square up from hem marks.
- Draw new legline as shown. (Shaded area is original legline.)
- Cut pants from paper.

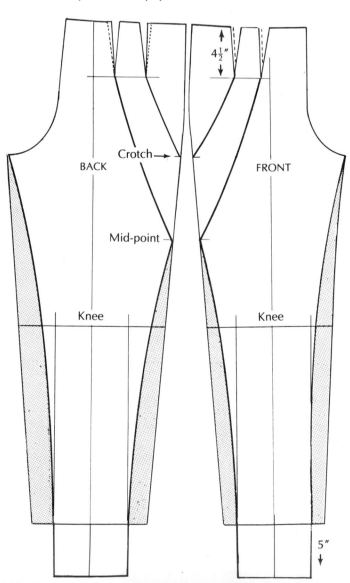

FIGURE 3 *Pant front:*
- Cut slash lines to, not through, side.
- Place on paper and spread dart points 1 inch. Secure pattern.
- Extend grainline 3 inches up from waist (label A) and square out.

FIGURE 4
- Place pushpins where shown.
- Separate pattern at side seam and spread until side waist touches square line. Label B. Space sections equally and tape. Label D and E.
- Length from B to C equals A to B. Square down from C, touching D, and draw outward curve from D, touching E, ending at knee level. Blend.
- Repeat for back.

FIGURE 5
- Notch for front and back pleats. Raise pleat centers $\frac{1}{8}$ inch and connect to notches.

FIGURES 6 and 7
- Complete front and back patterns pattern for test fit.

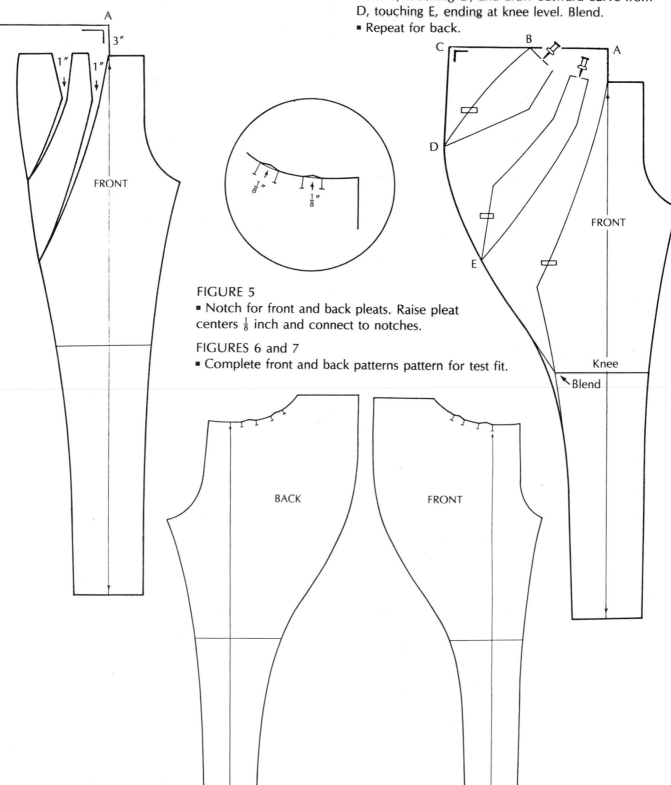

CLOWN PANT

Design Analysis
A stylized pant with added fullness is gathered evenly into the waistband, giving a puffy effect, tapering to a narrow hemline at ankle level. Scarf is pulled through a stylized waistband. The clown pant can be developed on the trouser or slack foundation (trouser is illustrated).

FIGURE 2 *Belt:*
- Mark buttonholes of basic belt 3 inches out from center, spaced 2 inches apart for pull-through scarf. A regular belt may replace stylized version shown.
- Draw continued grainline through pant and complete pattern for test fit.

Measurement needed
- (32) Ankle/heel _____.

Pattern plot and development
FIGURE 1
- Trace trouser front and back, and grainline from knee to hem level.
- Taper hemline by subtracting ankle/heel measurement equally from hemline measurement.
- For a tighter hemline, an opening for a zipper or button is required for foot entry (unless stretch knit is used).
- Cut patterns from paper.
- Cut slash lines from darts to knee, and from knee to inseams and outseams (hinge effect).
- Place slashed pattern on paper, spreading upward at knee as shown. Spread approximately 5 inches (may be more or less).
- Square up from side seam at hip level for additional fullness as shown.
- Retrace outline of pant. Blend across waistline.

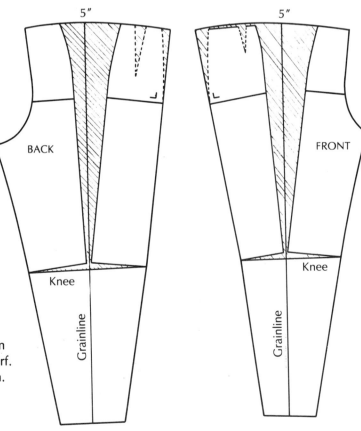

GEOMETRIC-DRAPED PANT

Design Analysis
Two designs are featured, with cowl folds appearing on the inside legline of Design 1 and on the outside of Design 2. Design 1 only is discussed. Design 2 should be developed using the same concept.

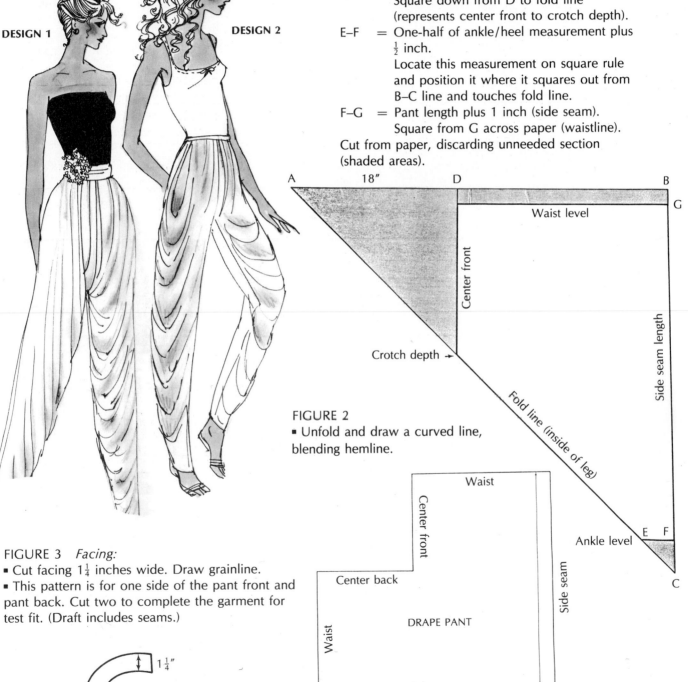

DESIGN 1

DESIGN 2

Measurements needed
- (32) Ankle/heel _____.
- (27) Pant length _____.

Paper needed: 45-inch square. Fold paper to form a triangle.

Pattern plot and development

FIGURE 1
Label corners of triangle A, B, and C as shown.
A–D = 18 inches.
Square down from D to fold line (represents center front to crotch depth).
E–F = One-half of ankle/heel measurement plus $\frac{1}{2}$ inch.
Locate this measurement on square rule and position it where it squares out from B–C line and touches fold line.
F–G = Pant length plus 1 inch (side seam).
Square from G across paper (waistline).
Cut from paper, discarding unneeded section (shaded areas).

FIGURE 2
- Unfold and draw a curved line, blending hemline.

FIGURE 3 *Facing:*
- Cut facing $1\frac{1}{4}$ inches wide. Draw grainline.
- This pattern is for one side of the pant front and pant back. Cut two to complete the garment for test fit. (Draft includes seams.)

FACING

PANT DERIVATIVES

Pant derivative is a term used to describe the length of a pant whenever its original hemline is raised or lowered. Pant lengths can be changed on any of the foundation patterns; however, the slack and jean are the ones most commonly used for this purpose. For convenience, it is recommended that pant length markings be placed on all foundation patterns. When developing the pedal pusher, toreador, and Capri lengths, provide an opening in the side seam at the ankle for ease of foot entry if the circumference at the hem is less than the ankle/heel measurement. Illustrated below are some of the more common pant lengths, along with their style names, which have been derived from pant foundations .

Shorty-short. 1½ inches below crotch at inseam, ending 1 to 1½ inches above crotch level at side seam (broken line).
    Short. 2 inches below crotch level.
    Jamaica. Midway between crotch and knee.

Bermuda. Between Jamaica and knee.
Pedal pusher. 2 inches down from knee.
Toreador. Between knee and ankle.
Capri. 1 inch above ankle.

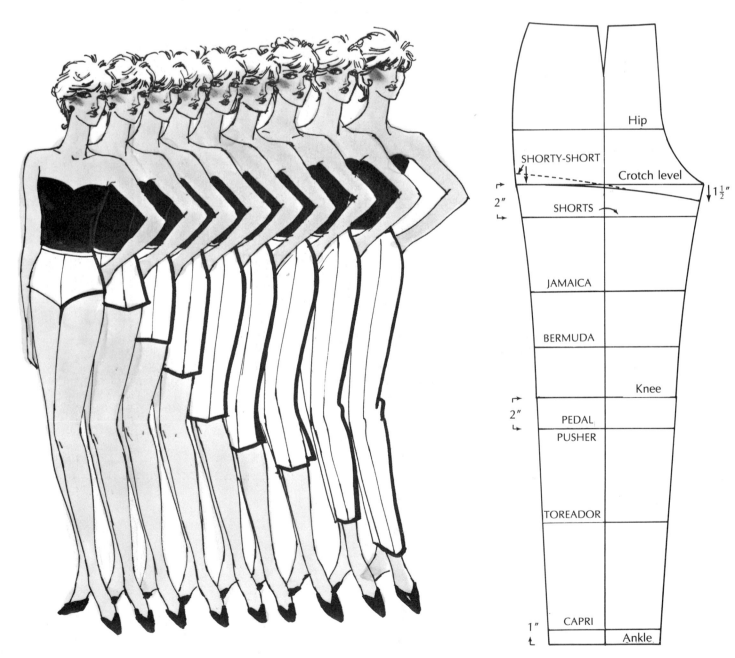

SHORTY-SHORTS

FIGURES 1 and 2
- Trace front and back to shorty-short styleline. Crossmark. Use pushpin to transfer the curve of legline within the pattern frame.
- Remove pattern and pencil in curve line.
- Draw slash line, starting 3 inches from inseam.
- Cut from paper.

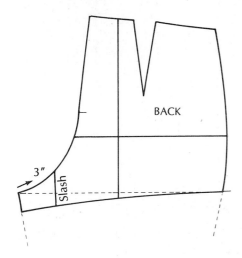

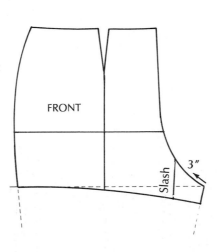

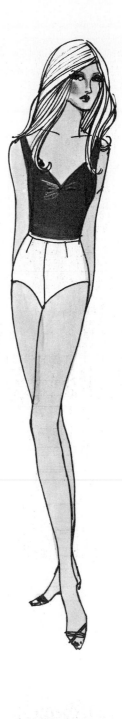

FIGURES 3 and 4
- Cut slash from leg to, not through, crotch curve.
- Overlap ½ inch. Tape.
- Place on paper and trace. (Broken lines indicate original pattern.)
- Blend new legline and crotch curve. Reduce side seams ¼ inch. Mark notches as shown.

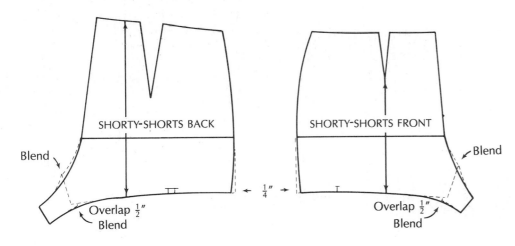

FIGURES 5 and 6
- Develop facings as shown.

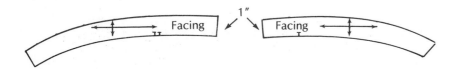

SHORTS

FIGURES 1 and 2
- Trace front and back pant to shorts length. Include all markings.
- *Inseam:* Measure in $\frac{1}{4}$ inch.
- *Outseam:* Measure in $\frac{1}{2}$ inch and blend with hipline.
- *Foldback:* Add 1 to $1\frac{1}{2}$ inches to length of pant. Fold along hemline and trace sides. Unfold and pencil in shape.
- Complete pattern for a test fit. (Adjust legline on figure, if required.)

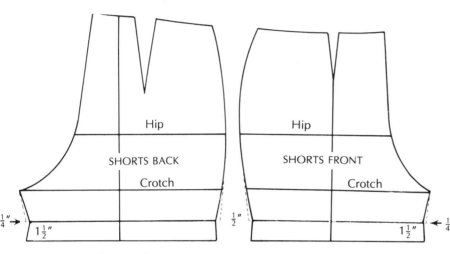

SHORTS   JAMAICAS   BERMUDAS

JAMAICAS

FIGURE 1
Instructions apply to front and back. Front only is illustrated.
- Trace front and back to Jamaica length. Include all markings.
- *Inseam:* Measure in $\frac{1}{4}$ inch.
- *Outseam:* Measure in $\frac{3}{8}$ inches. Redraw legline to crotch level.
- *Foldback:* Add $1\frac{1}{2}$ inches to length of pant. Fold along hemline and trace sides. Unfold and pencil in shape.
- Complete pattern for a test fit. (Adjust legline on figure, if required.)

BERMUDAS

FIGURE 1

Instructions apply to front and back. Front only is illustrated.

- Trace front and back to Bermuda length. Include all markings.
- *Inseam:* Measure in $\frac{1}{2}$ inch.
- *Outseam:* Measure in $\frac{1}{2}$ inch. Redraw legline to crotch level.
- *Foldback:* Add 1 to $1\frac{1}{2}$ inches to length of pant. Fold along hemline and trace sides. Unfold and pencil in shape.
- Complete pattern for test fit. (Adjust legline on figure, if required.)

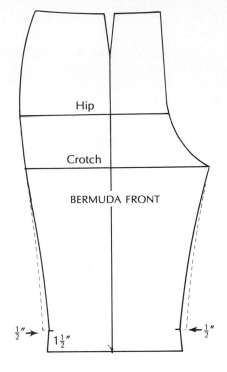

Hip

Crotch

BERMUDA FRONT

$\frac{1}{2}''$ $1\frac{1}{2}''$ $\frac{1}{2}''$

PEDAL PUSHERS   TOREADOR   CAPRI

PEDAL PUSHERS

FIGURE 1

- Trace front and back to pedal pusher length. Include all markings.
- *Inseam:* Measure in $\frac{1}{2}$ inch.
- *Outseam:* Measure in $\frac{1}{2}$ inch. Redraw legline to crotch level.

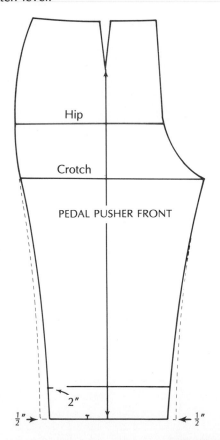

Hip

Crotch

PEDAL PUSHER FRONT

$2''$

$\frac{1}{2}''$ $\frac{1}{2}''$

(Continued on next page)

• *Hemline:* Place notch at least 2 inches up from outseam for opening for bent knee action. Add 1 to 1½-inch hem. For fold-back facing see instructions given for Bermuda pant, or make separate facing, as follows:

FIGURE 2

▪ *Facing:* Make facing by placing front and back inseams together and tracing legline 2½ inches up from hem. Remove pattern. To finish facing, draw line parallel with hem.

▪ Complete pattern for test fit. (Adjust legline on figure, if required.)

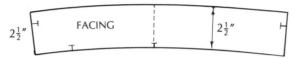

TOREADOR

FIGURE 1

Instructions apply to front and back. Front only is illustrated.

▪ Trace front and back to toreador length. Include all markings.

▪ *Inseam:* Measure in 1 inch.

▪ *Outseam:* Measure in 1 inch. Redraw legline to crotch level.

▪ For fold-back or separate facing, see instruction given for the Bermuda or pedal pusher.

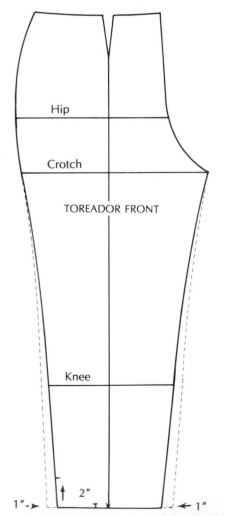

CAPRI

FIGURE 1

Instructions apply to front and back. Front only is illustrated.

▪ Trace front and back to Capri length.

▪ *Inseam:* Measure in 1 inch.

▪ *Outseam:* Measure in 1 inch. Redraw legline to crotch level.

▪ For fold-back or separate facing, see instruction given for the Bermuda or pedal pusher.

▪ Complete pattern for test fit. (Adjust legline on figure, if required.)

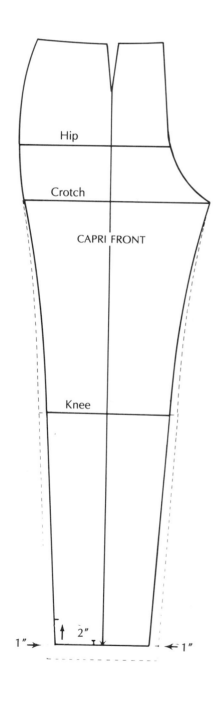

DESIGN VARIATIONS

The following practice designs are included to stimulate the imagination of the designer and the patternmaker. Each design utilizes concepts and instructions from previously developed skirt and pant designs. For example, Design 1 is based on a flared skirt and Design 8 on the baggy pant. Each pant design may be developed to any length desired. If the finished design looks like the sketch it represents, the pattern was correctly developed.

DESIGN 1

DESIGN 8

JUMPSUIT FOUNDATIONS

The jumpsuit can be based on any of the four pant foundation patterns (or any pant design). It can be developed as a one-piece or two-piece jumpsuit foundation (seamed at waistline) or as a combination of both. Once developed, this foundation should *not* be altered but used as a base for other designs. Jumpsuit designs with sleeves are developed from the basic or dartless sleeve. Some suggested styles are illustrated at the end of the jumpsuit series.

TROUSER/SLACK JUMPSUIT FOUNDATIONS

Note: The instructions apply to both the trouser and slack jumpsuit foundations. Trouser pant is illustrated. (See jumpsuit sketch, page 576.)

FIGURES 1 and 2
▪ Trace front and back torso and all markings. Crossmark midway between waist and hip. Allow room for pant length and width.
▪ Place pant front and back on traced torso, matching hip level and a point midway between crotch and waist at the center lines of the torso.
▪ *Important:* Creaseline of pant *must* be parallel with the center front and center back of torso. If not, place pushpin on pant at crossmark and pivot pattern, raising or lowering pant until creaseline grain is parallel with center front and back of torso (not illustrated).
▪ Trace pant pattern from hem to hipline. Transfer creaseline of pant to paper underneath with a pushpin. (Broken line indicates untraced pant pattern above hip level.)
▪ Remove pattern. Draw grainline through pant and torso.
▪ Lower front and back crotch ½ inch. Blend crotch and hipline of pant with torso.
▪ For convenience, draw bust circumference and contour lines on bodice (see Chapter 9).
▪ Hipline of torso extending beyond hipline of pant is trimmed (shaded area). Blend.
▪ Complete pattern for test fit. (Draw hip, crotch, and knee lines on muslin.)

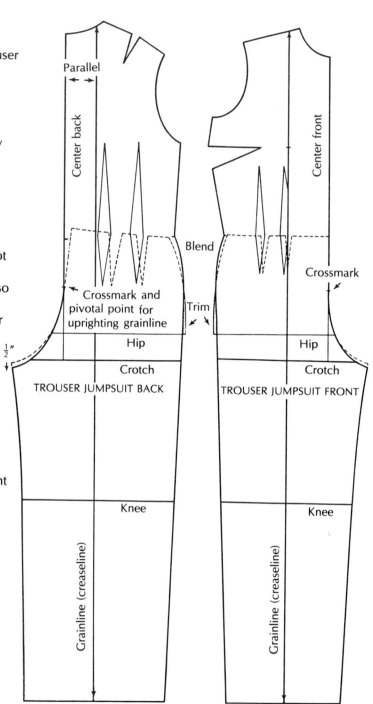

JEAN/JUMPSUIT FOUNDATION

The jean foundation has a very high pitch in back. This pitch (seating room) is removed through overlapping when the pant is aligned with the torso, causing a loss in the overall crotch length. For this reason, the jean jumpsuit should be cut in a firm knit (double knit) or spandex to provide ease of movement. When cut in a rigid fabric, the back should be developed in two pieces as a separate jean pant back and bodice back (not illustrated).

FIGURES 1 and 2

- Trace torso front and back, omitting one dart (broken line). Locate midpoint between waist and hip at centerlines. Crossmark 1 inch below. Allow room for pant length and width.

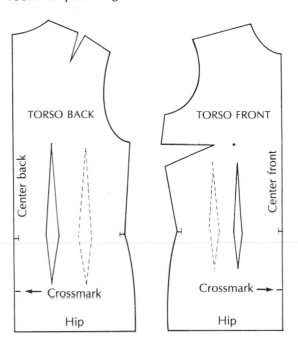

- Remove ¼ inch (ease) from the side and blend with the hipline of the pant as shown.
- For convenience, draw bust circumference and contour lines on bodice (see Chapter 9).
- Complete pattern for test fit. (Draw hip, crotch, and knee lines on muslin.)

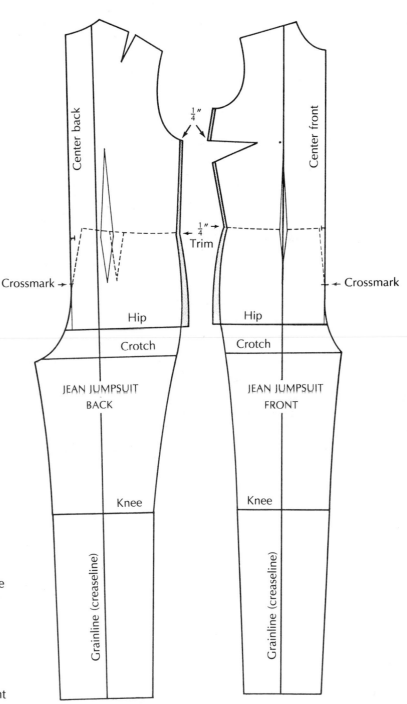

FIGURES 3 and 4

- Place jean pant front and back on paper, matching hip level, and touching centerlines at crossmarks.
- *Important:* Creaseline of pant *must* be parallel with center front and center back of torso. If not, place pushpin on pant at crossmark and pivot pattern, raising or lowering pant until creaseline line grain is parallel with center front and back (not illustrated).
- Trace pant pattern from hem to hipline. Transfer creaseline of pant to paper underneath with a pushpin. (Broken line indicates untraced pant pattern above hip level.)
- Remove pant pattern. Draw grainline through pant and torso.

CULOTTE JUMPSUIT FOUNDATION

FIGURES 1 and 2

■ Trace torso front and back, allowing ample paper for culotte foundation. Include all markings. Label A and B as shown.

■ Place culotte on torso, matching hip and center lines. Draw centerline and crotch extensions of the culotte. Crossmark at centerline at hem.

■ For flare at centerlines, place pushpin at the center front and center back (between crotch and waist), and swing pattern out 2 inches from crossmark at hem. Redraw crotch extension. Remove pattern and blend hemline.

■ Add for additional flare at side seam if desired.

■ For convenience, draw bust circumference and contour lines on bodice (see Chapter 9).

■ Complete pattern for test fit. (Draw hip, crotch, and knee lines on muslin.)

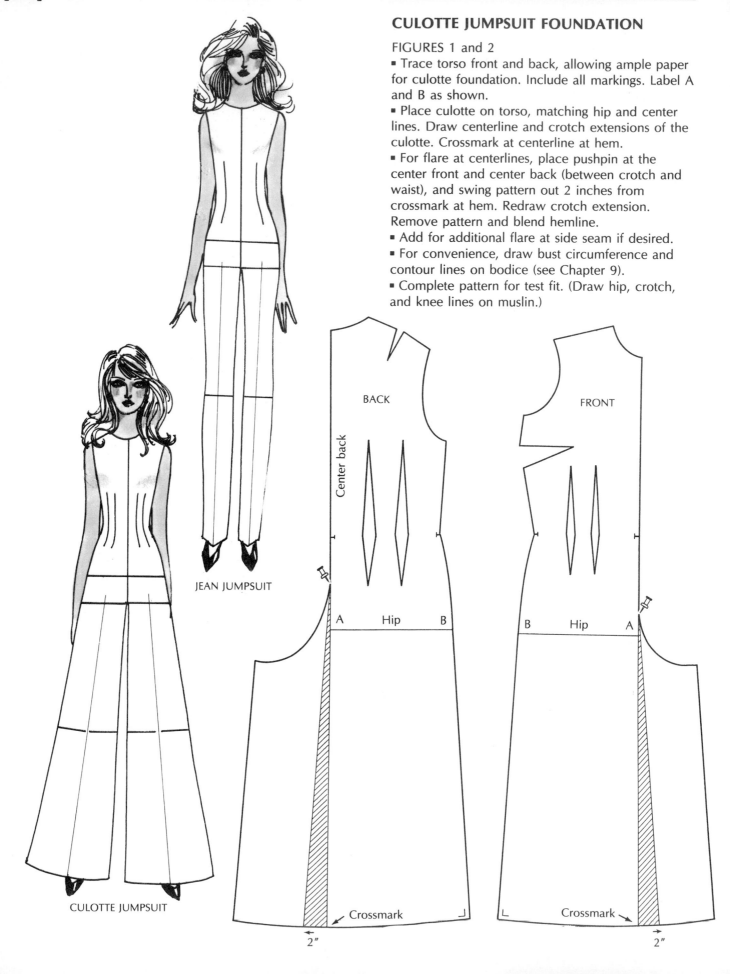

JEAN JUMPSUIT

CULOTTE JUMPSUIT

BACK

FRONT

Center back

A   Hip   B

B   Hip   A

Crossmark

Crossmark

2"

2"

GREAT COVERALL

The original coverall referred to a loose-fitting work garment worn over regular clothing as a protection against dirt. It became an inspiration for other designs and won a place in fashion history as an item designed to be worn separately. An example is the shirtmaker coverall, a garment in which a top is attached to a pant with either a belted or elasticized waistline.

Design Analysis

The coverall has a trouser bottom and shirtmaker top, with large patch pockets, yoked back, and shirtmaker sleeve. Waistline gathers are controlled by an inserted elastic (stitched partially above and below the waistline) drawn through a pleat-like opening slit where it is attached to a tab that buttons in front. Center front has zipper to waistline. Design is based on the shirtmaker (Chapter 18), and the trouser foundation (page 536); however, any pant and any top can be combined to achieve the jumpsuit effect.

Measurement needed
- (2) Waist measurement _____.

Pattern plot and development

FIGURES 1 and 2
- Trace front and back trouser. Mark notch placements for first dart leg, but omit tracing darts. (Broken lines indicate original pattern.)

Modifying trouser pant:
- Square up from hiplines at the side of the front and back trouser.
- Add $\frac{1}{2}$ inch to the center back. Draw line to blend with crotch.
- Blend line across the waistline. (For wider leglines add to side seams.)
- *Front pant:* Draw a 1-inch line down notch placement of first dart leg parallel with the center front.

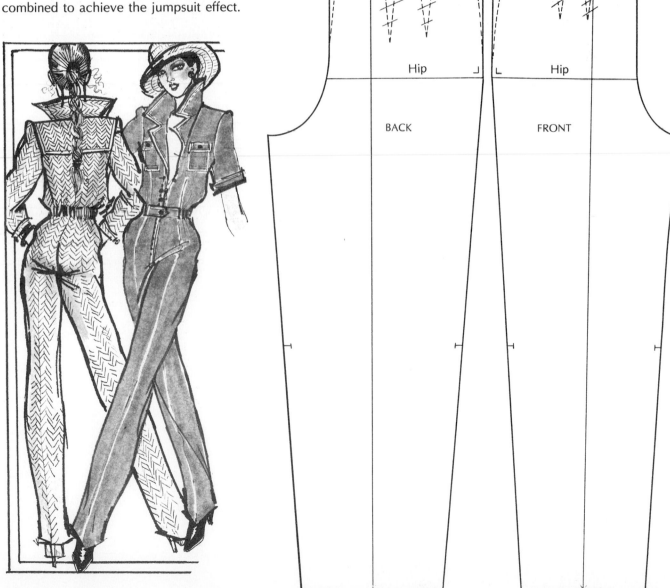

(Continued on next page)

FIGURES 3 and 4 *Modifying shirt:*
- Trace front and back shirt. Trace collar with stand and shirt sleeve. (Set aside for use with the completed pattern—not illustrated.)
- *Front shirt:* Square a line $\frac{1}{2}$ inch below waist, starting from facing and ending 4 inches past center front. Draw a blending curve line from this point, ending 1 inch below waist at side.
- Square a 1-inch line up from new waistline equal to slit placement on pant. (Measure in from the center front for slit placement.) Slit opening is cut $\frac{1}{16}$

inch wide. Notch across end of slit by folding pattern.
- Adjust width of waistline to equal width of front pant. Blend line to armhole at side. (Broken lines show original pattern.)
- *Back shirt:* Square a line 1 inch below waist of the center back, ending at the side.
- Adjust new waistline to equal width of the back pant. Blend line to armhole. (Broken lines show original pattern.)

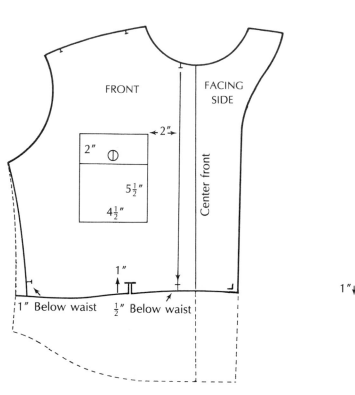

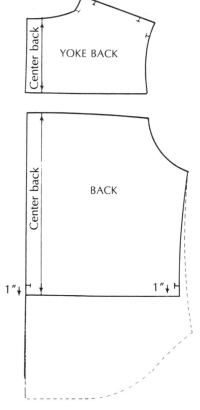

FIGURE 5 *Pocket:*
- Place paper under draft of shirt and trace pocket. Add flap to traced copy, or draft pocket using measurements given.

POCKET

FIGURE 6 *Belt tab:*
- Width = $1\frac{3}{4}$ inches. Length = Fold-back of facing to slit, plus 1-inch extension. Draw point as shown. *Special information:* Elastic length = 7 to 8 inches less than waist measurement. Elastic can be attached in one of two ways:

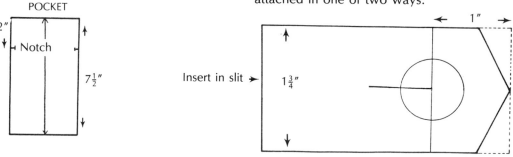

FIGURE 7
- Elastic may be slipped through casing placed and stitched above and below the waist.

Method 1

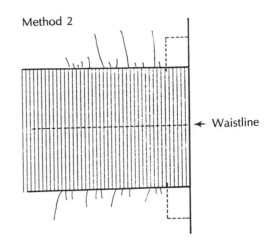

← Waistline
Opening for elastic insertion

FIGURE 8
- Elastic can be centered between waistline, stretched and zigzagged to the edge of the garment.
- Tab is inserted in slit and stitched after elastic is attached.

Method 2

← Waistline

JUMPSUIT DESIGN VARIATIONS

The following designs are given as practice problems. Develop patterns for each design, or design other variations. The finished garment should look like the design. If it does not, locate the problem and try again.

BODYSUITS AND LEOTARDS

Actionwear is a classification of garments designed to allow complete freedom of movement when worn for physical activities and sports. This chapter concentrates on those garments worn specifically for dancing and exercising. The bodysuit and leotard are ideal for such purposes. To be functional, the bodysuit and leotard should be cut in two-way stretchy knits that have 100% stretch and recovery in one direction and 50 to 100% in the other. Suitable knit fabrics are those combined with spandex (synthetic), and latex (rubber). Popular choices are nylon/spandex, cotton/spandex, nylon/latex, and cotton/latex. A study of Chapter 25 is recommended before purchasing knits for these garments.

The bodysuit and leotard foundations are based on the dartless knit top and sleeve. (See Chapter 18 for dartless knit development.) The foundation patterns are developed to compensate for the stretch factor of the knit used for the design. This ensures that the garment will cling to the figure without looseness.

BODYSUIT FOUNDATION

The completed draft includes stretch reduction, $\frac{3}{8}$-inch seam allowance and fold-back for hemline. Use the measurements that apply to the specific knit used for the foundation pattern or design being developed.

Note: If any part of the centerline of the traced copy is to be cut on fold, trim $\frac{3}{8}$ inch (seam allowance) from the pattern in that section. Examples will be given.

BODYSUIT DRAFT

Measurements needed
- (19) Front waist _____.
- (27) Waist to ankle _____.
- (30) Straight knee _____.
- (24) Crotch depth _____.
- (32) Ankle _____.
- (38) Elbow (straight) _____.
- (39) Wrist _____.

FIGURE 1   (opposite page)
- Trace back dartless knit pattern. Place front on top of back, matching hip and centerlines. Trace front, mark waistline, neckline and remove. Label armhole X. (Front and back are drafted together.)
- Raise bust point $\frac{3}{8}$ inch and draw bust circumference (example: $2\frac{1}{2}$ inches—allowing for stretch—for standard measurement). Use the circumference line as a guide when placing stylelines on pattern.

Body dimensions

FIGURE 2   (opposite page)
To reduce the length of the pattern for stretchy knits, place the adjusted waistline above the original waist, using the measurements given below that apply to the type of knit being used. Label adjusted waistline A.
Nylon/spandex—$1\frac{1}{8}$ inches above original waist.
Cotton/spandex—$1\frac{1}{2}$ inches above original waist.
Knits with 50% stretch—$\frac{3}{4}$ inch above original waist.
A–B = Front waist measurement, less $\frac{1}{2}$ inch. (Broken lines indicate original waist.)
C–D = Front hip measurement, less 1 inch.

Measure in $\frac{1}{2}$ inch and up 1 inch from point X. Mark. From this point draw new side seam, allowing curve below armhole for bust room (broken lines indicate original pattern). Blend line to armhole. For clarity of draft instruction, erase unneeded side seam.

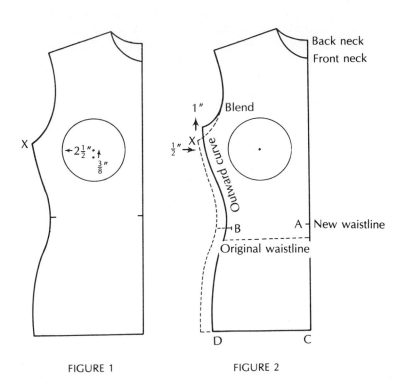

FIGURE 1 FIGURE 2

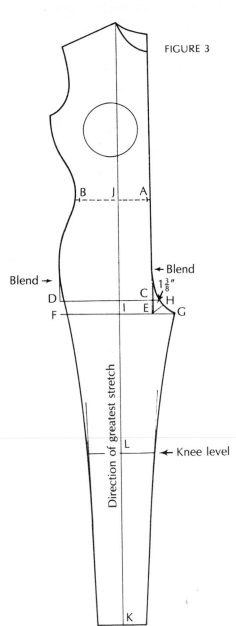

FIGURE 3

FIGURE 3 *Crotch and legline development:*

A–E = Crotch depth, minus the following measurement that applies to the knit being used.
Nylon/spandex—minus $1\frac{3}{4}$ inches.
Cotton/spandex—minus 2 inches.
Knits with 50% stretch—minus 1 inch.

E–F = C–D, squared from E.

E–G = One-third of E–F, less $\frac{3}{4}$ inch.
Draw a $1\frac{3}{8}$-inch diagonal line from E. Label H.
With French curve touching points G, H, and approximately $1\frac{1}{2}$ inches above point C at center front, draw crotch.

G–I = One-half of G–F.
Square line up and down from I. (Line may cross shoulder and waist at a different location than that of the illustration.) Label J at waist.

J–K = Waist length to ankle, minus the following measurement that applies to the knit being used.
Nylon/spandex—minus 2 inches.
Cotton/spandex—minus $2\frac{3}{4}$ inches.
Knits with 50% stretch—minus 1 inch.
The above measurements allow 1 inch for fold-back at hem.

I–L = One half of I–K, less $\frac{1}{2}$ inch (knee level).
Square out one-fourth of knee and ankle measurements, less $\frac{3}{8}$ inch, from each side of line at knee mark and at ankle.
Draw straight lines from ankle to just beyond knee level.
Draw curves slightly inward from G and D, blending with knee.
Blend hipline at point D as shown.

FIGURES 4 and 5 *Separate pattern:*
- Cut pattern from paper.
- Trace pattern and label. Trim bulge at side as shown on back pattern.
- Trim front neckline from the original pattern and label. Record type of knit used to develop pattern.

FIGURE 6 *Sleeve:*
- Trace knit sleeve, and label biceps X.
- Measure out one-half of elbow and wrist measurement less $\frac{1}{2}$ inch from each side of grain. Mark.
- Measure in $\frac{1}{2}$ inch and up 1 inch from point X. Mark and blend cap.
- Draw new underseam connecting with marks as shown. Fold-back for hem equals $1\frac{1}{8}$ inch allowance.
- Cut sleeve from paper and discard unneeded sections .

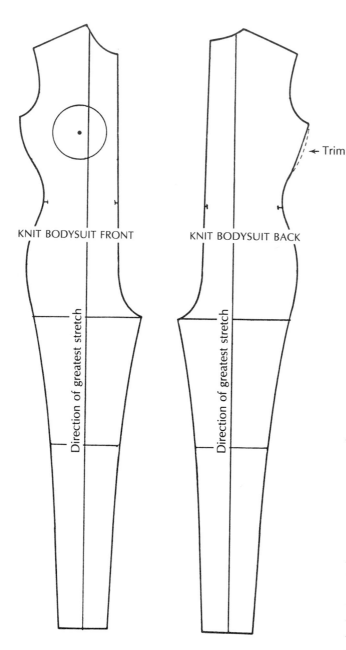

KNIT BODYSUIT FRONT   KNIT BODYSUIT BACK

Direction of greatest stretch

← Trim

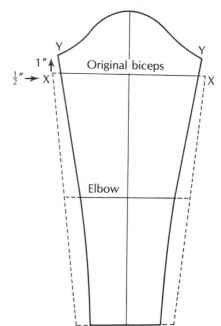

Test fit
- Place length of pattern on knit in the direction of greatest stretch.
- Overlock seams together, except for 10-inch opening at center back (for entry).
- Stitch sleeves to garment.
- For instruction on attaching elastic, see Chapter 24.
- Place leotard on form or figure and pin center back. If too loose around the figure, pin excess at the side seam and/or the center back. If length is too long, take up the excess along the waistline and the knee (if necessary).
- Check depth of neckline, and armhole—raise or lower as needed.
- Mark bust point, and verify location on the pattern. Redraw circumference line around the new bust point if required.
- Correct pattern.
- Trace this foundation for all designs cut in knit having the same stretch factor.

Note: There are two types of notching styles for knits: (a) notch to the depth of $\frac{1}{8}$ inch, and (b) cut pyramid shapes out from the seam edge $\frac{1}{8}$ inch wide and $\frac{1}{8}$ inch high. ($\triangle$)

BODYSUIT DESIGN VARIATIONS

Designs illustrated for the leotard and maillot can also be adapted to the bodysuit.

BODYSUIT WITH SCOOPED NECK AND CUTOUTS

Design Analysis

Design 1 has a scooped neckline with cut-out side sections touching above and below bust arc and waist. The front and back have same stylelines. Seam allowances of $\frac{3}{8}$ inch are included.

Pattern plot and development

FIGURE 1

- Trace front pattern. Mark bust point. Draw bust circumference with compass.
- Draw stylelines using measurements given.
- Cut pattern from paper. Discard unneeded sections (shaded areas).
- Draw grain in direction of greatest stretch.

FIGURE 2

- Retrace for back pattern.
- For elastic instruction, see Chapter 24.
- To develop stirrup, see page 587.

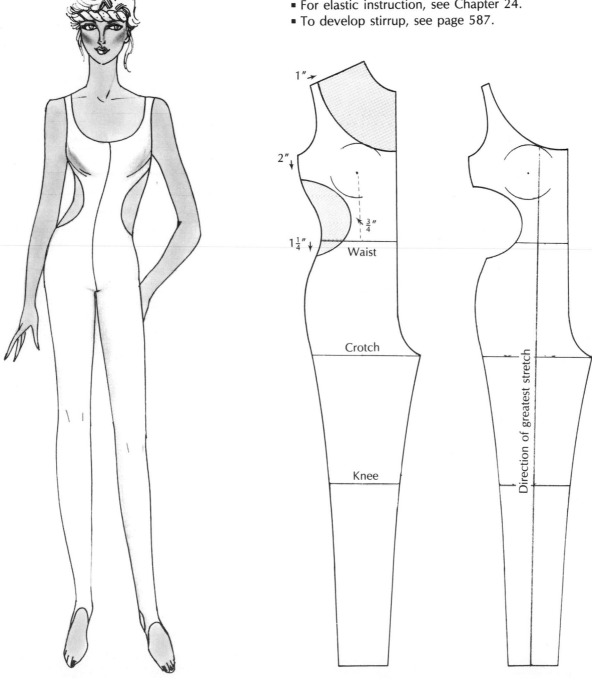

BODYSUIT WITH HIGH-NECKED HALTER TOP

Design Analysis
The halter top has a high neck extending above the natural neckline in front and back. A torso styleline gives a two-piece effect. Front and back have the same stylelines. The neckband has loops and buttons on one side for entry. Seam allowances of $\frac{3}{8}$ inch are included.

Measurement needed
- (12) Neck _____
(one-fourth of neck circumference).

Pattern plot and development

FIGURE 1
- Trace front pattern. Mark bust point. Draw bust circumference with compass.
- Extend line 4 inches up at center front neck and square a line equal to recorded neck measurement. Square down to shoulder and crossmark midpoint for fold-over facing.
- Draw halter styleline from shoulder to side, $\frac{1}{2}$ inch away from circumference line.
- From styleline at side seam, measure in $\frac{1}{2}$ inch and blend to waist.
- Square a line from center front midway between waist and crotch level (where pattern separates).
- Cut and separate patterns. Discard unneeded sections (shaded area).

FIGURES 2 and 3
- Retrace patterns with centerlines of torso back and front extending $\frac{3}{8}$ inch from fold. (Patterns for front and back are identical.)
- Cut from paper.
- Draw grainline in direction of greatest stretch.
- For elastic instruction, see Chapter 24.

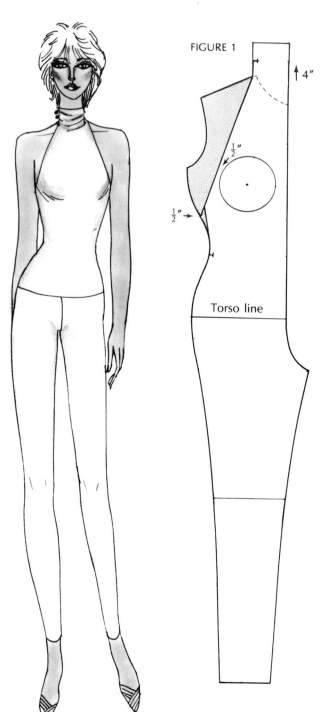

FIGURE 1

Torso line

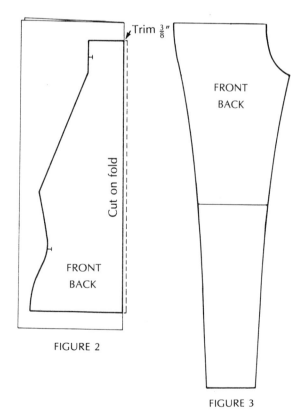

Trim $\frac{3}{8}$"

Cut on fold

FRONT BACK

FRONT BACK

FIGURE 2

FIGURE 3

TIGHTS

FIGURE 1

- For leggies, trace bodysuit from $1\frac{1}{2}$ inches above waist to ankle.
- *Elastic:* Width, $\frac{3}{4}$ to 1 inch. Length, 1 inch less than waist (overlap $\frac{1}{2}$ inch to secure ends). Fold waist to form casing.
- Draw grainline in direction of greatest stretch.
- Patterns for front and back are identical. Hip, crotch, and knee guides are optional.
- $\frac{3}{8}$-inch seams are included. (Design not shown.)

STIRRUPS

FIGURE 1

- For bodysuit designs with stirrups (rings extending around and under feet), cut out leg at ankle as shown.
- Hemlines at each side of front and back pant are stitched together. (This section lies at the bottom of the foot's instep.)
- $\frac{3}{8}$-inch seams are included.

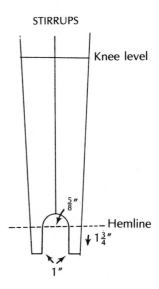

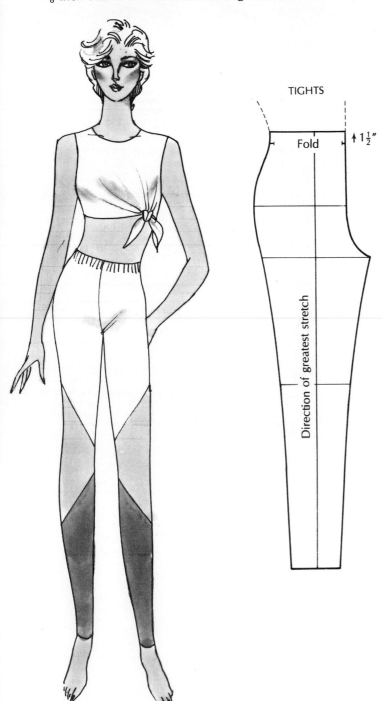

LEOTARD FOUNDATION

LEOTARD DRAFT

The leotard covers the figure's contours from neck to crotch and is used for dancing, exercising, and as a fashion item to be worn under skirts and pants.

Measurements needed
▪ (19) Front waist _____.
▪ (23) Front hip _____.
▪ (28) Crotch length _____.

The completed draft includes pattern reduction, $\frac{3}{8}$-inch seam allowance and fold-back for hemline. Use the measurements below that apply to the specific knit used for the foundation pattern or design being developed.

FIGURE 1
▪ Trace back dartless knit pattern. Place front pattern on top of back, matching hip and centerlines. Trace front neckline and remove. Label armhole X. (Front and back are drafted together.)
▪ Remove $\frac{3}{8}$ inch from the centerline. (Broken line indicates original centerline.)
▪ Raise bust point $\frac{3}{8}$ inch and draw bust circumference (example: $2\frac{1}{2}$ inches—allowing for stretch—for standard measurement). Use the circumference line as a guide when placing stylelines on pattern.

Body dimensions

FIGURE 2
▪ To reduce the length of the pattern for stretchy knits, place the adjusted waistline above the original waist using the measurements that apply to the specific knit being used for the design. Label adjusted waistline A.
▪ Nylon/spandex—$1\frac{1}{8}$ inches above original waist.
▪ Cotton/spandex—$1\frac{1}{2}$ inches above original waist.
▪ Knits with 50% stretch—$\frac{3}{4}$ inch above original waist.
A–B = Front waist measurement, less $\frac{1}{2}$ inch. (Broken lines indicate original waistline.)
C–D = Front hip measurement, less 1 inch.

> Measure in $\frac{1}{2}$ inch and up 1 inch from point X. Mark. From this point draw new side seam allowing curve below armhole for bust room. (Broken lines indicate original side seam.)
> For clarity of draft instructions, erase unneeded side seam and C–D line.

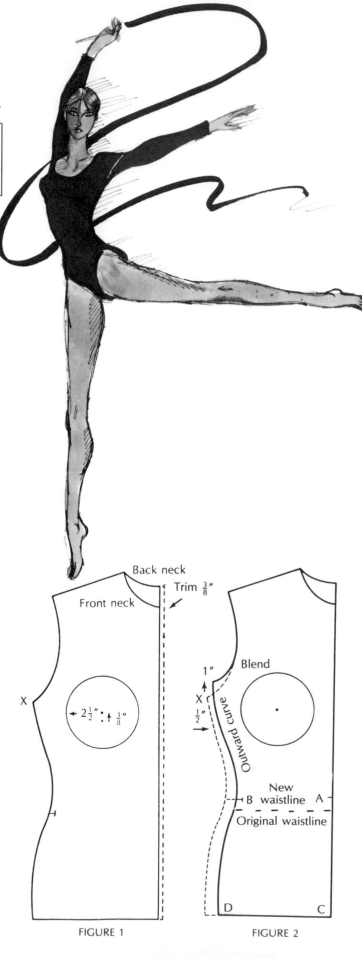

FIGURE 1   FIGURE 2

FIGURE 3 *Legline development:*

A–E = One-half of crotch length minus the following measurement that applies to the knit being used:
Nylon/spandex—minus $1\frac{3}{4}$ inches.
Cotton/spandex—minus 2 inches.
Knits with 50% stretch—minus 1 inch.

E–F = 2 inches.

E–G = One-half of E–A, plus 1 inch.
Square from G to side seam. Label H.

G–I = $1\frac{5}{8}$ inches.
Square down from I to E–F line. Label J.

I–K = One-half of I–H.

K–L = One-half of K–H.

L–M = $\frac{3}{8}$ inch, squared up from L.

I–N = One-half of I to J.

N–O = One-half of N to J.

N–P = I to L

O–Q = I to K.
Draw diagonal lines as follows:
$1\frac{3}{4}$ inches from I. Label R.
$1\frac{3}{8}$ inches from O. Label S.
(Subtract $\frac{1}{4}$ inch from measurements for petite sizes.)

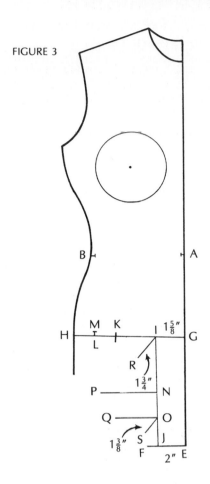

FIGURE 3

FIGURE 4 *Guidemarking front and back leg openings:*

▪ *Front:* Connect points H, M, K, R, and $\frac{1}{4}$ inch out from N, touching O and ending at F.

▪ *Back:* Connect points H, P, Q, and S, ending at F. Crossmark midpoint between H and P. (Broken lines indicate original guideline.)

FIGURES 5 and 6 *Shaping front and back leg openings:*

▪ Use measurements given to blend legline (bold line). If the shape of the leglines do not look like the illustrations, reshape until they do.

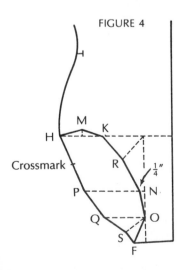

FIGURE 4

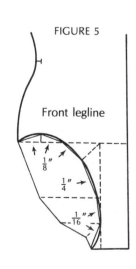

FIGURE 5

Front legline

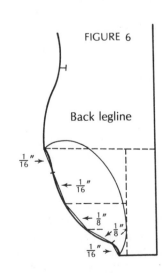

FIGURE 6

Back legline

(Continued on next page)

FIGURE 7

▪ This completes the leotard draft. Draw grain in direction of greatest stretch as shown.

▪ Use sleeve instructions given for the bodysuit (see page 584).

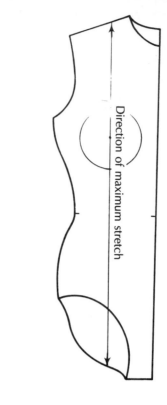

FIGURES 8 and 9   *Separate patterns:*

▪ Cut pattern from paper.

▪ Trace pattern for back copy. Blend as shown. Label back leotard.

▪ Trim original pattern to front neck and legline. Label front leotard. Record type of knit used to develop pattern.

  Note: To use this pattern for designs with center front and back seams, add $\frac{3}{8}$ inch to the center front and back patterns.

▪ Review notch information, page 584.

Test fit for the leotard

▪ Place length of pattern on knit in the direction of the greatest stretch.

▪ Overlock seams together, leaving 10 inches at the center back for entry.

▪ Stitch sleeves to garment.

▪ For instruction on elastic, see Chapter 24.

▪ Place leotard on form or figure, pinning center back together.

If too loose around the figure, pin in along the side seams and/or the center back.

If too long in length, take up the excess along the waistline.

▪ Check depth of neckline and armhole—raise or lower as needed.

▪ Check shape of leg openings.

▪ Mark bust point and verify location on pattern. Redraw circumference line around new bust point if required.

▪ Correct pattern.

▪ Trace leotard foundation for pattern manipulation. Use this foundation for all designs cut in knit with the same stretch factor when modifying the pattern.

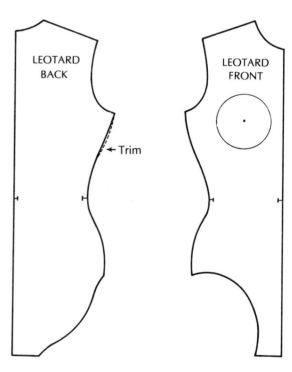

LEOTARD DESIGN VARIATIONS

EMPIRE-CUT LEOTARD

Design Analysis
The design has a stylized Empire cut (V-neckline in front and bateau In back) with shirring at the center front held in place by a separate fold-over band.

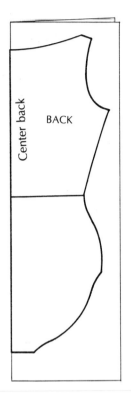

Pattern plot and development

FIGURES 1 and 2
- Trace front and back, include all markings.
- Plot as shown.
- Cut and separate patterns. Discard unneeded section (shaded areas).

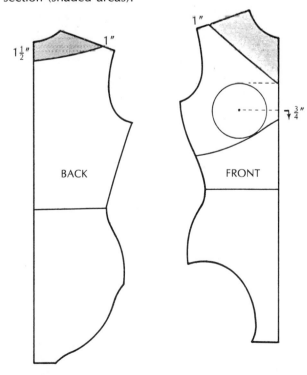

FIGURES 3, 4, and 5
- Retrace on fold. Add $\frac{3}{8}$-inch seam allowance at neckline and Empire stylelines.
- When cutting, place length of pattern in the direction of greatest stretch.

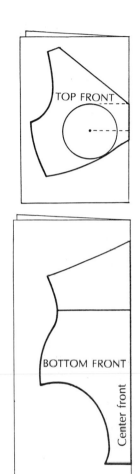

FIGURE 6
- Tab: 2 inches $\times$ 2 inches
- Wrap tab over fabric at center front. Stitch into seam to hold fullness.
- *Crotch lining and elastic instructions:* See Chapter 24.

LEOTARD WITH ASYMMETRIC TOP

Design Analysis

The leotard has an asymmetrical Empire cut in front and a low, squared back. The crossed-over wrapped front gathers at one side.

Pattern plot and development

FIGURES 1 and 2

- Trace a full leotard front, including bust arc as a guide for stylelines. Trace back and plot as shown.
- Cut and separate pattern sections, discarding unneeded sections (shaded areas).

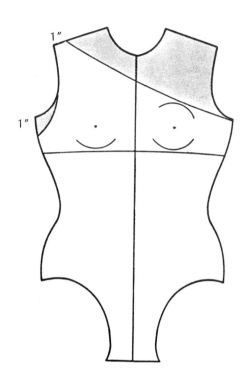

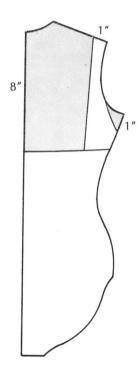

FIGURES 3, 4, 5, and 6

- Retrace all sections, cutting back on fold. Add $\frac{3}{8}$-inch seam allowance at neckline and where pattern separates.
- *Special notation:* Style cut of neckline in front ends at normal armhole, while the opposite side and back armhole is dropped (controls gathers at side).

   Note: Undersection of top front can be darted at side to take up excess, replacing gathers (not illustrated).

- When cutting, place length of pattern in direction of greatest stretch.
- *Crotch lining and elastic instructions:* See Chapter 24.

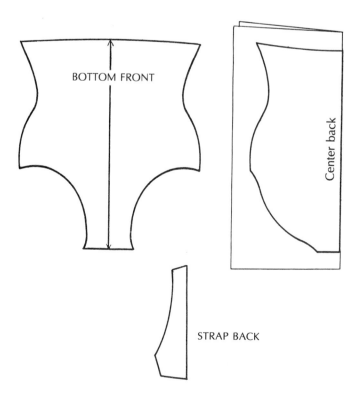

BOTTOM FRONT

Center back

STRAP BACK

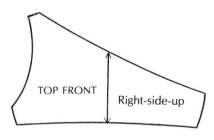

TOP FRONT

Right-side-up

STRIPED LEOTARD WITH SCOOPED NECK AND SHORT SLEEVES

Design Analysis

Leotard has a low, scooped neck, short sleeves, mitered center front and back seams, and a high legline.

Pattern plot and development

FIGURES 1 and 2
- Trace front and back leotard.
- Plot as shown.
- Add $\frac{3}{8}$-inch seam allowance at neckline and center front.
- *Grainline:* Draw grainline at a true 45° angle to the center front and center back when using striped fabric.
- Cut patterns from paper. Discard unneeded sections (shaded areas).

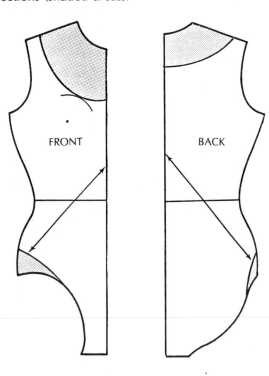

FRONT

BACK

FIGURES 3 and 4
- The completed front and back pattern shapes are illustrated at right.

FIGURE 5   *Sleeve:*
- Trace sleeve to biceps line. Measure down approximately $3\frac{1}{2}$ inches from cap. Measure down 1 inch from underseam. Draw curved line as shown. Use straight grain on sleeve.
- *Crotch lining and elastic instructions:* See Chapter 24.

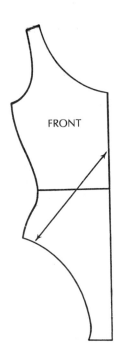

FRONT

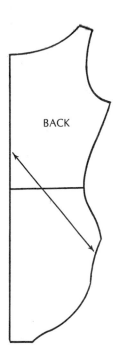

BACK

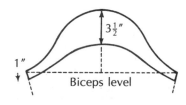

$3\frac{1}{2}''$

$1''$

Biceps level

LEOTARD WITH BATEAU NECK AND FLARED SLEEVES

Design Analysis
The leotard has a wide, shallow neckline in front extending to the shoulders and a low back scooped to the waist. Short sleeves are flared.

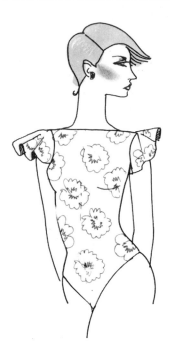

FIGURE 5 *Sleeve:*
- Trace sleeve to ¾ inch below biceps level.
- Draw slash lines as shown.

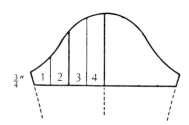

FIGURE 6
- Cut sleeve from paper and separate at center.
- Cut slash lines from hem to, not through, cap.
- Place on fold of paper and spread.
- When cutting, place length of patterns in direction of greatest stretch.
- *Crotch lining and elastic instructions:* See Chapter 24.

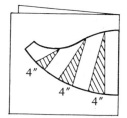

Pattern plot and development

FIGURES 1 and 2
- Trace front and back leotard.
- Plot as shown.
- Add ⅜-inch seam allowance at neckline.
- Cut patterns from paper. Discard unneeded section (shaded areas).

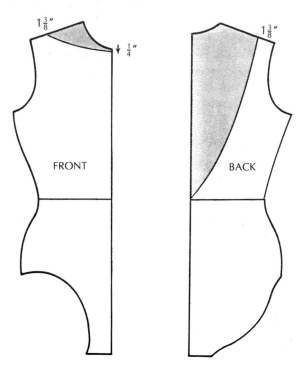

FIGURES 3 and 4
- The completed front and back patterns are illustrated.

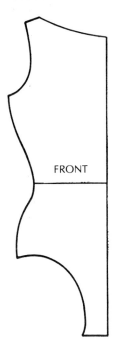
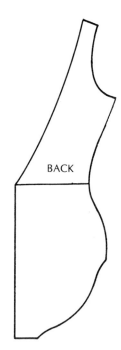

23

SWIMWEAR

SWIMWEAR TYPES 596
MAILLOT FOUNDATION 597
Maillot draft 597
MAILLOT DESIGN VARIATIONS 598
Princess-line Maillot 598
Maillot with inset bra 599
Asymmetric Maillot 600
BIKINI FOUNDATION 601
Bikini bottom draft 601
BIKINI BOTTOM VARIATIONS 602
Bikini without center seams 602
All-in-one bikini 602
Diaper-tie bikini 603
Drawstring bikini 603
Bikini with clasp closure 603
BIKINI TOP VARIATIONS 604
Princess-line bikini top 604
Strap variations 605
Bra top with horizontal styleline 606
String-a-long bikini top 607
Bandeau bikini top 608
LITTLE-BOY LEGLINE FOUNDATION 608
Little-boy legline draft 609
LITTLE-BOY LEGLINE VARIATIONS 610
Slit legline 610
FULL-FIGURE SWIM FOUNDATION 612
Full-figure swim draft 612
Swimsuit with skirt front 613

SWIMWEAR TYPES

In the nineteenth century, swimwear covered the female figure from neck to lengths that fluctuated between the knee and ankle. These suits were not always conducive to swimming. Today's swimwear fashions cover much less and allow complete freedom of movement. They are designed in a variety of fabrics, prints, and textures, ranging from cotton to stretchy knits.

The four swimsuit foundations illustrated in this chapter have distinct characteristics and differ from each other in a number of ways: the cut of the legline, the type of bust support, the type of fabric in which the suit can be cut, and the silhouette desired.

Maillot foundation. The cut of the legline encircles the leg starting at crotch level, and ends at varying distances above crotch level at the side. This one-piece suit is usually cut in stretchy knits, and clings closely to the figure's contours. The maximum stretch goes around the figure rather than up and down. Very little stretch is required in the length of the garment. The maillot has little or no bust support.

Bikini foundation. The cut of the legline of the two-piece bikini encircles the leg starting at crotch level, and ends at varying distances above crotch level at the side. It can be cut in any fabric. The bra top has little or no bust support.

Little-boy legline foundation. A one-piece or two-piece (separated at or just below the waistline) foundation has legline ending at the shorts or shorty-short length. Since the foundation is developed with waist and side dart control, the bust shape can be defined. Bust cups can be added for support, if desired. It can be cut in rigid fabrics or firm knits (little stretch). This foundation is also an excellent base for tennis garments and sun suits.

Full-bodied foundation. The one-piece foundation has legline ending at crotch level. Since the foundation is developed with waist and side dart control, the bust is defined through the use of darts. This foundation is often used as the base for full-bodied or mature figures. Bust cups are inserted. It can be cut in all fabrics, except stretchy knits. The legline is often disguised by the application of a short skirt that stretches across the legline just below crotch level.

Important: When cutting in knits, the maximum stretch goes around the figure, rather than up and down the body. Knits combined with spandex or latex are best.

LITTLE-BOY LEGLINE

MAILLOT

BIKINI

FULL-BODIED

MAILLOT FOUNDATION

The maillot is usually designed as a strapless or optionally strapless swimsuit. Without support at the shoulderline, the maillot will droop downward if too much stretch is removed from the length of the pattern. When wet, stretchy knits tend to hold water and also cause the swimsuit to droop. These factors should be considered when developing the maillot pattern.

MAILLOT DRAFT

FIGURES 1 and 2
▪ To develop the maillot, use instructions given for the leotard draft (Chapter 22). Use reduction measurements given for knits with 50% stretch when developing the maillot. The draft includes seam allowance.

Modifications to the draft
▪ Remove $\frac{3}{8}$ inch from the side seam of the front and back patterns.
▪ Raise bust point $\frac{1}{2}$ inch and redraw bust circumference.
▪ Separate patterns by tracing a copy. Mark back. Trim to front neck and legline of original pattern and mark front.

Test fit
▪ Place width of pattern on knit in direction of greatest stretch.
▪ Overlock garment together, except for one shoulder (for entry).
▪ For elastic and crotch lining instructions, see pages 616 and 617.
▪ Place on form or figure.
▪ Pin shoulder.
▪ If too loose around the figure, pin in along side seam and/or center back.
If too long in the length, pin along the waistline. Care must be taken not to remove too much stretch (garment may pull downward).
▪ Check fit of legline.
▪ Correct pattern if necessary.
▪ Trace maillot foundation for pattern manipulation.

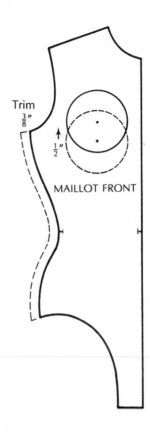

Trim $\frac{3}{8}''$

$\frac{1}{2}''$

MAILLOT FRONT

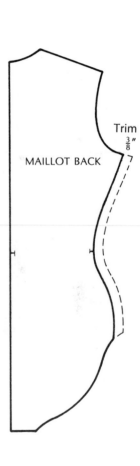

Trim $\frac{3}{8}''$

MAILLOT BACK

MAILLOT DESIGN VARIATIONS

PRINCESS-LINE MAILLOT

Design Analysis

Maillot has a deep-cut V-neckline, front and back, that ties at the shoulder. The princess line starts at mid-shoulder and extends over bust to legline.

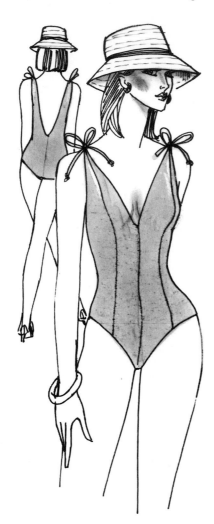

Pattern plot and development

FIGURES 1 and 2

• Trace front and back patterns separately as shown, and all markings.

• *Princess line:* Start at mid-shoulder, continue over bust to waist (3 inches in from center front). Draw an outward curve to hip (approximately 4 inches from center front), ending at legline.

• Draw remaining stylelines as shown.

• Cut and separate patterns, discarding unneeded sections (shaded area).

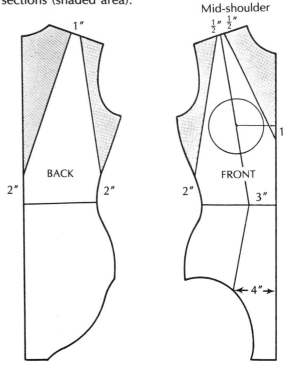

FIGURES 3, 4, and 5

• Retrace patterns. Add $\frac{3}{8}$-inch seams to styleline and at the centerlines. Cut from paper.

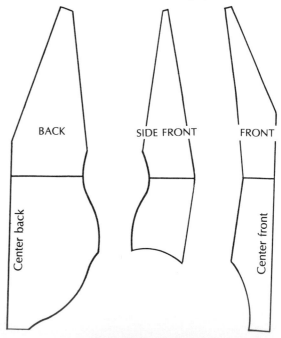

FIGURE 6

• *Tie:* Length = 8 inches. Width = 1 inch (finished width = $\frac{1}{2}$ inch).

• *Crotch lining and elastic instructions:* See Chapter 24.

MAILLOT WITH INSET BRA

Design Analysis
Maillot has a set-in bra and self-loop at center front that forces folds in the fabric, creating a gathered effect.

Pattern plot and development

FIGURES 1 and 2
- Trace front and back maillot foundation, including all markings.
- Plot as shown. (Broken lines indicate original patterns.) (The distance from the squared line above and below the bust circumference provides fullness for center front gathers on the bra and eliminates the necessity of spreading the pattern.)
- Cut and separate pattern sections. Discard unneeded sections .

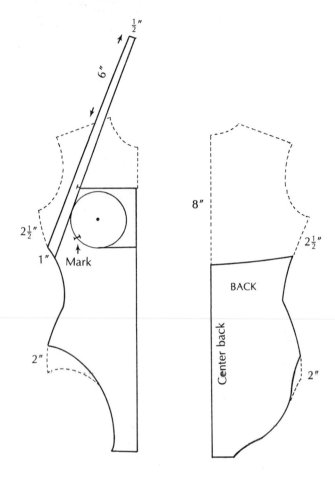

FIGURES 3, 4, 5, and 6
- Trace patterns on fold as shown. Add $\frac{3}{8}$-inch seams at stylelines, and at cut line of bra and strap.
- Cut patterns from paper.

BRA INSET

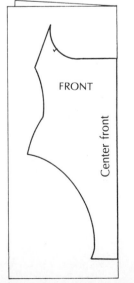

FRONT

Center front

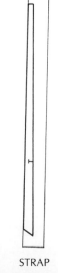

STRAP

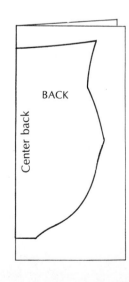

BACK

Center back

FIGURE 7
- Draw loop tab 3 × 1$\frac{1}{2}$ inches (finished width $\frac{3}{4}$ inch).
- *Crotch lining and elastic instructions: See Chapter 24.*

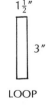

LOOP

ASYMMETRIC MAILLOT

Design Analysis

Maillot has an asymmetric styleline from the shoulder, across bust, to a point below armhole. Added fullness (principle #2) is shirred into one side of front.

Pattern plot and development

FIGURES 1 and 2

- Trace a full front and full back pattern.
- Plot as shown.
- Draw slash lines in the direction gathers radiate from side seam.
- Cut pattern from paper. Discard unneeded sections (shaded areas).

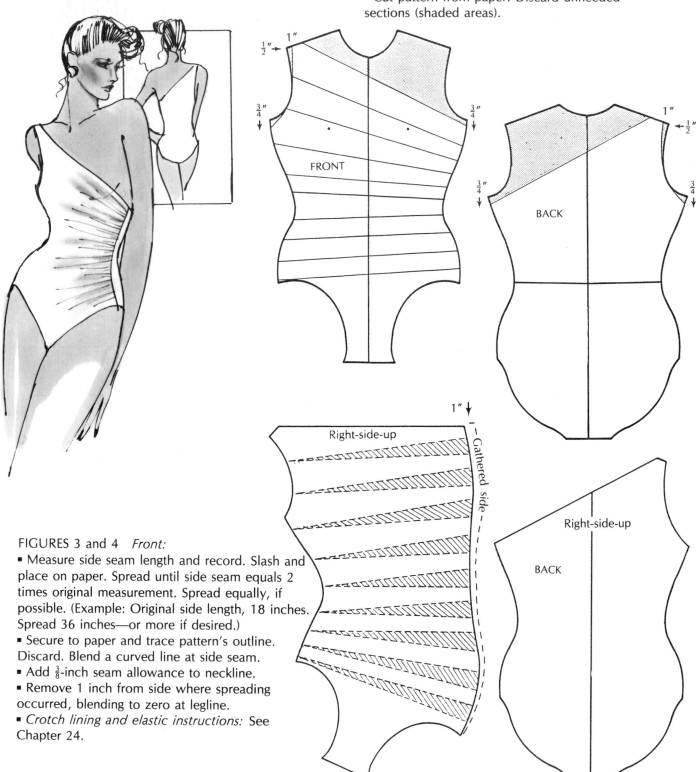

FIGURES 3 and 4 *Front:*

- Measure side seam length and record. Slash and place on paper. Spread until side seam equals 2 times original measurement. Spread equally, if possible. (Example: Original side length, 18 inches. Spread 36 inches—or more if desired.)
- Secure to paper and trace pattern's outline. Discard. Blend a curved line at side seam.
- Add ⅜-inch seam allowance to neckline.
- Remove 1 inch from side where spreading occurred, blending to zero at legline.
- *Crotch lining and elastic instructions:* See Chapter 24.

BIKINI FOUNDATION

The bikini is a brief two-piece swimsuit distinguished by its low-cut waistline, high-cut legline, and bra-like top. Bikini styles range from modest to extreme, depending on fashion trends and personal preference, and can be cut in rigid fabrics or knits. Two methods for developing the bikini bottom are given—one based on the maillot (or leotard), the other developed from the basic skirt front. The bikini top is developed from the Contour Guide Pattern. Four of these designs are illustrated and should be used as a guide for developing other similar designs.

BIKINI BOTTOM DRAFT

Develop the bikini using either of the two methods shown. Use this foundation as a base for the designs that follow.

Bikini based on maillot or leotard foundation

FIGURES 1 and 2
- Trace front and back maillot (leotard) patterns from waist to legline (broken lines show untraced sections).
- Square a line from center front and center back, midway between waist and legline at side as shown.
- Cut bikini bottom from paper. Label for *Knits only*.
- Trace another copy, adding $\frac{1}{2}$ inch to side seam, plus $\frac{3}{8}$ inch for seam allowances. Label for *Wovens only* (not illustrated).

Bikini based on front skirt foundation

Measurement needed
▪ (28) Crotch length _____.

FIGURES 1 and 2
- If the maillot or leotard foundation patterns are not available, trace the front basic skirt from waist to hip level. Square a line 4 inches down from front.
- Label center front waist A and follow instructions for the leotard (see page 589).

Adjustments after completing the draft:
- Trim $\frac{1}{4}$ inch from front and back side seams and cut from paper.
- Label *Wovens only*.
- Trace another copy. Trim $\frac{1}{2}$ inch from side seams. Label *Knits only*. (Seams are included.)

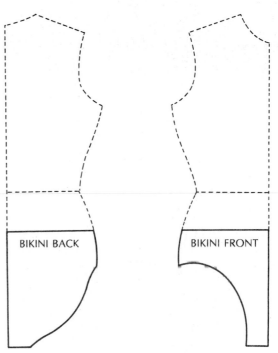

Front and back patterns separated:

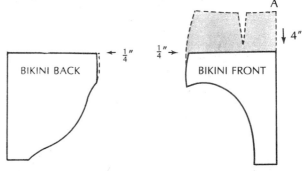

BIKINI BOTTOM VARIATIONS

BIKINI WITHOUT CENTER SEAMS

Pattern plot and development

FIGURES 1 and 2
- Trace pattern with center front and back on fold.
- Add $\frac{3}{8}$ inch if cut in wovens.
- Cut from paper and duplicate for lining.

FIGURES 3 and 4
- Unfold pattern and add grainline (straight or bias) as shown.
- *Crotch lining and elastic instructions:* See Chapter 24.

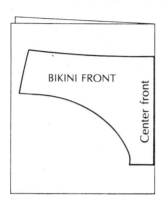

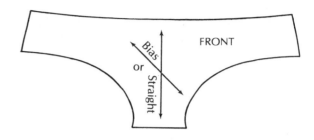

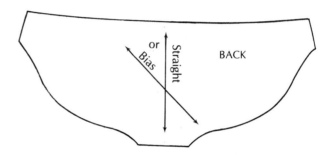

ALL-IN-ONE BIKINI

FIGURE 1
- Place front and back patterns on paper with crotch seams together. Trace.
- Draw grainlines (straight or bias). Add $\frac{3}{8}$-inch seams if cut in wovens.
- Cut from paper and duplicate for lining.
- *Crotch lining and elastic instructions:* See Chapter 24.

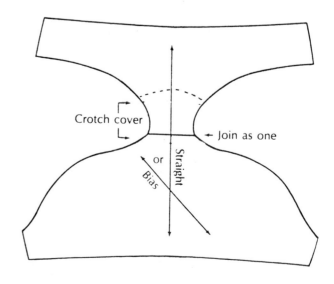

DIAPER-TIE BIKINI

Pattern plot and development

FIGURE 1 *Front:*
- Trace front bikini patterns.
- Locate midpoint at sides of front and back bikini. Label A. Square a line from center, extending line 5 inches beyond A.
- Shape tie, using illustration as a guide.
- Repeat for back.
- Draw grainline.

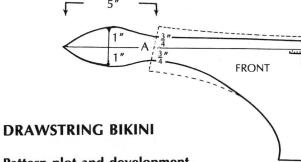

DRAWSTRING BIKINI

Pattern plot and development

FIGURE 2 *Front:*
- Trace front bikini pattern.
- Add $\frac{3}{4}$ inch to front and back side seam (folded back and stitched. Tie cord is pulled through and knotted at each end).
- Repeat for back.
- Draw grainlines.

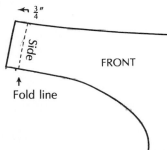

BIKINI WITH CLASP CLOSURE

FIGURE 3 *Front:*
- Trace front bikini pattern.
- Subtract width of closure (less $\frac{1}{2}$ inch for fold-back) from side of front bikini.
- Subtract to length of inside closure equally on each side of midpoint as shown.
- Reshape waist and legline.
- Repeat for back.
- Draw grainlines.

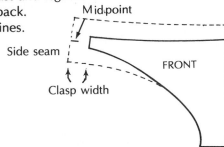

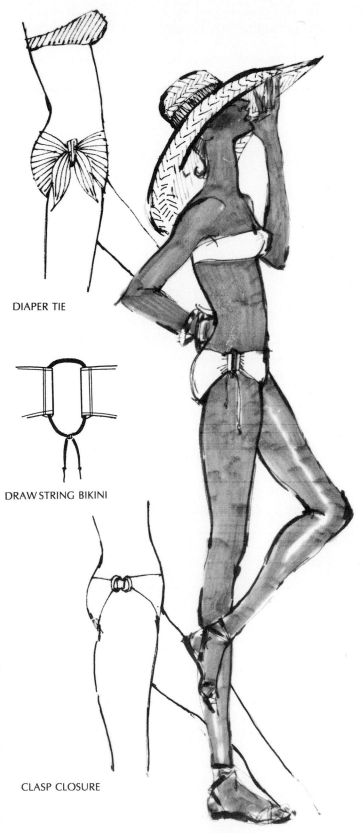

DIAPER TIE

DRAWSTRING BIKINI

CLASP CLOSURE

BIKINI TOP VARIATIONS

The brief bikini top covers the bust much like a bra and is the perfect complement for the bikini bottom. The four tops illustrated should be used as a guide for developing other similar bra designs. Bikini tops are based on the Contour Guide Patterns. The bust circumference is a reference for styleline placement while the reduction guidelines on the Contour Guide Patterns enables the patternmaker to accurately contour the bust closely (shaded areas in illustrations). Refer to Chapter 9 for instruction on contouring. If not using the Contour Guide Pattern, follow illustrations and measurements given as a guide for pattern development. Bikini straps can be developed for stitching directly to the top or pulled through a casing, such as spaghetti straps. They can extend around the neck, over the shoulders, be tied or buttoned. Three back strap variations are given, and it is suggested that the one best suited to the design be used.

PRINCESS-LINE BIKINI TOP

Design Analysis
The bikini has a styleline crossing over bust point from top to bottom (princess line).

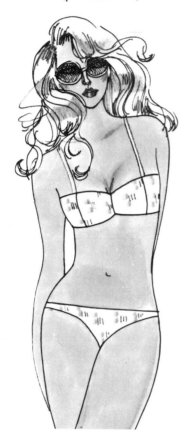

FIGURE 2
• Cut and separate bikini bra from pattern. Shaded areas are discarded.

FIGURE 3
• Close open area as shown. To provide room for the bust mound, draw $\frac{1}{16}$-inch outward curved lines above and below bust point, blending with top and bottom of the bra as shown.
• Draw grain.

Pattern plot and development

FIGURE 1 *Bikini bra:*
• Trace front Contour Guide Pattern. Use pushpin to transfer Guidelines 2 (over-the-bust contour), 5a and b (under-the-bust contour), and 6 (between-the-bust contour). Connect guidelines to bust point.
• Draw line $\frac{3}{8}$ inch in from side seam to remove ease.
• Draw bust circumference (example: 3 inches), and bra stylelines using measurements given.
• *Note:* For neck strap, see Figure 7 on opposite page.

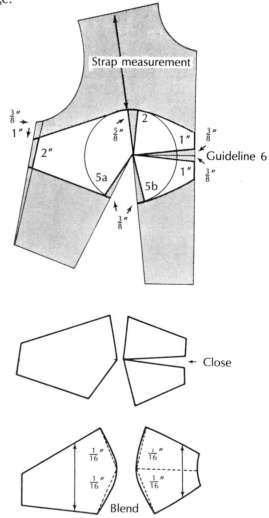

FIGURE 4 *Back strap:*
- Draw line $\frac{3}{8}$ inch in from side seam to remove ease.
- Mark width of strap at side using measurement given. Label A and B as shown.
- Square a line from center back touching point B.
- Mark width of band, and draw curved line to point A.
- Remove $\frac{3}{4}$ inch from strap at center back.

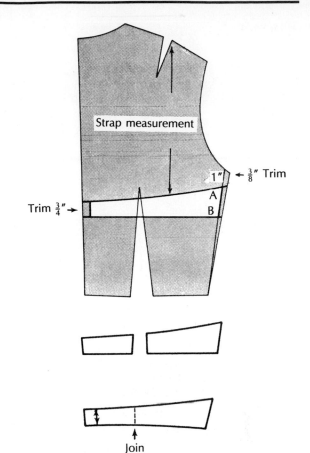

Strap measurement

1" ← $\frac{3}{8}$" Trim

Trim $\frac{3}{4}$" →

A
B

FIGURE 5
- Cut straps from pattern. Discard unneeded sections (shaded areas).

FIGURE 6 *Strap frame (base for strap variations):*
- Join strap sections and retrace.
- To complete the bra patterns, draw grainlines, retrace, and add seams. Cut from paper for test fit. Cut lining from these patterns. Choose back strap from variations shown to complete garment. If bra cup is desired, see Chapter 24.

Join

FIGURE 7 *Neck strap:*
- *Length:* Measure from front bra to mid-shoulder to back strap, and add 3 inches.
- *Width:* As desired. Example: Length, 20 inches; width, 2 inches (finishes to $\frac{3}{4}$ inch).
- Mark buttonhole 3 inches up and space up and down $\frac{1}{2}$ inch for buttonhole placement.

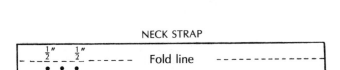

NECK STRAP

$\frac{1}{2}$" $\frac{1}{2}$" - - - - - Fold line - - - - - - - - - - - -

→ 3"

STRAP VARIATIONS

Tie strap

FIGURE 8
- Trace strap frame on fold (full strap shown).
- Extend 10 inches and shape tie end.
- Draw grainline and add $\frac{1}{4}$-inch seams. Cut from paper.

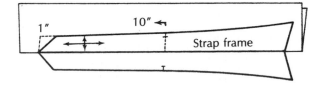

1"   10" ↰   Strap frame

Button control with elastic

FIGURE 9
- Trace strap frame on fold (full strap shown).
- Extend $2\frac{1}{2}$ inches. Mark 1 inch in from A (indicates center back). Mark 5 inches in from A. Label B.
- Mark buttonhole and button placement.
- Cut two elastic strips $\frac{3}{4}$ inch × 4 inches. (Elastic is attached at A and stretched to point B between the folds.)

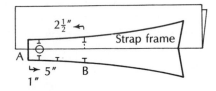

$2\frac{1}{2}$" ↰   Strap frame

A
→ 5"   B
1"

Elastic and hook strap

FIGURE 10

Note: This type of closure requires a bra design with ½-inch-wide side seams.

- Draw a strip 1½ inches × 12 inches (cut two).
- Cut two elastic strips ½ inch × 6 inches. (Stretch elastic when inserted between folds and stitch.)
- Fold strap to make loop and stitch. Other strap is folded over the hook and stitched. (Hook is inserted into the loop to secure the garment.)

Loop formed by fold-over

BRA TOP WITH HORIZONTAL STYLELINE

Design Analysis
The bikini top has a styleline crossing bust points from center front to side seam.

Pattern plot and development

FIGURE 1

- Trace front Contour Guide Pattern and include the following:
- Bust point and bust circumference (example: 3 inch radius).
- Use pushpins to transfer Guidelines 2 (over-bust contour), 5 (under-bust contour), and 6 (contour between the bust).
- Draw line $\frac{3}{8}$ inch in from side seam, ending at waist to remove ease. Connect guidelines to bust point.
- Use personal measurements, or those given.
- Square a line from center front to side, touching bust point.
- Draw bra stylelines using measurements given.

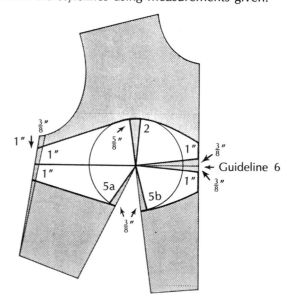

FIGURE 2

■ Cut bikini bra from pattern. Shaded areas are discarded.

FIGURE 3

■ Join pattern sections as shown. To provide room for the bust mound, draw outward curved lines and blend to bust points and sides of patterns as shown.
■ Retrace, draw grainlines, and add seams. Cut from paper. Trace bra patterns for lining.
■ Bra cups (optional); see Chapter 24.
■ Bra strap; see princess bikini top, Figure 7, page 605.
■ Back strap; see pages 605–606. Figures 4 through 10.

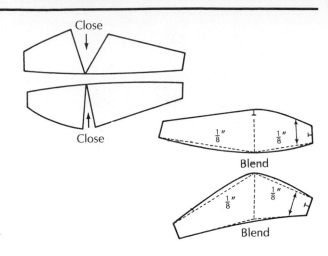

STRING-A-LONG BIKINI TOP

Design Analysis

Bikini top is shaped like a triangle. Straps attached to the bra tie at the back neck with spaghetti strap pulled through folded-hemline casing and ties in the back. Top is darted under the bust and is self-faced or lined.

Bra to neck strap: Cut two pieces 1 inch × 18 inches. (Ties attached to bra top.)
Pull-through strap: 1 inch × 40 inches. (Tie is pulled through casing at hem of bra and tied in back.)

Pattern plot and development

FIGURE 1

■ Trace the front Contour Guide Pattern. Mark bust point and draw bust circumference (3 inches).
■ Square a line out from each side of dart leg at the bust circumference, ending at center front and side.
■ Label A and mark B, 1 inch from side as shown.
■ Draw a guideline from bust point to corner of neck. Mark midpoint on line. Square out $\frac{1}{4}$ inch from each side of mark for top of bra. From these points, draw straight lines to points A and B.
■ Shape side of bra by drawing an inward curve line to within $\frac{1}{8}$ inch of bust circumference as shown.
■ Blend across open dart (see Figure 2).

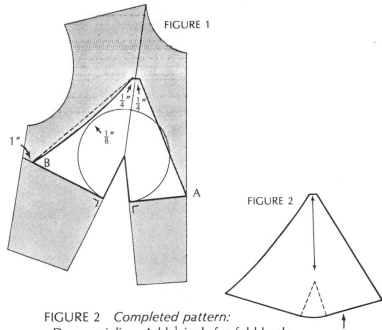

FIGURE 2 *Completed pattern:*
■ Draw grainline. Add $\frac{1}{2}$ inch for fold-back. All other seams $\frac{3}{8}$ inch. Cut from paper.
■ Trace pattern for lining.
■ Bra cups (optional); see Chapter 24.

BANDEAU BIKINI TOP

Design Analysis

The bandeau-effect bikini top is supported by a spaghetti strap pulled through a fold-back (casing) at the sides. The strap goes around the neck and ties in back.

Pattern plot and development

FIGURE 1
- Trace front Contour Guide Pattern.
- Mark bust point and draw bust circumference (3 inches).
- Square a line from center front, touching the top, bottom, and sides of circumference line (indicated by broken lines).

Options:
- Use squared lines to form bandeau, or measure down 1 inch and up 1 inch from squared lines at center front and mark.
- Measure in $\frac{1}{2}$ inch from each end at corners. Mark.
- Draw curved lines touching each mark as shown. The dart excess is absorbed into the design's feature.
- Cut bandeau from pattern. Discard unneeded sections (shaded areas).

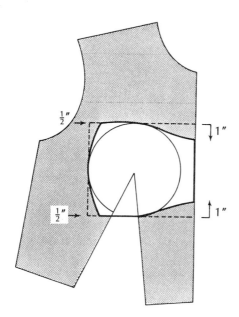

FIGURE 2
- Retrace on fold. Draw grainline and add seam allowance. Cut pattern paper. Full pattern shape is shown. (Broken line indicates optional shape.)
- Trace pattern for lining.
- Draw grainlines (straight or bias). Add $\frac{1}{2}$ inch for fold-back (casing). All other seams $\frac{3}{8}$ inch.
- Cut bias strap: 1 inch $\times$ 60 inches.

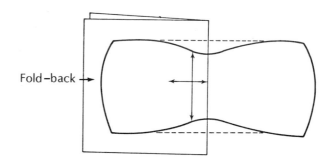

Fold—back

LITTLE-BOY LEGLINE FOUNDATION

The little-boy foundation is developed from the slack jumpsuit. If that is not available, see jumpsuit instructions (Chapter 21) and develop jumpsuit to knee level.

LITTLE-BOY LEGLINE DRAFT

Pattern development

FIGURES 1 and 2

- Trace front and back slack jumpsuit to $1\frac{1}{2}$ inches below crotch point on inseam of front and back. Draw a blending line to side seam at crotch level, or draw legline parallel with crotch level for a modest cut (broken lines).
- From crotch point, measure up $2\frac{1}{2}$ inches along crotch curve. Mark and draw a slash line to legline as shown.

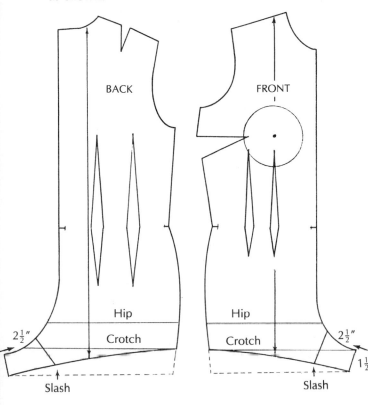

FIGURES 3 and 4

- Cut slash line to, not through, crotch curve.
- Overlap $\frac{1}{2}$ inch and tape. (Tightens legline.)

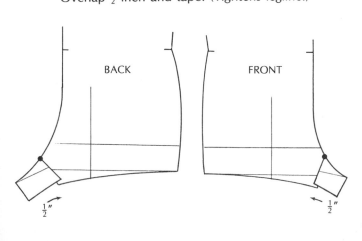

FIGURES 5 and 6

- Raise crotch point $\frac{1}{4}$ inch.
- Measure in $\frac{3}{8}$ inch at side seams.
- Blend leg and crotch areas.

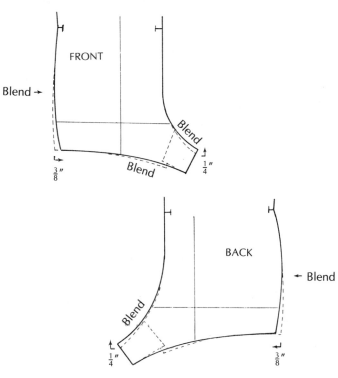

FIGURES 7 and 8

- Figures show completed foundation. If cut in a stable knit, remove $\frac{1}{2}$ inch from sides and 1 inch at waist.

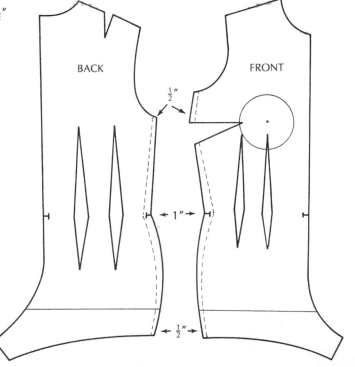

LITTLE-BOY LEGLINE VARIATIONS

The two designs that follow show the versatility of this foundation, which can also be used to develop tennis and sun suits. Design 1 features a little-boy slit legline while Design 2 features a princess-line overdress to which is attached an underframe, darted to control fit. The legline is gathered and used as bloomers. Design 1 is illustrated. Design 2 is a practice problem.

SLIT LEGLINE

Design Analysis

The little-boy legline (Design 1) is cut in cotton and is lined. It features an Empire cut with stylized neckline and lowered back. The bra section (bust cups are optional) has folded darts that point away from bust point. The legline is slit. Darts in front and back control fit. Straps follow the lowered armhole and have button adjustments.

Pattern plot and development

FIGURES 1 and 2
- Trace front and back Contour Guide Patterns. (See Chapter 9.)
- Mark bust point and draw bust circumference (example: 3 inch radius).
- Use pushpin to transfer Guidelines 2 (over-bust contour), 5 (under-bust contour), and 6 (contour between the bust). Connect guidelines to bust point.
- Use personal measurements, or those given.
- Draw Empire styleline and styled neckline, lower back, and widen legline as shown. Notch as shown.
- Continue dart intake (of lower section), ending at waist dart (shaded area of front pattern).
- Transfer one-half of the dart excess to center front and back and at the sides as shown (shaded areas).
- Measure in an additional $\frac{1}{2}$ inch at center back of swimsuit, blending to zero at crotch for a tighter fit.
- Cut and separate pattern. Discard unneeded sections (shaded areas). Cut slash lines to bust point.

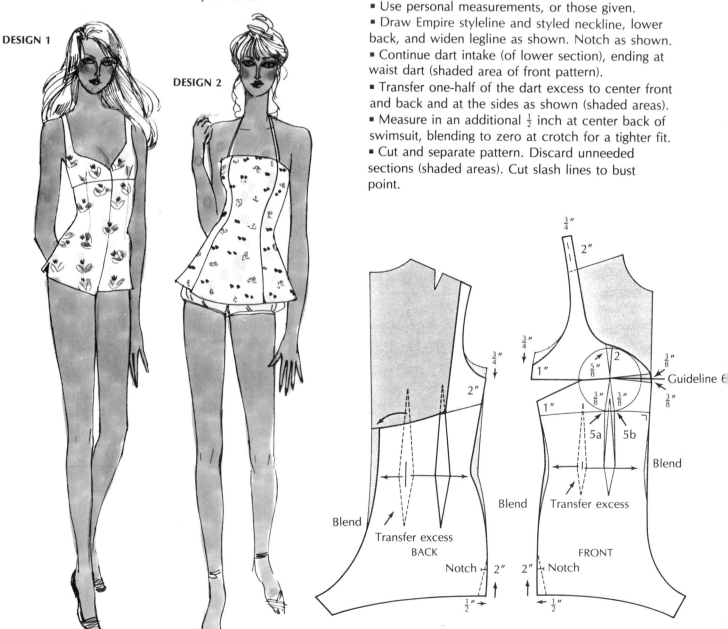

FIGURE 3 *Bra top:*
- Close side dart and Guidelines 2 and 6. Retrace.
- Measure out 1 inch from each side of bust point (new dart points). Label A and B. Mark center of open dart. Label C.

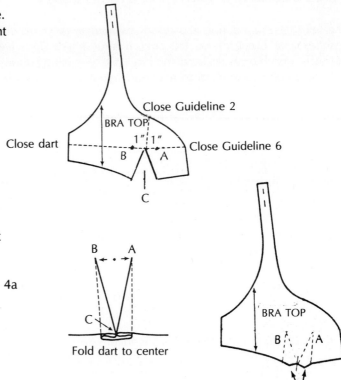

FIGURE 4
- Crease-fold dart legs to point C, and direct dart points to marks A and B. Use tracing wheel to transfer style line to folded darts underneath. Unfold and pencil in perforated lines. (See Figure 4a for dart shape.)
- Draw grainline.
- Bra cup information: see Chapter 24.

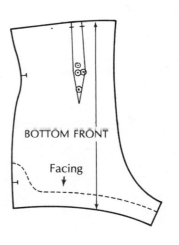

Fold dart to center

Shape of dart legs

FIGURES 5 and 6
- Trace patterns for lining. For facing, draw line 1 inch above legline as indicated by broken lines. Trace facing shape to paper.
- Add seams. Mark for button and buttonholes. Punch and circle darts as shown.

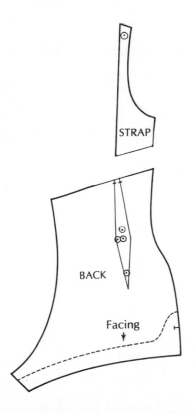

FULL-FIGURE SWIM FOUNDATION

The full-figure foundation is used for swimwear garments cut in rigid fabrics or knits such as latex and spandex. When cut in knit, the pattern is modified. Darts are needed to control the fit of the garment through the waist and bust areas, and the bra cups give extra support for the bust. A traced copy should be used to develop design patterns from this foundation. This pattern is seamless.

FULL-FIGURE SWIM DRAFT

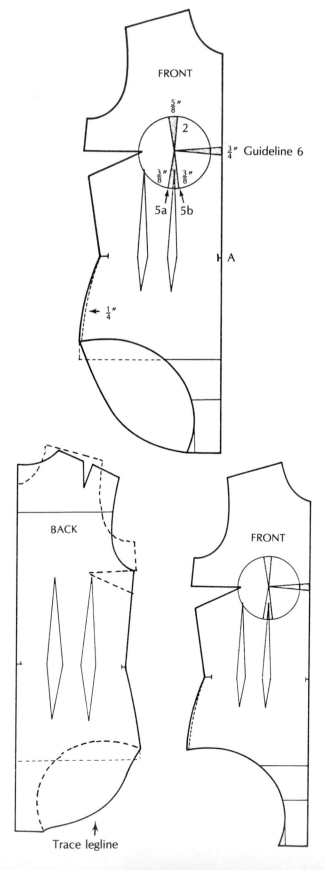

Measurement needed
▪ (28) Crotch length _____.

Patterns needed: Torso front and torso back patterns, with legline instructions from the leotard draft.

Pattern plot and development

FIGURE 1
▪ Trace torso front and torso back patterns.
▪ Mark bust point and bust circumference. Use pushpin to transfer Guidelines 2 (over-bust contour), 5 (under-bust contour), and 6 (contour between the bust). Connect guidelines to bust point.
▪ Measure out $\frac{1}{4}$ inch at front hip. Draw new hipline for front and back torso, ending at waist as shown (broken line indicates original hipline).
▪ Label center front waist A.
▪ The torso front is used for developing the front and back legline. Use the instructions given for the leotard draft, page 589, Figures 3 through 6. Follow instruction for knits with 50% stretch.
▪ After the legline is complete, cut pattern from paper.

FIGURE 2   *Back foundation:*
▪ Place front on top of torso back, matching hip levels and center front and back.
▪ Trace back legline. Remove pattern and cut from paper.

FIGURE 3   *Front foundation:*
▪ Trim to front legline.

Trace legline

FIGURES 4 and 5 *Leglines for skirted swimwear:*
- Square out from center front and center back at hip (A) and crotch (B) equal to hip measurement. Label C. Square up from C to side hip.
- Draw legline as shown (broken line indicates original legline).

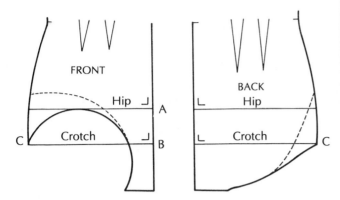

Reduction of the full-figure foundation
Use reduction instructions when cutting in firm knits.

FIGURES 6 and 7
- Trace front and back patterns.
- Measure in ½ inch at side at armhole.
- Measure in 1½ inches at waist.
- Measure in 1¼ inches at side leg.
- Draw a blending line for new side seam. (Shaded area to be discarded.)

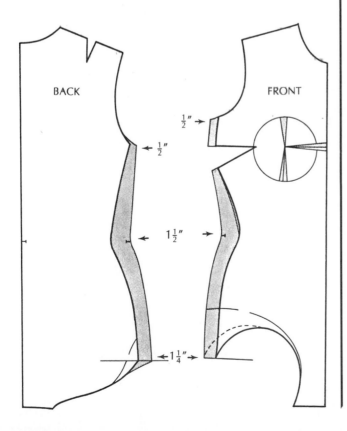

SWIMSUIT WITH SKIRT FRONT

Design I is cut in spandex and is based on the full-figure swim foundation. The traced pattern should be reduced for stretch before the pattern is developed, using instructions given on Figures 6 and 7. Remember: The width of the pattern should lie on the fabric in the direction of the greatest stretch. Design 2 is given as a practice problem.

Design Analysis
The Empire cut, with styleline of bra crossing bust points, has spaghetti straps that tie in back. The bra top is supported by bra cups, and the lower skirted section covers the legline. The underneath section is lined in tricot or power knit while the crotch section (visible on the right side of garment) is self-lined.

(Continued on next page)

Pattern plot and development

FIGURES 1 and 2

- Trace modified front and back full-figure foundation and include all markings. Use instructions for modified legline for skirted designs (Figures 4, 5, 6, and 7, page 613).
- Use personal measurements for contouring, or those given.
- Draw stylelines, using illustration and measurements as a guide.

  Note: Trim bottom section at side equal to dart intake so that patterns will true when joined together along Empire styleline (Figure 2).
- Cut and separate patterns, discarding unneeded section (shaded areas).

FIGURES 3, 4, 5, and 6

Bra top:
- Join sections and blend as shown. (Broken lines indicate original pattern.) Retrace. (Figure 3).
- Trace patterns with front cut on fold. (Figures 4 and 5).

Skirt pattern:
- Trace front lower section on fold and square from center front at crotch level to side. (When adding seams, add 1 inch to hem for attachment of 1-inch-wide elastic cut to skirt pattern width.) (Figure 6.).
- Add seams, and cut from paper.

Straps (not illustrated):
Cut bias strip 1 inch × 36 inches. Cut in half to make two straps.

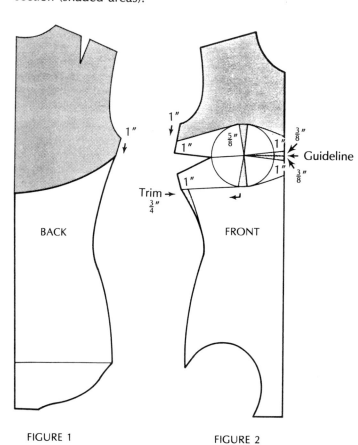

FIGURE 1   FIGURE 2

Note: For elastic and bra cup instruction see Chapter 24.

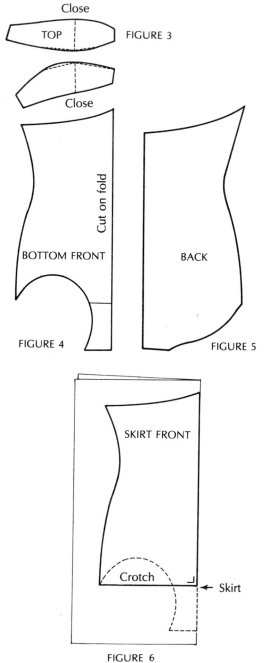

FIGURE 3
FIGURE 4   FIGURE 5
FIGURE 6

SUPPLIES AND SPECIAL INFORMATION 616
Use of elastic 616
Finishing crotch and shoulder 617
Bra cups for swimwear 617

24

ELASTIC, CROTCH LINING, AND BRA CUPS

SUPPLIES AND SPECIAL INFORMATION

The following general information and illustrations should be used to complete patterns for actionwear garments. Also included is special information relating to the garment construction for use wherever appropriate. Needed:

- Needles. Use ball point, sizes 9 to 11, and 10–12 stitches per inch.
- Thread. Corespun (nylon or polyester) or cotton.
- Bra cups, with or without power-knit frame. Purchase at fabric stores, notions counter, or supply houses catering to manufacturers of mass-produced garments.
- Power knit or nylon tricot for bra cup frames and crotch and/or swimsuit lining.
- Elastic. ¼ inch (⅜ inch is easier for beginners to handle). For bra frame, use ¼-inch lace elastic and ½-inch felt-back elastic, if available. Use 1-inch elastic for skirted-front swimsuits.

USE OF ELASTIC

Elastic is attached to all raw edges of the garment, whether it is cut in rigid or knit fabrics, except where seams are joined together or faced. This helps the garment cling to the figure, especially where stylelines cross the hollows of the body—above, below, or between the bust mounds; under the buttocks; and where cutouts cross through a part of the waistline. It is also used around lowered waistlines of the bikini pant.

Elastic guidelines

An elastic ratio of 1:1, as given in the examples, means that when the elastic is attached it is not stretched. Elastic is attached to the garment with a zigzag, overlock, or straight stitch. The elastic is placed on the wrong side of the garment (see shaded areas, Figures 1 and 3), stitched, folded over, and restitched. It should be stretched evenly while being stitched.

Elastic measurements

FIGURES 1, 2, and 3
- *Front neckline:* Cut elastic 1 inch less than neckline.
- *Back neckline:* Cut elastic, using 1:1 ratio.
- *Cutout armholes:* Cut elastic ½ inch less than armhole. Use 1:1 ratio for regular armhole.
- *Legline:* Cut elastic 1½ inches less than front and back legline (½ inch used for overlap). Stretch elastic across back and continue 1½ inches past crotch seam of front leg. Use 1:1 ratio on the remaining front legline.

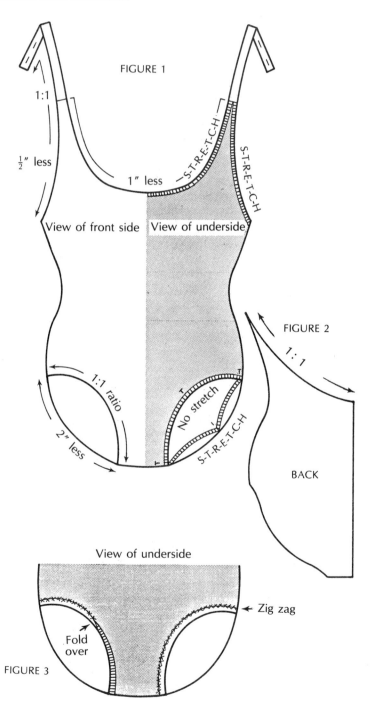

FIGURE 1

1:1

½" less

1" less

S-T-R-E-T-C-H

View of front side

View of underside

1:1 ratio

2" less

No stretch

S-T-R-E-T-C-H

FIGURE 2

1:1

BACK

View of underside

Fold over

Zig zag

FIGURE 3

FIGURE 4
- *Cutout waist:* Cut elastic $1\frac{1}{2}$ inches less than length of style cut, stretching $\frac{3}{4}$ inch under bust and $\frac{3}{4}$ inch along remaining styleline.
- *Straps:* Cut elastic using a 1:1 ratio.

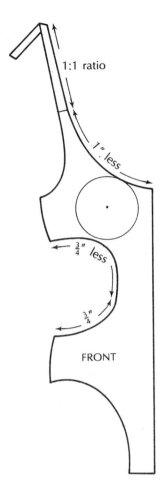

FIGURE 5
- *Bikini:* Cut elastic $1\frac{1}{2}$ inches less than total waist.

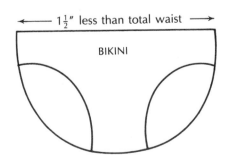

FINISHING CROTCH AND SHOULDER

Crotch lining pattern
FIGURE 6
- Trace front pattern from crotch to approximately 6 inches up (1 inch past crotch level).
- Remove pattern. Draw curved line to leg as shown.

FIGURE 7
- Cut from paper, place on fold, and retrace. (Full pattern shown.)
- Cut in self-fabric or nylon tricot.
- Place on the underside of the garment and stitch in with legline elastic.

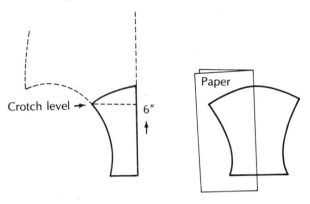

Shoulder tape
FIGURE 8
- Cut tape equal to shoulder length of pattern. Use along shoulderline of bodysuits and leotards to prevent stretching.

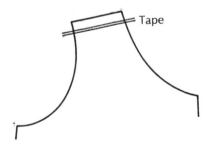

BRA CUPS FOR SWIMWEAR

Two types of bra frames are illustrated, with instructions for attaching each to the garment. Bra Frame 1 should be used for garments *without* stylelines crossing under the bust mound (example: the Empire styleline). The bra cup is attached to a frame that hangs free of the garment, except at the top and sides. Bra Frame 2 is used for garments *with* stylelines crossing under the bust; however, a free-hanging frame can also be used. The complete frame is attached to the garment.

(Continued on next page)

Bra frame 1

FIGURE 9

> **Measurement needed**
> ▪ (10) Bust span _____.

▪ Cut power knit, nylon tricot, or self-fabric equal to the length and width of the pattern from the strap to just under bust level, plus 2 inches.
▪ Draw a chalk line through center, and a horizontal line 4 inches up from the bottom.
▪ Locate bust points on the horizontal line (out from center) and mark.
▪ Place bra cups on fabric, aligning bust points of bra cup with bust marks. Pin cups to fabric.

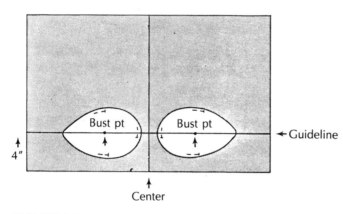

FIGURE 10

▪ Turn fabric over and trim excess from around bra cups to within $\frac{1}{2}$ inch. Place on form or figure and adjust cup position if necessary.

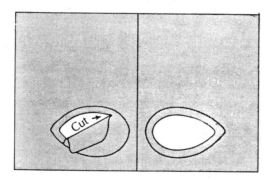

FIGURE 11

▪ *Bra cup attachment guidelines:* Stitch to garment with a zigzag or straight stitch. Trim excess to within $\frac{1}{4}$ inch.
▪ Attach $\frac{1}{4}$-inch lace elastic on the stitchline around bra cups on the underside of the garment.
▪ Cut $\frac{1}{2}$-inch-wide elastic (felt-back, if possible), $\frac{1}{2}$ inch less than width of frame. Attach along bottom of frame just under bust level, stretching evenly. Trim excess to bottom of elastic.
▪ Pin or stitch bra frame to wrong side of garment and attach with elastic to garment.

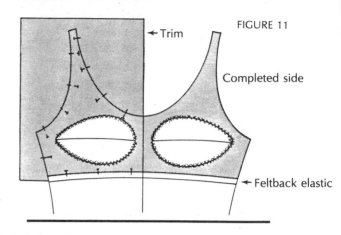

FIGURE 11

Bra frame 2

FIGURE 12
▪ Trace pattern for bodice front (section for bra insert).
▪ Cut in fabric and stitch. (Bra with Empire styleline shown as the example.)

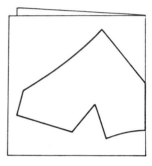

FIGURE 13
▪ Place stitched frame on form or figure. Put bra cups over fabric and the bust mound. Pin in place on fabric.
▪ Pencil in cup outline.
▪ Remove bust cups from garment. Remove stitched top from form.

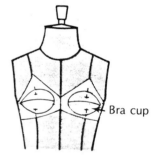

FIGURE 14
▪ Remove dart stitches from frame and trace pattern on fold, transferring penciled outline of bra cup. Allow $\frac{1}{4}$ inch for attaching bra cups. Cut from paper.
▪ Cut in power knit, nylon tricot or self-fabric.
▪ Stitch frame together at bottom. Follow instructions for bra cut attachment for Bra Cup 1. Felt-back elastic can be attached along styleline for comfort.

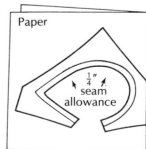

part Seven

PROBLEMS AND SOLUTIONS

Introduction 622
Stretch and recovery factor 622
Classification of knit fabrics 622
Direction of stretch 622
ADAPTING PATTERNS TO KNITS 623
Method 1: Shrinkage factor 623
Stretch/recovery gauge 624
Method 2: Stretch/recovery factor 624

KNITS—STRETCH AND SHRINKAGE FACTORS

INTRODUCTION

Knits are one of the most popular fabrics in the market today, primarily for the following reasons:
- *Structure:* Knit fabrics are made of natural and synthetic fibers.
- *Versatility:* Knits are suitable for dressy, daytime, and active wear.
- *Stretchability:* Knits have the capacity to stretch in length and/or width (in addition to the bias stretch common to all fabrics).

Many manufacturers and designers devote part or all of their lines to knit designs. The patternmaker should be knowledgeable about the special characteristics of knits and their stretch/recovery factors so that a good fit can be achieved with a minimum number of corrections. This is accomplished by modifying the pattern before cutting it in knit.

STRETCH AND RECOVERY FACTOR

The ability of a knit fabric to stretch and return to its original shape (length and width) is referred to as the fabric's *memory.* (See the Stretch/Recovery Gauge, page 624.)

The *stretch factor* is the amount of stretch per inch that occurs when the knit is stretched to its maximum length and width. The stretch factor of knits ranges anywhere from 18 to 100% or more.

The *recovery factor* is the degree to which a knit will return to its original shape after being stretched. Knits with good recovery are those that return to their original length and width when released. If the fabric does not return to its original dimension, or close to it, the garment will eventually sag on the body and lose some of its original shape.

There is a variance in the *degree of stretch among knits* and the *degree of stretch between the length and width of each specific knit.* Knits that stretch in both directions are two-way stretch knits.

CLASSIFICATION OF KNIT FABRICS

Knits come in many fibers; cotton, antron, and nylon to name a few. When combined with Lycra/spandex, or Lastex/latex, the fabric will vary in weight, texture, direction, and degree of stretch and shrinkage. There are single-knit and double-knit fabrics; however, knits can generally be classified in the following ways:

Stable (firm) knits. 18% stretch factor on the crosswise grain (Example: 5 inches will stretch to $5\frac{7}{8}$ inches.) This type knit has a limited degree of stretch and will retain its original shape well. Fit is similar to that of a garment cut in a woven fabric. Example: Double knit in any fiber.

Moderate-stretch knits. 25% stretch factor on the crosswise grain. (Example: 5 inches stretches to $6\frac{1}{4}$ inches.) Combines both characteristics of stable and stretchy knits. Generally used for sportswear where stretch is used for comfort and a close fit, but should not be used for garments contouring the figure. Example: Nylon tricot.

Stretchy knits. 50% stretch factor on the crosswise grain with 18 to 50% on the straight grain. (Example: 5 inches will stretch to $7\frac{1}{2}$ inches.) Because it is stretchy and lightweight, stretchy knit drapes well and is used for garments that contour the figure. This type knit is suitable for bodysuits, leotards, maillots, clinging dresses and tops

(provided the knit has an excellent recovery factor). Example: cotton/spandex, nylon/spandex, cotton/latex, nylon/latex. Any fabric containing spandex or latex.

Super-stretch knit. 100% stretchability factor in the lengthwise and crosswise grain. (Example: 5 inches stretches to 10 or more inches.) Its excellent stretch and recovery make it suitable for bodysuits, leotards, and skiwear, as well as tops. (Examples: Any fiber blended with spandex or latex.) The elastic fibers of this type knit can stretch many times its length and yet return to its original measurements.

Rib knits. 100% stretch factor (1 × 1 ribs will stretch less than 2 × 2 or 3 × 2). Used for tops and banding. (Example: The ''knit two, purl two'' traditional wristband stitch.) Rib knits are dependent on the *knit pattern* used, as well as fibers.

DIRECTION OF STRETCH

To utilize the built-in stretch of knits, the maximum stretch should *encircle* the figure when knits are used for dresses, jackets, pants, and tops. The maximum stretch should go *up and down* the figure for bodysuits, leotards, jumpsuits and skiwear to allow for maximum mobility.

ADAPTING PATTERNS TO KNITS

There are two different methods used for adapting a pattern to knit fabrics. One takes into consideration the shrinkage factor and the other the stretch factor of the knit. The choice between the two methods is determined by the type of knit and use of the garment.

METHOD 1—SHRINKAGE FACTOR

(Using Shrinkage Factor) This method is preferred for loosely fitted garments. Shrinkage is considered to be the most important factor; therefore, the pattern is enlarged to compensate for shrinkage. To do this, the shrinkage factor must be known.

Enlarging the pattern

FIGURES 1 and 2
- Cut garment parts. (The torso and sleeve are used as the example.)
- Wash and dry the fabric. Place on top of the pattern, aligning the centerline and waist of the torso, and the grainline and biceps line of the sleeve. [Shaded area indicates the garment part (A), the white area the original pattern (B), and the lined area the new enlarged pattern (C).]
- Enlarging the new pattern: Draw guidelines out from the corners of the fabric pattern and working patterns as shown. Measure the distances from the cloth pattern and the working pattern at each guideline. Use these measurements to mark the distances out from the working pattern at each location. Draw new pattern by connecting lines from one mark to the next, blending curved lines as shown. True patterns when cut.

  Note: Placement of garment parts on pattern may look different from the illustrations, but the process for developing the enlarged pattern remains the same.

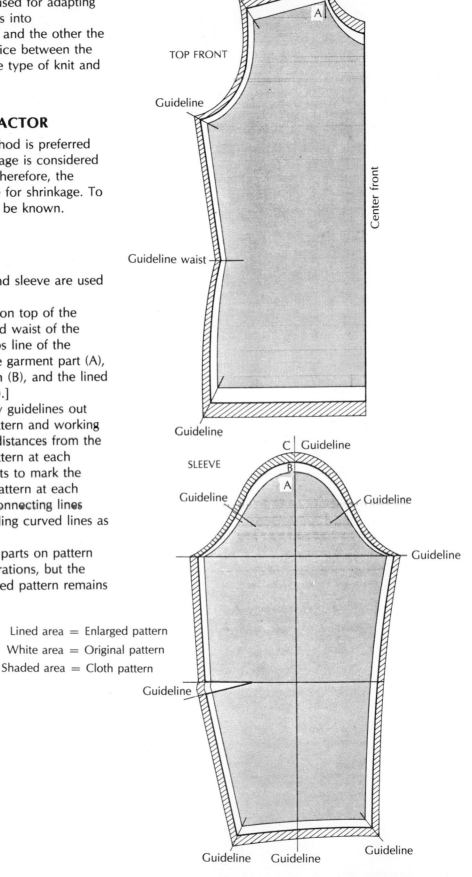

Lined area = Enlarged pattern
White area = Original pattern
Shaded area = Cloth pattern

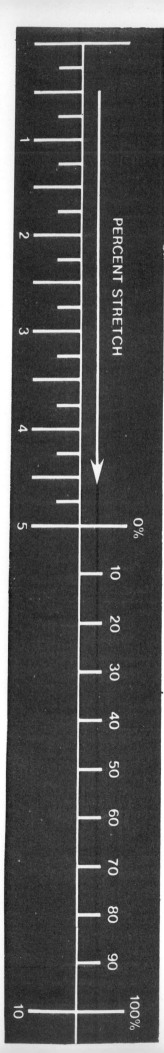

STRETCH/RECOVERY GAUGE

Ruler at edge of page is used to determine the stretch/recovery factor of knits. *Suggestion:* Xerox ruler, glue on cardboard, and take with you when testing and buying knits. To use stretch gauge ruler, follow instructions:

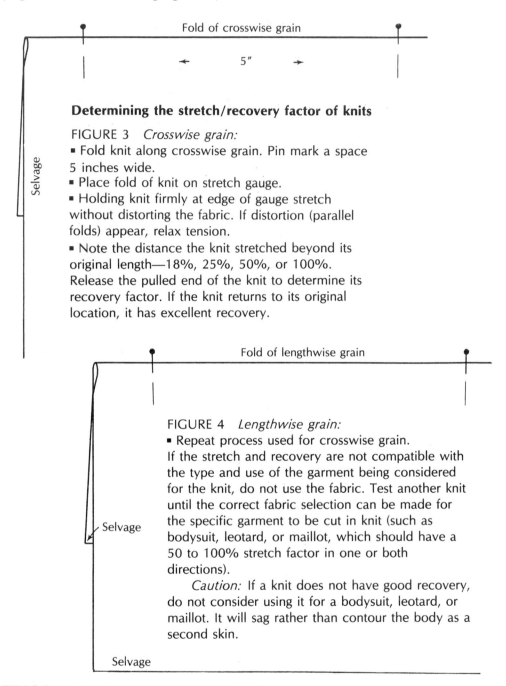

Fold of crosswise grain

← 5″ →

Selvage

Determining the stretch/recovery factor of knits

FIGURE 3   *Crosswise grain:*
- Fold knit along crosswise grain. Pin mark a space 5 inches wide.
- Place fold of knit on stretch gauge.
- Holding knit firmly at edge of gauge stretch without distorting the fabric. If distortion (parallel folds) appear, relax tension.
- Note the distance the knit stretched beyond its original length—18%, 25%, 50%, or 100%. Release the pulled end of the knit to determine its recovery factor. If the knit returns to its original location, it has excellent recovery.

Fold of lengthwise grain

FIGURE 4   *Lengthwise grain:*
- Repeat process used for crosswise grain.
If the stretch and recovery are not compatible with the type and use of the garment being considered for the knit, do not use the fabric. Test another knit until the correct fabric selection can be made for the specific garment to be cut in knit (such as bodysuit, leotard, or maillot, which should have a 50 to 100% stretch factor in one or both directions).

Selvage

   Caution: If a knit does not have good recovery, do not consider using it for a bodysuit, leotard, or maillot. It will sag rather than contour the body as a second skin.

Selvage

METHOD 2—STRETCH/RECOVERY FACTOR

(Using Stretch/Recovery Factor) This method is used for close-fitted and contour-type garments in which stretch is the most important factor (bodysuit, leotard, swimwear). The original pattern is modified (reduced in length and width) to compensate for the stretch. How much stretch is removed depends on the stretch factor of the knit. For knits with stretch factor from 18 to 25%, use reductions given on Figures 6, 7, 8, and 9. For knits with stretch factor of 50 to 100%, see page 582 (bodysuit) page 588 (leotard).

Length and width reduction of pattern

To determine how much a pattern's length and width should be reduced, follow the examples and measurements given for knits with a stretch factor from 18 to 25%. *For knits stretching beyond 25% but less than 50%, add $\frac{1}{8}$ inch to all measurements given below.* The measurements given are general and may require additional adjustments at time of fitting. Remember that knits do shrink when washed; this should be considered before fitting garments close to the figure. The basic front bodice, skirt, sleeve, and pant are illustrated and should be used as a guide for all similar pattern modifications. Broken line indicates original patterns.

FIGURES 6, 7, and 8 *Bodice, skirt, and pants:*
- *Neckline:* Raise $\frac{1}{4}$ inch. Blend. Back neck is not adjusted unless neckline is deeply cut.
- *Side seams:* Remove $\frac{1}{4}$ inch (parallel with original line of pattern). Repeat for back. Remove $\frac{1}{4}$ inch from inseam of pant.
- *Armhole:* Raise $\frac{1}{2}$ inch. Blend. Repeat for back.
- *Dart points:* Raise $\frac{1}{4}$ inch where shown.
- *Hemlines and waistline:* Remove $\frac{1}{4}$ inch (parallel with original hem or waist of pattern).
- *Crotch:* Raise $\frac{1}{4}$ to $\frac{1}{2}$ inch. (Amount depends on style of pant.) Example: $\frac{1}{2}$ inch for trouser, $\frac{1}{4}$ inch for slack or jean. Repeat for back.

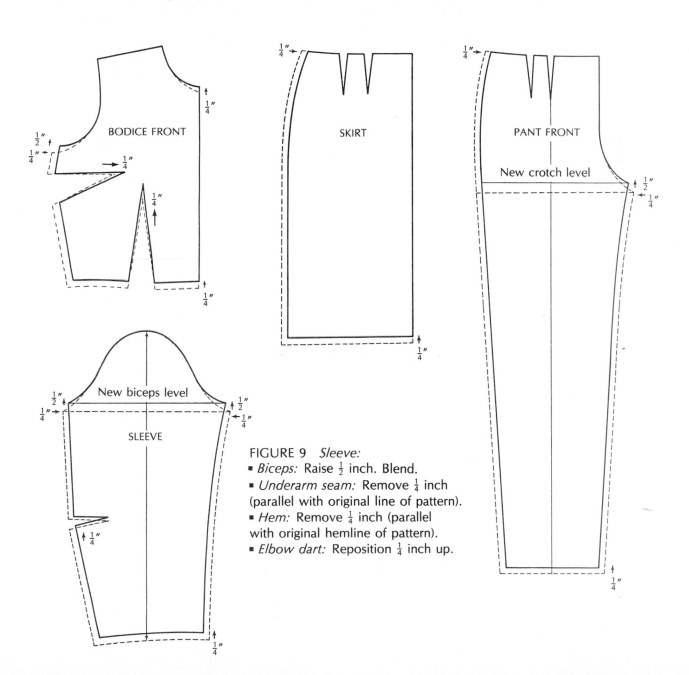

FIGURE 9 *Sleeve:*
- *Biceps:* Raise $\frac{1}{2}$ inch. Blend.
- *Underarm seam:* Remove $\frac{1}{4}$ inch (parallel with original line of pattern).
- *Hem:* Remove $\frac{1}{4}$ inch (parallel with original hemline of pattern).
- *Elbow dart:* Reposition $\frac{1}{4}$ inch up.

REQUIRED PANT DRAFT ADJUSTMENTS 628
Adjustments to figure shapes 628
Waist, abdomen, and hip adjustments 629
Crotch adjustments 632

26

PANT DRAFT ADJUSTMENT FOR PERSONAL FIT

REQUIRED PANT DRAFT ADJUSTMENTS

Pant adjustments must be made before the creaseline and leglines are drafted. Read through the series. Apply pant adjustments to the draft that are appropriate for the specific problems of the figure as recorded on the Measurement Chart, omitting all others. When adjustments are completed, you will be instructed to return to the draft to complete the pant. For clarity, use a sharpened red pencil to make adjustments wherever needed.

ADJUSTMENTS TO FIGURE SHAPES

R-shape adjustment for trouser only
Realignment of F/B crotch extensions.

FIGURE 1
- Reposition I by reducing G–I line $1\frac{1}{2}$ inches.
- Reposition M by extending K–M line by $1\frac{1}{2}$ inches.
- Subtract $\frac{1}{8}$ inch from G–g line.
- Add $\frac{1}{8}$ inch to K–k line.
- Reshape crotch curve, as shown.

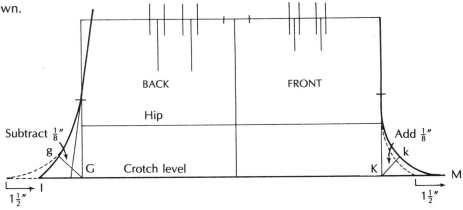

S-shape, O-shape, oval-O-shape, or protruding thighs
Extension of line at M to compensate for large thighs and abdomen.

FIGURE 2
- Reposition M by extending K–M line 1 inch.
- Add $\frac{1}{8}$ inch to K–k diagonal line.
- Reshape crotch curve, as shown.

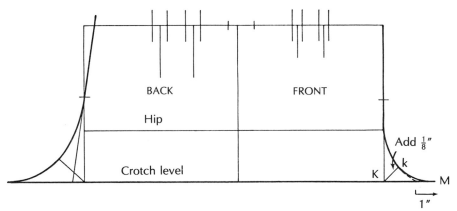

WAIST, ABDOMEN, AND HIP ADJUSTMENTS

Tilting waistlines
Repositioning point L (trouser) and point T (jean).

Measurements needed
• (25) Hip depth: CF _____, CB _____.

FIGURE 3
• It may be necessary to extend or reduce the length of the centerlines to establish personal measurements. Relocate letters as follows:
• Measure up from hip at center back, relocating point S (CB Hip depth).
• Measure up from hip level at center front (CF Hip depth) relocating point L (trouser) or point T (jean).

Note: The example illustrates a tilting waist with a low front and high back.

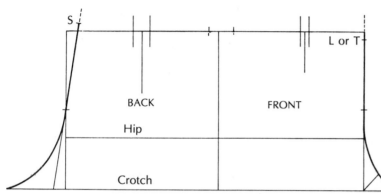

FIGURE 4
If the center front of the *trouser or slack* extends more than $\frac{1}{2}$ inch up from waist level, make the following additional adjustment:
• Square a line $\frac{1}{2}$ inch in from new point L. From L draw a straight line to crotch level, touching point X.
• Relocate P, $\frac{1}{2}$ inch toward point A.

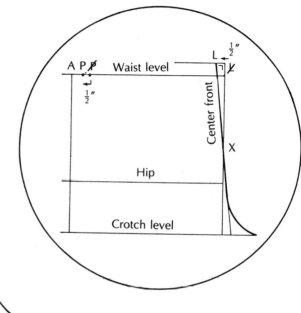

Points N and P
If points N and P are within $\frac{1}{4}$ inch of or touch point A, this will cause the hipline curves to overlap each other on the draft. This poses a problem when separating the front and back pants. Trace the back pant on paper placed underneath the draft before cutting the patterns apart, or cut patterns apart and mend hipline (not illustrated).

When points N and P overlap point A
Use red pencil to shape front and blue pencil to shape back.

FIGURE 5
• Draw a straight line from point C to point N (pant back) and to point P (pant front). Crossmark each line equal to the A–C measurement. Reposition letters N and P.
• Draw hipline curve from N and P to C.
• Connect waistline from S to N and L to P.

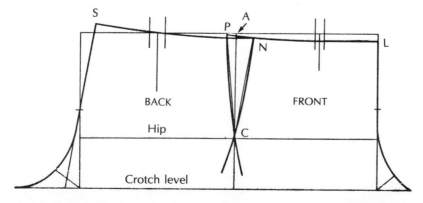

When abdomen replaces hip measurement

Adjust points C and D on draft.

FIGURE 6

A–X = One-third of A–D (original D).
F–C = Back hip plus $\frac{1}{8}$ inch. Mark new location for C.
G–D = Same as F–C, less $\frac{1}{4}$ inch. Mark new location for D.
J–C = Front hip plus $\frac{1}{8}$ inch. Mark new location for C.

K–D = Same as J–C, less $\frac{1}{4}$ inch. Mark new location for D.
- Draw outward curve from N to X to slightly beyond C.
- Draw inward curve from D, blending with C.
- Repeat for back hip. Blend at point D when legline is developed, if necessary.

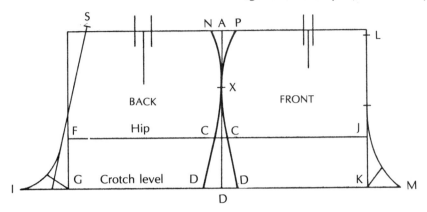

Waistline and darts

FIGURES 7, 8, and 9

Follow the appropriate illustration for your figure type when shaping the waistline curve, as shown below. Draw dart legs from curve of the waistline to the dart ends. True dart legs by adding to the shorter leg. Blend with the waistline.

Use vary curve or skirt curve to shape inward and outward curves of waistline.

- *High front, low back.*

- *Low front, high back.*

- *Low front, low back.*

Hipline curve

- Choose the tool appropriate for the hip type of model.

FIGURES 10, 11, and 12

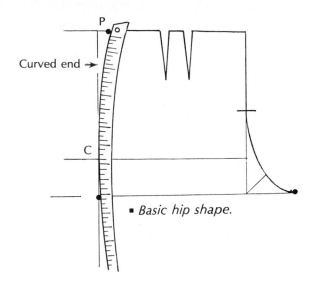

- *Basic hip shape.*

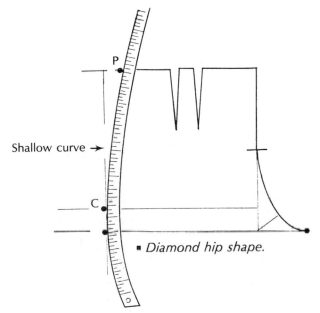

- *Diamond hip shape.*

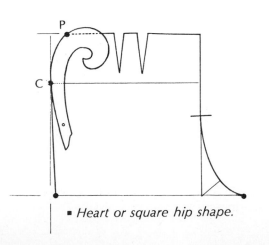

- *Heart or square hip shape.*

Abdominal adjustment

FIGURES 13 and 14

- Measure draft across abdomen level. If it does not equal personal abdominal measurement, adjust by adding to or subtracting equally from the hipline as shown. The broken lines indicate the original side seam. Repeat for back (not illustrated).

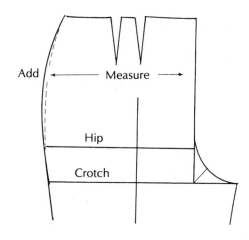

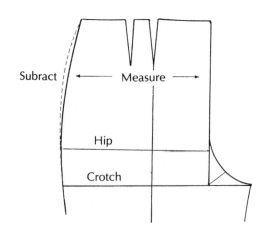

(Continued on next page)

CROTCH ADJUSTMENTS

Crotch level adjustment

FIGURE 15

▪ Line I–M should measure more than upper thigh as follows:

Trouser: I–M should measure at *least* 4 inches more.

Slack: I–M should measure at *least* 3 inches more than upper thigh.

Jean: I–M should measure at *least* 2 inches more.

▪ If it does not, extend line equally on each side of I and M until it does. Reposition letters.

   Note: Above measurements will finish approximately $\frac{1}{2}$ inch less when legline is developed.

Crotch length reference

▪ The front and back crotch length should measure *at least* as much as the recorded personal measurement of the model. However, this measurement tends to be elusive due to crotch depth variations, stretch of the fabric, and figure bulges. Measure and record for use as a reference when correcting the draft.

If crotch length does not equal personal or form measurement, adjust the pant as follows:

▪ *Trouser:* Extend crotch points I and M equally until it does.

▪ *Slack:* Extend crotch point I and point S (center back at waist) equally until it does.

▪ *Jean:* Extend point S (center back at waist until it does.

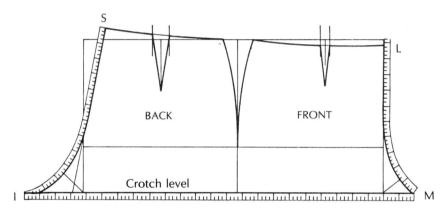

Legline development

After you have modified the pattern for a personal fit, refer to the draft for legline development instructions:

▪ Trouser, see page 539.

▪ Jean, see page 544.

   Note: Figures having knock-knees or bowlegs should develop the draft using the basic legline. Adjustments, if needed, will be done at the time of fitting.

27

FITTING PROBLEMS AND PATTERN CORRECTION

Introduction 634
A good fit 634
A poor fit 634
Terms relating to fit 635
METHODS FOR CORRECTING PATTERNS 635
Method 1: Using the muslin 635
Method 2: Using L-, W-, and X-guidelines 636
How to use the guidelines 636
GARMENT ADJUSTMENT 638
Strain and tightness along seamlines 638
Strain and tightness within the garment 638
Looseness and gapping 639
ANALYZING FIT 639
Sequence for correcting fitting problems 639
INITIAL CORRECTIONS 640
BODICE CORRECTIONS 641
Neckline area 648
SHOULDERLINE AREA 651
Chest and bust area 653
Armhole area 654
Waistline area 658
Darts 659
SKIRT CORRECTIONS 661
SLEEVE CORRECTIONS 666
Equalizing front and back armholes 666
Sleeve rotation 666
Puckering 668
Other sleeve fitting problems 670
PANT CORRECTIONS 674
Test fitting 674
Guidemarking pant front and back 675
Pant fitting problems 676

INTRODUCTION

After the basic pattern has been developed, it should be cut in muslin (or other woven fabrics) and placed on the form or figure for a test fit. This will indicate how accurately measurements were taken, how well the pattern was developed, and whether instructions were followed. In order to test fit the muslin and make the required pattern corrections, you must be able to recognize the differences between a good fit and a poor fit. Fitting errors if not corrected will be incorporated in the basic pattern. A perfect basic pattern is required for future designs that are based on it. Those adjusting the fit of pants should read the following information before turning to page 674.

A GOOD FIT

A garment that fits well will hang from the shoulder to the hemline without the appearance of strain, tightness, gapping, or looseness. The sleeve will be in perfect alignment with the arm. The garment will appear neither too short nor too long from neckline to waistline and from waistline to hemline. It will appear neither too tight nor too loose for comfort. The hemline and horizontal balance lines (HBL) will be parallel with the floor. The centerlines of the garment will be in perfect alignment with the figure regardless of body symmetry, proportions, and stance. That is, the figure need not be perfectly symmetrical, the proportions and stance may be less than ideal, but the garment will still align properly when well fit.

A POOR FIT

A garment with a poor fit is caused by the curves of the body displacing the natural hang of the garment. Fitting problems occur when the pattern shapes do not conform to the body's dimensions (excluding a normal amount of ease), symmetry, or stance. These conditions are identifiable by any one of the following conditions:

• The centerline of the garment is out of alignment with the figure.

• When the garment is on the figure, the hemline and horizontal balance lines are not parallel with the floor.

• The garment is too long or too short from neck to waist and/or from waist to hem.

• The sleeve is out of alignment with the arm,

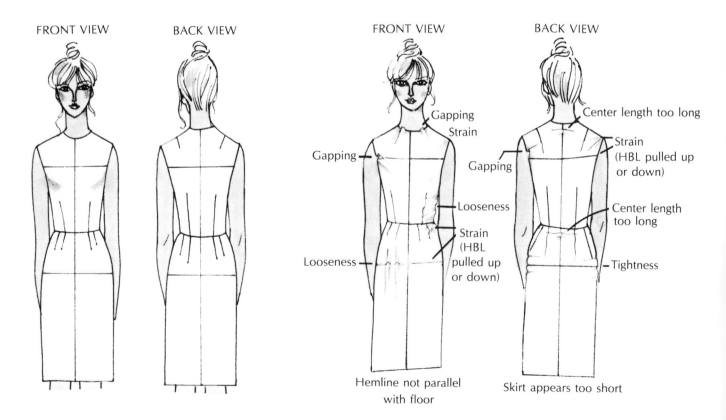

FRONT VIEW   BACK VIEW

FRONT VIEW   BACK VIEW

Gapping
Strain
Gapping
Gapping
Center length too long
Strain
(HBL pulled up or down)
Looseness
Center length too long
Strain
(HBL pulled up or down)
Looseness
Tightness

Hemline not parallel with floor

Skirt appears too short

causing strain, and/or puckering appears along the cap.
- Strain lines, tightness, gapping, or looseness appears in the garment.

A poor fit is usually caused by one of the following reasons:
- Careless work habits.
- Not following instructions accurately.
- Using incorrect measurements.
- Making the wrong adjustments for figure type. (This usually results from an inaccurate figure analysis and incorrect pattern adjustment.)
- Poor sewing or cutting. (Sewing should always be checked before pattern corrections are made.)
- Using steam on muslin causes the garment to shrink.

TERMS RELATING TO FIT

Strain. Strain is characterized by slight folds that begin and end within the garment's outline, such as those created by pulling fabric taut from two opposite ends. Strain results from using insufficient fabric for the dimensions of the form or

figure, thereby restricting movement or stretching the fabric beyond its normal limits.

Tightness. Tightness is characterized by a garment that fits too closely to the figure. Tightness results from using insufficient fabric in one part of the garment, or in the whole garment. Tightness can but does not always cause strain folds to appear. This usually means that more ease is required in the garment.

Looseness. Looseness is characterized by a garment that fits too loosely around the figure, causing the shoulderlines of the garment to droop over the shoulder tip of the form or figure, or by excessive looseness around the bust, waist, and/or hips.

Gapping. Gapping is characterized by misplaced excess around the neckline and/or armhole causing looseness. Gapping can be identified by its cone-like shape, with the widest part of the cone at the outline of the garment, and the end in direction of the bust or shoulder blade mound. Gapping occurs when the shoulder and/or side seams are out of alignment. It can also be caused by fabric that has stretched along cut line.

METHODS FOR CORRECTING PATTERNS

Two methods are illustrated for correcting patterns—one using guidelines and the other using the muslin. Fitting problems requiring other pattern correcting techniques will be illustrated under the appropriate fitting problem.

METHOD 1: USING THE MUSLIN

- After adjusting the garment, remove from figure or form. Release all seams and press the muslin flat without steam. True and blend all markings on muslin for new stitching lines (Figure 1).
- Muslin can remain as is, or be trimmed to new seam lines.
- Place marked muslin directly on top of the pattern or on a traced copy and secure with pins. Trace or pencil in markings to pattern underneath.
- Cut-out sections of the original garment can also be used as a guide for correcting the pattern (Figure 2). Place muslin section on pattern and pencil in new shape (Figure 3). Trim traced section from pattern.

FIGURE 1

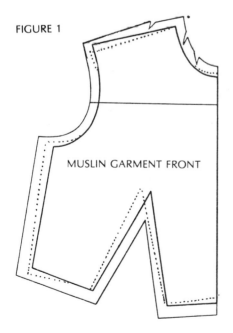

MUSLIN GARMENT FRONT

FIGURE 2

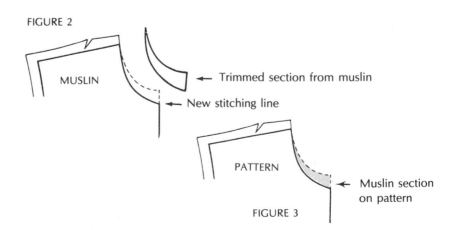

MUSLIN
← Trimmed section from muslin
← New stitching line
PATTERN
← Muslin section on pattern
FIGURE 3

METHOD 2: USING L-, W-, AND X-GUIDELINES

Fitting problems are corrected by adding to or subtracting from the length (L) and/or width (W) at specific locations within the "five-piece" pattern, or at its outline. (Pant guide marks are illustrated in pant sequence.) The use of guidelines helps to simplify (see examples) pattern correction. Using the symbols W (for width), L (for length), and X (for relocating armhole and sleeve cap area, the pattern should be coded as illustrated.

W-guidelines

- Mark and label pattern guidelines W as follows:
- *Back:* Mark $1\frac{1}{2}$ inches in from shoulder tip. Draw a line parallel with the center back.
- *Front:* Mark $1\frac{1}{2}$ inches in from shoulder. Draw line parallel with the center front and continue the line parallel with the dart leg as shown.
- *Skirt:* Repeat for front and back as shown.
- *Sleeve:* Mark a point in between underseam and grain on each side of sleeve on biceps line. Square a line up and down (through the pattern) from each mark as shown.

L-guidelines

- Mark and label pattern guidelines L-1, L-2 and L-3 as shown.
- Square lines from center front and center back to mid-armhole and above the waistline on the bodice, and below the waistline of the skirt, or use the existing horizontal balance line (hipline).
- *Sleeve:* Draw lines above and below the elbow, parallel with biceps line, and across cap.

X-guideline

- Mark and label pattern guidelines W as follows:
- Square a line from W-guideline to side seam, 1 inch below armhole (shaded area).
- *Sleeve:* Square a line from guideline to the underseam, 1 inch above elbow level (shaded area).

HOW TO USE THE GUIDELINES

- *X-guideline areas* are cut from the patterns and spread, overlapped, raised, or lowered along the W-guideline to increase or decrease width of the patterns (Figures 1 and 2); and to change the position of the armhole and biceps of the sleeve (Figures 3 and 4). Sleeve not illustrated.

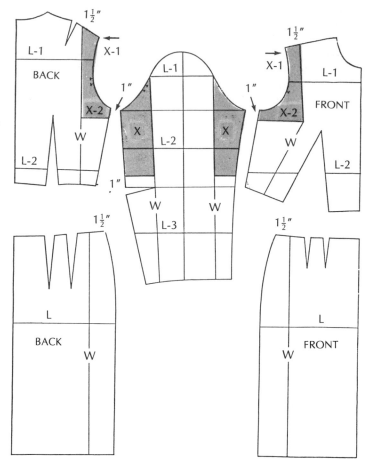

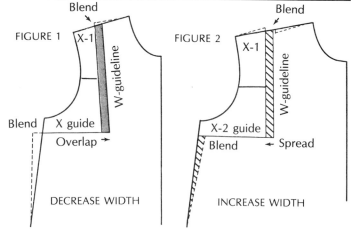

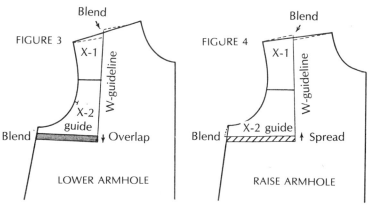

■ *L- and W-Guidelines:* To correct patterns requiring length and/or width adjustment, cut through guidelines, completely separating pattern sections. The pattern sections are overlapped to decrease the pattern's length and/or width (Figures 1 and 3) or spread to increase the pattern's length and/or width (Figures 2 and 4).

Note: To add width and/or length, cut a piece of paper wider or longer than the required pattern adjustment. Draw vertical guidelines on the paper and pattern. Place paper under the sections to be spread, matching guidelines.

The adjusted sections must be parallel with the cut lines when spreading or overlapping the pattern. Secure by taping both sides of the pattern. Blend for a smooth continuous line where correction took place.

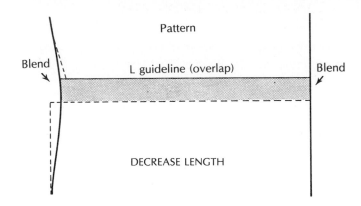

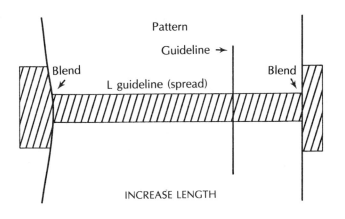

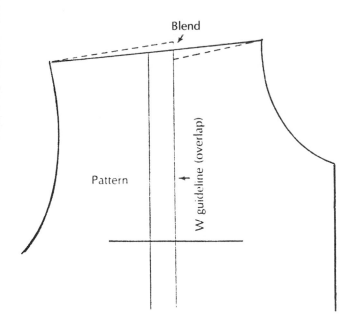

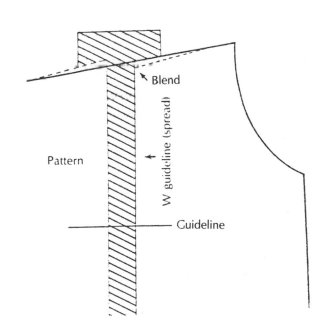

GARMENT ADJUSTMENT

Before the pattern can be adjusted, the patternmaker should know where adjustments are required on the garment and how these adjustments are used to correct the pattern. To help make this assessment, the muslin must be adjusted while on the form or figure, and information translated onto the pattern. This requires releasing seamlines to eliminate strain, pinning in folds to take up excess, cutting into the garment to determine additional fabric needed for prominent mounds (such as bust and shoulder blade areas), and placing strips of fabric underneath open sections wherever there is insufficient fabric provided to make the correction. The released and pinned sections are measured for pattern correction. Use the following examples as a guide:

STRAIN AND TIGHTNESS ALONG SEAMLINES

- Locate strain (Figure 1).
- Release the stitches along the seamline (Figure 2).
- Pin sections together along new seamline, allowing sufficient fabric to eliminate strain (Figure 3).

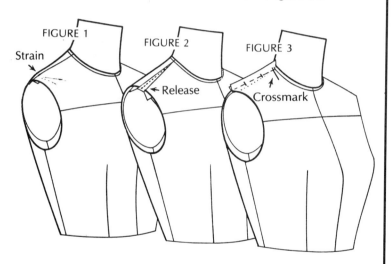

- Crossmark muslin at the location where pinned section joins the original stitchline.
- Measure the distance from the original stitchline to the widest point of the pin line (Figure 4).

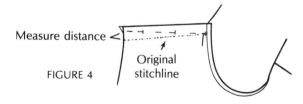

- Indicate new seamline by rubbing side of pencil lead across pins (Figure 5).
- Use muslin or measurement when making the pattern correction.

STRAIN AND TIGHTNESS WITHIN THE GARMENT

- To relieve strain caused by a large bust, prominent shoulder blades, thigh, and/or abdomen, cut through the muslin from within the garment as illustrated. (This will cause the garment to spread apart the amount necessary to relieve strain.)
- Place a strip of fabric underneath the open space, pinning at each side, and measure the distance.
- Use this measurement when making pattern correction.

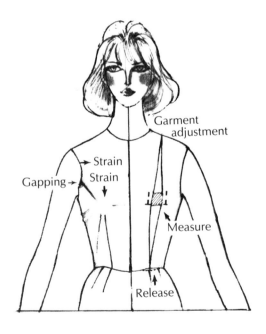

LOOSENESS AND GAPPING

- Pinch excess together between two fingers and pin, allowing for ease. Continue pinning until excess is absorbed.
- Rub pencil lead across pins on both sides of the garment.
- Use muslin to correct pattern, or measure the distance from pinmarks to the fold. Mark these measurements on pattern where they occur on the garment. If pinning occurs within the garment, and not at a seam, mark and unfold to measure distance.
- Use this measurement when making pattern correction. (Always blend pin line marks on pattern.)

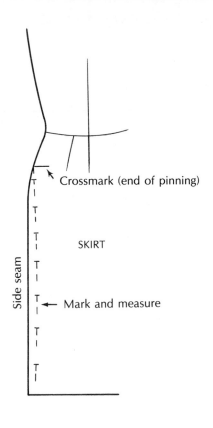

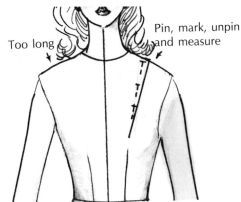

ANALYZING FIT

Skill in analyzing fitting problems improves with constant practice. Achieving a good fit requires the ability to identify strain, looseness, and gapping in the garment, to know what is causing the problem, and to adjust the pattern in order to resolve it. What may appear to be a fitting problem in one part of the garment may be automatically corrected by an adjustment to another part. For example, if the bodice is too short, the skirt stitched to it will be pulled upward. Once the bodice is corrected, the skirt may not need correction. Tightness across the abdomen can result from darts stitched too long as well as from insufficient side seam ease allowance, and so on.

The following sequence of fitting problems has been developed to minimize the possibility of correcting the wrong problem. When analyzing the fit, mark an *X* on the muslin wherever strain, tightness, looseness, or gapping appear. Then make adjustments in the order shown. It may be necessary to make a correction and recut the muslin before continuing the fitting process as indicated in the instructions. It is not practical to make all corrections at one time on the muslin, as this tends to create additional fitting problems.

SEQUENCE FOR CORRECTING FITTING PROBLEMS

Broken lines indicate original pattern shape.
First: Correct overall looseness.
Second: Correct overall tightness.
Third: Correct overall length too long or too short.
Fourth: Correct strain within the garment (from prominent bust, chest, or shoulder blades).
- *Fitting Problems* are illustrated as follows: The

sketch is divided in the center. The fitting problem is shown on the left side and the garment adjustment on the right side of the center line. For clarity, most illustrations show an exaggeration of the fitting problem. Illustrations should be used as a guide when adjusting the muslin or correcting the pattern. For pant adjustments, refer to page 674.

INITIAL CORRECTIONS
Broken lines indicate original pattern.

1. Overall looseness or tightness
Adjustment is made only on a garment which is too loose or too tight in width across the shoulder, bust, waist, and hips. Tightness or looseness in separate areas is illustrated in other examples later.
■ *Garment Adjustment for Looseness:* Pin in excess down center front and back. Measure for pattern correction. If neckline is too wide, see Problem 12.
■ *Pattern Correction:* Cut through front and back W-guidelines and overlap as shown (back not illustrated).

■ *Garment Adjustment for Tightness:* Release side seams. Pin. Measure from stitchline to pinmarks.
■ *Pattern Correction:* Cut through front and back W-guideline. Spread as shown (back not illustrated).

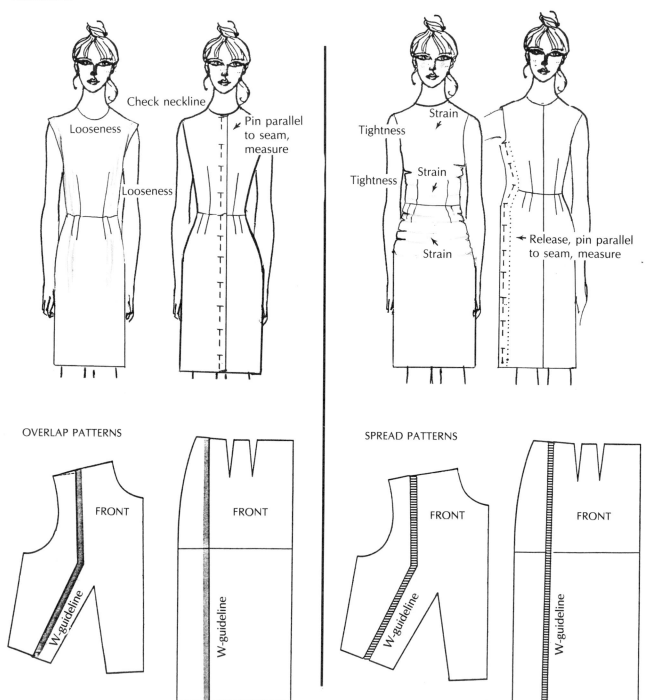

BODICE CORRECTIONS
Broken lines indicate original pattern.

2. Overall bodice too long or too short
Adjustment used only if length is too long or short at front, back, and sides. (Looseness appearing only along the side seam or centerline areas is a fitting problem which is illustrated later.)

- *Bodice Adjustment If Too Long:* Pin horizontal folds across front and back bodice. Measure for pattern correction. (If armhole is too low, see Problem 13.)
- *Pattern Correction:* Cut through front and back L-2 guidelines and overlap.

- *Bodice Adjustment If Too Short:* Release waistline and allow skirt to fall to natural waistline. Measure distance between bodice and skirt. (If armhole is too high, see Problem 30.)
- *Pattern Correction:* Cut through front and back L-2 guidelines. Spread tape and blend (back not illustrated).

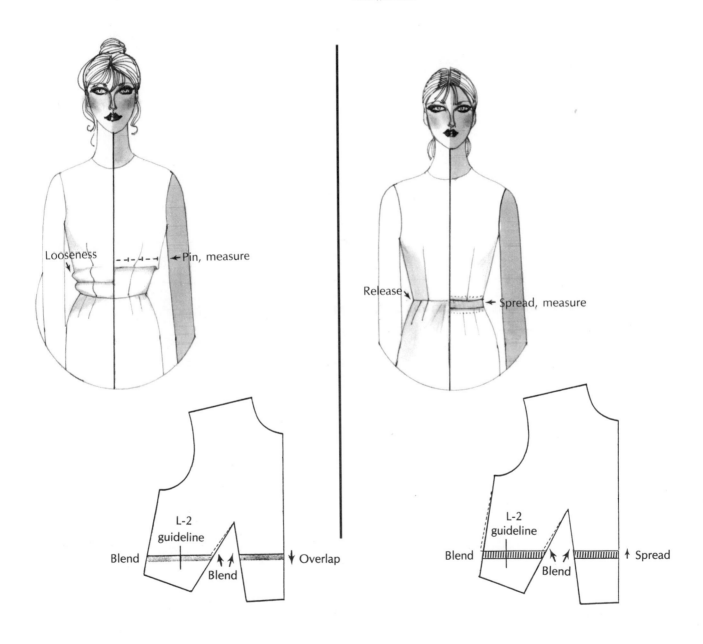

3. Strain around bust area

Waist may pull upward, and/or gapping may appear at mid-armhole. (Gapping usually disappears when additional cup room is provided.) Adding to the side seam will not correct the fitting problem. The strain is the result of insufficient dart intake which controls the degree of cupping within the garment. If tightness appears across the chest, use correction A. Use correction B if chest area fits well.

▪ *Bodice Adjustment:* If waist lifts upward, release waist allowing skirt to return to natural waistline.

Cut through dart just above waist at stitchline to mid-shoulder, if chest area is tight (A); or slash to mid-armhole (B) if chest area fits well. Allow fabric to spread for bust room. Measure distance between opening at bust point level.

▪ *Pattern Correction:* Slash from bust point to mid-shoulder (A) or to mid-armhole (B) and spread amount needed. True dart by adding to shorter leg. Add to waist as shown. Before continuing, recut front and stitch to back. Recheck fit and continue with fitting.

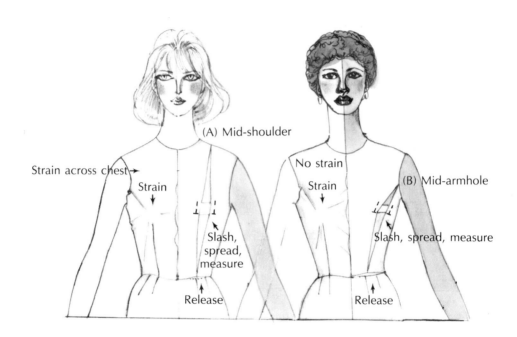

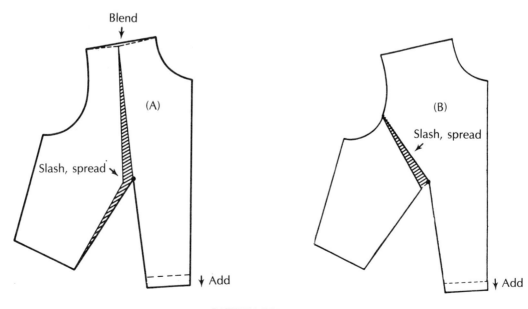

PATTERN CORRECTIONS

4. Looseness across bust level

Dart intake is too great for size of bust mound. If chest area is too wide, use correction A. If chest area fits well, use correction B.

- *Bodice Adjustment:* Pin excess at bust point (allow ease) to zero at waist dart. Continue pinning to mid-shoulder if chest area is loose (A) or to mid-armhole (B) if across chest fits well. Measure excess at bust level only.

- *Pattern Correction:* Slash from bust point to mid-shoulder (A) or mid-armhole (B) and overlap pattern at bust. Mark bust point in between overlapped section. True dart legs by subtracting from longer leg. Trim excess from waist and blend. Before continuing, recut front and stitch to back. Recheck fit and continue.

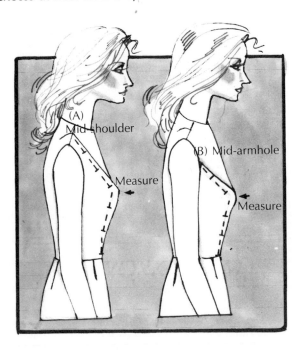

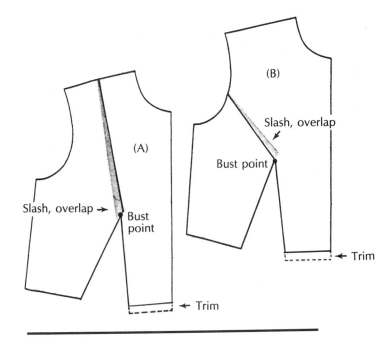

5. Strain at shoulder blade

Back waist may rise and gapping may appear at mid-armhole and neckline. It should disappear with the following correction.

- *Bodice Adjustment:* Slash across back, ending at stitchline of armhole, allowing waistline of bodice to fall to waist. Measure open space for pattern correction.

- *Pattern Correction:* Cut guideline L-1 and spread. Extend center back line and blend with neckline (increases neckline). If neckline is too loose, treat as gapping excess and transfer excess to shoulder dart, see Problem 15. Recut back and stitch to front. Refit and continue with fitting.

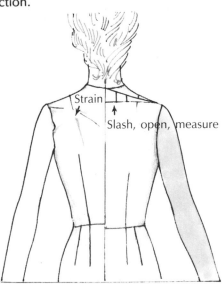

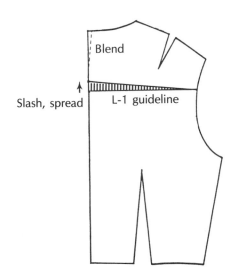

6. Horizontal folds above bust

Excess appears across chest ending at armhole (A), or includes armhole (B). Check for strain across back shoulder blade and armhole. See Problem 5 for correcting back pattern.

▪ *Bodice Adjustment:* Pin excess across chest, ending at mid armhole (A), or include armhole if loose (B).

▪ *Pattern Correction:* To correct problem A, slash from center front neck to, not through, shoulder tip. Overlap. Tape. Blend neck and continue fitting. To correct problem B, cut through L-1 guideline. Overlap and blend armhole. Recut front and stitch to back. Recheck fit and continue fitting. This may require repositioning shoulderline and adjusting cap ease. (See rotating sleeve before attaching sleeve, page 666.)

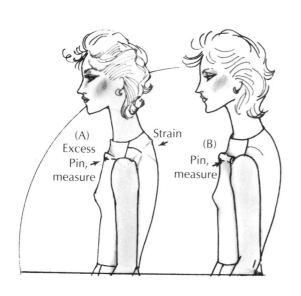

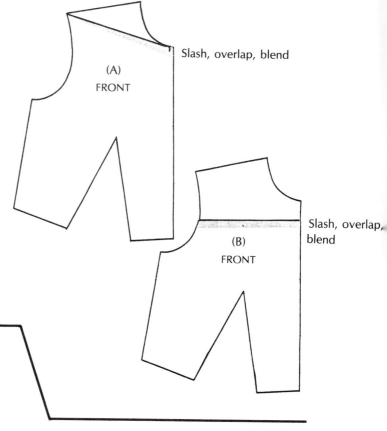

7. Horizontal folds below bust

▪ *Bodice Adjustment:* Pin excess from center front to side seam. If strain appears across back shoulder blade, see Problem 5.

▪ *Pattern Correction:* Slash from center front to, not through, side seam. Overlap pattern, blending center front. Redraw dart legs to bust point and true by adding to shorter leg. Blend waist.

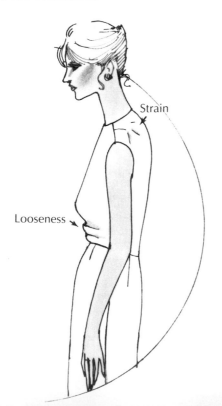

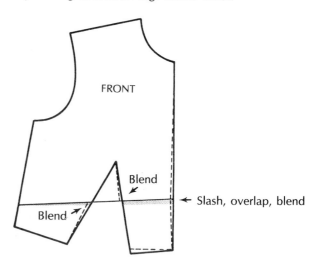

8. Horizontal folds above shoulder blades

■ *Bodice Adjustment:* Pin in excess. Measure for pattern corrections.

■ *Pattern Correction:* Slash from center back to, not through, mid-armhole and overlap pattern amount needed. Draw line up center back. Add needed amount to shoulder at neck to retain neck measurement. Blend neck to center back. Recut back and stitch to front. Recheck fit and continue fitting.

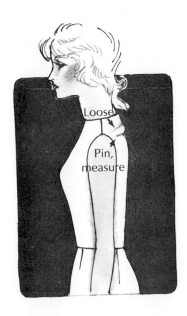

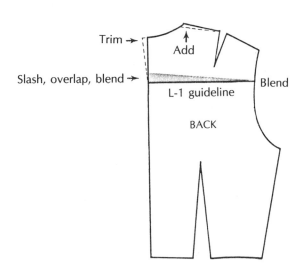

9. Strain at center of mid-chest (pigeon chest)

■ *Bodice Adjustment:* Slash muslin as shown. Pin and measure opening at neck.

■ *Pattern Correction:* Slash from neck to bust point and spread. (Neckline is increased and should be eased into adjusted facing or collar.) Recut front and stitch to back. Continue fitting.

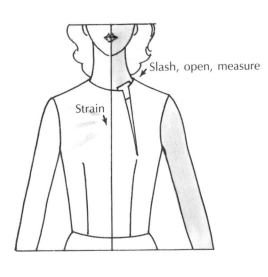

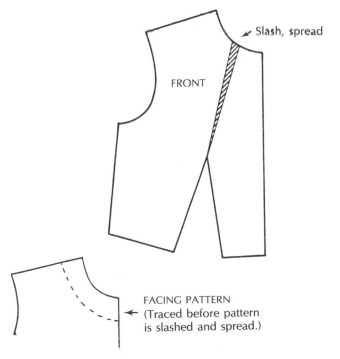

10. Hemlines not parallel with floor

If skirt is tight it will ride up, causing the hemline to tilt. Hemline tilt may also be the result of a tilting waistline or high/low hip.

▪ *Bodice Adjustment:* Release front and back waistline and side seam to hip level. Pin new waistline, keeping hemline parallel with floor. Smooth excess out at side seam and pin to hip level. If side seam curves too much (rippling along seam), unpin side seam and increase dart intake at front and back. Repin side seam. Pencil mark, remove skirt and bodice. True lines and use for correcting pattern.

▪ *Pattern Correction:*

Illustrated are corrections for tilting waistlines:

▪ See pattern correction A for asymmetric hips (high/low hip).
▪ See pattern correction B for high waist front, low waist back.
▪ See pattern correction C for low waist front, high waist back.

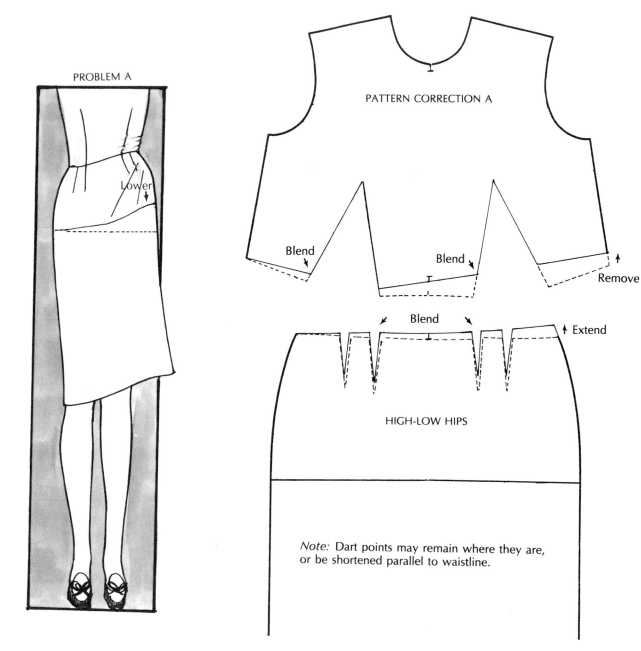

PROBLEM A

PATTERN CORRECTION A

Blend

Blend

Remove

Blend

Extend

HIGH-LOW HIPS

Note: Dart points may remain where they are, or be shortened parallel to waistline.

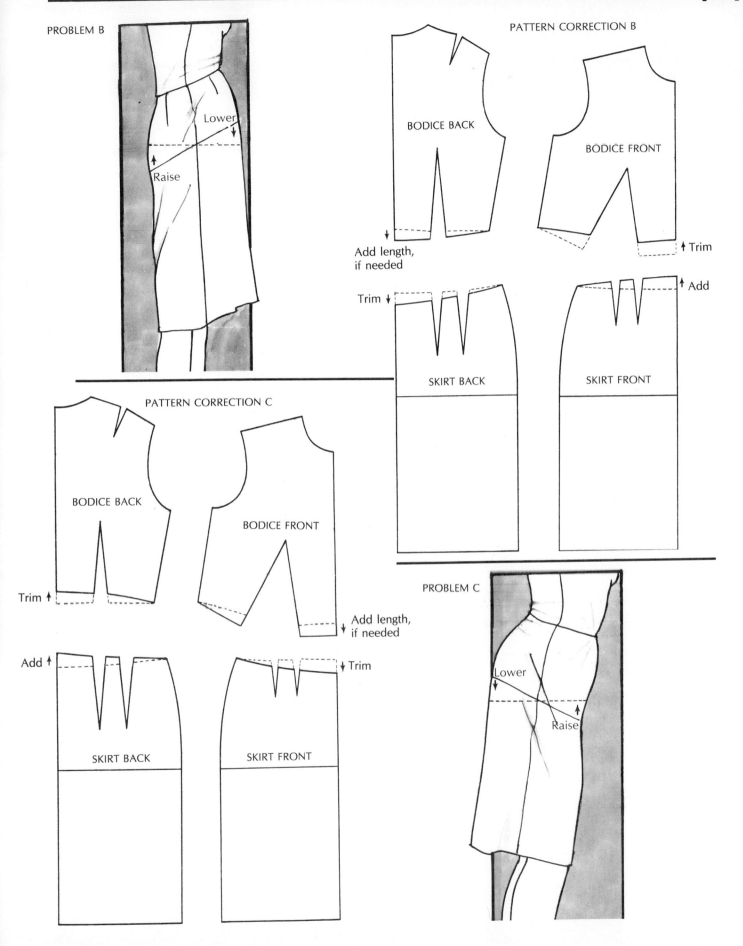

PROBLEM B

PATTERN CORRECTION B

BODICE BACK

BODICE FRONT

Lower

Raise

Add length,
if needed

Trim

Trim

Add

SKIRT BACK

SKIRT FRONT

PATTERN CORRECTION C

BODICE BACK

BODICE FRONT

Trim

Add length,
if needed

Add

Trim

SKIRT BACK

SKIRT FRONT

PROBLEM C

Lower

Raise

NECKLINE AREA
Broken lines indicate the original pattern.

11. Neckline too high in front and/or back
▪ *Bodice Adjustment:* Draw correct neckline. Trim. Use cut section of muslin to correct pattern.

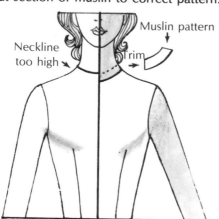

▪ *Pattern Correction:* Place cut section of muslin on pattern and trace. Blend lines and trim from pattern.

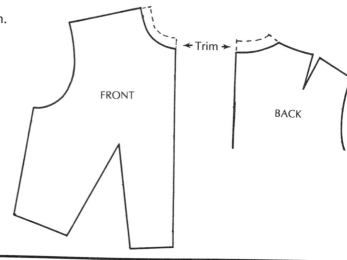

12. Neckline too low and/or too wide
▪ *Bodice Adjustment:* Measure up from stitched edge at center front and corner of neck (and center back, if necessary) to mark for correct neckline.

▪ *Pattern Correction:* Using measurements taken, add needed amount to pattern.

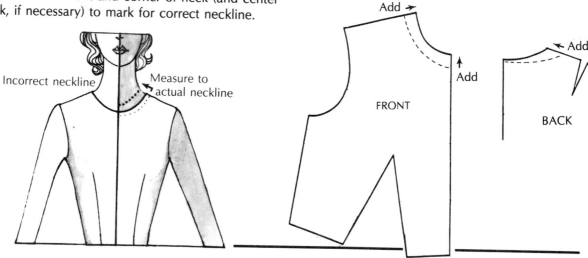

13. Neckline too loose
▪ *Bodice Adjustment:* Pin excess and measure.

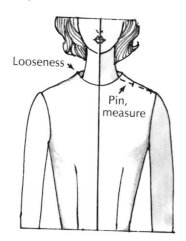

▪ *Pattern Correction:* Measure in at neck and draw line to shoulder tip as shown. True dart legs by adding to shorter leg of back pattern. Blend to neck.

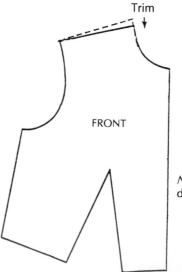

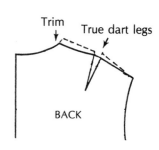

Note: Dart may be folded, with a line drawn from mark to shoulder tip.

14. Strain at neck
■ *Bodice Adjustment:* Release shoulder line. Adjust, pin, and measure.

■ *Pattern Correction:* Add to front and back neck. Draw line from new neck to shoulder tip. True dart legs by adding to shorter leg. Blend shoulder with neck.

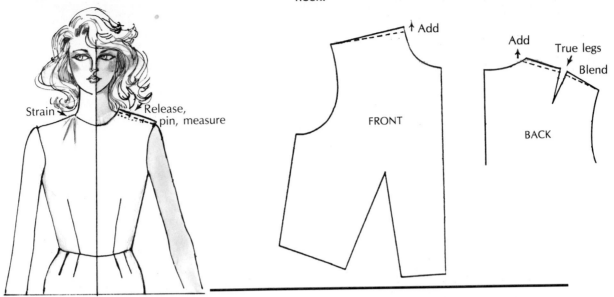

15. Gapping neckline, front and/or back
Gapping indicates front and/or back shoulders out of alignment.

■ *Bodice Adjustment:* Pin excess and measure.

■ *Pattern Correction:* Slash from neck to bust point (front), and/or dart point of shoulder dart (back). Overlap, transferring excess to dart as shown. Blend neckline.

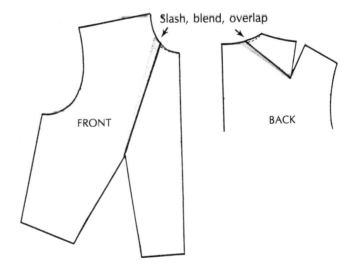

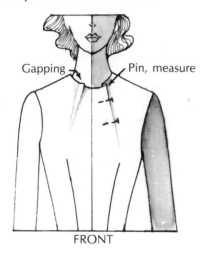

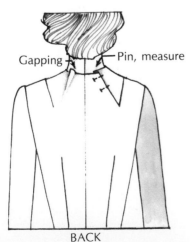

16. Strain around neck, front and/or back

▪ *Bodice Adjustment:* Release shoulder first. If back seam does not move, the correction is to the front garment only. After pinning shoulder, if neck is still too tight, slash to bust point and measure space.

▪ *Pattern Correction:* Add to shoulder at neck, ending at shoulder tip, if required. Repeat for back, if required. Slash from neck to bust point, and spread if required. Blend neckline. (Broken line original shoulder.)

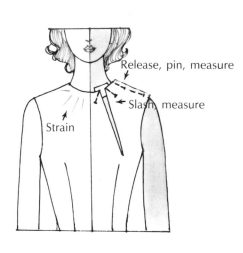

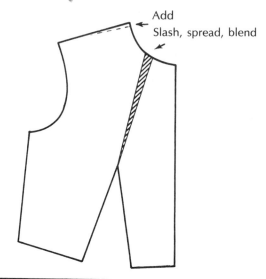

17. Neckline offcenter—excess on one side of neck

▪ *Bodice Adjustment:* Slash garment at neck to conform to actual neckline. Mark new neck and trim neckline. Use muslin to trim pattern.

▪ *Pattern Correction:* Use muslin pattern to trim neckline. Add to opposite neckline by equal amount and blend. Repeat for back neck (not illustrated).

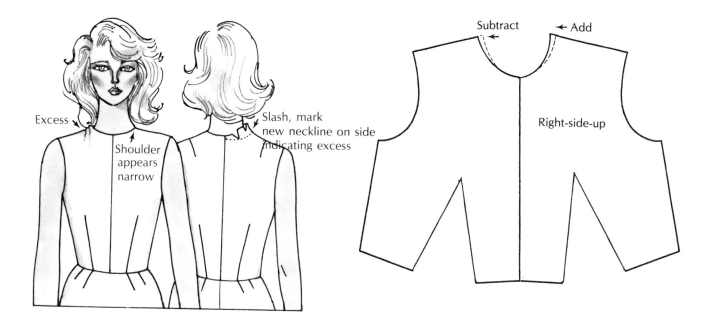

SHOULDERLINE AREA
Broken lines indicate original pattern.

18. Strain at shoulder tip
▪ *Bodice Adjustment:* Release shoulder. Pin (if possible) or add a strip of cloth to join sections and measure.

▪ *Pattern Correction:* Add to shoulder tip. Draw line to neck. Blend to armhole. True dart legs by adding to shorter leg and blend shoulder.

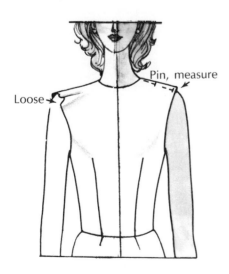

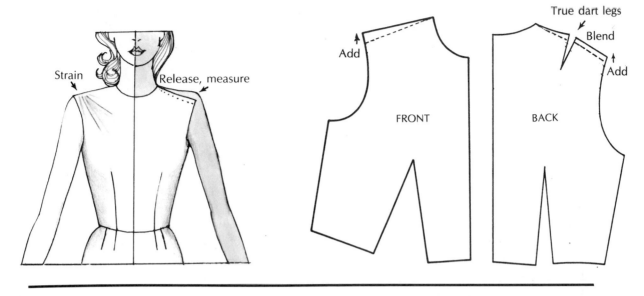

19. Looseness at shoulder tip
Looseness may appear only on front or back, or on both sides.
▪ *Bodice Adjustment:* Pin excess. Mark and measure.

▪ *Pattern Correction:* Measure down from shoulder tip. Draw line from shoulder mark to neck. True dart legs by adding to shorter leg and blend shoulder.

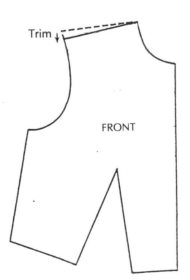

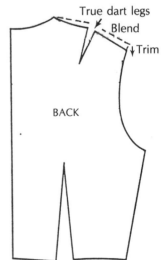

20. Shoulderline too narrow

▪ *Bodice Adjustment:* Measure from stitchline of fabric at shoulderline to shoulder tip of form or figure.

▪ *Pattern Correction:* Cut and spread section X-1. Draw straight line from shoulder tip to neck. Blend armhole. Repeat for back.

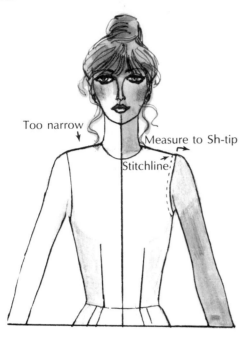

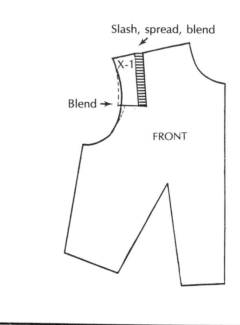

21. Shoulderline too long

▪ *Bodice Adjustment:* Pin vertical fold at shoulderline, ending at bust point to bring dropping shoulder to natural armhole of form or figure. Mark on both sides of pin at shoulder (avoid back shoulder dart). Unpin and measure. Repin and continue with fitting.

▪ *Pattern Correction:* Cut through X-1 section; overlap. Draw straight line from shoulder tip to neck. Blend armhole. Repeat for back.

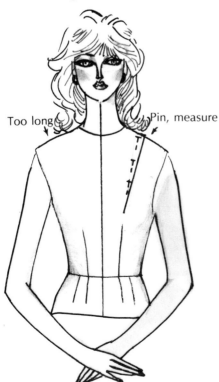

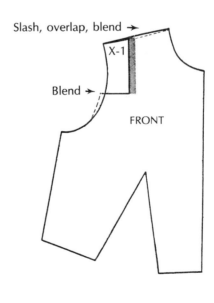

CHEST AND BUST AREA

22. Bodice circumference too tight

- *Bodice Adjustment:* Release side seam. Pin, allowing ease. If waistline fits well, taper side from armhole to waist. If waistline is tight, release side seam, adjust, pin, and measure. If bust area appears strained after adjustment is made, see Problem 3.

- *Pattern Correction:* Cut through front and back X-2 guideline, and spread. Draw straight line from armhole to waist. Blend armholes.

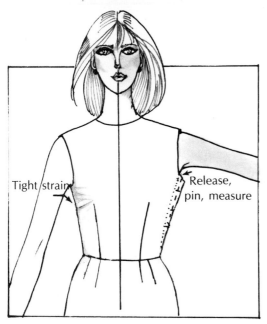

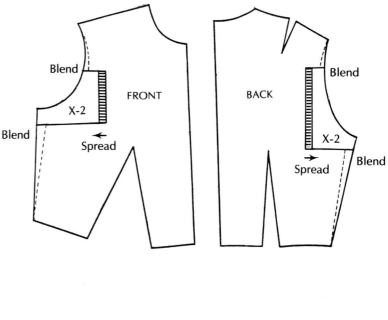

23. Bodice circumference too loose

- *Bodice Adjustment:* If shoulder and armhole droop, see Problem 21 for correction. If waist fits well, pin excess at side seam from armhole to waist. Measure. (If waistline is loose, see Problem 31.)

- *Pattern Correction:* Cut and overlap X-2 guidelines of front and back patterns. Blend armhole and draw line from armhole to waist.

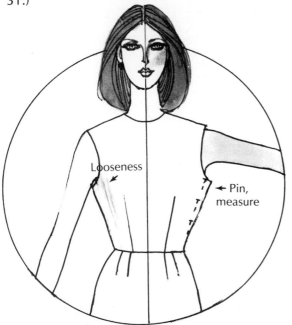

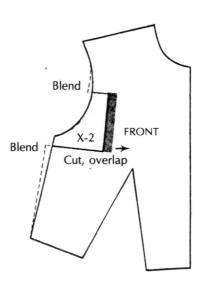

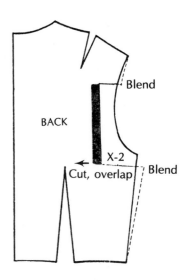

24. Fullness under arms

Side seam may be too long, and/or shoulders may slope.

• *Bodice Adjustment:* If shoulder is sloped, you may use shoulder pads to minimize slope before adjusting muslin. Pin excess at side seam. Mark, release pins, and measure.

• *Pattern Correction:* Cut sections X-1 and X-2. Move section down to overlap patterns. Draw straight line at shoulder to blend. True dart legs by adding to shorter leg. Cut and stitch new muslin from corrected pattern. Recheck fit before continuing with fitting.

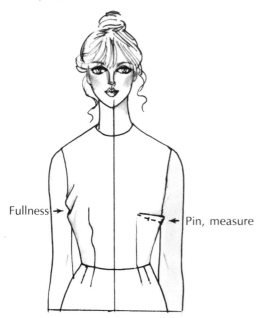

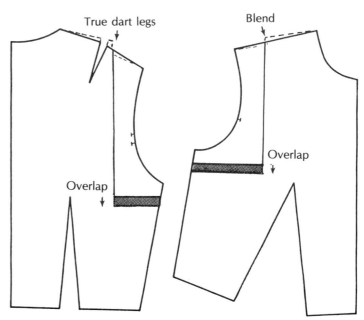

ARMHOLE AREA

Check armhole area for gapping or strain as indicated in illustrations. If armhole is adjusted, the sleeve may also need correction.

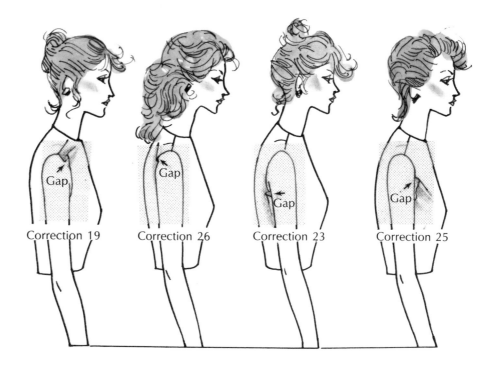

Correction 19   Correction 26   Correction 23   Correction 25

25. Gapping (front mid-armhole)

▪ *Bodice Adjustment:* Pin excess from armhole to bust point. Measure.

▪ *Pattern Correction:* Slash from mid-armhole to, not through, bust point. Overlap at armhole. Blend.

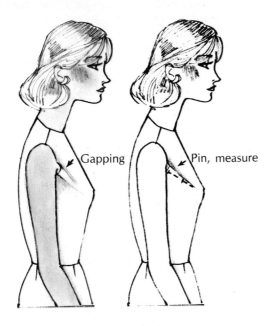

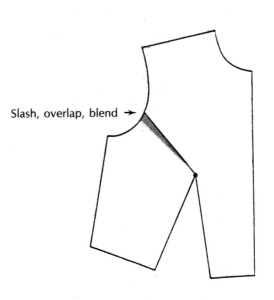

26. Gapping (back armhole)

▪ *Bodice Adjustment:* Pin excess to dart point of shoulder dart.

▪ *Pattern Correction:* Slash from armhole to dart point. Slash through center of dart to, not through, dart point. Overlap at armhole. Blend. If dart intake is too great ($\frac{3}{4}$ inch or more), decrease intake ($\frac{1}{4}$ to $\frac{1}{2}$ inch) and hold excess as ease along shoulderline.

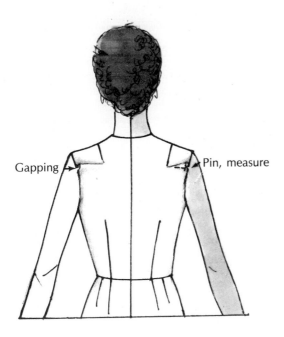

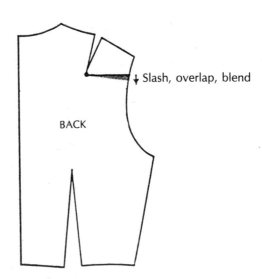

[656]

27. Inaccurate armhole shape (outside natural armhole curve)

Verify front and back armhole curve on garment.

■ *Bodice Adjustment:* Mark true armhole on muslin. Allow an extra $\frac{1}{4}$ inch out from mid-armhole at back for forward movement. Remove and true armhole curve. Broken line is original armhole (back not illustrated).

■ *Pattern Correction:* Use muslin to correct armhole. Blend armhole with French or vary curve.

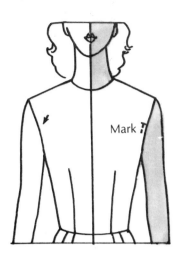

Mark

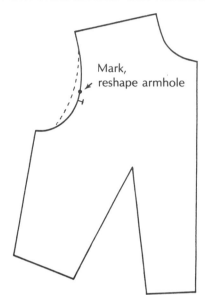

Mark, reshape armhole

28. Inaccurate armhole shape (inside natural armhole curve)

Verify front and back armhole curve on garment.

■ *Bodice Adjustment:* Measure from shoulder tip and mid-armhole of form or figure to stitchline on muslin. Allow $\frac{1}{4}$ inch for ease in back only.

■ *Pattern Correction:* Use French curve and measurement to correct shape of armhole.

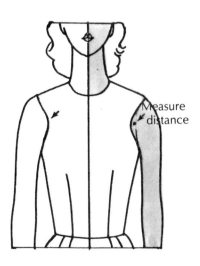

Measure distance

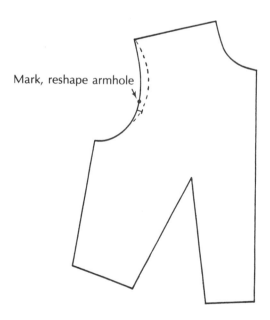

Mark, reshape armhole

29. Strain at front armhole

(Model to move arm forward. If armhole feels binding, make the following corrections.)

▪ *Bodice Adjustment:* Slash from mid-armhole to bust point. Measure space.

▪ *Pattern Correction:* Slash pattern to, not through, bust point. Spread. Blend armhole. Recut front. Stitch to back. Continue fitting.

30. Armhole too low or too high

▪ *Bodice Adjustment:* Recheck side seam measurement. Measure up from stitchline of armhole to height needed if armhole is too low. Measure down from stitchline of armhole to depth required if armhole is too high.

▪ *Pattern Adjustment:* Cut section X-2 and raise for Figure A or lower for Figure B by amount needed. Blend armhole and side seam.

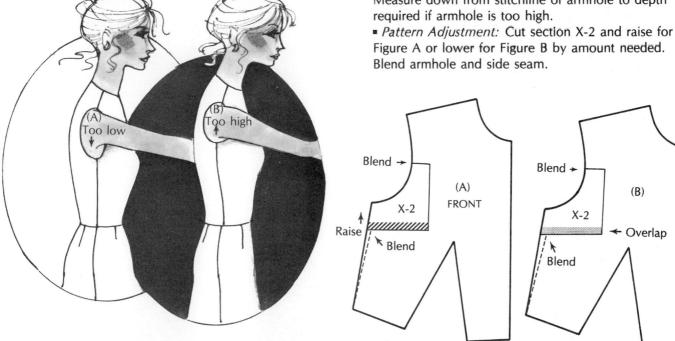

WAISTLINE AREA
Broken lines indicate original pattern.

31. Waistline too loose
A loose waistline requires both the bodice and skirt to be adjusted.
- *Bodice Adjustment:* Pin excess at front and back side seam. Adjust, measure, and pin (allow for ease).

- *Pattern Correction:* Trim excess from side seam of front and back bodice, and skirt (back not illustrated).

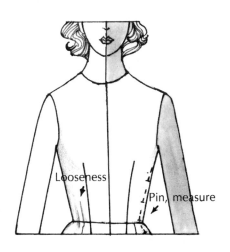

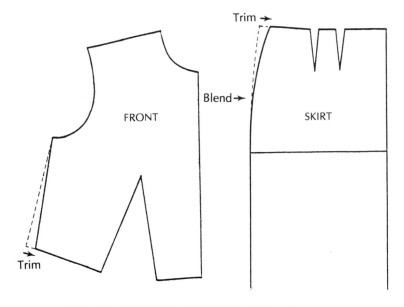

32. Waistline too tight
A tight waistline requires both the bodice and skirt to be adjusted.
- *Bodice Adjustment:* Release side seam, adjust, pin, and measure.

- *Pattern Correction:* Add to side seam of front and back bodice, and skirt. Blend hip area (back not illustrated).

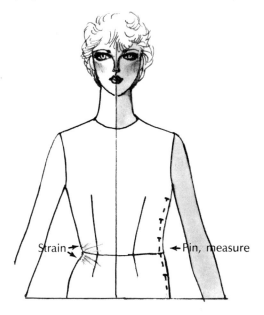

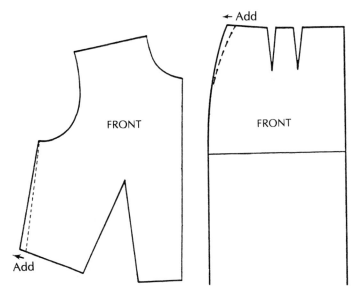

33. Strain at corner of dart front and/or back

Strain indicates too much dart intake.

- *Adjustment:* Release waist, part of side seam, and dart. Decrease dart intake so that strain lines disappear. Smooth remaining excess out at side seam. Repin. Pencil mark location of new dart and side waist. Measure or use muslin to correct pattern (back not illustrated).

- *Pattern Correction:* Mark new dart and side seam. Draw line to armhole and dart point.

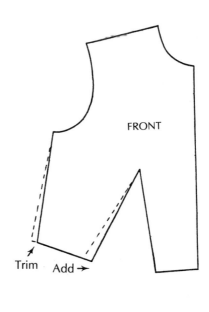

FRONT

Trim   Add →

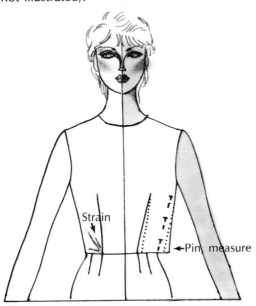

Strain

← Pin, measure

DARTS

Study the example for possible dart realignment. Bodice and skirt shown. Broken lines indicate original pattern. To adjust unaligned darts on skirt section, see Problem 47 (A), (B), and (C); on bodice, see Problem 36.

34. Dart point not directed to bust point

- *Bodice Adjustment:* Crossmark correct placement. Measure distance.

- *Pattern Correction:* Mark new bust point and redraw dart legs. True dart legs, adding to shorter leg. Blend with waistline.

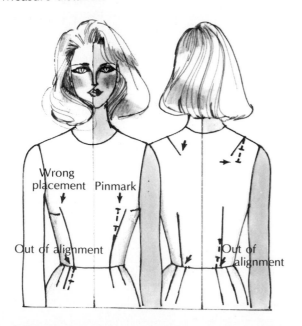

Wrong placement   Pinmark

Out of alignment

Out of alignment

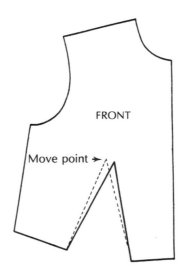

FRONT

Move point →

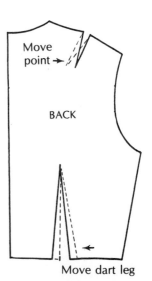

Move point →

BACK

Move point →

Move dart leg

35. Dart points too high or too low

▪ *Bodice Adjustment:* If too high, release dart; adjust, pin, and measure distance from original point. If too low, pin dart to eliminate excess. Measure distance up from original mark.

▪ *Pattern Correction:* Raise dart point (see Figure A), or lower dart point (see Figure B).

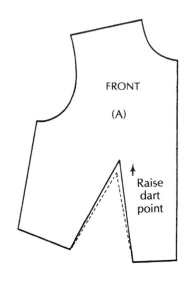

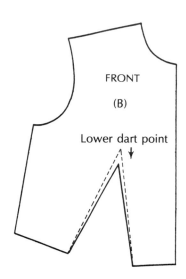

36. Side dart: Changing dart location and dart point

▪ *Bodice Adjustment:* Mark bust point and draw line in the direction of bust. Mark location along side seam where dart is to start. (See Problem 34.)

▪ *Pattern Correction:* Draw new dart legs on pattern. Figure A illustrates dart point raised in the direction of bust point. Figure B illustrates new location of dart legs along side seam. Pattern is folded along the dart legs and a straight line is drawn from side waist to armhole to true dart legs, and to establish new side seam. (See page 10, Trueing.)

DART WEDGE:

Trace and cut dart wedge from pattern. Place for new dart location and trace (shaded area).

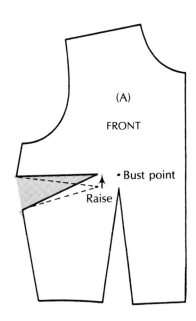

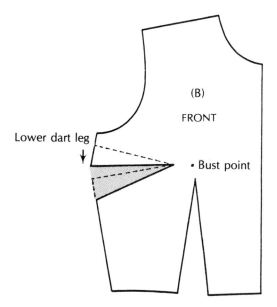

SKIRT CORRECTIONS

Based on skirt attached to bodice, or for separate skirt. Broken lines on pattern indicate original pattern shape.

37. Skirt too loose below waistline to hem
▪ *Skirt Adjustment:* Pin excess along side seam. Allow ease. Measure.

▪ *Pattern Correction:* Remove excess from side of front and back pattern ending at waist (back not illustrated).

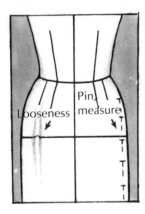

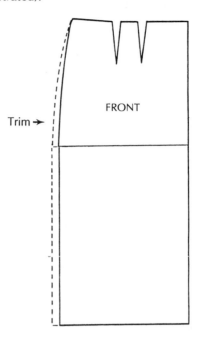

38. Looseness along side seam above hip level
▪ *Skirt Adjustment:* Pin excess at side seam between waist and hip, following hipline curves. Mark along new hip curve.

▪ *Pattern Correction:* Use muslin or measurement to reshape hip curve. Blend abrupt curves. Two examples are shown (back not illustrated).

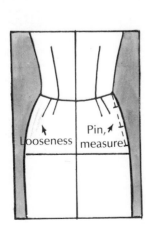

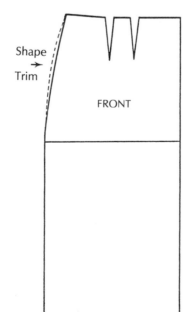

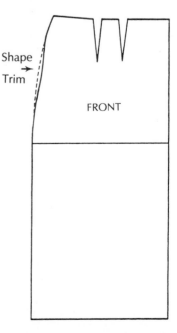

39. Skirt too tight

Tightness indicated by cupping under buttocks and/or abdomen, strain lines across hip and thighs. Hips may be too tight and/or darts stitched too long. (See Problem 40 on how to release and repin darts.)

- *Skirt Adjustment:* Release side seam. Allow ease and pin as shown. Measure, or use muslin to adjust pattern.
- *Pattern Correction:* Add to side seam as illustrated, ending at waist.

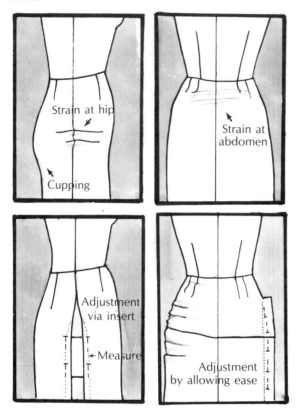

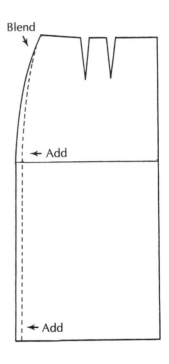

40. Strain at side near waist

Strain may occur only on one side of the figure. If so, a full pattern is required.

- *Adjustment:* Release front and back side seams. Pin new hipline (waist may drop slightly). If still tight, release darts and shorten. (Curved darts help the fit.) Pin. Mark the adjusted dart legs and side seam.

- *Pattern Correction:* Use garment or measurements for reshaping hip curve, waist, and dart. Blend and true dart legs. Adjust back hipline and waist (not illustrated).

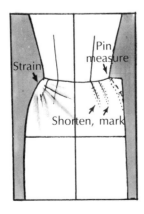

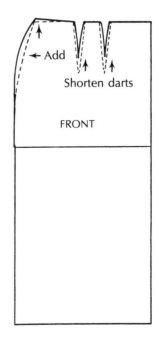

41. Folds across center back or front

- *Skirt Adjustment:* Release side seam. If fold remains, release waist. Smooth muslin upward from centerlines. Slash along waistline to relieve muslin. Mark new waist. Measure distance at center to stitchline of skirt. Remark dart location if not in line with waist dart. *Note:* Hemline must remain parallel with floor.

- *Pattern Correction:* Use muslin to reshape skirt waistline. True darts and blend with waist. Use same instruction if folds appear in front skirt (not illustrated).

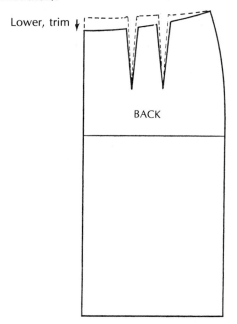

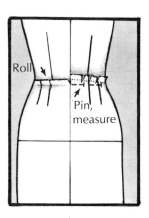

42. Drooping across back hip level

- *Skirt Adjustment:* Release waist and raise muslin, keeping hemline parallel with floor. Slash to relieve muslin. Pin to waist. Increase dart intake equally, to adjust waist measurement, if necessary. Mark and measure. For pattern correction, see Problem 41.

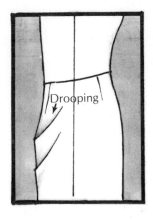

43. Strain around dart area

- *Skirt Adjustment:* Release waistline and darts. Repin darts, shortening dart point and curving darts, allowing room for bulge. Pin waist. If still tight, release side seam for additional ease. Pencil mark new darts and side seam.

- *Pattern Correction:* Use muslin or measurements for shaping darts and side seam of pattern. Blend.

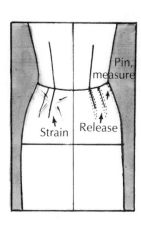

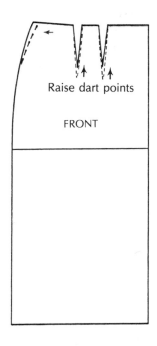

44. Excess at dart points

Several choices are given. Use adjustments that apply to the fitting problem.

▪ *Darts Too Short:* Pin in excess, lengthening short darts.

▪ *Flat Abdomen:* If abdominal area is flat, release darts and smooth part of the dart's excess out at side seam. Pin in one dart, absorbing remaining excess. Mark new side seam. (See example below.)

▪ *Excessive Dart Intake:* Release side seam, waist, and darts. Repin, using less intake. Smooth muslin to side seam to remove excess. Repin side seam.

▪ *Pattern Correction:* Darts too short: Mark new dart point, punch and circle. See Figure A. Flat abdomen: Use garment to correct pattern. See Figure B. Excess dart intake: Use garment to correct pattern. See Figure C.

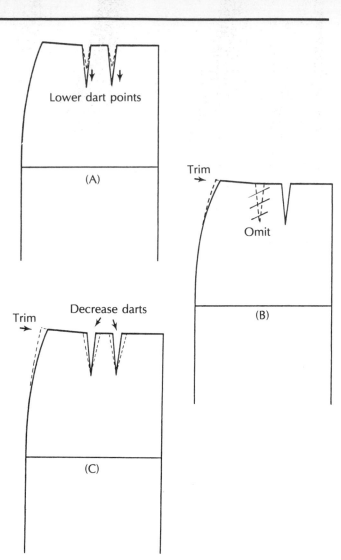

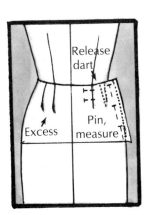

45. Diagonal strain at back darts toward side seam

Strain is caused by insufficient dart intake.

▪ *Skirt Adjustment:* Release waist and side seam to hip level. Increase dart intake until strain disappears. Shorten dart length ½ inch. Mark. Repin side seam.

▪ *Pattern Correction:* Use muslin to reshape pattern. (See uprighting darts, Problem 47, to complete pattern correction.)

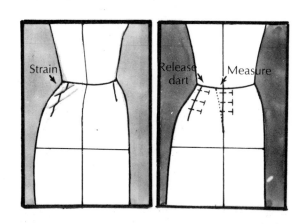

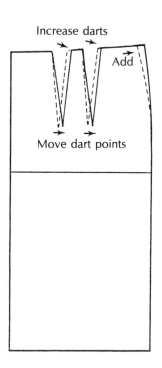

46. Diagonal strain at front dart

▪ *Garment Adjustment:* Release waist, darts, and part of side seam. Repin darts, taking in less dart excess. Smooth muslin to side and repin side seam. Mark new dart legs and side seam.

▪ *Pattern Correction:* Use muslin or measurement for correcting pattern.

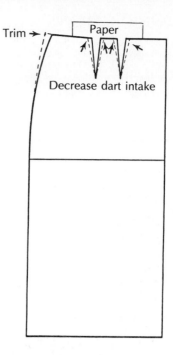

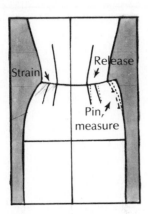

47. Dart correction series (front or back)

Choose the appropriate correction that applies to fitting problem.

▪ *Skirt Adjustment:* Mark correct placement for darts on garment. Measure. Darts may be too close, spread too far apart, not aligned with bodice, or dart points misplaced. Garment not illustrated. See sketch in Problem 34.

▪ *Pattern Correction:* Trace and cut a copy of the dart wedge. Place dart wedge where needed and trace (shaded areas).

See Figure A for darts placed too close.

See Figure B for darts spaced too far apart.

See Figure C for upright darts. (See page 12.)

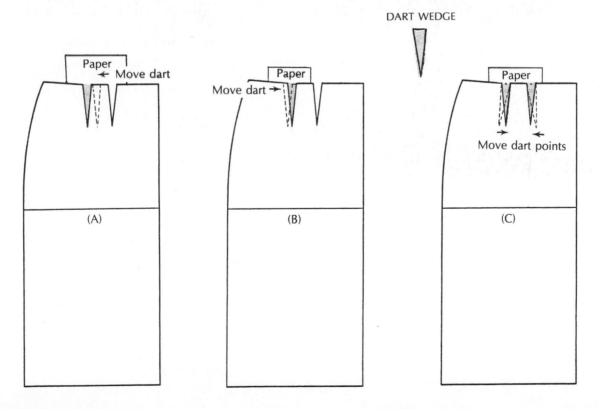

SLEEVE CORRECTIONS

In preparation for setting sleeve to armhole of garment, review pages 76 through 79. Special adjustments to the sleeve and/or armhole may be required if: *a*) the measurements of front and back armholes differ more than $\frac{3}{8}$ inch, see Equalizing the armholes, Figures 1 and 2; *b*) the angle of the relaxed arm is too far in front of or behind the side seam of the garment, see Rotating the sleeve, Figures 3 through 13. If neither is a problem, stitch sleeve to armhole and refer to page 688 for the fitting series.

EQUALIZING FRONT AND BACK ARMHOLES

- Measure back armhole (ex. 8 inches).
- Measure front armhole (ex. $7\frac{1}{2}$ inches).
- Subtract the measurements (ex. $\frac{1}{2}$ inch).
- Divide in half (ex. $\frac{1}{4}$ inch).
- Divide again (ex. $\frac{1}{8}$ inch).
- Adjust larger, and smaller, armholes as shown.

SLEEVE ROTATION

- *Bodice:* Fold and crease seam allowance around armhole from mid-armhole on front to mid-armhole on back (Figure 3).
- *Sleeve:* Sleeve should have two rows of gathering stitches—one at stitchline and the other parallel with it, $\frac{1}{4}$ inch away toward the raw edge. Shirr gathers equal to the distance from front to back mid-armhole on bodice (not illustrated).
- Slip sleeve onto arm of figure.
- Rotate sleeve in either direction until it aligns with the angle of the arm. Sleeve grain and underseam may not align with shoulderline of bodice and side seams. Slip gathered sleeve under fold-back of armhole.
- Place first pin at shoulderline and mid-armhole of front and back bodice, and one pin holding sleeve and bodice under the arm (Figures 4 and 5).
- Mark sleeve and bodice garment as follows:
- *Bodice:* Crossmark where grainline of sleeve and underseam are located on the bodice armhole. Measure distance between points A and B.
- *Sleeve:* Crossmark (use red pencil) where shoulderline and side seam of bodice are located on the sleeve (Figures 6 and 7).
- Stitch sleeve to garment. Recheck alignment. If strain appears on either side of sleeve, release and rotate again. Restitch.

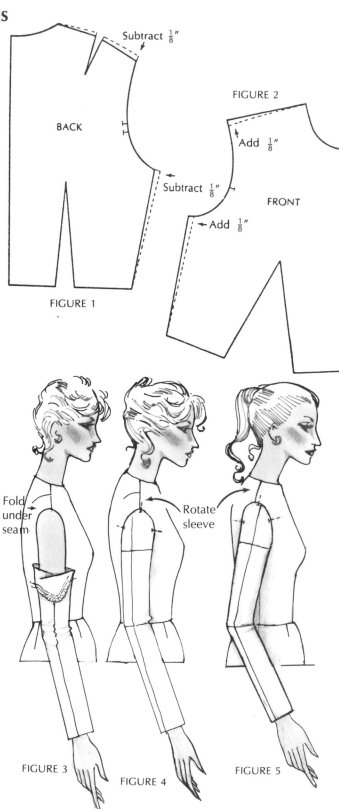

FIGURE 1

FIGURE 2

BACK

FRONT

Subtract $\frac{1}{8}$"

Add $\frac{1}{8}$"

Subtract $\frac{1}{8}$"

Add $\frac{1}{8}$"

Fold under seam

Rotate sleeve

FIGURE 3

FIGURE 4

FIGURE 5

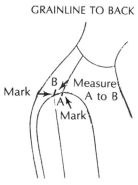

GRAINLINE TO BACK

Mark

B

A

Measure A to B

Mark

FIGURE 6

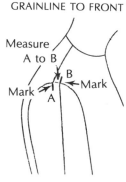

GRAINLINE TO FRONT

Measure A to B

Mark

B

A

Mark

FIGURE 7

Pattern adjustments

Three methods are given for adjusting the sleeve to the armhole. Choose the method that best satisfies the needs of the garment.

FIGURES 8 and 9

▪ *Method 1—Realigning shoulder and side seam:* Use A–B measurement to mark down from shoulder tip, and out from side seam at armhole. Draw lines from marks to neck and side waist. (What is added or removed from one side of the pattern must be removed or added to the joining pattern.) Realignment should not affect the overall front and back armhole measurement.

FIGURES 10 and 11

▪ *Method 2—Establishing new notch marks:* If the shoulderline and side seam are in perfect harmony with the figure, place notches on the armhole (indicating sleeve grain and underseam), using A–B measurement. When stitching sleeve to garment, the grain of the sleeve cap and underarm seam should be placed at the new notch locations on armhole. This correction is for personal fit only.

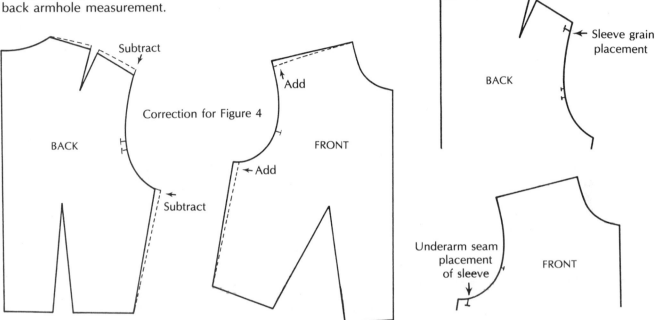

FIGURES 12 and 13

▪ *Method 3—Adjusting sleeve:* Rather than changing the location of the shoulderline and side seam, adjust the sleeve as follows:

▪ Cut through biceps line of sleeve. Using A–B measurement, shift biceps line forward or backward to decrease or increase front and back cap measurements. Correct notch placements to true to bodice. Blend sleeve cap. This correction is for personal fit only.

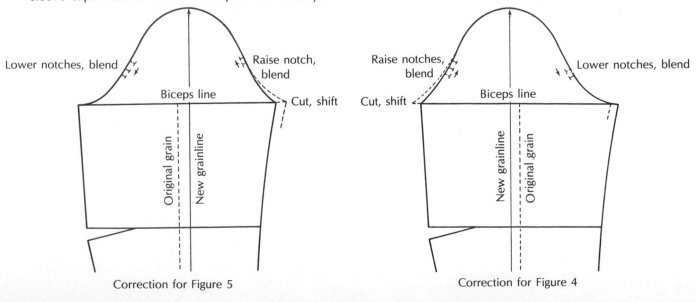

PUCKERING

Puckering around the sleeve cap indicates excessive fullness. This may be the result of the following: careless distribution of excess when stitching sleeve to bodice; front and back armholes differing more than $\frac{3}{8}$ inch; sleeve too large for armhole. Before adjusting patterns, check stitching and the distribution of excess. If sleeve has been correctly stitched, follow instruction given.

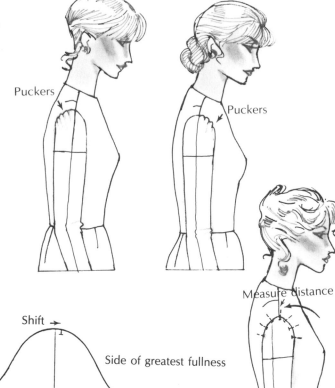

48. Puckering on one side of sleeve cap

▪ Release cap to mid-armhole and distribute the excess evenly. Repin. Mark sleeve where shoulder ends.

▪ If new cap notch is shifted more than $\frac{3}{16}$ inch past shoulder tip, equalize front and back armholes (page 666, Figures 1 and 2).

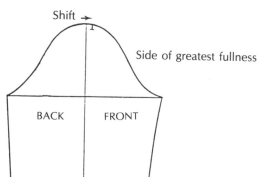

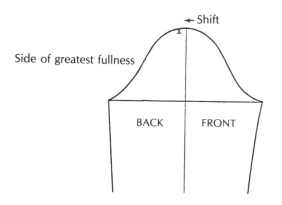

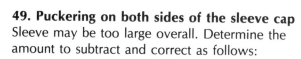

49. Puckering on both sides of the sleeve cap

Sleeve may be too large overall. Determine the amount to subtract and correct as follows:

FIGURE 3

▪ *Too large overall:* Cut through pattern on W-guideline. Overlap one-half the amount on each side of sleeve grain as shown. Tape and blend sleeve cap as shown. Add to wrist level if too tight (see page 673).

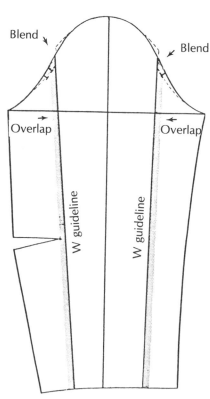

FIGURE 4
▪ *Too large from biceps to cap:* Cut X-guidelines from cap to, not through, underseam. Overlap one-half the amount on each side of sleeve grain. Tape and blend sleeve cap as shown.

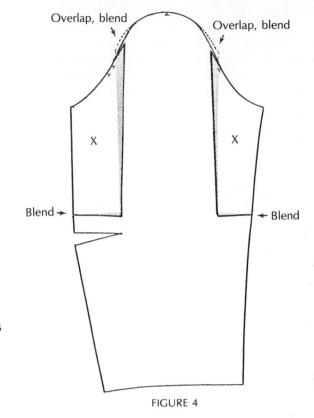

FIGURE 4

50. Sleeve too tight (little or no cap ease)
Sleeve may be too tight overall, or tight from biceps to cap. Determine amount needed and correct as follows:

FIGURE 5
▪ *Too tight overall:* Cut through pattern on W-guideline. Spread one-half the amount on each side, as shown. Blend.

FIGURE 6
▪ *Too tight from biceps to cap:* Cut X-guideline from cap to, not through, underseam. Spread one-half the amount. Blend cap and underseam.

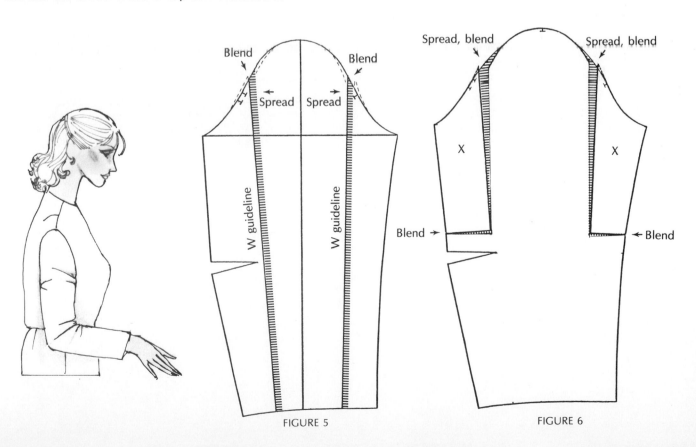

FIGURE 5

FIGURE 6

OTHER SLEEVE FITTING PROBLEMS

51. Sleeve drops off shoulder
■ Pin a vertical fold at mid-shoulder, bringing muslin stitchline to shoulder tip of form or figure. See correction given for Problem 21, Figure 2.

52. Strain across chest and armhole
■ Release sleeve, measure distance from stitchline of sleeve to armhole of form or figure. See correction given for Problem 28.

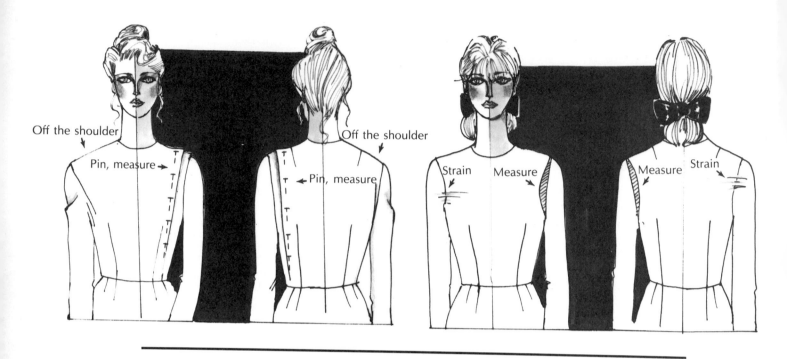

53. Diagonal strain at ball-of-arm
■ *Garment Adjustment:* Release sleeve from shoulder tip to mid-armhole (or lower). Repin seam, allowing room for ball-of-arm.
■ *Pattern Correction:* Use garment (or measurements taken) to correct pattern (Figure 1).

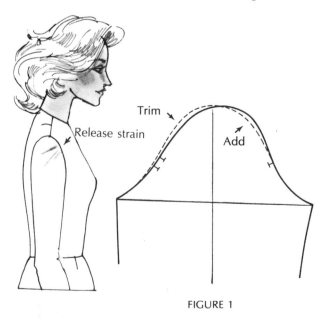

FIGURE 1

Note: If a diagonal strain appears between sleeve cap and biceps line (out from the under curve of the front, or back sleeve, Figures 2 and 3), the sleeve should be released and rotated to fit the correct angle of the arm. See page 666, Figures 3 through 13 for guidance.

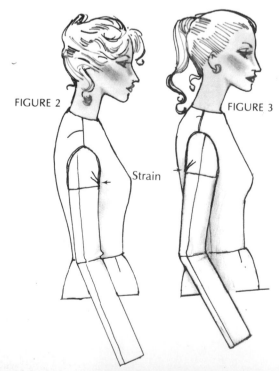

FIGURE 2

FIGURE 3

54. Diagonal strain lines directed to cap

Strain indicates sleeve cap is too short.

▪ *Garment Adjustment:* Release muslin across cap. Allow sleeve to fall. Measure from stitchline of shoulder to stitchline of cap.

▪ *Pattern Correction:* Cut through L-guideline and spread sleeve cap. Blend cap.

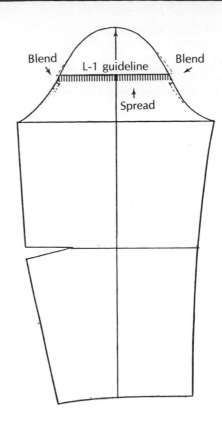

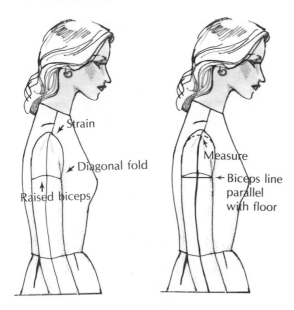

55. Cap extends above shoulder of bodice

Looseness indicates cap too high.

▪ *Garment Adjustment:* Pin cap excess at grain and measure.

▪ *Pattern Correction:* Cut through L-guideline and overlap sleeve cap. Blend cap.

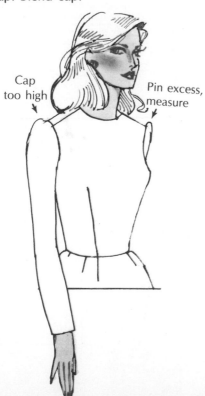

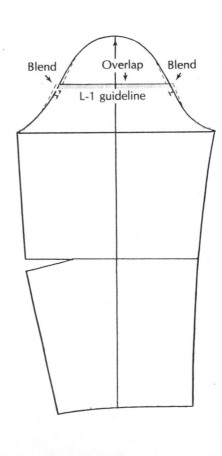

56. Difficulty in raising arm

If armhole is too low, see bodice Problem 30. If sleeve needs lift, follow correction shown.

▪ *Pattern Correction:* Cut X-section. Raise biceps level $\frac{1}{2}$ inch. Blend sleeve and underseams. Retest fit.

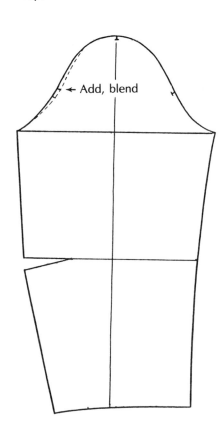

57. Armhole binds when arm in forward movement

See correction given for Problem 29.

58. Strain across back when arm in forward movement

▪ *Garment Adjustment:* Release back sleeve from cap to just below mid-armhole. Bring arm partially forward. Measure open space (not illustrated).

▪ *Pattern Correction:* Add to back armhole and sleeve cap.

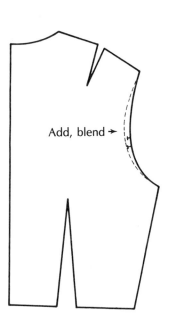

59. Sleeve too long or too short
- *Garment Adjustment:* For sleeve that is too long, pin sleeve to length needed.
- *Pattern Correction:* Cut L-2 and L-3 guidelines and overlap. Blend underseams.

- *Garment Adjustment:* Measure from sleeve to length desired for sleeve too short.
- *Pattern Correction:* Cut L-2 and L-3 guidelines and spread. Blend underseam.

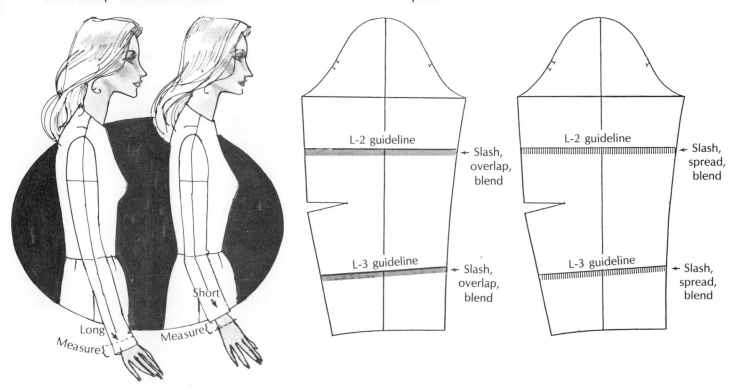

60. Wrist too tight or too loose
- *Garment Adjustment:* If too loose, pin in excess and measure. If too tight, release underseam and repin. Measure (not illustrated).
- *Pattern Correction:*

Wrist too tight: Add to wrist at both sides of underseams equally. Blend to elbow level.
Wrist too loose: Subtract from wrist at both sides of underseams equally. Blend to elbow level.

61. Elbow dart misplaced
- *Garment Adjustment:* Mark sleeve for correct location (not illustrated).
- *Pattern Correction:* Cut guideline section from sleeve pattern. Raise or lower needed amount. Blend underarm seams.

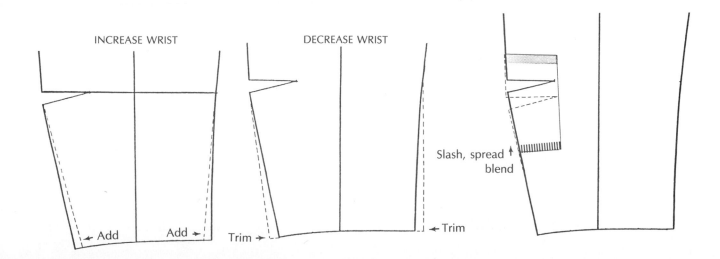

PANT CORRECTIONS

A pant that fits well on the figure and is comfortable will not hinder the movement of the legs. Fitting problems that interfere with comfort and movement are usually centered around the front and back crotch area. Strain lines, tightness, and looseness distort the appearance of the pant and indicate areas that need corrections.

TEST FITTING

Use a firm fabric to test fit the pant. However, each time a fabric with a different texture is used, the pattern should be test fit in that fabric. Any change in firmness or looseness of the yarn will cause the pant to fit and hang differently on the body.

Stitching

Stitch pant legs together before stitching around crotch seam. Press. Attach waistband and place zipper at center back or leave open. (Pin together when fitting.)

The model

The model should wear her regular foundation garments. She should stand in a natural position with feet spread apart approximately 5 inches, weight equally distributed and arms by her side, looking ahead. Place X-marks where strain or fullness appears on the pant.

Walking (front view)

Crease folds at crotch level are normal. If there are deep folds or tightness across thighs, these indicate crotch depth is too low or crotch extension is insufficient.

5" apart

Walking (back view)

Crease folds appearing under buttocks are natural and not necessarily a fitting problem.

Bending

Vertical folds indicate crotch curve is too flat, and/or inseam needs to be more curved.

Sitting

Waistband pulling down in back more than $\frac{1}{2}$ inch indicates crotch extension or crotch length is insufficient. This will cause a feeling of tightness at waist and across thighs.

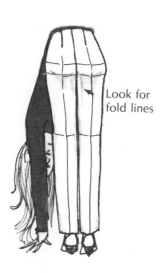

Look for fold lines

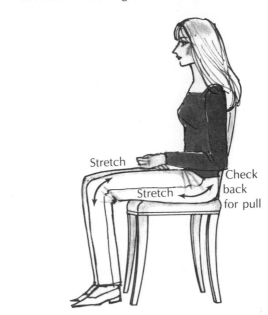

Stretch

Stretch

Check back for pull

GUIDEMARKING PANT FRONT AND BACK

Mark guidelines on pattern, as shown.
Use the following guidelines to help simplify pattern correcting. Review instructions given for use of guidelines and other patternmaking techniques on pages 634–636.

W-guideline (width)

- Use grainline (W-guideline) for increasing and decreasing pattern width.

L-guideline (length)

- Use hipline (L-guideline) for increasing and decreasing pattern length and crotch depth.

X-sections

- Label shaded areas X as shown. This section is used for adding and subtracting width at crotch level. It is also used to raise or lower crotch depth.

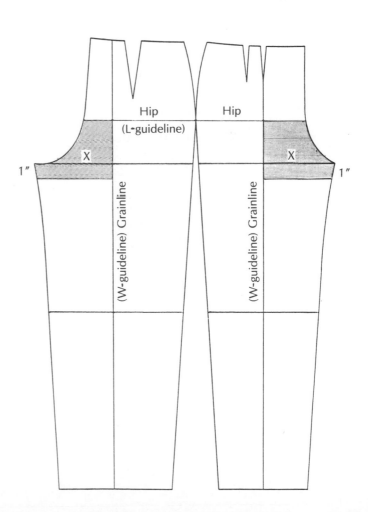

PANT FITTING PROBLEMS

Broken lines indicate the original pattern in the illustrations. Recheck waist and hip measurements on patterns. Fitting Problems 5 through 9 are based on skirt adjustments. Study skirt problems for other possible adjustments not covered in this section.

1. Pant too tight

▪ *Pant Adjustment:* Release side seam first. Allow pant to relax on the figure. Repin. (Add fabric if space is too wide for repinning.) Measure.
If strain still appears at center front around the crotch area, release center front from approximately hip level to within 2 inches of crotch point. Pull down on the pant leg at hem and allow pant to spread apart at center front. Measure this distance. Use one-half this amount for pattern correction.
▪ *Pattern Correction:* Cut W-guideline from hem to, and across, hip to side seam and spread. Cut across hip to center front and spread to add width, if needed. (Both adjustments are shown in the illustration.) Blend pattern to waistline. Repeat for back.

2. Pant too loose around hip (and hollow areas) or legline

▪ *Pant Adjustment:* Pin excess at the side seam first. If excess still appears at the center front and/or inseam, pin excess. Measure.
▪ *Pattern Correction:* Cut W-guideline from hem to, and across, hip to side seam. Move pattern section inward from side seam to reduce width. Cut across hip to center front and overlap to reduce width, if needed. Both adjustments are shown in the illustration. Blend pattern to waistline. Repeat for back.

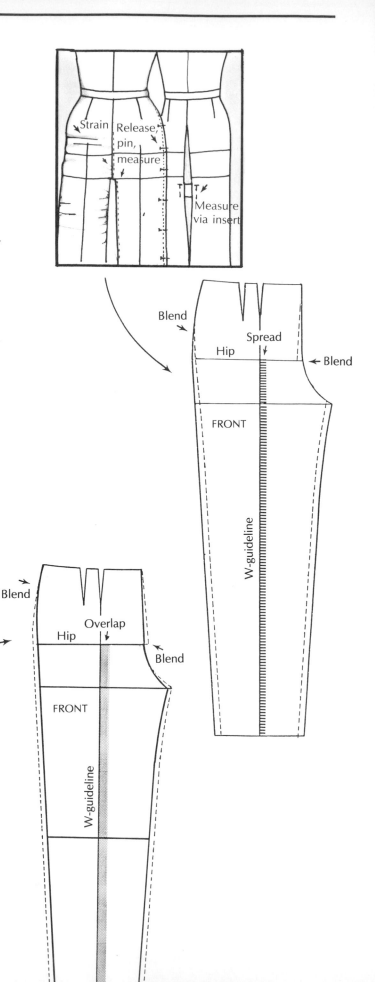

3. Crotch depth too long

▪ *Pant Adjustment:* Pin up excess to allow for a comfortable crotch depth. Pin excess evenly around hip. Have model bend and sit. Adjust depth if necessary.

▪ *Pattern Correction:* Cut X-guide section and raise. Blend crotch and inseam. Repeat for back. This adjustment will not affect the original length of the pant.

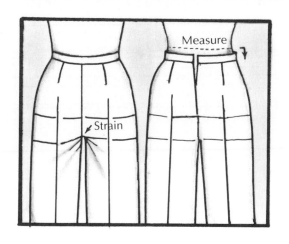

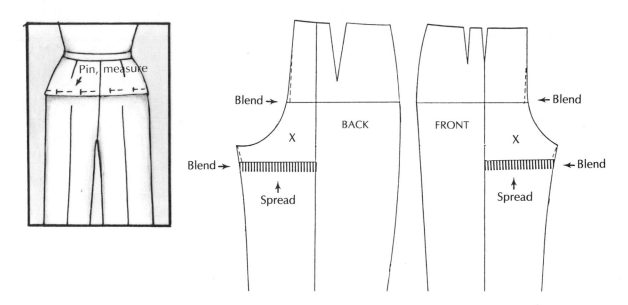

4. Crotch depth too short

Diagonal strain lines appear from hip to crotch. Crotch feels snug.

▪ *Pant Adjustment:* Release center front waist. Let pant fall to a level where crotch feels comfortable. Measure from below waistband to waist level.

▪ *Pattern Correction:* Cut X-guideline and lower crotch as required. Blend crotch and inseam. Repeat for back. This adjustment will not change the original length of the pant.

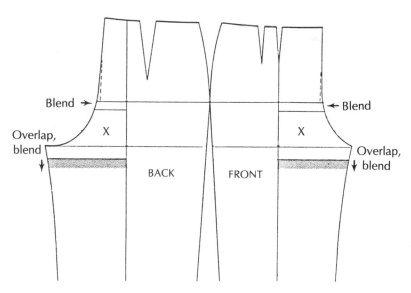

5. Excess along side seam at hip or thigh area
See skirt Problem 38 for correction.

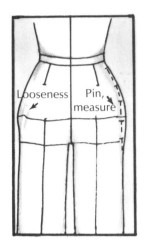

6. Drooping at center front or center back
See skirt Problem 41 for correction.

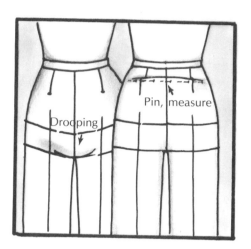

7. Diagonal strain toward side seams from darts
See skirt Problem 45 for correction.

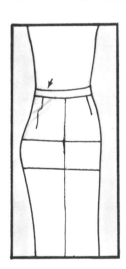

8. Diagonal strain lines from dart
See skirt Problem 46 for correction.

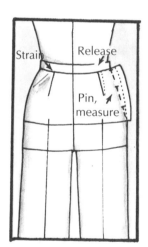

9. Other dart problems
- Strain around dart area, see Problem 43.
- Excess at dart points, see Problem 44.
- Diagonal strain at front dart, see Problem 46.
- Shifting dart locations, or dart points, see Problem 47.

10. Strain from a dominant hip bulge or high/low hip

▪ *Pant Adjustment:* Release side seam above hip, waist, and darts. Repin, allowing ease for bulge. Mark new dart, waist and hip.

▪ *Pattern Correction:* Use pant to correct pattern as shown.

▪ Label *Right-side-up* on both front patterns.

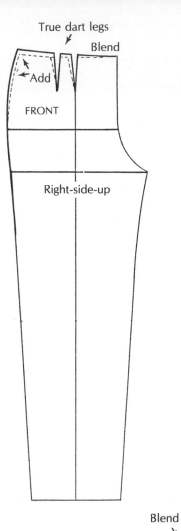

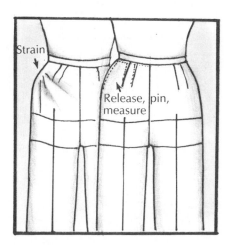

11. Strain at abdominal area (prominent bulge)

▪ *Pant Adjustment:* Release center front seam from waist to just above hip level. Slash from center front to side seam. Let pant fall until hip level is parallel with floor. Measure space.

▪ *Pattern Correction:* Slash pattern from center front to, not through, side. Raise to spread section. Blend center front.

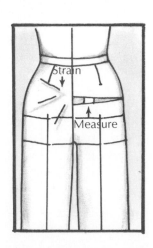

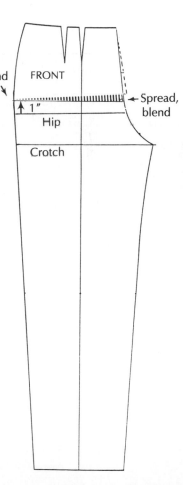

12. Strain lines between hip and crotch at center front

▪ *Pant Adjustment:* Release center front from abdomen to below hip level. Tug on hem of pant and center will open needed amount. Crossmark at widest point. Measure. Use one-half this measurement for pattern correction. Adjust and restitch pant and continue with fitting if additional adjustment is not needed.

▪ *Pattern Correction:* Cut X-section from pattern and spread. Blend center front, and from crotch point to knee level.

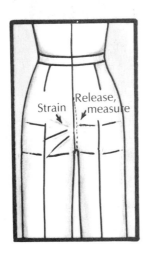

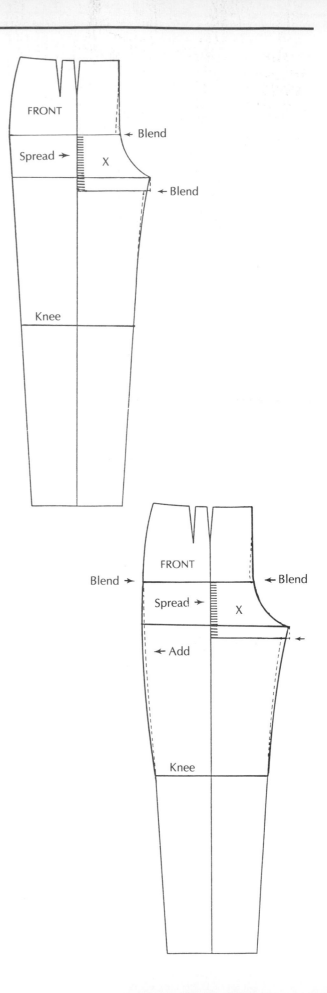

13. Diagonal strain lines from thigh to center front crotch

▪ *Pant Adjustment:* Release center front from abdomen to crotch curve. Release side seam from hip to upper thigh. Tug on hem of pant, side and center will open needed amount. Repin side seam allowing room for thigh bulge. Repin center front. Adjust and restitch pant and continue with fitting.

▪ *Pattern Correction:* Cut X-section and spread. Blend center front and from crotch point to knee level. Add the needed amount to front and back side seam. (Back not illustrated.)

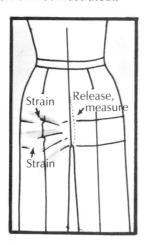

14. Diagonal strain lines to crotch point of back

Strain in this area indicates insufficient crotch point extension. This is a difficult area to fit. It is best to add to crotch point of pattern, using measurement given below. Adjust pant and continue with fitting.

• *Pattern Correction:* Add ½ inch to crotch point, blend line to crotch, and end at knee level.

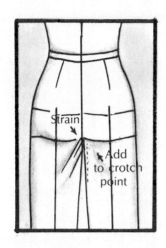

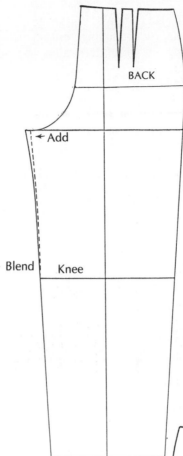

Note: If strain still appears after adjustment, add another ½ inch to crotch point and blend to knee.

15. Diagonal strain lines to crotch point of front

Apply the same instruction given for Problem 14.

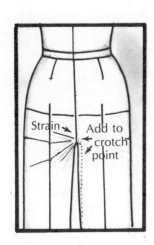

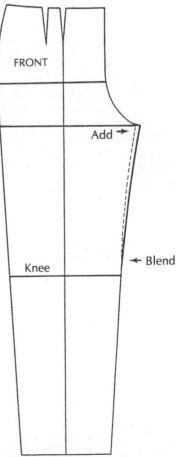

16. Strain radiating from prominent thigh to inseam

▪ *Pant Adjustment:* Release outseam and inseam to crotch point. Repin, allowing room for thigh bulge. Add ½ inch to front crotch point when correcting pattern. Restitch pant and continue fitting if no further adjustment is needed.

▪ *Pattern Correction:* Cut X-section. Spread ½ inch. Blend crotch extension. Add to front and back side seams. Blend at center front and from crotch point to knee level. (Back not illustrated.)

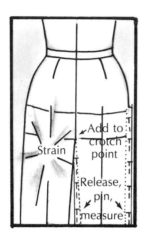

17. Vertical folds at center front crotch

▪ *Pant Adjustment:* Pin excess (allow ease). Measure widest part.

▪ *Pattern Correction:* Cut and overlap X-section. Blend center front and from crotch point to knee level.

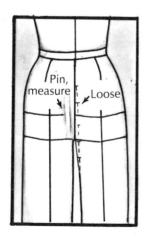

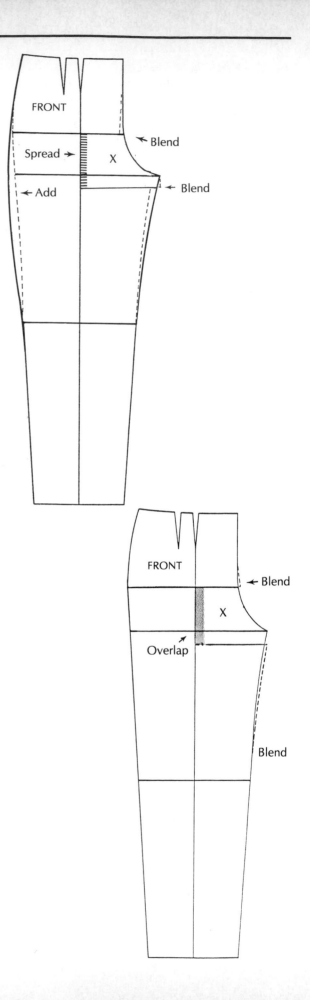

18. Band dips down in back

▪ *Pant Adjustment:* Release waistline to side seam. Let pant fall downward. Measure distance from band to stitchline at waist.

▪ *Pattern Correction:* Add to center back waist and draw new waist to side. True dart legs, adding to shorter leg. Blend waistline and center back.

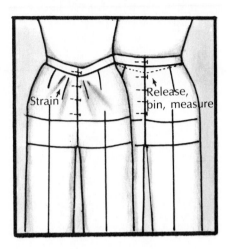

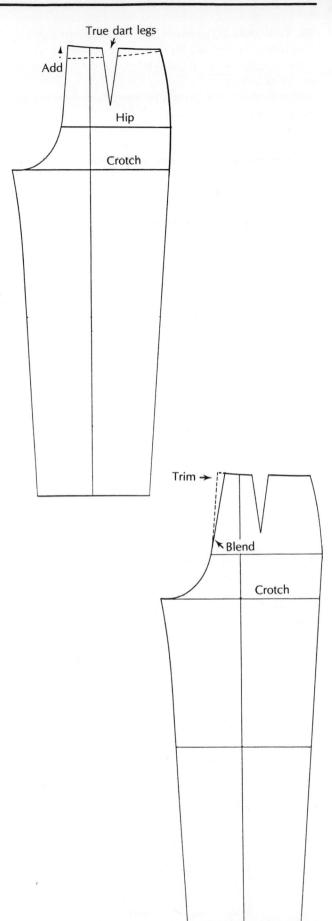

19. Band falls away from center back

(Hollow area of back)

▪ *Pant Adjustment:* Remove band. Pin excess at center back. Measure.

▪ *Pattern Correction:* Trim center back and blend with crotch curve. Shorten length of belt by equal amount.

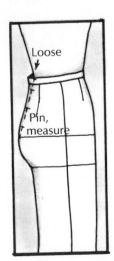

20. Pant dips downward too much when sitting

Strain may be felt across waist and abdomen. Two adjustments are given. Use adjustment best suited to the problem.

▪ *Pant Adjustment:* Measure from band to waistline (while seated). Subtract $\frac{1}{2}$ inch.

▪ *Pattern Correction:* For slack or jean pant, follow instruction for pattern A. Slash pattern from center at hip level to, not through, side seam. Swing pattern upward amount required. Blend center back and side seam. For trouser pant follow instruction for Pattern B. Cut X-guide section. Spread and blend center back and inseam.

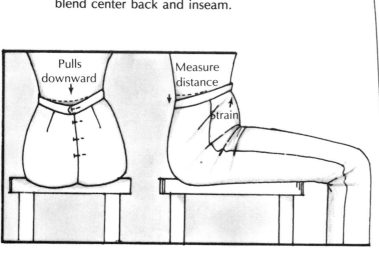

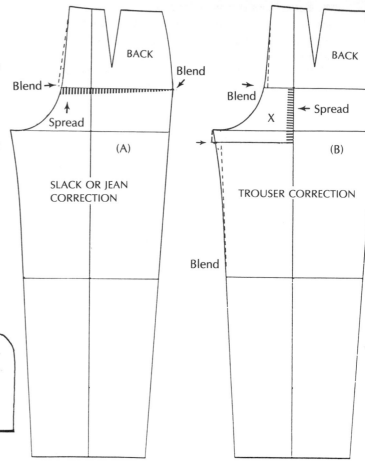

21. Sides differ from right to left

Folds on one side of front or back at hipline are caused by buttocks and/or abdomen being smaller on one side.

▪ *Pant Adjustment:* Pin excess on side indicated. Measure.

▪ *Pattern Correction:* Trim excess on front and back pattern. A full front and back pattern is required. Label all pattern sections *Right-side-up*. (Back not illustrated.)

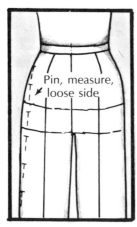

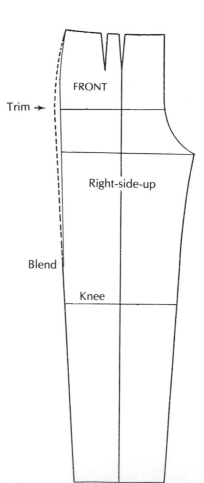

22. Side seam out of alignment

Side seams are too far forward or backward.

▪ *Pant Adjustment:* Draw correct line. Measure distance.

▪ *Pattern Correction:* Subtract from one side of pattern, adding an equal amount to the other side. Blend side seam. (See pattern correction A for problem A, and pattern correction B for problem B.)

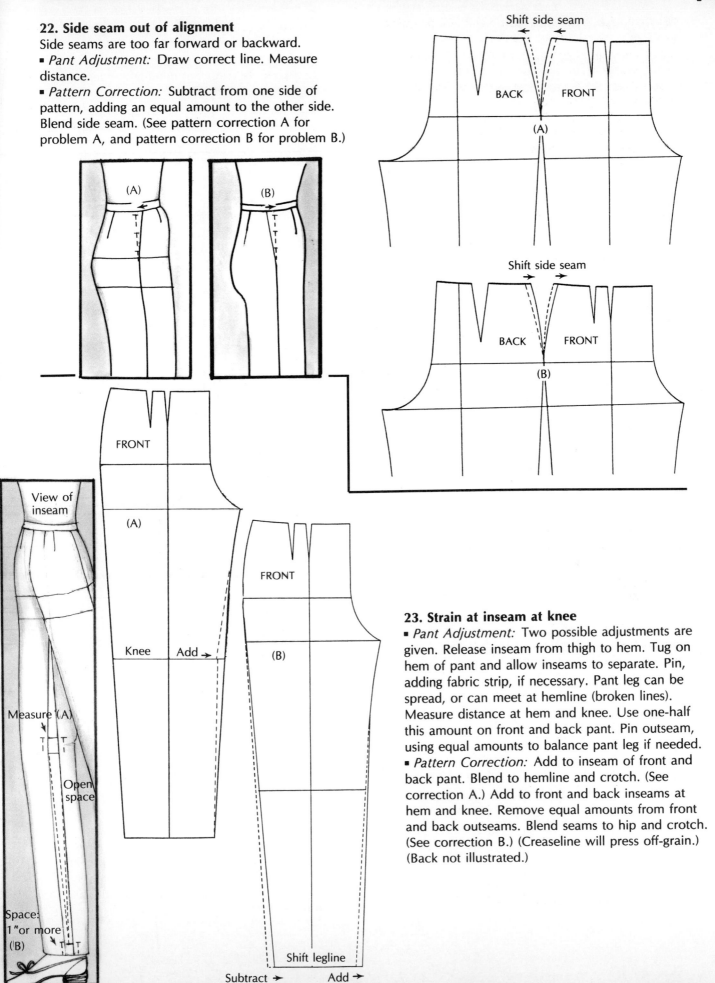

23. Strain at inseam at knee

▪ *Pant Adjustment:* Two possible adjustments are given. Release inseam from thigh to hem. Tug on hem of pant and allow inseams to separate. Pin, adding fabric strip, if necessary. Pant leg can be spread, or can meet at hemline (broken lines). Measure distance at hem and knee. Use one-half this amount on front and back pant. Pin outseam, using equal amounts to balance pant leg if needed.

▪ *Pattern Correction:* Add to inseam of front and back pant. Blend to hemline and crotch. (See correction A.) Add to front and back inseams at hem and knee. Remove equal amounts from front and back outseams. Blend seams to hip and crotch. (See correction B.) (Creaseline will press off-grain.) (Back not illustrated.)

24. Diagonal strain lines directed toward thigh and calf

Widen front at thigh area, and back leglines at calf.

▪ *Pant Adjustment:* Release side and inseam from thigh to just above knee and release muslin at side and inseam from just below knee to just above hem. Repin, allowing ease.

▪ *Pattern Correction:* Correct pattern using muslin as a guide.

25. Twisting legline

Two of the possible causes of this problem are:

▪ Garment is cut off-grain, or crosswise grain and straight grain have shrunk at different percentages, such as in untreated denim.

▪ *Correction:* Preshrink fabric and recut pattern. Refit.

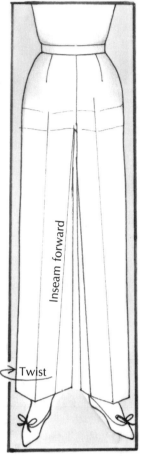

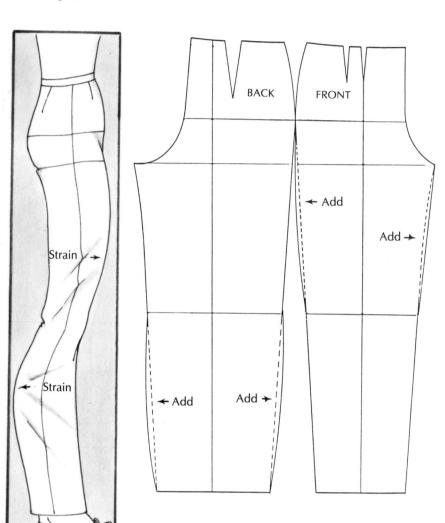

Pants too long or too short

Add to or subtract from hemline of pant as needed (not illustrated).

Modifying legline circumference

▪ *Trouser and Slack:* Pin excess equally on inseam and outseam of hemline, ending at hip level and crotch point (not illustrated).

▪ *Jean Pant:* Pin excess equally on inseam and outseam of back legline. If pant is to be tapered close to the leg and under buttocks, pin outseam and inseam equally. If a lighter or more snug fit under buttocks is desired, pin in more on the inseam in the upper thigh area.

METRIC CONVERSION TABLE

(INCHES TO CENTIMETERS)

(1 inch, U.S. standard = 2.540005 centimeters)

The centimeter equivalent to the inch measurement is to the nearest tenth in this text. It is an accepted general practice to measure to the nearest half centimeter for major measurements when using the metric system of measurement exclusively.

Inches	0	1/16	1/8	1/4	3/8	1/2	5/8	3/4	7/8	Inches
0	0.0	0.2	0.3	0.6	1.0	1.3	1.6	1.9	2.2	0
1	2.5	2.7	2.9	3.2	3.5	3.8	4.1	4.4	4.8	1
2	5.1	5.2	5.4	5.7	6.0	6.4	6.7	7.0	7.3	2
3	7.6	7.8	7.9	8.3	8.6	8.9	9.2	9.5	9.8	3
4	10.2	10.3	10.5	10.8	11.1	11.4	11.7	12.1	12.4	4
5	12.7	12.9	13.0	13.3	13.7	14.0	14.3	14.6	14.9	5
6	15.2	15.4	15.6	15.9	16.2	16.5	16.8	17.1	17.5	6
7	17.8	17.9	18.1	18.4	18.7	19.1	19.4	19.7	20.0	7
8	20.3	20.5	20.6	21.0	21.3	21.6	21.9	22.2	22.5	8
9	22.9	23.0	23.2	23.5	23.8	24.1	24.4	24.8	25.1	9
10	25.4	25.6	25.7	26.0	26.4	26.7	27.0	27.3	27.6	10
11	27.9	28.1	28.3	28.6	28.9	29.2	29.5	29.8	30.2	11
12	30.5	30.6	30.8	31.1	31.4	31.8	32.1	32.4	32.7	12
13	33.0	33.2	33.3	33.7	34.0	34.3	34.6	34.9	35.2	13
14	35.6	35.7	35.9	36.2	36.5	36.8	37.1	37.5	37.8	14
15	38.1	38.3	38.4	38.7	39.1	39.4	39.7	40.0	40.3	15
16	40.6	40.8	41.0	41.3	41.6	41.9	42.2	42.5	42.9	16
17	43.2	43.3	43.5	43.8	44.1	44.4	44.8	45.1	45.4	17
18	45.7	45.9	46.0	46.4	46.7	47.0	47.3	47.6	47.9	18
19	48.3	48.4	48.6	48.9	49.2	49.5	49.8	50.2	50.5	19
20	50.8	51.0	51.1	51.4	51.7	52.1	52.4	52.7	53.0	20
21	53.3	53.5	53.7	54.0	54.3	54.6	54.9	55.2	55.6	21
22	55.9	56.0	56.2	56.5	56.8	57.2	57.5	57.8	58.1	22
23	58.4	58.6	58.7	59.1	59.4	59.7	60.0	60.3	60.6	23
24	61.0	61.1	61.3	61.6	61.9	62.2	62.5	62.9	63.2	24

(Continued on next page)

					Fractions					
Inches	0	1/16	1/8	1/4	3/8	1/2	5/8	3/4	7/8	Inches
25	63.5	63.7	63.8	64.1	64.5	64.8	65.1	65.4	65.7	25
26	66.0	66.2	66.4	66.7	67.0	67.3	67.6	67.9	68.3	26
27	68.6	68.7	69.0	69.2	69.5	69.9	70.2	70.5	70.8	27
28	71.1	71.3	71.4	71.8	72.1	72.4	72.7	73.0	73.3	28
29	73.7	73.8	74.0	74.3	74.6	74.9	75.2	75.6	75.9	29
30	76.2	76.4	76.5	76.8	77.2	77.5	77.8	78.1	78.4	30
31	78.7	78.9	79.1	79.4	79.7	80.0	80.3	80.6	81.0	31
32	81.3	81.4	81.6	81.9	82.2	82.6	82.9	83.2	83.5	32
33	83.8	84.0	84.1	84.5	84.8	85.1	85.4	85.7	86.0	33
34	86.4	86.5	86.7	87.0	87.3	87.6	87.9	88.3	88.6	34
35	88.9	89.1	89.2	89.5	89.9	90.2	90.5	90.8	91.1	35
36	91.4	91.6	91.8	92.1	92.4	92.7	93.0	93.3	93.7	36
37	94.0	94.1	94.3	94.6	94.9	95.3	95.6	95.9	96.2	37
38	96.5	96.7	96.8	97.2	97.5	97.8	98.1	98.4	98.7	38
39	99.1	99.2	99.4	99.7	100.0	100.3	100.6	101.0	101.3	39
40	101.6	101.8	101.9	102.2	102.6	102.9	103.2	103.5	103.8	40
41	104.1	104.3	104.5	104.8	105.1	105.4	105.7	106.0	106.4	41
42	106.7	106.8	107.0	107.3	107.6	108.0	108.3	108.6	108.9	42
43	109.2	109.4	109.5	109.9	110.2	110.5	110.8	111.1	111.4	43
44	111.8	111.9	112.1	112.4	112.7	113.0	113.3	113.7	114.0	44
45	114.3	114.5	114.6	114.9	115.2	115.6	115.9	116.2	116.5	45
46	116.8	117.0	117.2	117.5	117.8	118.1	118.4	118.7	119.1	46
47	119.4	119.5	119.7	120.0	120.3	120.7	121.0	121.3	121.6	47
48	121.9	122.1	122.2	122.6	122.9	123.2	123.5	123.8	124.1	48
49	124.5	124.6	124.8	125.1	125.4	125.7	126.1	126.4	126.7	49
50	127.0	127.2	127.3	127.6	128.0	128.3	128.6	128.9	129.2	50
51	129.5	129.7	129.9	130.2	130.5	130.8	131.1	131.5	131.8	51
52	132.1	132.2	132.4	132.7	133.0	133.4	133.7	134.0	134.3	52
53	134.6	134.8	134.9	135.3	135.6	135.9	136.2	136.5	136.9	53
54	137.2	137.3	137.5	137.8	138.1	138.4	138.8	139.1	139.4	54
55	139.7	139.9	140.0	140.3	140.7	141.0	141.3	141.6	141.9	55
60	152.4	152.6	152.7	153.0	153.4	153.7	154.0	154.3	154.6	60

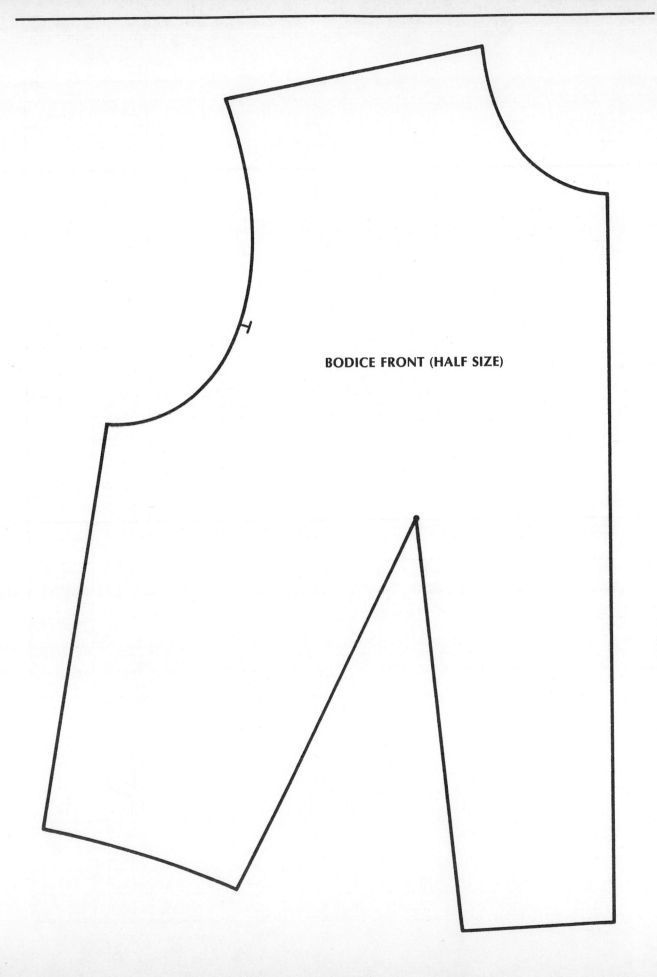

BODICE FRONT (HALF SIZE)

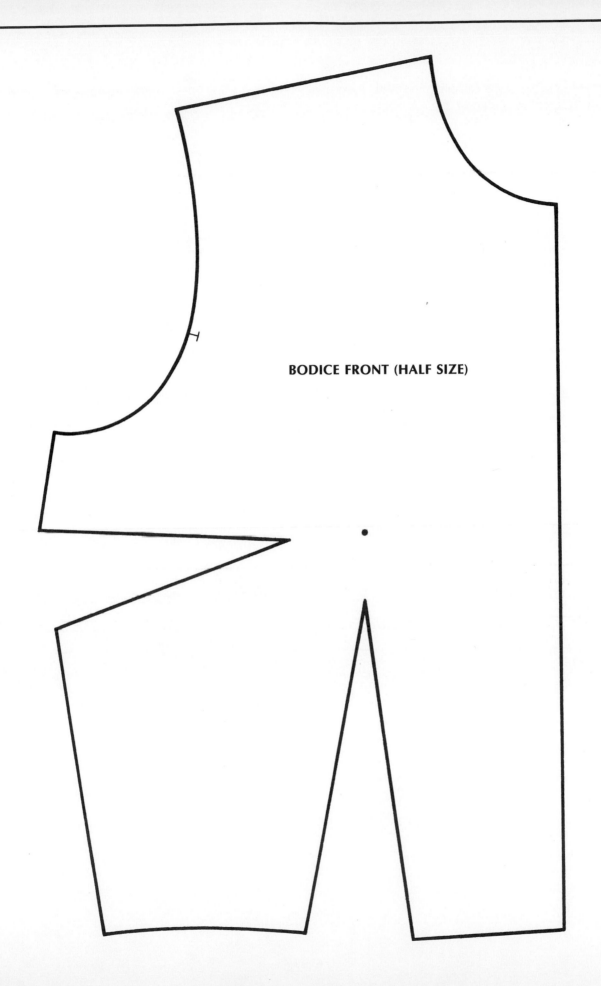

BODICE FRONT (HALF SIZE)

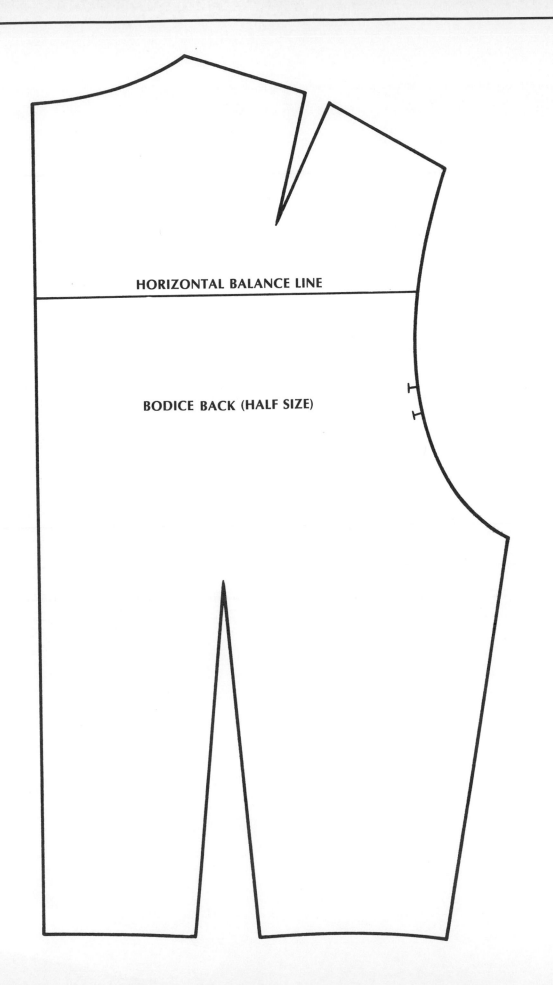

HORIZONTAL BALANCE LINE

BODICE BACK (HALF SIZE)

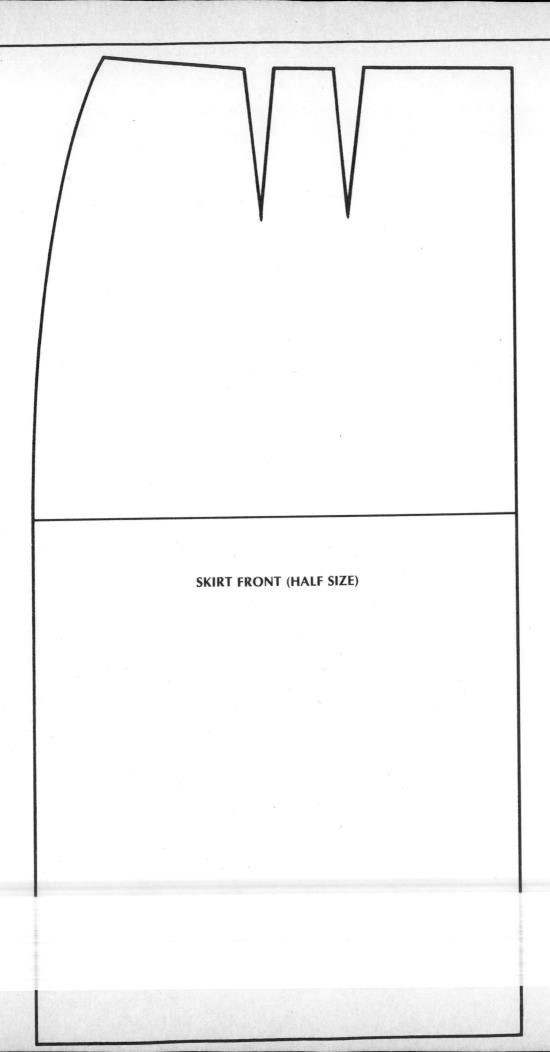

SKIRT FRONT (HALF SIZE)

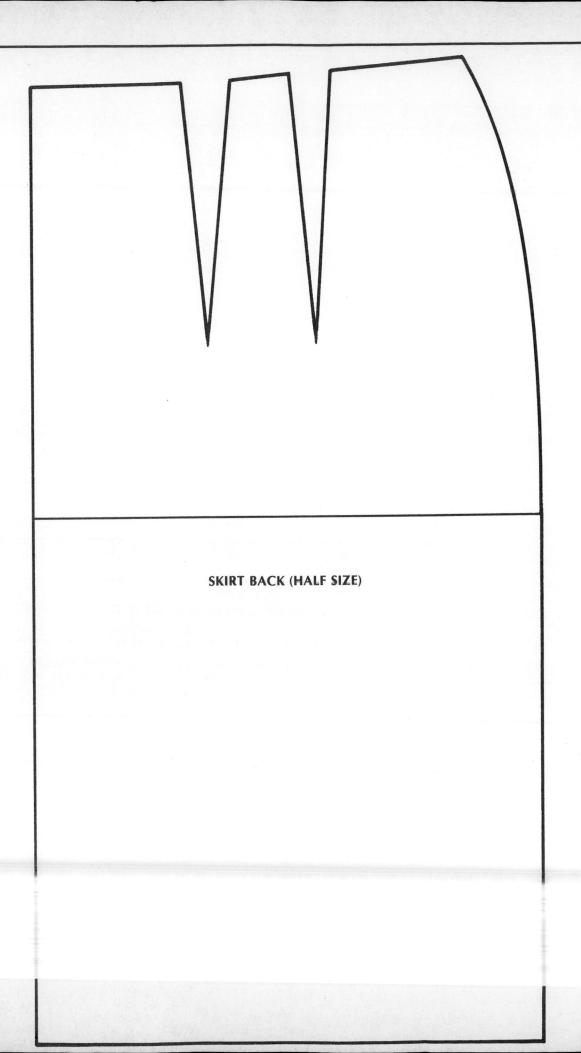

SKIRT BACK (HALF SIZE)

SLEEVE (HALF SIZE)

JOIN LOWER

SEC

WRIST LEVEL

VE

JOIN LOWER | SECTION HERE

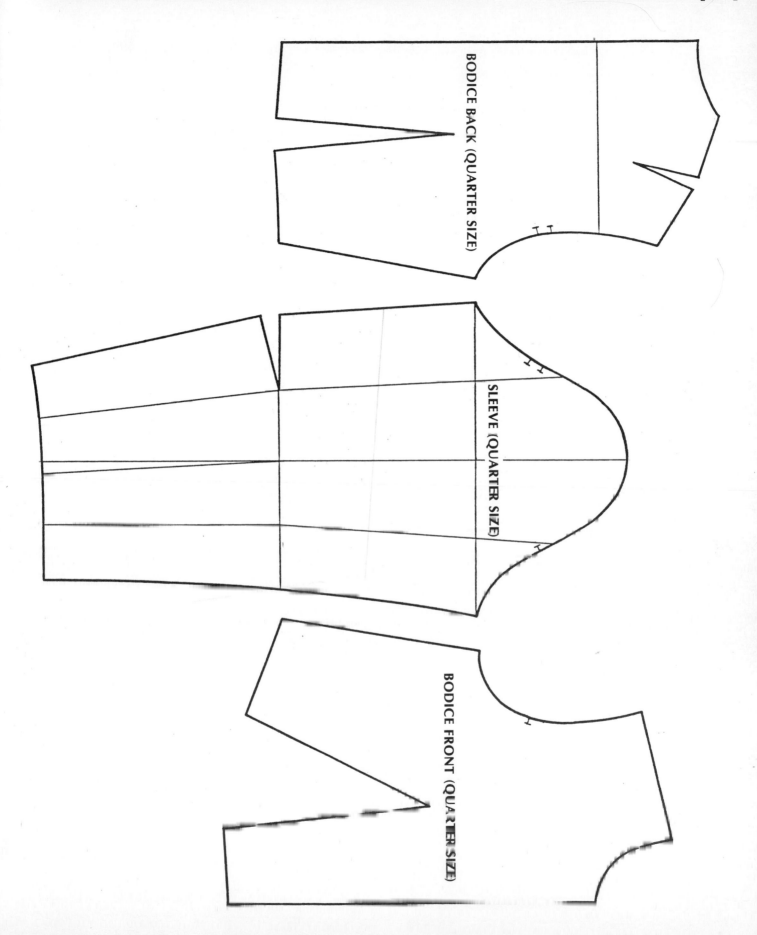

BODICE BACK (QUARTER SIZE)

SLEEVE (QUARTER SIZE)

BODICE FRONT (QUARTER SIZE)

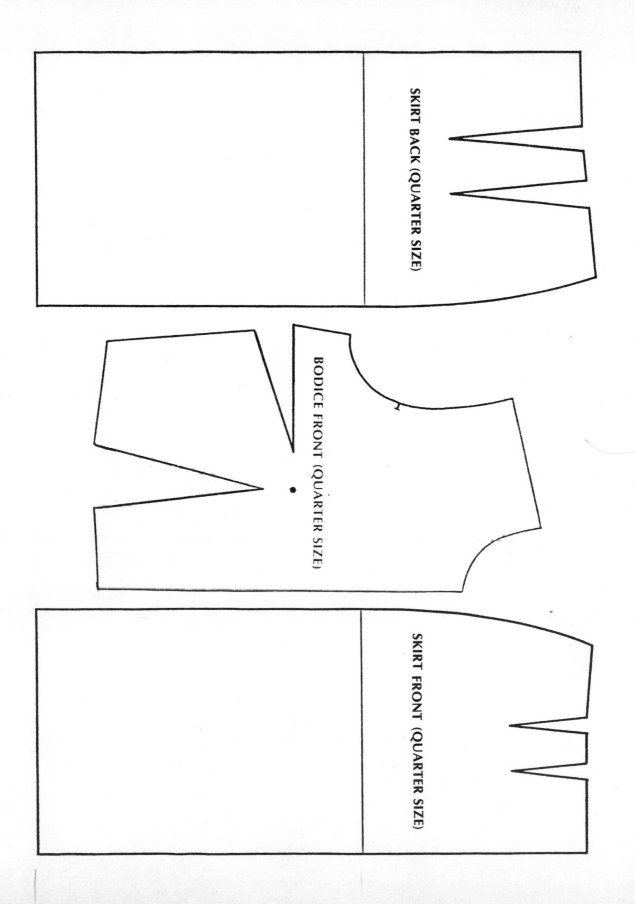

SKIRT BACK (QUARTER SIZE)

BODICE FRONT (QUARTER SIZE)

SKIRT FRONT (QUARTER SIZE)

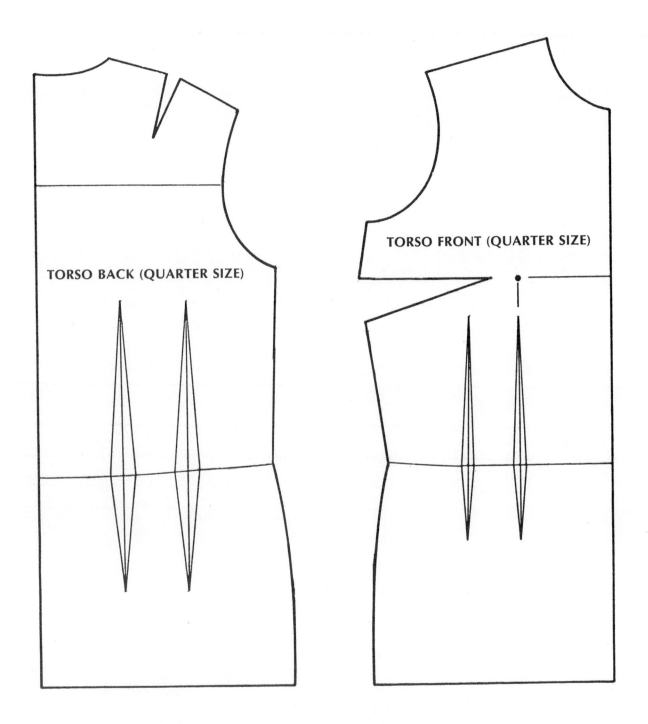

TORSO BACK (QUARTER SIZE)

TORSO FRONT (QUARTER SIZE)

FRENCH CURVE

General index

Added fullness (Principle #2)
  introduction, 112, 180–181, 186
    above bust, 183
    along princess line, 185
    around neckband, 184
    at dart leg, 182
Armhole adjustments, 80–81

Balance, 12–13
Balance line terms
  asymmetric lines, 12
  balancing a pattern, 13
  horizontal balance line, 12–13
  perpendicular line, 12
  plumb line, 12
  right angle, 12
  vertical line, 12
Basic pattern set
  introduction, 64
  pattern parts, 65
  shaping process, 65
  see also Drafting, Draping, and
      Commercial pattern adjustments
Bifurcated garments, 530–531
  see also Pants
Bikinis. See Swimwear
Blouson, 190
  increased fullness, 192
  modified, 191
Bodice draft
  back bodice, 68–69
  front bodice, 66–67
  measurements needed, 66, 68
Bodice drape, 88–92
Bodysuits
  foundation, 582–584
    halter neck, 586
    scooped neck, 585
  stirrups, 587
  tights, 587
  see also Leotards
Bra cups, 617–618
Buttonholes
  closure, 415–416
  placement guide, 416–417
  types, 415
Buttons, 414–415

Capes
  A-line foundation, 516–517
  flared foundation, 518–519
Charts
  armhole depth/cap height, 60
  bra cup adjustment, 103
  circle-cascade radius, 332–336
  cost sheet, 18
  dart intake on skirts/pants, 62
  dart locations, 115
  industrial form measurement, 45
  metric conversion, 687–688

pattern, 19
personal measurement, 46
sleeve draft measurement, 73
tools, 4–6
Coats. See Jackets
Collars
  all-in-one, 271
  basic shirt collar, 256
    corrections, 259
    folded, 258
    straight, 256
    undercollar, 257
  introduction, 254–255
  mandarin, 268–269
  Peter Pan, 260–263
  roll, 272–273
  sailor, 264–266
  square neck, 267
  with stand, 270–271
  terms, 254–255
  turtle neck, 272–273
  variations, 274
  V-neck, 267
  wing, 426–427
  see also Jackets
Commercial pattern adjustments
  asymmetricity, 104–106
  bra cup sizes, 102–103
  conversion to one dart, 108
  other adjustments, 107
Contouring (Principle #3)
  contour guide pattern, 206–212
  figure vs. basic garment, 205
  introduction, 204
  see also Empire, Halters, Off-shoulder
      designs, Strapless, Surplice
Cost sheet, 18
Cowls
  armhole, 243
  deep, 239–240
  exaggerated, 246–247
  high back, 240–241
  high horizontal, 232–233
  high relaxed, 234–235
  inset, 248–249
  introduction, 232
  low, 238
  low back, 242
  mid-back, 242
  mid-depth, 236–237
  pleated, 244–245
  sleeve, 379
Cuffs, 352–355
Cupping, 12, 24

Dart equivalents, 138
  flare, 139
  gathers, 140–143
  pleats, 139, 146–148
  tuck-darts, 138, 146–148

Dartless knit foundation, 470–472
Dart manipulation (Principle #1), 112,
  114–115
Darts
  asymmetric, 156, 160
    curved, 159
    radiating, 157–158
    squared, 156–157
  back neck, 165
  back shoulder, 164, 166
    eliminating via multi-dispersion, 165
    transferring excess to armhole, 166
  cluster
    bust, 148
    darts, 144–146
    pleat, 144–146
    shoulder, 147
    tuck-dart, 144–146
    waist, 144–146
  completing, 23–26
  cupping, 24
  direction of darts excess, 24
  graduated, 149, 150
  intersecting, 161, 164
    with gathers, 163
    shoulder, 161
    waist, 162
  manipulation, 112, 114–115
  parallel, 151, 155
    cape effect, 154
    French, 152
    neck, 153
  pencil marking, 25
  radiating, 149–150
  shaping, 26
  sleeve, 351
  terms, 11
  tissue copy, 26
  uprighting, 12
  see also Single-dart series, Two-dart
      series
Department store standard measurements.
    See Standards
Drafting basic patterns, 66–85
Draping basic patterns
  bodice drape
    back bodice, 90–92
    front bodice, 88–89
    preparation, 87
  introduction to draping, 86
  pinning bodice to skirt, 98
  skirt drape
    back skirt, 95–98
    front skirt, 94–95
    preparation, 93
  transferring muslin drape to pattern
    paper, 99–101
Dresses
  basic foundations, 448–449
  caftan, 467

Dresses (*Continued*)
   categories, 448
   empire foundation, 456–457
      with slinky skirt, 458–459
   jumper, 463
   oversized, 462
   panel dress foundation, 454–455
   princess-line foundation, 450
      A-line, 451–452
      stylized, 452–453
   styleline problems, 464–466
   tent foundation, 460–461
   variations, 468

Empire designs, 213–216, 456–459

Fabric terms
   bias, 14
   bowing, 15
   grains, 14–15, 22
   muslin, 14
   selvage, 14
   warp, 14
   weft, 14
Facings, 418–422
Figure analysis, individual, 32–41
Flange, 197, 202
   dart, 197
   inset, 200–201
   to waist, 198–199
Flat patternmaking system. *See*
      Patternmaking methods
French curve, 707
   see also Tools

Grainline, 22

Halters, 224, 586
Hoods, 520–525

Industrial form, 7–8
Industrial form measurement chart. *See*
      Charts

Jackets
   double-breasted, 500
   foundations, 486–487
   interconstruction, 506–513
   introduction, 486
   lapels
      basic notched, 492–495
      low-notch, 496–497
      portrait, 498–499
   shawl foundation, 502
      collar variations, 503–505
   sleeve enlarging, 488–489
      two-piece, 490–491
   terms, 486
   variations, 501
Jog seams, 20–21

Knits
   adapting patterns to, 623–625
   dartless foundation, 470–472
   dresses, 448
   introduction to, 622
   shrinkage factor, 623
   stretch and recovery factor, 624, 625

Labeling pattern pieces, 27–28
Landmarks, 8
Leotards
   draft, 588–590
      asymmetric top, 592
      bateau neck, 594

empire-cut, 591
scooped neck, 593
see also Bodysuits

Measuring
   human figure
      arc measurements, 57
      arm measurements, 60
      bodice measurements, 58–59
      circumference measurements, 57
      horizontal balance line, 56
      measuring for symmetry, 55–56
      pant draft, 61
      preparation, 54–55
   industrial form
      circumference measurements, 48
      horizontal balance line, 49
      horizontal measurements, 51
      pant draft, 52
      preparation, 47
      verifying shoulder/side seam
         alignment, 48
      vertical measurements, 50
   tools required, 44
Metric conversion tables, 687–688

Necklines
   built-up
      bateau, 228–229
      introduction, 226
      stovepipe, 226–228
   inset bands, 230–231
Notches, 20–21
   see also Cowls, Collars

Off-shoulder designs, 222–223

Pants
   adjustments for personal fit, 628–632
   analysis, summary, 532–533
   baggy, 554
   Bermuda, 568, 571
   Capri, 568, 572
   clown, 566
   completing the pattern, 545–546
   contour, 560
   culotte, 532–533, 534–535
      box-pleated, 547–548
      tiered, 551
      wide-sweeping hemline, 550
   curved hemline, 562
   draped, 564–565, 567
   flare, 560, 561
   gaucho, 548–549
   high-waisted, 556
   hip-hugger, 557
   Jamaica, 568, 570
   jean, 532–533, 541–544
      with back yoke, 558–559
   knickers, 563
   pedal-pusher, 568, 571
   pull-on, 555
   short, 568, 570
   shorty-short, 568, 569
   slack, 532–533, 540
   terminology, 531
   toreador, 568, 572
   trouser, 532–533, 536–539
      pleated, 552–553
Pattern chart. *See* Charts
Pattern industry standard measurements.
   See Standards
Patternmaking methods
   adjusting commercial basic patterns,
      102–108

drafting basic patterns, 66–85
draping basic patterns, 86–101
flat patternmaking system
   introduction, 112
   techniques, 112
   terms, 113
   test fit, 113
Patternmaking terms
   apex, 11
   basic pattern set, 9
   blend, 10
   bust point, 11
   darts, 11–12
   drafting, 9
   draping, 9
   ease, 12
   marking, 10
   trueing, 10
   working pattern, 9
Pattern set
   half-size, 689–699
   quarter-size, 701–705
Peplums, 319
Personal measurement chart. *See* Charts
Pin tucks, 187, 189
Plackets
   wing collar, 426–427
   with facing-in-one, 424–426
   with slit opening, 428
Pleat tucks, 187–188
   see also Yokes
Pockets
   classification, 429
   in-one with seam, 432–434,
      435–437
   inserted, 431–432, 437
   outside, 430, 431
   patch, 429, 430
   welt, 435
Principle #1. *See* Dart manipulation
Principle #2. *See* Added fullness
Principle #3. *See* Contouring
Production terms
   cutter, 17
   first patterns, 15
   grading, 16
   marker, 17
   production pattern, 15
Punch circles, 20–21

Reference areas, 8

Seam allowance, 20–21
Shoulder pads, 352
Single-dart series
   pivotal-transfer technique
      mid-armhole, 124
      mid-neck, 121–122
      shoulder-tip, 125
      side, 123
   slash-spread technique
      center front neck, 118
      center front waist, 116–117
      French, 120
      mid-shoulder, 119
Skirts
   A-line, 282–283
   basic skirt draft
      measurements needed, 70
      skirt back type 1, 70–72
      skirt back type 2, 72
      skirt front, 70–72
   circular
      circle measuring tool, 336
      full-circle, 338–339

half-circle, 342
quarter-circle, 343
three-quarter, 340–341
darts, 278, 286
draped, 309
see also Draping basic patterns
flared
added flare, 288–289
basic, 284–285, 287
clinging hipline/slinky, 290–291
gathered waist, 293
graduated, 304–305
foundation, one-dart, 286
with gathered waistlines
dirndl, 292
flare, 293
godets, 327–329
gored
eight-gore flare, 299
four-gore flare, 294–295
six-gore flare, 296–298
ten-gore flare, 300–302
twelve-gore, 303–306
high-waisted, 280
introduction, 276–277
lengths, 276
low-waisted, 279
pegged
with gathers, 307
with pleats, 308
pleats
all-around, 323–324
box, 322, 324–326
inverted, 320, 322, 324–326
kick, 321–322
knife, 320
pegged, 308
sunburst, 320
terminology, 321
silhouettes, four major, 277
tiers, 314–320
with uneven hemlines, 345–347
variations, 348
waistband, basic, 281
wrap, 330–331
with yokes
flared skirt, 312–313
gathered skirt, 310–311
Sleeve/bodice combinations
dolman, 390, 393
drop-shoulder, 386, 408–409
exaggerated armhole
introduction, 386
square, deep-cut, 404–406
square, gathered, 406–408
kimono
basic, 387–389
full-sleeved, 392
with gusset, 394–397
introduction, 386
tapered, 391, 393
variations, 393
raglan
armhole-princess, 401
basic, 398–400
bell, 402
deep armhole, 403

introduction, 386
one-piece sleeve, 400
variations, 402
yoke, 402
Sleeves
adjustments, 76–79
see also Armhole adjustments
bell, 363
bishop
basic, 360–361
exaggerated, 362
cap
close-fitting, 356
jutting, 356
circular
full-circle, 368–369
half-circle, 367
see also Charts, circle-cascade radius
cowl, 379
dartless, 357
draft, 73–75
elbow darts, 351
extended caps
crescent-shaped, 376–377
darted, 375
introduction, 350
lantern
long, 372–373
short, 374
leg-of-mutton, 378
lift, 382–383
lowered armhole, 384–385
measurement chart. *See* Charts
petal, 370–371
puffed, 364–366
set-in, 350
shirtmaker, 358–359
terminology, 351–352
wedding, 380–381
Slits, 20–21, 358, 359
Squaring a line, 6
Standard ideal figure. *See* Standards
Standards
department store measurements, 31
ideal figure, 30–31
pattern industry measurements, 31, 33–37
Strapless designs, 217–219
Stylelines, 168, 175, 464–466
armhole princess, 172–174
classic princess, 168–171
panel, 176–178
Surplice designs, 220
Swimwear
bikini foundation, 596, 601
bottom variations, 602–603
top variations, 604–608
bra cups, 617–618
crotch finishing, 617
elastic, use of, 616–617
full-figure foundation, 596, 612–613
with skirt front, 613–614
little-boy legline foundation, 596, 609
variations, 610–611
maillot foundation, 596, 597
asymmetric, 600

inset bra, 599
princess, 598
shoulder, finishing, 617

Test fitting patterns
asymmetric shoulder/hip, 84
muslin preparation, 85
trueing basic patterns, 82–83
see also Chapter 27
Tools and equipment
awl, 4
chalk, 5
compass, 6
cutting board, 5
elastic, 6
erasers, 4
French curve, 4
hooks, hangers, 5
notcher, 4
paper
carbon, 6
pattern, 9
pens, pencils, 4, 44
pins, 5, 44
punch, 5
pushpins, 5
rulers, 5–6, 44
shears, 5
stapler, 5
tailor's square, 6
tapes (masking, measuring, metal), 6, 44
template, 4, 12
tracing paper, 5
tracing wheel, 5
vary form curve, 5
weights, 5
Tops
dartless foundation, 470–472
peasant blouse, 482–484
shirt
basic, 473–476
large, 479–481
oversize, 478
without yoke, 476–478
variations, 484
Torso foundation draft, 442–445
Trueing. *See* Test fitting
Two-dart series
pivotal-transfer technique
center front neck and waist, 135
mid-neck and waist, 133
shoulder-tip and waist, 134
slash-spread technique
mid-armhole and waist, 132
mid-shoulder and waist, 131
waist and side, 129–130
working pattern, 129

Wrap designs. *See* Surplice designs

Yokes, 193, 196
with action pleat, 196
back yoke, 194–196
front yoke, 193
pivotal-transfer, 194–195
slash-spread, 193

FITTING PROBLEMS AND PATTERN CORRECTION (CHAPTER 27)

Bodice corrections
  armhole corrections, 654–657
  bust/chest corrections,
    653–654
  dart corrections, 659–660
  horizontal folds, 644–645
  length, 641
  looseness across bust level, 643
  neckline corrections, 648–650
  shoulderline corrections,
    650–651
  strain around bust, 642
    at mid-chest, 645
    at shoulder blade, 643
  waistline corrections, 646–647,
    658–659

Garment adjustment
  gapping, looseness, 639
  strain, tightness, 638

Initial corrections, 640
Identifying good fit and poor fit,
  634–635

Methods for correcting patterns
  using L-, W-, and X-guidelines,
    636–637
  using muslin, 635

Pant corrections
  band corrections, 683
  crotch depth, 677
  downward pull when sitting,
    684
  drooping, 678
  guidemarking, 675
  looseness, 676
  side seam corrections,
    684–685
  strain
    at abdomen, 679
    at hip, 679
    between hip and crotch, 680
    at knee, 685
    diagonal, 678, 680–681, 686
    thigh to inseam, 682
  test fitting, 674–675
  tightness, 676

twisting, 686
vertical folds, 682

Skirt corrections
  dart excess, 664
    relocation, 665
    strain, 663–665
  folds, drooping, 663
  hemline not parallel floor, 646–647
  looseness, 661
  tightness, 662
Sleeve corrections
  cap too high, 671
  diagonal strain at biceps, 670
  length, 673
  puckering at sleeve cap, 668–669
    across sleeve, 668
  rotation, 666–667
  sleeve drops off shoulder, 670
  strain at ball-of-arm, 670
    across back, 672
    at cap, 671
    in raising arm, 672
  wrist, 673